MODERN ARCHITECTURE AND THE MEDITERRANEAN

This collection of essays seeks to explore the vernacular dialogues and contested identities that shaped a complex cultural and architectural phenomenon like Mediterranean modernism. The authors bring to light the debt twentieth-century modernist architects owe to the vernacular building traditions of the Mediterranean region, a geographical area that touches three continents – Europe, Africa and Asia.

This book is subdivided into two sections of essays by an international group of scholars who adopt a number of different methodological perspectives. The first part discusses architects who lived and worked in Mediterranean countries. It examines how they (and their designs) addressed and negotiated complex politics of identity as a constituent of a multilateral vision of modernity against the prevailing "machine age" discourse that informed canonic modernism at the time. Some of the best-known exponents of Mediterranean modernism discussed here are Josep Coderch, Sedad Eldem, Aris Konstantinidis, Le Corbusier, Adalberto Libera, Dimitris Pikionis, Fernand Pouillon, and Josep Lluis Sert. The second part maps the contributions of architects of non-Mediterranean countries who travelled and occasionally practiced in the Mediterranean region, as well as those who took a radical stand against Mediterranean influences. This group includes Erik Gunnar Asplund, Erich Mendelsohn, Bernard Rudofsky, Bruno Taut, Aldo van Eyck, and Paul Schulze-Naumburg. Collectively, the twelve essays situate Mediterranean modernism in relation to concepts such as regionalism, nationalism, internationalism, critical regionalism, and postmodernism. What all of the essays share in common is their investigation of the impact of the natural and vernacular built environment of the *Mare Nostrum* upon the interwar (1920–40s) and postwar (1945–70s) experiences of major European architects.

Jean-François Lejeune is a Professor of Architecture and History at the University of Miami School of Architecture.

Michelangelo Sabatino (Ph. D) is an Assistant Professor of Architectural History in the Gerald D. Hines College of Architecture at the University of Houston.

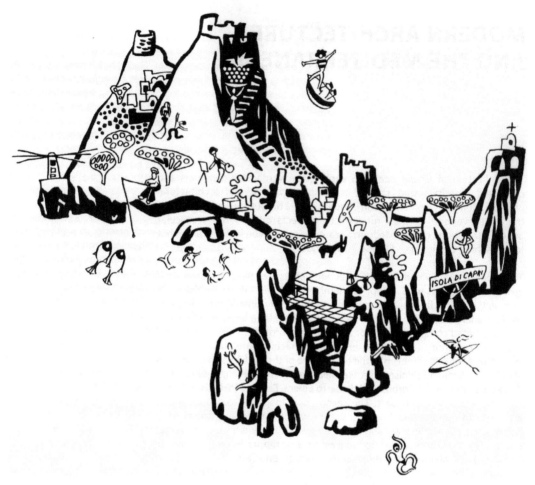

Bernard Rudofsky.
Caricatural drawing of the
island of Capri, 1933.
Source: *Die Insel der
Verrückten*, The Bernard
Rudofsky Estate, Vienna.
© Ingrid Kummer.

Like the best cultural history of our day, this book follows people and forms, ideals and myths, across distances large and small. I have no doubt that this will quickly become a key book among architectural historians, as well as geographers and cultural historians. It will also have great appeal for present-day architects and landscape architects, all of whom are grappling with these themes.

Gwendolyn Wright, Professor of Architecture,
Columbia University

This extensively-illustrated collection, which ranges across well-known and little-known cases (from Le Corbusier, Dimitri Pikionis and Louis Kahn, to Luigi Figini, Aris Konstantinidis or Sedad Eldem), summarizes existing research and opens new avenues, thereby establishing itself as a critical reference point not just for the architectural notion of the Mediterranean, but for modernist architecture in general.

J.K. Birksted, The Bartlett School of Architecture,
University College London

MODERN ARCHITECTURE AND THE MEDITERRANEAN

Vernacular Dialogues and Contested Identities

Edited by Jean-François Lejeune and Michelangelo Sabatino

Routledge
Taylor & Francis Group

LONDON AND NEW YORK

First published 2010
by Routledge
2 Park Square, Milton Park, Abingdon, Oxon OX14 4RN

Simultaneously published in the USA and Canada
by Routledge
711 Third Avenue, New York, NY 10017, USA

Routledge is an imprint of the Taylor & Francis Group, an informa business

© 2010 selection and editorial matter, Jean-François Lejeune
& Michelangelo Sabatino; individual chapters, the contributors
Reprinted 2010

Text design by
Ivonne Delapaz
Typeset in Corbel by
Florence Production Ltd, Stoodleigh, Devon

British Library Cataloguing in Publication Data
A catalogue record for this book is available from the British Library

Library of Congress Cataloging in Publication Data
Modern architecture and the Mediterranean: vernacular dialogues
and contested identities/edited by Jean-François Lejeune &
Michelangelo Sabatino.
       p. cm.
    Includes bibliographical references and index.
  1. Modern movement (Architecture).   2. Vernacular architecture –
  Mediterranean Region – Influence.   I. Lejeune, Jean-François.
  II. Sabatino, Michelangelo.   III. Title: Vernacular dialogues and
  contested identities.
   NA682.M63M62 2010
  720.9182'20904 – dc22   2009008117

ISBN10: 0–415–77633–3 (hbk)
ISBN10: 0–415–77634–1 (pbk)
ISBN10: 0–203–87190–1 (ebk)

ISBN13: 978–0–415–77633–2 (hbk)
ISBN13: 978–0–415–77634–9 (pbk)
ISBN13: 978–0–203–87190–4 (ebk)

CONTENTS

CONTRIBUTORS

Jean-François Lejeune (editor) is a Belgian-born architect who graduated from the University of Liège. He is Professor of Architecture at the University of Miami School of Architecture, where he is also Director of Graduate Studies. His research focuses on the history of Caribbean and Latin American cities as well as on twentieth-century urban discourses in Europe. He has published essays in *Rassegna*, *Stadtbauwelt*, *Journal of Decorative and Propaganda Arts*, and exhibition catalogues. He is the author or editor of many books, including *Miami Architecture of the Tropics* (2001, with Maurice Culot), *The New City: Modern Cities* (1996), *The Making of Miami Beach 1933–1942* (2001, with Allan Shulman), *Sitte, Hegemann and the Metropolis* (2009, with Chuck Bohl), and *Cruelty and Utopia: Cities and Landscapes of Latin America* (2003), winner of the Julius Posener CICA Award for Best Architecture Exhibition Catalogue in 2005. Lejeune is a founder and Vice-President of DOCOMOMO-US/Florida and was an Affiliated Fellow at the American Academy in Rome.

Michelangelo Sabatino (editor) is Assistant Professor of Architecture, in the Gerald D. Hines College of Architecture, at the University of Houston. He holds a Ph.D. from the University of Toronto. He has lectured widely and contributed to journals and co-authored publications in the field (*Casabella, Cite, Harvard Design Magazine, Journal of Architecture, Journal of Design History, Journal of the Society for the Study of Architecture in Canada, Places*). His forthcoming book is entitled *Pride in Modesty: Modernist Architecture and the Vernacular Tradition in Italy* (2010). Sabatino has received fellowships and grants from Harvard University's Graduate School of Arts and Sciences, Graham Foundation for Advanced Studies in Fine Arts, Georgia O'Keeffe Research Museum, the Wolfsonian-FIU, SSHRC (Social Sciences and Humanities Research Council of Canada), and the Japan Foundation.

Esra Akcan holds a Ph.D. in Architectural History from Columbia University and is an Assistant Professor in the Department of Art History of the University of Illinois at Chicago. Akcan has published extensively in Turkish and English in journals such as *Centropa, Domus, New German Critique*, and *Perspecta*. Akcan has published a number of essays in multi-authored books and her forthcoming book is entitled *Modern Architecture in Turkey: From the First World War to the Present* (co-authored with Sibel Bozdogan). Akcan has received fellowships from the Getty Research Institute in Los Angeles and the Canadian Centre for Architecture in Montreal.

Tom Avermaete is an Associate Professor of Architecture at the Delft University of Technology in the Netherlands, where his work concerns the public realm and the architecture of the city. He is the author of *Another Modern: the Post-war Architecture and Urbanism of Candilis-Josic-Woods* (2005) – which was based on his Ph.D. Dissertation at Delft University – and the editor of *Wonen in Welvaart (Dwelling in Welfare)* (2007) on the architecture of the welfare state in Belgium. He is an editor of *OASE Architectural Journal*, and is working on a research project entitled "Migration in Post-war Architecture: Shared Stories on the Architecture of Dwelling in North Africa and Europe."

Barry Bergdoll is the Philip Johnson Chief Curator of Architecture and Design at the Museum of Modern Art and Professor of Modern Architectural History at Columbia University. Holding a Ph.D. from Columbia University, his broad interests center on modern architectural history with a particular emphasis on France and Germany since 1800. Bergdoll has organized, curated, and consulted on many landmark exhibitions of nineteenth- and twentieth-century architecture, including "Home Delivery: Fabricating the Modern Dwelling" at MoMA (2008); "Lost Vanguard: Soviet Modernist Architecture, 1922–32" at MoMA (2007); "Mies in Berlin" at MoMA (2001, with Terence Riley); "Breuer in Minnesota" at the Minneapolis Institute of Arts (2002); "Les Vaudoyer: Une Dynastie d'Architectes" at the Musée D'Orsay, Paris (1991). He is author or editor of numerous publications, including *Mies in Berlin*, winner of the 2002 Philip Johnson Award of the Society of Architectural Historians and AICA Best Exhibition Award, 2002; *Karl Friedrich Schinkel: An Architecture for Prussia* (1994), winner of the AIA Book Award in 1995; and *Lèon Vaudoyer: Historicism in the Age of Industry* (1994); and *European Architecture 1750–1890*, in the Oxford History of Art series. He served as President of the Society of Architectural Historians from 2006 to 2008.

Andrea Bocco Guarneri is an architect and holds a Ph.D. degree in Architecture and Building Design. He is Assistant Professor at the Politecnico di Torino, where he teaches Fundamentals of Building Technology and Participatory Design for Urban Regeneration. He has been working on Bernard Rudofsky since 1990, and he is the author of the only monograph so far published (*Bernard Rudofsky. A Humane Designer*, 2003). He was also curator of the section dedicated to Rudofsky in the *Visionäre und Vertriebene* exhibition (Vienna, 1995); and author of an essay in *Lessons from Bernard Rudofsky* (2007 – the exhibition was shown in Vienna, Montreal and Los Angeles in 2007–08). He also catalogued the Berta and Bernard Rudofsky Estate (Vienna, 2006–07), and has published many articles in international magazines.

Sibel Bozdogan holds a professional degree in Architecture from Middle East Technical University, Ankara, Turkey (1976) and a Ph.D. from the University of Pennsylvania (1983). She has taught Architectural History and Theory courses at Rensselaer Polytechnic Institute (1986–91), MIT (1991–99), and the GSD/Harvard University (part-time since 2000). She has also served as the Director of Liberal Studies at the Boston Architectural Center (2004–06) and currently teaches in the new Graduate Architecture Program of Bilgi University during Spring semesters. Her interests range from cross-cultural histories of modern architecture in Europe, the USA, the Mediterranean, and the Middle East to critical investigations on modernity, technology, landscape, regionalism, and national identity in Turkey and across the globe. She has published articles on these topics, has co-authored a monograph on the Turkish architect Sedad Hakki Eldem (1987) and co-edited an interdisciplinary volume, *Rethinking Modernity and National Identity in Turkey* (1997). Her *Modernism and Nation Building: Turkish Architectural Culture in the Early Republic* (2001) won the 2002 Alice Davis Hitchcock Award of the Society of Architectural Historians and the Koprulu Book Prize of the Turkish Studies Association.

Sheila Crane is Assistant Professor of Architectural History in the School of Architecture at the University of Virginia and holds a Ph.D. from Northwestern

University. Her research focuses on twentieth-century architecture and urban history in France and Algeria. Her publications have addressed questions of memory, urban representation, the movements of architects, and translations of built forms and have appeared in *Future Anterior* and the *Journal of the Society of Architectural Historians*. She has also contributed essays to *The Spaces of the Modern City* (2008) and *Gender and Landscape* (2005). Her research has been supported by fellowships from the Shelby Cullom Davis Center for Historical Studies at Princeton University, the Canadian Centre for Architecture, and the Graham Foundation. Crane has completed a book manuscript entitled *Mediterranean Crossroads: Marseille and the Remaking of Modern Architecture.*

Benedetto Gravagnuolo is Professor of History of Architecture and former Dean of the Faculty of Architecture at the Università di Napoli dal Federico II. The author of many essays, he wrote or edited books including *Adolf Loos. Theory and Works* (New York, 1982), *Design by Circumstance: Episodes in Italian Architecture* (1981), *Gottfried Semper. Architettura, Arte e Scienza* (1987), *La progettazione urbana in Europa, 1750–1960. Storia e teorie* (Roma-Bari, 1991), *Il Mito Mediterraneo nell'architettura contemporanea* (1994), *Le Corbusier e l'Antico. Viaggi nel Mediterraneo* (1997), *Le Teorie dell'Architettura nel Settecento. Antologia critica* (1998), and *Napoli del Novecento al futuro: architettura, design e urbanistica* (2008).

Kai K. Gutschow is an architectural historian working in the professional, five-year Bachelor of Architecture (BArch) program at Carnegie Mellon University in Pittsburgh. He holds a Ph.D. from Columbia University and his research has focused on the complex and controversial history of modern German architectural culture. He has published on a variety of topics, including the work of the German architectural critic Adolf Behne, on Bruno Taut's Glashaus as "Installation Art," on the East African colonial architecture of the German modernist Ernst May, and on the German patriotism and Jewish heritage of Walter Curt Behrendt. With funding from a Getty Research Fellowship, he is currently preparing a book manuscript titled *Inventing Expressionism: Art, Criticism, and the Rise of Modern Architecture*, a thematic and cross-disciplinary look at the origins of Expressionism in architecture in the years before and after World War I.

Ita Heinze-Greenberg holds a Ph.D. from the Technische Universität in Munich, and has worked and taught at various institutions including the Faculty of Architecture and Town Planning at Technion Haifa, and the Faculty of Art History at the University of Augsburg, Germany. Her research project "Europe in Palestine: The Zionist Project 1902–1923" was funded by a Gerda Henkel grant under the auspices of the ETH Zurich. Since 2006, she has led the research project "The European Mediterranean Academy Project (1931–1934)" under the auspices of the Zentralinstitut für Kunstgeschichte in Munich. Her work on Erich Mendelsohn and twentieth-century modern architecture and urbanism in Palestine has been published in many books and exhibition catalogues.

Francis E. Lyn received his Master of Architecture from Princeton University in 1995 and his Bachelor of Architecture from the University of Miami in 1990. Since 1995 he has taught at various institutions in the areas of design, drawing, and architectural theory. At Florida Atlantic University, he is currently Assistant Professor of Architecture. His architectural work has received national recognition and has been included in national and international exhibitions. His research and writing deal with drawing and Scandinavian modernism, with a particular focus on the work of Erik Gunnar Asplund. He has published various essays in conference proceedings around the world.

Ioanna Theocharopoulou received her Ph.D. in Architecture (History and Theory) at Columbia University. Her research focuses on urbanization and informal development particularly in twentieth-century Greece, and more recently, on the history and theory of sustainable design. She has participated in numerous academic conferences. Her publications include contributions to *Paradigmata*, 9th International Architectural Exhibition, Venice Biennale (Hellenic Ministry of Culture, 2004); *Negotiating Domesticity: Spatial Productions of Gender in Modern Architecture*, edited by Hilde Heynen and Gulsum Baydar (Routledge, 2005) and to *Landscapes of Development: The Impact of Modernization on the Physical Environment of the Eastern Mediterranean*, edited by Pani Pyla and Hashim Sarkis (2008). She is now Assistant Professor at the School of Constructed Environments, Parsons The New School for Design.

ACKNOWLEDGMENTS

This book has two distinct origins. The first one was the seminar *The Other Modern – On the Influence of the Vernacular on the Architecture and the City of the Twentieth Century* that the University of Miami School of Architecture held at Casa Malaparte in Capri on March 8–15, 1998, under the direction of Professor Jean-François Lejeune. Forty students and guests attended the event, while twenty experts (historians and architects) were invited from around the world to lecture. The second moment of origin was the encounter at the Wolfsonian-FIU in 2005 between the future book editors, Jean-François Lejeune and Michelangelo Sabatino. At that time Sabatino was a Research Fellow at the Wolfsonian-FIU, located in the heart of Miami Beach, a "modern vernacular" city in its own right. The meeting and the many conversations that ensued were the genuine starting point for this book. Accordingly, the final table of contents groups four essays that were based on lectures originally presented in Capri (Benedetto Gravagnuolo, Jean-François Lejeune, Andrea Bocco Guarneri, Kai K. Gutschow), and a larger series of essays specifically commissioned for this project (Michelangelo Sabatino, Sheila Crane, Ioanna Theocharopoulou, Sibel Bozdogan, Ita Heinze-Greenberg, Esra Akcan, Francis E. Lyn, Tom Avermaete).

Modern Architecture and the Mediterranean has been a labor of love, not only for the field of architectural and cultural history that we both practice, but even more so for the Mediterranean whose cities, landscapes, art, architectures, people, food, and myths have for centuries continued to attract and inspire millions of informed travelers, students, and scholars. Among many places, the book reflects our shared love for the island of Capri and particularly for the Casa Malaparte, an icon of modern architecture that symbolizes the union between building and landscape, tradition and modernity, architecture and literature.

First of all, Jean-François Lejeune thanks the Florence-based Giorgio Ronchi Foundation, Niccolò Rositani, and the architect Marco Broggi, for granting access to the Casa Malaparte and making it an unforgettable week. Lejeune extends his special thanks to all the undergraduate and graduate students who made the event possible by attending the seminar in the sun and rain of March 1998, as well as to all the lecturers present in Capri whose talks did not make it into the book including: Silvia Barisione (Genoa), Roberto Behar (Miami), Mathias Boeckl (Vienna), Jaime Freixa (Barcelona), Miriam Gusevich (Washington), Marianne Lamonaca (Miami Beach), Nicholas Patricios (Miami), Gabriele and Ivo Tagliaventi (Bologna), Hartmut Frank (Hamburg), and Wolfgang Voigt (Frankfurt).

Additional credit goes for the following institutions and persons: the University of Miami School of Architecture and Dean Elizabeth Plater-Zyberk for her continuous support; Gilda Santana and the library staff; the School of Continuing Studies at the University of Miami; the Wolfsonian-FIU, and especially Cathy Leff, Marianne Lamonaca, and the library staff; Roselyne Pirson; and Prof. Ann Cederna at Catholic University in Washington without whom we might never have been allowed to use the Casa Malaparte. For the preparation of the manuscript and its illustrations, the editors thank Silvia Ros, Andrew Georgadis, Maria Bendfeldt, Andrea Gollin, Maria Gonzalez, and Sara Hayat, for their tireless work and enthusiasm; for the compilation of the index, Sibel Veziroglu; and Ivonne Delapaz whose graphic design skills were invaluable to the visual success of this book.

Furthermore, Michelangelo Sabatino would like to extend personal thanks to Jean-François Lejeune for making the experience of co-editing this book memorable. A number of colleagues and friends also deserve special mention for helping in different ways during the preparation of this book: Prof. Barry Bergdoll, Prof. Emily Braun, Prof. Karla Britton, Dean Joe Mashburn, Prof. Francesco Passanti, Prof. Emmanuel Petit, Dean Robert A. M. Stern, and Prof. Gwendolyn Wright. Special thanks are for Serge Ambrose for assisting with imaging and sharing in the day-to-day joys and difficulties that accompanied the production of this book.

Likewise, Jean-François Lejeune would like to thank Michelangelo Sabatino for his friendship and the relentless energy he deployed to get this time-consuming and difficult project going. He also thanks the Fondazione CE.S.A.R. (Rome) and its President Cristiano Rosponi for their financial support of his Spanish research. Special credit also goes to Prof. Vittorio Magnago Lampugnani, Prof. Barry Bergdoll, Prof. Gwendolyn Wright, Prof. Eric Dluhosh, and Prof. Peter Lang for writing essential letters of support. Last but not least, Lejeune thanks Petra Liebl-Osborne, architect, historian, and artist from Munich and Miami, whom he met at Casa Malaparte in Capri in 1998 and has become a very dear friend; and his wife, Astrid Rotemberg, for her love, her patience and never-ending enthusiasm.

This book has been made possible through a grant from the Graham Foundation for the Advancement of the Arts, Chicago.

(*Right*) Karl Friedrich
Schinkel. View of
Amalfi on the Gulf
of Salerno, 1804.
Source: © Bildarchiv
Preußischer Kulturbesitz/Art
Resource. Photo J. P. Anders.

Città di Amalfi al golfo di Salerno.

FOREWORD

Barry Bergdoll

Waves of Mediterraneanism have lapped at the development of modern architecture since the Enlightenment, reshaping its contours often as self-conscious initiatives to redefine or redirect prevailing styles, discourses, or practices. Like tides, the pull has been in at least two directions: towards radical change and towards a sense of atemporal fullness. Influence has ebbed and flowed. Following Fernand Braudel, the great historian of the Mediterranean between the Renaissance and the Enlightenment, one might speak of different time frames of modern Mediterreaneanism from the practices of interwar and postwar modernism in the twentieth century studied in the vibrant array of case studies assembled here by editors and essayists Jean-François Lejeune and Michelangelo Sabatino, to the longer and more complex development of the theme over the two and a half centuries of modern architecture's longer *durée* from the Enlightenment celebration of the historical primacy of the classical replete with the primitive Doric encountered at Paestum to the embrace of a more particularized vernacular in the critical regionalism of the late twentieth century from Hassan Fathy in Egypt in the 1970s to Alvaro Siza in Portugal of the 1990s. The modern movement's polemical and instrumental engagement with the warming waters of the Mediterranean, and with the everyday vernacular on its shores, was, at once, the symptom and the agent of one of the movement's leitmotifs: the attack on inherited academicism, on the hold of Graeco-Roman canons for architectural expressionism, and on the inherent historicism that prevailed in so much of the architectural culture of the eighteenth and nineteenth centuries. One wave of Mediterraneanism thus set out to wipe away traces of preceding ones.

The Mediterranean had become a destination of cultural pilgrimage in the mid-eighteenth century, the aim to recover the purity of antique classicism often in explicit and self-conscious critique of Baroque and Rococo practice, beginning with the renowned voyage of the French architect Jacques-Germain Soufflot in 1749, as tutor of the future aristocratic patron the Marquis de Marigny, and the rediscovery of Grecian purity in the archeological voyages and publications of Julien David Le Roy (1758) and James Stuart and Nicholas Revett (1762), which made the second half of the eighteenth century a golden period of Mediterraneanism. The English Society of Dilettanti even restricted membership to men who had made a substantial voyage distant from London in a southerly direction (the rediscovery of Scotland would need to wait for several decades). The development of European neoclassicism is inextricably tied up with the Mediterranean culture of the Grand Tour, at once focused on the canons of Graeco–Roman classicism and enhanced by the exoticism of discoveries of the "Orient" at the edges of the Roman Empire.

It would be a wholly different experience of the Mediterranean that would, beginning in the 1890s, serve as a leitmotif for architectures born of the rejection

(*Left*) Gottfried Semper. Villa Garbald, Castasegna (Switzerland), 1863–65. Source: Photo Ruedi Walti, Basel.

of the logics of academic imitation – first exalted by Johann Joachim Winckelmann in his mantra that the "only way for us to be great, inimitable even, is the imitation of the ancients" (1755) – and of historicist understanding of the present. Yet even the tonic effect of the anonymous vernacular of the Mediterranean was not wholly the discovery of Josef Hoffmann, who recorded the "authorless" houses of south Italy, and of Capri and Ischia in particular, as an attack on the culture of imitation of a distant past rather than a response to local tradition. Hoffmann was not, however, the first northern European architect to discover the whitewashed vernacular of the houses of the islands in the Bay of Naples as an architecture devoid of the canonic columnar expression of the classical ruins carefully measured and studied on the nearby shoreline. An undercurrent of primitivism, of autochthonous authenticity, and of rootedness can be detected in the modern adoption of the Mediterranean both by architects from north of the Alps and by the architects who sought to work in harmony with the surroundings of their native soil already in the early years of the nineteenth century. From early on, then, the tensions that surface in this volume's essays were at play: the capacity of the local – usually domestic – vernacular to sustain both discourses of transcendent timelessness and of nationalist specificity, of both rootedness and regionalism and of innocence or freedom from learned and cultured symbolism, of a quest for abstraction and of the search for meaning.

While the background vernacular architecture of the Italian countryside had long been a mainstay of artistic inspiration for painters – one has only to think of the landscapes of Nicolas Poussin or of Claude Lorrain – it was around 1800 that architects began to find inspiration in the duality between the columnar expression and proportional order of architect-designed temples, palaces, and villas, and the seeming organic relationship to the land and to local materials, climate, and habits in rural farm structures and in the simple houses of the Italian countryside. From Charles Percier and Pierre-François Léonard Fontaine in Paris to Mathurin Crucy in Brittany, and from John Nash in England to the circle around Friedrich Gilly in Berlin and Friedrich Weinbrenner in Karlsruhe, the embrace of the rural vernacular of Italy was an integral part of the picturesque quest to use architecture in evocative ways, as a tool of associationism, of pastoral literary meaning, and this in ways that extended beyond the imitation of high styles, particularly in the settings of landscape parks and gardens. But it was Karl Friedrich Schinkel who seems to have been the first influential architect to have made the study of the vernacular an integral part of the dialectics of architectural composition in his analysis of the farmhouses encountered on his Italian journey of 1803–05. Already in his twenties, Schinkel explored the margins of the classicism he had learned in the newly formed studios and classrooms of the Berlin Bauakademie, to seek an alternative order, a play between typological regularity and topographic adjustment, between innovation and tradition, between notional symmetry and programmatic accommodation. From this he was to build a mode of composition, particularly for suburban and rural compositions, a mode that was to form a veritable movement by the 1830s, carried forth in the work of a so-called "Potsdam School," – or what Henry Russell Hitchcock and other historians dubbed "romantic classicism" – including Ludwig Persius, Friedrich August Stüler, Ludwig Hesse, Friedrich von Arnim, and others. They developed a form of romantic asymmetrical composition, interweaving indoor and outdoor spaces, sheer volumes and unadorned walls which eschewed the classical orders or even sometimes moldings, the blocky massing in turn unified and enlivened by open trellises and pergolas. This villa style was at once evocative of Mediterranean vernacular sources and the springboard for a freedom of composition in counterpoint to the neoclassical norm, the means to an evocative architecture freed of the historical specificity of the period's revivalist styles. Under the patronage of the Prussian crown this mode was given its *titres de noblesse*. It teetered for decades between the logic of Mediterranean evocation and the freedom of abstract composition freed of time and place even as it emphatically created a new place, a transplanted Prussian vernacular with etymological roots on the other side of the Alps.

The Mediterranean vernacular as one half of a dialectical pair was already signaled by Schinkel's notes for a projected but unpublished textbook *Das architektonische Lehrbuch*, c.1820–1830 on the tectonic and compositional bases of all architecture. "Every object with a specific function demands a correspondingly specific order. That order is either symmetry, which everybody understands, or relative order which is understood only by those who know its principle." For Schinkel, for the first time, vernacular architecture contained an order under picturesque asymmetry which demanded further investigation and was worthy of the respect and emulation of high art.

By the end of the nineteenth century the idea of the vernacular as a more authentic expression of locality, whether tied to nationalist or regionalist arguments, had fully emerged, reinforced by the theories of the relationship of architectural expression to lifestyle, to climate, and to local custom, even to geology, in the writings of John Ruskin, in the later writings of Viollet-le-Duc, in Charles Garnier's exhibition and book *L'Histoire de l'Habitation Humaine* (1875), and in particular in the anthropologically intoned theories of Gottfried Semper, whose Villa Garbald of 1864 in Castasegna in the Swiss Ticino achieves a level of abstraction uncommon in the architect's built work, at the same time as it is rooted in his ideas of the auto-generation of style from factors of materials, social use, and family structure, all intimately linked to place.

But at the same time as the Mediterranean was the source of images of a rooted architecture which sponsored notions of the intimate relationship of architectural expression and spatial configurations to local birth of cultural forms, the nineteenth century also witnessed the first formulations of a geo-politics of Mediterraneanism. It was in the circles of utopian socialism, and in particular in the milieu of French Saint-Simonianism, that the first syncretic views of Mediterranean culture as the result of admixtures, of filtering and absorption, and of progressive synthesis were first formulated as comprehensive theories of cultural development. The Saint-Simonians thus coined the dialectic between the concept of the avant-garde – a term first used in cultural rather than military connotation in the 1820s – and the concept of a geo-politics of historical development. In his 1832 *Système de la Méditerranée*, Saint-Simonian economist and cultural theorist Michel Chevalier first expounded the idea of the Mediterranean as the crucible in which diverse cultural traditions were mixed, synthesized even, in a process which led to continual transmission, hybridism, and the sponsorship of new inventions. His was a theory of cultural interchange and dialectic formation that was to be given architectural form in such programmatic buildings as Léon Vaudoyer's great Cathedral of Marseille (1855–93). Vaudoyer sought to give visual form to the idea of the Mediterranean as the veritable crucible in which the cultures of Occident and Orient met, resolving in peaceful synthesis the opposed terms of religious and cultural conflict in the Mediterranean into an admittedly nationalist-intoned synthesis. Similar ideals obtained in John Ruskin's *Stones of Venice* (1851–53), with its image of the Venetian lagoon as a system for the gradual merging of the diverse currents of cultural expression flowing into the complex hydraulics of the Mediterranean, a veritable figure then of the nineteenth century's search for a science of history that could accommodate, rather than flatten or reduce, the dynamics of cultural progress. Mediterraneanism through much of the nineteenth century could be said to have offered one of the most sophisticated of historicist modes of explanation, and one that served as the matrix for some of the most sophisticated exercises in syncretic design from Léon Vaudoyer and Henri-Jacques Espérandieu in mid-nineteenth century Marseille to the *modernismo* of Antonio Gaudí, Puig i Cadafalch, and their contemporaries in turn-of-the century Catalonia. But like earlier waves of Mediterraneanism, this deployment of a theory of the cultures of Europe's sea was to be gradually replaced by another as the century came to a close, even if the geo-politics of Saint-Simonianism was to continue to echo in many theories of the racial interactions, of economic axes and poles of transmission, well into the twentieth century, from Tony Garnier to Le Corbusier in France, from Erik Gunnar Asplund to Alvar Aalto in the Nordic countries, and from Camillo Boito to Giuseppe Pagano in Italy.

The tension between place and abstraction, between rootedness and exportable lessons resurfaces in the engagement of the architects of the Viennese Secession with the vernacular of Capri and Ischia. In this seminal episode of the architectural avant-gardes of the modern movement the dialetic relationship of the vernacular to concepts of modernity is clear. "[P]easant styles were already secessionist, for they know nothing about academic theory," Olbrich and Hoffmann's supporter Ludwig Hevesi declared. The avant-garde break with academic conventions, rules and historicist structures of thought and practice, was now provocatively linked with the supposed naivety, naturalness, and non-self reflexive invention and problem solving of the indigenous builder. For the next century it might be said that the vernacular would continually oscillate between its role as modernism's other and its foundation myth.

It is the understanding of this duality which constitutes the originality of the most recent generation of scholarship on the complexities of the modern movement and its legacy. Inspired by our own early twenty-first-century moment with evident tensions around the world between the forces of globalization and the assertive renaissance of regionalist identities and particularisms, the history of twentieth-century modernism in architecture appears to us more and more as shot through not with a single teleological line of development but with a complex cat's cradle, palimpsest even, of dualities and desires. A radical reappraisal of the most influential thinkers and form givers of the modern movement architecture, and their relationship to both the classical and the vernacular centered on the Mediterranean basin, has been a key force in a revised cartography of architectural modernism. Emerging is a map in which cosmopolitan and internationalizing centers share space with regional centers anchored in the politics of identity, in which canons and polemically rudimentary definitions have been broken down. The photographs of cars, ships, and machine parts, *and* the diagrams of the Acropolis and sketches of Pompeian villas in Le Corbusier's *Vers une architecture* (1923) take on equal significance. Just as later the aesthetic position of Robert Venturi can take in both Le Corbusier and Armando Brasini and their very different brands of Mediterraneanism. The old periodization – in which a purely rational, machine imagery based, abstract International Style emerged in the 1920s in sharp reaction to the pre-World War I neo-vernaculars of the German *Heimatstil*, the French neo-Regionalisms, or the English Arts and Crafts, only in turn to be overtaken by a new wave of primitivism and vernacularism in the 1930s in response to the political and economic storm clouds of the time – has been eroded. Not only is periodization distinctly out of favor, but the diversity of the modern movement is now embraced as evidence both of its historical complexity and its continued relevance. The early careers of Alvar Aalto, of Mies van der Rohe, and of Le Corbusier are no longer viewed simply as talented training periods in the dominant taste of neo-traditionalism, but as experimental early careers with lasting legacies in the strident avant-garde moments of the 1920s. Integral to this reevaluation of the place of the vernacular has been the understanding of the role of theories of the vernacular in late nineteenth-century anthropology and in early twentieth-century cultural theory which were applied equally to a reevaluation of the indigenous forms of rural architectures throughout Europe in the years on either side of World War I and to the "anonymous" design of machines and new modes of transportation which were transforming the daily landscape of the metropolis and of the increasingly interconnected landscapes of Europe and America. A decade ago, in a seminal article "The Vernacular, Modernism, and Le Corbusier" published in the *Journal of the Society of Architectural Historians* (1997), Francesco Passanti offered a close reading of the parallelisms between Le Corbusier's fascination with what the Viennese Secession had labeled peasant architectures and the machines which *L'Esprit nouveau* had reified as a modern vernacular. Just as fifty years earlier Colin Rowe had erased the oppositional reading between classicism and purism in his influential interpretation – in "The Mathematics of the Ideal Villa" (1947) – of Le Corbusier's villas of the 1920s, so Passanti debunked for good the opposition between a precisionist and *sachlich* embrace of modern machinery and an admiration for the anonymous production of the countryside as twin sides of a single vernacular coin. Indeed in Le Corbusier the opposition between the Mediterraneanism of the Grand Tour and that of the peasant vernacular might likewise be consigned to the waste-bin of monolithic dualisms that reduce complex and subtle architectural creations to polemical manifestos. While Passanti's work on Le Corbusier, reinforced by a generation of colleagues including Stanislaus von Moos, Arthur Rüegg, Jean-Louis Cohen, and Mary McCleod, among others, has focused on a fine-grained reassessment of the complex world of layered dualisms at play in the Franco-Swiss master's work, it has also opened an invitation to a fundamental reappraisal of the modern movement on both sides of World War II. The cut-and-dry periodization of the Weimar Bauhaus into a primitivist craft early phase and a machinist age of maturity is likewise undergoing fundamental revision. A figure such as Marcel Breuer – who moved within a handful of years from the creation of the so-called "African chair" (1921), recently rediscovered, to the postulation of a modern prefabricated vernacular of all-steel studio houses that might be serially produced, to an architecture in which steel-framed cantilevers can be juxtaposed with rugged self-supporting masonry walls in projects such as the Ganes Pavilion in Bristol, England (1936 with F. R. S. Yorke), or the Chamberlain Cottage in Massachusetts (1943, with Walter Gropius) – likewise found both formal and intellectual matrices in which seeming oppositions could be brought into dialogue as equal partners. Just as the work of key modern architects from the well-known masters who have dominated accounts of modernism since its inception, such as Mies van der Rohe or Breuer, to figures who have yet to be fully integrated, such as Giuseppe Pagano or Sedad Eldem (both featured in this anthology), is given a richer interpretation by shifting the lens from the metaphors of the machine to those of the anonymous vernacular, so the overall shape of modernism in architecture achieves a new subtlety and complexity in the essays brought together in this volume. The layered nature of architectural history is revealed, even as the practices brought under the lens of the historians gathered here are given a new vitality and a new relevance. ∎

NORTH *VERSUS* SOUTH

Introduction

Jean-François Lejeune and Michelangelo Sabatino

Technically, modern architecture is in part the result of the contribution of Northern countries. But spiritually, it is the style of Mediterranean architecture that influences the new architecture. Modern architecture is a return to the pure and traditional forms of the Mediterranean. It is the victory of the Latin sea![1]

The complex relationship between Modern Architecture and the Mediterranean, a "meeting place" in the words of Fernand Braudel, of diverse cultural, economic, and social realities, is the common theme of the essays in this collection.[2] A fountainhead of classical and vernacular traditions, the Mediterranean basin not only inspired native artists and architects of this southern region to delve into its visual, spatial, and material history for creative renewal, it also attracted individuals from northern countries who traveled to its shores in pursuit of education and recreational escape. As Barry Bergdoll outlines in the Foreword, this North–South relationship that brought northern artists, architects, and intellectuals to the "land where the lemon trees bloom" (as Wolfgang von Goethe described it) in search of classical proportions and new experiences began to change with the radical social and economic paradigm shifts that came with urbanization and industrialization of the northern countries. A growing belief that cultural and material progress was dependent

[1] Josep Lluís Sert, "Raices Mediterráneas de la arquitectura moderna," *AC* 18 (1935), pp. 31–33. Republished in Antonio Pizza (ed.), *J. LL. Sert and Mediterranean Culture*, Barcelona, Colegio de Arquitectos de Cataluña, 1997, pp. 217–219.
[2] Fernand Braudel, *The Mediterranean and the Mediterranean World in the Age of Philip II*, London, Collins, 1972–73, p. 231.

0.1 (*Far left*) Curzio Malaparte (with Adalberto Libera). Rooftop terrace of Casa Malaparte, with painting installation by Petra Liebl-Osborne, *Fixierte Orte* [Fixes Sites], 1994–99.
Source: Photo Petra Liebl-Osborne, Munich-Miami.

0.2 (*Left*) Tony Garnier. Residential quarter, perspective drawing, *Une cité industrielle*, 1918.
Source: Tony Garnier, *Une cité industrielle: étude pour la construction des villes*, Paris, 1918.

0.3 André Lurçat. Hotel
    Nord-Sud (Hotel North-
    South), Calvi, 1931.
Source: Fonds André Lurçat,
Institut Français
d'Architecture.

on technology began to upset the balance between humanist inquiry and science that had traditionally played an important role in art of architecture from the Renaissance onward.

Many of the critics and commentators from the North who wrote about the rise of modernism and its expression as the New Architecture (*Neues Bauen*) defined it as a movement based upon a break with academic culture and historicist design prevalent in the nineteenth century. Ethnographers and geographers who drew public attention to vernacular architecture and shared vernacular traditions among agrarian cultures during the nineteenth and early twentieth centuries furthered the ideologically driven pursuit of national identity. Their activity played a leading role in the transformation of architectural practice at precisely the moment when industrialization began to radically alter relationships between countryside and city.

The German architect and writer Hermann Muthesius distinguished between "Style-Architecture" and "Building-Art" as early as 1902.[3] Muthesius's study, *Das englische Haus* (1904–05), made the new spirit explicit.[4] Describing the English house and its functionalist design inspired by farmhouses and other English vernacular elements, he wrote:

> In England too vernacular architecture had been disregarded and scorned, just as Gothic churches had been dismissed during the period of Italian domination. But the inherent artistic charm of these buildings was now recognised and with it the qualities they had to offer as prototypes for the smaller modern house. They possessed everything that had been sought and desired: simplicity of feeling, structural suitability, natural forms instead of adaptations from the architecture of the past, rational and practical design, rooms of agreeable shape, colour and the harmonious effect that had in former times resulted spontaneously from an organic development based on local conditions.[5]

[3] Hermann Muthesius, *Style-Architecture and Building-Art: Transformations of Architecture in the Nineteenth Century and its Present Condition*, Santa Monica, CA, The Getty Center for the History of Art and the Humanities, 1994.
[4] Hermann Muthesius, *The English House*, Dennis Sharp (ed.), New York, Rizzoli, 1987. Originally published in three volumes as Hermann Muthesius, *Das englische Haus: Entwicklung, Bedingungen, Anlage, Aufbau, Einrichtung und Innenraum*, Berlin, E. Wasmuth, 1904–05.
[5] Hermann Muthesius, *The English House*, pp. 15–16.

Renewed interest in the vernacular and its role in undermining the dichotomy between "cultivated" and "spontaneous" art forms originated in England during the nineteenth century. The first Industrial Revolution had a traumatic impact on the development and quality of life of cities and on the conditions of workers' housing, thus engaging architects, social scientists and artists in attempting a return to the sources. In England, and later in France, the medieval Gothic vernacular and the structural principles of Gothic construction became the sources of inspiration for a new architecture that defined itself in opposition to the neo-Palladian (Italian and Mediterranean) principles that dominated much of the eighteenth and the first decades of the nineteenth centuries. John Ruskin and William Morris were the proponents of the Arts and Craft Movement and the spiritual fathers of the Garden City, two deeply interconnected movements that relied upon the vernacular as catalyst and which were to spread across Europe and the United States in the first decades of the twentieth century.

The German–English axis initiated by Muthesius resurfaced in the program of the Staatliches Bauhaus, which opened in Weimar in 1919. It relied on two apparently contradictory tendencies: that of the pre-World War I Deutscher Werkbund (with Muthesius as one of its founders) and the "organic" Expressionist medievalism epitomized by Bruno Taut, Erich Mendelsohn, and Hans Poelzig. Both approaches were partially in thrall to the concept of vernacular. Within the Werkbund, Muthesius hinted early at the idea of standardized machine-made production, whereas Gropius's medievalism akin to the Arts and Crafts was unequivocally suggested in the program for the Bauhaus: "Architects, sculptors, painters, we all must return to the crafts!"[6] During the tenure of Walter Gropius, Hannes Meyer, and Ludwig Mies van der Rohe at the helm of the Bauhaus in Dessau, the postwar craft-oriented approach gave way to machine-oriented design practices and to the agenda of industrialization understood as the necessary form of modern-day vernacular.

Nikolaus Pevsner's influential *Pioneers of the Modern Movement*, published in 1936, acknowledged and emphasized the contribution of vernacular traditions of the English countryside to the reformist program of William Morris's Arts and Crafts Movement and, ultimately, the development of the modern movement.[7] Yet, as Maiken Umbach and Bernd Hüppauf point out in their introduction to *Vernacular Modernism*, if traditional scholars such as Pevsner and others "helped wipe away the aesthetic 'clutter' of historicist revival styles of the nineteenth century, and thus prepared the ground for modern functionalism . . . [t]hey reduced the role of the vernacular in modernism to a purely transitory one, which ceased to be relevant as soon as high modernism developed."[8] As a result, such interpretations overlooked both socio-political context and a "sense of place" in favor of a purely formal interpretation that led to the schematic tendencies of modern abstraction. *Mechanization Takes Command* (to use the title of Sigfried Giedion's book of 1948) became the mantra of modernist architects who believed in combining anonymity and industrialization to erase artistic individuality in order to promote a collective identity. At that time, the resolutely anti-classical stance and overwhelming influence of Pevsner and Giedion, both northern-based historians and critics, interrupted and potentially inverted the pluri-secular exchange between North and South that flourished from the Renaissance until the beginning of the twentieth century in the form of the Grand Tour.[9] Only grudgingly did Sigfried Giedion make a small concession to the classical tradition:

> Tony Garnier felt an attraction to the classical, as the modeling of his
> buildings shows. He broke through this attachment, however, in many

[6] Walter Gropius, "Programme of the Staatliches Bauhaus in Weimar," in Ulrich Conrads (ed.), *Programs and Manifestoes on 20th-Century Architecture*, Cambridge, MA, The MIT Press, 2002, pp. 49–53.
[7] Nikolaus Pevsner, *Pioneers of the Modern Movement from William Morris to Walter Gropius*, London, Faber & Faber, 1936.
[8] Maiken Umbach and Bernd Hüppauf (eds.), *Vernacular Modernism: Heimat, Globalization, and the Built Environment*, Stanford, CA, Stanford University Press, 2005, pp. 13–14.
[9] Guido Beltramini (ed.), *Palladio nel Nord Europa: Libri, Viaggiatori, Architetti*, Milan, Skira, 1999. Also see Fabio Mangone, *Viaggi a sud: gli architetti nordici e l'Italia, 1850–1925*, Napoli, Electa Napoli, 2002.

[10] Sigfried Giedion, *Space, Time and Architecture – The Growth of a New Tradition*, Cambridge, Harvard University Press, 1941, p. 693.
[11] Panayotis Tournikiotis, *The Historiography of Modern Architecture*, Cambridge, MA, The MIT Press, 1999; Maria Luisa Scalvini and Maria Grazia Sandri, *L'immagine storiografica dell'architettura contemporanea da Platz a Giedion*, Rome, Officina, 1984.
[12] Maiken Umbach and Bernd Hüppauf (eds.), pp. 1–23.
[13] See Jean-Louis Cohen, *André Lurçat: 1894–1970: Autocritique d'un moderne*, Liège, Mardaga, 1995, pp. 110–120.
[14] Gio Ponti, "Esempi da fuori per le case della Riviera – una interessante costruzione mediterranea a Calvi in Corsica," in *Domus*, November 1932, pp. 654–655.
[15] The Hungarian émigré architect Marcel Breuer also employed rubble stone walls as his trademark in many of his postwar domestic designs in America. See Barry Bergdoll, "Encountering America: Marcel Breuer and the Discourses of the Vernacular from Budapest to Boston," in Alexander von Vegesack and Mathias Remmele (eds), *Marcel Breuer: Design and Architecture*, Weil am Rhein, Vitra Design Shiftung, 2003, pp. 260–307.
[16] Bruno Reichlin, "'Cette belle pierre de Provence' La Villa De Mandrot," in *Le Corbusier et la Méditerranée*, Marseilles, Parenthèses, 1987, pp. 131–136. On Corbusier and the vernacular see Gérard Monnier, "L'architecture vernaculaire, Le Corbusier et les autres," in *La Méditerranée de Le Corbusier*, Aix-en-Provence, Publications de l'Université de Provence, 1991, pp. 139–155.

details of his Cité Industrielle. Its houses, with its terraces and the gardens on their flat roofs are a sound combination of modern construction and the old tradition of the Mediterranean culture.[10]

With the exception of Bruno Zevi's *Storia dell'architettura moderna* (1950), until well into the 1960s, most major surveys of modern architecture were written by German, British, Swiss or American scholars who showed little if any interest in the Mediterranean basin as a locus of modern architecture.[11] Even though they recognized the value of Northern vernaculars, they ignored those of the South and made little if any reference to the experiences of Josef Hoffmann and Adolf Loos, both of whom studied the vernaculars of the Mediterranean basin.[12] Likewise they ignored the leaders of the rising trend of "Mediterranean modernism" such as Josep Lluís Sert, Adalberto Libera, Giuseppe Terragni, and Dimitris Pikionis. One of the primary reasons for suspicion of a Mediterranean modernism is that it often flourished in countries that were under right-wing dictatorships, which outside observers tended to condemn, even if the architects were engaged in designing social housing, as they often were. Moreover, Mediterranean vernacular buildings were often based upon a tectonics of stereotomic solid walls that echoed the sculptural qualities of reinforced concrete whereas Northern vernaculars were associated with the framed systems of construction that could be extrapolated to concrete and steel.

Mediterranean modernism was eclipsed not only in Pevsner's *Pioneers*, which barely acknowledged Le Corbusier, but in other influential narratives of the 1930s as well. Philip Johnson and Henry-Russell Hitchcock's 1932 exhibition and supporting publication *The International Style: Architecture since 1922* is a case in point. Although the authors published André Lurçat's evocatively named Hotel Nord-Sud completed in 1931 in Calvi on the island of Corsica, they failed to acknowledge the architect's explicit engagement with a Mediterranean vernacular tradition characterized by smooth whitewashed surfaces, unadorned, simple volumes and flat roofs.[13] Contrast this attitude with the "Southern" commentator, Italian architect and designer Gio Ponti, who was quick to notice the "perfect Mediterranean character" of Lurçat's hotel.[14] In Ponti's estimation, engaging context and culture was not at odds with the "straightforward modern style" of the work. Likewise, built on the French shores of the Mediterranean only three years after Villa Savoye, Le Corbusier's Mandrot villa of 1931 challenged militant critics who sought to undermine the complexity of Le Corbusier's modernity by reducing it to his "Five Points." In place of the pilotis that lifted the Villa Savoye above the ground, the villa at Le Pradet was anchored to its site by rubble stone walls typical of the Mediterranean region, serving as a reminder of the role that nature and the vernacular could play in an organic modernism.[15] In lieu of the Villa Savoye's smooth surfaces and ribbon windows, the Mandrot villa introduced the "primitive" texture of the Provençal *genius loci*.[16] Following the example of Le Corbusier, Adalberto Libera and Curzio Malaparte would rely on the expertise of stonemasons to design the modernist masterpiece in Capri, the Villa Malaparte, completed between 1938 and 1942 (plates 1, 2 and 3). Even though Johnson and Hitchcock included the Mandrot villa in their publication, their omission about the Mediterranean-ness of these buildings is not surprising in light of the fact that they were not really interested in recognizing the regional or national iterations of modernity, because it did not reinforce their curatorial argument that modern architecture constituted an international style. What they failed to acknowledge is how the shared heritage of the vernacular helped Mediterranean modernists identify with a collective ethos without necessarily forgoing national or pan-regional identities.

0.4 Le Corbusier. Villa Mandrot in Le Pradet, France, 1931.
Source: Henry-Russell Hitchcock and Philip Johnson, *The International Style*, New York, 1966.

More than any other modernist interested in the Mediterranean classical and vernacular environment, Le Corbusier's complex positioning posed serious challenges to the Anglo-German axis. Le Corbusier's epistemological shift from an arts and crafts exordium in La Chaux-de-Fonds and his machine-oriented modernism of the mid-1920s (Plan Voisin, 1925) to a southern version where the vernacular was substituted for the discursive role performed by the machine was also a direct response to a series of events, both personal and global, that put Le Corbusier's original position into crisis: the Great Depression and the critique of industrial capitalism in the 1930s, the rise of German right-wing parties and the ascent of National Socialism, which made northern-based modernist arguments dangerously ambiguous, and finally the intellectual consequences of his loss at the Palais des Nations competition in Geneva. The impact of these events coincided with Le Corbusier's first encounter with Josep Lluís Sert in Barcelona and the subsequent journey aboard the ship *Patris II* from Marseilles to Athens as part of the fourth CIAM meeting at which German architects were noticeably absent. Sert's writings regarding the vernacular and modernity made this global positioning of the Mediterranean clear:

> Every country has a timeless architecture which is generally termed vernacular, not in the sense as understood in architecture schools, which means regional, but rather vernacular of the lowest class, classified according to the economic means at their disposal. (. . .) The pure functionalism of the "machine à habiter" is dead. (. . .) Architects and theorists, above all Germanic, carried functionalist experiments to absurd extremes.[17]

Le Corbusier's famous letter to the mayor of Algiers, published in *The Radiant City*, summarized the international and political context of his perspective in the 1930s:

[17] Josep Lluís Sert, "Arquitectura sense 'estil' i sense 'arquitecte,'" *D'Ací i d'Allà* 179, December 1934.

[18] Cited in Mary McLeod, "Le Corbusier and Algiers," in *Oppositions* 19–20, Winter/Spring 1980, pp. 55–85; idem, "Le Corbusier – L'appel de la Méditerranée," in Jacques Lucan (ed.), *Le Corbusier: une Encyclopédie*, Paris, Éditions du Centre Pompidou/ CCI, 1987, pp. 26–31. The periodical *Plans* campaigned for a new European order. The old continent was to be divided into three vertical north–south sections: West = Latin federation; Center = Mittel Europa/ Germans; East = Russians and Slavs.
[19] On the debate over function see Adrian Forty, *Words and Buildings – A Vocabulary of Modern Architecture*, London, Thames & Hudson, 2000, pp. 174–195.
[20] Wolfgang Voigt, *Atlantropa – Weltbauen am Mittelmeer: ein Architektentraum der Moderne*, Hamburg, Dölling und Galitz, 1998.

The economy of the world is upset; it is dominated by the incoherence of arbitrary and harmful groups. New groupings, and regroupings, new units of importance must come into being which will give the world an arrangement that is less arbitrary and less dangerous. The Mediterranean will form the link of one of these groupings, whose creation is imminent. Races, tongues, a culture reaching back a thousand years – truly a whole. An impartial research group has already, this year, through the organ *Prélude*, shown the principle of one of these new units. It is summed up in four letters, laid out like the cardinal points: Paris, Barcelona, Rome, Algiers.[18]

Within these new geographical coordinates the Northern axis between Berlin and London was marginalized, as was the important role of function in modernism typically associated with Nordic modernism.[19] Interestingly, it is around the end of the 1920s that Herman Sorgel's technical-architectural utopia – Atlantropa – of lowering the level of the Mediterranean Sea came to the fore. In 1932, Erich Mendelsohn, one of the German architects involved in the project along with Peter Behrens and Hans Poelzig, argued in a speech in Zürich that in order to establish a peaceful coexistence between the nations a supranational New Deal had to be established, which was able to combine the European nations to "productive technical world tasks." Atlantropa, the huge hydro-electrical project to connect Europe and Africa would have created a North–South Super-Continent as dominant a power as America and Asia.[20]

Post-World War II historiography – the book and its structure

Modern Architecture and the Mediterranean aims to bring to light the creative debt that twentieth-century modernist architecture owes to extant vernacular traditions of the Mediterranean region. By exploring the impact of the vernacular buildings of stonemasons and craftspeople on the rise and diffusion of modernism, the twelve essays in this collection take a novel look at the moment when professionally trained architects began to project modern values onto anonymous building traditions that had flourished for millennia among the pre-industrial cultures of the Mediterranean basin. During the first three-quarters of the twentieth century, architects in the North and the South deeply engaged elements of the context – climate, geography, materials, and culture – in the search for solutions to contemporary problems of housing and urban planning.

Although a number of the architects featured in this collection have been the subject of in-depth analysis, there has been no overview of the overlaps between the strategies of protagonists practicing throughout different countries of the Mediterranean and their potential interaction. *Modern Architecture and the Mediterranean* is the first book to study the work of these architects as part of the collective phenomenon of what we have defined as "Mediterranean modernism" – modern architecture that responds to program with cues derived from vernacular buildings so as to infuse spatial and material concerns with context and culture.

The first group of essays, titled "South," discusses architects who lived and worked in Mediterranean countries; it examines how they and their designs addressed and negotiated complex politics of identity as a constituent of a multilateral vision of modernity against the prevailing "machine age" discourse that informed canonical modernism at the time. The second group of essays, titled "North," maps the contributions of architects from non-Mediterranean countries who traveled and occasionally practiced in Mediterranean countries.

What distinguishes the two groups is the different ways in which each negotiated issues of cultural identity and professional demands. If the first group of essays discusses architects who engaged with traditions that were familiar insofar as they were part of their own national or pan-regional cultures (i.e., the Mediterranean Sea), the second group of architects were "outsiders" who appropriated a tradition that, although foreign, resonated within them. This Mediterranean modernism debate involved the architects Sedad Eldem, Erich Mendelsohn, Bernard Rudofsky, Bruno Taut and Aldo van Eyck, as well as Sert, Aldo Rossi and several others. Whatever the point of view, national or transnational, insider or outsider, these different psychological and cultural perspectives weighed on personal experiences of discovery and appropriation of vernacular traditions.

The continuity in the approaches of Mediterranean modernist architects who reassessed the importance of the vernacular during the interwar years and pursued their interests after World War II is particularly significant for the historiography of twentieth-century architecture and urbanism. Although the exploitation of classicism in the volatile relationship between nationalism and architecture has been closely studied, the pan-regional, transnational "progressive" phenomenon of Mediterranean modernism has been neglected in most monographic studies of individual architects as well as comprehensive surveys of twentieth-century architecture and urbanism. A number of individuals tried to react to this status quo. For example, the Italian architect Luigi Figini, a founding member of the Italian Gruppo Sette, wrote an essay on the architecture of Ibiza (1950) in which he complained that Giedion's *Space, Time and Architecture*, attributed far too much importance to the machine-age and abstraction as the primary source of modern architecture. Figini vindicated the equally important contribution of the whitewashed walls of Mediterranean vernacular buildings to the development of modern architecture.[21] The fact that he did not praise Italian but Spanish and Mediterranean vernacular architecture is indicative of the pan-regionalist approach to a phenomenon that many critics overlooked. Significantly, Figini was a long-time member of the Italian delegation to the Congrès Internationaux d'Architecture Moderne (CIAM), and in that capacity was able to witness the tensions over the definition of modern architecture and urbanism that surfaced among its northern and southern members during the 1930s and continued to exist well into the 1950s.[22]

A "tipping point," to use Malcolm Blackwell's metaphor, was the Italo-Swiss Rationalist architect and critic Alberto Sartoris's *Encyclopédie de l'architecture nouvelle* (1948–57). His three-volume overview, in which climate and geography were the framework for presenting the development of the New Architecture, distinguished between the "Mediterranean climate and order" (vol. 1), that of the Northern countries (vol. 2), and that of the Americas (vol. 3) (plate 19):

> The inevitable differences that are indeed justified, between city and countryside, mountains and plains, the North and the South, never fade, even in architecture whose style has crossed all boundaries and consequently penetrates everywhere.[23]

Hubert De Cronin Hastings, who also wrote under the name Ivor de Wolfe, contributed to the growing awareness of the Mediterranean and "vernacular modernism" during the critical years of post-World War II reconstruction. This was made possible thanks to his development of the concept of "townscape," which Gordon Cullen popularized in his book *Townscape* of 1961 interpreting Hastings's ideas through his talent as an inspired draughtsman. Two years

[21] Luigi Figini, "Architettura naturale a Ibiza," *Comunità* 8, May–June 1950, pp. 40–43.
[22] Eric Mumford, *Defining Urban Design – CIAM Architects and the Formation of a Discipline, 1937–69*, New Haven, CT, London, Yale University Press, 2009; see also, Eric Mumford, *The CIAM Discourse on Urbanism, 1928–1960*, Cambridge, MA, The MIT Press, 2000.
[23] Alberto Sartoris, *Encyclopédie de l'Architecture Nouvelle*. Vol. 1, *Ordre et climat méditerranéens*, Milan, Ulrico Hoepli, 1948; Vol. 2., *Ordre et climat nordiques*, 1957; Vol. 3, *Ordre et climat américains*, 1954. The quote is taken from Vol. 2, p. 4 (our translation).

LETTER TO A MAYOR:

TO MONSIEUR BRUNEL,
MAYOR OF ALGIERS.

"Paris, December, 1933

"With a firmness and broad-mindedness which have earned you as much admiration as envy, you govern a city of great destiny.

"The economy of the world is upset; it is dominated by the incoherence of arbitrary and harmful groups. New groupings, and regroupings, new units of importance must come into being which will give the world an arrangement that is less arbitrary and less dangerous. The Mediterranean will form the link of one of these groupings, whose creation is imminent. Races, tongues, a culture reaching back a thousand years – truly a whole. An impartial research group has already, this year, through the organ *Prélude*, shown the principle of one of these new units. It is summed up in four letters, laid out like the cardinal points:

$$\begin{array}{c} P \\ B \quad\quad R \\ A \end{array}$$

Paris, Barcelona, Rome, Algiers. A unit extending from north to south along a meridian, running the entire gamut of climates, from the English Channel to Equatorial Africa, embracing every need – and every resource.

"Algiers ceases to be a colonial city; Algiers becomes the head of the African continent, a capital city. This means that a great task awaits her, but a magnificent future too. This means that the hour of city planning should strike in Algiers.

0.5 Le Corbusier. Cardinal Points, 1933.
Source: Le Corbusier, *La Ville radieuse* (The Radiant City), Paris, 1933.

later, in 1963, Hastings/de Wolfe published *Italian Townscape*, a study of Italian medieval cities observed through the prism of the picturesque. Hastings did not advocate imitation of vernacular towns and building types but rather their use as models of collective form for contemporary reconstruction and urban design. A similar interest developed in Italy with Ernesto Rogers's discussion on "continuity" and Giancarlo De Carlo's concept of the "hill town reconsidered," with the city of Urbino as his paradigm. In De Wolfe's *Italian Townscape*, North and South meet to some extent through a modern reinterpretation of Uvedale Price's original foray into the question of the picturesque.[24]

A significant impetus to changing perceptions in non-Mediterranean countries after World War II about the constructive role that vernacular buildings of the South could play in shaping postwar modernism was Bernard Rudofsky's 1964 exhibition and publication *Architecture Without Architects* at the Museum of Modern Art and Myron Goldfinger's 1969 book *Villages in the Sun: Mediterranean Community Architecture*, both of which stressed how Mediterranean vernacular builders prefigured industrially produced housing while still engaging with context and culture. The issue of "repetition without monotony," implying type and serial production in the studies of Goldfinger and Rudofsky, was key to designers whose identity was heavily invested in Mediterranean modernism.

Recent overviews of world architecture have taken up where authors like Sartoris left off to explore how geography shaped twentieth-century architecture and urbanism.[25] A number of publications have increasingly become more explicit about the interplay of architecture, modernity, and

[24] See M. Christine Boyer, "An Encounter with History: the Postwar Debate between the English Journals of *Architectural Review* and *Architectural Design* (1945–1960)," pp. 136–163, accessed on the Internet at: www.team10online.org/research/papers/delft2/boyer.pdf.
[25] Kenneth Frampton (ed.), *World Architecture 1900–2000: A Critical Mosaic*, Vienna, New York, Springer, 1999–2000, and in particular, Vittorio Magnago Lampugnani (ed.), *Mediterranean Basin*, vol. 4.

geopolitics.[26] Yet, for the most part, these studies stand as isolated instances. While surveys of twentieth-century architecture tend to address nationalism, they rarely deal with the transnational phenomenon of Mediterranean modernism that existed within, rather than in opposition to, modernism. *Modern Architecture and the Mediterranean* sets out to redress this gap in the literature and to contribute to the "many voices" of a multilateral and multifaceted modernity.[27]

It is precisely this multiplicity, and the tensions that this approach generates, that the subtitle of the book suggests. Dialogues about the vernacular and contested identities were instrumental in shaping Mediterranean modernism. They were at the centre of debates between critics and historians who disagreed about the role that nationalism and regionalism should play in the emergence of an international, even universal, language of modernism that could unite rather than divide. Building upon what architectural and cultural historians such as Jean-Louis Cohen, Benedetto Gravagnuolo, Vittorio Magnago Lampugnani, Vojtech Jirat-Wasiutynski, and Jan Birksted have already accomplished, this book explores the fascination modern architects and urban planners had with Mediterranean traditions.[28] The authors' contributions take into account a number of different methodological perspectives. Some frame their research with the help of theories of translation, while others opt to use architectural type as a basis for analysis. Others explore the impact of literary debates on architectural and artistic culture. What all of the essays share in common is their investigation of the impact of the natural and built environment of the

[26] See for instance Thomas Da Costa Kaufmann, *Toward a Geography of Art*, Chicago, IL, Chicago University Press, 2004, and Eeva-Liisa Pelkonen, *Alvar Aalto: Architecture, Modernity, and Geopolitics*, New Haven, CT, London, Yale University Press, 2009.
[27] On Fernand Braudel's notion of "many voices" see Iain Chambers, *Mediterranean Crossings – The Politics of an Interrupted Modernity*, Durham, NC, London, Duke University Press, 2008, pp. 1–22.
[28] See for instance Jean-Louis Cohen and Monique Eleb, *Casablanca: Colonial Myths and Architectural Ventures*, New York, Monacelli Press, 2002; Benedetto Gravagnuolo, *Le Corbusier e l'antico: Viaggi nel mediterraneo*, Napoli, Electa Napoli, 1997; Vittorio Magnago Lampugnani, *Die Architektur, die Tradition und der Ort – Regionalismen in der europäischen Stadt*, Stuttgart, München, Deutsche Verlags-Anstalt, 2000; Vojtech Jirat-Wasiutynski and Anne Dymond (eds.), *Modern Art and the Idea of the Mediterranean*, Toronto, Buffalo, The University of Toronto Press, 2007; Jan. K. Birksted, *Modernism and the Mediterranean: The Maeght Foundation*, Aldershot, Burlington, Ashgate, 2004.

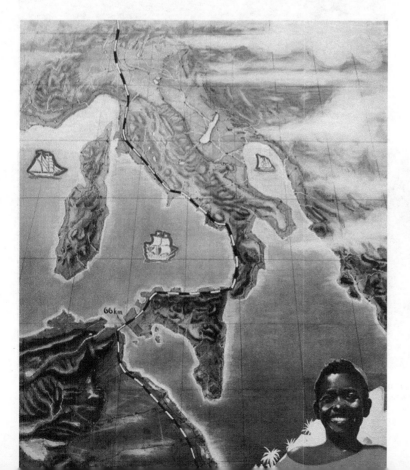

0.6 Herman Sörgel. "New Geography for the Middle Section of the Mediterranean. Italy connected with Sicily and filling up of the Adriatic. Railroad connection from Middle Europe to Capetown." Collage, c. 1931.
Source: From Herman Sörgel, *Verirrungen und Merkwürdigkeiten im Bauen und Wohnen*, Leipzig, 1929.

Mediterranean basin upon the interwar (1920–1940) and postwar (1945–1970s) experiences of architects working in a number of different countries.

Not all the architects who participated in this broad phenomenon have been included in this collection of essays nor have we endeavored to address the phenomenon as it resurfaced in other parts of the world. Opportunities for further studies in Europe, in Africa, the United States and Latin America abound. In the 1960s Yona Friedman collaged one of his urban megastructures on top of a photograph of a vernacular village published in Rudofsky's *Architecture without Architects* (see illustration 12.7). Hassan Fathy, a major advocate of the

0.7 José Luis Fernández del Amo (I.N.C.). Houses in Vegaviana, Cáceres, c.1956.
Source: *Fernández Del Amo: Arquitecturas 1942–1982,* Madrid, 1983. Photo Joaquín del Palacio "Kindel."

0.8 José Luis Sert. Perspective, Fondation Maeght, St-Paul-de-Vence, France, 1958.
Source: The Josep Lluis Sert Collection, Francis Loeb Library Special Collections, Graduate School of Design, Harvard University.

0.9 Alvaro Siza. Housing
quarter, Quinta da
Malagueira, Évora,
Portugal, from 1977.
Source: *El Croquis*, 68–69.
Photo Luis Ferreira Alves.

use of vernacular traditions in the modern Egyptian town of New Gourna completed in 1948, collaborated with Constantinos Doxiadis, who fueled his creative practice by way of lifelong interest in Mediterranean vernacular. The domestic architecture of Irving Gill in California during the 1910s and 1920s paralleled some of the concerns of Josef Hoffmann and Adolf Loos in Austria. Likewise, it would be difficult not to see how Mediterranean modernism – through the influence of Italian Rationalism and the analogies between the Mare Nostrum and the Atlantic coast of South America – helped shape the Brazilian architectures of Lucio Costa and Oscar Niemeyer. During those same years Louis I. Kahn traveled to southern Europe and produced a series of masterful sketches of Capri, Positano and the Amalfi coast (plate 4). Vincent Scully has explained the importance of Kahn's drawings:

> Kahn broke the hold of the International Style on modern architecture and opened the way for the revival of the vernacular and classical traditions of architecture which has been going on during the past generation and was initiated by Robert Venturi, along with Charles Moore and Aldo Rossi, each indebted to Kahn in fundamental ways.[29]

In 1966, not long after Kahn completed his Richards Medical Centre (1961) which echoed the medieval towers he had studied in Tuscany, Robert Venturi's *Complexity and Contradiction in Architecture* and Aldo Rossi's *L'architettura della città* were published on both sides of the Atlantic. Produced under the patronage of the American Academy and published with the Museum of Modern Art in New York, Robert Venturi's "gentle manifesto" became, in Scully's analysis, the indispensable complement – and contradictor – of Le Corbusier's *Toward an Architecture* (1923):

> The older book demanded a noble purism in architecture, in single buildings and in the city as a whole; the new book welcomes the contradictions and complexities of urban experience at all scales.[30]

[29] Vincent Scully, Introduction to Jan Hochstim, *The Paintings and Sketches of Louis I. Kahn*, New York, Rizzoli, 1991, p. 16.
[30] Vincent Scully, Introduction to Robert Venturi, *Complexity and Contradiction in Architecture*, New York, The Museum of Modern Art, 1966, pp. 11–12.

[31] Ibid.
[32] Peter Eisenman, "The Houses of Memory: The Texts of Analogy," preface to Aldo Rossi, *The Architecture of the City*, Cambridge, MA, The MIT Press, 1982, p. 4.
[33] Rafael Moneo, *Theoretical Anxiety and Design Strategies in the Work of Eight Contemporary Architects*, Cambridge, MA, The MIT Press, 2004, pp. 102–143. For a firsthand account, see Aldo Rossi, *Architetture Padane*, Modena, Edizioni Panini, 1984, pp. 11–14. Also see Maurice Halbwachs, *On Collective Memory*, Chicago, IL, University of Chicago Press, 1992.

For Scully, Venturi's inspiration did not come from Le Corbusier's Greek temple, but from its opposite, "the urban facades of Italy, with their endless adjustments to the counter-requirements of inside and outside and their inflection with all the business of everyday life."[31] In Rossi, Peter Eisenman saw "an attempt to build a different kind of castle from that of the moderns. It is an elaborate scaffold erected for and by someone who can no longer climb its steps to die a hero's death." Rossi proposed "an *other* architecture, an *other* architect, and most importantly, an *other* process for their understanding."[32] Critical to Rossi's theories were the typological studies of the urban vernacular of Rome and Venice initiated by his teacher Salvatore Muratori, as well the thesis of Maurice Halbwachs on "Collective Memory." Rossi's interest in extant vernacular architectures has been discussed in Rafael Moneo's overview of contemporary theoretical anxieties and design strategies: the Spanish architect stresses Rossi's "nostalgia of the rational construction of vernacular architecture" in relation to a 1973 project in Borgo Ticino influenced by indigenous lake dwellings. Moneo goes on to discuss Rossi's interest in the "anonymous architecture" that led him to embrace urban spaces, ranging from a courtyard in Seville to houses on the Po River delta.[33] Rossi's cabanas also reflect his interest in the vernacular (plate 22).

We hope this book, as incomplete as it may be, will open up new avenues of future research. ■

Part I
SOUTH

1

FROM SCHINKEL TO LE CORBUSIER

The Myth of the Mediterranean in Modern Architecture

Benedetto Gravagnuolo

When we say Mediterranean we mean above all the solar stupor that generates the panic-stricken myth and the metaphysical immobility.[1]

It is with these words pregnant with esoteric suggestions that Massimo Bontempelli attempted an acrobatic definition of the "myth of the Mediter-ranean" – a myth that exercised a notable magnetic force on the artistic, literary, and architectonic debate in Italy, Spain, and France in the first decades of the 1900s.[2] Carlo Belli, a witness and actor of the period, wrote:

> The theme of "Mediterranean-ness" and "Greek-ness" was our navigational star. We discovered early that a bath in the Mediterranean would have restored to us many values drowned under gothic superimpositions and academic fantasies. There is a rich exchange of letters between Pollini, Figini, Terragni and myself on this subject. There are my articles in various journals, especially polemical with Piacentini, Calza Bini, Mariani and others embedded in Roman fascism . . . We studied the houses of Capri: how they were constructed, why they were made that way. We discovered their traditional authenticity, and we understood that their perfect rationality coincided with the optimum of aesthetic values. We discovered that only in the ambit of geometry could one actuate the perfect *gemütlich* of dwelling.[3]

Without a doubt, *mediterraneità* – not to be confused with *romanità* to which it was often polemically counterpoised – represented an explicit font of inspiration from which a small circle of initiates, mostly French and Italian, drew. Yet, before entering into an evaluation of the merit of this ideology – and analyzing the verbal and visible alchemies of the "disquieting muses" – it may be useful to pose a few basic questions.[4] Does there exist a "Mediterranean culture of living"? And, if it exists, in what measure is it recognizable as a historical phenomenon? And lastly, is it possible to reassert it in terms of a collective design ethos? It is not easy to respond to these questions, but it is worth reducing the discourse to its schematic essence.

The *mare nostrum* or Mediterranean has represented for centuries a privileged cradle of commercial exchange, bellicose conflicts, and cultural transmissions. On its shores ancient historical civilizations flowered – including Egyptian, Cretan-Mycenaean, Phoenician, and Greek – and on its waters the first empires were founded – Carthaginian, Roman, Byzantine, and Islamic. Many affinities of climate, traditions, topography, and even ethnic traits are visible along the coastlines of countries facing the Mediterranean. Among the various anthropological manifestations, the one that best registers and preserves the

[1] Massimo Bontempelli, *Introduzioni e discorsi*, Milano, Bompiani, 1945, p. 171. Bontempelli was the founder and the director of two periodicals: *900*, in collaboration with Curzio Malaparte (1926–29) and *Quadrante*, in collaboration with Pier Maria Bardi (1933–36). In these periodicals and his numerous books, he established the theoretical basis of "magical realism." In so doing, he became a pole of reference for the "classical" and "metaphysical" cultural movements.

[2] For a more extensive bibliography, see Carlo Enrico Rava, *Nove anni di architettura vissuta, 1926–1935*, Roma, Cremonese, 1935, and, in particular, the essay titled "Architettura 'europea,' 'mediterranea,' 'corporativa,' o semplicemente italiana," pp. 139–150. Also see Carlo Belli, "Lettera a Silvia Danesi," in Silvia Danesi and Luciano Patetta (eds.), *Il razionalismo e l'architettura in Italia durante il Fascismo*, Venezia, Biennale di Venezia, 1976, pp. 21–28; Benedetto Gravagnuolo, "Colloquio con Luigi Cosenza," in *Modo* 60, June–July 1983.

[3] Carlo Belli, "Lettera a Silvia Danesi," p. 25.

[4] See Manfredo Tafuri, "Les 'muses inquiétantes' ou le destin d'une génération de 'maîtres'", in *L'architecture d'aujourd'hui*, 181, 1975.

1.1 (*Far left*) Karl Friedrich Schinkel. Farmhouse in Capri, 1804.
Source: © Bildarchiv Preußischer Kulturbesitz/ Art Resource, Inv. SM 5.31. Photo J. P. Anders.

[5] See Fernand Braudel, *La Méditer-ranée et le Monde méditerranéen à l'époque de Philippe II*, Paris, Armand Collin, 1949. In English, *The Mediter-ranean and the Mediterranean World in the Age of Philip II*, London, Fontana/Collins, 1972.
[6] Fernand Braudel, *La Méditerranée, l'espace et l'histoire*, Paris, 1977, p.7 [Editor's translation]. In the chapter "Novecentismo e opzione classica" of his monograph on *José Luis Sert, 1901–1983*, Milano, Electa, 2000, Rovira discusses Braudel's research and book as an attempt to counteract the simplistic and propagandistic mythification of the Mediterranean. He also sees the timing as important, at the moment of the post-World War II political and physical recon-struction.
[7] Massimo Bontempelli, "Realismo magico," in *900*, July 1928; also in Luciano Patetta (ed.), *L'architettura in Italia, 1919–1943. Le polemiche*, Milano, Clup, 1972, p. 90.

signs of a transnational civilization is architecture. Not the cultured or high architecture but rather the vernacular architecture, an expression of constructive, repetitive, and choral techniques sustained by a collective culture of living that settled over the course of centuries.

However, once the legitimacy of the "civilization of the Mediterranean" has been recognized as a subject of historical analysis – particularly in the pioneering work of Fernand Braudel – it remains to be asked whether and up until what point does such a civilization demonstrate unifying features?[5] For it is clear that – despite both the presence of a cradle of communal exchange and the permanence of techniques and forms tied to a *longue durée* – the towns and buildings along the Mediterranean coasts have not only developed in relation to different local specificities but also have incurred in time many transformations that cannot be underestimated. Braudel asked the question:

> What is the Mediterranean? It is one thousand things at the same time. Not one landscape but innumerable landscapes. Not a sea, but a succession of seas. Not a civilization, but civilizations amassed on top of one another. To travel within the Mediterranean is to encounter the Roman world in Lebanon, prehistory in Sardinia, the Greek cities in Sicily, the Arab presence in Spain, Turkish Islam in Yugoslavia. It is to plunge deeply into the centuries, down to the megalithic constructions of Malta or the pyramids of Egypt. It is to meet very old things, still alive, that rub elbows with ultra-modern ones: beside Venice, falsely motionless, the heavy industrial agglomeration of Mestre; beside the boat of the fisherman, which is still that of Ulysses, the dragger devastating the sea-bed, or the huge supertankers. It is at the same time to immerse oneself in the archaism of insular worlds and to marvel in front of the extreme youth of very old cities, open to all the winds of culture and profit, and which, since centuries, watch over and devour the sea.[6]

This plurality of cultures, languages, and ethnicities – woven into tight and complex knots – can then be disentangled in a historical setting. But in the field of design, *mediterraneità* can only be re-proposed – or, at least, it has always been re-proposed that way – through a mytho-poetic transfiguration and an acknowledged invention. Massimo Bontempelli clarified this mechanism in his typical Machiavellian mysticism:

> It is necessary to invent. The ancient Greeks invented beautiful myths and fables that humanity has used for several centuries. Then Christianity invented other myths. Today we are at the threshold of a third epoch of civil humanity. And we must learn the art of inventing new myths and new fables.[7]

The deceit that the Mediterranean myth dispenses is, in fact, the transhistorical representation of the past as present. It insinuates the elegant assumption of the *eternal*, beyond the cyclical mutation of the seasons, beyond the perennial alternating of day and night, and the infinite forms across which time shows itself, almost as if the art of each epoch were measured with a unique theme: the desire for harmony. And it is exactly as *myth*, as a desire for simple and harmonious construction, as a simulacrum of absences of decorum and pure Euclidean volumes, as symbolic expression of the arithmetic canons of "divine proportion," as a shade of Apollonian beauty and as an echo of sirens transmitted on the waves of the sea, that the concept of *mediterraneità* can and must be evaluated beyond its objective verifiability.

In European culture this myth has exercised an extraordinary evocative force on some of the theories of "rational" architecture, beginning with the eighteenth-century rediscovery of the *goût grec*.[8] It is often said that it was the discovery of a statue of Hercules by the Austrian prince d'Elboeuf in the year 1711 at Herculaneum that the enthusiastic re-evaluation of the "noble simplicity and calm greatness" of the classical ancient civilization of the Mediterranean began.[9] Besides, we know that Anton Raphael Mengs, who jokingly passed off a false representation of *Giove e Ganimede* (Jupiter and Ganymede) as a Herculaneum original, was responsible for one of Johann Joachim Winckelmann's most passionate pages on the sublime and sensual beauty of ancient art.[10] Anecdotes aside, it is certain that, from the early 1700s, the best part of Europe turned its historic gaze to the south.

The voyage to Italy became one of the obligatory stops in the cultural formation of young French, English, and German people. Montesquieu went as far south as Naples in 1729.[11] Twenty years later de Vandières arrived and established the rules of the grand tour.[12] They were followed by the architect Soufflot, the future author of the Pantheon of Paris, the draftsman Cochin, and later the abbot of Saint-Non – who would engrave his romantic transfiguration in the *Voyage picturesque* – and many others, including the "sublime marquis" de Sade.[13] Around the Academy of France in Rome, a genuine group of artists gathered – including Louis-Joseph Le Lorrain, Joseph-Marie Vien, and others. They established tight relations with Giovanni Battista Piranesi, whose incisions of the ruins that survived the shipwreck of the classical world were largely known in Parisian intellectual circles.[14] Moreover, it should be remembered that in the formation of that movement of taste, so-called "revolutionary" but codified afterwards in the revisionist Empire style, the thirty-four plates engraved by Piranesi and dedicated to the minute representation of objects of daily life in Pompeii and in Herculaneum played a primary role. The companion volume of *Antiquités d'Ercolanum*, of 1780, richly illustrated with graphic reproductions of antique house furnishings in the style of David, was equally influential.[15]

On the other side of the channel, the same mystic infatuation with the ancient culture of the south was crucial in the formation of the English neoclassical architects: in particular, the brothers Adam, with Robert coming to Italy in 1764, and George Dance the Younger following ten years later.[16] There again, it is above all in the *intérieur* of the private homes that the echo of a faraway nostalgia resonated. One thinks of the house of Sir John Soane, built on Lincoln's Inn Fields in London (1792–1824). It provides exemplary proof of the importation to northern Europe of typological, compositional, and decorative norms of the Latin *domus* – with sunlight raining from above in a vestibule reminiscent of the ancient *impluvium*, the Pompeian frescoes of the dining room, and the great gallery on three floors crowded with heroes, gods, and every sort of marble findings from the great classical ruins.[17]

How can we forget the Neapolitan salon of Sir William Hamilton where Lady Emma, in the presence of illustrious guests from every part of Europe, displayed herself in seductive *tableaux vivants* inspired by the Herculaneum paintings? Wolfgang Goethe was among the many who went there, and with his enthusiastic graphic and verbal descriptions of his voyage to Italy, exported to Germany the Mediterranean cult of Apollonian serenity. In a letter from Rome to his friend Humboldt, Goethe confessed that the desire to contemplate the solar quiet of the Italian countryside had become for him a "malady from which I could recover only with admiration."[18] It is the same "incurable" illness

[8] See Joseph Mordaunt Crook, *The Greek Revival: Neo-classical Attitudes in British Architecture, 1760–1870*, London, J. Murray, 1972; Dora Wiebenson, *Sources of Greek Revival Architecture*, London, A. Zwemmer, 1969.

[9] See *Civiltà del '700 a Napoli, 1734–1799*, Firenze, Centro Di, 1979; Mario Praz, *On Neoclassicism*, London, Thames and Hudson, 1969; Cesare De Seta, *Architettura, ambiente e società a Napoli nel '700*, Torino, Einaudi, 1981; *Pompéi. Travaux et envois des architectes français au XIX siècle*, Paris, Ecole Nationale des Beaux-Arts, 1981; *The Age of Neoclassicism*, London, Arts Council, 1972.

[10] See Johann J. Winckelmann, *Lettere italiane*, Milano, Feltrinelli, 1961, and Cesare De Seta, op. cit.; Peter H. Werner, *Pompeji und die Wanddekoration der Goethezeit*, München, Fink, 1970; Massimiliano Pavan, *Antichità classica e pensiero moderno*, Firenze, La nuova Italia, 1977.

[11] Charles de Montesquieu, *Viaggio in Italia*, Bari, Laterza, 1971. See Cesare De Seta, *L'Italia del Grand Tour da Montaigne a Goethe*, Napoli, Electa, 1992; Andrew Wilton, *The Lure of Italy in the Eighteenth Century*, London, Tate Gallery, 1996.

[12] Daniel Rabreau, "Autour du Voyage d'Italie (1750). Soufflot, Cochin et M. de Marigny réformateurs de l'architecture théâtrale française," in *Bollettino del Centro Internazionale di Studi di Architettura Andrea Palladio*, 17, 1975.

[13] Jean Claude Richard (Abbé) de Saint-Non, *Voyage pittoresque ou Description des royaumes de Naples et de Sicile*, Paris, 1781–86, reprint Napoli, Electa Napoli, 1995.

[14] See J. G. Legrand, *Notice historique sur la vie et les ouvrages de J. B. Piranesi*, Paris, 1799, and Georges Brunel, op. cit.

[15] *Piranesi, Incisioni, rami, legature, architetture*, Venezia, Pozza, 1978; Mario Praz, "Le antichità di Ercolano," in *Civiltà del '700 a Napoli*, op. cit., vol. 1.

[16] See David Irwin, *English Neoclassical Art: Studies in Inspiration and Taste*, London, Faber and Faber, 1966; Robert Rosenblum, *Transformations in Late Eighteenth Century Art*, Princeton, Princeton University Press, 1967; Georges Teyssot, *Città e utopia nell'illuminismo inglese: George Dance il giovane*, Roma, Officina Edizioni, 1974.

[17] See Margaret Richardson and Mary Anne Stevens (eds.), *John Soane Architect – Master of Space and Light*, London, Royal Academy of Arts, 1999; Georges Teyssot, "John Soane et la naissance du style," *Archives d'architecture moderne*, 21, 1981.

[18] See Annalisa Porzio and Marina Causa Picone (eds.), *Goethe e i suoi interlocutori*, Napoli, Macchiaroli, 1983.

[19] See Oswald Zoeggeler, "L'immersione nel passato classico: il viaggio in Italia nella formazione artistica degli architetti tedeschi," in Augusto Romano Burelli (ed.), *Le epifanie di Proteo: la saga nordica del classicismo in Schinkel e Semper*, Fossalta di Piave, Venezia, Rebellato, 1983, pp. 25–44.
[20] On Schinkel's works, see in particular, Paul Ortwin Rave, *Schinkels Lebenswerk*, Berlin, Deutscher Kunstverlag, 1941–62; Nikolaus Pevsner, "Schinkel," in *RIBA Journal* LIX, January 1952; Michael Snodin, *Karl Friedrich Schinkel: An Universal Man*, New Haven, Yale University Press, 1991; Barry Bergdoll, *Karl Friedrich Schinkel: An Architecture for Prussia*, New York, Rizzoli, 1994; Emmanuele Fidone (ed.), *From the Italian Vernacular Villa to Schinkel to the Modern House*, Siracusa, Biblioteca del Cenide, 2003.
[21] See Felice Fanuele, "Il trapianto di un tipo architettonico: il padiglione napoletano di Charlottenburg," in Augusto Romano Burelli, pp. 65–78.
[22] See Gottfried Riemann, "Karl Friedrich Schinkel. La vita e le opere," in Luigi Semerani (ed.), *1781–1841: Schinkel, l'architetto del principe*, Venezia, Albrizzi Editore, 1982, pp. 35–37; Italo Prozzillo, "Schinkel in Italia," in *Civiltà del Mediterraneo*, 1, January–June 1992.

that would compel the painters Koch and Carstens to never abandon Rome and that would lead many young German architects to elect Italy to the promised land of Art.[19]

For Karl Friedrich Schinkel (who made his grand tour from 1803 to 1805 as well as for Gottfried Semper (who arrived thirty years later) the voyage to Italy was above all a voyage into the classical.[20] Yet Schinkel did not limit himself to drawing and reinventing the ruins of Roman magnificence. His gaze also stopped on the anonymous Mediterranean vernacular of the south, investigating its logic and its constructive systems. In 1823, when he received from Friedrich III the task of redesigning an existing pavilion in the royal park of Charlottenburg, he carried out a virtual "transplant" of a Neapolitan architectonic typology, importing into the cold Berlin climate its balconies, louvers, flat roofs, white plaster walls, and overall cubic massing.[21] Even more emblematic of Schinkel's fascination for the simplicity of the minor rural buildings were his drawings of the farmhouses of the Roman countryside or the island of Capri. His sketches showed a minute attention to the constructive details, the relationship with the countryside, and the compositional game of pure Euclidean volumes.[22] It is thus Schinkel who rigorously occasioned the first European re-evaluation of the most ancient, authentic, and elementary Mediterranean culture of vernacular building, distinct in many aspects from the more academic and monumental culture of Roman grandeur (plate 7).

1.2 Karl Friedrich Schinkel. Charlottenburg Pavilion in Berlin, 1824.
Source: Photo Jean-François Lejeune.

However, it is important to clarify that the relation initiated by Schinkel was deeply idealized, imaginative, and mytho-poetic, impregnated by a romantic culture that had already wrapped in its cloak the writings of Goethe, Schiller, or Hölderlin, as well as the timeless landscapes of Caspar David Friedrich. In Schinkel's projects, the classical and Gothic worlds, the solar muses from the Olympian Mediterranean and the lunar fates of the forests of the Nibelungen, as well as the reason of Eupalinos and the soul of Faust, coexist eclectically. It is an evocative architecture, complex, polyphonic, constantly tuned to the sublime, much like the music of Richard Wagner (plate 7).

In contrast, the studies of Gottfried Semper were marked by an analytic detachment and a rigorous and severe historical selectivity. For his generation, Greco-Roman antiquity was no longer an object of ecstasy but rather of philological and scientifically founded research. Semper explored the excavations of Pompeii and the Sicilian valleys to find confirmation for his thesis on the importance of polychrome coverings in the dwellings and temples of Magna Grecia. He put forth his polemic theory in his essay *Vorläufige Bemerkungen über bemalte Architektur und Plastik bei den Alten* (1834) and then in his fundamental text *Der Stil in den technischen und tectonischen Künsten* (1860).[23] In this later volume, Semper developed a "theory for architectonic invention," which moved away from a logical-philosophical standpoint of a positivist nature. The basic principles were the investigation of the evolution of the architectonic typologies (*Typenlehre*), as well as those needs and reasons of use that determine such evolution. From here, he derived the centrality of the problem of "technique," "competence," and "know-how" (*Können*).[24]

In 1896 Joseph Hoffmann returned in Schinkel's and Semper's footsteps, pursuing an itinerary analogous to that completed two years earlier by his friend and teacher, Joseph Maria Olbrich.[25] Two years earlier, Olbrich had sent a letter to his young friend in Vienna, in which he extolled the lessons of the "old ruins." Hoffmann's beautiful watercolor drawing of the Forum of Pompeii (plate 5), which "transfigured" the two columns framing the scene in pure white cylinders on red bases silhouetted against the blue of the sky, is testimony of his emotional voyage into antiquity. However, more than the archeology and the classical monuments – obligatory stops on the grand tour – it is, above all, the anonymous Mediterranean architecture of the islands and the southern coast that attracted, like Schinkel, the attention of the young Viennese architect. Hoffmann did not limit himself to an attentive analysis of the compositional interplay of the pure volumes (which he fixed in around two hundred drawings), but published upon his return a significant piece on the architecture of the island of Capri in the pages of *Der Architekt*.[26] There is one drawing in particular that is symptomatic of the design process that leads from the analysis to the project: it is a sketch of a terraced house in Pozzuoli which has in the lower left corner the rough drawing of a villa of his invention. This "bath in the Mediterranean" – to use Hoffmann's language – may possibly have spawned the process of architectonic simplification that would reach its apex in the pure stereometry of the Purkersdorf Sanatorium in Vienna (1903–08). Conventionally read as "the anticipation of rationalism" this work revealed many features that recall the graphic elaboration of the voyage to Italy. An indirect confirmation of the decisive role played by the *Italienische Reise* in the formation of Hoffmann comes from the brief but dense article that Adolf Loos dedicated to his contemporary on the pages of *Dekorative Kunst* in 1898:

It is difficult for me to write about Josef Hoffmann. I am in stark opposition to that tendency that is represented, not only in Vienna, by the young

[23] Gottfried Semper, *Vorläufige Bemerkungen über bemalte Architektur und Plastik bei den Alten*, Altona, Hammerich, 1834, and *Der Stil in den technischen und tectonischen Künsten*, Frankfurt, 1860. In English translation, Gottfried Semper, *The Four Elements of Architecture and other Writings*, Cambridge, Cambridge University Press, 1988; Harry Francis Mallgrave and Michael Robinson (eds.), *Style in the Technical and Tectonic Arts, or Practical Aesthetics*, Los Angeles, Getty Research Institute, 2004.

[24] See Benedetto Gravagnuolo, "Gottfried Semper, architetto e teorico," in Benedetto Gravagnuolo (ed.), *Architettura Arte e Scienza: Scritti scelti di Gottfried Semper, 1834–1869*, Napoli, Clean, 1987.

[25] See Giovanni Fanelli and Ezio Godoli, *La Vienna di Hoffmann, architetto della qualità*, Roma-Bari, Laterza, 1981, pp. 32ff.; Eduard Sekler, *Joseph Hoffmann. The Architectural Work*, Princeton, Princeton University Press, 1985; Giuliano Gresleri (ed.), *Joseph Hoffmann*, New York, Rizzoli, 1981.

[26] Joseph Hoffmann, "Architektonisches von der Insel Capri," in *Der Architekt* III, 13, 1897.

1.3 *Top*: Josef Hoffmann.
House in Capri,
preliminary drawing for
Der Architekt, 1898.
Bottom: House in
Pozzuoli and sketch for a
villa inspired by it
(*bottom left*).
Source: Eduard Sekler, *Josef
Hoffmann: The Architectural
Work*, Princeton, 1985.

artists. For me tradition is everything; the free work of fantasy comes only second in line. But in this case we are dealing with an artist who, from the space of his exuberant imagination, brought to life ancient traditions.[27]

Loos had already, and polemically, moved away from the free "imagination" so dear to Art Nouveau, in two articles significantly published in July of 1898 in *Ver Sacrum*, the mouthpiece of the Viennese Secession.[28] However, the few elective affinities (unconfessed but unequivocal) that he shared with Hoffmann can be found in their common admiration for the simple and anonymous architecture of the South. Here again, the common source was Schinkel, recognized in the various writings by Loos as his chosen mentor.

Loos completed his first voyage to Italy in January of 1906, traveling to Massa Carrara in search of marble for his Kärntner Bar in Vienna.[29] In 1910, the manifesto-essay *Architektur* made explicit his ties with the territories of classicism:

From the moment that mankind has understood the grandeur of classical antiquity, a sole thought unites the great architects among themselves. They think: like I build, the Ancients would have built as well.[30]

[27] Adolf Loos, "Ein wiener Architekt," in *Dekorative Kunst* 12, 227, September 1898.
[28] Adolf Loos, "Unsere jungen Architekten" and "Die potemkinsche Stadt," in *Ver Sacrum* 7, July 1898.
[29] "Here I am, happy, in Massa Carrara, under a mass of marble of Carrara. Everything is Carrara here. Even the posts to which the vines are attached are from Carrara marble" (from a postcard, dated January 17, 1906, within the Loos-Archiv in the Albertina, Vienna).
[30] In English in Adolf Loos, *Spoken in the Void: Collected Essays, 1897–1900*, Cambridge, The MIT Press, 1982. For more on the theme of *classicità* in the works of Loos, see Benedetto Gravagnuolo, *Adolf Loos*, New York, Rizzoli, 1988.

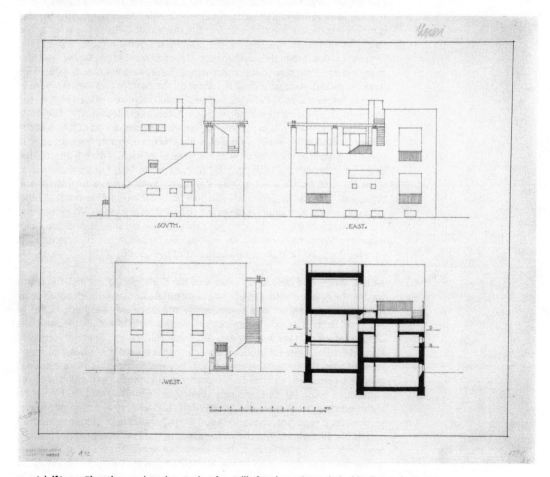

1.4 Adolf Loos. Elevations and section, Project for a Villa for Alexander Moissi, Lido di Venezia, 1923.
Source: © Albertina, Architektur Sammlung, Vienna, ALA 207.

³¹ Among his other trips, Loos's sojourn in Venice in April 1913 along with Karl Kraus and Peter Altenberg was particularly important. A little later, his wife Bessie and the poet Georg Trakl joined him. See Hans Joachim Malberg, *Winderhall des Herzens*, Münich, 1961, p. 116.
³² Cristina Nuzzi (ed.), *Arnold Böcklin e la cultura artistica in Toscana*, Roma, De Luca, 1980.
³³ Sepp Kern, "Adolf von Hildebrand," *Grove Dictionary of Art On Line*, Internet resource.

The same year he returned to Italy, staying in Naples upon his return from the Greek island of Skyros, where he had gone to choose the stone block for the cladding of his Goldman and Salatsch store on the Michaelerplatz in Vienna. Subsequently, his "Italian voyages" became more frequent, until the last one, taken in 1930 as a guest of his student and friend Giuseppe De Finetti.[31]

Beyond the biographical data, the sequel of these experiences can be traced in Loos's projects on the Mediterranean shores: the Villa Verdier at Le Lavandou near Toulon (1923), the nucleus of the "twenty Villas with terraces" on the Côte d'Azur (1923), the Villa Moissi on the Lido of Venice (1923), and the Villa Fleischner in Haifa, Israel (1931). Among these, the work most emblematic of the dialectic tradition versus innovation that distinguishes the entire parabola of Loos's architecture is the unrealized project for the Venetian home of the actor Alexander Moissi. At first sight, the model appears to reveal an almost "vernacular" declination of the Mediterranean culture of building, with its unequivocal open staircase leading to a terrace covered by a pergola placed on simple pilasters with square bases, and around which the rooms of the house rotate, similar to an ancient *impluvium*. Yet, a more detailed examination reveals that the line incisions in the compact white walls precisely follow a sophisticated regulating pattern founded on the "golden rectangle." The design of the façades is in fact not casual: it is the nature of the place that dictates the rules of the game. The light and the sea are the primary elements of composition. The terrace is dislocated in the southeastern corner, in front of the lagoon, in order to take in the rising sun. To the south, where the rays are warmer, the openings have minimal dimensions. They are wider on the eastern and western sides in order to follow the solar cycle until sunset. Small apertures, placed high on the northern side, guarantee a perfect and natural ventilation. But the most suggestive innovation is in the interior, where the complex articulation of the *Raumplan* is illuminated by a radiant light, which penetrates from an oblique aperture placed at the floor level of the terrace-solarium. Like a leitmotiv, the theme of "the terrace with pergola" dominates, in fact, Loos's entire work, from his first building – the Villa Karma on Lake Geneva in Switzerland (1904–06), inspired by Schinkel's villa built for Wilhelm von Humboldt at Tegel (1820–24) in the surroundings of Berlin – to one of his last works, Villa Fleischner on the Israeli coast. For Loos as for Schinkel, the geraniums and the white volumes did not have climatic or regional limits, but rather represented the "modern" epiphany of the eternal present of the classical.

At this stage, and before we enter into the Corbusian labyrinth, it is worth tracing the Ariadnean thread of a line of pictorial elaboration with noteworthy historical importance – one nourished by the so-called "aesthetic circle" of Florence, formed by nineteenth-century German artists and art theoreticians of the stature of Hans von Marées, Adolf von Hildebrand, Theodor Heyse, or Konrad Fiedler.[32] The theoretical connection that bound them was a common reflection on the immutable laws of art, beyond changeable manifestations over the centuries. Central to sculptor von Hildebrand's thinking was the concept of form, which starts from reality but simplifies it. Like Fiedler he assumed that chaos preceded form, which explains his rejection of Impressionism as "apparent chaos."[33] Accordingly, the group demonstrated an ostensible alienation from the movements of the first avant-garde. Instead, they kept an eye on a historical, immobile space that was in ceaseless movement, like the waves of the Mediterranean that Böcklin observed for hours and hours while sitting on a parapet of Castel dell'Ovo in Naples, not to paint but only to understand the laws and the meaning of it.

Architecture was a topos of their collaboration in Italy. In 1873, Hans von Marées was commissioned by the German zoologist Anton Dohrn to decorate the newly established Zoological Station in Naples (plate 8). Marées collaborated on the project with Hildebrand, who designed and painted the trompe l'oeils of the architectural decoration, while Marées himself contributed five large scenes, showing the life of the fishermen in the Bay of Naples, groups of male and female figures in the orange groves of Sorrento, and the self-portrait of the artist with his friends Dohrn and Hildebrand seated beneath a trellis (*Scena di pesca*). Such scenes were intended by Marées to serve as exemplary images of human life conducted in a world of perfect economic, social, and emotional relations. One year later von Hildebrand was able to buy and install his studio and family in the former monastery of San Francesco di Paola near Florence, where von Marées worked as well until 1875. Here, the deceiving song of the sirens, which promises a happy homecoming to a past without crises, still seems to resonate in the rooms. The photos as *tableaux vivants* of the artist's daughters who pose for their father, covered by a few white cloths and some acanthus leaves, against a background of a neoclassical fireplace, recount it to us – even better than the bas-relief of Dionysus, which closes the quiet perspective sequence from the entrance.[34]

In 1883 Max Klinger was commissioned to decorate the Villa Albers in Steglitz-Berlin. There, his admiration for the Impressionists and the work of Arnold Böcklin (whom he met in 1887) is especially clear. On the walls of the villa, he realized his ideas of *Raumkunst*, derived from Pompeian mural art and iconically inspired by Böcklin's mythological scenes. In 1894 Böcklin himself acquired the Villa Bellagio in San Domenico near Fiesole, where he also carried out wall decorations in the Pompeian style. Likewise, when he enrolled, in 1907, at the Akademie der Bildenden Künste in Munich, the young De Chirico (who departed from Greece one year earlier) became fascinated by the uncanny narratives of Klinger's prints, such as *The Glove Cycle* that anticipated Surrealism in its combination of reality and dream, while reflecting the contemporary beginnings of psychoanalysis. De Chirico's early work, however, owed most to the mythological and symbolic paintings of Böcklin.

And so it is that the works of von Hildebrand, von Marées, and Böcklin are tied together by a thin thread of poetic evocation, to those following shortly by Max Klinger. And with the last rings of this visual chain – Giorgio de Chirico and Alberto Savinio – we reach our time.

Magical Realisms

In the Italian and French cultures of the 1930s – or rather in a small refined and elite part of it – we discover again, distilled and mixed together, suggestions of both a pictorial thread and an architectonic seam to the Mediterranean. Directed by Jolanda and Mario Pelegatti from 1933 to 1936 and from 1939 to 1943, the *Rivista bimestrale d'arte, letteratura e musica* was specifically dedicated to "Mediterranean Art," as were numerous pages of the magazine *Colonna*, directed and published in Milan by Alberto Savinio in 1933–34.[35] Likewise, among others, Gio Ponti wrote many articles, including a pamphlet of 1941 titled "Architettura mediterranea."[36] The seeds of this Mediterranean flowering had been sown in the first years of the 1920s by the magazine *Valori Plastici*. Thanks to the mediation of its main instigator and extraordinary ambassador of Italian art to Paris, Gino Severini, the magazine, from the very first issue, featured interventions of Jean Cocteau, Paul Dermée, André Breton, and Louis Aragon, in addition to an essay by Carlo Carrà on Pablo Picasso.[37]

[34] See Christian Lenz, "Hans von Marées," Elizabeth Clegg, "Arnold Böcklin," *Grove Dictionary of Art On Line*, Internet resource. Christiane Groeber, *The Naples Zoological Station at the Time of Anton Dohrn*, Naples, The Station, 1975.
[35] The *Rivista bimestrale* was published under a new cover between 1939 and 1943. Only five issues of the periodical *Colonna, Periodico di civiltà italiana* were published between 1933 and 1934. The main collaborators were Carlo Carrà, Libero De Libero, Gino Levi Montalcini, Leonardo Sinisgalli, and others. In issue no. 1 of 1934, one can find a reproduction of the Pompeian painting *Ulysses and Penelope*, with a significant declaration of "affinità" by Alberto Savinio, painter and writer of great talent, and brother of Giorgio de Chirico.
[36] Giò Ponti, "Architettura mediterranea." *Stile* 7, July 1941, p. 1.
[37] *Valori Plastici: Rassegna d'arte* was one of the most influential periodicals of the early 1920s. It was published monthly from 1918 to 1922. Collaborators included Theo van Doesburg, Giorgio de Chirico, Filippo De Pisis, Alberto Savinio, Ardengo Soffici, and others. See the catalogue of the XIII Quadriennale di Roma, *Valori Plastici*, Roma, Skira, 1999. Among the many bonds that linked the Spanish artist and his oeuvre to the historical culture of the *mare nostrum*, the visit which Picasso made, with Sergej Djaghilev, to Naples and Pompeii is said to have arguably played a significant role in the pictorial rethinking that led him to a return to classical figuration. See *Picasso e il Mediterraneo*, Roma, Villa Medici, 1983.

1.5 Giorgio de Chirico.
Mythologie, 1934.
These two drawings
are part of a series
of ten lithographs
accompanied by a text
of Jean Cocteau.
Source: Giorgio de Chirico
and Jean Cocteau, *Mythologie*,
1934, Paris, Editions des
Quatre Chemins, author's
collection.

In his own way, Gino Severini made himself the interpreter of the new course with the pamphlet *Du Cubisme au Classicisme*, published by Povolozky in Paris in 1921.[38] Here is not the place to analyze the theoretical themes generated from this important text. Its words cross in Pindaric flight the blue skies of aspiration to harmony, skipping the conventional rails of chronology without ever hiding the sources. On the contrary, the author enumerates them with infantile enthusiasm for discovery – from Plato to Leon Battista Alberti, Luca Pacioli, Leonardo da Vinci and Albrecht Dürer to Jules-Henry Poincaré and Henri-Louis Bergson. It is also important to remember that those reflections on the "aesthetics of the number and of the compass" were translated into pictorial forms in Severini's *Affreschi con maschere*, a cycle of frescoes realized in 1921–22 for Sir George Sitwell in the medieval castle of Montegufoni near Florence. Painted in accordance with mathematical calculations of harmonic rapports, these scenes from the *Commedia dell'arte* – "between the human and the abstract, between the real thing and the invented one" – transformed those simple rooms into *camere sonore* (sound chambers) – to use Savinio's words.[39]

[38] Gino Severini, *Du Cubisme au Classicisme*, Paris, 1921, republished in Piero Pacini (ed.), *Gino Severini: Dal cubismo al classicismo e altri saggi sulla divina proporzione e sul numero d'oro*, Firenze, Marchi and Bertolli, 1972.
[39] Alberto Savinio, *Scatola Sonora*, Torino, Einaudi, 1977. See also Carlo Cresti, "Geometria per Montegufoni," in Renato Barilli (ed.), *Gino Severini*, Firenze, Electa Firenze, 1983.
[40] Gino Severini, *Tutta la vita di un pittore*, Milano, Garzanti, 1983, p. 278.

In any case it is undeniable that Severini's little volume exercised a major influence on the Parisian intellectual culture of the time and, in particular, on Amédée Ozenfant and Le Corbusier. As Severini himself recalled, an initial encounter with the "Dioscuri of Purism" took place in 1921 through the mediation of their mutual friend, Paul Dermée:

> We talked a lot about the relationships of harmony, geometry, and mathematics applied in general to the arts. And hearing that I had given a book to Povlozky on this subject, they seemed afflicted. They wanted me to take it back to publish it in *L'Esprit nouveau*, but I refused absolutely.[40]

A relationship of reciprocal esteem – which gave way to the collaboration of the Tuscan artist in the pages of *L'Esprit nouveau* – degenerated later into open confrontation. Le Corbusier and Ozenfant accused Severini of surrendering to a "damaging mystical spirit" and of having excessive faith "in the ecstasy of virtues of the golden section."[41] Paradoxically, from that moment on, the same magazine dedicated much attention to the *tracés régulateurs* and the arithmetic canons of harmony – whether in painting or in architecture. Severini had anticipated the thematic that Matila C. Ghyka stirred up later in his *Esthétique des proportions dans la nature et dans les arts* (1927) and then in the more fortunate volume *Le nombre d'or* (1931), introduced by Paul Valéry. Of particular interest is the third chapter of *Le nombre d'or*, titled "Le canon géométrique dans l'art méditerranéen."[42] It is also noteworthy that Ghyka did not mention Severini's volume in the ample bibliography, which stretched from ancient time to the modern age. Neither does he name it in the generous acknowledgments that range from *Eupalinos ou l'Architecte* and *L'Âme et la Danse* by Valéry to *Vers une architecture* by Le Corbusier.[43]

In its turn, Valéry's language was a beacon of orientation for the dangerous course of thought across the Mediterranean. From his early essay *Introduction à la méthode de Léonard de Vinci* (1894), Valéry discovered an esoteric fascination with mathematics that would lead him to submit the irrational to the metric and phonetic rules of the "difficult poetic game."[44] Then came the masterpieces *La jeune Parque* (1917), *Album de vers anciens* (1920), and

[41] On this theme, read the correspondence between Ozenfant, Le Corbusier, and Severini, conserved in the Severini Archives and published in *L'Esprit Nouveau* 17, 1922.
[42] M. C. Ghyka, *Esthétique des proportions dans la nature et dans les arts*, Paris, Gallimard, 1927, and *Le nombre d'or; rites et rythmes pythagoriciens dans le développement de la civilisation occidentale*, Paris, Gallimard, 1931.
[43] See Paul Valéry, *Eupalinos ou l'Architecte*, Paris, Gallimard, 1921, and idem *L'Âme et la Danse*, Paris, Gallimard, 1921. In English, *Eupalinos or the Architect*, London, Oxford University Press, 1932.
[44] Paul Valéry, *Introduction to the Method of Leonardo da Vinci*, London, Rodker, 1929.

1.6 *Left*: Matila C. Ghyka. Pythagorean intervals. *Right*: Le Corbusier. Regulating lines of Villa Garches, 1927.
Source: Matila C. Ghyka, *Le nombre d'or; rites et rythmes pythagoriciens dans le développement de la civilisation occidentale*, Paris, 1931.

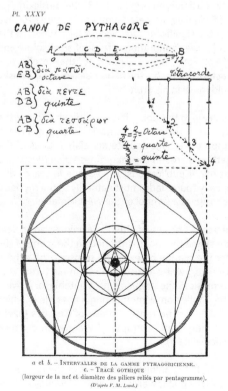

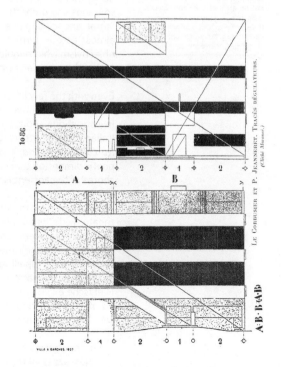

45 Paul Valéry, *Cahiers: Notebooks*, vol. 2, Brian Stimpson (ed.), New York, P. Lang, 2000.
46 Walter Benjamin, *Schriften*, Frankfurt, Suhrkamp Verlag, 1955. Italian translation, "Avanguardia e rivoluzione", Torino, 1973, p. 45.
47 Ibid. Italian translation, "Avanguardia e rivoluzione", Torino, 1973, p. 42.
48 See "Erik Satie," in *Enciclopedia della musica*, Milano, Rizzoli Ricordi, 1974, p. 510.
49 Alberto Savinio, *Nuova Enciclopedia*, Milano, Adelphi, 1977, p. 375.
50 Fausto Melotti, *Sculture astratte*, Milano, All'insegna del pesce d'oro, 1967.
51 Massimo Bontempelli, *Introduzione e discorsi*, p. 171.
52 Giorgio de Chirico, "Estetica metafisica," in *Valori Plastici*, April–May 1919; also in Massimo Carrà, *Metafisica*, Milano, Mazzotta, 1968, p. 150. English translation, *Metaphysical Art*, New York, Praeger, 1971.
53 See Cesare De Seta, *La cultura architettonica in Italia tra le due guerre*, Bari, Laterza, 1972, and *L'architettura del Novecento*, Torino, UTET, 1981; Giorgio Ciucci, "Il dibattito sull'architettura e la città fasciste," in *Storia dell'arte italiano: Il Novecento*, Torino, 1982; Richard Etlin, *Modernism in Italian Architecture, 1890–1940*, Cambridge, The MIT Press, 1991.
54 See Luigi Ferrario, D. Pastore, and Stefano Casciani (eds.), *Giuseppe Terragni. La Casa del Fascio*, Roma, Istituto MIDES, 1982, pp. 68ff.; Vittorio Savi (ed.), *Luigi Figini e Gino Pollini: architetti*, Milano, Electa, 1980, p. 12.
55 Carlo Belli, "Dopo la polemica," *Quadrante* 3, no. 35, October 1936; Luigi Figini, "Novocomum," *Natura* 1, 1930.

Le Cimetière marin (1922). "Art" – wrote Valéry – "is a language that has music on one side and algebra on the other."[45] Walter Benjamin echoed him when he affirmed, in his splendid essay dedicated to the French poet:

> The sea and mathematics: they appear in one of the most beautiful things that [Valéry] wrote, in the episode of Socrates who tells Fedro what he found on the seashore, with a chain of fascinating ideas. It is an uncertain object – ivory or marble or even a bone of an animal – that the surf tossed on the shore and that appears almost as a head with the features of Apollo. And Socrates wonders if it is a work of the waves or of the artist. He reflects, 'How much time does the ocean need before among millions of forms chance will produce another like this, how much time would the artist need?' And he can well say that an artist is worth a thousand centuries or one hundred thousand or even many more than that. This becomes a particular criterion for gauging works of art.[46]

And Benjamin continued:

> If we wanted to surprise the author of this grandiose work, *Eupalinos, or the Architect*, for his sixtieth birthday, giving him as a gift an *ex libris*, it would represent a potent compass with one leg planted at the bottom of the ocean and the other stretched far on the horizon.[47]

It is not – it cannot be – happenstance that at the threshold of the 1920s different minds met in a common reflection on the meaning of "order," in the search for "rules," and on the magic of the "number." There is a kind of historical determination in this return to the "soul," to the eurythmics of an Apollonian dance after the inebriation of the Dionysian orgy. In 1918, the musician Erik Satie, friend of Picasso and of Djaghilev, wrote a "symphonic drama for five sopranos and orchestra" – with the significant title, *Socrates* – attuned to the "total renunciation of every subjective connotation in favor of an absolute and almost ascetic formal rigor." For Satie, it was a mark of "that intellectual objectivism which would characterize, later on, the neoclassicism of Stravinsky and of the musicians who would move in his orbit."[48]

Even with the few allusions made up to this point, it is not difficult to intuit the substantial "elective affinity" and reciprocal osmosis between French investigations and the contemporary artistic and literary elaborations of the Italian circle of intellectuals gathered around the magazines *Valori Plastici, La Raccolta, La Ronda*, and other minor publications. The voyage in search of a poetic dimension that is chemically "pure" led almost naturally to the mythical shores of the ancient Hellas, chosen as a symbol of the West's infancy.

"All of Greece is in the shape of a shell," observed Alberto Savinio. As an ancient theater with "its back to the West and the mouth introducing the scene of the East," Greece seems to gather the marine breezes and transmit the echo.[49] "We believe in the order of Greece," writes Fausto Melotti in his turn.[50] And Massimo Bontempelli suggests music as the language most suitable for arriving at the absolute harmony of the Apollonian, remembering a passage in which Nietzsche exalts the solar and the "Mediterranean" music of Georges Bizet's *Carmen*, contrasting it to the "undone and corrupting" Wagnerian drama.[51] De Chirico wrote in *Valori Plastici* (plate 9):

> In the construction of the city, in the architectural forms of the houses, of the piazzas, of the gardens, of the public walkways, of the doorways, of the

train stations, etc. . . . are the primary fundamentals of a great metaphysical aesthetic. The Greeks had a certain scruple in such constructions, guided by their aesthetic-philosophic sense: the porticoes, the shaded promenades, the terraces were built like stages in front of the great spectacles of nature.[52]

In the 1930s the studies of the golden section, the "cubic laws," and other neo-Pythagorean canons on proportionality became the latent *trait d'union* between the Italian pictorial and architectonic experiments. A kind of "mystic halo" seems to wrap in a single cloak the abstract *archipitture* of Licini, the "musical" sculptures of Melotti, the "magical realism" of Carrà, the melancholic Italian piazzas of De Chirico, and the "rational" constructions of Terragni, Figini, Pollini, Sartoris, Banfi, Belgioioso, Peressutti, Rogers, Albini, Libera, Bottoni, Cosenza, Pagano, and Nizzoli.[53]

Let us start with two "supreme" examples of this relation: the Mediterranean aura that insinuates itself in the harmonic lines regulating the perforations of the four walls of Terragni's Casa del Fascio, and the unsurpassed, abstract game of geometrical planes, levels, floors, and bundles of sunlight in the patio of Figini and Pollini's villa-studio for an artist (plate 16, figure 2.1).[54] In that spirit, Carlo Belli regarded the Casa del Fascio (1932–36) as the extreme point of arrival of the rational attitude, derived from "Greece, Mediterranean, Magna Grecia," while Luigi Figini extolled the "Mediterranean", "solar," and "serene" character of an earlier work by Terragni in Como: the *Novocomum* of 1927–29.[55] In relation to their own villa-studio for an artist at the V Triennale of Milan of 1933, Figini and Pollini spoke unequivocally of the patio as a "Pompeian impluvium."[56] Likewise, in the descriptive summary of the project, one reads that rhythm is determined by constant intervals – that is by the numbers.[57]

In fact, it should be remembered that, in the Italian architectonic debate of the interwar period, the theme of *mediterraneità* was developed with explicit theoretical awareness. Following the seminal text of *Presentazione* at the second Exposition of the MIAR (Movimento Italiano per l'Architettura Razionale, 1931), the rationalist architects elected the "Mediterranean tendency" as a Trojan horse for the victory of modernity against the tinsel of equivocal historicist academic culture.[58] As it is noted, Carlo Enrico Rava, who in the first years had represented in a certain sense the theoretical soul of Gruppo 7, did not participate in this Second Exposition. But the divergences of opinion did not regard the concept of *mediterraneità* of which, on the contrary, Rava was the most obstinate observer.[59] Already in an essay of 1927, he had defended rational Italian architecture from the "accusation of imitation of foreigners," underscoring how "the natural propensity towards a balance of planes and towards the relaxed symmetry of volumes, a quality of our race . . . profoundly distinguishes us from other nations."[60] This very same essay argued for a return to the "complete relaxation of forms" and to the "happy creation, that is the heritage completely classical and ours," in polemic contrast with various attempts to elect copies of Roman architecture as expressions of the "spirit of Imperial Italy."[61]

The calls for the "Hellenic spirit" assumed, moreover, a desire for simplicity, harmony, and an equilibrium of Euclidean, archaic, and primordial volumes. In short, there was no lack in these assertions of chauvinistic motives, but these were not to be confused with the historicism of the Italian academic architects. One could argue that these positions were nothing but subtle differences within a common conservative culture, but on these differences played a battle of language that often assumed the violent tones of an ideological conflict,

[56] Interestingly, the first reference to Le Corbusier in Italy was made by Marcello Piacentini in "Notiziario di arte moderna," *Architettura e Arti decorative* 2, 1921. Yet, it was the architects of the Il Gruppo 7 (founded in Milan in October 1926) who literally exalted the Swiss maestro as "one of the most remarkable initiators of a rational architecture": in English translation, Il Gruppo 7, "Architecture"; "Architecture (II): The Foreigners" in *Oppositions* 6, September 1976, 89–102. On the relationship with Le Corbusier, see the entry "Italie," in *Le Corbusier: une encyclopédie*, Paris, Centre Georges Pompidou, 1987, pp. 206–209. Also see Michelangelo Sabatino's essay in this book.
[57] Luigi Figini and Giorgio Pollini, "Villa-studio per un artista," *Catalogo della V Triennale di Milano*, Milano, 1933, also in Vittorio Savi, p. 12.
[58] The MIAR (Movimento Italiano per l'Architettura Razionale) was founded in 1928. See Michele Cennamo (ed.), *Materiali per l'analisi dell'architettura moderna, il MIAR*, Napoli, Società editrice napoletana, 1977. The first exhibition was held in Rome in April 1928, with the support of the Sindacato Nazionale Fascista Architetti. The second exhibition took place in the gallery of Pietro Maria Bardi in Via Veneto. It had a stronger polemical character, with a direct attack to the architecture of Armando Brasini, Gustavo Giovannoni, and Piacentini expressed in the famous photomontage "Tavolo degli orrori". In the *Presentazione* to the second exhibition: "It is overall correct to recognize that this character of '*latinità*' – which had allowed this architecture to be defined as Mediterranean – is becoming more and more accentuated": see *Casabella* 40, April 1931.
[59] See Carlo Enrico Rava, *Nove anni di architettura vissuta*, op. cit.
[60] Carlo Enrico Rava, "Dell'europeismo in Architettura," in *Rassegna Italiana*, December 1927, also in Luciano Patetta, *L'architettura in Italia*, p. 146.
[61] Ibid., pp. 147–148.

[62] Carlo Enrico Rava, "Premessa" in *Nove anni di architettura vissuta*, p. 7.
[63] Giorgio Ciucci, "Il dibattito sull'architettura e le città fasciste", p. 328.
[64] See Brian McLaren, *Architecture and Tourism in Italian Colonial Libya: An Ambivalent Modernism*, Seattle, University of Washington Press, 2006.
[65] "Un programma di Architettura," *Quadrante* 1, May 1933, also in Luciano Patetta, pp. 227–229. *Quadrante* was a monthly periodical directed by Massimo Bontempelli and Pietro Maria Bardi. Published from 1933 to 1936, it also saw the collaboration of Carrà, Giedion, Gropius, Léger, Le Corbusier, Lurçat, Mussolini, Melotti, Nervi, Pound, Sartoris, Severini, Terragni, and others.
[66] Alberto Sartoris, "Avvenire del funzionalismo," in *Quadrante* 1, May 1933.

and at times was more than verbal. According to his own declarations, the reasons that led Rava to dissociate himself from the Gruppo 7 and to adhere – along with his friend Sebastiano Larco – to RAMI (*Raggrupamento Architetti Moderni Italiani)*, founded by the Sindacato degli Architteti in 1931) are to be sought in the critique leveled at the errors and the dangers of a rationalism too often reduced to a sterile dogma.[62]

The divisiveness of this critique is obvious. Beyond verbal enunciations, it is Rava's own architectonic production that demonstrates how his poetic, originally based on an intransigent purism, evolved towards the "search for a modern colonial setting," elaborated on "an anti-Novecento base of Mediterranean rationalism and therefore essentially Italic." Interesting examples of this position can be seen in Rava's projects for the Church at Suani Ben-Adem (1930), Tripoli's Arch of Triumph (1931), or the Pavilion of Eritrea and Somalia (1933–34), all done in collaboration with Sebastiano Larco. These projects not only prefigured the "colonial architecture" exported from Italy into the North African countries and some Greek islands like Rhodes, but also represented – as Giorgio Ciucci recalls – an original architectonic research on the theme of *mediterraneità*.[63] This experiment became even more evident in the construction of the hotel at the archeological site of Leptis Magna near Tripoli (1933) and in the hotel in Mogadishu (1935).[64]

Clearly, the Mediterranean theme was not the exclusive perquisite of this or that architecture, but rather the object of a collective reflection on the part of the rationalist movement. The "Programma di Architettura," published in the first issue of the magazine *Quadrante* of May 1933, articulated the following sixth theorem:

> Clarification of the characteristics of the Italian rationalist tendency. Affirmation of classicism and of Mediterranean-ness – understood in the spirit and not in the forms and in the folklore – in contrast with Nordism, with Baroque-ism, or with the romantic arbitrariness of a part of the new European architecture.[65]

Among the signatories we read the names of Bottoni, Figini, Pollini, Lingeri, the members of the BBPR group, and others. In the same issue of *Quadrante*, the Hellenic spirit was re-evoked by Alberto Sartoris in his essay "Avvenire del funzionialismo," in which he maintained that:

> The Greeks employed in their architectonic and plastic modulations, based on the movement and on the stasis of dynamic rectangles, geometrical markings rigorously exact and in some sense identical to those that inform the compositions of the rationalist Europeans and the characteristic proportions revealed by the framework of their works. [...] These postulates on the new architecture also derive from antique notions that had, particularly in Mediterranean art, an imprint of imperative origin. These organic structures show up in the famous *golden number*, which was indispensable at that time for anyone wanting to create and establish in the work plastic forms that were consonant with the sensibility and spirit of the period. This kind of harmonious growth in space and dynamic succession in time have been transmitted down to us and today, more than ever, modernist architects have been won over by a plastic beauty, that cannot be a mirage, but is perhaps the eternal possibility of developing a work of art into absolute perfection, into a higher serenity, into something never thought of.[66]

Concordant to these considerations, Alberto Sartoris, who had in 1925 re-evoked antiquity with his Theater Gualino in Turin, proposed in the pages of *La Casa Bella* his intent to pursue "beauty and solemnity" and – this should not be a surprise – classical art in his project for a house/studio for the painter Jean-Saladin van Berchen in Paris. He elaborated on this aim in the second version of the house for the winegrower Morand Pasteur in Saillon in Switzerland (1933), played out on the ample terraces and with evident neo-Hellenic, rational purism.[67]

In the Footsteps of Janus: Le Corbusier's Mediterranean Odyssey

Le Corbusier's *Oeuvre complète* is a genuine encyclopedia – an *Encyclopédie*.[68] The scholarly angle of approach of the – often – contradictory adventure of his ideas is thus significant and determinant. As a result, it is not surprising that the theme of his relationship with the antique has been for a long time the most neglected. Not that Le Corbusier was ever parsimonious of explicit declarations. But the evidence was fogged for too long by the smokescreen of the banalizing interpretations of the modernist vulgate, raised to hide any interpretative attempt that would put into doubt the absolute coherence of his "progressive" way of thinking. Few understood the profound value and the inescapable complexity of a double-sided protective mask, a mask divided between the joyful crown of the solar rays and the dolorous spiral of the serpents, between Cartesian order and chaotic emotionality, between the faith in industrial progress and the melancholy in front of the collapse of the archaic civilizations, between Apollo and Dionysus, between the Moderns and the Ancients.[69]

"From now on, I will speak only with the Ancients; the Ancients respond to those who know how to question them" – the young Charles-Edouard Jeanneret wrote emphatically to Charles L'Eplattenier in a letter of 1908.[70] The voyage to Italy, initiated between September and October of the preceding year along an itinerary established with his master at the Ecole d'Art de la Chaux-de-Fonds,

[67] See *La Casa Bella* 3, October 1930, pp. 78–80. On the works of Alberto Sartoris, see Jacques Gubler (ed.), *Alberto Sartoris*, Lausanne, Ecole polytechnique d'architecture, 1978; Alberto Cuomo, *Alberto Sartoris, L'architettura italiana tra tragedia e forma*, Roma, Edizioni Kappa, 1978; Alberto Sartoris, *Progetti e assonometrie di Alberto Sartoris*, Roma, Officina, 1982. On the Casa Morand-Pasteur, see *Alberto Sartoris – La Casa Morand-Pasteur*, Roma, Veutro, 1983, with an essay by Sartoris titled "Architettura rurale moderna."
[68] Jacques Lucan (ed.), *Le Corbusier: une Encyclopédie*, Paris, Editions du Centre Pompidou, 1987. This section of the essay recapitulates the theme of my introduction to Benedetto Gravagnuolo (ed.), *Le Corbusier e l'Antico. Viaggi nel Mediterraneo*, Napoli, Electa Napoli, 1997. Also see Giuliano Gresleri's contribution to the above mentioned *Encyclopédie*, "Antiquité," pp. 40–45.
[69] The famous drawing of the solar mask dates from 1948.
[70] Charles Edouard Jeanneret, "Letter à L'Eplattenier," Vienna, 1908, Fonds Le Corbusier of the Library of La Chaux-de-Fonds. All translations by editor unless otherwise noted.

1.7 Le Corbusier. A Stamboul street scene, "tier upon tier of endless wooden houses submerged in greenery," 1911.
Source: © 2009 Artists Rights Society (ARS), New York/ADAGP, Paris/FLC.

71 The voyage in Italy was part of the canonic tradition of the Ecole d'Art de La Chaux-de-Fonds. See Giuliano Gresleri, *Le Corbusier. Il viaggio in Toscana. 1907*, Venezia, Marsilio, 1987. Also see Harold Allen Brooks, *Le Corbusier's Formative Years: Charles-Edouard Jeanneret at La Cahux-de-Fonds*, Chicago, University of Chicago Press, 1997; Paul V. Turner, "The Beginnings of Le Corbusier Education 1902–1907," in *The Art Bulletin* 2, 1971; and Stanislaus von Moos and Arthur Rüegg, *Le Corbusier Before Le Corbusier: Applied Arts-Architecture-Painting-Photography-1907/1922*, New Haven, Yale University Press, 2002.

72 The French version of John Ruskin's *Morning in Florence* (*Les matins en Florence*) and the *Voyage d'Italie* by Hippolyte Taine were the two "bed" books that Jeanneret packed with him to follow his Tuscan itineraries. See *Le Corbusier. Il viaggio in Toscana*, op. cit.

73 The first edition of *Le voyage d'Orient*, Paris, Edition Forces, 1966, was prepared by Jean Petit. See the edition overseen by Giuliano Gresleri, *Voyage d'Orient: Carnets/Jeanneret Le Corbusier*, Milano, Electa, 1987. In English, see Giuliano Gresleri (ed.), *Les voyages d'Allemagne [Voyage d'Orient]: Carnets/Jeanneret Le Corbusier*, New York, Monacelli Press, 1995 and Ivan Zaknic (ed.), *Journey to the East*, Cambridge, The MIT Press, 2007.

74 Le Corbusier, "Confession," in *The Decorative Art of Today*, Cambridge, The MIT Press, 1987, pp. 206–207; in French, *L'Art Décoratif d'Aujourd'hui*, Paris, Editions Cres, 1925, pp. 210–211.

75 On the tradition of the voyage to Italy, see Cesare de Seta, *L'Italia del Grand Tour, da Montaigne a Goethe*.

76 The itinerary along the visited houses can be followed with the pencil annotations he made in the Baedeker volume *L'Italie des Alpes à Naples*, Paris, 1909.

77 On that theme, see *Pompéi. Travaux et envois des architectes français au XIXème siècle*, Paris-Rome, Ecole nationale supérieure des Beaux Arts/Ecole française de Rome, 1981.

78 See the pencil and watercolor drawing on hard paper, dated and signed *Pompéi 1911*, Charles Edouard Jeanneret in the Fondation Le Corbusier (no.2859; folder *Language des pierres*, XII), also reprinted in *L'Esprit Nouveau*, no.15. A similar drawing can be found in the Carnet no. 4 of *Carnets de Voyage d'Orient*.

79 See Antoine Chrysostone Quatremère de Quincy, *Le Jupiter Olympien: ou l'Art de la Sculpture antique considéré sous un nouveau point de vue*, Paris, Editions De Bure Frère, 1815. In English, see *Essai sur la nature, le but et les moyens de l'imitation dans les beaux arts*, New York, Garland, 1979; Samir Younès (ed.), *The True, The Fictive and the Real: The Historical Dictionary of Architecture of Quatremère de Quincy*,

represented in his formation something far beyond the ritual "petit-grand tour."[71] The attentive visit of the antique monuments, pushed as far as the tactile observation of the grain and color of the materials in the light of their natural setting, produced the effect of a cleansing bath that was to purify him from the late romantic scoria of Ruskin's teaching, even if the master continued to guide his footsteps along the "matins de Florence."[72]

Even more determinant was the following *Voyage d'Orient*, launched from Berlin in May 1911 and that was to lead him to Naples in October of the same year after having visited the Balkans, Turkey, and Greece.[73]

> I embarked on a great journey, which was to be decisive, through the countryside and cities of countries still considered unspoilt. From Prague I went down the Danube, I saw the Serbian Balkans, then Rumania, then the Bulgarian Balkans, Adrianople, the Sea of Marmara, Istanbul (and Byzantium), Bursa in Asia.
> Then Athos.
> Then Greece.
> Then the south of Italy and Pompeii.
> Rome.
> I saw the grand and eternal monuments, glories of the human spirit.
> Above all, I succumbed to the irresistible attraction of the Mediterranean. And it was high time, after ten years' work (published in all the reviews) on German decorative art and architecture.
> The Turkey of Adrianople, Byzantium, of Santa Sophia or Salonica, the Persia of Bursa, the Parthenon, Pompeii, then the Coliseum. Architecture was revealed to me.
> Architecture is the magnificent play of forms under the light.[74]

According to the letter of this autobiographical confession, the ruins, the only survivors of the wreckage of classical antiquity, played a decisive role in his fulgurating intuition of the "*jeu magnifique.*" The scientific rigor of the nineteenth-century travelers gave way to an unequivocally emotional approach to archeology, quite distant from the romantic contemplation and esthetic of the ruins.[75] In Pompeii, the young Le Corbusier recorded in his *carnet* the variations in the composition and organization of the Italian *domus*.[76] His quick but incisive sketches reveal his fascination for the gardens and the pergolas, but also his attempt at confronting, in his own way, the technique of the *restauration*, which had characterized the *envois de Rome* at Villa Medici.[77] In this spirit, one of the most fascinating examples is the idealized completion of the colonnade of the Temple of Jupiter in Pompeii, which frames, from the elevated terrace of the temple, the urban scenario of the Forum and, in the background, the green silhouette of the Mount Lattari rhythmically cadenced by the intercolumniation (plate 10).[78] The ultimate end of such mental games was no longer an archeological dispute about polychromy or the philological precision of the *anastylosis*, but the discovery of the "eternal laws" of architecture.[79] Le Corbusier wrote in *Vers une architecture*:

> One must go and see Pompeii, which is moving in its rectitude . . . Outside of Rome, where there was air, they built Hadrian's Villa. There you meditate on Roman grandeur. There they imposed order. It is the first grand ordonnance of the West . . . But careful, architecture is not just ordonnance. Ordonnance is one of the fundamental prerogatives of architecture. To walk about Hadrian's Villa and say to oneself that the

modern power of organization that is "Roman" has yet to do anything: what a torment for a man who feels himself party and accomplice to this confounding mess!

[. . .] Strength of intention and classification of elements, that is proof of a turn of mind: strategy, legislation. The architecture is responsive to these intentions, *it renders*. The light caresses the pure forms: *it renders*.[80]

In the footsteps of Janus, the Mediterranean god with two faces, Le Corbusier constantly kept the dialectical relationship between the antique and the modern, between the echo of an ancestral harmony that derives from the remote classical past and the will to understand and to dominate the new force of the industrial universe. Paradoxically, Le Corbusier never ceased to repeat that it was the very anti-academic "re-reading" of the antique that revealed to him the foundational principles of modernity.

Furthermore, it would be easy to retrace the network of fine threads that linked the observation upon the ruins to the very conception of his projects. It is enough to think about the pergolas of the Casa Sallustio, photographed and drawn in October 1911 in Pompeii, then re-proposed (the year after), almost faithfully – as Gresleri noted – in the garden of the Jeanneret House in La Chaux-de-Fonds.[81] Equally convincing is the analogy – signaled by Kurt Forster – between the composition of the Maison La Roche Jeanneret and the sketches for the *Casa del Poeta Tragica*, also in Pompeii.[82] It is in the same way that the memory of the white volumes of rural architecture would return in the projects of the "purist" phase of the 1920s, giving even more credence to the individuation of a genealogical ascendancy of an esthetic abstracted from the "Mediterranean myth." Yet, what matters most is the *visual* legacy of the travels, which remained engraved in the deepest of his memory and kept resurfacing, as a karstic river, throughout the entire adventure of his ideas.[83]

Likewise, one must start from Le Corbusier's expressed doubts, from his disquieting interrogation about what we call "progress," to understand the authentic meaning of his "modernity" and the challenge launched by a David against the gigantic forces of the machinist civilization in order to submit them to a cultural project. In 1911 he wrote in Pompeii:

> Why is our progress so ugly?
> Why is it that those who still have a virgin blood like to take the worst from us? Does one have taste in art? Isn't it dry Theory than to do more of it? Will one ever do Harmony again? [. . .] We have sanctuaries left to go and cry and doubt forever. There, one knows nothing of today, one lives in the old days; there the tragic comes close to exultant joy; one is completely shaken because the isolation is complete . . . It is on the Acropolis, on the steps of the Parthenon, it is in Pompeii, along its streets.[84]

His passion for the archaic civilizations never fell into a regressive nostalgia, or, worse, into the mimesis of the past that often ends in parody. Even more interesting was the conceptual distance that separated the "modern" vision of Le Corbusier from the visceral "anti-past" attitude of the most radical avant-garde. From the same Venice that Marinetti had earlier described, without periphrasis, as the "*cloaca massima del passatismo*" (great sewer of traditionalism), Le Corbusier extracted in the summer of 1923 an extraordinary lesson on the "visible," or, as Stanislaus von Moos demonstrated, on the relationship between the perception of the architectural form and the hourly variation of the solar intensity.[85]

London, A. Papadakis, 1999. Also see Jacques-Ignace Hittorff, *L'architecture polychrome chez les Grecs*, Paris, 1830; 1815 first edition.
[80] Le Corbusier, *Toward an Architecture*, Los Angeles, Getty Research Institute, 2007, pp. 198–200. Also see Giuliano Gresleri, "Il silenzio delle pietre, le parole dei numeri, la solitudine, il 'deflagrante ricordo,'" in Benedetto Gravagnuolo (ed.), *Le Corbusier e l'Antico*, pp. 71–83.
[81] Giuliano Gresleri, "Il poema orientale," in *Le Corbusier. Il linguaggio delle pietre*, Venezia, Marsilio, 1988, p. 34.
[82] Kurt W. Forster, "Antiquity and Modernity in the La Roche-Jeanneret Houses of 1923," in *Oppositions* 15–16, 1973, pp.131ff.
[83] See Mogens Krustrup, "Tutto è questione di perseveranza, di lavoro e di coraggio," *Le Corbusier. Il Linguaggio delle pietre*, pp. 41ff.
[84] Le Corbusier, note dated from Pompeii on October 8, 1911, in Giuliano Gresleri, *Les Voyages d'Allemagne-Carnets/Voyage d'Orient-Carnets*, Carnets d'Orient no. 4, p. 137.
[85] See Stanislaus von Moos, *Le Corbusier. Album La Roche*, New York, Monacelli Press, 1997, pp. 24–40. Also see Stanislaus von Moos, "La leçon de Venise," in *Le Corbusier e l'Antico*, pp. 84–97.

86 The complete photographic corpus of the young Jeanneret during his 1911 journey was curated by Giuliano Gresleri in the exhibition at the Palazzo Reale di Napoli in 1996–97. See also, Leo Schubert, "Jeanneret, the City, and Photography," in *Le Corbusier Before Le Corbusier*, pp. 54–67.
87 See the above-mentioned *Il Linguaggio delle pietre* (note 80).
88 See Jean Petit, *Le Corbusier lui-même*, Genève, Rousseau, 1970; *Le Corbusier pittore e scultore*, Milano, Mondadori, 1986; Heidi Weber (ed.), *Le Corbusier. The Artist. Works from Heidi Weber Collection*, Zürich, 1988.
89 See Benedetto Gravagnuolo, "Viaggi nelle classicità: da Schinkel a Semper," in Carlo Cresti (ed.), *Gottfried Semper. Aggiunte e digressioni*, Firenze, Pontecorboli, 1995.

In fact, the juvenile "vibrations" of the *Voyage d'Orient* had already been fixed on the four hundred photographic plates made with his rudimentary camera Cupido 80, and in the drawings and writings of his *Carnets*, later re-elaborated upon his return to Switzerland.[86] In April of 1912, Charles-Edouard Jeanneret exhibited in Neuchâtel a series of watercolors, grouped under the title *Language des Pierres*, and partly re-presented the year after in the prestigious exhibition of the Salon d'Automne in Paris,[87] five years before he painted *La cheminée* (1918) in a celebrated episode of the purist period. It was the first exhibition where he declared his passion for painting – a never appeased passion that would develop during his entire life.[88] The osmosis between these two forms of "visible thinking" was so continuous along his career that Theodor Fontane's metaphor about Karl Friedrich Schinkel seems entirely appropriate to Le Corbusier's own career: "he painted as an architect, and he built as a painter."[89]

This sensibility to color induced the young Jeanneret to put the constructions of architecture in close relationship with the chromatic context of their *locus*. As a result, the landscape, the intensity of light and the climatic temperature, along with the colors of the stones, the trees, the skies and other natural elements, became decisive corollaries of the beauty of architecture beyond the measurable proportions of the academic tradition. Yet it would be eminently reductive to interpret these works as simple analytical exercises about the relationship between architectonic *text* and landscape *context*. The pictorial research surged with a relative formal autonomy from the representative content, delivering in the figuration of the landscapes along the "road to Eleusis" genuine summits of absolute lyricism. Leaning even more toward new emotional horizons is the transfiguration of the hills of Pera and Istanbul into mauve or rotten-green blemishes that detach themselves from the backdrop of the Sea of Marmara. In the memory of the painter, the drawings of the things observed merge with the things imagined, and they acquire the taints of dreamy colors, fresh and "fauve": they vibrate from the blood red to the cobalt blue in the celebrated variations on the oblique views of the Parthenon (plate 12). The stones of architecture seem to speak the Homer-like language of the trees, within the metaphysical immobility of the "unspeakable space." Everything is improbable and, at the same time, deeply real, as a journey in time, replete with colored spectra and, further inside, with the darkest ink which frequently dominates the serene and blue scintillation of the Mediterranean waters.

The journey faraway is by definition the movement of the self toward an *elsewhere*, toward another *locus* far from one's homeland and cultural traditions. The photographs, the drawings, the annotations, and sketches of the *Carnets* reveal the interest of the young Jeanneret, not only for the sacred precincts of architecture but also for the handcrafted objects, for the country vases, for the clothes, faces, and bodies of the peoples; in other words, for the anthropological culture in its largest sense. Suffice to allude to the drawings *View of the seraglio from the Bosphorus*, with its depiction of colored sails caught in the wind; or *Garden of an interior courtyard*, which shows rural artifacts in the surroundings of Kazanlak; or the photographs *Fountain of Istanbul, with woman, child and dog*, the *Tomb cippus with character seen from behind at Eyüp*, or *Cart pulled by ox* showing hieratic monks with their large black tunics, immobile in the silence of Mount Athos.

Before becoming notorious under the pseudonym of Le Corbusier, the young student interpreted, with "eyes that know how to see" the latent correlation between the *culture de l'habiter* (culture of living) and the *culture du construire* (culture of building). This association surfaced with "magisterial simplicity" during the four months spent in the Orient – in the West, it was being lost under the Babel-like blanket of styles, packed one on top of the other or confused together in "dubious, horrendous and disgusting conglomerates."[90] This notwithstanding, this aptitude to "know how to see" beyond architecture always remained the tenuous yet traceable thread that interconnects his "mental journeys" into the labyrinth of heterogeneous civilizations, even after his decision to abandon the camera for the pencil, more adept at forcing the mind to interpret the visible than the mechanical shutter. *Les femmes d'Alger*, sketched with all the sensual fascination of their "abundant curves" suggests one source of inspiration for the fluidity of the Plan Obus.[91] Likewise, the great gestures at the regional scale for Montevideo, Buenos Aires, São Paulo, and Rio de Janeiro derived unequivocally from the "view from above" that he experienced from the aircrafts of Mermoz and Saint-Exupéry.[92] As for the *hybris* of the Chandigarh Capitol, it cannot be understood without recalling Le Corbusier's discussion of the rediscovery, amidst the faraway *terres d'Orient*, of "the fundamental human activities, linked to cosmic elements like the sun, the moon, the waters, the seeds, the fructification."[93] That the Mediterranean represented a polar star in the design journey of Le Corbusier is thus undeniable. A further proof can be found in the autobiographical notes written in the *cabanon* during the month of July 1965, a couple of days before the fatal drowning in the waters of Cap-Martin:

> Along those years I have become a man of everywhere. I have traveled across the continents. Yet, I have only one deep attachment: the Mediterranean. I am a Mediterranean, strongly . . . Mediterranean, Queen of form and light. Light and space. . . . My recreations, my roots, they must be found in the sea that I have never ceased to like. . . . The sea is movement, and endless horizon.[94]

What thus is the legacy of these reiterated odysseys in the Mediterranean? The key of the enigma can very probably be found in the prologue, apparently out of context, that Le Corbusier pronounced in Athens on August 3, 1933, in front of the Congrès International d'Architecture Moderne (CIAM) members:

> I have attempted to act and create a work of harmony and humanity. I have done it with the Acropolis deep inside me, in the stomach. My work has been honest, loyal, obstinate, sincere. It is the essential truth that made me a challenger, somebody who proposes something else . . . One has accused me of being a revolutionary . . . It is the Acropolis, which made me a rebel . . . The Greek spirit has remained the symbol of control: mathematical rigor and law of numbers bring us harmony . . . And now, to get it over with the Acropolis, in the name of harmony, we must in the whole world, without weakness and with a valiant soul, create harmony. The word truly expresses the *raison d'être* of the present times. In the name of the Acropolis, a strong harmony, triumphant, unfailing, invulnerable.[95]

Harmony and not symmetry: the word has a wide significance, irreducible to the banal academic exercises of bilateral and axial symmetry. The rediscovery of the *esprit grec* was to become an initiation voyage across the secrets of the numbers that explain the beauty of the visible forms. Major steps in this pilgrimage will be the neo-Pythagorean principles of the *tracés régulateurs*, the esoteric fascination for the golden section, and their extreme logical conclusion:

[90] *Le Corbusier. Voyage d'Orient*, English edition, p. 347.
[91] This hypothesis was first suggested by Stanislaus von Moos in his essay "Les femmes d'Algers," in *Le Corbusier et la Méditerranée*, Marseille, Ed. Parenthèses, 1987, p. 195.
[92] See Le Corbusier, *Precisions on the Present State of Architecture and City Planning*, Cambridge, The MIT Press, 1991.
[93] Le Corbusier, *L'échelle humaine* (The Human Scale), speech at the VIII CIAM of Hoddesdon. See *CIAM 8: The Core*, CIAM, 1951.
[94] Le Corbusier, handwritten note transcribed in *Le Corbusier et la Méditerranée*, p. 7.
[95] Le Corbusier, "Air, son, lumière," (Air, Sound, Light), speech held on August 3, 1933, at CIAM IV, in *Texnica Xeonika*, B IV no. 44–45–46, 1933. Also see Eric Mumford, *The CIAM Discourse on Urbanism 1928–1960*, Cambridge, The MIT Press, 2000.

96 Le Corbusier, *The Modulor: A Harmonious Measure to the Human Scale, Universally Applicable to Architecture and Mechanics*, Cambridge, The MIT Press, 1968 [1954]. Also see the discussion about Severini, Ghyka, and Valéry in the section Magical Realisms of this essay.
97 Le Corbusier, *Sur les quatre routes*, Paris, Gallimard, 1941.
98 The drawing is from Auguste Choisy, *Histoire de l'architecture*, Paris, Gauthier-Villars, 1899, p. 415.
99 Auguste Choisy, p. 419.
100 Gino Pollini, "Il IV CIAM," in *Parametro*, no. 52, December 1976. On the congress, see *Texnika-Xeonika*, op. cit.; *Quadrante* 5, September 1933, and *Quadrante* 13, May 1934.
101 Gino Pollini, "Cronache del quarto Congresso Internazionale di Architettura Moderna e delle vicende relative alla sua organizzazione," in *Parametro* 52, December 1976, pp. 19–21.

the theory of the Modulor.[96] Yet, the extraordinary pages that Auguste Choisy dedicated to the Acropolis may very well have been the true catalyst for Le Corbusier's reassessment of the complex game of calibrated "asymmetries." Every architecture is rational and symmetrical, but their disposition on the ground, out of axis and in apparent autonomy, can be read in a "picturesque" manner as one proceeds along the emotional sequence of perspectival stations.[97] In 1922 he had borrowed Choisy's drawing of the Acropolis as the frontispiece of his "third advertisement to the architects."[98] The parallelism of thought between the architect and the historian can be read in Choisy's following lines:

> And so behaves nature: the leaves of a plant are symmetrical, the tree is a balanced mass. Symmetry dominates its every part, but the whole merely follows the laws of harmony, of which the word *balance* translates both the image and the physical expression.[99]

Voyages into Harmony

The Mediterranean echo found further international resonance in the CIAM congress of 1933, "taking place aboard a beautiful ship, the *Patris II*, on a cruise from Marseille to Athens."[100] Not to be underestimated is the symbolic value of this itinerary in *mare nostrum*, whose final destination was the mythical Athens. The voyage started on July 29 at the port of Marseille, wrapped that day in an exotic halo imprinted on the film shot on board by Laszlo Moholy-Nagy. Gino Pollini remembers:

> The meetings took place on the decks, sheltered by the curtains, in a ventilated atmosphere, full of light and sun, on a calm sea. Gropius, Breuer, and almost the whole German group were absent . . . On the afternoon of August 1, we disembarked in Athens; the following day was dedicated to visiting the city. So we went up to the Acropolis – us, with emotion, as it was our first time – with Le Corbusier who recalled the twenty-one days he had passed up there many years ago. With this memory, he introduced the following day his discourse *Air, sound, and light* [. . .] The Temple to Athena Nike, the Parthenon, everything appeared regulated by laws not taken for granted . . . At Cape Sunio, in Delphi, in Epidauro, we were able in the following days to find an ulterior confirmation . . . Even in the islands, architecture appeared marked by valid rules, even if not always evident, deriving from typology and, among other things, the factors of climate and the ways in which single edifices were grouped and placed in relation to the site. The Mediterranean population appeared to have expressed in this way a rapport between their very poverty and an essentially rational action. The feeling of ancient tradition was certainly in their consciousness, but it could not blossom on the surface of the Congress' works. This would have been, aside from being out of the theme, irreconcilable with a general diffuse restraint of the time.[101]

From the direct testimony of a participant, we find confirmed the influence that an indiscrete fascination with the Hellenic myth exercised, even on this intransigent Congress, which sanctioned the principles of the "modern functional city." Yet that "diffuse restraint" would surrender a little afterwards to an undisclosed apology of ancient Mediterranean civilization. The animator of this infatuation was principally Le Corbusier, who was a collaborator in those years of *Plans*, an unequivocally "rightist" magazine (1930–33) and of *Prélude*, another French organ of "regionalist action" ambiguously placed along a "line of demarcation between fascism and collectivism" (1933–35). And it is precisely from the cultural alliance between *Prélude* and the Italian magazine *Quadrante* that the idea was born for a "plan d'organisation européenne" among France, Italy, Spain, and Algeria on the basis of acknowledgment of climatic axes.[102] When Le Corbusier was invited to give two lectures at the Roman *Circolo delle Arti e delle Lettere* in July 1934, he proclaimed, "Rome is the highest potential of Latin and Greco-Latin cultures, under the sky of a Mediterranean fatality." And he added, "Rome is still today, amidst the universal tumult, at the place that its authority conquered, an authority that is capable of claiming its message in the face of the whole world."[103]

Yet, one cannot discard a possible premeditation in attempting to capture the benevolence of Mussolini, a personification of the mythified "authority," in order to obtain the commission to design Pontinia, the third new town in the reclamation program of the Pontine Marshes. In November of the same year Le Corbusier sent the Duce a dedicated copy of the second volume of the *Oeuvre complète*, and two years later he proposed a project of transformation of Addis Ababa into a large "garden city."

Edoardo Persico's disdain is more than understandable, when in an incisive essay from 1934 entitled "Punto a capo per l'archittetura," he expressed a severe and sarcastic judgment against the equation *latinità = mediterraneità* – acted out opportunistically by the Italian rationalists in order to sanction the cachet of their own "tendency" of "art of the State" – and against the charming thought of *climats* and *cultures* brought up by Le Corbusier.[104] His scorn came undoubtedly from his distinctly "religious" and authentically anti-fascist point of view.

It would be mistaken, however, to keep evaluating an "aesthetic" formulation in "ethical" terms. At least as originally intended, *mediterraneità* was prevalently a poetic game, a literary metaphor, a neo-Pythagorean allegory of number and cosmic rhythm, a metaphysical desire to rediscover, through the proportional relationships of the golden section, the abstract and mathematical laws of beauty. It was a fantastic pretext for ungluing from the skies Icarus's wings and re-plunging them into the Homeric waters of Ulysses's peregrination.

It was not by chance that Le Corbusier dedicated some extraordinarily fascinating watercolors to the illustration of the *Iliad* in February of 1955 (plate 11). Recluse in the spiritual cave of the Cap-Martin *cabanon*, he applied sanguine colors to the eighteenth-century neoclassical designs of John Flaxman chosen by the publishing house Les Portiques to illustrate the pages of the *Iliad*.[105] The conflict between the pale serenity of Arcadia and the chromatic passion of tragedy is unequivocal. The vivifying breath of the fight between Eros and Thanatos, understood in the Homeric song, is re-evoked in unparalleled Dionysian inebriation. In these apparently minor drawings, Le Corbusier revealed symptomatically the most secret aspects of his psyche, perennially oscillating between extreme poles – a desire for harmony on the one hand and a phobia of silence on the other. If we ignore this intimate and perennial tension between order and chaos, sphere and labyrinth, classicism and avant-garde, we cannot understand the authentic sense of his poetics. "I think that if one recognizes some meaning in my work as an architect, it is to this secret labor that one should attribute a profound value" – these were the words suggested by Le Corbusier to accompany his famous drawing of 1948, which depicts the timeless mask of solar rays and knots of serpents.[106]

[102] For a further discussion of the CIAM IV and, in particular, of the influence of José Luis Sert on Le Corbusier, see Antonio Pizza, "The Mediterranean: Creation and Development of a Myth," in *J.LL. Sert and Mediterranean Culture*, Barcelona, Collegi d'arquitectes de Catalunya, 1977, pp. 12–45; and in the same work, Josep Rovira, "Arquitectura: El Mediterráneo es su cuña," pp. 46–79. Also see the monograph by Rovira, *José Luis Sert, 1901–1983*.

[103] Le Corbusier, "Urbanismo e architettura secondo Le Corbusier," in *Quadrante* 13, May 1934.

[104] Edoardo Persico, "Punto e a capo per l'architettura," in *Domus*, November 1934, also in Giulia Veronesi (ed.), *Edoardo Persico. Tutte le opere (1923–1935)*, Milano, Edizioni di Comunità, 1964. The essay can be considered as a fundamental bibliographical source on the theme of the *mediterraneità*.

[105] Those drawings remained unpublished for a long time; they were finally discovered and subtly interpreted by Danish scholar Mogens Krustrup in an edition of 1986. See Mogens Krustrup, *Le Corbusier, l'Iliade, Dessins*, Copenhagen, Krustrup, 1986; also in Mogens Krustrup, *Le Corbusier et la Méditerranée*, pp. 200–209.

[106] See Bruno Salvatore Messina, *Le Corbusier. Eros e Logos*, Napoli, Clean, 1987.

[107] Gino Severini, *Ragionamenti sulle arti figurative*, Milano, Hoepli, 1936, p. 154.
[108] Waldemar George, *Profits et pertes de l'art contemporain*, Paris, Editions Chroniques du jour, 1933.
[109] Edoardo Persico, *Relazione per il concorso del Salone d'Onore*, Milano, 1935.
[110] Giuseppe Pagano and Guarniero Daniel, *Architettura rurale italiana*, Milano, Hoepli, 1936, p. 76.

Contemporary Mediterranean mythology does not lack an esoteric tension, pagan and mystical in its own way, which should not be confused with Christian spirituality. As Gino Severini clarified:

> One can say that there exists a diabolical spirituality as well as a religious spirituality. The first can be directed towards magic, a sense of the hidden and the mysterious, the demonic, the sensual. For example, certain Greek hermaphroditic idols, certain idols and black masks, and numerous cases in the Italian Renaissance.[107]

The predilection for the classical narcotic, for Apollonian ecstasy, for the abandonment to the sensual call of the Mediterranean's hermaphroditic idols is a piece of historical fact widespread in the culture of those years. It spread well beyond the French and Italian boundaries, where it had found fertile ground from which to draw nourishment. "The European spirit can find consciousness of its own apostolate only if it can recognize the legitimacy of its own Hellenic and Latin affiliation" – one reads in an essay by Waldemar George, which was promptly translated into Italian in 1933 by Ardengo Soffici.[108] And Persico, having overcome the contingent motivations of the polemic, would realize in the Salone d'Onore at the VI Triennale of Milan (in collaboration with Marcello Nizzoli and Giancarlo Palanti, and with the insertion of figurative sculpture by Lucio Fontana) an installation that "re-exalts, in a new aspect, the ancient principle of the '*colonnato*' (colonnade)." In relation to the project, he added that "the classical taste of the composition is legitimate in its addressing of the rationalist movement for whom the aspiration for a new European renaissance has always been alive."[109]

It should not be forgotten, however, that the International Exposition of Architecture of that same VI Triennale of 1936 was dominated by the exhibition *L'architettura rurale nel bacino del Mediterraneo* (Rural architecture in the cradle of the Mediterranean), curated by Guarniero Daniel and Giuseppe Pagano – the latter was Persico's significant road companion. The exhibition represented in a certain sense the synthesis of the studies on the "anonymous" constructions of vernacular architecture. One reads in the description of the exhibit,

> It should not surprise us then if, from the study of the casual rural Mediterranean and particularly the Italian Mediterranean, some of the most intelligent architects from northern Europe . . . have discovered the emotional power of the poet/builder, substituting it to the craft of the conventional set designer. The flat roof, the pure blocks with a minimum of decorative objects and accidents, the horizontal window, the non-symmetrical composition, the expressive force of the flat wall, the influence of the surrounding countryside and above all the unprejudiced functional coherence and technique are evidently readable in these works of rural architecture. Functionality has always been the fundamental logic of architecture. Only the presumption of a society in love with appearances could forget this law that is both external and human at the same time. Today this law has been re-discovered and is now defended not only for aesthetic reasons, but also for the moral necessity of clarity and honesty.[110]

1.8 Luigi Cosenza. *Top right*: Patio of Villa Cernia, Capri, 1966–67.
Bottom right: Patio of the Olivetti factory, Pozzuoli, 1951–54.
Source: *Luigi Cosenza. L'opera completa*, Naples, 1987.
Photo Mimmo Jodice.

The cultural priority characterized by "Mediterranean" architecture in confrontation with European Rationalism for the definition of a purist language had been alleged in the preceding year by Enrico Peressutti in the pages of *Quadrante* and even earlier by Gio Ponti in articles published in *Domus* and collected in 1933 in the brief volume *La casa all'italiana*.[111] Ponti would further

[111] "Architectures of white walls, rectangular or square, horizontal or vertical; architectures of voids and solids, of colors and forms, of geometries and proportions . . . an heritage that, discovered by Gropius, Le Corbusier, and Mies van der Rohe, was camouflaged as a novelty of Nordic origin, as an invention of the twentieth century." From Enrico Peressutti, "Architettura mediterranea," in *Quadrante* 21, January 1935; Gio Ponti. See Giò Ponti, *La casa all'italiana*, Milano, 1933, pp. 9–11; see reprint in Fulvio Irace, *La casa all'italiana*, Milano, Electa, 1988.

[112] Gio Ponti, *Architettura mediterranea*, Milano, 1941. See Lisa Licitra Ponti, *Giò Ponti: The Complete Work, 1923–1978*, Cambridge, The MIT Press, 1990.

[113] On colonial architecture, see Riccardo Mariani, "Trasformazione del territorio e città di nuova fondazione," in *Gli Anni Trenta*, pp. 285–299. From the same author, see *Fascismo e città nuove*, Milano, Feltrinelli, 1976, which analyzes the theme of the "rural" ideology in new foundations. Also see Giuliano Gresleri, Pier Giorgio Massaretti, and Stefano Zagnoni (eds.), *Architettura italiana d'oltremare, 1870–1940*, Venezia, Marsilio, 1993.

[114] On Luigi Cosenza's research on Mediterranean architecture, see Benedetto Gravagnuolo, "Colloquio con Luigi Cosenza," in *Modo* 60, Giugno-Luglio 1983. Also see Gianni Cosenza and Franscesco Domenico Moccia (eds.), *Luigi Cosenza. L'opera complete*, Napoli, Electa, 1987. On Bernard Rudofsky see Andrea Bocco Guarneri's essay in this book and *Bernard Rudofsky: A Humane Designer*, Wien/New York, Springer, 2003.

[115] See Cherubino Gambardella, *Case sul Golfo: abitare la costa napoletana 1930–1945*, Napoli, Gambardella, 1993.

[116] "I designed the landscape" responded Malaparte, as a rhetorical paradox, to Marshall Rommel during the visit to the villa, described in *La Pelle*, Roma/Milano, 1949. English translation: *The Skin*, Boston, Houghton Mifflin, 1952.

[117] "The day I started to build a house, I did not think that I would have designed a self-portrait." From Curzio Malaparte, "Ritratto di pietra" (Capri, 1940), first published in Proceedings of the Conference *First Soviet–Italian Symposium on Macromolecules in the Functioning Cells*, Capri, 1978, New York, Plenum Press, 1979. On Casa Malaparte see Marida Talamona, *Casa Malaparte*, New York, Princeton Architectural Press, 1992; see also Gianni Pettena, *Casa Malaparte Capri*, Firenze, Le Lettere, 1999.

[118] Manfredo Tafuri, "L'ascesi e il gioco. Il metaforico naviglio di Malaparte e Libera a Capri," in *Gran Bazar* 15, 1981, pp. 92–99.

experiment in the villa in Bordighera of 1938 with the operative and anti-picturesque reinterpretation of the canons of traditional construction, polemically writing in his essay *Architettura mediterranea* against the mimetic vulgarity and the false historicalness of the contemporary French productions in "style provençal."[112] If one considers that *Quadrante* of Bardi and Bontempelli, *Casabella* of Pagano, and *Domus* of Ponti were the most culturally established magazines in those years, one can understand the impact that the Mediterranean question had on the Italian architectonic debate, beyond such inevitable divergences of opinion or maybe because of them.

So many partisans of anti-north provincialism or exalted nationalism would eventually adhere to such lines of inquiry that they found their ideological outlet, after the Mussolini proclamation of May 9, 1936, on the conquest of the "Empire," in colonial building exported to Libya, Ethiopia, Somalia, and in other northeastern areas of Africa.[113] More than unjust, it would be wrong, however, to express a liquidating judgment on the entire thematic without deepening the analysis and making the necessary distinctions between the different and often hurriedly conflated positions. One thinks, for instance, of the depth of the architectonic thought of Luigi Cosenza, who knew how to immerse himself in a profound analysis of the typological characteristics of the vernacular building of Capri, Ischia, Procida, and the Sorrentian and Amalfitan coast. He rediscovered the essentialness of that ancient simplicity, without drowning in the vulgar copy of local folkloric elements.[114] Special mention must be made for the Villa Oro (1936–37, designed with Bernard Rudofsky) and, after the war, for the Villa Cernia in Anacapri (1966–67), where he transformed the theme of the Pompeian *impluvium* in a "modern" key.[115] Likewise, in the Olivetti factory at Pozzuoli (1951–54), he used the "Pompeian" courtyard to great effect.

Yet, it is the house of the writer Curzio Malaparte built in Capri between 1937 and 1942 that is without a doubt one of the highest peaks of the constructive lyricism inspired by *mediterraneità*. Perhaps it is the exceptional natural scenery that transcends the inimitable perfection of the "metaphysical" game (plates 1, 3).[116] Cave-like with its red mass floating between the gray of Cape Massullo and the blue of the sky, this "*ritratto di me stesso*" which the arch-Italian Malaparte wanted to construct, was not by chance the center of international critical attention.[117] The thirty-three steps of the staircase, which widens toward the top as an inclined plane of Pythagorean ascendance, lead with mystical crescendo to the *solarium*, which is suspended without protection and dominated by a hermetic white veil petrified in windless Olympus. As Manfredo Tafuri noted,

> [the] Greek absoluteness of the architecture of Libera [and Malaparte] becomes a *simulacrum* of a *ratio* that has become elliptical, which resolves perfectly in itself, which has severed every bridge with the world of utility and action [. . .] A timeless, archaic swimmer that oscillates between memories of Mediterranean building and games of abstraction, are paginated on its facades.[118]

Even in the interior of this home/refuge, allegories weave together in enigmatic reflections: beginning with the great room, with its floor that evokes the ancient Appian way, from which rise the false bases of Doric columns supporting singular wooden tables, and a fireplace that "perforates" the wall in front of the sculpture of Pericle Fazzini, allowing a view of the distant movement of the sea which mixes with the flames of fire. Finally, in the studio, with its floor designed by Alberto Savinio in the form of a lyre, the Roman bath with its tub carved into the marble, and the room of the "favorite," with tiles and traditional decorations that climb the walls in order to cover the fireplace corner.[119]

All of this complex and ambiguous fermentation of ideas found an inevitable end with the beginning of the war. After the conflict the new ideological winds of reconstruction definitively swept away the ashes of this esotericism. Only Giò Ponti and especially Alberto Sartoris would return to the theme in 1948 with *Ordre et climat méditerranéens*, the first volume of the *Encyclopédie de l'architecture nouvelle* (plate 19).[120] But the attention of the theoretical debate was already focused elsewhere.

What remains today of that mythology? Apparently nothing! Even the postmodern tendencies that are decidedly inspired by the past are inclined to a spectacular, ironic, and self-publicizing use of stylistic elements borrowed from the roof of history, rather than to a search for the magical and rarefied atmospheres of the neo-Pythagorism of those years. It is nevertheless not to be excluded that the echo soaked in that ancient nostalgia could return to exercise its magnetic call, because the need for harmony seems to be a kind of ancestral instinct, stronger than its own functional needs. ■

[119] On Libera, see Giulio Carlo Argan, *Adalberto Libera*, Roma, Editalia, 1975; Vieri Quilici, *Adalberto Libera. Architettura come ideale*, Roma, Oficina, 1981; *Adalberto Libera. Opera completa*, Milano, Electa, 1989.
[120] Alberto Sartoris, *Encyclopédie de l'architecture nouvelle. Ordre et climat méditerranéens*, vol. 1, Milano, Hoepli, 1948.

1.9 Curzio Malaparte. Rooftop terrace of Casa Malaparte, Capri.
Source: Photo Petra Lieb-Osborne, Munich-Miami.

2

THE POLITICS OF *MEDITERRANEITÀ* IN ITALIAN MODERNIST ARCHITECTURE

Michelangelo Sabatino

The political landscape of Italy as an emerging nation state in the early twentieth century was shaped by a complex interplay of reactionary and democratic forces.[1] Palmiro Togliatti, the leader of Italy's Communist Party from 1927 to 1964, once described Fascism as an "eclectic ideology" in which a social democratic agenda could coexist with totalitarian ideals.[2] In this complex political context, from the late 1920s into the early 1970s, the notion of a "Mediterranean ideal" functioned as a creative catalyst for modernist architects in Italy. The ideal of Mediterranean-ness or *Mediterraneità* was grounded in a dialogue with Italy's classical past as well as its pervasive vernacular architecture, the anonymous building traditions that have persisted over centuries across the diverse regions of the Italian peninsula (and the Mediterranean basin). Many of the architects who dedicated themselves to the perpetuation of *Mediterraneità* during the Fascist period subscribed to a design approach that rejected a priori styles typical of nineteenth-century historicism in favor of a "rational" approach that took program, context, and site as the catalysts for design. It has been argued that the question of *Mediterraneità* ceased to be a force in Italian architecture with the fall of Mussolini's regime.[3] While it is true that the terms of the debates surrounding *Mediterraneità* with all of its attendant regional, national, and transnational implications shifted significantly between the 1920s and the 1970s, there was renewed interest in vernacular traditions among architects working in Italy after the Second World War. The Rationalist movement galvanized during those "reconstruction years" laid the groundwork for the *Tendenza* or Neorationalist movement of the 1970s, spurring a critical reassessment of the Rationalist legacy in Italy and beyond in an exhibition at the XV Triennale of Milan in 1973.[4] In reviews of the exhibition, ironically, it was not Italian but rather foreign commentators who were quick to notice formal continuities between the "new" Rationalists (Aldo Rossi et al.) and certain strains of Fascist architecture.[5] During those same years, Peter Eisenman assimilated the architecture of Rationalist architect Giuseppe Terragni to his own formal metaphysics.[6] I would argue that such appropriation – whether it involves classical or vernacular precedents – points to *continuity* rather than rupture during a historical period characterized by such complexity and conflict.[7]

Immediately after the war, peasants of rural Italy began abandoning the countryside and moving into cities; this great influx of a new labor force enabled the "Italian miracle," an industrial boom that brought prosperity during the 1950s, especially to the major cities of the North. Architects continued to engage issues that had incubated during the interwar years in the hands of forward thinkers, especially those on the Left; these included the relationship between tradition and modernity, the interplay between rural and urban values and conditions, and building types for housing, public buildings, and urban infrastructure. This essay looks at how an enduring interest in the forms and

[1] See Norberto Bobbio, *Ideological Profile of Twentieth-Century Italy*, Princeton, Princeton University Press, 1995; Martin Clark, *Modern Italy, 1871 to the Present*, New York, Pearson Longman, 2008.

[2] Palmiro Togliatti, *Lectures on Fascism*, New York, International Publishers, 1976, pp. 1–12.

[3] See Rolando Scarano and Antonietta Piemontese, "La ricerca dell'identità mediterranea italiana degli anni Trenta," in Paolo Portoghesi and Rolando Scarano (eds.), *L'Architettura del mediterraneo – Conservazione, Trasformazione, Innovazione*, Rome, Gangemi, 2003, pp. 27–96.

[4] Ezio Bonfanti, Gianni Braghieri, Rosaldo Bonicalzi, Franco Raggi, Aldo Rossi, Massimo Scolari, and Daniele Vitale (eds.), *Architettura razionale*, Milan, Franco Angeli Editore, 1973.

[5] Charles Jencks, *The Language of Post-Modern Architecture*, London, Academy Editions, 1978.

[6] Peter Eisenman, "From Object to Relationship II: Giuseppe Terragni's Casa Giuliani Frigerio," in *Perspecta* 13–14, 1971, pp. 36–65.

[7] Writing in his opening editorial for the relaunch of *Casabella-Continuità* Ernesto Rogers defined "continuity" in postwar Italy as "historic conscience" of the events that surfaced during Fascism: *Casabella-Continuità* 199, December–January, 1953–54, p. 2. Manfredo Tafuri was the first to raise the issue in "Design and Technological Utopia," in Emilio Ambasz (ed.), *Italy: The New Domestic Landscape: Achievements and Problems of Italian Design*, New York, Museum of Modern Art, 1972, pp. 388–404.

2.1 (*Far left*) Luigi Figini and Gino Pollini. Period photo, "Villa-studio per un artista" (Villa-studio for an artist), Milan, V Triennale, 1933.
Source: *Catalogo della V Triennale*, Milan, 1933.

[8] Cesare De Seta was the first to publish an overview of architecture and urbanism under Fascism: *La cultura architettonica in Italia tra le due guerre*, Bari, Laterza, 1972. Two other important monographs that give an overview of the entire Italian context even while focusing on specific contributions are: Ezio Bonfanti and Marco Porta, *Città, Museo, e Architettura, Il Gruppo BBPR nella cultura architettonica 1931–1970*, Florence, Vallecchi, 1973; and Manfredo Tafuri, *Ludovico Quaroni e lo sviluppo dell'architettura moderna in Italia*, Milan, Edizioni di Comunità, 1964.
[9] Marco De Michelis, *Fascist Architectures in Italy* in Hubert-Jan Henket and Hilde Heynen (eds.), *Back from Utopia. The Challenge of the Modern Movement*, Rotterdam, 010 Publishers, 2002, pp. 86–91. See also Ruth Ben-Ghiat, *Fascist Modernities, 1922–45*, Berkeley, University of California Press, 2004; Sergio Poretti, *Modernismi italiani*, Roma, Gangemi, 2008.
[10] See the anthology by Giorgio Ciucci, Francesco Dal Co (eds.), *Architettura italiana del '900 – Atlante*, Milan, Electa, 1993. In particular see chapter 2, "Razionalismo architettonico e impegno politico fra arte e urbanistica," pp. 97–123. For an English translation of "The Rationalist Manifesto" presented to Mussolini on the inauguration day of the Second Exposition of Rationalist Architecture in Rome see Bruno Zevi, "Gruppo 7: the Rise and Fall of Italian Rationalism," in *Architectural Design* 51 1/2, 1981, pp. 40–43.
[11] Adalberto Libera, "Arte e razionalismo," in *La rassegna italiana*, March 1928, pp. 232–236. Republished in Luciano Patetta (ed.), *L'Architettura in Italia 1919–1943. Le polemiche*, Milan, Clup, 1972, pp. 149–151.
[12] Edoardo Persico, "Punto ed a capo per l'architettura," in *Domus*, November, 1934. Republished in Giulia Veronesi (ed.), *Edoardo Persico – Scritti d'architettura (1927/1935)*, Florence, Vallecchi editore, 1968, pp. 153–168. Cited in Bruno Zevi, "The Italian Rationalists" in Dennis Sharp (ed.), *The Rationalists – Theory and Design in the Modern Movement*, London, Architectural Press, 1978, pp. 118–129.

materiality of vernacular buildings shaped the Rationalist movement and the ideal of *Mediterraneità* under Fascism, how traditional buildings realized by anonymous masons or peasants were "rediscovered" or revalued and appropriated by professionally trained architects to construct Italy's modernist image during the 1950s, and how this movement morphed into Neorationalism during the 1960s and 1970s. In this sense, more broadly, it tracks the complex history of a nation struggling to come to grips with its preindustrial heritage as it embraced a new identity forged in the throes of industrialization after the Second World War and right through the deep-seated social turmoil that led to the widespread protests of workers against industrialists which started during the *Autunno caldo* or Hot Autumn of 1969.

Writing about the past inevitably betrays present-day concerns, and it is no coincidence that the "culture" of Italian architecture during the interwar years and its relationship to politics were reassessed during the late 1960s and 1970s when unrest surfaced among a younger generation of architects and intellectuals.[8] A critical mass of publications and exhibitions challenged the perception of Fascist architecture as a monolithic phenomenon in favor of a more porous and heterogeneous one.[9] On one hand, ideologically driven architectural concepts developed under Fascism, such as *Stile Littorio*, *Latinità*, and *Romanità* based on the exploitation of history for propagandistic ends, were dismissed. On the other hand, interwar Rationalism was saved from the wrecking ball of history because it was associated with architects who worked against literal and historicist classicism during the Fascist years.

Rationalism, Mediterraneita, and the Vernacular

From the late 1920s, architects in Italy used the term "Rationalism" to describe a movement in modern architecture that prioritized functional or technical requirements as well as spiritual qualities having to do with tradition and identity. Between 1928 when the first exhibition of Rationalist architecture was promoted by the *Movimento Italiano per l'Architettura Razionale* (MIAR), and 1931, the year of the second and final exhibition of the Rationalism group, debates raged over the agenda and validity of the movement with respect to the Fascist political agenda.[10] Adalberto Libera defended it against critics who accused the Rationalists of "internationalism" at the expense of nationalist ideals, asserting that,

> It might seem that Rationalism in architecture is synonymous with internationalism. However, even though qualities associated with commonly accepted international standards regarding technology, comfort, and culture are intrinsically part of Rationalism, those associated with nationalism like climate and ethics will also continue to exist alongside these.[11]

Although the critic Edoardo Persico endorsed Rationalism as a broader, European phenomenon, he criticized Italian Rationalists for their opportunism and what he perceived as ethical compromise with the nationalistic and self-aggrandizing agenda of the Fascist regime. Persico viewed *Romanità* or Romanness with the same disdain as *Mediterraneità*:

> Italian Rationalism is unable to absorb the lesson of European architecture because it lacks the faith necessary to do so. And so, moving from the dubious "Europeanism" of early "Rationalism", the Italians moved, with cold calculation regarding practical circumstances, from the "Roman" and the "Mediterranean", right down to the recent endorsement of corporative architecture.[12]

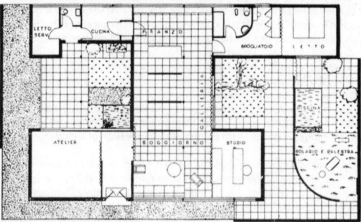

2.2 Luigi Figini and Gino
Pollini. Period photo
of the patio and plan,
"Villa-studio per un
artista" (Villa-studio
for an artist), Milan,
V Triennale, 1933.
Source: Alberto Sartoris,
*Encyclopédie de l'architecture
nouvelle*, vol. 1, Milano, 1948.

Shortly before this statement was published, Alberto Sartoris employed the
terms "modern," "functional," and "rational" almost interchangeably in the
introduction to his 1932 survey of functional architecture.[13] He defined
Rationalism in this way:

> In contrast to what one might expect, European Rationalism is not only
> about mechanics, statics, or dynamism. It is also about sculptural ideas
> that reflect timeless desires for lyricism and spirituality that can easily be
> fulfilled within the framework of Rationalism.[14]

For Sartoris, Rationalism was grounded in a complex attitude toward design,
one that embraced spiritual, lyrical as well as practical concerns. Just a year
before Sartoris's book appeared, Giuseppe Pagano and co-authors of a plan for
Via Roma in Turin proclaimed that "the architecture of the new street should
be rational but even more than that, it should be resolutely modern."[15]

From the extreme right wing, Ardengo Soffici lashed out at the Rationalists
with vitriol:

> Architectural Rationalism, not unlike other pseudo-artistic expressions, is
> of German and Anglo-Saxon derivation, and thus protestant. Rationalism
> and everything that resembles it is nothing other than an expression of

[13] Alberto Sartoris, *Gli elementi
dell'architettura funzionale*, Milan,
Hoepli, 1932.
[14] Reprinted in Giorgio Ciucci,
Francesco Dal Co (eds.), *Architet-
tura italiana del '900 – Atlante*,
pp. 114–116.
[15] Giuseppe Pagano Pogatschnig,
Gino Levi Montalcini, Umberto Cuzzi,
Ottorino Aloisio, and Ettore Sottsass,
"La Via Roma di Torino," *Per Vendere*,
June, 1931, republished in Cesare De
Seta (ed.), *Pagano – Architettura e
città durante il fascismo*, Bari and
Rome, Laterza, 1990, pp. 217–233.

[16] Ardengo Soffici, "Bandiera gialla," *Il Selvaggio*, May 30, 1931.
[17] Piero Bottoni, Mario Cereghini, Luigi Figini, Gino Frette, Enrico Griffini, Piero Lingeri, Gino Pollini, Gian Luigi Banfi, Ludovico di Belgiojoso, Enrico Peressutti, and Ernesto N. Rogers, "Un programma d'architettura," in *Quadrante*, May, 1933, 1. Republished in Luciano Patetta (ed.), *L'Architettura in Italia 1919–1943*, pp. 227–229.
[18] An exception is found with Richard A. Etlin, *Modernism in Italian Architecture, 1890–1940*, Cambridge, The MIT Press, 1991: see chapter "A Modern Vernacular Architecture", pp. 129–161.
[19] For an overview of classicism in Italian architecture see: Giorgio Ciucci, "Italian Architecture During the Fascist Period: Classicism between Neoclassicism and Rationalism: The Many Souls of the Classical," in *Harvard Architectural Review 5*, 1987, pp. 76–87.
[20] This issue is addressed in depth in the introduction of my forthcoming book: Michelangelo Sabatino, *Pride in Modesty: Modernist Architecture and the Vernacular Tradition in Italy*, Toronto and Buffalo, University of Toronto Press, 2010.
[21] Annegret Burg, *Novecento Milanese. I novecentisti e il rinnovamento dell'architettura a Milano fra il 1920 e il 1940*, Milan, Federico Motta Editore, 1991; Rossana Bossaglia, *Il Novecento Italiano*, Milan, Edizioni Charta, 1995.
[22] Alberto Asor Rosa, "Selvaggismo e novecentismo. La cultura letteraria e artistica del regime," in *Storia d'Italia*, vol. IV: *Dall'Unità a oggi*, Turin, Giulio Einaudi editore, 1975, pp. 1500–1513; Laura Malvano, *Fascismo e politica dell'immagine*, Turin, Bollati Boringhieri, 1988, in particular, see "Il fascismo rurale", pp. 144–151.
[23] Maurizio Fagiolo dell'Arco (ed.), *Carlo Carrà: The Primitive Period, 1915–1919*, Milan, G. Mazzotta, 1987.
[24] On Ferrand Braudel's observation of "many voices," see Iain Chambers, *Mediterranean Crossings: The Politics of an Interrupted Modernity*, Durham, NC, and London, Duke University Press, 2008, pp. 1–22.
[25] For an overview of the Mediterranean's complex history see: David Abulafia (ed.), *The Mediterranean in History*, London, Thames and Hudson, 2003.

aggression on the part of northerners and Protestants against Rome and Latin-ness.[16]

At the heart of this debate between North and South and scrambling to defend Rationalism from nationalistic attacks, like those perpetrated by Soffici, the authors of the *"programma"* published in the first issue of *Quadrante* (whose editors were Pier Maria Bardi and Massimo Bontempelli) managed to promote the "intransigent Rationalism" of Le Corbusier, Walter Gropius, and Mies van der Rohe, while defending classicism and its roots in southern *Mediterreaneità*.[17]

At this point of the essay it is essential to underline that during those same years the concept of the Mediterranean was fast expanding beyond the classical heritage to include the vernacular tradition. And although classicism's impact on core issues of twentieth-century Italian architecture and urbanism has been thoroughly examined, the equally important contribution of the vernacular has been in fact overlooked. In particular, the role that vernacular architecture played toward shaping Rationalism and the evolving concept of *Mediterraneità* has been little studied,[18] whereas the rhetorical and representational power associated with classical architecture has preoccupied historians anxious to deconstruct the difficult relationship between architecture and politics in Italy.[19] Unlike the vernacular, which has only been recognized as a category by historians for less than a century (in spite of its importance in the works of major figures such as Sebastiano Serlio, Andrea Palladio, and Karl Friedrich Schinkel), classicism consolidated its meanings in theory as well as practice over centuries in parallel with the rise of the profession of architecture.[20]

If geometric proportions and the Golden Mean resurfaced seductively in classical modernism (*Novecento* and Rationalism) in Italy during the 1920s and 1930s, appropriation of the "primitive" vernacular of Italy's various regions generated unease.[21] Mino Maccari's journal *Il Selvaggio* (The Savage), published between 1924 and 1943, and Leo Longanesi's journal *L'Italiano* both promoted an anti-urban, anti-modern agenda based on rural values that stood in contrast to the European and cosmopolitanism of the short-lived rival journal of the *Stracittà* movement, *900 Cahiers d'Italie et d'Europe*.[22] While the two movements *Strapaese* and *Stracittà* are typically discussed as diametrical entities, some architects and artists like Carlo Carrà associated classicism with the primitivism of rural buildings to express a certain solemnity.[23]

During the charged years between the two World Wars when Fascism dominated the Italian political sphere, Rationalist architects who embraced *Mediterraneità* did so in contrast to narrow nationalist agendas espoused by some members of Mussolini's regime. The transnational cultural heritage of the Mediterranean basin is characterized by "many voices" and architectural traditions, and as such offered Rationalist architects a wide cultural horizon on which to forge their brand of Mediterranean modernism.[24] Before the rise of nation states in the nineteenth century and the reconfiguration of the European geopolitical landscape, the Mediterranean basin was the theatre of successive empires, from Roman to Ottoman, each of which attempted to consolidate (typically more coercively than voluntarily) highly diverse traditions. The monumental as well as the vernacular buildings of Greco-Roman antiquity across a region extending west as far as Portugal, east as far as Turkey, and south as far as Africa inspired Italian Rationalists as diverse as Giuseppe Pagano and the *Gruppo Sette*, seven architects who banded together in 1926 just out of school to promote a modern architecture that creatively embraced tradition and tempered the universal qualities of the machine with the poetic qualities of context and culture.[25]

Although Italian Rationalist architects and their contemporaries throughout the Mediterranean region embraced tradition, with the inevitable "misprisions" that operative uses of the past risk, they rejected the mere imitation of historical styles promoted by exponents of the Fascist regime in the name of a chauvinistic Italianess or *Italianità*. Just as the Amsterdam School, Alvar Aalto, the German Expressionists and other modernist movements across Europe sought ways to combine traditional materials and building technologies with modern ones, and embraced both figuration and abstraction, the Rationalists approached traditional forms with a progressive agenda. Unlike their conservative counterparts in Italy and elsewhere, they looked to tradition as a source of invention, neither slavishly imitating it nor resisting progress in the name of past glories. In a bid to win Mussolini over to a modernist aesthetic, the militant critic Pier Maria Bardi assailed historicist architects as "*culturalisti*" with his *Tavolo degli orrori* or Panel of Horrors, a montage of historicist buildings realized in Italy.[26]

A case in point is Armando Brasini's Italian pavilion at the 1925 Paris Exposition Internationale des Arts Décoratifs et Industrials Modernes. Compared with Le Corbusier's Pavillon de l'Esprit Nouveau, with its Mediterranean-inspired patio and coloring, Brasini's pavilion is exposed as historicist pastiche.[27] Rather than simply embracing a bombastic or baroque classicism with rigid symmetries, stylized orders, clumsy massing, and indiscriminate use of opulent materials, the Rationalists harked back to a more elusive *Mediterraneità* that coalesced around architectural building types or elements such as open-air terraces, rooftop gardens, balconies, porticoes, patios, and courtyards. These constituted the places and spaces of the Mediterranean lifestyle lived as much outdoors as indoors. To be sure, northern Italy has less tangible connections with the Mediterranean Sea than affinities with building traditions of the Alpine regions. As the Italian leisure class emerged in the 1950s and 1960s as a result of industrial prosperity, architects designed hotels, ski resorts, and youth hostels in Alpine regions using local materials and techniques to achieve a provocative synthesis of tradition and modernity, for instance Franco Albini's Pirovano Youth Hostel (1949–51) and Carlo Mollino's Casa del Sole (1947–55) in the alpine town of Cervinia.[28]

Even though most of the Rationalists active during the 1920s and into the late 1930s were involved with projects for public buildings and housing,

[26] Bardi first used the expression "*culturalisti*" to refer to nineteenth-century architects: Pier Maria Bardi, *Rapporto sull'Architettura (per Mussolini)*, Rome, Critica fascista, 1931. The term is echoed in Sigfried Giedion, "Situation de l'architecture contemporaine en Italie," in *Cahiers d'art* 9–10, 1931, pp. 442–449.

[27] Mario Pisani, *L'Onta di Parigi – Il Padiglione Italiano di Armando Brasini all'Expo di Parigi del 1925*, Melfi, Edizioni Libria, 1996.

[28] Luca Moretto (ed.), *Architettura moderna alpina in Valle d'Aosta: Albini, BBPR, Cereghini, Figini e Pollini, Melis, Mollino, Muzio, Ponti, Sottsass Senior, Sottsass Junior*, Aosta, Musumeci, 2003.

2.3 Luigi Piccinato. Period photo of the patio and axonometric view, "Casa coloniale" (Colonial house), Milan, V Triennale, 1933.
Source: *La casa coloniale*, Milan, 1933.

[29] Vittorio Magnago Lampugnani, "Razionalismo e Italianità – L'architettura italiana moderna tra cosmopolitismo e nazionalismo (1926–1936)," in Max Seidel (ed.), *L'Europa e l'arte italiana*, Venice, Marsilio Editore, 2000, pp. 563–573.
[30] See for example Jean-Claude Vigato, *L'architecture régionaliste: France, 1890–1950*, Paris, Editions Norma, 1994. On the topic of regionalism in Europe and Italy see my contribution in the forthcoming Leen Meganck and Linda Van Santvoort (eds.), *Regionalism and Modernity in the Interwar Period*, Leuven, Leuven University Press, 2009.
[31] Matthias Schirren, *Bruno Taut – Alpine Architektur*, Munich/New York, Prestel, 2004.
[32] A similar dualistic phenomenon defined the arts in France: see Romy Golan, *Modernity and Nostalgia: Art and Politics in France Between the Wars*, New Haven, Yale University Press, 1995.
[33] See Manfredo Tafuri, "Modern Architecture and the Eclipse of History," in Manfredo Tafuri, *Theories and History of Architecture*, New York, Harper and Row, 1980, pp. 11–77.
[34] Alan Colquhoun, "From Rationalism to Revisionism: Architecture in Italy 1920–65," in Alan Colquhoun, *Modern Architecture*, Oxford and New York, Oxford University Press, 2002, pp. 182–191.
[35] Herbert Read, *Art and Industry: The Principles of Industrial Design*, London, Faber and Faber, 1934.
[36] Marco Mulazzani, "Il dibattito sulle arti applicate e l'architettura" in Giorgio Ciucci and Giorgio Muratore (eds.), *Storia dell'architettura italiana – Il Primo Novecento*, Milan, Electa, 2004, pp. 100–125.

the Mediterranean ideal allowed most of them to oppose the Fascist regime's manipulative rhetoric and "aestheticization of politics" with anthropologically layered notions of dwelling tailored for a specific climatic and geographic area. Whether for single or multi-family patio houses in Italy and its colonies, new towns on the Roman littoral, or seaside colonies for youth, these projects gave "progressive" Fascist architects with socially conscious aspirations opportunities to assert "Italian" as well as international values as they forged a Mediterranean modernism.[29] It is worth pointing out how this ambitious Mediterranean modernism with transnational and pan-regional implications shared little with the competitive spirit of regionalism that had surfaced in Italy and across Europe as a reaction to nationalism.[30] In this sense, it is possible to draw a parallel between the Mediterranean modernist phenomenon and the moral and aesthetic dimensions of Bruno Taut's transnational, pan-regionalist utopia sketched out in his *Alpine Architektur* published in 1918, immediately after the end of the First World War.[31]

The dialectic between tradition, whether inspired by nostalgia or reason, and modernity is key to understanding an Italian modernism that comprised movements as diverse as Rationalism, *Novecento*, Neorealism, and *La Tendenza* or Neorationalism.[32] The Mediterranean ideal was based on a dialogue with history at a time when an "eclipse of history" was dominant.[33] As such, it functioned as an important concept of "resistance" for Italian architects and helped them to achieve their distinctive contribution to European and North American twentieth-century architecture and urbanism. As Alan Colquhoun has recently written about Italy in a chapter on its architectural development from 1920 to 1965:

> The strong connection between the architectural avant-garde and Fascism in Italy during the "heroic" period of modern architecture has always been an embarrassment to architectural historians. . . . The Modernist architects, for their part, sympathized wholeheartedly with a movement that shared their dislike of nineteenth-century liberalism and their desire simultaneously to modernize and return to ancient roots.[34]

North and South

The modernity of the North that flourished in Germany, at least until the Nazi regime thwarted its development and made a spurious distinction between "modernization" and "modernism," was conceptualized around *Industriekultur*, a project that brought together art and industry.[35] In Italy – like in most countries of the Mediterranean region including Spain, Greece, and Southern France – modernity was shaped less exclusively by this sort of faith in technology. Although they embraced innovation, leading Italian Rationalists like Giuseppe Terragni, Luigi Figini and Gino Pollini, and Adalberto Libera (whom I will often refer to as "Mediterranean modernists" in this essay), tended to employ both new materials and building technologies and traditional ones. Aside from Antonio Sant' Elia's short-lived futurism, a movement interrupted by his premature death and the absence of compelling heirs to his visionary ideas, these Mediterranean modernists were less anxious to break altogether with craft and traditional modes of making.[36] Their decision was as much a result of theoretical propositions as real possibilities available to them at the time, given the different speeds at which Mediterranean countries embraced industrialization and the building industry was able to introduce these changes into practice. Moreover, the southern methods of construction favored masonry and load-bearing walls in contrast to traditional wood construction that relied on more "modern" (at least in the sense of a critic like Sigfried Giedion) posts and beams techniques.

In the less-industrialized South where labor was relatively cheap, architects tended to explore the sculptural qualities of reinforced concrete or "liquid stone" instead of its more expensive counterpart, steel.[37] Not only did reinforced concrete echo the stereotomic masses of vaulted stone construction typical of the Mediterranean basin, but it emphasized stability and sturdiness over transparency, thus turning on end one of modernism's core ambitions. In a discussion of Le Corbusier's Unité d'Habitation in Marseille, Reyner Banham pointed out how

> The Brutalists were not alone in seeing that in this building, modern architecture had finally come to terms with what northern Europe loosely calls "The Mediterranean tradition", a consummation humorously expressed in the form "the first modern building that has room for cockroaches". . . . Right or wrong, Le Corbusier had vouchsafed his younger readers a vision of a grandiose Mediterranean architectural tradition.[38]

Other subtle yet important differences distinguish architects working in the North from their counterparts working in the South, particularly the use of technology to address the growing preoccupation with hygiene for modern dwelling. While slogans such as "light, air, and openness" gave northern functionalists many opportunities for architectural expression (i.e., large plate-glass surfaces), in the South, the pursuit of light and shadow was less materialistic and technocratic, thus more spiritual. The glow of natural light that bathed the Mediterranean shores starkly contrasted with the gleaming

[37] See Jean-Louis Cohen and G. Martin Moeller, Jr. (eds.), *Liquid Stone: New Architecture in Concrete*, New York, Princeton Architectural Press, 2006.
[38] Reyner Banham, *The New Brutalism – Ethic or Aesthetic?*, New York, Reinhold, 1966.

2.4 Gio Ponti and Bernard Rudofsky. Drawing of the Room of the Doves, Hotel San Michele project, Capri, 1938.
Source: © Archivio Ponti, CSAC, Parma.

[39] See Paul Overy, *Light, Air and Openness: Modern Architecture between the Wars*, London, Thames and Hudson, 2007. On the pursuit of light and "whiteness" see Cherubino Gambardella, *Il sogno bianco – Architettura e "mito mediterraneo" nell'Italia degli anni '30*, Naples, Clean, 1989.

[40] Kenneth E. Silver, *Making Paradise: Art, Modernity, and the Myth of the French Riviera*, Cambridge and London, The MIT Press, 2001; Marisa Vescovo (ed.), *Luci del Mediterraneo*, Milan, Electa, 1997; Claudio Crescentini (ed.), *Mediterraneo d'arte – il mare e la pesca da Giorgio de Chirico all'era della globalizzazione*, Rome, Errecienne, 2005; Steingrim Laursen (ed.), *Picasso and the Mediterranean*, Humlebaek, Louisiana Museum of Modern Art, 1996

[41] Hans Sedlmayr, *Art in Crisis: The Lost Center*, Chicago, H. Regnery, 1958, (recently republished with new introduction by Roger Kimball, New Brunswick, NJ, Transaction Publishers, 2007). On Sedlmayr and light see Roberto Masiero (ed.), *Hans Sedlmayr – La Luce nelle sue manifestazioni artistiche*, Palermo, Aesthetica edizioni, 1989.

[42] Le Corbusier, "A Coat of Whitewash: The Law of Ripolin," *The Decorative Art of Today*, Cambridge and London, The MIT Press, 1987, pp. 185–192.

electric light of the machine age, and carried a number of symbolic associations for southern architects who looked at the Mediterranean basin as the birthplace of classicism as well as the site of mythological events.[39] It is no coincidence that art historians and critics have written extensively on the topic of southern light and the Mediterranean landscape in painting from Paul Cézanne to Pablo Picasso, Giorgio de Chirico, and beyond.[40]

For modernists in search of a spiritual light, religion was not an issue; nor did they wish to restore the "lost center" much lamented by the Catholic art and architectural historian Hans Sedlmayr.[41] Instead, they related to a new secular spirituality based on enlightened rationalism. And yet, there were fundamental differences in how they experienced modernity. Whereas architects in the North interpreted unornamented volumes as a rejection of culture and style, Le Corbusier's journey to the Eastern Mediterranean led him to discover that simplicity also carries cultural values:

> Whitewash exists wherever peoples have preserved intact the balanced structure of a harmonious culture. Once an extraneous element opposed to the harmony of the system has been introduced, whitewash disappears. Hence the collapse of regional arts – the death of folk culture.[42]

The choice of color and whitewash not only echoes vernacular and classical traditions anchored in the past (and in nature), but also finds parallels in contemporary designs of German expressionists such as Bruno Taut who used color to express drama and creativity. On the other hand, the use of primary colors by De Stijl architects such as Theo van Doesburg and Gerrit Rietveld is altogether different because it seeks to heighten abstraction by using colors not necessarily found in nature. When he used deep red stucco on the walls of his villa in Capri (1937–42), Curzio Malaparte (with Adalberto Libera) likely intended to forge a direct with the not-too-distant ruins of Pompeii and the multi-colored houses of the island of Procida. This was a far cry from the

2.5 Virgilio Marchi.
   "Primitivismi capresi"
   (Capri Primitivisms).
Source: *Cronache d'attualità*
6–10, 1922.

abstraction of pure red, blue, and yellow of the Rietveld–Schroeder house in Utrecht (1924). In sum, for Mediterranean modernists who espoused Rationalism, tradition tempered the machine with poetry and lyricism.[43] It is due to the anti-materialist bias of many Italian architects trained in schools marked by Benedetto Croce's neo-idealism that the Rationalist movement was distinguished from functionalism.[44] These were the anti-functionalists Adrian Forty has identified: "The liberation offered by 'functionalism' was short-lived: by the late 1930s most of the first generation of European modernists were anxious not to produce anything that could be describe as 'functionalist.'"[45] Although they shared some similarities, functionalism was dismissed because it was perceived as a term that described the response to the program whereas Rationalism was ideally linked to the "first moderns" and implied a trajectory that went from the French Revolution to Le Corbusier.[46]

During the postwar years, the Mediterranean ideal resurfaced amongst Italian architects, most of whom identified with Rationalism and were already practicing under the Fascist regime. Instead of seaside youth colonies and Fascist new towns, housing estates for the proletariat posed new challenges to the profession. The differences in opinions that had developed during the 1920s between the architects of the North and the South toward the role of technology and tradition continued to define postwar production. In fact, signs that the debate was expanding to include different generations of architects started to appear in books and journals. The vernacular of the southern Mediterranean started to be discussed as a source of modernism *tout court* during those years. For example James Stirling's seminal essay on *Regionalism and Modern Architecture* (1957) asserted that: "The most visually stimulating chapters of Kidder-Smith's recent book *Italy Builds* were not those on Italian Modern and Italian Renaissance, but that on the anonymous architecture of Italy."[47]

Stirling's essay on regionalism must be understood in the context of his earlier articles on Le Corbusier in which the English architect examined Corbusier's Ronchamp chapel in relationship to a purported "crisis of rationalism."[48] Faced with perplexity regarding Le Corbusier's Mediterranean vernacular references in his Ronchamp chapel, Stirling asks: "If folk architecture is to re-vitalise the movement, it will first be necessary to determine what it is that is modern in modern architecture." The debate over the "crisis of rationalism" jump-started by the "irrational" Ronchamp (with its hybrid structure and material "primitive" palette) opened up new possibilities to redefine the relationship between modernity and tradition that shaped the direction of *La Tendenza* (Neorationalism) shortly thereafter.

In the postwar era, under the newly installed democratic Republic, *Mediterraneità* was strategically revisited and transformed so as to rid it of its association with Fascist initiatives. It was thus also subsumed into debates concerning "continuity" and "Neorealism." Different forms of continuity were hardly surprising given that, unlike Germany whose progressive architects left to go to England and the United States, most architects working in Fascist Italy continued to practice during the postwar years. Some Fascist-era projects like Marcello Piacentini's Via della Conciliazione in Rome were actually completed during the postwar years.[49] Although some postwar housing estates reintroduced types associated with the Mediterranean ideal (between 1950 and 1954 Adalberto Libera, formerly a *Gruppo Sette* member, designed the INA-Casa Tuscolano housing in Rome based on one-story courtyard houses), most architects abandoned classical vernaculars and looked to the formal variety and density of the Italian hill town to express a new postwar

[43] On this difficult dialogue see Jean-Louis Cohen, *Le Corbusier, 1887–1965: The Lyricism of Architecture in the Machine Age*, Köln and Los Angeles, Taschen, 2004.

[44] For a discussion on the difference between rationalism and functionalism in Italy during the 1930s see Paolo Nicoloso, "Le parole dell' architettura. Il dibattito terminologico. 1929–1931," in Giulio Ernesti (ed.), *Costruzione dell'Utopia – Architetti e urbanisti nell'Italia fascista*, Rome, Edizioni lavoro, 1988.

[45] Adrian Forty, *Word and Buildings – A Vocabulary of Modern Architecture*, London, Thames and Hudson, 2000, pp. 174–195; Stanford Anderson, "The Fiction of Function," *Assemblage* 2, February 1987, pp. 18–31; Tim Benton, "The Myth of Function," in Peter Greenhalgh (ed.), *Modernism in Design*, London, Reaktion Books, 1990, pp. 41–52; Bruno Reichlin, "L'infortune critique du fonctionnalisme," in Jean-Louis Cohen (ed.), *Les années 30 – L'architecture et les arts de l'espace entre industrie et nostalgie*, pp. 186–195.

[46] Emil Kaufmann, *Von Ledoux bis Le Corbusier. Ursprung und Entwicklung der Autonomen Architektur*, Leipzig – Vienna, Verlag Dr. Rolf Passer, 1933, Italian trans. 1973; Joseph Rykwert, *The First Moderns: The Architects of the Eighteenth Century*, Cambridge, The MIT Press, 1980.

[47] James Stirling, "Regionalism and Modern Architecture," in *Architects' Year Book* 7, 1957, pp. 62–68. Republished in Vincent Canizaro (ed.), *Architectural Regionalism: Collected Writings on Place, Identity, Modernity, and Tradition*, New York, Princeton Architectural Press, 2006, pp. 327–330.

[48] James Stirling, "Ronchamp – Le Corbusier's Chapel and the Crisis of Rationalism," in *Architectural Review* 119, March 1956, pp. 155–161.

[49] Terry Kirk, "Framing St. Peter's: Urban Planning in Fascist Rome," in *Art Bulletin* 88, 4, December 2006, pp. 756–776.

50 See, for instance, Bruno Reichlin, "Figures of Neorealism in Italian Architecture (Part 1)," in *Grey Room* 5, Fall 2001, pp. 78–101; "Figures of Neorealism in Italian Architecture (Part 2)," in *Grey Room* 6, Winter 2002, pp. 110–133.
51 Marcia Landy, *The Folklore of Consensus: Theatricality in the Italian Cinema, 1930–1943*, Albany, State University of New York, 1998; Gian Piero Brunetta, *Cent'Anni di Cinema Italiano*, Bari, Editori Laterza, 1991; Peter Bondanella, *Italian Cinema From Neorealism to the Present*, New York, Frederick Ungar, 1983.
51 Ernesto N. Rogers, "L'evoluzione dell'architettura. Risposta al custode dei frigidaires," originally published in *Casabella-Continuità*, June 1959; republished in Ernesto N. Rogers, *Editoriali di Architettura*, Turin, Giulio Einaudi Editore, 1968, pp. 127–136.
52 Benito Mussolini, "Arte e civiltà" (1926), in Edoardo and Duilio Susmel (eds.), *Opera omnia di Benito Mussolini*, vol. XXII, Florence, La Fenice, 1957, p. 230.
53 See Claudio Fogu, *The Historic Imaginary: Politics of History in Fascist Italy*, Toronto and Buffalo, University of Toronto Press, 2003; Claudio Fogu, "To Make History Present," in Roger Crum and Claudia Lazzaro (eds.), *Donatello Among the Blackshirts: History and Modernity in the Visual Culture of Fascist Italy*, Ithaca, Cornell University Press, 2005, pp. 33–52; Giorgio di Genova, *L'uomo della provvidenza – Iconografia del duce 1923–1945*, Bologna, Edizioni BORA, 1997; Laura Malvano, *Fascismo e politica dell'immagine*, 1988.
54 Luca Somigli and Mario Moroni (eds.), *Italian Modernism: Italian Culture Between Decadentism and Avant-Garde*, Toronto and Buffalo, University of Toronto Press, 2004; Emilio Gentile, *The Struggle for Modernity: Nationalism, Futurism, and Fascism*, Praeger, Westport, CT, 2003; Walter Adamson, *Avant-Garde Florence: From Modernism to Fascism*, Cambridge, Harvard University Press, 1993.
55 Elias Canetti, *Crowds and Power*, New York, Farrar, Straus and Giroux, 1984, pp. 177–178.

rapprochement between the "people" and designers.[50] The workers benefited from housing realized under Fascism, but it was always a top-down (paternalistic) power relationship and not grass-roots collaboration that characterized the exchange. This type of changed power relationship was also evident in the new cinema of neorealism that featured the lives of ordinary people and not simply the bombast of Roman epics and other forms of propaganda.[51]

From the analysis of words and concepts in the historiography and criticism of Italian modernism, this essay will now focus on types of buildings and settlements where the concept of *Mediterraneità* flourished through the vernacular tradition and which became major references for Mediterranean modernists in Italy: the *patio house* reconsidered from the 1920s to the 1960s; *Capri and the Mediterranean hill towns* of the Gulf of Naples and their influence on the Futurist movement during the interwar period; *villas and rural cottages*; the *Italian hill town* revisited after World War II with Urbino as the new paradigm.

The Patio House Reconsidered

As Benito Mussolini's nationalistic agenda for the arts emerged in the late 1920s and consolidated in the late 1930s, he encouraged architects to avoid imitating the past and to use their creativity to surpass it:

> On top of the fertile ground of the past a new and great art can be reborn that is both traditionalist and modern. We must create, otherwise we will just be exploiting our heritage. We must create a new art for our time, a Fascist art.[52]

His vision of an art that was both traditionalist and modern was grounded in building upon the remains of the past, and as such went against the grain of a radical *tabula rasa* approach.[53] In fact, avant-garde impulses were anything but absent in Fascist art and architecture, despite the regime's instrumental use of the past.[54] In *Crowds and Power*, Elias Canetti observed that

> Italy may serve as an example of the difficulty a nation has in visualizing itself when all its cities are haunted by greater memories and when these memories are deliberately made use of to confuse its present.[55]

In the 1930s, a number of Italian architects expressed interest in the Mediterranean (and thus Italian) patio house. Belonging as much to the Classical tradition as the vernacular, the patio house proved to be adaptable to the functional requirements of modern dwelling, but it also facilitated a traditional Mediterranean lifestyle that involved spending parts of the day outdoors. Primarily the domain of wealthy and upper-middle-class clients, with its common elements (atrium and blank external walls that serve to protect the house rather than represent its owners through an elaborate façade), the patio house type lent itself to repetition and anonymity. For rationalist architects, the patio house was an expression of effective planning with limited space; for the nationalists and historicists (Bardi's "*culturalisti*"), it was an expression of *Italianità* that could be flaunted to the rest of the world. By comparing the appropriation of the patio house one can easily understand the different strands of Italian modernism during the 1920s well into the 1940s before the end of the war.

Writing in the early 1930s for the short-lived periodical *Arte Mediterranea*, architect Giovanni Michelucci stressed how the design of the Pompeian house

2.6 Giuseppe Pagano,
Franco Diotallevi, and
Irenio Marescotti. "Città
orizzontale" (Horizontal
City), 1940.
Source: *Costruzioni-Casabella*,
148, 1940.

was based on a humanist sense of scale. He went on to criticize Pompeian revivalism, which he called "*Pompeianismo*," as being more about style than the experience of space. Michelucci stressed the rational or logical dimension over the ideological: "As man felt the need for shelter, he created an environment that responded to his needs. Humanist principles of design are the key to Pompeian architecture."[56] Although Michelucci did not design a patio house himself, his appreciation for the basic principles of its design reveal that he was not interested in Pompeian style but rather, how architecture could facilitate lifestyle.

Although it remained only a prototype, the Villa-studio for an artist designed by Luigi Figini and Gino Pollini for the Fifth Milan Triennale in 1933 was one of the first examples of rationalist architecture that revealed the designers' commitment to realizing a Mediterranean modernism that was "Italian" and rational (plate 16 and figure 2.1). To be sure, Milan is closer to the Alps than the Mediterranean Sea, so one needs to suspend disbelief. Figini and Pollini's one-story, flat-roof building was organized around several open-air courtyards that could give the inhabitant opportunity to enjoy external spaces as extensions of the interiors. Significantly, their plan did not replicate the axial symmetrical qualities of a typical *domus*, with its atrium as the dominant spatial element. The architects recreated spaces that gave the inhabitant exposure to open-air and shaded outdoor spaces, one of which contained an *impluvium*.[57] Whitewashed surfaces on the exterior elevation are juxtaposed with exposed brick and a number of painted walls (light-blue, brown, peach) echo the sky and the earth. Figini and Pollini achieved a synthesis of modern building technologies with traditional models for dwelling in the patio house. Only three years later, the team designed an "Environment with living room and terrace" (1936), which they described as an established conciliatory position between the organic (vernacular) and the machine-age aesthetic.[58] Coherent with this conceptual description of the project, the designers employed a floor-to-ceiling glass wall along with a rustic flagstone floor and anonymous vernacular objects like basic reed and wood table and chairs.

[56] Giovanni Michelucci and Roberto Papi, "Lezione di Pompei," in *Arte Mediterranea: Rivista Bimestrale di arte, letteratura, e musica* 2, 1, 1934, pp. 23–32.
[57] Cherubino Gambardella, "Il patio e l'impluvium: nuovo frammenti di una architettura classica," in *Il sogno bianco*, pp. 94–100.
[58] Luigi Figini and Gino Pollini, "Ambiente di soggiorno e terrazzo," in *Catalogo della VI Triennale di Milano*, Milan, Hoepli Editore, 1936, also in Vittorio Savi, *Figini e Pollini – Architetture 1927–1989*, Milan, Electa, 1990, p. 39.

59 Luigi Figini, "Architettura naturale
ad Ischia," in *Comunità* 3, May–June,
1949, pp. 36–39; Luigi Figini, "Architettura naturale a Ibiza," in *Comunità*
8, May–June, 1950, pp. 40–43.

Some fifteen years later, Figini's writings on Italian and Mediterranean vernacular demonstrate "continuity" between interwar and postwar interests. In two articles on natural architecture in Ischia and Ibiza, the author seized the opportunity to reflect on recent trends in the historiography of modern architecture.[59] Citing Sigfried Giedion's *Space, Time and Architecture – The Growth of a New Tradition* (1941), Figini pointed to the tendency of many commentators on modern architecture to overemphasize the contribution of technology and that of avant-garde painting movements such as Cubism and Purism. Figini reproached critics for their reluctance to acknowledge what he felt was the equally significant contribution of the South. Examining the intellectual premises of *Mediterraneità* in the development of Rationalism, Figini sees it as instrumental in the "*smeccanizzazione*" or de-mechanization and "*sgelo*" or defrosting of modernism. He concludes his essay with a reminder of the fundamental value of vernacular architecture:

**2.7 Adalberto Libera.
View of courtyard
houses, Tuscolano,
Rome, 1950–54.**
Source: *Casabella-Continuità*
207, 1955.

A lesson of morality and of logic (simplicity, sincerity, modesty, humility, adherence to necessity, renunciation of the superfluous, adaptation to human scale, adaptation to local and environmental conditions). A lesson of life (vast employment of "intermediary" elements between open-air and indoor living: loggias, terraces, porticoes, pergolas, patios, walled gardens, etc.). A lesson of style (anti-decorativism, love of smooth surfaces, and for elementary sculptural solutions, the site and "framing" of buildings in the landscape).[60]

If Figini and Pollini's design for the Villa-studio appropriates the Italian or Mediterranean patio house, with its mixture of classical and vernacular elements, feeling no compulsion to overtly classicize it, Gio Ponti's design for a one-story "Villa alla pompeiana" (1934) is altogether different (plate 15). With its perfectly square plan, central patio, Pompeian-red stucco façade, and low-incline roof, Ponti's villa is closer to the classical spirit typical of *Novecento* than the vernacular–classical of Figini and Pollini's Villa-studio.[61] Ponti's approach to the Italian domestic interior comes across as more pragmatic than ideological (plate 13).[62] In the opening editorial of *Domus*, he wrote:

> The Italian-style house is not a crammed and closed refuge against the harshness of the climate, as it is for those who live on the other side of the Alps, where for many long months people seek to conceal themselves from inclement weather. The Italian house is made for us to enjoy the beauty that our land and our sky bestow upon us during the long seasons.[63]

To be sure, the Pompeian patio house was of interest to traditionalists and modernists in northern and southern countries alike.[64] For example, in his *Une cité industrielle* (1918), Tony Garnier adopted the patio house.[65] Drawing from his journey to the Mediterranean in *Toward an Architecture* (1923), Le Corbusier projected modern *Existenz minimum* values onto the Casa del Noce in Pompei he had visited and sketched (plate 21):

> Out of the clatter of the swarming street which is for every man and full of picturesque incident, you have entered the house of *a Roman*. Majestic grandeur, order, a splendid amplitude: you are in the house of *a Roman*. What was the function of these rooms? That is outside the question. After twenty centuries, without any historical reference, you are conscious of Architecture, and we are speaking of what is in reality a very small house.[66]

Le Corbusier's interest in the Pompeian house is especially significant in the context of Figini and Pollini's Villa-studio. Both designers were founding members of the *Gruppo Sette* and had collectively drafted the first manifestos published in 1926 and 1927.[67] Their writings were largely indebted, both in style and content, to Le Corbusier's *Vers une architecture*, and heralded the advent of a *nuova epoca arcaica* (new archaic era).[68] These writings powerfully endorsed Le Corbusier's rejection of academic historicism and embrace of a "living" relationship with the architectures of the past.[69] This conciliatory attitude is key to understanding why Le Corbusier was so important a mentor for Italian architects who sought to rethink and not merely to reject the past. A passage from the *Gruppo Sette's* 1926 manifesto *Architettura* reads:

> Here, in particular, there exists a classical foundation. The spirit (not the forms, which is something different) of tradition is so profound in Italy that evidently, and almost mechanically, the new architecture will preserve a

[60] Luigi Figini, "Architettura naturale a Ibiza," pp. 40–43.

[61] Gio Ponti, "Una Villa alla Pompeiana," in *Domus* 79, July, 1934, p. 19.

[62] Maristella Casciato, "The Casa all'Italiana and the Idea of Modern Dwelling in Fascist Italy," in *Journal of Architecture* 5, 4, 2000, pp. 335–353; Annalisa Avon, "La casa all'italiana," in Giorgio Ciucci and Giorgio Muratore (eds.), *Storia dell'architettura italiana – Il Primo Novecento*, pp. 162–179.

[63] Gio Ponti, "La Casa all'Italiana," in *Domus* 1, January 1928, p. 7; republished in Giovanni Ponti, *La casa all'italiana*, Milan, Edizioni Domus, 1933, pp. 7–11. English translations in Gio Ponti, *In Praise of Architecture*, New York, F. W. Dodge, 1960, pp. 91–93.

[64] See Carlo Cresti, "Segni e soggezioni di paternità Latina nell' architettura italiana degli anni Venti e Trenta," in Marilena Pasquali (ed.), *Pompei e il recupero del classico*, Ancona, Galleria d'arte moderna, 1980, pp. 120–135.

[65] Pierre Pinon, "Calcestruzzo e Mediterraneo," in *Tony Garnier 1869–1948*, Milan, Mazzotta, 1990, pp. 102–135.

[66] Maria Salerno, "Mare e memoria: la casa mediterranea nell'opera di Le Corbusier," in Benedetto Gravagnuolo (ed.), *Le Corbusier e l'Antico – Viaggi nel Mediterraneo*, Naples, Electa, 2000, pp. 107–113; see also Gerard Monnier, "L'architecture vernaculaire, Le Corbusier et les autres," in *La Méditerranée de Le Corbusier*, Aix-en-Provence, Publications de l'Université de Provence, 1991, pp. 139–155.

[67] The four foundational writings of the *Gruppo Sette* were published in *La rassegna italiana* between December 1926 and May 1927. English translations of "Architecture" and "Architecture II: The Foreigners" are in *Oppositions* 6, Fall 1976, pp. 85–102; English translations for "Architecture (III): Unpreparedness–Incomprehension–Prejudices" and "Architecture (IV): A New Archaic Era" are in *Oppositions* 12, Spring 1978, pp. 88–105.

[68] Marida Talamona, "Primi passi verso l'Europa (1927–1933)," in Vittorio Gregotti and Giovanni Marzari (eds.), *Luigi Figini. Gino Pollini. Opera Completa*, Milan, Electa 1996, pp. 55–81.

[69] Kurt Forster, "Antiquity and Modernity in the La Roche-Jeanneret Houses of 1923," in *Oppositions* 15–16, Winter/Spring 1979, pp. 131–153.

2.8 Giuseppe Vaccaro.
Agip Recreation Colony,
Cesenatico, 1938.
Source: © Archivio Giuseppe
Vaccaro.

70 Gruppo 7, "Architettura," December 1926.
71 Since its first issue in 1933, the journal was the center of the debate over the Mediterranean ideal. By including poetry, literature, and art in addition to architecture, the editors aimed to emulate journals such as *Cahiers d'art* and attract a broad readership. Franco Biscossa, "'Quadrante': il dibattito e la polemica," in Giulio Ernesti (ed.), *Costruzione dell'Utopia – Architetti e urbanisti nell'Italia fascista*, pp. 67–89.
72 The program of *Quadrante* was endorsed by Piero Bottoni, Mario Cereghini, Luigi Figini, Gino Frette, Enrico A. Griffini, Pietro Lingeri, Gino Pollini, Gian Luigi Banfi, Lodovico B. Belgioioso, Enrico Peressutti, and Ernesto N. Rogers.
73 Reprinted in Luciano Patetta (ed.), *L'architettura in Italia 1919–1943*, pp. 227–229.
74 Giovanni Denti, Andrea Savio, and Gianni Calzà (eds.), *Le Corbusier in Italia*, Milan, Clup, 1988.
75 On the CIAM see Eric Mumford, *The CIAM Discourse on Urbanism, 1928–1960*, Cambridge, The MIT Press, 2000; Sara Protasoni, "Il Gruppo Italiano e la tradizione del moderno," in *Rassegna* 52, December 1992, pp. 28–39.
76 Letter of Carlo Enrico Rava to Le Corbusier dated March 1927, in Maria

stamp which is typically *ours*. And this is already a great force, since tradition, as we said, does not disappear, but changes appearance.[70]

Tradition and "lyricism" was what allowed these rationalists to go beyond functionalism. Lyricism was also closely associated with the concept of *Mediterraneità* espoused by members of the *Gruppo Sette* during the late 1920s, who later went on to endorse the "*pensée midi*" of the journal *Quadrante*.[71] Though the *Gruppo Sette* had dissolved by 1930, its founding members were joined by several other architects in clarifying and defending their approach to Rationalism in the "*Programma*," published in the first issue of *Quadrante*. During a time when they were being questioned by Fascist officials for betraying *Italianità*, the group advanced their own design agendas including an anti-academic response to classicism and *Mediterraneità*:[72]

> A clarification is required about the characteristics of Italian rationalism. We appreciate classicism and "*Mediterraneità*" on the grounds of their spiritual dimension and not merely as tools for stylistic exercises or picturesque revival. We view classicism and "*Mediterraneità*" as antagonistic to certain approaches of Northern architects, Baroque revivals and arbitrary romanticism, which also characterize some of the new European architecture.[73]

The architects working in the circle of *Quadrante* wanted to engage the powerful, dream-like visual qualities of the sun-drenched Mediterranean environment and cultural heritage that had already fascinated artists. In 1933, several Italian delegates of the Congrés International d' Architecture Moderne (CIAM) such as Giuseppe Terragni, Figini and Pollini met Le Corbusier onboard the *Patris II* as it sailed from Marseille to Athens.[74] From 1928, the year of its founding, to 1959, when it was disbanded, CIAM offered important opportunities for Italian architects who identified with Rationalism and *Mediterraneità* to build alliances with like-minded colleagues outside of Italy.[75] After reading Le Corbusier's *Vers une architecture* (1923), members of the *Gruppo Sette* like Carlo Enrico Rava wrote to the Franco-Swiss architect: "The origin of our ideas is to be found within yours; consequently, our intellectual debt is to you."[76] It is not surprising that these Italians in thrall to Rationalism would revere the Franco-Swiss architect who fused antiquity and *art paysan*, and whose villa for CIAM patron Madame de Mandrot in France (1930–31) synthesized *Mediterraneità*.[77]

Rationalist architects found themselves under constant attack by historicist and nationalistic architects on the grounds that their designs were inspired by non-Italian sources. Enrico Peressutti, a member of the Studio Architetti BBPR founded in 1932 and a partner of the *Quadrante* milieu, responded to such claims by stressing the Italian and trans-national heritage of the Mediterranean vernacular. In his article "Mediterranean Architecture," published in *Quadrante* in 1935, Peressutti wrote:

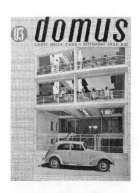

2.9 Giuseppe Terragni, Casa Rustici, Milan, 1933–35.
Source: *Domus* 13, 1935.

> Here they all are, recreated in the houses of Biskra, in the houses of Libya, in the houses of Capri. Here is a heritage that we Italians all too often ignore, or want to ignore; a patrimony which we have confined to the archives, a patrimony which we have neglected, as if it were merely a document which has only historical value. . . . A patrimony which, rediscovered by Gropius, Le Corbusier, Mies van der Rohe, has been disguised as an innovation of northern origin, as a twentieth-century invention. And many have been deceived. Many have mistaken this disguise for a real novelty, for a universal law. Without realizing that this novelty lacks the life, lacks the language, lacks the song of the Mediterranean.[78]

Peressutti was writing to defend the "authentic" origins of the shared vernacular heritage and its role in a Mediterranean modernism that responded to site and context. Peressutti was venting his concerns at a time when discussions concerning Italy's Mediterranean colonies raised the spectres of hybridity and authenticity. Recall Luigi Piccinato's Rationalist design for a Casa Coloniale based on a courtyard house typology and displayed at the 1933 Milan Triennale.[79] Comments from critics outside Italy supported Peressutti's claim that the Mediterranean vernacular, with its flat roof and "cubist" volumes, was viewed as a source of *Mediterranean modernism* that in turn influenced northern European modernist movements.

Paul Schultze-Naumburg's comparison of a village on the Greek island of Santorini with the Weissenhof in his *Das Gesicht des Deutschen Hauses* (The Face of the German House, 1929) is a case in point, as is the much more aggressive (and racist) 1941 collage of the German Heimatschutzbund in which the Weissenhof housing estate was compared with an Arab village.[80] Unlike these racist assignations, Peressutti's observation showed a deep understanding of pan-Mediterranean architecture with its attention to the relationship between site, climate, and building. This is the position that Gio Ponti repeated some years later when he expanded his previously more narrow vision to espouse a more inclusive, shared Mediterranean heritage:

> The Mediterranean is large and its shores along the coasts of Morocco, Spain, France, Sardinia, Sicily, Italy, the Tyrrhenian and the Adriatic, Greece, Anatolia, Palestine, Egypt, Libya, Tunisia, and Algeria have washed over many different histories, civilizations and climates.[81]

Lamberti, "Le Corbusier e l'Italia (1932–1936)," in *Annali della Scuola normale superiore di Pisa*, 1972, p. 827. Marida Talamona, "Primi passi verso l'Europa (1927–1933)," in Vittorio Gregotti and Giovanni Marzari (eds.), *Luigi Figini. Gino Polllini*, pp. 55–81.
[77] Luisa Martina Colli, *Arte artigianato e tecnica nella poetica di Le Corbusier*, Bari/Roma, Laterza, 1982; Le Corbusier's *L'Etude sur le mouvement d'art décoratif en Allemagne* (1911) and *Les Arts décoratifs d'aujourd hui* (1925) dedicates ample space to "*l'art paysan*." On Corbusier and the vernacular see Francesco Passanti, "The Vernacular, Modernism, and Le Corbusier," *Journal of the Society of Architectural Historians*, 4, 1997, pp. 438–451.
[78] Enrico Peressutti, "Architettura mediterranea," in *Quadrante* 21, 1935, pp. 40–41. English translation published in Stefano de Martino and Alex Wall (eds.), *Cities of Childhood: Italian Colonies of the 1930s*, London, Architectural Association, 1988, p. 78.
[79] Giuliano Gresleri, Pier Giorgio Massaretti, and Stefano Zagnoni (eds.), *Architettura italiana d'oltremare, 1870–1940*, Venice, Marsilio, 1993. For an overview of colonialism see Mia Fuller, *Moderns Abroad – Architecture, Cities and Italian Imperialism*, London/New York, Routledge, 2007.
[80] For a detailed analysis of these episodes see Kai K. Gutschow's essay in this volume. See also Richard Pommer, "The Flat Roof Controversy in Germany," in *Art Journal*, Summer 1983, pp. 158–169.
[81] Gio Ponti, "Facciamoci una coscienza nazionale della architettura mediterranea," in *Lo Stile nella Casa e nell'arredamento* 7, July 1941, p. 1.

82 Lisa Licitra Ponti, *Gio Ponti, L'opera*, pp. 96–97.

83 Gio Ponti "Una casa al mare" in *Domus, 138*, June 1939, p. 34. See the essay by Andrea Bocco Guarneri in this book.

84 See Fabio Mangone, *Viaggi a sud. Architetti nordici in Italia, 1850–1925*, Naples, Electa, 2002).

85 On Capri as a pilgrimage site for architects, see Fabio Mangone, *Capri e gli architetti* (Naples: Massa, 2004). On the broad range of artists and intellectuals who visited and lived on the island, see Lea Vergine, ed., *Capri 1905–1940*, Milan, Skira, 2003 On Cerio, see "Edwin Cerio" in *Dizionario biografico degli italiani*, Rome, Istituto della enciclopedia italiana, 1979, pp. 745–47.

86 Filippo Tommaso Marinetti, "Il discorso," *Il convegno del paesaggio*, Edwin Cerio (ed.), Naples, Gaspare Casella, 1923. Capri, Edizioni la Conchiglia, 1993.

87 Apollonio, *Futurist Manifestos*, 19–24. See R. Warren Flint, ed., *Marinetti: Selected Writings*, New York: Farrar, Straus and Giroux, 1971, pp. 39–44; on Futurism, see Enrico Crispolti, *Storia e critica del futurismo*, Bari-Rome, Laterza, 1986; Ezio Godoli, *Il futurismo*, Bari and Rome, Laterza, 1983.

88 Filippo Tommaso Marinetti, "Elogio di Capri," *Natura* 1, January 1928, pp. 41–48; Francesco Cangiullo, *Marinetti a Capri: Blu Marino*, Naples, Gaspare Casella Editore, 1922.

89 See Alessandro d'Amico and Silvia Danesi (eds.), *Virgilio Marchi architetto, scenografo, futurista*, Milan, Electa, 1977; Enrico Crispolti, "Virgilio Marchi architetto futurista ed espressionista," *Il mito della macchina e altri temi del futurismo*, Trapani, Celebes, 1971, pp. 343–361; Ezio Godoli, "Virgilio Marchi e l'architettura futurista nella prima metà degli anni Venti," *Il Futurismo*, pp. 44–49.

90 Virgilio Marchi, "Primitivismi capresi," *Cronache d'attualità 6–10*, June–October 1922, pp. 49–51. On avant-garde journals in Rome during the 1920s see also Elisabetta Mondello, *Roma futurista. I periodici e i luoghi dell'avanguardia nella Roma degli anni venti*, Milan, Franco Angeli, 1990.

91 Virgilio Marchi, "Quadro della capacità architettonica," in *Architettura futurista*, Foligno, Franco Campitelli, 1924, pp. 26–34; republished in vol. 1 of Ezio Godoli and Milva Giacomelli, *Virgilio Marchi. Scritti di architettura*, Florence, Octavo, 1995, pp. 57–61.

It is not unlikely that his design collaboration with Bernard Rudofsky for an extensive hotel on Capri with numerous whitewashed and flat-roofed vernacular "case-stanze" or room-like houses led Ponti to rethink his former dependency on the classical language of *Novecento*.[82] Following this collaborative experience with Rudofsky, Ponti conceived projects for vacation villas in seaside settings. Together, the whitewashed surfaces and flat roofs and the colorful interiors echoed the modesty of extant Mediterranean vernaculars while promoting "a luxury of the spirit."[83]

Capri and the Futurists

By the early 1920s Capri had become an important pilgrimage site for artists and architects who looked with interest to its vernacular forms for a number of different reasons.[84] Capri's climate, the interaction of architecture and landscape, coupled with its remote qualities inspired and relaxed world travelers. After the First World War, owing to the efforts of Capri's charismatic mayor Edwin Cerio, an engineer-turned-politician, the island (like the French Riviera and other Mediterranean destinations including Ibiza) became a haven for artists, architects, intellectuals, and preservationists from around the world.[85] In an address delivered to the 1922 *Convegno del Paesaggio* (Symposium on Landscape) in Capri, Filippo Tommaso Marinetti praised the *"stile pratico* (practical style)" of indigenous architecture. He celebrated the island's local vernacular architecture for its rational rather than picturesque qualities, and asserted:

> I believe that this is a Futuristic island; I feel that it is full of infinite originality as if it had been sculpted by Futurist architects like Sant'Elia, Virgilio Marchi, painted by Balla, Depero, Russolo, Prampolini, and sung and made musical by Francesco Cangiullo and Casella![86]

Despite his war cry in the *Manifesto of Futurism* of 1909 to "free this land [Italy] from its smelly gangrene of professors, archaeologists, *ciceroni* and antiquarians," more than ten years later he exonerated vernacular architecture and folk art, sparing it his anti-historicist wrath and proclaiming them to lie outside the flux of the history of style.[87] Marinetti saw beauty and freedom in the dramatic and unpredictable landscape of Capri because it rejected "any kind of order reminiscent of classicism."[88]

The Futurists were, paradoxically, interested in both the myth of the machine and the "primitive" character of vernacular architecture and peasant art. The use of the vernacular did not imply an end to the avant-garde, but rather a reframing of its objectives; the seemingly opposed mass-produced a-contextual machine and historically charged landscape in fact coincided and mutually influenced each other. In 1922, Virgilio Marchi (1895–1960), an architect and set designer who was known for his Futurist-expressionist style, lauded the vernacular architecture of Capri and the Amalfi coast as a source for contemporary designers in "Primitivismi capresi (Capri Primitivisms),"[89] a short, illustrated essay he published in *Cronache d'attualità*, Anton Giulio Bragaglia's avant-garde journal.[90]

Two years later, in his *Architettura futurista* (1924), Marchi elaborated on the "innate virtue of primitive builders" in his discussion of the relationship between the vernacular tradition and contemporary design.[91] On the cover he reproduced a design for a hydroelectric station – one of the most modern of twentieth-century architectural types – that echoes the sculptural, stereotomic qualities of the Capri and Amalfi coast vernacular he had recorded in a drawing a few years earlier of the Hotel Luna (Amalfi). In this book as well as his *Italia nuova architettura nuova* of 1931, Marchi expressed admiration for the "ingenious spontaneity" of the architecture of Capri.[92] With *Architettura futurista* and *Italia nuova architettura nuova*, Marchi tried to position himself as the living heir to Sant'Elia as promoter of futurist architecture after the latter's premature death.

The dialogue between classical and vernacular traditions among artists and architects shaped interwar Italian modernism in thrall to *Mediterraneità*. For example, the influential artist and writer Carlo Belli working in the circle of *Quadrante* reflected on the interest in *Mediterraneità* and classicism (which he calls *Grecità*):

> The theme of *Mediterraneità* and *Grecità* [Greek-ness] was our navigational star. . . . We studied the construction techniques of the vernacular of Capri, in order to understand why houses were built that way. We discovered their traditional authenticity and we understood that their perfect rationality coincided with optimum aesthetic values.[93]

Despite their common platform and appreciation for the classical and vernacular traditions, there are substantial differences between the approaches of rationalists such as Giuseppe Pagano and Edoardo Persico, who openly criticized the *Quadrante* milieu on the basis of their "excess" lyricism (in other words, their lack of adherence to the New Objectivity of the New Architecture). Although Pagano's promotion of Italian and Mediterranean vernacular traditions via his exhibition *Architettura rurale italiana* at the Milan Triennale in 1936 also projected issues of nationalism onto modernity, his approach toward the patio house was more straightforward and less self-consciously "poetic." Giuseppe Pagano, Franco Diotallevi, and Irenio Marescotti's schemes for a "Città orizzontale" or Horizontal City (1940) employed courtyard housing extensively.[94] In these examples of urban planning, the patio house was the template for multiple-unit housing.

After the end of the Second World War, Adalberto Libera designed a housing estate in the Tuscolano neighborhood of Rome (realized under the aegis of INA casa) on the basis of the patio house.[95] Libera embedded his configuration of interlocking patio houses into its irregular site, inspiring Bruno Zevi to describe it as a *"grattacielo sdraiato"* or reclining skyscraper, and a "horizontal Unité d'Habitation."[96] This horizontal village was designed as a self-contained community in which basic services were provided alongside the domestic units. By abandoning the urban tactic of the classical grid, like the Horizontal City of Pagano, Diotallevi, and Marescotti, Libera was able to achieve a sense of community without succumbing to the trope of classical visual and spatial order which had fallen into disrepute with the Fascist regime.

[92] Virgilio Marchi, "Primitivismi Capresi" and "Priorità futuriste," in *Italia nuova architettura nuova*, Rome-Foligno, Franco Campitelli Editore, 1931, pp. 19–23, 25–32; republished in vol. 2 of Ezio Godoli and Milva Giacomelli, *Virgilio Marchi*, Florence, Octavo, 1995, pp. 31–34, 35–40.

[93] Silvia Danesi, "Aporie dell'architettura italiana in periodo fascista—mediterraneità e purismo," in Silvia Danesi and Luciano Patetta (eds.), pp. 21–28.

[94] Massimiliano Vittori and Giorgio Muratore (eds.), *Angiolo Mazzoni: architetto futurista in Agro Pontino*, Latina, Novecento, 2000; *Angiolo Mazzoni: architetto ingegnere del Ministero delle comunicazioni*, Milano, Skira, 2003.

[95] Marco Zanuso "Unità d'abitazione orizzontale nel quartiere Tuscolano a Roma," in *Casabella-Continuità* 207, September–October, 1955, pp. 30–37; Angela Argenti, "Adalberto Libera, l'insula-Casa al Tuscolano," *Rassegna di Architettura e Urbanistica* 117, September–December, 2005, pp. 86–97.

[96] Bruno Zevi, "Il grattacielo sdraiato," *L'Espresso* 8, February 22, 1955, pp. 28–29, republished in Bruno Zevi, *Cronache di Architettura* vol. 1, Rome and Bari, Editori Laterza and Figli, 1971, p. 300

2.10 View of Sabaudia, c. 1936.
Source: © Archivio Storico TCI, Milan.

97 Cherubino Gambardella, "Un ara arcaica tra roccia e mare: Villa Malaparte," in Cherubino Gambardella, *Il sogno bianco*, pp. 106–114.
98 Renato De Fusco, "Mediterraneità minimalista," in Francesco Domenico Moccia (ed.), *Luigi Cosenza scritti e progetti di architettura*, Naples, Clean, 1994, pp. 20–23; Jean-Louis Cohen, "La Villa Oro, o tre miti moderni," in Alfredo Buccaro and Giancarlo Mainini (eds.), *Luigi Cosenza oggi*, Naples, Clean, 2006, pp. 116–117.
99 Cherubino Gambardella, *Case sul Golfo – Abitare lungo la costa napoletana 1930–1945*.
100 Enrico A. Griffini and Luigi M. Caneva (eds.), *36 Progetti di Ville di Architetti Italiani*, Milan and Rome, Casa editrice d'arte Bestetti e Tumminelli, 1930, pp. 33–37. Also see Giancarlo Consonni, Lodovico Meneghetti and Graziella Tonon (eds.), *Piero Bottoni – Opera Completa*, Milan, Fabbri Editori, 1990, pp. 166–167.
101 Gian Carlo Jocteau (ed.), *Ai monti e al mare. Cento anni di colonie per l'infanzia*, Milan, Fabbri Editori, 1990; Stefano de Martino and Alex Wall (eds.), *Cities of Childhood: Italian Colonies of the 1930s*, London, Architectural Association, 1988.
102 Umberto Cao (ed.), *Giuseppe Vaccaro: Colonia marina a Cesenatico (1936–38)*, Rome, Clear, 1994.
103 See Benito Mussolini, *Fascist Agrarian Program*, January 1921, republished in Charles F. Delzell (ed.), *Mediterranean Fascism, 1919–1945*, New York, Walker, 1971, pp. 18–21; Carlo Cresti, "Mediterraneità e ruralità," in Carlo Cresti, *Architettura e fascismo*, Florence, Vallecchi, 1986, pp. 95–144.
104 On the relationship between politics, propaganda, and rural culture, see Laura Malvano, *Fascismo e politica dell'immagine*, pp. 144–151.
105 Walter L. Adamson, *Avant-garde Florence: From Modernism to Fascism*, Cambridge, Harvard University Press, 1993; Walter Adamson, "The Culture of Italian Fascism and the Fascist Crisis of Modernity: The Case of Il Selvaggio," in *Journal of Contemporary History*, 20, 1995, pp. 555–575; Luciano Troisio (ed.), *Le riviste di Strapaese e Stracittà – Il Selvaggio – L'Italiano*, Treviso, Canova, 1975; Emily Braun, "Speaking Volumes: Giorgio Morandi's Still Lifes and the Cultural Politics of Strapaese," in *Modernism/Modernity* 2–3, 1995, pp. 89–116.

Villas and *Casa Coloniche*: Elitism versus Populism

While Adalberto Libera's *insula* in Tuscolano shares little with his dramatic Villa Malaparte completed years earlier (1938–42), his renewed commitment to the vernacular links these two projects and creates a bridge between his interwar and postwar design tactics.[97] Continuity within minimalist Mediterranean modernist design is also self-evident in the designs of Luigi Cosenza during this period. Cosenza's Villa Oro (designed in collaboration with Bernard Rudofsky and completed in 1937) shares much of the Mediterranean character of the Olivetti factory and grounds in Pozzuoli he designed years later (1951–54; 1970).[98] The vernacular thus functioned as an underground stream that continued to traverse and feed into Italian modern architecture during Fascist and Democratic Italy.

Despite their allusions to extant Mediterranean vernacular, both the Villa Malaparte and the Villa Oro are single-family villas designed for elite clients who were able to afford them.[99] Piero Bottoni's acclaimed "Villa Latina" or "Villa al Mare," presented at the Fourth Milan Triennale in 1930, also belongs to this group of elite vacation retreats geared toward enjoyment of the Mediterranean Sea (plate 18).[100] To be sure, enthusiasm for the Mediterranean was spurred primarily by Italy's "leisure class," who commissioned weekend and vacation homes along the Adriatic, Ionian, Mediterranean, and Tyrrhenian seas. The most important examples of Italian domestic architecture that invoked *Mediterraneità* were designed with these sites in mind. An exception to these private retreats that were also geared toward enjoyment of the Mediterranean were the numerous "cities of childhood," recreational and sun therapy colonies for youth, realized under the auspices of the Fascist regime.[101] The sweeping monumentality of Giuseppe Vaccaro's Agip Colony in Cesenatico (1938) or Giuseppe Terragni's extensive use of outdoor corridors (*ballatoio*) in the Casa Rustici (Milan, 1933–35) are just some of many such examples in which the open-air terraces and balconies allowed Fascist youth to experience the visual and sensual spectacle of the Mediterranean.[102]

While the villa continued to carry with it associations of prestige, one of the types with which Italian (and thus Mediterranean insofar as Italy is part of the basin) vernacular was most associated is the *casa colonica*, a two-story dwelling whose program combined domestic and agrarian functions. A *colono* was a tenant farmer who worked the land, but did not own it. All too rarely have scholars discussed *Mediterraneità* as a function of Mussolini's "ruralism," belonging to his economic and social plans based on revitalizing Italy's agricultural resources and his desire to celebrate "the *Homo rusticus* as the most dependable type of *Homo sapiens*."[103] During the 1930s Rationalist architects and urbanists looked to the "*casa colonica*" because it provided a cost-efficient, easily repeated model for domestic architecture and could be offered to tenant farmers either in the outskirts or within new towns like Sabaudia, Littoria (present-day Latina), and Aprilia. The concerted attention to the design of company towns for agriculture demonstrated Benito Mussolini's plan to re-establish Italy's agricultural primacy.[104]

With their characteristically strong sense of regional pride, Tuscan intellectuals (mainly in Florence) saw in the "*casa colonica*" a fusion of tradition and modernism and staked claims to its paternity. Their zeal was fueled by competition between rural (*Strapaese*) and metropolitan (*Stracittà*) values espoused by Maccari.[105] Writers like Curzio Malaparte eventually abandoned Massimo Bontempelli's cosmopolitan journal *900 Cahiers d'Italie et d'Europe* to

FONTI DELLA MODERNA ARCHITETTURA ITALIANA

Poiché viva è sempre fra il pubblico la discus- sione sui caratteri della nuova Architettura, ci piace presentare due esempi di case coloniche, delle quali è stato rifatto lo schema disegnativo, a dimostrare come « nuovissime » forme, quelle che il pubblico poco attento definisce nordiche o, per essere più pre- cisi « tedesche », hanno pure radici da noi, nella chiara serena nostrana tradizione e della logicità funzionale di questi esempi sono lo sviluppo.

Queste fotografie e questi disegni dicono, più di qualunque commento, in quale errore si cada con- dannando delle costruzioni che differiscono dalle au- tiche o comunque da quelle generalmente accettate ed ammirate soltanto per la sostituzione della terrazza.

elemento antichissimo, elemento mediterraneo. Un molti casi più pratical al tetto e per un maggior nitore o senso di pulizia che dir si voglia, che tanto offende gli amatori del vecchio ad ogni costo.

GIOVANNI MICHELUCCI

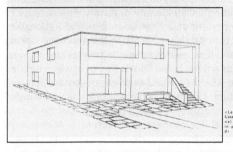

«Lo Panzer Casa colonica nel Chianti in provincia di Firenze

Casa colonica nella villa Salviati ora Hagermann nei dintorni di Firenze

2.11 (*Top* and *Bottom*)
Giovanni Michelucci.
"Fonti della moderna
architettura" (Sources
of Modern
Architecture).

Source: *Domus* 50, 1932.

adhere to Maccari's platform and promoted the values of a "primitive" Italian peasantry.[106]

The debate over the *casa colonica* polarized the attention of Tuscan architects, artists, and critics like Giovanni Michelucci, Corrado Pavolini, Ardengo Soffici, and Mario Tinti. Different positions surfaced. Soffici argued that classical influences helped shape the *casa colonica*, an argument that minimized the contribution of the anonymous builder, whether artisan or peasant, whom progressive architects like Pagano did much to celebrate. Ardengo Soffici's complaints that the anonymous builders were being fetishized, and that many of the examples cited were actually "designed" by architects fell upon deaf ears.[107] Even so, Soffici looked almost exclusively to the Tuscan hill towns and agrarian landscapes where such buildings were found in constructing his own paintings,[108] and Pavolini and Tinti hailed the Tuscan *casa colonica* as a legitimate source of contemporary design.

In 1935 Mario Tinti published an important text entitled *L'architettura delle case coloniche in Toscana* with thirty-two commissioned drawings by the Roman artist Ottone Rosai.[109] Rosai would continue to explore the mesmerizing pull of the "primitive" archetypes of reed haystacks and the Italian cottage throughout his artistic life. Other critics and artists, like Pagano in Milan, discussed the appropriation of the *casa colonica* in relation to contemporary criticism of the Rationalist movement in architecture and with respect to the problem of *Italianità*.[110] Thus Corrado Pavolini argued in 1933:

> When a rationalist architect will search in his work to be originally inspired by these concepts, that is, to understand the admonition of a good realistic

[106] Fabrizio Brunetti, *Architetti e fascism*, Florence, Alinea, 1993; in particular see chapter entitled "La polemica di Strapaese", pp. 217–237.
[107] Ardengo Soffici, "Neoprimi- tivismi," in *Selva Arte*, Florence, Vallecchi, 1943, pp. 323–326.
[108] See Luigi Cavallo (ed.), *Ardengo Soffici*, Milan, Mazzotta, 1992.
[109] *Ottone Rosai nel centenario della nascita – Opere dal 1919 al 1957*, Flo- rence, Edizioni Pananti 1957; Luigi Cavallo (ed.), *Ottone Rosai*, Milan, Mazzotta, 1995.
[110] When in 1936 Pagano would gather images of Tuscan farmhouses for his *architettura rurale* exhibition he asked a local architect Pier Niccolò Berardi who had already spent years in the pursuit of this interest. Recently these photos have been republished in Giovanni Fanelli and Barbara Mazza, *La casa colonica in Toscana. Le fotografie di Pier Niccolò Berardi alla Triennale del 1936*, Florence, Octavo, 1999.

[111] Corrado Pavolini, "Case toscane," *Illustrazione toscana e dell'Etruria*, 1933, pp. 20–24.

[112] Giovanni Ceas, *Capri – Visioni architettoniche di Gio. Batt. Ceas*, Rome, Biblioteca d'arte editrice, 1930.

[113] Giovanni Michelucci, "Contatti fra architetture antiche e moderne (I)" *Domus*, 50, 1932, pp. 70–71; "Contatti fra architetture antiche e moderne (II)," in *Domus*, 51, 1932, pp. 134–136; "Fonti della moderna architettura italiana," in *Domus*, 56, 1932, pp. 460–461.

[114] Paolo Portoghesi, *After Modern Architecture*, New York, Rizzoli, 1982, p. 36.

[115] Vittorio Gregotti, *New Directions in Italian Architecture*, New York, George Braziller, 1968, pp. 54–56.

[116] See Eugen Joseph Weber, *Peasants into Frenchmen: The Modernization of Rural France, 1870–1914*, Stanford, Stanford University Press, 1976, and Silvio Lanaro, "Da contadini a Italiani," in Piero Bevilacqua (ed.), *Storia dell'agricoltura italiana in età contemporanea*, vol. 3, Venice, Marsilio Editori, 1991, pp. 937–968.

sense and of ideal warmth that comes from the Tuscan house, I will say then that he will have made a rational work (conceived according to reason) or functional (responding to function): because he will have made a work that is alive, natural and beautiful.[111]

But Pavolini did not limit his analysis to Tuscany; he also praised a recent book by Giovanni Ceas on the vernacular architecture of Capri. He declared it a triumph of "*razionalismo spontaneo* (spontaneous rationalism)" because it was not "designed" by architects but rather built by masons in situ.[112] Thus, despite the focus on Tuscany, most of the protagonists of vernacular architecture looked to examples across the regions of the Italian peninsula. This allowed for the emergence of an Italian "*casa colonica*" that was both national and regional. This was also the position espoused by the architect Giovanni Michelucci, who added to the choir of voices of those who saw in the Tuscan farmhouse a model of contemporary design that could fulfill functional requirements without obliterating Italian identity or history. This defense of Italian-ness was especially important at a time when critics of Rationalism claimed that modern architects in Italy were betraying the nation by looking to examples of international and Bolshevik avant-garde architecture. In 1932, Michelucci published a series of articles in Gio Ponti's *Domus* in which he tried to mollify critics by discussing what he viewed as points of contact between ancient and modern architecture. The most significant of these was entitled "Sources of Modern Italian Architecture," in which he celebrated the Tuscan farmhouse as an Italian model for modern architecture.[113] Michelucci's discussion of tradition and modern Italian architecture was directed toward operative concerns with the intent of establishing a genealogy that could subsume both the Tuscan vernacular and contemporary Italian modernism. He illustrated his point by redrawing the *casa colonica* without the typical pitched roof and by introducing a rooftop garden used by Le Corbusier. Michelucci argued that the core elements of vernacular buildings could undergo transformations such as substitution of materials (reinforced concrete in the place of masonry) and still reflect Italian-ness because they continued to resemble the forms and spatial configurations of extant traditional buildings even though they might look like abstract German modernism.

Urbino and the Italian Hill Town Revisited

Paolo Portoghesi described "peasant culture" as an "old passion" of Italian architects during the twentieth century.[114] Echoing this enthusiasm and asserting the continuity between interwar and postwar architecture, Vittorio Gregotti stated:

> Interest in spontaneous architecture had long existed in Italy. Since Giuseppe Pagano and Guarniero Daniel's book *Architettura rurale italiana* (1936), this architecture had been seen as naturally connected with rationalist architecture, inasmuch as it related the natural and functional styles of building. Its extraordinary formal repertory had, for many years, a direct influence on Italian architects attempting to make contact with the working class.[115]

For postwar architects of Gregotti's generation working under the influence of Neorealism, the rediscovery of the vernacular was essential in order to engage with the reality (and innate poetry) of a peasantry that had been gradually transformed into proletariat citizens over the course of the first half of the twentieth century.[116]

Carlo Levi's *Christ Stopped at Eboli*, an autobiographical account of his forced exile in the "godforsaken" region of Lucania, was published in 1945, immediately after the end of the Second World War. In his autobiographical account he wrote, apropos the Mediterranean qualities of the hill town he visited during his time in southern Italy:

It had been hard at first. Grassano, like all the villages hereabouts, is a streak of white at the summit of a bare hill, a sort of miniature imaginary Jerusalem in the solitude of the desert.[117]

His gripping yet poetic tale of the year he spent amongst the unschooled, often illiterate peoples of the South served to reignite interest in artisanal practices among "book-fed" intellectuals, artists, and architects. Levi's fascination with the natural and built environment of the South was captured in the ethereal palette of whites and pinks of paintings such as his *Aliano sul burrone* (1935) (plate 23).[118] The first architecture to take its cue from Levi's poetic rendering of southern Italy and its culture was La Martella, a new town completed in 1954 near the town of Matera. It was one of the first postwar experiments in which vernacular models like the *casa colonica* were employed to create an autonomous village for peasants who formerly inhabited troglodyte dwellings or *sassi*. Ludovico Quaroni led the team of designers. The completion of the village fell shortly after the opening of the *Mostra di architettura spontanea* (Spontaneous Architecture) exhibition curated by Giancarlo De Carlo, Enzo Cerutti, and Giuseppe Samonà. This exhibition promoted the high density and social heterogeneity of the vernacular of Italian villages, towns, and cities. Reviewing this contribution to Italian architectural culture, De Carlo openly praised the "realism" underlying the conception and realization of La Martella:

The urban planners that designed this village did not think about realizing a dream of utopian ideal city. But rather, in front of the problem of having to build an organism that could provide housing for a group of peasants originally living in the sassi of Matera, they began their work thinking about the real limits of this problem.[119]

Thus, for De Carlo, the strategic adoption of extant architecture as part of a comprehensive idea of the town as village, in which domestic architecture coexisted with small artisanal *bottege* or workshops, a church, and other communal buildings to create an autonomous and self-sufficient community reflected a response to real conditions with concrete proposals that avoided abstract utopianism. It was from this materialist understanding that the notion of Neorealist architecture arose.[120] De Carlo would soon offer his own take on Neorealist architecture in his mixed-use public housing project for Matera (1956–57).

Although Quaroni's La Martella shares some point in common with experiments conducted in the mid-1930s in the new towns along the Roman coast such as Sabaudia and Littoria, the political and economic conditions that made these projects possible during the interwar years changed radically with the fall of Fascism (plate 20). The Fascist initiatives were focused upon reclaiming marshlands with the nation's economic prosperity in mind, whereas Quaroni's La Martella was more an existentialist experiment in rethinking conditions of dwelling. While new towns tended to fuse grid plans and winding streets, this postwar example steered completely away from any trace of orthogonality.

[117] Carlo Levi, *Christ Stopped at Eboli*, New York, Farrar, Straus and Co., 1947, p. 5; originally published as *Cristo si è fermato a Eboli*, Turin, Einaudi, 1945.
[118] On Levi as painter during his period of exile, see Pia Vivarelli (ed.), *Carlo Levi e la Lucania: Dipinti del confino 1935–1936*, Rome, De Luca Edizioni d'Arte, 1990.
[119] Giancarlo De Carlo, "A proposito di La Martella," in *Casabella-Continuità* 200, February–March 1954, pp. v–viii.
[120] On the concept of realism in modern architecture, see Manfredo Tafuri, "Realismo e architettura," in Vittorio Magnago Lampugnani (ed.), *Architettura moderna: L'avventura delle idée, 1750–1980*, Milan, Electa, 1985, pp. 123–145; Bruno Reichlin, "Figures of Neorealism in Italian Architecture (Part 1)," in *Grey Room* 5, Fall 2001, pp. 78–101; "Figures of Neorealism in Italian Architecture (Part 2)," in *Grey Room* 6, Winter 2002, pp. 110–133. See Amerigo Restucci, *Matera: I sassi*, Turin, Einaudi, 1991.

121 See Lamberto Rossi, *Giancarlo De Carlo. Architetture* (Milan: Arnoldo Mondadori Editore, 1988); Francesco Cellini and Claudio D'Amato, *Le architetture di Ridolfi e Frankl*, Milano, Electa, 2005; Paola Di Biagi (ed.), *La grande ricostruzione: il piano INA-Casa e l'Italia degli anni Cinquanta*, Roma, Donzelli, 2001.
122 Ernesto De Martino, *Sud e magia*, Milan, Feltrinelli, 1959; Ernesto De Martino, *The Land of Remorse: A Study of Southern Italian Tarantism*, London, Free Association, 2005; originally published as *La terra del remorse*, Milan, Saggiatore, 1961.
123 See introduction to Rita Devos and Mil de Kooning (eds.), *L'architecture moderne à l'Expo 58*, Brussels, Fonds Mercator et Dexia Banque, 2006.
124 For an analysis of the Italian contribution see Geert Bekaert, "'Un volto sincero' – Le Pavillon Italien," in Rita Devos and Mil de Kooning (eds.), *L'architecture moderne à l'Expo 58*, pp. 131–143.
125 Ernesto Rogers, "The Future Was Not to Be Seen at Brussels" in *Architects Year Book* 9, 1959, pp. 132–139. It is no coincidence that Rogers used the term "experience" in the title of his anthology of writings published in the same year as the pavilion in Brussels: Ernesto N. Rogers, *Esperienza dell'architettura*, Turin, Giulio Einaudi editore, 1958.

Despite the picturesque character of the winding streets, the repetitive quality of the homes recall the overlap between "authentic" rural vernacular and a machine-made factory-produced vernacular. Much like the new towns that embraced the *casa colonica* as a conventional, serially reproduced type of housing for rural peasants flooding into urban areas, the architects of La Martella also hoped to offer living conditions that were at once hygienic and with which the peasants could still identify culturally as a community. The elimination of those spaces associated with agrarian work was aimed at sanitizing scarcely hygienic conditions of the previously inhabited *sassi*, in which residents and animals shared living space.

During the post-war years, the focus shifted from single rural buildings and from the vernacular of Capri (now being discredited by the ascent of tourism) to the vernacular and the urban structure of the hill town. The understated quality of medieval domestic architecture, especially of central Italy in towns like Urbino and Siena lent itself to rethinking the pros and cons of the legacy of rationalism as it had developed during the inter-war years. Giancarlo de Carlo took the lead in the revival of the hill-town model with his extensive design work for Urbino. The housing for University workers (1955) followed by his terraced Collegio del Colle (1962–66) are de Carlo's first important realizations in Urbino. The student housing villages simultaneously embrace and facilitate communal student life by using the Italian hill town as urban model. De Carlo's contribution is especially important if one considers his active role in dismantling the CIAM, which would lead to foundation of the Team X. Thanks to medieval hill-town urbanism imported by De Carlo to the renewed post-CIAM debate, modern urban planning had a new impetus. Other examples of contemporary design in which local vernacular traditions resonate were the Quartiere Tiburtino (1950–54) designed by Quaroni in collaboration with Mario Ridolfi; in northern Italy, the experimental housing estate by Piero Bottoni known as the QT8 in Milan, and the INA village in Cesate including low-cost housing by architects such as Albini, Albricci, the BBPR (Belgioioso, Peressutti, and Rogers), and Gardella.[121]

As disparities between the industrial North and the agrarian South became more and more exaggerated, and as television exercised its capacity to diffuse information, Italians became increasingly aware of social inequities, and tensions grew. Even for those acting in good faith, this top-down paternalism was especially characteristic of architects and intellectuals from central and northern Italy attempting to address the so-called "*questione meridionale*," or Southern Question that had been denounced by communist intellectual Antonio Gramsci whose critique had been echoed after the war by the work of Ernesto De Martino.[122] The disparity between the rich and industrial North and the poor and agrarian South was ever more apparent especially during the years of Italy's "economic miracle."

Perhaps the most cohesive and "anachronistic" experiment with the hill town as a national model is found in the Italian pavilion at the Brussels World Fair of 1958.[123] In the shadow of the Atomium by André Waterkyn, this self-consciously modest "Italian village," designed by architects Ignazio Gardella, BBPR (Belgiojoso, Peressutti, and Rogers), and Ludovico Quaroni, was a homage to the understated, yet thoroughly urban, qualities of the Italian hill town, and a reaction to the typical excess of much exhibition architecture.[124] It was by way of the "experience" of architecture, learned through the phenomenological teachings of Antonio Banfi and Enzo Paci, that Rogers and others helped to counteract a naïve celebration of the atomic age (plate 17).[125]

2.12 Ludovico Quaroni and
collaborators (Federico
Gorio, Michele Valori,
Piero Maria Lugli,
Michele Agati). Centre
of La Martella village,
Matera, 1954.
Source: IN-ARCH, Rome.

It was on these premises of "continuity" that Aldo Rossi established the foundations of the *Tendenza* movement. In his series of cabana drawings of the 1970s Rossi celebrated ordinary maritime objects, redolent of archetype and awaiting transformation into architecture.[126] In a recent overview of contemporary anxieties and design strategies, Spanish architect Rafael Moneo stressed Rossi's "nostalgia for the rational construction of vernacular architecture" in relation to a 1973 project in Borgo Ticino influenced by indigenous lake dwellings. Moneo went on to discuss Rossi's interest in the "anonymous architecture" of the Mediterranean and elsewhere, which led him to embrace urban spaces ranging from a courtyard in Seville to housing in the Po River delta.[127] Significantly, the river dear to Rossi originates in Emilia Romagna and traverses the Veneto region, where Andrea Palladio's Renaissance villas combine "the portico and the farmyard," representing, respectively, the classical and vernacular traditions.[128] Rossi and contemporaries such as Giorgio Grassi applied Palladio's synthesis of the mundane functions of a working farm and learned aspirations to civic representation in elements such as the covered entryway in an attempt to rethink the obvious.[129] Rossi's use of the two-story portico to span the façades of his housing estates in Pegognaga (Mantua, 1979) and Grassi's student housing at Chieti (1976–78) eloquently express an interest in the two traditions filtered through the lens of Rationalism (plate 6). These projects moreover embody the creative tension between urban and rural types that characterizes so much of twentieth-century Italian architecture. In his attempt to circumvent "naïve functionalism," Rossi (and Grassi) reconsidered preindustrial urban environments to create new hybrid forms of architectural identity for a twentieth-century Italy struggling to redefine itself.[130] Rather than ignore the vestiges of an agrarian world defined by the Mediterranean Sea and threatened by dissolution in the wake of industrialization, Italian architects sought new forms of creative dialogue between the city and the countryside. In recent years, however, "spontaneous" urbanism (in Italian, "*abusivismo*" or abusivism) – a term that has come to mean "vernacular" building without permits, informal sprawl that occurred off the grid, so to speak – has led Italian cities and suburbs away from rethinking extant vernacular models and toward embracing hybrid *villini* (small villas) as surrogates of the American-style single-family house. If Rationalism and *Mediterraneità* helped define Mediterranean modernism in Italy up until these recent developments by providing the guideposts for a complex political context, the vernacular and classical traditions functioned at once as muse and master. ∎

[126] See Morris Adjmi and Giovanni Bertolotto (eds.), *Aldo Rossi: Drawings and Paintings*, New York, Princeton Architectural Press, 1993, pp. 145–159.
[127] Rafael Moneo, *Theoretical Anxiety and Design Strategies in the Work of Eight Contemporary Architects*, Cambridge, The MIT Press, 2004, pp. 102–143. For a firsthand account, see Aldo Rossi, *Architetture padane*, Modena, Edizioni Panini, 1984, pp. 11–14.
[128] See Howard Burns et al., *Andrea Palladio, 1508–1580: The Portico and the Farmyard*, London, Arts Council of Great Britain, 1975.
[129] See Giorgio Grassi, "La licenza dell'ovvio, nota sull'architettura rurale," in *Lotus* 15, 1977, pp. 22–29, republished in Giorgio Grassi, *L'architettura come mestiere e altri scritti*, Milan, Franco Angeli Editore, 1980, pp. 197–199. See essay entitled "'*Rurale*' e '*urbano*' nell'architettura," in *L'architettura come mestiere e altri scritti*, pp. 140–156.
[130] See Aldo Rossi, "Critique of Naïve Functionalism," in *The Architecture of the City*, Cambridge, MA, The MIT Press, 1982, pp. 46–48 (trans. Diane Ghirardo).

3

THE MODERN AND THE MEDITERRANEAN IN SPAIN

SERT, CODERCH, BOHIGAS, DE LA SOTA, DEL AMO

Jean-François Lejeune

I have run across the Spanish land and have learnt, in all its corners, what an anonymous architecture could teach me. I have filled my eyes with all what man makes for oneself, with the wisdom of necessity supported by the tradition of the place. Going from surprise to surprise, I have learnt to guess the measure and the function of the spaces that man built to shelter his life and his work, and how he set up an environment for social life. So were born and were made the villages and small towns that I admire and from which I learnt the hidden laws of spontaneous organization.[1]

The origin of the Spanish intellectual quest toward a "re-discovery" of the Mediterranean can be located at the beginning of the twentieth century, when the major protagonists of Catalan modernity, industrialist Eusebi Güell and philosopher Eugeni d'Ors, embraced a cultural and political project for Catalonia that would be based upon the return to a mythical Mediterranean classicism dominated by the Greek ideal – "a metaphor of progress, sea, commerce and opening of the borders."[2] D'Ors titled the movement Noucentisme. His writings about the new Catalonian cultural identity defended the classical, Greco-Roman, inheritance as well as unequivocal "imperial" aspirations. For d'Ors, the goal was "to discover the Mediterranean in ourselves and to affirm it, in imperial work, among men."[3] The intellectuals supporting Noucentisme actively engaged in the new institutional and political context issued from the elections of 1901 and the pivotal victory by the Catalan nationalist parti, the *Lliga Regionalista* [Regionalist League], dominated by industrialist Francesc Cambó and the theoretician of Catalan nationalism Enric Prat de la Riba. Culturally, it was the Mediterranean that was to anchor the legitimacy of the new parti, allow Catalonia to re-discover itself, and establish the system of reference for the concept of *Catalunya Ciutat* [Catalonia-City] – the Noucentiste vision of Catalonia as an "ideal city" of sort, embracing a new civic ethos of collective life at once urban and modern. It is significant that, from 1908 onwards, Josep Puig i Cadafalch had been leading the excavation works at Ampurias (in Catalan, Empúries), a Greco-Roman town in proximity to Cadaqués whose discovery nurtured the roots of the *Renaixança* in the Mediterranean:

> Emporium . . . Ampurias . . . It is a blue horizon that extends its serenity to the Mediterranean father, Mare Nostrum! . . . Sometimes I think that the ideal ambition of a redeeming Catalonian gesture would come down nowadays to discovering the Mediterranean.[4]

Aesthetically, Noucentisme was opposed to Modernisme and advocated a return to Mediterranean classicism based on order, proportion, moderation, and civic awareness. The Noucentiste artists stressed those Mediterranean

[1] José Luis Fernández del Amo, "Del hacer de unos pueblos de colonización," *Palabra y Obra: Escritos Reunidos*, Madrid, COAM, 1995, p. 77. All translations are by the author, unless otherwise noted.
[2] Josep Rovira, *José Luis Sert: 1901–1983*, Milan, Electa, 2000, p. 197.
[3] Quoted by Alícia Suàrez and Mercè Vidal, "Catalan Noucentisme, the Mediterranean, and Tradition," in William Robinson, Jordi Falgàs, and Carmen Belen Lord (eds.), *Barcelona and Modernity: Picasso, Gaudí, Miró, Dalí*, New Haven-London, Yale University Press, p. 230, from Eugeni d'Ors, "Emporium," *Glosari 1906–07*, pp. 31–32. Also see Teresa Camps, "Critical Theories of Noucentisme, Classicism and the Avant-garde in Catalonia, 1906–1930," in *On Classic Ground: Picasso, Léger, De Chirico, and the New Classicism 1910–1930*, Elizabeth Cowling and Jennifer Mundy (eds.), London, Tate Gallery, 1990. On Eugeni d'Ors, see Norbert Bilbeny, *Eugeni d'Ors I la ideologia del Noucentisme*, Barcelona, La Magrana, 1988. For this introduction I am indebted to Olivier Thomas Kransch, "Towards the 'Ideal City' of Noucentisme: Barcelona's Siren's Song of Cosmopolitan Modernity," in *Journal of Cultural Spanish Studies* 4, no. 2, 2003, pp. 225ff.
[4] Eugeni d'Ors, "Emporium," pp. 31–32.

3.1 (*Far left*) Alejandro de la Sota (INC). Pedestrian street, Esquivel, Sevilla, 1952.
Source: © Fundación Alejandro de la Sota, Madrid.

[5] Quoted by Alícia Suàrez and Mercè Vidal, "Catalan Noucentisme, the Mediterranean, and Tradition," p. 226, from Joaquín Torres-García, "La nostra ordinació i el nostre cami," *Empori*, April 1907.
[6] See Jordi Falgás, "The Almanach dels Noucentistes: A Hybrid Manifesto," *Barcelona and Modernity*, pp. 233–235. The Almanach was published once only, in 1911.
[7] William Curtis, *Modern Architecture Since 1900*, 3rd edition, London, Phaidon, 1996, p. 60.
[8] On Gaudí and the Mediterranean, see Juan José Lahuerta, *Antoni Gaudí, 1852–1926*, Milan, Electa, 1992, pp. 143–171; quote on p. 155, from V. M. Gilbert, *Gaudí, músico potencial*. Also see Josep Rovira, "La possessió del Mediterráneo," *Urbanización en Punta Martinet, Ibiza, 1966–1971*, Almería, Colegio de Arquitectos de Almería, 1996, pp. 7–32.
[9] Josep M. Rovira, "The Mediterranean is his Cradle," *J.LL. Sert and Mediterranean Culture*, Barcelona, Colegio de Arquitectos de Cataluña, 1995, p. 47.
[10] See Olivier Thomas Kramsch, "Towards the 'Ideal City' of Noucentisme: Barcelona's 'Sirens' Song of Cosmopolitan Modernity," pp. 225ff.
[11] For this section, see Antonio Pizza, "The Mediterranean: Creation and Development of a Myth," *J.LL. Sert y el Mediterranéo*, p. 23.

virtues in contrast to Modernisme that Joaquín Torres-García dubbed as a phenomenon typical of "the people of the north."[5] Contrary to the exaltation of individualism in Modernisme, Noucentisme was seen as a social and public art, more intent to support the Catalan nationalist project than importing modernist ideals from afar. In 1911, d'Ors published the *Almanac dels Noucentistes*, a collection of texts, drawings, and poems that had in common a return to classicism, a particular interest in urban life, and a special concern for the determining aspects of private life.[6]

In reality, the opposition with Modernisme was not as clear-cut as its detractors would argue. Modernist artists like Gaudí and Puig i Cadafalch attempted to update Catalan arts and architecture so as to uplift Catalan culture to a par with other European countries and regions. They articulated Modernisme as a critical and unambiguous instrument of Catalan Renaissance (Renaixança) and linked it to the search for a style that would better express the revendication of Catalonian culture and politics. Ruskin was the major inspiration for Gaudí's return to principles of medieval architecture and construction techniques to which he attempted to give a genuine Catalan character – see his use of the Catalan vault – while at the same time demonstrating his interest for Arab architecture as a fundamental constant of Spanish architecture. As William Curtis wrote about Gaudí,

> it was a matter of understanding local structural types and construction techniques in brick and ceramic, but also of reacting poetically, not to say mystically, to the hedonistic Mediterranean landscape and vegetation, as well as to the maritime character and traditions of Barcelona.[7]

Besides, as José Lahuerta has discussed, Gaudí and Eugenio d'Ors already approached the theme of the Mediterranean in the planning of the Parque Güell between 1900 and 1914, and in particular the archaic Doric hypostyle hall imagined by Güell as a Greek theatre:

> The temple where songs would be sung in praise of Apollo . . . was not only the domed living room in the Güell Palace: there was another location. . . . That of the Parque Güell, the theatre of Appolo, and the temple of the God.[8]

City and Country

Summarizing the complex and often contradictory aspirations of the Noucentistas, Josep Rovira argued that the return to Mediterranean classicism and tradition was in fact an ideological mask, "an ideological covering for the programs, urban strategies and technological advances necessary to tackle the problems to be solved by the industrial metropolis in times of modernity and of the presence of the masses in the streets."[9] Noucentistas pressed for an orderly vision of Catalonia in which urban life would eclipse ruralism. Yet, this collective ambition was not devoid of ambiguity, for d'Ors and his colleagues affirmed a notion of "tradition" that was rooted both in a classical, urban Mediterranean ideal, and in popular, rural communitarian values.[10] As a result, within the process of modernization of the Catalonian metropolis, the forms of the countryside could equally be called upon to solve the problems of urban architecture. In the words of architectural historian Antonio Pizza, it was "a process of symbolic unification in which not only architecture would become 'telluric' and the countryside acquire an architectural sheen, but the woman would also have to be natural and *ben plantada*, spontaneous and constructed"[11]

Thus, it is not surprising that the Mediterranean and his vernacular architecture framed the human geography of d'Ors's seminal novel:

> now I would like to speak to you about the *Ben Plantada*, who has blossomed, taller than the rest, during these days of heat and gold, in a very humble summer village, small and white, close to the wide blueness of the Mediterranean.[12]

And further:

> You see, then, that there is nothing particular about the tiny village in which the *Ben Plantada* spends the summer. It is neither rustic, nor crude, nor picturesque. It looks neither fashionable nor wild. But we must love it by virtue precisely of its humility, in which the secret resides of its profound grace and truth.[13]

Joaquim Folch i Torres, author of *Meditaciones sobre la arquitectura* (1916) and a major Catalan art historian, also emphasized the harmony of the traditional houses in the landscape when he wrote, "houses in a landscape are like the eyes of a face and a kind of splendour on earth, just as the human eyes are a kind of spiritual splendour in the body."[14] Likewise, in a poem published in the *Almanach dels Noucentistes* by Josep Pijoan, one could read:

> Minorca, your white houses, the labyrinthine walls of the entire island, all painted white, make even more clear the grey sponge of the flat rock that rises out of the sea.[15]

This ongoing dialectic between the renewed *civitas* and a countryside arcadia was important for the development of an independent Catalonian identity. As Pizza wrote, "it is the rural world that is presented as the depositary of the new collective values which will be needed to construct the modern city, seen as the culminating moment of 'artistic' investment on the part of a bourgeois nationalism which would thus claim recognition of its role as a driving force at the core of the political movements of the time."[16] This assertion was clearly at the basis of one of the manifestoes of Noucentisme and Catalan autonomy, Prat de la Riba's *La Nacionalitat Catalana* of 1906. His vision referred to the organic nature of the nation and was imbued with Hippolyte Taine's theory of race, milieu, and moment, which, according to Prat, could be considered as the "foundations and roots of regionalism."[17] Prat de la Riba himself expressed its mistrust of the classical agenda, defending instead the architecture that originated from the countryside:

> The appearance of the country folk on the Catalonian public stage signalled the beginning of the *renaixença*. The accumulated vigor of so many generations could not remain unused and dead to the society. The sons and heirs of the *masía* owners are now renewing and strengthening, with their new blood, the population of our cities and towns.[18]

For the Noucentiste, the *masía* – a type of rural construction connected to a large estate, often fortified, which had its origins in the antique Roman villas and was also influenced by the Palladian types – became a fundamental symbol of Catalan identity. Like so many artists, Joan Miró used it as a major source, as in his famed work of 1921–22, *La Masia* (plate 26).[19] Joaquim Sunyer's paintings such as the *Pastoral* built up the image of an Arcadia for a Catalan nation; likewise, the *Cala Forn* of 1917, with its background of urbanization,

[12] Quoted by Pizza, p. 20, from Eugeni d'Ors, *La Ben Plantada*, Barcelona, Ed. Selecta, 1958, p.15. A subsequent passage from d'Ors sets up true vernacular versus "regionalist": "The rest of the village will also remain white, provided it is not vulgarly colored and sugared-over by the rubbish that architects and master builders are propagating all over Catalonia in the abominable style that has degraded our Tibidabo," ibid.
[13] Quoted by Pizza, p. 21, from Eugeni d'Ors, p. 32.
[14] Quoted by Pizza, p. 23, from J. Folch i Torres, "Record d'una masía," *La Veu de Catalunya*, no. 210, December 27, 1913, also quoted in R. S. Lúbar, "La carn del paisatje: tradició popular i identitat nacional en el noucentisme," in *El Noucentisme. Un projecte de modernitat*, op. cit.
[15] Josep Pijoan, "De les terres Velles," *Almanach dels Noucentistes*, 1911.
[16] Antonio Pizza, p. 19. Also see note 10.
[17] Alícia Suarez and Mercè Vidal, p. 226. Quote from Enric Prat de la Riba, *La Nacionalitat Catalana*, Barcelona, Biblioteca Popular, 1906, p. 53.
[18] Enric Prat de la Riba, p. 20; quoted by Josep Rovira, *Urbanización en Punta Martinet*, p. 15.
[19] On the Catalan masía, see Joaquím de Camps i Arboix, *La masía catalana: Historia-Arquitectura-Sociología*, Barcelona, 1969.

[20] Antonio Pizza, p. 22.
[21] Jordana Mendelson, *Documenting Spain: Artists, Exhibition Culture, and the Modern Nation, 1929–1939*, University Park, Pennsylvania State University Press, 2005, p. 12.
[22] Jordana Mendelson, p. 15.
[23] Dalí was one of the first artists to live in Cadaqués, which attracted many others like Picasso, Miró, etc. On Dalí and Buñuel, see Matthew Gale, *Dalí & Film*, New York, Museum of Modern Art, 2007.
[24] See Jordi Carreras, "Noucentisme between Architecture and the Art of the Object," in *Barcelona and Modernity*, pp. 281–293.
[25] See *Josep Puig i Cadafalch: la arquitectura entre la casa y la ciudad*, Barcelona, Centro cultural de la Fundación Caja de Pensiones, 1990. On the 1929 Exposition, see for instance Josep M. Rovira, *La arquitectura noucentista*, Barcelona, Universitat Politècnica de Barcelona, 1983; *Exposición Internacional de Barcelona*, Barcelona, 1929.

brought together "the perilous dichotomy between the natural and the man-made, governed wisely by the controlled, progressive evolution of the times."[20] Under the impulse of Prat, three major ethnographic archives (one of which was specially dedicated to the *Estudi de la Masia Catalana*) were established in Barcelona, whose focus would be to document scientifically "not only that a specific Catalan culture existed but also that it was different from the rest of Spain."[21] The most important collection, the *Arxiu d'Etnografía I Folklore de Catalunya* (AEFC), made an innovative and pioneering use of photography and advanced classification to record all aspects of the region's traditional culture and folklore, including architecture, labor, trade, and types of inhabitants. Context and truth, provided by the new medium, were "crucial to the Noucentiste notion of photography and archives."[22]

For Miró – but also for the younger Salvador Dalí – the passage from Noucentiste realism to surrealism would be swift, but the Catalonian countryside would be equally important for the new aesthetic. In 1924, the twenty-year-old Dalí painted an enigmatic portrait of Luis Buñuel, then 24, shown as a very solemn Spanish man looking into the distance while, in the background, the cubic volumes of a village seem to anticipate the architecture of the new towns built by the Instituto Nacional de Colonización (INC) in the 1950s and 1960s (plate 24). It is also near Cadaqués, a vernacular white town on the edge of the Mediterranean, that Dalí and Buñuel would script and shoot their manifesto, *L'âge d'or* (1930).[23]

In architecture, the Noucentistas lacked the range and overall impact of their Modernist counterparts. The houses of Rafael Masó, the leading spirit of the Girona Athena Society, exemplified the step from Modernisme to Noucentisme; in Barcelona Josep Goday was the author of the measured "baroquism" of various municipal school groups.[24] But it was Puig i Cadafalch who evolved from Modernisme to Noucentisme (his white period inspired by the Viennese Secession) like the Company House of 1911 and then, in the 1920s, to a more monumental classicism, at once, urban, civic, and expressive of collective enterprise (yellow period) of which the 1929 International Exposition, originally scheduled to open in 1917, was the masterwork.[25] Under the dictatorship of Primo de Rivera – who was supported at first by Puig and the Catalan elite in exchange for a simulacrum of Catalan autonomy – the

3.2 Pueblo Español, Barcelona, 1929.
Source: *Pueblo español*, 1929, pamphlet, author's collection.

Exposición Universal of Barcelona of 1929 was reconceived as a propaganda means "to reaffirm the central government's power over both its internal and external satellites, its own 'regions' as well as its past colonies."[26] The Exposition celebrated the metropolitan achievements of Catalonia and Spain, but its most popular attraction was the *Pueblo Español*. Most accounts make the Pueblo the collaborative work of art historian Miguel Utrillo, visual artist Xavier Nogués, and architects Ramon Reventós and Francesc Follguera – the latter two acted as photographers during the more than 6,000 miles that the team traveled across the cities, towns, and villages of Spain to bring back the accurate documentation. One hundred and seventeen buildings and places were selected from the photographic *moisson* and picturesquely reassembled to become, themselves, "photogenic."[27] Visitors of the exhibition were encouraged to take the place of the original rural subject, thus fulfilling the Noucentiste aspiration to achieve a fusion between city and country, a "new relationship between Spain's rural architecture and its now urban inhabitants."[28]

Contrary to other ethnographic exposition "collages" (for instance in Chicago, Paris, or Rome), the vernacular fabric of the Pueblo Español was here arranged to form urbanistically correct urban spaces, without distortion or downscaling. Culturally and sociologically part of the countryside, the exposed vernacular was typologically urban. The *plaza mayor*, approximately 200 by 150 feet, gave the feel of a true small city, while the Andalucian section of the Pueblo was the recreation of a *barrio* whose very urban structure was the reason of its success. Its houses, patios, and narrow streets like the "Calle de los Arcos" projected a recognizable image of southern Spain, the one that most influenced writers, musicians, painters, philosophers, and others from Bizet to Nietzsche to Picabia to Man Ray.[29]

Vernacular and Worker Housing

From the end of World War One onwards, the study of popular architecture was seen as the basis for a new Spanish architecture of low-cost houses for the working class. In 1918, following the Interallies Conference on the Reconstruction in Paris, Amós Salvador argued that industrialization and normalization (building materials, windows, furnishings . . .) was necessary to economic construction. This reflection was essential in order to respond to the increasing migratory flux from the countryside toward urban centres as well as to respond to the substandard conditions of life in cities and towns, and to major urban transformations such as the opening of the Gran Vía in Madrid that destroyed thousands of dwellings. Yet, in contrast to the developing debate in advanced industrial countries like Germany, in Spain, architects and housing advocates argued that low-cost construction would best be served by the normalization and the standardization of the extant production in order to conserve the traditional systems of production and to adopt solutions confirmed by tradition and the availability of abundant and qualified manpower.[30]

[26] Jordana Mendelson, p. 9.
[27] Jordana Mendelson, p. 23. Also see Jordana Mendelson, "From Photographic Fragments to Architectural Illusions at the 1929 Poble Espanyol in Barcelona," in Medina Lasansky and Brian McLaren (eds.), *Architecture and Tourism: Perception, Performance and Place*, Oxford-New York, Berg, 2004, pp. 129–147
[28] Jordana Mendelson, *Documenting Spain*, p. 25.
[29] See for instance Agnès Rousseaux, *La nuit espagnole: flamenco, avant-garde et culture populaire, 1865–1936*, Paris, Paris-Musées, 2008; on Nietzsche and the south, see Martine Prange, *Lof der Méditerranée: Nietzsches vrolijke Wetenschap tussen noord en zuid*, Kampen, Klement, 2005.
[30] See Carlos Sambricio, "La normalización de la arquitectura vernácula: un debate en la España de los veinte," in *Revista de Occidente*, no. 235, December 2000, pp. 21–44; here pp. 23–24. Also see Federico López Valencia, *Las casas baratas en España*, Madrid, Establecimiento tipográfico, 1928; Paloma Barreiro Pereira, *Casas baratas: la vivienda social en Madrid, 1900–1939*, Madrid, Colegio Oficial de Arquitectos de Madrid, 1992.

3.3 Manuel Cases Lamolla, J. M. Monravà Lòpez y Francisco Monravà. *Casas Baratas* [low-cost houses], Tarragona, 1928–35.
Source: Ayuntamiento de Tarragona, Spain.

31 Carlos Sambricio, *Cuando se quiso resucitar la arquitectura*, Murcia, Comisión de Cultura del Colegio Oficial de Aparejadores y Arquitectos Técnicos, 1983, p. 29. For the influence of Otto Bauer in Vienna, see Eve Blau, *The Architecture of Red Vienna, 1919–1934*, Cambridge, The MIT Press, 1999. See Otto Bauer, *Der Weg zum Sozialismus*, Wien, Ignaz Brand, 1919 [in English, *The Road to Socialism*, 1919].
32 Carlos Sambricio, "La normalización de la arquitectura vernácula," p. 36.
33 Ibid., p. 44.
34 Ibid., p. 41.

This policy implied the development of specialized workers' neighborhoods in the periphery of major cities. Under the influence of the English Garden City theorized by Ebenezer Howard, the laws of *Casas Baratas* were promulgated in 1911, revised in 1921, and extended to the middle class in 1925 under the dictatorship of Primo de Rivera. The typological model was the small vernacular house of the countryside, one or two floors high, usually detached, and built in non-urbanized or poorly urbanized areas on the fringes of Madrid, Zaragoza, Tarragona, and other middle and large cities. These districts were usually managed by housing cooperatives or specific public institutions like municipalities, or political parties, etc. In 1926 the Socialist Parti and its leader Julián Besteiro saw strong convergences between Primo de Rivera's policies of low-cost vernacular houses, and their own assumptions based upon the Austro-marxist principles of Otto Bauer, whose *Der Weg zum Sozialismus* [The Road to Socialism, 1919] was published in Spain in 1920.[31] The economic houses – or *casas baratas* – became the point of departure for a program of participation of the Socialists to the De Rivera government.

The movement of the *casas baratas* changed the conditions of the debate about a new "national architecture" – debate that had started after 1898 and the crisis following the loss of American colonies. The concept of "national" was progressively replaced by the study of the vernacular and it increasingly dissolved in the study and use of regional styles perceived as more authentic and in fact more modern. For Torres Balbás, Balbuena, and Salvador, the study of the vernacular was to become a system of reference in order to solve concrete housing problems, thus shedding away any remnant of a romantic vision of craft (*artesano*). The study of the popular presupposed to precisely analyze the constructive elements in order to search for the optimal conditions of standardization, normalization, and implementation.[32] As Carlos Sambricio has written:

> To normalize meant to standardize the vernacular; it meant to look for a solution to the problem of building low-cost and hygienic dwellings; it became the action plan to establish a new policy of housing in a city which was being transformed into a metropolis.[33]

In this fundamental debate one must emphasize the role of Luis Lacasa Navarro, later to be co-designer with José Luis Sert of the Spanish Pavilion in Paris in 1937. In 1921 he went to study urbanism in Germany and, at his return, helped propagate the terms of the German context within Spain through the works of Tessenow and Muthesius – that he translated in Spanish – and their role within the Werkbund.[34]

Overall, the question of popular housing in the 1920s marked the genuine renewal in the architectural debate. Against the defenders of a nostalgic-monumental architecture connected to history and the international Beaux Arts tradition – see the works of Antonio Palacios and Leonardo Rucabado – the proponents of change adopted two converging axes of reform. The first and earlier one centered, as we have just seen, on the concept of standardization of housing, a rational approach that used the vernacular as point of departure and was linked to the *Heimatsbewegung* of regional identity. Torres Balbás, a great proponent of that regionalist, vision saw it as a way to rejuvenate the discussion about national identity by opening it up to foreign (mostly German) influences:

> There exists a type of architectural "chauvinism" that scorns the trivial and rather searches for the essence of buildings, and, with confidence, does

not fear the contact with all foreign art that could fertilize it. Our task is to propagate that type of healthy "chauvinism," open to all occurrences; and to do so we must study the architecture of our country, travel across its cities and countryside, and draw and measure the old buildings.[35]

In his short essay "Nuevas casas antiguas" José Ortega y Gasset saw progress in the construction of these new houses "in estilo." For the Madrid philosopher, they marked a return to a necessary concept of beauty, but he lamented that they were copied and selected from a catalogue rather than invented. "Those who claim tradition," Ortega wrote, "are precisely the ones who do not follow it, for, who talks about tradition means change."[36] It is Ortega's point of view that would frame the second and more radical direction of architectural change. Rejecting the regionalist mask, Fernando García Mercadal, José Luis Sert, and the architects of GATCPAC saw in the reinterpretation and abstraction of the vernacular aesthetic and tectonics (Ibiza in particular) the means to "mediterraneanize" the modern.

Mercadal, GATCPAC, and the Lesson of Ibiza

From 1927 onwards Fernando García Mercadal was the most distinguished and traveled architect in the campaign to link Spanish architecture with modern developments in Europe.[37] He was a founding member of the Congrés International d'Architecture Moderne (CIAM), and organized a number of conferences in Madrid, inviting some of the most notable contemporary architects, including Erich Mendelsohn, Theo van Doesburg, Walter Gropius, and Le Corbusier. He also took an interest in vernacular, mainly Mediterranean, architecture, which had been a focus of his studies in Rome and was reflected

[35] Torres Balbás, quoted by Carlos Sambricio, "La normalización de la arquitectura vernácula," pp. 41–42; the article gives no reference to sources.

[36] Quoted by Carlos Sambricio, "L'architecture espagnole entre la IIè république et le franquisme," in *Les années 30 – L'architecture et les arts de l'espace entre industrie et nostalgie*, Paris, Editions du patrimoine, 1997, p. 181. See José Ortega y Gasset, "Nuevas casas antiguas [1926]," *Obras completas*, Madrid, Revista de Occidente, 1957, vol. 2 (*El Espectador*, 1916–1934), pp. 549–551.

[37] See Juan Daniel Fullaondo, *Fernando García Mercadal: arquitecto aproximativo*, Madrid, Colegio Oficial de Arquitectos de Madrid, 1984; Carlos Sambrico, *Cuando se quiso resucitar la arquitectura*, op. cit.

3.4 *Left*: Raul Haussman, photographer. House in Ibiza, c. 1933–36. Source: Archives Raoul Haussman, Limoges. *Right*: Fernando García Mercadal. Sketch of a Street in Amalfi, 1924. Source: Fernando García Mercadal, *La casa mediterránea*, Madrid, 1984.

38 Fernando García Mercadal, "Arquitectura Mediterránea," in *Arquitectura*
85, May 1926, pp. 192–197; "Arquitectura Mediterránea II," in *Arquitectura*
97, May 1927, pp. 190–193. See
Augustin Bernard, *Enquête sur
l'habitation rurale des indigènes de
l'Algérie*, Algiers, Fontana frères,
1921.
39 Fernando García Mercadal, *La
casa popular en España*, Madrid,
Espasa-Calpe, 1930; reprinted,
Barcelona, Gili, 1981, p. 54. Overall,
Mercadal's works have been overlooked, yet he built some of the first
examples of rationalist architecture,
such as the *Rincón de Goya* (1927–
28; remodeled) in Saragoza and the
series of houses he built in 1930 in
the Colonia Residencia de Madrid.

in a 1926 article published in *Arquitectura* titled "Arquitectura mediterránea,"
and a second one a year later. In the first article he mentioned the studies of
Albert Demangeon on rural habitat and of Augustin Bernard in indigenous
Algeria to argue for a unity of purpose and construction rationalism that tie the
rural houses throughout the Mediterranean. He accompanied the text with his
drawings for the Casa a la Orilla del Mar and the Casa in Sicilia, both of them
showing influences from Karl Friedrich Schinkel and Adolf Loos. In the second
article he used the title *Arquitectura mediterránea* to promote his project for a
Club Naútico and the Casa para el ingeniero, the latter showing influences
from Mendelsohn and Loos again.[38] In 1930 Mercadal published *La casa popular
en España*, the first book of its type in Spain, which discussed most regional
vernaculars of the country. There he wrote about the Mediterranean island of
Minorca: "Mahón, which is all geometry, might easily fulfil the aspirations of
the most fanatical Cubists."[39]

El Rincón de Goya (1928) – one of the very first buildings of the modern
movement in Spain – and his other built or unbuilt projects demonstrate that
Mercadal had not waited for the Catalans to adapt the Mediterranean ideal to
modern architecture. Nor had other Madrid architects such as Bergamín and

3.5 Rafael Bergamín.
Houses in the Colonia
El Viso, Madrid, c.1934.
Source: Blanco-Solar,
Bergamín, Abril, *Los
arquitectos Blanco-Soler y
Bergamín*, Madrid, 1933.

Luis Blanco Soler. The new middle-class single-family districts to the north of Madrid such as Colonia Parque Residencia (planned by Bergamín and Luis Soler, 1931–34) and Colonia El Viso (planned by Bergamín, 1934), with houses by Mercadal, Bergamín, and Luis Gutiérrez Soto, among others, became the showpieces of the new Mediterranean-inspired rationalist architecture in the capital. El Viso, which housed some of the most important professionals and intellectuals of the period (Ortega y Gasset, Salvador de Madariaga, etc.), showed strong influences from modern German Siedlungen in terms of morphology and typology. The colonies were the middle-class version of the *casas baratas*, but in the mid-1930s their planning had taken a turn toward modernity.

Through his critical role of mediator between a modernized tradition (Torres Balbás) and modernism (CIAM), Mercadal embraced Le Corbusier's ideas, but remained wary of the consequences of an "international agenda" on national values:

> [The] intellectual spirit of the southern people and its manifestation in civic art are today under threat. Our modern *Zeitgeist* tends to level and standardize all the ways of life; likewise, modern architecture, which should aim at the synthesis of all creative elements, turns out, with its powerful means of expression, to overturn and neutralize the sacred laws derived from the land and the race.[40]

It is at Mercadal's invitation that Le Corbusier came to lecture in Madrid. On May 15, 1928, at a stopover of the train in Barcelona, Le Corbusier was literally "intercepted" at the station:

> In Madrid I received a telegram signed by José Luis Sert (whom I did not know at the time) who said he would meet me at 10 o'clock in the evening in Barcelona station, an intermediate stop for the Madrid–Port-Bau express, and rush me off without delay to give a talk somewhere in the city. At Barcelona station I was received by five or six youths, all short but full of fire and energy.[41]

Le Corbusier lectured on his way back in Barcelona. This was a moment of frustration and crisis in Le Corbusier's career after his failure at the competition for the Palais des Nations. In his speech he was shifting away from the analogy of the machine toward an architecture where classical proportions, references, and harmony could be harnessed to redefine modernity and new architecture.[42] After listening to Le Corbusier, Sert and his colleagues realized that there were therefore neither real contradictions nor oppositions between modernity and tradition, and it was possible to be truly modern without losing their Spanish roots. At the same time, they prepared to demonstrate that they were the heirs of an "autochthonous culture whose roots revealed the same preoccupations as those concerning Europe in the years immediately before," and that gave them the right to be now, albeit belatedly, at the forefront of the modernist movement.[43] In working together on the mythification of the Mediterranean and of its vernacular as the primary sources of modern architecture, Le Corbusier, Sert, and others, particularly in Italy, attempted to substantiate the myth of the origins beyond the machine and other technological analogies.[44]

In the late 1920s, Sert and his classmate at the School of Architecture, Germán Rodríguez-Arias, embarked on a series of journeys in the south of Spain to

[40] Fernando García Mercadal, *Casa Mediterránea*, Madrid, Dirección General de Bellas Artes y Archivos, p. 16.
[41] Le Corbusier, quoted by Josep Rovira, "The Mediterranean is his Cradle," p. 49. See Juan José Lahuerta, *Le Corbusier e la Spagna*, Milan, Electa, 2006; and Le Corbusier, *Espagne: Carnets*, Milan-Paris, Electa, Fondation Le Corbusier, 2001.
[42] Le Corbusier, *Une maison, un palais – A la recherche d'une unité architecturale*, Paris, G. Crès, 1929.
[43] Josep Rovira, "The Mediterranean is his Cradle," pp. 63–64.
[44] The process bears some analogy with Abbé Laugier's relationship to the vernacular and the primitive hut. See in particular Alan Colquhoun, "Vernacular Classicism," *Modernity and the Classical Tradition–Architectural Essays 1980–1987*, Cambridge, The MIT Press, 1989, p. 30.

SAN POL DE MAR

EN IBIZA NO EXISTEN LOS "ESTILOS HISTÓRICOS"...

3.6 *Left*: pages from *AC 2*, 1931: J. L. Sert's comparison between fishermen's houses on the Catalonian Coast (San Pol de Mar) with J. P. Oud's housing complex at the Weissenhofsiedlung in Stuttgart, 1927. *Right*: *AC 6*, 1932: "In Ibiza there are no historical styles."
Source: *AC*, 1931 and 1932.

discover the vernacular architecture of its towns and villages.[45] Ibiza was the next step and there they joined a small crowd of intellectuals who, like in Capri in Italy, saw in the "primitive" rural architecture and quasi-virginal culture of the island the values of modernity.[46] Among the visitors were Albert Camus, Man Ray, Tristan Tzara, Raoul Hausmann, and also Walter Benjamin, who stayed on the island twice, in 1932 and 1933, and left his impressions in his correspondence:

> We were then put ashore in a hidden bay [of Ibiza]. And there we were presented with an image of such immutable perfection that something strange but not incomprehensible took place within me: namely, I actually did not see it at all; it made no impression on me; because of its perfection, it existed on the very brink of the invisible.[47]

And further:

> The interiors are likewise archaic. These chairs along the wall of the room opposite the entrance greet the stranger with assurance and weightiness, as if three works by Cranach and Gauguin were leaning against the wall; a sombrero over the back of a chair is more imposing than a precious Gobelin tapestry. . . . The end of all these things is unfortunately to be feared because of a hotel being built in the port of Ibiza.[48]

On October 25, 1930, Sert, Subino, García Mercadal, and others officially launched the group GATCPAC, and announced the publication of their periodical *AC*.[49] The GATCPAC's manifesto, published in *AC 1*, reflected the ambiguity of the group's position. On the one hand, it advocated that "this new architecture is fruit of the machine age" and the need for industrialization and mass production; on the other hand, it claimed the "full Latinism" of modern architecture and the direct reference to Mediterranean architectures. Attacked by conservative architects, the manifesto also saw strong reactions from Joaquín Torres-Garcia, former Noucentiste who had just created a constructivist group with Mondrian, who criticized the lack of spiritual expression of an architecture that required "standardized mannequins" to inhabit them.[50]

45 See Josep Rovira, "Ibiza y la mirada de la vanguardia," in *Urbanización en Punta Martinet, Ibiza, 1966–71*, pp. 33–54; also see Josep Rovira, *José Luis Sert*, op. cit.
46 See Michelangelo Sabatino's essay in this volume.
47 Walter Benjamin, *The Correspondence of Walter Benjamin, 1910–1940*, Gershom Scholem and Theodor W. Adorno (eds.), Chicago, University of Chicago Press, 1994: letter to Gretel Adorno, June 1933, p. 420. The German interest for Spanish vernacular has been extensively studied in Joaquín Medina Warmburg, *Projizierte Moderne: Deutschsprächige Architekten und Städtebauer in Spanien (1918–1936) – Dialog, Abhängigkeit, Polemik*, Frankfurt am Main, Vervuert Verlag, 2005. Of particular interest is the third section of the book, titled "Inseln" [Islands].
48 Walter Benjamin, *The Correspondence of Walter Benjamin*: letter to Gerhard Scholem, April 22, 1932, p. 340.
49 *AC (Documentos de Actividad Contemporánea)* was published from 1931 to 1937 with a total of

The first issue of *AC* further set the tone for the series of twenty-five issues published between 1930 and 1937. Next to photos of modern architecture in San Sebastián and Barcelona, a discussion of the future urbanization of Barcelona and the Green City in Moscow, it featured a double page that focused on traditional fishermen's houses on the Mediterranean coast and compared them dramatically (using large arrows and red crosses not unlike Paul Schulze-Naumburg in his *Kulturarbeiten* series) to J. P. Oud's row of houses at the Weissenhofsiedlung of 1927.[51] Opposed to the architectonic eclecticism of various regionalisms reduced to exterior signs of decoration, they saw in the sobriety of the white volumes of the peasant and fishermen's houses as well as in the strict functionality of their constitutive elements a genuine model for a new modern and social-oriented architecture. In the second issue, the editors made clear that "respetamos la buena arquitectura del passado": not unlike the declarations of the Italian Gruppo Sette in 1927 in the periodical *Rassegna* the editors argued about the value of good historical architecture (Santa Maria del Mar in Barcelona, the Catalan, Monasterio de Pedralbes, all Romanesque buildings studied by Domènech y Montaner and Puig i Cadafalch earlier in the century) as roots for the new architecture that the new social conditions required.[52] Clearly the Catalonian environment dominated the magazine but the first issues again made clear that the new modern conditions were rising throughout the country: for instance, the masterplan for the extension of the Paseo de la Castellana in Madrid by Herman Jansen and Secundino Zuazo (1929–30), and the new campus of the Ciudad Universitaria in Madrid (1927–). Overall, *AC* was the publishing platform for Sert, his friends, Le Corbusier, and CIAM. Of his own work, Sert gave special attention to the apartment house at Calle Muntaner (# 4), his summer resort near Barcelona in collaboration with Torres Clavé (# 7, # 13), the plan Macià (# 13) and the Casa Bloc for the revision of the Ensanche (# 10), and the Week End house in Garraf also with Torres Clavé (# 19), a modern Mediterranean project which Sert would take over and adapt thirty years later for the Ibiza development of Punta Martinet (1966–74).

twenty-five issues. It was the theoretical organ of GATCPAC or GATEPAC (Grupo de Artistas y Técnicos Españoles Para el Progreso de la Arquitectura Contemporánea), founded by Sert and Subiño (who were co-authors of the founding manifesto), along with Antoni Bonet Castellana, Josep Torres Clavé, José Manuel Aizpurúa and Fernando García Mercadal. See *A.C.: la revista del G.A.T.E.P.A.C., 1931–1937*, Barcelona, Museo Nacional Centro de Arte Reina Sofía, 2008.
50 See Enrique Granell Trías, "Impossible not to Succumb to the Song of the Sirens. Parallel 1933," in *J.LL. Sert and the Mediterranean*, pp. 126–137.
51 See Kai K. Gutschow's essay in this volume.
52 *AC* 2, 1931, p. 22.

3.7 José Luis Sert and J. Torres Clavé. House "Week-End," type A, Costas de Garraf, Barcelona, 1935.
Source: *AC* 19, 1935.

53 José Luis Sert, "Raíces mediterráneas de la arquitectura moderna,"
AC 18, 1935; reprinted in Antonio
Pizza, J.LL.Sert y el Mediterráneo,
pp. 217–218, quote on p. 217.
54 Bartomeu Marí, Jean-Paul Midant
et.al., Raoul Hausmann, Architect.
Ibiza 1933–1936, Brussels, Archives
d'Architecture Moderne, 1990.
55 Raoul Hausmann, "Ibiza et la maison méditerranéenne," L'architecture
d'aujourd'hui, no 1, 1935, p. 33.
56 Raoul Hausmann, "Elvissa I l'ar-
quitecture sense arquitecte," D'Aci I
d'Allà 184, 1936. Here quoted from
the French translation in Bartomeu
Marí, Jean-Paul Midant et. al., Raoul
Hausmann, p. 28.
57 On the impact of the Civil War on
architects, see Sofía Diéguez Patao,
La generación del 25: primera arquitectura moderna en Madrid, Madrid,
Catédra, 1997. Interestingly, Aizpúrua
was a member of GATEPAC and
a close friend of Federico Garcia
Lorca. On Aizpúrua, see José Ángel
Sanz Esquide, Real Club Náutico de
San Sebastián, 1928–1929, Almería,
Colegio de Arquitectos de Almería,
1995.
58 Enrique Granell Trías, p.136.

The AC # 18 (1935) was entirely dedicated to popular culture and contained Sert's renowned essay "Raíces mediterráneas de la arquitectura moderna" where he wrote those important lines:

Technically, modern architecture is mostly a discovery of the Nordic countries. Yet, spiritually, it is the "style-less" Mediterranean architecture which has influenced this new architecture. Modern architecture is a return to the pure, traditional forms of the Mediterranean. It is a victory of the Latin Sea.[53]

Besides two small articles on "popular" industry and the paintings of Joan Miró, the issue focused mainly on Mediterranean towns and cities, emphasizing the rationality of their streets and building types, in particular the casa-patio of various dimensions. It was, indeed, a surprising analysis, one that emphasized the urban vernacular of the Mediterranean and would characterize the distinctly urban, Spanish approach to the Mediterranean and its vernacular. The twenty-first issue (1936) continued the survey, this time on the rural side, in the form of a survey of the traditional Ibiza rural house done by Raoul Hausmann, and Erwin Heilbronner, the first an architect and photographer who was then active as a dadaist artist, and the second an architect who remained on the island permanently after changing his name to Broner.[54] In this article, accurate floor plans and sections, along with remarkable photos of peasant houses in Ibiza, were published for the first time. Hausmann recorded his impressions in a series of articles as a correspondent.[55] He shared the same fascination as the architects, yet his glance was more scientific, even ethnological:

These primitive conditions and the patriarchal structure of the family are reflected in an architecture that is especially attractive to us due to the purity of its lines and cubic volumes. It appeals to our love for truth and simplicity . . .
Ibiza is by excellence the land of architecture without architects. The houses that the peasants build there have such a pure style and such a harmonious expression, that they can perfectly sustain the comparison with more mature and more designed works of modern architecture. As soon as one leaves the city and enters the interior of the island, one goes from surprise to surprise; everywhere the same plastic expression, everywhere the same noble forms of dwellings.[56]

A couple of weeks later the Civil War erupted. Most modernist architects – including José Luis Sert, Felix Candela, and Luis Lacasa, – took the road of exile. However, modern architecture could not be exclusively associated with left-orientated political sympathies: a major pioneer of Spanish modernism, Basque architect José Manuel Aizpúrua, embraced the Falangist cause and was executed by the Popular Front in 1936, while other modern architects like Luis Guttíerez Soto and Secundino Zuazo remained in Spain for similar political reasons.[57] Before leaving for the United States, Sert and his colleague Lacasa designed the Spanish Pavilion for the Paris World's Fair of 1937 and brought the spirit of the Mediterranean to the heart of the French metropolis. In contrast to the massive symbolism of the German and Italian pavilions, Sert and Lacasa's work was light, open-air and organized around an open patio covered with a sail-like canopy. "This pavilion" – Enrique Granell Trías wrote – "was a reliquary, a Noah's Ark, a kind of artificial Ibiza where the 'degenerates' could seek refuge: Picasso, Miró, Alberto and Julio Gonzalez, among others, would be present there."[58] The pavilion plan encouraged movement in a continuous way. Following the entrance through the grand patio, a series of ramps and rooms defined a path not unlike an urban corridor, with an ingenious sequence that allowed the visitor to see the two upper floors before descending into the amenities of the ground floor. Jaime Freixa has interpreted this layout as "a metaphor of the city, with shelves and display cases that replicated the linear contemplation of storefronts in the city streets." Here, it seems,

> the urban planner met the Mediterranean: the memories of the old medinas and historic quarters with their web of tight corners and narrow streets filled with intense life, alleviated finally by the splendid breadth of the plazas.[59]

As Jordana Mendelson has shown, photography and graphic arts had an equivalent, possibly even bigger, role on the image of the Spanish pavilion. Along the architectural promenade and on some exterior façade panels as well, the large photomurals, conceived by Valencian artist Josep Renau, used the most advanced techniques of photomontage, collage, and other contraposition to present Spain's diverse regional geography, the social advancement of the Republic such as land reform, the *Misiones pedagogicas* to bring art and culture to the countryside, as well as the wealth and diversity of Spanish popular arts and crafts.[60]

The Escorial or the Vernacularization of the Classical

Between General Franco's uprising of July 1936 and the fall of Madrid in 1939, combatants of both sides of the Civil War and their international allies totally destroyed one hundred and ninety-two villages, towns, and districts. Although there were urgent needs in rebuilding the metropolitan peripheries, the reconstruction focused on the rural "front." The main rationale was Franco's economic policy to bolster new agrarian development in order to allow the necessary reorganization of private capital, at that time without opportunities for rapid investment. The implicit objective was to stabilize the impoverished rural population away from the big cities and thus prevent rural flight, excessive urban expansion, and potentially explosive socio-economic conditions.[61] Propaganda was also instrumental in this policy: the schematic – and at times simplistic – pre-war partition of the country between the Republican industrial cities and the Falangist small towns remained in the memory of the victors. The "New Spain" not only thanked the "agrarian man," but also took pains at presenting him as the model of the New Spaniard, long-suffering and reserved, anchored in the old tradition of individual courage in the face of adversity and exacting daily labor:

> In Spain nowadays many towns and villages survive whose laments, curses, and tears tell us of a past of squalor and poverty. Spain used to live at the expense of its villages. At the best they served as the set design for a picturesque drama, glimpsed through the window of a train or of an automobile. . . . It is the war itself that eventually brought the city dwellers nearer to the countryside.[62]

Reconstruction was the central theme of the First National Assembly of Architects held on June 26–29, 1939, in the Teatro Español of Madrid under the presidency of Pedro Muguruza Otaño. Muguruza gave confidence to his colleagues and rallied them to the task of reconstructing towns and cities, as well as solving the problems of housing for the poorest classes in the country.[63] The premises were clearly stated:

[59] From the unpublished lecture notes of Jaume Freixa "From Ibiza to America: Josep Lluis Sert's Modern Reinterpretation of the Mediterranean Vernacular," at the University of Miami School of Architecture "The Other Modern" conference at Casa Malaparte, Capri, March 8–13, 1998. On Sert abroad, see for instance Josep Rovira, *José Luis Sert*, op. cit.; Xavier Costa and Guido Hartray (eds.), *Sert: arquitecto en Nueva York*, Barcelona, ACTAR, 1997.

[60] See Jordana Mendelson, "Josep Renau and the 1937 Spanish Pavilion in Paris," *Documenting Spain: Artists, Exhibition Culture, and the Modern Nation, 1929–1939*, pp. 125–183.

[61] See Lluís Domènech, *Arquitectura de Siempre: Los años 40 en España*, Barcelona, Tusquets, 1978, pp. 23–24.

[62] "Muerte y reconstrucción de unos pueblos," *Reconstrucción* X, 8, 1949.

[63] Lluís Domènech, pp. 18ff.

It is absolutely indispensable to think that one critical element [to eliminate the condition of poor housing] is to get rid of the purely material concept of making the housing unit a "machine for living." This idea cannot but annihilate or negate the concept of place.[64]

Likewise, the speech by architect Luis Gutiérrez Soto reflected a functionalist attitude, devoid of any international "rigidity" or formalism, and anchored in a serious understanding of working-class life in poor families. For Soto, styles were to be used as pure instruments of design in order to wrap up the logical structure of the architecture. To the excessive decomposition of functions advocated by the Bauhaus, he opposed simple arrangements inspired by the national and regional and argued "that the minimum dwelling does not depend on size and dimensions of rooms, but on a good organization of space."[65]

The historiography has generally presented Muguruza's and other attacks against Internationalism and the Republican-period avant-garde as reactionary statements by conservative pro-regime architects. Yet, in recent years, historians such as Carlos Sambricio have started to dismantle the comfortable myth of an epistemological rupture between the Republican period and Franco's regime.[66] Sambricio has put into question the so-called "Bohigas' axiom" that the architecture of the 1930s had been marked by an orthodox avant-garde, which was culturally monolithic, formally coherent, and "politically correct."[67] He argued that the different architectural options proposed at the beginning of the 1940s were "the fruitful outcome of heterogeneous ideas, whose gestation can be traced back to the decade preceding the Civil War."[68] Although Muguruza was clearly a conservative architect, his speech oddly echoed José Luis Sert's declarations in 1934 at the time that the monolithic image of the avant-garde was already shattered by both ideological developments and political complexities:

> The pure functionalism of the "machine à habiter" is dead. . . . Architects and theorists, above all Germanic, carried functionalist experiments to absurd extremes.[69]

As Sola-Morales wrote, the Spanish situation of the immediate post-Civil War corresponded in fact to a "reinterpretation of the methodological postulates and goals of the 'principles of modern architecture,' [mostly] in matters of housing."[70] The autarchic regime inherited both the situation and the ideology based upon the social-democratic reformism of Germany and Central Europe: building in the periphery, cooperativism, architectural alternative to the bourgeois residence both in terms of type and methods of construction, state and municipal control, etc.[71] In 1939, the newly created National Institute of Housing directed by José Fonseca, active in a similar position during the Republican period, enacted the *Ordenanzas de la Vivienda*, a set of regulations based upon pre-Civil War research that established all technical conditions necessary for the new worker dwelling unit and colonist house, including number and dimensions of rooms, orientation, preferred materials, and ventilation systems.[72]

The task of reconstruction was entrusted to the Department General of Devastated Regions, created within the Ministry of the Interior before the end of the war, on March 25, 1938. A large staff of architects, engineers, and other professionals (reaching more than two hundred in 1945) was assembled to design, control, and direct the process. Planned in Madrid, but subdivided

[64] *Sesiones de la I Asamblea Nacional de Arquitectos*, Madrid, Servicios técnicos de FET y de las JONS, 1939, p. 4.
[65] Lluís Domènech, pp. 33–34.
[66] See for instance Carlos Sambricio, "L'architecture espagnole entre la Deuxième République et le Franquisme," p. 181.
[67] Ibid.
[68] Ibid.
[69] Josep Lluis Sert, "Arquitectura sense 'estil' i sense 'arquitecte'", *D'Ací i d'Allà* 179, December 1934, reprinted in Antonio Pizza, *J.LL.Sert and the Mediterranean*, p. 210.
[70] See the very important essay by Ignasi Sola-Morales, "La arquitectura de la vivienda en los años de la Autarquia, 1939–1953," in *Arquitectura* 199, April 1976, p. 20.
[71] Ignasi Sola-Morales, p. 22. All of these issues were integrated in the prologue to the law of 1939.
[72] José Fonseca, Director of the National Institute of Housing, was an important link between the pre-Civil War era and the reconstruction: see José Fonseca, "La vivienda rural en España: estudio técnico y jurídico para una actuación del Estado en la material," *Arquitectura* XVIII, no. 1, 1936, pp. 12–24. On the Housing Ordinances of 1939, see Manuel Calzada Pérez, "La vivienda rural en los pueblos de colonización," *PH. Boletín del Instituto Andaluz del Patrimonio Histórico* XIII, no. 52, 2005, pp. 55–67; Ignacio Sola-Morales, "La arquitectura de la vivienda," pp. 19–30.

3.8 *(Far left)* José Luis Sert and Luis Lacasa. Covered patio of the Spanish Republic Pavilion at the Paris Exposition, Paris, 1937 ["Le Pavillon de l'Espagne. Guernica, par Picasso. Fontaine de Mercure, par Alexander Calder"].
Source: *Cahiers d'Art* 8–10, 1937. The New York Public Library/Art Resource, NY.
© 2009 Estate of Pablo Picasso/Artists Rights Society (ARS), New York.

73 The reconstruction was the subject of a large exhibition in 1987 and a catalogue titled *Arquitectura en Regiones Devastadas*, Madrid, MOPU, 1987; also see Lluís Domènech, *Arquitectura de siempre*, op. cit.; Jean-François Lejeune, "The Intellectual Pleasure of Ambiguity: The Reconstruction of Spain in the Years of Autarky (1939–1956)" in *The Venice Charter Revisited: Modernism and Conservation in the Post-War World*, London, INTBAU, 2009, pp. 196–207, and "Rationalism and Tradition in the New Towns of the Reconstruction in Spain," in *Oriental-Occidental, Proceedings ACSA International Conference Istanbul 2001*, Washington DC, ACSA, 2002, pp. 28–32.
74 José Moreno Torres, *La reconstrucción urbana en España*, Madrid, Artes Gráficas Faure, 1945, unpaginated. An order issued in 1938 forbade anyone to rebuild without prior authorization to be granted in accordance with the approved town-planning scheme of reconstruction or restoration. An efficient system of land redistribution permitted this complicated process of urban re-platting or transfer of property rights from the destroyed area to the new town.
75 José Moreno Torres, unpaginated.
76 Lluís Domènech, p. 23.
77 José Ortega y Gasset, "La meditación del Escorial," [1915]," *Obras completas*, Madrid, Revista de Occidente, 1957, vol. 2 (*El Espectador*, 1916–1934), p. 557.

3.9 *Left*: Plaza Mayor of the reconstructed Brunete, Madrid, 1943. *Right*: Plaza Mayor of the reconstructed town of Belchite, Zaragoza, c.1943.
Source: Departamento de las Regiones Devastadas, Archivo General de la Nación, Alcalá de Henares.

among thirty regional offices, the program included the reconstruction of devastated villages and towns, and a vast campaign of restoration of civic and religious public buildings. It had its own periodical, *Reconstrucción*, which in spite of its propagandistic overtones provided a well-documented review of the operation.[73]

In the short term, the return to tradition and to the vernacular forms of building was a pragmatic solution imposed by the economic shortages and technical obstacles endemic in the country. However, the architects benefited from a high degree of autonomy to improve the miserable conditions of housing, particularly in rural areas. This often included total reconstruction if deemed necessary.[74] Whether the town was rebuilt adjacent to the destroyed settlement (Belchite, Villanueva de la Cañada, Seseña) or superimposed over it (Guernica, Brunete), the orthogonal grid of elongated rectangular blocks was the common feature of the reconstructed towns.[75] In all cases, this modern and rational morphology strongly contrasted with the medieval, often irregular and chaotic, organization of the blocks and lots in the destroyed towns and cities. A limited amount of party-wall types, generally organized around a patio, make up the fabric of the towns. Houses were rationally conceived behind a vernacular mask. Designers systematically documented the architectonic elements of tradition (ironwork, balconies, doors, arches, etc.), and catalogued the different typologies in relation to the climate and other regional characteristics. This scientific labor could be found on the pages of *Reconstrucción* between 1940 and 1953 and was further supported by a series of publications such as *Construcciones rurales*, *La vivienda rural*, and *La vivienda de los pescadores*.[76]

The political ideal of civil life under the national-catholic regime could be summarized in the triad family/work/town; it was thus logical that the *plaza mayor* became the point of crystallization of the reconstructed urban context. Yet, in contrast to the traditional Spanish plaza carved out of the urban fabric, the plazas of the reconstruction were new and modern creations, defined by thin-bar buildings and assemblage of interconnected objects. Yet, their modernity was masked and, all around Spain, these plazas were built in the classical style, seen in this first phase of the dictatorship as most appropriate to define the grandeur and unity of Spain. Juan de Herrera's Escorial – in the words of Ortega y Gasset "an effort, a strenuous exertion, consecrated to effort itself"[77] – became the paradigm of the regime's architecture. To some extent, the Escorial was "vernacularized," and the new squares appeared like a

3.10 Aerial views of two
early towns of the
Instituto Nacional de
Colonización (INC).
Left: Guadiana del
Caudillo (Francisco
Giménez de la Cruz,
1948). *Right*:
Valdelacalzada (Manuel
Rosado Gonzalo, 1945).
Source: *I.N.C. – Memoria
octubre 1939–diciembre 1965*,
Madrid, 1967.

modernized recreation of the late sixteenth-century classical type later established by the same Herrera in Toledo and Valladolid.[78] As historian Lluís Domènech wrote in one of the first works to re-evaluate a long-neglected program, "Brunete, Seseña, Nules, Montarrón, Los Blázquez, or Villanova de la Barca [. . .] they were names dispersed across the geography of Spain, which revealed serious experiments, never repeated, of rigorous planning."[79]

Colonizing the Countryside

When Luis Buñuel shot his third film *Las Hurdes: Tierra sin pan* in 1933, the gap between Spain's urban life and the blighted countryside had reached dramatic and politically dangerous proportions, with growing poverty and social unrest. The "anarchist–surrealist" documentary about one of the poorest and most remote villages of Spain was immediately censored by the Republican government, intent as it was to promote a more optimistic vision of rural Spain through various projects of agrarian reform and propaganda.[80] In the footsteps of Mussolini in Italy and Roosevelt in the United States, large-scale irrigation, dam construction, electrification, and foundation of new rural settlements were necessary solutions to the improvement of rural life and overall political stability that the Second Republic studied, but had no time to implement.

At the outset of the Civil War, the *Instituto Nacional de Colonización* (National Institute of Colonization) (INC) was created in October 1939 to implement the proactive policy of land reclamation and rural foundation within the territory of six major river basins – the Guadalquívir, the Guadiana (Plan Badájoz), the Tagus and the Alagón, the Ebro, the Duero between Salamanca and Palencia, and the Segura River around Murcía.[81] Arguably, the program of colonization was not an experiment *ex novo*. From the Reconquista, Spain had forged a rich and brilliant tradition of urban foundation, both in America and in the Peninsula itself.[82] Architects and planners of the INC found a fertile ground in that heritage; likewise, they were unequivocally aware of modern town and regional planning in Germany, Palestine, Fascist Italy, and Anglo-Saxon countries.[83] Italian new towns like Sabaudia and Segezia, the 1933 *Concurso de Anteproyectos para la construcción de poblados en las zonas regables del Guadalquivir*, and the new town program in post-war England served as blueprints for the three hundred new towns, which between 1943 and 1965 sprang up from the drawing boards of a new generation of young architects-urbanists.[84] More than sixty-five thousand colonists and their families

[78] Catherine Wilkinson-Zerner, *Juan de Herrera, Architect to Philip II of Spain*, New Haven, Yale University Press, 1993.
[79] Lluís Domènech, p. 13. On the polemic between, on one side, Tomas Llorens and Helio Piñon who criticized the revived interest, and on the other side, Carlos Sambricio and Ignasi Sola-Morales, in *Arquitectura española contemporáneo. Documentos, escritos, testimonios inéditos*, Madrid, Colegio de Arquitectos de Madrid, 2002, pp. 253–280.
[80] See Jordana Mendelson, "Contested Territory: The Politics of Geography in Luis Buñuel's *Las Hurdes: Tierra sin pan*," *Locus Amoenus* II, 1966, pp. 229–242; Jordana Mendelson, *Documenting Spain: Artists, Exhibition Culture, and the Modern Nation, 1929–1939*, pp. 65–91.
[81] It is only after the establishment of the Department of Architecture at the INC in 1941, under the direction of José Matés Alarcón, that the first significant settlements were established (El Torno, Bernuy, Gimenells).
[82] See Javier Monclús and José Luis Oyon, *Políticas y técnicas en la ordenación del espacio rural*, Volume I of the *Historia y Evolución de la Colonización Agraria in España*, Madrid, MAP/MAPA/MOPU, 1988. Also see José Tamés Alarcón, "Proceso urbanistico de nuestra colonización interior," *Revista Nacional de Arquitectura*, November 1948, pp. 414–424; Graziano Gasparini, "The Spanish-American Grid Plan,

an Urban Bureaucratic Form," *The New City* I, 1991, pp. 6–17 and in the same volume "The Laws of the Indies of 1571," pp. 18–33.

[83] See José Tamés Alarcón, "Proceso urbanistico de nuestra colonización interior," op.cit.; and "Actuaciones del Instituto Nacional de Colonización 1939–1970," *Urbanismo*, COAM 3, 1988, pp. 4–18, where he referred to Sabaudia, Segezia, and Nahalal, the kibbutz-village designed in 1921 by Richard Kauffman.

[84] "Concurso de anteproyectos para la construcción de poblados en las zonas regables del Guadalquivir y del Guadalmellato," *Arquitectura* XVI, no. 10, 1934, pp. 267–298.

[85] See Alfredo Villanueva Paredes and Jesus Leal Maldonado, *Políticas y técnicas en la ordenación del espacio rural*, Volume III of the *Historia y Evolución de la Colonización Agraria in España*, Madrid, MAP/MAPA/MOPU, 1991.

[86] Manuel Calzada Pérez, p. 61.

[87] Alejandro de la Sota, "Vivienda agrupada. Pueblo de Gimenells," *Revista Nacional de Arquitectura*, November 1948, pp. 439–441.

[88] This section derives from my essays, Jean-François Lejeune, "Planned Cities in Spain, 1944–1969," Claudio D'Amato Guerrieri (ed.), *Cities of Stone: The Other Modernity, Xth Biennale of Venice*, Milan, Marsilio, 2006, pp. 158–167, and "Città di fondazione in Spagna, 1944–1969" in Jean-François Lejeune and Cristiano Rosponi (eds.), *Bollettino del CE.S.A.R.*, December 2006, unpaginated.

[89] See Antonio Pizza, "Die Dörfer Der Agrarkolonisation Im Spanien Francos," in Vittorio Magnago Lampugnani (ed.), *Die Architektur, Die Tradition Und Der Ort: Regionalismen in der Europäischen Stadt*, Ludwigsburg: Wüstenrot Stiftung, 2000, pp. 464–493. In my essays (see note 88), I mentioned the likely influence of the *Manifiesto de la Alhambra* on those new directions; reprinted in Angel Urrutia Núñez (ed.), *Arquitectura española contemporáneo. Documentos, escritos, testimonios inéditos*, pp. 356–383.

[90] Alejandro de la Sota, "El Nuevo pueblo de Esquivel, cerca de Sevilla," in *Revista Nacional de Arquitectura*, 133, December 1953, pp. 15–22; "Pueblo para el Instituto de Colonización, 1952–1956, Esquivel, Sevilla," *AV: Monografias (Alejandro de la Sota)*, 68, Nov.–Dec. 1997, pp. 38–45. Also see the transcription of a debate on the influence of traditional Andalucian towns on new urban design, Sesión de crítica de arquitectura celebrada en Sevilla, "Posibilidades que tienen los barrios típicos andaluces para el urbanismo actual," in *Arquitectura*, 155, 1954, pp. 19–48.

[91] William Curtis, "Dúas obras." *Grial*, 109, 1991, p. 17. Quoted in Pedro de Llano, *Alejandro de la Sota: O nacemento dunha arquitectura*, Pontevedra, Deputación Provincial de Pontevedra, 1994, p. 41.

– thus an estimated half a million of residents considering the size of rural families and their service employees – settled in the new towns built and integrated within new regional networks.

As a department of the Ministry of Agriculture, the INC was better sheltered from ideological pressure than the Department of Devastated Regions, and its architects were able to work according to more flexible architectural criteria.[85] Like their colleagues of the Devastated Regions they investigated the typologies of vernacular architecture – most types were organized around a large patio where tractors and other vehicles could be easily handled – but they did so increasingly in a stronger spirit of abstraction. The first generation of towns from 1944 to the early 1950s continued to display a regionalist character. Towns like Bernuy (1944, Manuel Jiménez Varea), Gimenells (1945, Alejandro de la Sota), Suchs (1945, José Borobio), Valdelacalzada (1947, Manuel Rosado Gonzalo), or Torre de la Reina (José Tamés, 1951) were planned rationally and systematically, albeit more picturesquely than the towns of the Devastated Regions. Each town was planned and built by a single architect as a unified project responding to a precise program. Given the amount of new foundations, the limited number of building types and their systematic repetition within the towns according to the 1939 regulations, standardization at the INC became "such a natural process that [architects] had to redouble their efforts to avoid it."[86] As Alejandro de la Sota wrote about Gimenells, it was important to achieve a variety of urban form that "without being overly irregular would be sufficient to evade the rigorous aspect of a town of grid-like pattern."[87] The town plans presented a lot of design diversity, and were generally planned around a vernacular-inspired *plaza mayor*, empty of references to the Escorial. The town edges provided spaces for parks, schools, or sports fields, while the peripheral blocks created a genuine urban façade fronting the fields. From the main roads, the towns appeared within the agricultural landscapes as compact white settlements dominated by a slender and modern bell tower.[88]

From the early 1950s and the foundation of Esquivel onwards, the second phase of INC towns sprang up from the drawing boards of Alejandro de la Sota, José Fernández del Amo, Miguel Herrero, Fernando Terán, and others like Antonio Fernández Alba. For this new generation of architects, the first principle was to follow the true nature of the Mediterranean vernacular and strip their houses from all stylistic reference, thus reconnecting with the GATCPAC's ambitions of the 1930s. At the same time, they intended to demonstrate that the grid and the block could lose their absolute character; accordingly they searched for a more abstract urban form that would establish new relationships between city and nature.[89]

Whereas his plan for Gimenells (1943) was loosely asymmetrical and centred on a relatively traditional plaza, de la Sota designed Esquivel as a symmetrical fan-shaped grid, whose apparent rigidity reflected that "it was born all at once on a flat terrain."[90] An extensive system of traffic separation was based upon pedestrian-only streets, alleys, and small squares which gave access to the front of the houses, whereas another system of streets, wider and bordered by high courtyard walls, concentrated all the agricultural traffic and the commercial movement. Overall, Esquivel's spaces were traditional, yet as William Curtis noted, "they were abstracted in order to adapt them to a new order and a new landscape."[91] For instance, the parish church and the town hall did not appear as the walls of a square, but rather rose as a corporeal, freestanding, and somewhat surrealist complex within the park that separated the curved town façade from the regional road. Esquivel and Entrerríos, also designed by de la

Sota near Merida in 1953, showed themselves as "utopian", introducing a subtle and playful commentary on the social or physical context within which they were inscribed. Their civic architecture reinterpreted, at times with a bit of irony, the simple white volumes of the private and public buildings of the region. Their low and sober houses were as close as could be to the vernacular models praised before the war by Sert and his friends, and which de la Sota investigated for himself thoroughly (plate 25).

José Luis Fernández del Amo developed further the vision of a modern urban form and the typological abstraction in San Isidro de Albatera (Alicante, 1953–56), Villalba de Calatrava (Ciudad Real, 1955–59), Cañada de Agra (1962) – whose center showed obvious influences from Alvar Aalto – and especially Vegaviana (Cáceres, 1956–58).[92] Planned by the INC as a settlement of three hundred and forty houses to accommodate six hundred agricultural workers and their families, Vegaviana was located in the midst of a thousand-year old

[92] For an overview see *Fernández Del Amo: Arquitecturas 1942–1982*, Madrid, Ministerio de Cultura, 1983; José Luis Fernández del Amo, *Palabra y Obra. Escritos Reunidos*, Madrid, COAM, 1995. On Vegaviana, see "Vegaviana: un poblado de colonización," *Revista Nacional de Arquitectura*, 202, 1958, pp. 1–14.

3.11 Alejandro de la Sota (INC). Sketch of the skyline and sketch plan of Esquivel, Sevilla, 1952.
Source: Fundación Alejandro de la Sota, Madrid.

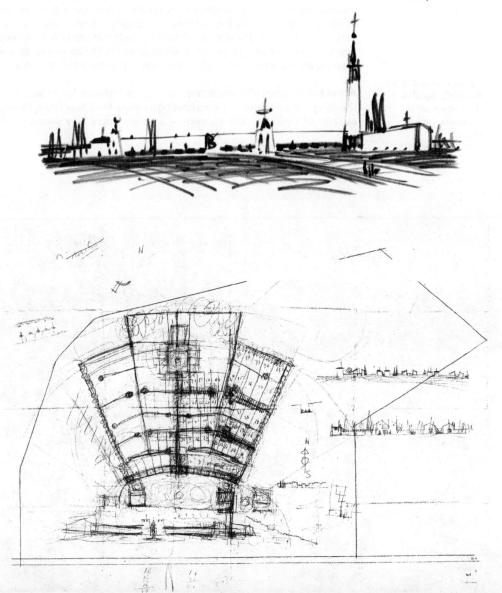

93 Quoted from Francisco Javier Saenz de Oiza, "El Pueblo de Vega-viana," *Arquitectura*, 7, 1959, pp. 25–28, reprinted in *Fernández Del Amo: Arquitecturas 1942–1982*, p. 46.
94 Oscar Niemeyer, catalogue of the 1961 Biennale of São Paulo where Del Amo received the Gold Medal, quoted by José de Castro Arines, "El hombre y la obra" in *Fernández Del Amo: Arquitecturas 1942–1982*, p. 16.
95 Ignasi Sola-Morales, p. 28.

landscape of oak trees. Aware that the countryside would disappear over time for cultivation, del Amo decided to conserve the oak groves throughout the town, as natural relics and first monuments of the foundation. He allowed the landscape to penetrate the whole organism, and made it indispensable to the loose definition of the streets and squares. At its geometric center he located the church, the town hall and tribunal, the post office, the cinema-library, and all the necessary commercial areas. The *plaza mayor* still came into view but its edges mutated into an informal and poetic mix of built fabric and landscape.

Displaying a new type of organic character, the plan consisted of fragments of urban fabric connected together by the landscape. The super-blocks were more loosely articulated than in Esquivel, and the automobile circulation was likewise separated from the pedestrian-oriented center. Located less than fifty kilometers southwest of the infamous Hurdes region, now part of the dammed basin of the Alagón river, Vegaviana was praised by Oscar Niemeyer as a work of "human, plastic, and social quality,"[93] "whose architecture derives from man and serves his vital fulfilment."[94] Yet the experiment of Vegaviana quickly fell into oblivion. Although the experience of the INC is now opening up new fields of research for historians, the official historiography has been mostly silent or perplexed. Yet, as Ignacio Sola-Morales wrote, "only a dogmatic position would lead us to undervalue an experience, which turned out to be, and for so many reasons, analogous to the one of the orthodoxy of the modern movement."[95]

About twenty years after Vegaviana, Portuguese architect Alvaro Siza started the design for a new working-class housing neighborhood near Évora, Portugal. In spite of their opposite contexts – a derelict periphery versus pristine

3.12 José Luis Fernández del Amo (INC). Aerial view of the new town of Vegaviana, Cacéres, 1954–58.
Source: INC, Ministerio de la Agricultura, Madrid.

agricultural landscapes – the parallels between Alvaro Siza's Quinta de Malagueira, del Amo's Vegaviana and de la Sota's Esquivel are astounding and deserve special consideration.[96]

Coderch and Grup R: From Rural to Urban Vernacular

The Fifth National Assembly of Architects of 1949 marked another seminal date for the Spanish architectural world. It opened to an international forum after ten years of relative isolation, and is generally seen as the starting point of the revival of modern architecture. In their speeches, guest lecturers Alberto Sartoris and Gio Ponti argued for a new architecture of "mediation" whose modernity would reflect "the rational and functional concept of the art of building . . . as old as the world and born on the coasts of the Mediterranean," thus reconnecting with the pre-Civil War debates in Spain.[97] Sartoris (who knew Spain during the 1930s through an exchange of publications with Fernando García Mercadal) delivered a lecture that reflected his recent publication of *Ordre et climat méditerranéen* (1948) and that presented together the architecture of Pier Luigi Nervi, Carlo Cattaneo, and Antoni Gaudí along with sketches of houses in Spanish fishing villages. Likewise, Ponti spoke of Antoni Gaudí and the traditional Catalan rural architecture – "the primitive popular house of Catalonia . . . that sprouts a fruit of spirituality of the greatest and most sacred importance" – as precursors and paradigms of a new modernity.[98] Back in Italy, he wrote in *Domus*:

> At times, thinking back to Ibiza and Benicarló, I ponder with some affliction how difficult it is for us architects, in spite of all our theoretical and polemical baggage . . . to achieve a result as natural as that "architecture without architects," that farmers and men of sea have always built with content unawareness.[99]

It is during that event that Coderch met Ponti and Sartoris, who invited him to publish in the Italian magazine *Domus*. It marked the grand entrance on the national and international scene of a Spanish architect of the post-Civil War era. Born in Barcelona on November 26, 1913, José Antonio Coderch de Sentmenat worked in Madrid from 1940 to 1942 for Secundino Zuazo. Back to Catalonia where he started his collaboration with Manuel Valls, he worked in Sitges and acquainted himself with the problems involved in the design of subsidized housing, an issue that will be at the heart of both his theoretical work and his professional activity. In 1945 he was appointed municipal architect in Sitges. To this period date projects such as the Obra Sindical del Hogar (1944) and the unrealized Les Forques neighborhood plan (1945), all projects whose clear typology and simple vernacular made reference to popular architecture of the coastal region. Likewise, the fishermen's houses built for Instituto Social de la Marina in the harbour of Tarragona (1949) were organized as a long "double crescent" with great formal economy and conceptual urban clarity bearing a strong resemblance with the fisherman's rowhouses individualized by set in the early 1930s.[100]

For Coderch and Vall's 1951 was a golden year. In May, the IX Triennale of Milan opened, with the Spanish pavilion designed by Coderch and Santos Torroella, "an exercise in synthesis intended to demonstrate the quintessence of Spanish 'modernity,' at least as Coderch understood it."[101] The left wall of the U-shaped 700-square-foot pavilion was made of a structure of wood shutters, within which Coderch inserted three rows of photographs of minor Ibizan architecture mixed with details of Gaudí's buildings, all of them by photographer Joaquín

[96] On the Quinta Malagueira, see Enrico Molteni, *Álvaro Siza: Barrio de la Malagueira, Évora*, Barcelona, Universitat Politècnica de Catalunya, 1997; Peter G. Rowe, *Prince of Wales Prize in Urban Design, 1988*, Cambridge, Harvard University, Graduate School of Design, 1988.

[97] Antonio Pizza, "The Tradition and Universalism of a Domestic Project," Antonio Pizza and Josep Rovira (eds.), *In Search of Home: Coderch 1940/1964*, Barcelona, Colegio de Arquitectos de Cataluña, 2000, pp. 89–90.

[98] For this section, see Josep M. Rovira, "The Sea Never Had a Dream," in *Coderch 1940/1964*, pp. 73ff. On the relationship between Spain and Italy, see Antonio Pizza and Josep Rovira, *In Search of Home*, op. cit., and María Isabel Navarro, "La crítica italiana y la arquitectura española de los años 50. Pasajes de la arquitectura española en la segunda modernidad," in Escuela Técnica Superior de Arquitectura, *Modelos alemanes y italianos para España en los años de la posteguerra*, U.N.A.V. 4, Actas del Congreso Internacional, March 2004, Pamplona, T6 Ediciones, 2004, pp. 61–100 (Internet edition).

[99] Gio Ponti, "Della Spagna," *Domus*, quoted by Luigi Spinelli, *José Antonio Coderch: La cellula e la luce*, Torino, Universale di architettura, no. 134, 2003, p. 14.

[100] On Coderch's early work, see Antonio Pizza and Josep Rovira, *In Search of Home*, and Luigi Spinelli, *José Antonio Coderch*, op. cit.

[101] For this section, see Antonio Pizza, "The Tradition and Universalism of a Domestic Project," p. 92ff., quote on p. 94.

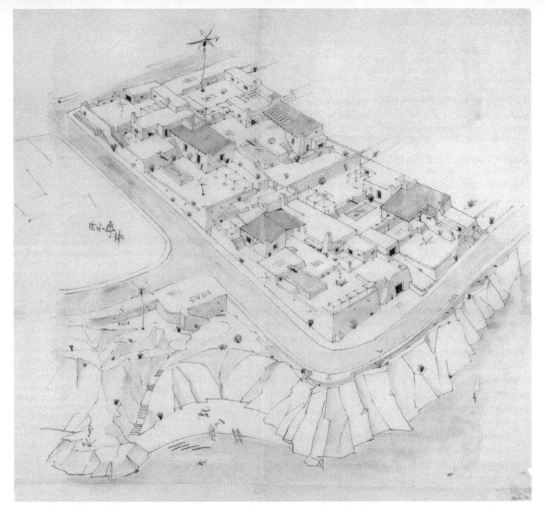

3.13 José Antonio Coderch. Las Forcas housing development, Sitges, 1945.
Source: © Arxiu Coderch, Escola Tecnica Superior Arquitectura Vallé (ETSAV), Sant Cugat del Vallés.

3.14 José Antonio Coderch and Santos Torroella. Partial view of the Spanish pavilion at the IX Triennale of Milan, 1951. Inserted within the Llambí louvers are photographs of Ibizan popular architecture and Antoni Gaudí's details of buildings (photos by Joaquín Gomis).
Source: *Spazio* II, 1951.

Gomis in association with Juan Prats Vallés. The opposite wall was covered with straw and displayed a painting by Ángel Ferrant, *Muchachas*, a *Composition* by Miró, along with a selection of objects (glass vase, popular ceramics and the maiolicas, etc.) selected by Torroela, one of the artisans of renovation of Catalan art. The red wall at the centre held a Romanesque painting of the Catalan School, a wooden Virgin Mary, and on an amoeba-shaped low table were exhibited the illustrated edition of García Lorca's works by Guinovart, ceramic pots, mantillas, and other handicraft objects. Commenting on the pavilion in the columns of *Spazio*, Luigi Moretti argued that "the vigor but also the terror and the liberating vehemence of Gaudí live from the same blood, and from the same substance that the men who have put up the walls of the houses on Ibiza." And he added:

> Both architectures are the extreme poles, linked by countless continuous passages, of the same drive that leads one to detach from, and to renounce, the things that are not completely controlled; in the case of Gaudí, renunciation to the voluble casuistry of nature, and refuge within the controlled world of the spirit; in the case of Ibiza, abandonment of the intellectual and spiritual casuistry in favour of traditional, as solid as the objects of nature. . . . In sum, a particular architecture rejects what the other one assumes. This is in fact the law of true architecture in all the places which truly bear the mark of the individual and the collective.[102]

The first phase of Coderch–Valls's oeuvre involved a series of relatively small non-permanent residences on the Catalan coast. The first one, Casa Ugalde en Calldes d'Estrac near Sitges, whose first sketches date from October 1951, became an instant icon of Spanish modernity. Ponti wrote in *Domus* about its "informal and disjointed plan, in which the Mediterranean principle of the encounter with the landscape has been pushed to its limits: almost to a labyrinth."[103] Casa Ugalde was followed by the Esteve house in Garraf, the extension of the Torrents house in Sitges, and the Casa Catasús (1956–59) also in Sitges, all projects that show an increasing typology-driven approach to the program and site, and the strong influence of Richard Neutra's Californian houses of the same period. Beautifully photographed by Català-Roca, these buildings acquired an iconic aura that was for the early 1950s in Barcelona what the photographs of Julius Shulman were for the California of the Case Study Houses. With their white walls, their large sliding glass doors and sliding shutters, and their "cell-like" typology (not unlike the way Ibiza houses grew by addition of well-defined rooms), those houses exalted "the syncretism they longed to illustrate between Mediterranean tradition and avant-garde culture."[104]

However, Coderch's work was not limited to the "recreation" of the Catalonian bourgeoisie along the Mediterranean shores. To the contrary, during the same period, the firm pursued various works, in the very core of Barcelona, whose importance cannot be overemphasized. At a time of general urban crisis in Europe and the United States, Coderch–Valls's works respected the urban traditions and rules of the city, while at the same time developing a unique urban approach to the modernization of the vernacular. Their first building was a project of 150-working class units for the Instituto de la Marina in the highly popular district of La Barceloneta. Amidst the very narrow eighteenth-century streets, they designed an urban block centered on a large planted courtyard. In order to provide views toward the sea, the courtyard, faced by the living rooms, was open on one of its narrow sides while the bedrooms facing the streets projected out as triangular loggias with their windows oriented to the

[102] Luigi Moretti, "Tradizione muraria a Ibiza," *Spazio* II, 1951, 5, pp. 35–42. It is interesting to note that Sert, from the other side of the Atlantic, was equally interested in Gaudí, see José Luis Sert and James Johnson Sweeney, *Antoni Gaudí*, London, Architectural Press, 1960. Two years earlier, Le Corbusier prefaced a book dedicated to the Catalan architect with photographs by Joaquín Gomis and Juan Prats, *Gaudí*, Barcelona, Editorial RM, 1958.
[103] "Casa sulla costa spagnola," *Domus* 289, December 1953.
[104] Carlos Flores, "La arquitectura de José Antonio Coderch y Manuel Valls, 1942–60," in *De Roma a Nueva York: Itinerarios de la nueva arquitectura española 1950/1965, UNAV* 1, Actas del Congreso International, October 1988, Pamplona, T6 Ediciones, pp. 67–77, quote on p. 69, Internet version.

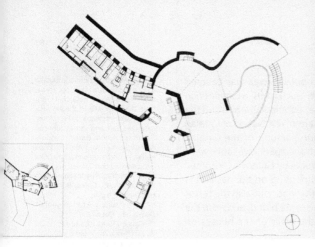

3.15 José Antonio Coderch.
Plans and views of
Casa Ugalde, Caldes
de Estrach, 1951.
Source: © Arxiu Coderch,
ETSAV. Photographer
F. Català-Roca.

water. For the same Instituto de la Marina, Coderch and Valls would build
their masterwork in 1952–53: the apartment house for the Institute's
employees, again at the heart of La Barceloneta on the Passeig de Joan de
Borbó. In response to the tight site, a double street corner with three short
façades, the architects made the upper floors float and "undulate" freely above
the ground floor aligned with the rest of the block. With its glazed plinth, its
light façades of wood louvers and ceramic tiles, and its projecting attic, the
apartment house was praised by Gio Ponti for its architecture "born from
the interior" which proceeds from rational necessity and not from "odd and
imitative spirits."[105]

The apartment house can also be seen as a kind of environmental "manifesto"
which inaugurated Coderch and Valls's approach to dealing with modern
materials – large glazed windows – while responding to the extreme conditions of the climate. Whether in the city (see the apartment building at Calle
Bach of 1958, the house for Tapiés of 1958, or Coderch's own townhouse in
Cadaqués of 1956) or in the countryside (Casa Urlach, Casa Ugalde, etc.) they
would, repeatedly and for almost two decades, use the so-called Llambí shutters
to screen the interiors from the sun, and thus develop a sort of modern
"vernacular skin" whose mix of vertical divisions and horizontal louver lines
facilitated the integration in many historic contexts independently from
the structural system and materials. The patent for the modern *persiana*
was filed in March 1953 by Coderch, Valls, and Juan and José Llambí, the owners
of the Llambí company. Originally founded in 1940 as a wood carpentry
shop, it gradually evolved towards what became its main activity from 1950:
the manufacture of wooden shutters, with both fixed and tiltable horizontal
wood slats.

The *persiana* or louvers has a rich Hispanic tradition, whose origin can be
traced back to the Arab dwelling and the mashrabiya (moucharabieh). Rare in
the countryside, the *persiana* remains a defining element of the urban
vernacular landscape in Spain, where it contributes greatly to creating
"a metaphysic of the Mediterranean notion of intimacy."[106] In contrast,
the vernacular peasant houses – documented in the periodical *AC* by
Haussmann, Baeschlin and others – do not use wood louvers but display
small openings, thick walls, loggias and other terraces to screen the rooms
from excessive light. Interestingly, *AC* had precisely documented those
differences in the 1930s, particularly in the issue # 18. For instance, a set of six
photographs from the streets of Tarifa and San Fernando in Andalucia
emphasized the variety and rhythm of the windows screened with *persianas*.
The text read:

[105] Gio Ponti, "Casa a Barcelona,"
Domus 306, May 1955, pp. 7–10. The
concrete engineer for the project
was Eustequio Ugalde, owner of the
Ugalde house.
[106] Carlos Garrido, "Paisaje de persianas," *Diario de Mallorca*, Feb. 21,
2008 (accessed on the Internet).

3.16 José Antonio Coderch.
Apartment for the
Instituto de la Marina,
La Barceloneta,
Barcelona, 1951.
Source: © Arxiu Coderch,
ETSAV, Collegi d'Arquitectes
de Catalunya. Photographer
F. Català-Roca.

The *standard* elements, repeated to the infinite, instead of creating monotony – the one for which the professors of academic schools are so afraid – give a great impression of unity and ensemble to the Andalucian towns.[107]

Another important event took place in Barcelona in 1951: the foundation of Grup R, composed by Coderch and Valls, along with José Pratmasó, Joaquín Gili, Antoni De Moragas, Josep Maria Sostres (Casa Agustí in Sitges, 1953–55), and Oriol Bohigas. The group, mostly a loose association of two generations of architects – the first one around Coderch, Gili, Sostres; the younger one around Bohigas, Martorell, Ribas, etc. – was essentially an intellectual center of resistance, whose members intended to reconnect with the spirit of GATCPAC. Grup R never issued any theoretical platform or manifesto, but organized four architectural exhibitions that presented photographs of Catalá-Roca, models, drawings, and in some cases ceramics, sculptures, and other subjects. Next to the cited works of Coderch–Valls, the MMI and Agustí houses by Sostres displayed the clearest Mediterranean-modern image marked by clear white volumes and the intensive use of louvers.[108]

[107] See AC 18, 1935, p. 19.
[108] See Gabriel Ruiz Cabrero, *The Modern in Spain: Architecture after 1948*, Cambridge, The MIT Press, 2001; Carmen Rodríguez and José Torres, *Grup R*, Barcelona, Gili, 1994.

109 Miguel Fisac, "Estética de la Arquitectura," quoted by Antonio Pizza,
"Italia y la necesidad de la teoría en
la arquitectura catalana de la
postguerra: E. N. Rogers, O. Bohigas,"
in *De Roma a Nueva York: Itinerarios
de la nueva arquitectura española
1950–1965*, p. 100. In that essay,
Pizza stresses the role of Bruno Zevi
and Alvar Aalto who lectured in Spain
in 1950.
110 Gabriel Ruiz Cabrero, *The Modern
in Spain: Architecture after 1948*,
p. 13. Cabrero mentions Rafael
Aburto, Francisco Cabrero, Alejandro
de la Sota, Miguel Fisac. It is worth
noting that Coderch also fought on
the Falangist side during the Civil
War and was a dedicated Catholic
as well. As a counterpoint, see the
recent and aggressively one-sided
article by Josep Rovira, "Architettura
Popolare E Fascismo. Celebrazioni
Franchiste. Prima Fiera Nazionale
Dell'agricoltura. Casa De Campo.
Madrid, 1950," *Casabella 771*, November 2008, pp. 88–97.
111 Fernando Chueca Goitia et al.,
Manifiesto de la Alhambra, Madrid,
Dirección General de la Arquitectura,
1953; reprinted in Angel Urrutia
Núñez (ed.), *Arquitectura española
contemporáneo. Documentos, escritos,
testimonios inéditos*, pp. 356–383,
quote p. 361. For an analysis, see
Juan Calatrava Escobar (ed.), *El Manifiesto de la Alhambra 50 años después:
el monumento y la arquitectura contemporánea*, Granada, Patronato de
la Alhambra y Generalife, 2006.

The Catalonian sphere, however, did not have the monopoly on modernity. In his Fifth Assembly speech of 1949, Madrid architect Miguel Fisac paralleled the declarations of Sartoris and Ponti when he stated:

> We all agreed on the necessity to abandon the road that we had been following, because it lacked any vital content. . . . To copy the popular or classical Spanish art leads us to folklore or "espagnolades." To pull out its essence, to be able to extract the ingredients of truth, of modesty, of joy, of beauty – that is the way to open the path to a New Architecture.[109]

Fisac, known for his Swedish-influenced organic approach to architecture, also wrote an influential essay "La arquitectura popular española y su valor ante la del futuro," published in Madrid in 1952. With Rafael Aburto, Secundino Zuazo, Fernández del Amo, Alejandro de la Sota, Francisco de Asis Cabrero – to name a few – he belonged to the informal group of regime-supporting Catholic-oriented architects who had moved to Madrid to work on the reconstruction project. As Gabriel Cabrero wrote:

> A very strong link united them: they all belonged to one precise faction among the many that had constituted the self-styled "national" camp. These were the Catholics, who had taken arms to defend their religion, interpreting the war as a crusade, and emerged from it convinced that only on the basis of a Catholic perception of life could society be regenerated. For them, architecture was above all an instrument for building the spaces in which society's ethical necessities could be renewed.[110]

Beside de la Sota and del Amo whose work we have already discussed, Miguel Fisac and Francisco Cabrero understood, like Coderch, that a modern approach to the vernacular held the key to the reopening of the architectural culture: among their most notable realizations were the Instituto Laboral de Hellín (Fisac, 1954), the Colegio Apóstolico de los P.P. Dominicanos in Valladolid (Fisac, 1952), the social apartments of the Virgen del Pilar in Madrid (1948, where Cabrero used the traditional Catalan vaults), or the Recinto de la Fiera Casa del Campo (Cabrero, 1948). In 1953, Fisac and Cabrero were among the twenty-four signees of the *Manifiesto de la Alhambra*, written under the direction of Fernando Chueca Goitia following a long encounter in Granada. Whereas reference to the Escorial had dominated Spanish architecture during the 1940s, Chueca Goitia and his group saw in the Alhambra in Granada a more appropriate historical and multicultural reference to the modern condition and needs of post-war Spain:

> The relationship between this edifice of the fourteenth century and the most advanced contemporary architecture is, in many ways, astonishing. They concur in their acceptation of human module; in the manner, asymmetrical yet organic, to organize the plans; in the purity and the sincerity of the resulting volumes; in the manner to incorporate the garden and the landscape to the edifice; in the strict and economic use – without any plastic "fat" – of the materials, and in so many other things.[111]

"In Praise of the Shanty"

At the occasion of the First Hispano-American Biennale held in Madrid from October 1951 to February 1952, various architects including Mitjans, Sostres, and Coderch himself addressed the question of low-cost housing within the emerging context of renewed international relations, particularly with the

United States. Like in the 1920s and the immediate post-Civil War period the reality of the economic structure of Spain in the 1950s continued to favour standardization and relatively labour-intensive solutions. In their *Estudio sobre la vivienda económica en España*, Casadesús and Gaspar suggested the recourse to "simplicity in the composition of the projects, in the use of manpower and materials; simplicity which does not mean poverty, . . . proportions driven by simple masses, plays of voids and solids, rhythm of the building masses and open spaces."[112] Likewise, Coderch suggested the use of standardization and simple pre-stressed concrete techniques that would recreate the articulated image of a traditional village, evoking echoes of "primitive culture" in his vision of vernacular assemblages of simple volumes which he would illustrate in a later photomontage presented at the 1962 Team X meeting in Royaumont.[113]

To be sure, there was nothing explicitly new in these positions; one could argue that the contemporary works of Alejandro de la Sota, Fernández del Amo and other architects who worked for the INC responded directly to Coderch's statements, yet they were definitely ignored by the Catalan group. To their credit, the architects of Grup R were mainly interested in urban issues; the most fruitful Catalonian experiments and debates took place in the very context of the metropolis. A case in point were the early works of Oriol Bohigas who, in his early thirties, built a remarkable series of brick apartment buildings – among them, the block at Calle Pallars (1959–65) for metallurgy workers and the Casa Meridiana (1959–65). Erected at the heart of Barcelona in the Ensanche, they were Bohigas's counterpart to the contemporary Italian Neorealist movement (Ridolfi, Quaroni, etc.) and a demonstration of his deep interest in Ernesto Rogers's theory and writings.

Rogers believed in a double historical continuum: the tradition of the modern masters (Loos, Gropius, Le Corbusier, Mies), and the spontaneous and popular tradition that would allow the architects to get closer to the working class masses, which were becoming the new protagonists of history.[114] Bohigas followed Roger's position closely. Hence, his work was an extension of the "vernacular discourse" that had until then concentrated on the countryside or the remote peripheries. His aim was to define a strategy of an "urban

112 Antonio Pizza, "The Tradition and Universalism of a Domestic Project," pp. 103ff.
113 Ibid., p. 108, quoted from Giralt Casadesús and Maynés Gaspar, *Estudio sobre la vivienda económica en España*, Barcelona, Cuerpo de Arquitectos Municipales de España, 1950, p. 52.
114 See Antonio Pizza, "Italia y la necesidad de la teoría en la arquitectura catalana de la postguerra: E. N. Rogers, O. Bohigas," p. 107.

3.17 Photomontage by José Antonio Coderch.
Source: Cover of *Auca 14*, Santiago de Chile, 1969.

[115] Oriol Bohigas, "Elogi de la barraca," *Barcelona entre el Pla Cerdà
i el barraquisme*, Edicions 62,
Barcelona, 1963, pp. 154–155.
[116] O. Bohigas, "L'arquitectura entre
la indústria i l'artesania" en *Serra
d'Or* no.10, Barcelona, 1960. Quoted
by Antonio Pizza, "Italia y la necesidad
de la teoría en la arquitectura
catalana de la postguerra: E. N.
Rogers, O. Bohigas," p. 105.
[117] See Luis Fernández Galiano, Justo
F. Isasi, and Antonio Lopera (eds.),
*La quimera moderna – Los Poblados
Dirigidos de Madrid en la arquitectura
de los 50*, Madrid, Hermann Blume,
1989.

vernacular," linked to materials, urban typology, and a traditional manner of building. With their urban vernacular façade of traditional bricks and their careful insertion within the urban fabric, his buildings stood against the ideological tenets of the Modern movement by opposing traditional manpower to advanced technological structures and solutions, thus reconnecting with the experience of the *casas baratas* of the early decades and the first debate on industrialization vs. standardization. In 1963, Bohigas wrote his famous manifesto *Elogi de la barraca* [In praise of the shanty], which provocatively ennobled both traditional construction techniques and self-construction processes in contrast with the speculative blocks of the periphery:

> We think that it is possible to "redeem" the space of the shanties and add some value to it – an impossible task in our inorganic groups of mass housing. Likewise, we believe that the genuine qualities to be found in the shanties could offer lessons to our urbanists, and make them understand what are the authentic foundations and the sociological premises of a new neighbourhood.[115]

And in another text:

> One must remember that the immediate problem is to provide houses for the countless families that have been rejected by our social structure. And, for the sake of those families, it is critical to renounce, at least for the time being, to our constant discussions: what style, opinions, principles, forms, etc. Including, if necessary, step down from the pedestal of the technicians of the industrial era, in order to work, manually, with "medieval" craftsmen and craftswomen.[116]

In Madrid, the social crisis of 1956 in the *chabolas* [bidonvilles] of the periphery, the activism of a local priest, Padre Llanos, and the organizational energy of architect Julián Laguna converged to produce a short-lived experiment in public housing. Mixing vernacular-based techniques of auto-construction for single-family units and semi-industrial typologies of multi-family mid-rise blocks, the seven Poblados Dirigidos (Directed Districts) built from 1957 to the mid-1960s marked an abrupt departure from the design and construction methods of the INC.[117] Heavily influenced by the nascent brand of British brutalist functionalism, the experience resulted in very different districts, ranging from the alienating grid of Canillas (1957) to the more picturesque Almendrales (1959–66). The most successful of the seven quarters – the Caño Roto district (1957–63) – disclosed unmistakable influences from Italian neo-realism: the brick façades of the two-story houses, the narrow pedestrian lanes, and the metaphysical playgrounds populated by the sculptures of Angel Ferrant made it the most photogenic of all the Poblados (it is not surprising that its best interpreter was Joaquín del Palacio "Kindel," who was also the "official" photographer of Del Amo's works for the INC). In spite of their overall failure – the rapidity of design and construction, the lack of maintenance, and the isolation from the city resulted in rapid degradation – the seven Poblados were the last link in a continuous sixty-year chain of projects and experiments that connected the vernacular to the modern. The Francoist regime, now out of its international isolation, would soon embark upon a frenzy of industrial-based mass-housing that would irremediably endanger the urban peripheries and damage the Mediterranean shores.

In 1959 Coderch became a member of CIAM on the recommendation of José Luis Sert who had just completed his return to the Mediterranean with the

3.18 José Luis Iñiguez de Onzoño and Antonio Vázquez de Castro. View of a pedestrian alley in the Poblado Dirigido [Sponsored Settlement] of Caño Roto, Madrid, 1956–57.

Source: Luis Fernández-Galiano, Justo F. Isasi, and Antonio Lopera, *La quimera moderna: los Poblados Dirigidos de Madrid en la arquitectura de los 50*, Madrid, 1989.

Joan Miró studio on Palma de Majorca. He immediately joined, albeit not officially, the ranks of Team X after the Eleventh Congress of Otterlo. In 1961 Coderch wrote a manifesto-letter to the attention of secretary Jacob B. Bakema: in it he manifested his pessimism in the face of increased commercialism, the destruction of the coasts, and the degenerating quality of the urban and rural environment. Under the title "It is not geniuses that we need nowadays," he wrote:

> No, I do not believe that it is geniuses that we need today. I believe that geniuses just happened, they are neither means nor ends. Neither do I think that we need Popes of architecture, nor great doctrinaires and prophets (I am always doubtful of those) . . . I think that above all we need good schools and good professors. We must take advantage of what remains of our constructive tradition, and particularly of our moral one, in this epoch when our most beautiful words have lost their true meaning. . . . We must make it so that thousands and thousands of architects think less about Architecture, money, and the cities of the next millennium, and more about the very fact of being an architect. We need them to work with a rope attached to their feet, so that they cannot drift too far away from the land in which they have roots, nor from the men and women that they know best.[118]

With this statement a disillusioned Coderch summed up and reiterated the constant and critical role played by Spain's "constructive tradition" in order to frame an architectural modernity that challenged the status quo and the looming architectural prospects in the new capitalistic phase of Franco's regime. ∎

[118] Antonio Coderch, "No son genios lo que necesitamos ahora," published in *Domus* 384, November 1961, and *Arquitectura* no. 38, February 1962, pp. 21–26; reprinted Angel Urrutia Núñez (ed.), *Arquitectura española contemporáneo*, pp. 303–305; revised version of 1977, pp. 306–309.

4

MEDITERRANEAN DIALOGUES

Le Corbusier, Fernand Pouillon, and Roland Simounet

Sheila Crane

In August 1931, at the end of a two-month tour of Spain, Morocco, and Algeria, Le Corbusier created a series of drawings from the *Governor General Chanzy*, the boat that was to take him from Algiers to Marseille on his way back to Paris. As the boat pulled out of the harbor in Algiers and into Mediterranean waters, Le Corbusier sketched successive views of the city as its recognizable panorama faded from view. In the first of these drawings, the broad outlines of the city's landscape emerge from the distinctive arcades lining the port of Algiers (figure 4.2). The outlines of select landmarks defined the city's skyline, each clearly labeled in the drawing: the Citadel (where the Fort l'Empereur stood), the Casbah, the Governor's Palace, and the Marine Quarter. Each of the six successive sketches further distilled the essential outlines of the city as it receded further towards the horizon, even as the architect began defining the rough outlines of new buildings within the abstracted silhouette of the existing city. As Jean-Pierre Giordani has shown, this series of drawings defined the distinctive physiognomy of Algiers that Le Corbusier subsequently used as the conceptual and representational foundation of his new urban plans for the city.[1]

Near the end of his Mediterranean crossing, as the ship drew near the coast of France, Le Corbusier sketched the approaching port of Marseille (plate 27). This final drawing of the series begun in Algiers depicted Marseille's broad topographic outlines, punctuated by a line of distinctive buildings clustered around the old port: the Saint-Laurent Church, the seventeenth-century Saint-Jean and Saint-Nicolas forts, the Notre-Dame-de-la-Garde Basilica, and the transporter bridge spanning the mouth of the port. Viewed from the sea, with these monuments lined up in procession above the line of land and water, Le Corbusier's drawing defined a similarly iconic visage of Marseille. As with Algiers, this composition became Le Corbusier's personal, iconic representation of the city, one that was explicitly and experientially consolidated in relation to Algiers.

Le Corbusier frequently figured port cities following a similar formula, as he did, for example, in depictions of Istanbul, Rio de Janeiro, and Buenos Aires.[2] However, the specifically dialogic relationship he constructed in this sequence of sketches between Algiers and Marseille is unusual. When viewed in succession, these drawings not only record the architect's passage from Algiers to Marseille, but also, and even more crucially, they create a spatial and structural relationship between these two sites, founded on their proximity across the Mediterranean Sea and on the well-plied shipping route that ran between their ports. Le Corbusier's drawings were thus products of the history of colonization through which these cities were repositioned as key points of connection within the broader infrastructure of the French imperial system.

[1] Jean-Pierre Giordani, "Territoire: Nouveaux plans urbaines, les esquisses sud-américaines et le Plan Obus d'Alger," in Jacques Lucan (ed.), *Le Corbusier, une encyclopédie*, Paris, Éditions du Centre Pompidou/CCI, 1987, pp. 402–406, Jean-Pierre Giordani, "Le Plan Obus pour Alger," in *Le Corbusier et la Méditerranée*, Marseille, Éditions Parenthèses/Musées de Marseille, 1987, p.158, Jean-Pierre Giordani, "Le Corbusier et les projets pour la ville d'Alger, 1931–1942," Thèse du 3e cycle, Université de Paris VIII, 1987.

[2] Le Corbusier explicitly equated the landscape of Rio de Janeiro with Mediterranean port cities: "Rio-de-Janeiro is a celebrated site. But Algiers, but Marseille, but Oran, Nice and the entire Côte d'Azur, Barcelona and so many maritime or continental cities have wonderful landscapes!": from Le Corbusier and François de Pierrefeu, *La maison des hommes*, Paris, Librarie Plon, 1942, p. 69. See also Giordani, "Territoire," pp. 402–403, Hubert Damisch, "Modernité: Les tréteaux de la vie moderne," in Jacques Lucan (ed.), *Le Corbusier, une encyclopédie*, pp. 253–255.

4.1 *(Far left)* Fernand Pouillon. Model of the Climat de France quarter with the Square of Two Hundred Columns, Algiers, 1955–57.
Source: © Archives Fernand Pouillon, Association Les Pierres Sauvages de Belcastel.

3 Thierry Fabre, *La Méditerranée française*, Paris, Maisonneuve and Larose, 2000, pp. 28–38.

This important circulation route between Algiers and Marseille and the imagined map of connections it produced constitutes a significant terrain of Mediterraneanism in modern architecture. As numerous scholars have noted, "the Mediterranean" is a distinctly modern construct, one whose definition as concept and consolidation as image was itself the product of the history of imperialism and colonization that so profoundly restructured this region from the late eighteenth century onwards.[3] The Mediterranean claims of modern architecture were constructed through particular mappings and associative relationships that were themselves tied to localized histories of political and economic connections as well as to embodied experiences of travel, transit, and translation.

In order to unravel the "Mediterranean" forms and discourses of modern architecture, we must understand the conceptual mappings and political frameworks through which appropriations of vernacular forms were made possible. In what follows, I consider Le Corbusier's mapping of a direct connection between Algiers and Marseille in relation to subsequent architectural projects by Fernand Pouillon and Roland Simounet. Both Pouillon and Simounet worked in the shadow of their more famous predecessor, even as they articulated quite distinctive visions of Mediterranean modernism based on their own mappings of Marseille and Algiers as mirror reflections across the sea. My aim here is to examine one pathway of connections that might help us to consider more carefully the multi-directional dislocations of "the vernacular" and "the modern" in architecture.

Le Corbusier's Mirror Images

The formative effects of North African vernacular architecture on Le Corbusier's architectural practice are legendary and represent well-trodden ground in the voluminous writings on his work. Beginning in 1931, the architect spent a decade developing a series of proposals for the urban restructuring of the city of Algiers, which were ultimately rejected in 1942. In the summer of 1931, at the very beginning of his project for Algiers, Le Corbusier traveled through Spain, Morocco, and Algeria, with his cousin and collaborator Pierre Jeanneret, his brother the musician Albert Jeanneret, and his friend the artist Fernand Léger. At the end of this trip, the architect created the drawings of the ports of Algiers and Marseille with which this chapter began. This was also the occasion of the architect's famous discovery of the towns of the M'Zab, including the oasis of Laghouat and Ghardaïa. Upon his return to France, he published an

4.2 **Le Corbusier. Drawing of Algiers, August 1931.**
Source: © 2009 Artists Rights Society (ARS), New York/ ADAGP, Paris/FLC.

Plate 1 (*Previous page*) Curzio Malaparte (with Adalberto Libera). Cassa Malaparte, 1937–42.
Source: Photo Petra Liebl-Osborne.

Plate 2 (*Left*) Joseph Beuys. "Capri-Batterie," 1985.
© 2009 Artists Rights Society (ARS), New York/VG Bild-Kunst, Bonn. Sammlung Schlegel, Berlin. Photo Heiner Bastian.

Plate 3 (*Below*) Curzio Malaparte (with Adalberto Libera). Villa Malaparte, 1937–42. Staircase with installation *Fixierte Orte* [Fixed Sites] by Petra Liebl-Osborne.
Source: Photo Petra Liebl-Osborne.

Plate 4 Louis Kahn. *View of Town, no. 2, Positano, Italy,* **1929.**
Source: private collection.

Plate 5 Josef Hoffmann. *Pompeii*, 1896.
Source: private collection.

Plate 6 Giorgio Grassi. Perspective of the Chieti Students
Housing project, 1976–78.
Source: © Giorgio Grassi Architetti.

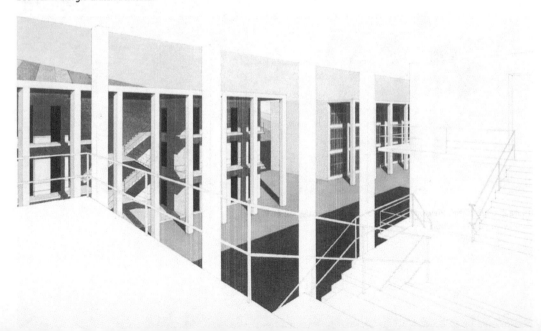

Plate 7 Franz Ludwig Catel. *Karl Friedrich Schinkel in Naples,* **1824.**
Source: Nationalgalerie, Staatliche Museen zu Berlin, Berlin. © Bildarchiv Preussischer Kulturbesitz/Art Resource, New York. Inv. Ng 1968 47/48. Photo: Joerg P. Anders.

Plate 8 Hans von Marées. *Pergola*, fresco on the east wall in the library of the Zoological Station (Aquarium), Naples, Italy, 1873. From the left, the three characters in the fresco are Anton Dohrn, founder of the Zoological Station, Adolf von Hildebrandt (standing) who was responsible for the architectonic structure of the frescoes, and Hans von Marées himself.

Source: © Archivio Stazione Zoologica, Naples. Photo: Ralph Goertz/IKS.

Plate 9 Giorgio de Chirico. *The Enigma of a Day*, early 1914.
Source: The Museum of Modern Art, James Thrall Soby Bequest. ©The Museum of Modern Art/Licensed by SCALA/Art Resource, New York. © 2009 Artists Rights Society (ARS), New York/SiAE, Rome.

Plate 10 (*Top left*) Le Corbusier. The forum in Pompeii (reconstruction), 1911.
Source: © 2009 Artists Rights Society (ARS), New York/ADAGP, Paris/FLC.

Plate 11 (*Bottom left*) Le Corbusier. Pastel drawings superimposed over John Flaxman's original illustrations of Homer's
Iliad (1793, first published in 1795). The drawings were executed by Le Corbusier at Cap-Martin in February 1955 and
were traced over a new publication of Flaxman's drawings in the series *Les Portiques*, no. 35, November 1954.
Here, the drawing illustrates a dialog between Paris and Helen, "Allons! Couchons-nous et goûtons le plaisir
d'amour" [Let's go. Let's lie down and taste the pleasure of love].
Source: Mogens Krustrup, *Le Corbusier: L'Iliade Dessins*, Copenhaghen, 1986. © 2009 Artists Rights Society (ARS), New York/ADAGP,
Paris/FLC.

Plate 12 Le Corbusier. *Athens*, panorama from the northwest side of the Parthenon, September 1911.
Source: Plate VIII, *Le Langage des pierres* [The Language of Stones], exhibition in Zürich in 1914. © 2009 Artists Rights Society
(ARS), New York/ADAGP, Paris/FLC.

Plate 13 Gio Ponti. "An Ideal Small House," 1939.
Source: From *Domus* 138, 1939.

Plate 14 (*Top right*) Luigi Figini and Gino Pollini. Perspective, "Electric House," IV International Exposition of Modern Decorative and Industrial Art, Monza, 1929–30.
Source: © Archivio Figini-Pollini, MART, Rovereto.

Plate 15 (*Bottom right*) Gio Ponti. Perspective, "Villa alla Pompeiana" (Pompeian-type Villa), 1934.
Source: From *Domus* 79, 1934.

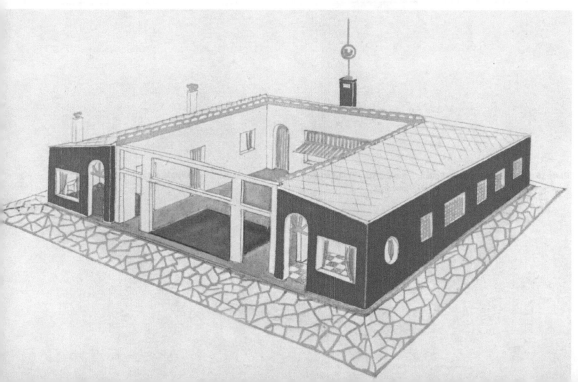

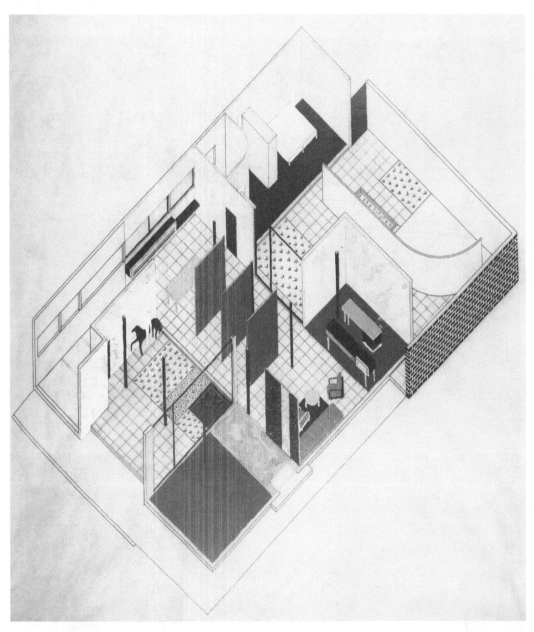

Plate 16 Luigi Figini and Gino Pollini. Axonometric, "Villa-studio per un artista," Milan, V Triennale, 1933.
Source: © Archivio Figini-Pollini, MART, Rovereto.

Plate 17 Ernesto Rogers et al. Perspective [partim], Italian
        Pavilion, Brussels, 1958.
Source: © Archivio BBPR, Milan.

Plate 18 Piero Bottoni. "Villa al mare," Milan,
        IV Triennale, 1930.
Source: © Archivio Piero Bottoni, Milan.

Plate 19 Alberto Sartoris. Cover of
        *Encyclopédie de l'architecture
        nouvelle: Ordre et climat
        méditerranéens*, Milan, 1948.
Photo: Michelangelo Sabatino.

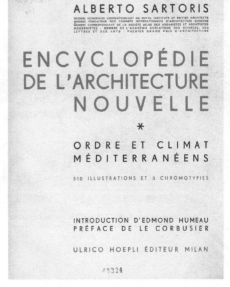

ALBERTO SARTORIS

MEMBRE HONORAIRE CORRESPONDANT DU ROYAL INSTITUTE OF BRITISH ARCHITECTS
MEMBRE FONDATEUR DES CONGRÈS INTERNATIONAUX D'ARCHITECTURE MODERNE
MEMBRE CORRESPONDANT DE LA SOCIÉTÉ BELGE DES URBANISTES ET ARCHITECTES
MODERNISTES - MEMBRE DE L'ACADÉMIE ADRIATIQUE DES SCIENCES, DES
LETTRES ET DES ARTS - PREMIER GRAND PRIX D'ARCHITECTURE

ENCYCLOPÉDIE
DE L'ARCHITECTURE
NOUVELLE

*

ORDRE ET CLIMAT
MÉDITERRANÉENS

510 ILLUSTRATIONS ET 3 CHROMOTYPIES

INTRODUCTION D'EDMOND HUMEAU
PRÉFACE DE LE CORBUSIER

ULRICO HOEPLI ÉDITEUR MILAN

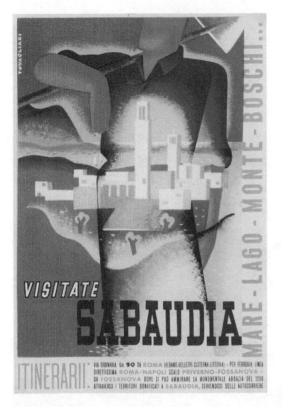

Plate 20 (*Left*) Sabaudia, Postcard "Visitate Sabaudia."
Source: The Wolfsonian-FIU, Miami Beach.

Plate 21 (*Below*) Le Corbusier, Casa del Noce, Pompeii
(*Carnet, Voyage d'Orient*, 1911, p. 113).
Source: © 2009 Artists Rights Society (ARS), New
York/ADAGP, Paris/FLC.

Plate 22 (*Right*) Aldo Rossi. *End of Summer*, 1980.
Photo: Jean-Claude Planchet.
Source: Musée National d'Art Moderne, Centre Georges
Pompidou. © CNAC/MNAM/Dist. Réunion des Musées
Nationaux/Art Resource, New York.

fine dell'estate
AR 80

Plate 23 Carlo Levi, "Aliano sul burrone" [Aliano on the Ravine], 1935.
Source: private collection. © SiAE, 2009.

essay describing this experience and what he understood to be the striking contrast between the grandeur of the architectural structures and simplicity of daily life that he observed in the towns of the M'Zab. Elaborating on notes scrawled in his sketchbooks, Le Corbusier emphasized the potent contrasts between the stark exterior walls and light-filled interior spaces of these buildings at the edge of the desert:

> The houses are completely closed off from the alleys. But, inside, opening onto the abundance of fertile stands of trees, is completely equipped, perfect, efficient, eminently functional, on a human scale.[4]

What is dramatized is the shock of discovery, as seemingly impenetrable walls revealed hidden interior spaces remarkably well adapted to the needs of everyday life, at least in the architect's impressionistic estimation.

While developing the early stages of his urban proposals for Algiers, Le Corbusier spent time visiting and sketching buildings and streets in the Casbah. An essay from 1933 describes his impressions of vernacular dwellings in the old city that became important touchstones for his subsequent architecture:

> In the Casbah of Algiers . . . every house . . . has its terrace at the summit, from where the view extends to the distant horizon. Where family life takes place in . . . its open air (the patio and its galleries), where one lives with the benefits of architecture – to be quite truthful, the benefits of Arab culture – which makes of us, colonizing architects, the barbarians.[5]

As Zeynep Çelik has argued, Le Corbusier's understanding of vernacular architecture in Algeria, and most particularly the Casbah in Algiers, was informed by a broader colonialist obsession with the indigenous house.[6] Like many of his peers, Le Corbusier was fascinated by the forms of roof terraces and interior courtyards that allowed buildings which seemed at first to be impenetrable fortresses to be remarkably open to light and air as well as to dramatic views of the surrounding urban landscape and the bay of Algiers. Despite striking differences amongst the architecture of M'Zab, buildings in the Casbah, and the free-standing dwellings built for leading members of the city's political elite during the Ottoman period in the Mustapha hills on the southern end of Algiers, Le Corbusier described all the structures in remarkably similar terms. Rather than recognizing the diversity of indigenous architecture in Algeria, Le Corbusier saw essential similarities instead. The architect's enthusiastic "discovery" of vernacular dwellings in North Africa ultimately served as a means of confirming pre-existing ideas that seemed to find their echo in unfamiliar landscapes. By drawing attention to the roof terraces, courtyards, the effects of light, and the importance of direct access to fresh air in vernacular dwellings in Algeria, Le Corbusier was able to re-articulate the key elements of his own established architectural repertoire – and thus his vision for modern architecture – as the culmination of a timeless tradition of Mediterranean architecture.

In the early 1930s, the Mediterranean associations of modern architecture held renewed interest. Unable to hold its third conference in Moscow as originally planned, in the summer of 1933 CIAM (International Congress of Modern Architecture) made the Mediterranean the literal forum for their meetings, enshrined in the subsequent publication of the *Athens Charter*.[7] Although the formal meetings were held in Athens, discussions regarding the principles of designing modern cities took place on the *Patris II*, the boat that

[4] Le Corbusier, "Retours . . . ou l'enseignement du voyage: Coupe en travers Espagne, Maroc, Algérie, Territoires du Sud," in *Plans* 8, 1931, pp. 104–105. Unless otherwise indicated, all translations are by the author.
[5] Le Corbusier, "Le Lotissement de L'Oued-Ouchaïa à Alger," in *Architecture d'Aujourd'hui* 10, no. 117, 1933.
[6] Zeynep Çelik, *Urban Forms and Colonial Confrontations: Algiers under French Rule*, Berkeley, University of California Press, 1997, pp. 97–103; Zeynep Çelik, "Le Corbusier, Orientalism, Colonialism," in *Assemblage* 17, 1992, pp. 59–77. See also Sherry McKay, "Mediterraneanism: The Politics of Architectural Production in Algiers during the 1930s," in *City and Society* 12, no. 1, 2000, pp. 79–102.
[7] Le Corbusier, *La Charte d'Athènes*, Paris, Plon, 1943.

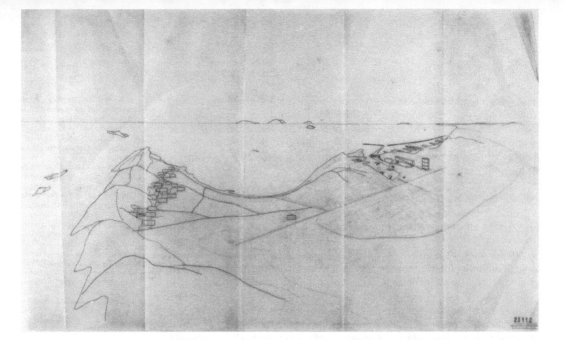

4.3 Le Corbusier, bird's-eye view of proposals for Marseille, *c.*1950.

took the delegates from Marseille to Athens and then back again to Marseille. As numerous scholars have recognized, this event marked a new investment in the Mediterranean sources of modern architecture, an association that Le Corbusier proclaimed to much fanfare in Athens.[8] However, if Greece was positioned at the very heart of the architect's affective Mediterranean map, another key axis was once again given potent visual form that same summer.

While visiting Algiers shortly before setting sail on the CIAM voyage, Le Corbusier depicted the city from the vantage point of the Fort l'Empereur erected in the mid-sixteenth century at the crest of the hills overlooking the bay (plate 28). The Fort l'Empereur was a strategic site within Le Corbusier's developing proposals for Algiers, as he proposed to erect a group of apartment buildings there.[9] The drawing, elaborated with colored pencils, explored the relationship of this structure to the topography and the view from this bluff onto the water below. Perhaps unremarkable in itself, the drawing appears quite differently when paired with another sketch created a few days later. After making his return voyage to France and landing in Marseille, Le Corbusier again shifted his vantage point from water to land. In Marseille, he recorded the blocky outlines of the Fort Saint-Nicholas at the mouth of the old port, as seen from above, with a narrow blue strip of the sea just visible in the distance (plate 29). By representing these two landmarks from similar vantage points with the same color palette and style of rendering, Le Corbusier dramatized the similarities between them and, by extension, the cities they guarded. Once again, Le Corbusier staged a visual dialogue of correspondence, seeing the built landscape of Marseille through the lens of Algiers. Stretching between them, the Mediterranean Sea functioned both structurally and metaphorically as a mirror, reflecting these two cities back onto one another across its shimmering surface.

Le Corbusier's designs for the Unité d'habitation in Marseille have long been understood as a project that effectively recuperated the architect's failed urban proposals for the city of Algiers. As many have noted, the *brise-soleil* at the Unité d'habitation derived from previous projects for Algiers in which the architect had adapted what he described as "a primary and fundamental

[8] See Jos Bosman, "Sur le *Patris II*: De Marseille à Athènes," in *Le Corbusier et la Méditerranée*, pp. 73–89, Eric Mumford, *The CIAM Discourse on Urbanism, 1928–1960*, Cambridge, The MIT Press, 2000.
[9] A series of related drawings depicting the hills surrounding the Fort l'Empereur were included with documents of the early Obus project for Algiers by Le Corbusier in Willy Boesiger (ed.), *Le Corbusier et Pierre Jeanneret: Oeuvre complète, 1929–1934*, Zürich, Éditions d'Architecture, 1964, pp. 140–141. The fort, named "the Emperor" because it was erected at the site where Charles V had set up camp in 1541, was erected as part of the elaborate new infrastructure bringing water into the city of Algiers constructed under Hassan Pacha. See Sakina Missoum, *Alger à l'époque ottomane: La médina et la maison traditionnelle*, Aix-en-Provence, Édisud, 2003, pp. 97–99.

element of regional North African architecture."[10] Mary McLeod has argued that Le Corbusier's designs for the Unité d'habitation in Marseille "changed the Algiers *brise-soleil* from a symbol of European-Muslim integration to one of European dominance."[11] From a somewhat different vantage point, Sherry McKay interpreted Le Corbusier's willful abstraction of elements of indigenous architecture in Algiers as a means of resisting the cultural complexity of the Mediterranean and attempting to rewrite the entire region as European.[12]

Building on these observations, I want to suggest that the process of abstracting, adapting, and translating the *brise-soleil* from Algiers to Marseille was founded on the conceptual equation of northern and southern shores of the Mediterranean Sea. In this regard, Le Corbusier's encounter with vernacular architecture in North Africa was shaped by the reigning assumption that the Mediterranean was a region defined "bio-geographically and thus as a landscape," a notion that Vojtech Jirat-Wasiutynski reminds us had long been a potent justification for imperialist ventures.[13] This idea was given most vivid form in an unrealized proposal for Marseille in which the city is restructured in the image of the architect's final plan for Algiers, with the old port recreated as commercial center, defined by the prominent tower of the *Cité d'affaires*. Once again, the architect was rereading Marseille as Algiers, seeing these urban landscapes as mirror images reflecting back on one another across the sea. Le Corbusier's vision of modern architecture's Mediterraneanism was thus an admixture of associations, projected expectations, and observed equivalences constructed over time, through the process of moving between Algiers and Marseille.

Pouillon's Mediterranean Dislocations

In 1953, Fernand Pouillon was invited to Algiers by the mayor Jacques Chevallier who had been impressed with the architect's contributions to the postwar rebuilding of Marseille and hoped he could be persuaded to design a series of new housing complexes for Algiers. Pouillon worked in the opposite direction from Le Corbusier, moving from Marseille to Algiers, and his impressions of these cities coalesced through the windows of airplanes and automobiles, rather than from the deck of a steamship. In his autobiography, *Mémoires d'un architecte*, published in 1968, Pouillon described this first trip to Algiers and the transformative experience of seeing the Casbah and the Fort l'Empereur:

> I felt a new architecture being born in me . . . I began to see how to create a link between the Casbah and my *cités*, thanks to the volumes seen in the hills long ago occupied by the Turks.[14]

Historians have invariably followed this formula, interpreting Pouillon's architecture as a sensitive synthesis between a distinctly classicizing modernism and a serious engagement with local vernacular forms. In her groundbreaking study of colonialism and urban form in Algiers, Zeynep Çelik described Pouillon's architecture as "a modernistic hybrid, learned from the local heritage and from classical antiquity."[15] Jean-Lucien Bonillo has suggested, in somewhat different terms, that Pouillon engaged the local not simply as a regionalist expression, but "in a modern posture," or, in Jacques Lucan's words, as "an 'other' modernity."[16]

I want to posit that Pouillon's architecture negotiates the vernacular and the modern in less neatly resolved ways. In this regard, Alberto Ferlenga's work is

[10] Le Corbusier, *Le Corbusier et Pierre Jeanneret: Oeuvre complète, 1929–1934*, p. 169. For the relationship between the Unité d'habitation in Marseille and the earlier proposals for Algiers, see Jean-Louis Cohen, "Le Corbusier, Perret et les figures d'un Alger moderne," in Jean-Louis Cohen, Nabila Oulebsir, and Youcef Kanoun (eds.), *Alger: Paysage urbain et architectures, 1800–2000*, Paris, Éditions de l'Imprimeur, 2003, p. 184; Jacques Sbriglio, *L'Unité d'habitation de Marseille*, Marseille, Editions Parenthèses, 1992, pp. 19–22; and Jacques Sbriglio, *Le Corbusier: The Unité d'habitation in Marseille*, Basel, Birkhäuser, 2004.
[11] Mary McLeod, *Urbanism and Utopia: Le Corbusier from Regional Syndicalism to Vichy*, Ph.D. dissertation, Princeton University, 1985, p. 420. See also Mary McLeod, "Le Corbusier and Algiers" in *Oppositions* 19–20, 1980, pp. 55–85.
[12] McKay, "Mediterraneanism," p. 93.
[13] Vojtech Jirat-Wasiutynski, "Modern Art and the New Mediterranean Space," in Jiarat-Wasiutynski (ed.), *Modern Art and the Idea of the Mediterranean*, Toronto, University of Toronto Press, 2007, p. 6.
[14] Fernand Pouillon, *Mémoires d'un architecte*, Paris, Seuil, 1968, p. 172.
[15] Çelik, *Urban Forms and Colonial Confrontations*, pp.145–146. For a similar assessment of Pouillon's work, see Bernard Félix Dubor, *Fernand Pouillon*, Milan and Paris, Electa-Moniteur, 1986, p. 56.
[16] Jean-Lucien Bonillo, *Fernand Pouillon: Architecte méditerranéen*, Marseille, Éditions Imbernon, 2001, p. 26; Jacques Lucan, "Le paysage intérieur de l'architecture, ou Fernand Pouillon comme problème théorique," in Jacques Lucan and Odile Seyler (eds.), *Fernand Pouillon, architecte: Pantin, Montrouge, Boulogne-Billancourt, Meudon-la-Forêt*, Paris, Éditions du Pavillon de l'Arsenal/Picard, 2003, p. 15.

4.4 Fernand Pouillon.
Cité of Diar el-Mahsul
(with the European
section in the
foreground and the
Algerian section in the
upper left corner),
Alpiers, 1954–55.
Postcard.
Source: http://diaressaada.
alger.free.fr/index.html
(accessed on October 9,
2009).

important, as he has provocatively argued that Pouillon's relationship to locality
was unusually complex. Particularly once the architect began developing his
designs for new housing in Algiers, he was almost constantly moving between
the cities of Marseille (and its surrounding region), Algiers, and Paris, notably
shifting his main residence amongst these locations at several key junctures.
In Ferlenga's eyes, Pouillon's willfully nomadic existence gave him an unusual
capacity for synthesis, so that past history and local place became formative
materials of his architecture.[17] Through an examination of Diar el-Mahsul, the
second housing complex Pouillon designed in Algiers, the significance of these
moves and the claims of locality and belonging forged by his work between
Marseille and Algiers might be better understood.

From the moment of its initial design in 1954, Diar el-Mahsul was heralded as
the first intentionally mixed housing development in Algiers, with sixty percent
of the apartments designated for Algerian residents. A broad avenue bisected
the complex, dividing it into two sections, one for Europeans and the other for
Algerians. Despite the rhetoric of integration repeatedly used to describe the
project, segregation was nevertheless spatially enforced. Like all of Pouillon's
projects in Algiers, Diar el-Mahsul featured monumental exterior walls,
constructed of pre-cut blocks of limestone shipped across the Mediterranean
Sea from a quarry near Arles. In the European section, apartment buildings of
varied heights defined a series of partially enclosed, expansive courtyards,
organized in terraces and linked by elaborate ramps and staircases. A ten-story
tower lent weight and focus to the central courtyard, while an arcaded passageway, called "the door to the sea," led to an esplanade that traversed the length
of the complex and framed a spectacular panoramic view of the city and the
sea below. By contrast, the Algerian section was set back behind the crest of
the hill and its smaller buildings crowded more closely together around
remarkably narrow courtyards. In comparison to the prominent balconies,
distinctive decorative embellishments, generous interior spaces, and modern
appliances in the European section, the apartments across the road were
extremely small, with only minimal kitchenettes and restrained fenestration.

As much as the staggered heights of terraced buildings in the European section
created the impression of variety within the regularized structural grid, projecting

[17] Alberto Ferlenga, "L'histoire comme
matériau," in Jean-Lucien Bonillo
(ed.), *Fernand Pouillon, architecte
méditerranéen*, Marseille, Éditions
Imbernon, 2001, pp. 118–123; Alberto
Ferlenga, "Fernand Pouillon (1912–
1986): New Foundation of the City,
New Foundation of a Discipline," in
New City 3, 1996, pp. 71–93.

4.5 Fernand Pouillon.
Cité of Diar-el-Mahsul
(social housing district),
Algiers, 1954–55.
Fountain at the foot of
the tower. Postcard.
Source: http://diaressaada.
alger.free.fr/index.html
(accessed on October 9,
2009).

embellishments of balconies and loggias worked to similar ends. One five-story block featured two horizontal ranges of cantilevered balconies stretching across the upper two floors of the building, with simple corbelled wooden supports that appeared to reference similar elements characteristic of buildings in the Casbah. The central tower had its own vertical bay of projecting loggias running its entire height to create open-air enclosures looking out to the sea. The tower's opposite wall facing the main courtyard broke with the ordered fenestration of the complex, instead combining irregularly projecting stone blocks and unframed square openings. Layered in front of the exterior wall of the building, the distinctive pattern of projections and apertures appeared as an abstracted and reinterpreted *mashrabiy'ya*, creating an elaborate sculptural wall as mediating screen. Near the summit of the tower, a dramatically projecting, two-tiered wooden structure was attached to the façade and provided an exoticizing pendant to the sculpted fountain at its base that featured the dramatic and distinctly classicizing scene of Neptune in his chariot drawn by horses.

At Diar el-Mahsul, the most spectacular gestures towards "local" architectural forms adorned buildings that housed Europeans. Across the road, the low-rise apartment buildings in the Algerian section featured smaller window openings, recessed balconies, and few of the sculptural flourishes seen across the road. There, the architecture of the Casbah was more obliquely referenced in the massing of the buildings and the self-conscious interiority of impenetrable walls. In effect, the vivid embellishments inspired by corbelled elements and *mashrabiy'ya* that animated exterior walls in the European section worked to confer authority on these buildings and their inhabitants by way of their distinctiveness. According to architect Jean-Jacques Deluz, who spent his career working in Algiers and has written extensively on the city's architecture, in Pouillon's projects,

> References to Turkish fortifications, to the corbelled structures of the Casbah . . . while claiming to manufacture an imaginary history for new quarters or new sites, register instead their artificiality.[18]

At Diar el-Mahsul, the constructed artifice of Pouillon's vernacular references seem intended to lend weight and a palpable sense of history to this new

[18] Jean-Jacques Deluz, "Alger 1962: L'Héritage," in *Techniques et Architecture* 328, 1980.

4.6 Fernand Pouillon. Tower at the center of Diar el-Mahsul, Algiers, 1954–55.
Source: Municipal periodical, *ALGER, ville-pilote*, special issue, May 1955; http://diaressaada.alger.free.fr/index.html.

Cette immense tour-immeuble a été construite en moins de deux mois. A ses pieds, s'étendra un bassin. Les plans inégaux ménagés sur l'un des pans de mur sont destinés à briser la lumière qui se réfléchira sur la surface de l'eau.

miniature city within the city. These formal gestures, however, were not simply products of Pouillon's encounter with the Casbah, but were also articulated in relation to his previous work in Marseille.

Numerous commentators have noted the similarities in materials, massing, organization of plan, and relationship to site that tied Pouillon's housing complexes in Algiers to his previous projects in Marseille.[19] While the architect insisted that the placement of Diar el-Mahsul at the crest of the hill was inspired by the Fort l'Empereur, the notion of housing as modern fortification had previously informed his design of La Tourette, the first housing complex he created as part of the postwar reconstruction of Marseille's Vieux-Port quarter. There, the hulking façade with narrow window openings looking out towards the Mediterranean Sea echoed the massive walls of the nearby fort guarding the entrance to the harbor. As his predecessor and nemesis Le Corbusier had done before him, Pouillon asserted a connection to vernacular architecture in North Africa as a means of authenticating and "localizing" a formula developed elsewhere. Pouillon's vernacular appropriations, however, took distinctly different form, as the increasingly industrialized prefabrication processes he developed to construct his buildings were tempered by their monumental stone façades and by the incorporation of uniquely crafted details.

[19] Ferlenga, "L'histoire comme matériau," p. 122, Alberto Ferlenga, "Fernand Pouilllon: Le pietre di Algeri," in *Casabella* 66, no. 706–707, 2002–03, pp. 49–51, Jean-Lucien Bonillo, "Fernand Pouillon in Algier", in *Bauwelt* 94, no. 26, 2003, pp. 50–59.

The dramatic embellishments that lent visual distinction to the European section at Diar el-Mahsul were not simply products of Pouillon's encounter with the Casbah upon his arrival in Algiers. In Marseille, the housing complex at La Tourette featured vertical bays of cantilevered balconies with distinctive enclosures formed by grill-like panels of thin wooden rods.[20] The loggia-balconies in Marseille were similar to those at Diar el-Mahsul, although the addition of corbelled supports to one of these at Diar el-Mahsul served to more forcefully anchor its association with buildings in the Casbah. Even more striking, however, were the two so-called *claustra* walls developed for the largest apartment block at La Tourette. Both of these attached panels were created with mass-produced ceramic squares; the one facing the central courtyard set the blocks on the diagonal, while the second embellished a section of the façade looking out towards the Mediterranean Sea. Visible from a distance, these elements provided visual orientation for the complex and worked to counteract its otherwise massive, homogenizing walls. Compared with the elaborate screen wall at Diar el-Mahsul, the *claustras* at La Tourette were created with inexpensive, mass-produced materials whose effects were much less sculptural or dramatic. Nevertheless, these elements at La Tourette likewise served as abstracted *mashrabiy'ya*.

Far from simply a product of his "discovery" of the Casbah, Pouillon's adaptation of elements inspired by North African vernacular architecture preceded his work in Algiers. My aim here is neither to substitute one account of architectural origins with another nor to displace the Casbah as the essential referent of Pouillon's architecture in order to claim such a role for Marseille. Rather, the fact that his buildings in Algiers were not simply generated from his initial encounter with this city, but also constructed in relation to an architectural imaginary of Marseille's own Mediterranean affiliations necessitates a more careful examination of the projections of place and claims for authenticity that the architect directed towards both cities. In this regard, Pouillon's observation that Marseille's Vieux-Port resembled the Casbah is significant:

4.7 Fernand Pouillon. *Claustra* facing the central courtyard at La Tourette, 1948–52. Photo by author.

> All of it terraced like an amphitheater, with its churches and its steeples, its low houses and its noble architecture, forming, like the Casbah of Algiers, a harmonious ensemble, ordered in its diversity.[21]

Pouillon's desire to clad modern dwellings in Marseille and Algiers in legible abstractions of North African architectural details reveals his interest in creating an architecture that might express a transcendent Mediterranean identity through contested and perhaps even contradictory processes of mimicry, distinction, and identification.[22]

Pouillon's architecture was founded on an imagined connection across the Mediterranean through which Marseille and Algiers were understood as mirror reflections of one another, as Le Corbusier's was before him. However, the very processes through which Pouillon negotiated modern and vernacular forms might help us to further question familiar assumptions about the static, timeless nature of the vernacular, its spatial boundaries, and indeed its very "located-ness." Pouillon's work between Marseille and Algiers reveals a desire to master vernacular architecture and to appropriate visible cultural signs of the colonized, effectively creating architecture that seems particularly fraught by a desire for identification. Pouillon's complexes thus allowed "modern" European inhabitants on both sides of the Mediterranean to identify with recreated elements of "traditional" Islamic architecture. In this way, the terms of the vernacular and the modern were negotiated through imagined and experienced connections across the Mediterranean Sea and through the design of buildings, whose ambiguous origins challenge familiar assumptions about locality, identity, and belonging in place.

[20] For an important discussion of these elements of Pouillon's work at La Tourette and their relationship to his broader interest in decorative elements and collaborative work with artists and artisans, see Sylvie Denante, "De la vertu de l'ornement", in Jean-Lucien Bonillo (ed.), *Fernand Pouillon, architecte méditerranéen*, pp. 138–148.
[21] Fernand Pouillon, *Mémoires d'un architecte*, p. 83.
[22] I have discussed these dynamics in further detail in "Architecture at the Ends of Empire: Urban Reflections between Algiers and Marseille," in Gyan Prakash and Kevin Kruse (eds.), *The Spaces of the Modern City: Imaginaries, Politics, and Everyday Life*, New York, Princeton University Press, 2008, pp. 99–143.

Simounet's *Nostalgérie*

In 1992, the National School of Dance (École Nationale Supérieure de Danse) was inaugurated in Marseille in the presence of the head architect, Roland Simounet, and President François Mitterand's Minister of Culture, Jack Lang. Erected in a small park on the southern end of the city not far from Le Corbusier's Unité d'habitation, the building's stark white walls vividly contrasted with the surrounding verdant landscape. Although the school was only two stories tall, its monolithic exterior conveyed a sense of unified mass that exceeded its relatively compact dimensions. The building appeared as an assemblage of stacked, cubic volumes, overshadowed by a narrow fly tower projecting high above the main rehearsal space. The fortress-like exterior walls were punctuated in a regular pattern of crenellations along the roofline, formed by narrow recessed bays crowned by small, hidden apertures that alternated with projecting, rectilinear hoods framing high windows. A broad ramp cutting through the front façade led into an enclosed courtyard and to the building's main entrance at its far end. Early commentators and critics repeatedly

4.8 a (*Right*) and b (*Below*) Roland Simounet. Djenan el-Hasan, Algiers, 1956–62.

Source a: *Techniques et Architecture* 329, February/ March 1980. Photo Jean de Maisonseul.
Source b: © Archives national d'outre-mer. Photo Girard.

compared the building to "a small Arab village," or a modern Casbah, either to suggest it was an exotic apparition within this small city park and its neighboring residential streets, or to assert that it was particularly at home in Marseille's Mediterranean landscape.[23]

Born in the town of Guyotville, on the western outskirts of Algiers, Roland Simounet traced his family's roots in Algeria back five generations, to a pharmacist attached to the French army who was among the first wave of settlers to arrive in Algeria shortly after the French invasion of 1830. Simounet briefly attended the École des Beaux-Arts in Algiers before leaving school to pursue his career in architecture. In the decade leading up to independence in 1962, he designed a wide range of projects in Algeria, including individual villas, mass housing prototypes, a cultural center in Chelff (then Orléansville) dedicated to his friend Albert Camus, and a new town erected near the vestiges of an ancient Roman settlement in Timgad. Shortly after independence, Simounet joined the mass exodus of European residents (subsequently known as the *pieds-noirs*) to France, where he reestablished his architectural practice in Paris. Until his death in 1996, Simounet designed a wide range of housing, university, and museum projects in France and abroad.[24]

The defining elements of Simounet's early work in Algeria are particularly evident in Djenan el-Hasan ("the beautiful gardens"), a housing development designed for the challenging site of a ravine in the western hills of Algiers. Built in two sections, the first in 1957 and the second shortly after independence in 1962, Simounet's modular dwellings, designed as temporary, transitional housing for Algerians, follow the dramatic contours of the topography. Each unit, with its own balcony and vaulted roof, was stacked in a staggered formation to provide an outdoor terrace for the apartment below. The housing model Simounet developed at Djenan el-Hasan self-consciously responded to Le Corbusier's earlier work in Algiers and, as Zeynep Çelik has shown, to Simounet's own detailed studies of architecture and social practices in la Mahieddine, then the largest shantytown in Algiers, that he presented at the 1953 meeting of CIAM in Aix-en-Provence.[25]

At Djenan el-Hasan, the interior courtyards that Le Corbusier had privileged as the structural and social heart of the North African house were transformed into external balconies, while terraced roofs were designed as outdoor living spaces, in reference to the architecture of the Casbah and to Simounet's observations of informal dwellings at la Mahieddine. More than simply the replication of select elements of indigenous architecture, however, at Djenan el-Hasan Simounet exploited contrasts between light and dark and the spatial possibilities of staggered massing to create temporary dwellings that featured expansive views of the surrounding landscape and protected interior spaces of refuge.

Simounet's Algerian origins and his experience working in Algeria have led scholars and critics of his work to emphasize his intimate knowledge of vernacular architecture in North Africa and thus to valorize his "authentic" connection to the Mediterranean landscape.[26] Accounts of Simounet's work concur that his sustained knowledge of vernacular architecture in Algeria profoundly informed his architecture and was evidenced in his repeated use of unfinished and durable materials, monolithic enclosures, interior courtyards, and roof terraces. In Marseille, however, the Mediterranean associations and vernacular references of Simounet's work were pushed to new heights and subject to distinctly different pressures.

[23] Barbara Shortt, "Roland Simounet: National Academy of Dance, Marseilles, France", in *Architecture* 82, no. 9, 1993, p. 84; Penny McGuire, "Dancing in Light", in *Architectural Review* 198, no. 1186, 1995, p. 61; Jean-Paul Robert, "D'une unité à l'autre," in *Architecture d'aujourd'hui* 287, 1993, p. 40.

[24] For an overview of Simounet's career and work, see Richard Klein (ed.), *Roland Simounet à l'oeuvre: Architecture 1951–1996*, Villeneuve d'Asq, Édition Musée d'art moderne Lille Métropole & Institut français d'Architecture, 2000; *Roland Simounet, d'une architecture juste*, Paris, Le Moniteur, 1997; *Roland Simounet, pour une invention de l'espace*, Paris, Electa-France, 1986.

[25] Zeynep Çelik has examined Simounet's works and excavated their formative influence on Djenan el-Hasan and other housing projects Simounet designed in Algeria. Zeynep Çelik, "Learning from the Bidonville: CIAM Looks at Algiers," in *Harvard Design Magazine* no. 18, 2003, pp. 71–74.

[26] See, for example, Maurice Besset and Jean Maisonseul in *Roland Simounet, d'une architecture juste*, pp. 15–16, 22.

[27] Centre des Archives du Monde du Travail, Roland Simounet collection (hereafter CAMT/RS), handwritten text by Roland Simounet, October 22, 1992.
[28] Annette Fierro, *The Glass State: The Technology of the Spectacle, Paris, 1981–1998*, Cambridge, The MIT Press, 2003.
[29] Roland Simounet, "Leçons d'Alger," in Richard Klein, *Roland Simounet: Dialogues sur l'invention*, Paris, Éditions du Moniteur, 2005, p. 160.
[30] At least one critic described Simounet's project in precisely these terms: Gilles Davoine, "École de danse Marseille," in *Moniteur Architecture AMC*, no. 39, 1993, p. 20.

What is most immediately striking about the School of Dance is the insistent interiority suggested by its monolithic, white exterior. The unifying wall mass belied the fact that the structure housed two separate but interdependent institutions, the ballet company and the school then directed by choreographer Roland Petit. As his designs for the school evolved, Simounet exploited the possibilities of sectional design to create intersecting paths of circulation and subsidiary spaces dispersed around the two dominant voids – the courtyard and the main rehearsal space. Exterior and interior walls worked together to isolate the rehearsal rooms from the outside both acoustically and visually in order to focus the attention of the dancers inward. By locating apertures near the meeting points between ceiling and wall, interlocking interior spaces allowed for the maximum provision of natural light to the dance studios and other important workspaces. In a text written for the building's inauguration, the architect emphasized this paradox, describing the school as "enclosed by high walls and glowing with light."[27]

The fortress-like exterior walls effectively masked the light-filled interior spaces and the spatial complexity of their organization. While elements drawn from Simounet's knowledge of North African vernacular architecture – including roof terraces, interior courtyards, and white walls – were immediately striking, upon closer examination the School of Dance reveals a much more subtle and sophisticated engagement with the tectonic logic and spatial complexity of buildings in the Casbah.

Although the National School of Dance in Marseille was included on President Mitterand's list of *grands projets* when it was first proposed in 1982, Simounet approached the design of this building as a self-conscious critique of the prevailing architectural rhetoric of transparency shared by the Parisian monuments at the center of Mitterand's building campaign, including Jean Nouvel's Institut du Monde Arabe (1981–87) and I. M. Pei's Grande Pyramide du Louvre (1983–89). As Annette Fierro has shown, Mitterand's *grands projets* shared an interest in articulating newly rationalized, high-tech systems of construction that exploited the possibilities of glass. Their refined details offered a spectacular display of constructive systems and of visitors passing through interior spaces that attempted to embody and symbolize a state ideology of openness and accessibility.[28] Simounet overtly opposed this tendency, asserting in an interview in 1995 that, "today, except for a few inimitable, beautiful achievements, transparency renders everything banal."[29]

In his designs for the National School of Dance in Marseille, Simounet articulated an alternative discourse of transparency, predicated on the tectonic possibilities of the wall. In numerous studies for the building, Simounet returned again and again to the careful elaboration of points of juncture, where walls and structural columns met floors, roofs, ceilings, and beams. One such drawing trained attention on the south-facing façade where administrative offices met the central dance studio. Here structural supports were set back from the wall surface, while a beam projected slightly beyond it, providing opportunities for hidden apertures at the junctions between interlocking interior volumes. With such details, Simounet manipulated the concrete wall mass and structural system to create recessed openings that provided an unexpected internal luminosity. By implication, Simounet's overt rejection of the high-tech possibilities of glass and steel ran counter to the centralizing aims of Mitterand's *grands projets*, an approach that resonated with the School of Dance's own project of "cultural decentralization," as a national institution located in Marseille.[30] When the School of Dance was inaugurated in October 1992, this move would have had new

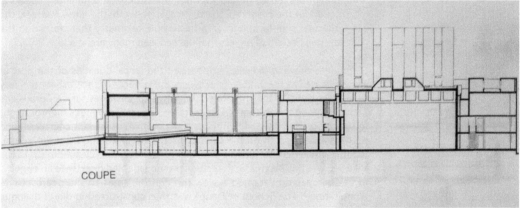

COUPE

4.9 *Top* and *Bottom*: Roland Simounet, National School of Dance, Marseille, 1985–92. Photo by author. *Bottom*: Section drawing of National School of Dance.
Source: Roland Simounet collection, Centre des Archives du Monde du Travail, Roubaix.

significance in the wake of Marseille's ambitious *Musée des Civilisations Europe Méditerranée* project, first articulated in a convention signed four months earlier.

When Simounet initially won the architectural competition for the School of Dance in 1985, however, he was at work on designs for a museum dedicated to "the Conservation and Development of the Cultural Patrimony of the French Natives of North Africa" that was to be erected in L'Estaque, a former fishing village turned industrial suburb on the coast north of Marseille. A product of a new effort to promote the culture and history of French settlers in Algeria, the museum aimed to represent the *pieds-noirs* as a model minority culture that, in the decades after Algeria's independence, had been successfully assimilated into the universalizing aims of the French Republic.[31] Simounet's design for the School of Dance drew on elements of the proposed museum, particularly the entrance sequence of ramp and enclosed courtyard. Here the gardens he designed at the entrance and in the interior courtyards were critical, as the proposed plantings of orange trees, cypresses, and olive trees were inspired by his grandfather's garden in Algeria and memories of its evocative perfumes.[32] Although the museum was never realized as planned, these ideas informed the garden created in the interior courtyard of the School of Dance. Simounet's

[31] See CAMT/RS, file P124/2: Association pour la Conservation et le Développement du Patrimoine Culturel des Français Originaires d'Afrique du Nord, *La mémoire des français originaires d'Afrique du Nord,* unpublished manuscript, September 24, 1984.
[32] See Roland Simounet, interview with Christian Devillers (1986), reprinted in Richard Klein, *Roland Simounet: Dialogues sur l'invention,* Paris, p. 84.

33 François Chaslin (ed.), *Corbu vu par*, Liège, P. Mardaga, 1987.
34 Roland Simounet, interview with Jean-Paul Dollé (1989), reprinted in Richard Klein, *Roland Simounet: Dialogues sur l'invention*, p. 118.
35 Simounet himself observed that Le Corbusier's notion of the "architectural promenade" was inspired by the Casbah in an interview from 1995. Roland Simounet, interview originally published in *La Ville* 1, 1995; reprinted in ibid., p. 150.
36 The term "*nostalgérie*" was coined by Henri Montherlant, in his romanticized, fictional accounts of *pied-noir* life before independence and the trauma of repatriation. See Henri de Montherlant, "La Rose de Sable," in Michel Raimond (ed.), *Romans*, Paris, Gallimard, 1982, p. 179.

project might then also be understood as a product of the architect's renewed engagement with his own Algerian past rediscovered in Marseille.

As construction advanced on the School of Dance, Simounet's reminiscences of Algiers were increasingly intertwined with musings about his mentor Le Corbusier. In 1987, Simounet participated in the exhibition "Corbu vu par . . ." in Brussels, contributing a drawing with accompanying text in which memories of his childhood and the landscapes of Algiers merged with a poetic lament for modern architecture as articulated in the city's palm trees which Simounet described as "the *pilotis* of my youth."[33] This drawing was part of a broader reassessment of the specifically Algerian roots of the modern movement that emerged in Simounet's writings and interviews during and after his work in Marseille. As he explained in an interview in 1989:

> The fundamental elements of the modern Movement in architecture were found in the region of Algiers, where I was born, and generally speaking throughout the Maghreb: the terrace, whitewash, the interior street, the vernacular side of things, with this simple geometry that we find in the Ottoman Casbah of Algiers that has seduced many architects.[34]

Simounet's drawing likewise emphasized the lyrical qualities of the port of Algiers as well as the whitewashed walls and terraces of the Casbah, the very aspects of the city that had been formative touchstones for Le Corbusier's architecture. In the School of Dance, references to Simounet's mentor might in turn be read in its stark white walls, its prominent interior courtyard, and perhaps most directly, in the curving interior ramp leading from the administrative offices to one of two accessible roof terraces. In a clear homage to the Villa Savoye, this playful "architectural promenade" led directly to an opening in the parapet that framed a view through the trees to the nearby Unité d'habitation.[35] The School of Dance was thus constructed in direct dialogue with Le Corbusier's looming legacy. In Marseille, then, a particular convergence of circumstances made the School of Dance as much an ode to the origins of Mediterranean modernism reimagined through the work of Le Corbusier, as it was an unusually nostalgic engagement with personal history and intimate knowledge of the built landscapes of Algiers. Founded on an imagined connection between Marseille and Algiers, the School of Dance expressed intersecting longings for a lost innocent past, a *nostalgérie* founded in the mythic Algerian origins of Simounet and of modern architecture.[36]

For Simounet, the city of Marseille provided resonant ground for a critique of the centralizing presumptions of Mitterand's *grands projets*, a renewed encounter with Le Corbusier's work and its legacies, and a more direct negotiation of the architect's own Algerian past, in the face of which clear distinctions between vernacular and modern effectively dissolved. Beyond the curving ramp that formed an evocative bridge to the Unité d'habitation, the "architectural promenade" structuring the School of Dance was not the same as Le Corbusier's. Unlike Le Corbusier and Pouillon, Simounet's experience of vernacular architecture in Algiers did not simply focus on the prominent landmarks of the Fort l'Empereur and the Casbah, but also included extensive studies of the informal settlement at La Mahieddine that were critical to his early work in Algiers, including Djenan el-Hasan. Simounet's engagement with North African "vernacular" extended to such modern constructions created by displaced rural residents, a landscape that was a direct product of the history of colonization and the more immediate effects of wartime violence. While the building's exterior appeared to simply mimic the stark white walls of the Casbah,

Simounet aimed most importantly to recreate the phenomenological and sensorial effects of built landscapes in Algiers. Rather than simply recreating interior courtyards, Simounet also drew inspiration from the *sqifa*, the L-shaped entrance found in buildings in the Casbah and the Mahieddine that created layered protection. The school was thus organized around the experience of space unfolding in time and through movement, where light-filled spaces for dance and movement alternated with shadowy places for rest and retreat. The intertwining threads of *nostalgérie* embedded in the School of Dance thus articulated Simounet's multifaceted experience of refinding Algiers in Marseille.

Whereas Le Corbusier's movement between Algiers and Marseille was organized around perceived similarities linking the urban landscapes of both cities, Pouillon forged an anticipatory connection across the sea. Through intersecting processes of mimicry and distinction, vernacular references in Pouillon's housing complexes were rearticulated as spectacular embellishments. By contrast, Simounet's Mediterraneanism delved beyond abstracted formula or external flourishes to engage the tectonic and phenomenological effects of urban landscapes, recreated on the scale of a single building. Despite these differences, the "Mediterraneanism" of all three architects was founded on remarkably similar translocal mappings and constructed through imagined and embodied dialogues across the sea, between Algiers and Marseille. ■

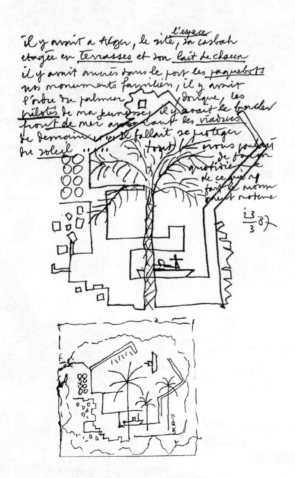

4.10 Roland Simounet. Study for the National School of Dance, March 1986.
Source: Roland Simounet collection, Centre des Archives du Monde du Travail, Roubaix.

5

NATURE AND *THE PEOPLE*

The Vernacular and the Search for a *True* Greek Architecture

Ioanna Theocharopoulou

"The history of man as a seeker of shelter is the history of his relationship to his environment," wrote Sibyl Moholy-Nagy in 1955.[1] Almost ten years before Bernard Rudofsky's influential *Architecture Without Architects* (1964), in a short text for *Perspecta* magazine, Moholy-Nagy outlined the ways in which "anonymous" architecture is "a carrier of life-continuity" that "tames" the environment with "humility and cunning." Rudofsky famously defined the vernacular as "architecture without architects," "non-pedigreed," and with some sense of discomfort, used the terms "vernacular, anonymous, spontaneous, indigenous and rural" to explain that which is still "so little known that we don't even have a name for it."[2] He saw the art of building as a quasi-universal phenomenon and thought that something important had been lost with the introduction of modernization.

The two influential thinkers and practitioners Dimitris Pikionis (1887–1968) and Aris Konstantinidis (1913–93), discussed in this essay, also expressed feelings of loss. At the same time they were committed to creating a new *modern* architecture using their studies of the vernacular as inspiration. They sought to create a modern analogue to the vernacular that would be "true" both in the sense of belonging to the present, and also deeply rooted to the specific climate, landscape, and culture of the geographical space of Greece. As we will see, the vernacular meant different things to Pikionis and to Konstantinidis, both of whom left numerous writings formulating their ideas and research initiatives. Another important figure in the exploration of the vernacular was Constantinos Apostolos Doxiadis (1913–75). This essay situates his contribution with regard to the work of Pikionis and Konstantinidis, whom he knew well and collaborated with at different stages of his career.

The term *vernacular* is used here to discuss primarily domestic buildings built without any involvement by architects. It is significant that there is no exact equivalent of the term "vernacular" in Greek.[3] The closest equivalent to the term, *popular* architecture (*laikí architektoniki*), has a different etymological root to the Latin *verna*. Related to *laòs* meaning "people," the Greek term renders "vernacular architecture" as *architecture of the people*, that is, built by those with little or no education, primarily in the countryside but also found in cities, well into the twentieth century.[4]

At some level, the appeal Greek architects felt towards the idea of a local/popular/vernacular architecture intimately linked to a particularly local landscape is similar to that of their colleagues in Northern Europe. As Germans discussed the rootedness of the *Volk* and Finns proclaimed the importance of Karelian fairy tales, so Greeks at a particular moment in time – during the early part of the twentieth century – began to recognize "true" Hellenism in popular

[1] Sibyl Moholy-Nagy, "Environment and Anonymous Architecture," *Perspecta* 3, 1955, pp. 3–8.
[2] Bernard Rudofsky, *Architecture Without Architects. A Short Introduction to Non-Pedigreed Architecture*, New York, Museum of Modern Art, 1964, p. 2.
[3] Some scholars translate the term *popular* as *folk* architecture. However *folk* has other, particularly Northern European, connotations that are not applicable to the Greek context (the idea of a romanticized "homeland" as well as links to totalitarian regimes). The issue of un-translatibility of certain key terms such as this one, highlights the very different experiences of Greek architects compared to their colleagues in Northern and Western Europe. Given the impossibility of an exact translation, this essay uses the two terms side by side, popular/vernacular, hoping to capture and convey some of the essence of both these meanings.
[4] The first public buildings post-Independence (1821) were designed by foreigners or foreign-educated Greeks. Throughout the nineteenth and early twentieth centuries, the majority of domestic buildings were designed by non-architects setting a precedence that, I argue, was influential in the development of the urban *polykatoikia*, the multistory domestic apartment block, primarily constructed without the involvement of architects that thrived after the Second World War. See Ioanna Theocharopoulou, "Urbanization and the Emergence of the Polykatoikia: Habitat and Identity. Athens, 1830–1974," Ph.D. Dissertation, Columbia University, 2007.

5.1 (*Far left*) Dimitris Pikionis. Entrance to the tourist center of San Dimitris Loumbardiaris, Acropolis Park, Athens, 1954–58.
Source: Alberto Ferlenga, *Pikionis, 1887–1968*, Electa, Milan, 1999.

5 Michael Herzfeld, *Ours Once More. Folklore, Ideology and the Making of Modern Greece*, New York, Pella, 1986, p. 13. It is also notable that unlike other young (Northern) nations such as Finland and Ireland where "folk" culture was used in order to support those nations' claims to independence, in Greece *laography* as an object of study and as an academic discipline begins almost a century *after* Independence. The first sustained scholarly study of *laography* by Nikolaos Politis – illustrated by Dimitris Pikionis – was published in 1918.
6 This claim has a long and complex lineage. See Stathis Gourgouris, *Dream Nation: Enlightenment, Colonization and the Institution of Modern Greece*, Stanford, Stanford University Press, 1996. See also Michael Herzfeld, *Ours Once More: Folklore and Ideology and the Making of Modern Greece*.

art and architecture and sought intimate links between "humble buildings" and the Greek landscape. Like their Northern European counterparts, the perceived connection with nature was what allowed them to talk about "timelessness" and "immutability" in respect to this vernacular. Greeks "found" their lost – or at least buried – past in the Hellenic landscape and they projected some of their history as well as their creative ideas onto their readings of the Hellenic landscape. But the similarities with Northern Europe end here. Rather than praising the great awe-inspiring forests, Greeks talked about a sun-drenched, bleached, harsh, and barren land in the midst of a gentle blue sea.

In actuality, the Greek architects' and other intellectuals' interest in studying indigenous shelter – not only formally interesting structures but even explicitly uninteresting ones as long as they were built by "the people" – began during the mid-nineteenth century. At that time there was a shared concern to safeguard the previously orally transmitted cultural artifacts produced and inherited from almost four centuries of Ottoman rule (1453–1821). The research conducted included gathering and transcribing fairy tales, songs, poems, and stories, as well as collecting, sketching, and photographing material drawn from regional arts and crafts, clothing, and by the early 1920s, dwellings. Those who studied these artifacts were called *laographers* (from *laòs* = people and *gràfo* = to write, to transcribe). Although essentially identical to ethnography, as "*èthnos*" means "nation" in Greek, *laography* rather than *ethnography* provided a new connection between the mostly uneducated *laòs* and the idea of new Hellenic state. In addition, as anthropologist Michael Herzfeld has pointed out, "*èthnos* did not need a branch of study of its own . . . [being] one of the eternal verities, an absolute moral entity against which the *laòs* could be matched and measured."[5]

Scholars have remarked extensively on the ideological project of Greek *laographers* as a way to bolster the claims for an "unbroken" cultural continuity between ancient and modern Greece.[6] Clearly there was a great deal of ideology there, but that was not all. Wishing to transcribe and record aspects of modern Greece was a timely quest, since there was extremely little information about the everyday life of occupied Greeks during Ottoman times. Until the 1940s – and despite the ample studies of classical Greece, primarily by non-Greeks – there were few scholarly studies of more recent geography, geology, population structure, religions, climate, etc. The wish on the part of Greek intellectuals to study ordinary people's lives and local vernacular architecture during the long centuries of Ottoman occupation also had to do with restoring a sense of history – as well as ascribing some dignity, elegance, and even wisdom – to these "dark ages" of Greece's past.

Pikionis and Konstantinidis discussed in this essay wrote about popular/ vernacular architecture, often in parallel with "popular art." What did these studies give to these architects and what might we learn from a close study of vernacular architecture today? In what follows I explore the ways in which Pikionis and Konstantinidis approached the issue of "anonymous" *laographic* research and discuss how it became a rich source of inspiration both in terms of theoretical work as well as building projects. By studying the relationship of buildings built by "men of the soil" to local land use and climatic conditions, these architects were able to learn by example, that is to imagine – primarily in texts as well as in projects, built and unbuilt – a new contemporary architecture, appropriate to local building materials, climate, and cultural life.

Dimitris Pikionis and the *Language* of Popular Architecture

Dimitris Pikionis's interest in the relationship of built form to nature and landscape is well known. In particular, his design for the topography of the walkway to the Acropolis at Athens and landscaping of nearby Philopappou Hill (1951–57) are widely considered masterpieces of modern landscape and architecture. In a catalogue accompanying an exhibition of Pikionis's work held at the Architectural Association School of Architecture in 1989, Kenneth Frampton wrote about Pikionis's "almost ecological insistence":

> Pikionis' importance today derives from what one might call his onto-topographical sensibility – that is, from his feeling for the interaction of the being with the glyptic form of the site. . . . It is this almost ecological insistence on the interdependency of culture and nature which gives Pikionis' work a critical edge that is as relevant today as it was thirty years ago. For it repudiates our habitual fixation on the freestanding technical and/or aesthetic object, not to mention our destructive, Promethean attitude towards nature that once was beneficial but now is assuming the ominous dimensions of a tragic legacy.[7]

Like many others of his generation, Pikionis began his studies in Athens but pursued some years of further education in Northern Europe before returning to practice in Greece. He completed his studies in engineering at the National Polytechnic School of Athens (there was no separate School of Architecture in

[7] Kenneth Frampton, "For Dimitris Pikionis," in *Dimitris Pikionis, Architect 1887–1968. A Sentimental Topography*, London, Architectural Association, 1989, p. 9.

5.2 The Rodakis house, Aegina.
Source: © Neohellenic Architecture Archives, Benaki Museum, Athens.

[8] Klaus Vrieslander and Julio Kaimi also collaborated with Pikionis in a progressive journal, perhaps the closest equivalent to an avant-garde publication in Greece at that time. *The Third Eye* [To Trito Mati] Journal (1935–37), was co-edited by Pikionis and the artist Nikos Chatzikyriakos-Gikas. As cited on the journal's cover page, *The Third Eye* published articles on "music, art, poetry, theater, ethnography, youth and philosophy."
[9] The example I have in mind, although not at all similar in scale or form or ambition, is the house of postman Cheval, built in stone carried mostly by hand by Ferdinand Cheval alone, between 1879 and 1892.

Greece until 1918) before setting off for Munich to study painting (1908–09), and Paris to study drawing and sculpture (1909–12). Pikionis's first in-depth studies of a popular/vernacular house, the Rodakis house on the island of Aegina, began almost immediately upon his return to Greece. He traveled to Aegina often, both on his own and later on with his students (he began teaching at the School of Architecture in 1921) to record this house in drawings and photographs.

Pikionis's studies of the Rodakis house were complex. At one level, he perceived the house with European eyes, obviously knowledgable of major artistic movements from the North, such as Cubism and Surrealism. For him this house was a "primitive" *other* – an *object trouvè*, as fascinating as some of the African masks "discovered" by Picasso and Giacometti in the Parisian flea markets – and Pikionis often used the terms *primitive* and *popular* interchangeably indicating how close he felt they were in meaning. Among the black and white photographs included in the book published by his friends the German painter Klaus Vrieslander and the writer and shadow-theater artist Julio Kaimi, are details of mysterious figures on the property wall: a pig, a clock, a snake, and a dove. According to Vrieslander and Kaimi they could symbolize "Luck, Time, Evil and Peace".[8] Other photographs show plaster busts "that look away with a mystical gaze" leaning against the corners of the roof – reminding us, at least in spirit, of other "naïf" eccentric architecture admired by André Breton and Pablo Picasso.[9]

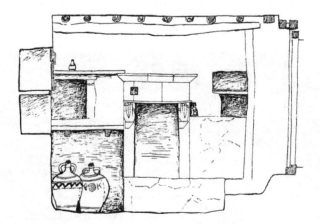

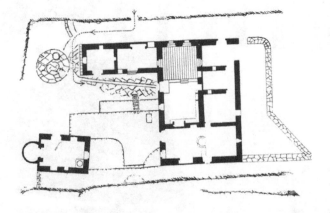

5.3 Dimitris Pikionis. House section and plan, Rodakis house, Aegina. Note the niches in the thick stone walls for storage, as well as the outstretched palms carved on either side of the fireplace. In plan, the threshold (*alòni*) is marked by the small stone-paved circle at the edge of the building.
Source: Klaus Vrieslander and Julio Kaimi, *Rodakis's House in Aigina (To spiti tou Rodaki stin Aigina)*, [1934], reprinted Athens, 1997.

At another level, the Rodakis house marked the beginning of a series of studies in popular/vernacular architecture that Pikionis was to continue throughout his life and that had a particularly local, ethnographic character. He was clearly not only interested in the appearance of the house and its many idiosyncratic details and decorative elements, but in how daily life was lived within it. In fact *laographic* research was treated by Pikionis as a repository of wisdom about how to go about building. He approached it with seriousness and a great deal of respect.[10]

The Rodakis house consisted of an L-shaped plan with a rather large courtyard surrounded by a high stone wall. The house was comprised of a series of four rooms, only three of which, apparently multi-use living areas, were connected together. Another L-shaped series of rooms directly adjacent and roughly as large as the main living areas, housed the animals. Cooking was done in a separate outhouse that contained a circular stone oven whose outline extended outwards from the otherwise orthogonal plan. The courtyard also contained its own threshing area (*alòni*).

Pikionis read this humble dwelling of Aegina as an extension of the island's landscape and nature, recognizing similar kinds of characteristics and qualities in both: a sense of absolute simplicity, the ruggedness of materials such as stone, the extremes of light and shade, strong contrasts in color. He wrote about the great richness found in the poverty of means, a characteristic of vernaculars everywhere. In the Greek context and within the history of centuries of foreign rule where the population experienced extreme material restrictions, this was particularly valid. For Pikionis, to evoke a phrase we may be more familiar with, this popular/vernacular was nothing less than a kind of "survival through design."[11]

Pikionis was not alone in evoking the interconnectedness of nature and culture, or the relationship between landscape (*topìo*), and place (*tòpos*) and the popular/vernacular buildings. The generation active during the 1930s, generally known as "The Thirties Generation" of high modernists, were particularly involved with evaluating Greek nature and talking about its specific qualities. The preceding decade, the 1920s, was marked by traumatic political events, including a disastrous war with Turkey. Encouraged by Greece's European allies, this war, which resulted in a flood of destitute refugees, has been known since as "The Catastrophe" in Greece. On the Turkish side, it was instrumental in bringing about the establishment of the Modern Turkish State. In the midst of a widely felt defensive sense and a painful population exchange with Turkey, there was a renewed interest in *laographic* studies, that some historians have called "a return to the roots."[12]

In addition, the men and women of the Thirties Generation were the first to travel freely in the Aegean. As Artemis Leontis has shown, at that point the notion of a Hellenic *tòpos* became particularly important in "mapping the homeland":

> A genealogy of the Greek usage of *tòpos* shows that the term receives its deceptively transparent referentiality during this [twentieth] century. Under certain conditions, *tòpos* becomes the preferred term – competing with *éthnos*, "nation," *yénos*, "nation, people, race" (Latin *genus*), *filí*, "race, nation," *laós*, "people," and *patrída*, "fatherland, homeland" – for invoking the self-presence of Hellenism.[13]

Pikionis drew and painted the Greek landscape throughout his life. Aside from the Rodakis house, Pikionis also published numerous sketches, drawings, and

[10] Even though he collaborated with *laographers* especially during the 1930s, 1940s, and 1950s, Pikionis did not think of his own studies as "ethnographic" but as part of his architectural work. It is my contention that the level of detailed analysis and interest in recording different aspects of how everyday life was lived within these anonymous buildings, including the material culture within it, from furnishings to cooking utensils, was more *akin* to ethnographic research than to architecture – or at least it was an architecture significantly informed by and engaged in ethnography.
[11] Richard Neutra, *Survival Through Design*, London/Oxford, Oxford University Press, 1969.
[12] Dimitris Philippidis, "A Return to the Roots," Chapter 5, *Modern Greek Architecture: Theory and Practice (1830–1980) As a Reflection of Ideological Choices of Greek Culture*, Athens, Melissa, 1984, pp. 149–181.
[13] Artemis Leontis, *Topographies of Hellenism: Mapping the Homeland*, Ithaca, Cornell University Press, 1995, p. 69.

14 A collected volume of Pikionis's texts used here as primary source material, *Dimitris Pikionis: Texts* [in Greek], Athens, National Bank Educational Institute, 1987, was published after his death, edited by his daughter Agni Pikionis and by Michalis Parousis.
15 Dimitris Loukopoulos, *Aetolian Dwellings, Utensils and Foods*, Athens, 1925.
16 An early mentor of Chatzimihali was the architect Aristotelis Zachos, who also published some studies of Greek *popular* architecture, in the early twentieth century, "Altere Wohnbauten auf griechischem Boden," *Wasmuths, Monatshefte für Baukunst* VII. However since these studies did not appear in Greek, his work, although well known among other intellectuals at that time, was not part of a more local discussion. Chatzimihali's own house, designed by Zachos in the Plaka area of Athens, now houses the National Laographic Museum.
17 Dimitris Pikionis, "Our Popular Art and Ourselves," *Dimitris Pikionis: Texts* (in Greek), p. 69.

texts about the vernacular and its relationship to the Greek landscape in various journals and newspapers.[14] In 1925 he wrote an important text that he intended as part of a theoretical trilogy on the popular/vernacular, "Our Popular Art and Ourselves." The same year there were two more significant publications about popular art and popular dwellings: Aggeliki Chatzimihali's book *Skyros*, a treatise on that Aegean island's locally produced arts, crafts, and architecture, and Dimitris Loukopoulos's *Aetolian Dwellings, Utensils and Foods*, exploring the architecture and the culinary culture of that region of Greece side by side, complete with recipes, and illustrated by Dimitris Pikionis.[15]

Whereas *Aetolian Dwellings* was the only book-length study by Dimitris Loukopoulos, a teacher in mainland Greece, Chatzimihali, authored several studies and was very active in organizing the study of popular arts and architecture before, during, and after the Second World War. An upper-middle class artist, Chatzimihali's work on vernacular architecture originated in her studies of material culture in isolated rural areas of Greece. Throughout her life she traveled all over Greece to live with her subjects of observation, whether they were Skyrian women or Sarakatsanian nomads living in tents, and was responsible for collecting a huge variety of artifacts from popular civilization that otherwise would have simply been lost and forgotten.[16]

In 1930 Pikionis and Chatzimihali were two of the founding members of the Association for the Study of Greek Popular Art [*Syllogos Elliniki Laiki Techni*], founded to document vanishing artifacts primarily from the Greek countryside. Some of the other members from a pool of well-known artists and architects included artists Nikolaos Chatzikyriakos-Gikas and Yiannis Tsarouchis, and architects Dimitris Moretis, Alexandra Paschalidou-Moreti, Giorgos Giannoullelis, and Maria Zagorisiou. In 1936 Pikionis became in charge of a systematic study of the Greek house. He organized a team of people who went on summer expeditions both to the mainland as well as to the islands to record local architectural culture. They held exhibitions of this work (Athens, 1938 and 1939) and intended a series of publications that remained largely unrealized until very recently, due to the onset of the Second World War.

It was Pikionis who introduced a sense of the vernacular closer to the European term. He discussed the vernacular was as a kind of language. The underlying idea was that like the Greek language, which has been alive for millennia, there could be built forms appropriate to the specific climate and landscape waiting to be revealed, or reactivated. If only one started to understand the different components properly, one could use them to construct a new, contemporary vocabulary of forms that would again be natural and indigenous, local to the Greek soil. Citing a fragment from the poet Dionysios Solomos, "first, learn to obey the language of the people, and then, if you are strong enough, conquer it," Pikionis wrote:

> as the people [*laòs*] give words to the writer, so they give us [the architects] shapes as if other kinds of words, those of our plastic language. If only we could appreciate the meaning of this gift.[17]

The idea that the study of the architectural vernacular is akin to a new plastic language, that of the people, was illustrated further by an example about woodcarving, accompanied by a black and white photograph inserted in the text:

> Look at the example of popular woodcarving. . . . Let us observe the influence that materials have in the creation of a plastic language. We can

5.4 Dimitris Pikionis.
Moraitis House,
Tzitzifies, Neo Faliro,
1921–23.
Source: © Neohellenic
Architecture Archives,
Benaki Museum, Athens.

carve wood with a tool [rural people] call *sgorpia*. The shapes emerge naturally from the use of this tool on the wood. These are the *elements*, the *words* of woodcarving.[18]

An important factor that contributed to Pikionis imagining a plastic language in parallel with or equivalent to a spoken language, was the larger intellectual context of his generation. At that time, the debates about architecture had as a constant backdrop the so-called "language question." At issue was in which language should Greeks speak: the *demotic* – everyday, popular, vernacular language – or the *katharevousa*, constructed by nineteenth-century intellectuals by adapting classical Greek to the Greek of their time and by "cleansing" it from traces of "foreign" (and particularly Turkish) words. The so-called language question was the overwhelming issue of the day during the 1930s; it passionately divided not only the intellectuals but also politicians and the press, and was constantly encountered in all aspects of everyday life.[19]

Another member of the so-called Thirties Generation, the poet Odysseas Elytis, took the analogy between landscape and language – in his case poetic language – further by claiming that one can actually read the Greek alphabet in the landscape, discussing "places here and there in the soils of the Aegean," bearing signs of the "many-century presence of Hellenism," which furnish their own spelling, and where

> each *omega*, each *ipsilon*, each accent mark or *iota* subscript is nothing but a small bay, a slope, the vertical line of a rock over the curved line of a boat's stern, winding grapevines, a decoration over a church door, red and white dotted here and there from pigeon houses and potted geraniums.[20]

Pikionis's way of viewing the relationship between language, architecture, and nature was complex. He tried to develop a poetics of reading the landscape and to create buildings as an extension of this landscape. By understanding the vernacular, Pikionis felt more able to compose new syntheses suitable for the contemporary world. In addition, he also experimented with different "languages" or idioms in his architecture, especially in his early works. His Moraitis House (Athens, 1921–23) was a homage to an Aegean island vernacular. A courtyard house built entirely of stone, it had arched lintels, asymmetrical openings, niches carved in the walls, and a flat roof, whereas his next commission, the Karamanos House (Athens, 1925), experimented with a Hellenistic building type, inspired by a contemporary discovery of a house in Priene.

Pikionis's first public building, an elementary school in Athens at Lycabettus Hill (1931–32), was part of the School Building Program initiated by the Eleftherios Venizelos government. As if wishing to learn from the modernist language – that as he wrote had "secret affinities" with the Greek vernacular – Pikionis's building was comprised of a series of unadorned, flat-roofed, startlingly white, interlinked cubes that followed the contours of the landscape. However, even before the CIAM IV meeting held in Athens in August 1933,

[18] Ibid., p. 64.
[19] On the persistence of the official and popular debates about language in Greek culture see Karen Van Dyck: "Ever since the War of Independence in the 1820s. . . . the question of language consumes Greeks [to this day] in their newspapers and everyday interactions. . . . the power of the word has a claim on the Greek national imagination which provides a striking contrast to the status of language in many other Western countries where linguistic issues are often debated only among small groups of intellectuals." From Karen Van Dyck, *Kassandra and the Censors, Greek Poetry Since 1967*, Ithaca/London, Cornell University Press, 1998, p. 14.
[20] Odysseas Elytis, *The Public and the Private* [Ta dimosia kai ta idiotika], 1990, pp. 8–9, translated by Artemis Leontis. Even though this particular collection of poems postdates Pikionis, Odysseas Elytis, winner of the Nobel Prize for Literature in 1979, often brought these kinds of analogies to his work.

5.5 Dimitris Pikionis.
Primary School,
Pefkakia, Lycabettus,
Athens, 1931–32.
Source: © Neohellenic
Architecture Archives,
Benaki Museum, Athens.

[21] The text makes several points why Pikionis thought it did not altogether make sense to hold CIAM IV in Athens. Among the reasons he cited was the terrible state of the city and the contrast it would make to the "ideal solutions" discussed by the delegates, and the fact that young Greek architects should not "succumb passively" to dogmas such as that about "contemporary mechanical conditions." "Thoughts About A Conference" [Gyro apo ena synedrio], 1933, *Pikionis: Texts*, pp. 168–170.

about which he wrote a critical text, Pikionis had begun to distance himself from the forms and the ideology of the modern movement and focused his attention on developing new ways in which to express age-old vernacular forms.[21]

A good example of his rather sudden turn away from the modernist idiom is the Experimental School in Thessaloniki (plate 33, 1935). Visibly influenced by his studies of the northern Greek vernacular, this building, situated in the midst of a busy urban area, has an L-shaped plan that creates an outdoor space for sports activities, and is designed to take full advantage of Thessaloniki's specific climatic conditions. The orientation, positioning of openings, and the shallow-pitched roofs with long overhangs render the building sunny in the winter and shaded during the summer.

Pikionis's interest in nature and the vernacular and the ways in which his studies informed his work transformed over time. Not only was he also interested in the architecture and philosophy of the Far East, and particularly of India and Japan, but as his work developed very direct associations with the Greek vernacular began to disappear. By the time Pikionis designed the remarkable Aixoni Protoype Housing (plates 34–35, 1950–54), even though the "lessons" from the vernacular were visible, particularly in the topography and landscaping of this unbuilt project, the building forms had no direct relation to either modernist or vernacular forms. Similarly, the Xenia Hotel in Delphi (1951–54) bears no clear resemblance to any existing tradition, vernacular or otherwise, but is rather a new synthetic work that is responsive to the existing topography of the site.

Pikionis's analysis of the relationship of nature to the vernacular provided ways for him to understand classical art and architecture and relate it to contemporary Greece. He noted that the ancient Greeks, too, adapted their buildings to climate and to qualities of light, working with shadows in order to create visual effects, texture, and delicate contoured graduations to provide surfaces that are constantly changing against the strong Greek sunlight. For Pikionis, the art of the ancient Greeks was "founded upon nature, upon her laws" and "a Doric column is for instance natural, not because of its type but due to the balance of its mass, its modeling. . . . it is natural . . . as natural as a simple plank of stone that the peasant puts down on the ground."[22]

Reading ancient art "as if" it were popular art, Pikionis looked for essential visual-poetic equivalences between these two worlds. In a particularly pertinent segment accompanied by a laconic line drawing, Pikionis made an analogy between a peasant woman's skirt as she dances and the fluting of an ancient column:

> The pleats and folds in the costume of this peasant woman undulate around her ankles, tracing mountain shapes upon the ground. The woven ornamentation around the hem of her skirt stands out as vividly as a frieze. The dance unfolds like a moving colonnade. The sound of the pipe, interwoven with the dancers' song, makes the mountaintops sway and the rivers flow. The rhythm of these draperies as they ripple around the body, the shape of this brow or forearm, the waves and curls of that hair – all of these explain the landscape.[23]

Pikionis perceived the popular/vernacular idiom as a language, one that was rich enough to overcome the dichotomies between ancient and modern, high and low, foreign and local, and even North and South. He never stopped thinking about nature, the particular forms of the Greek landscape and its importance in imagining a new architecture and culture in a broader sense (plate 36). One important postwar activity was his involvement in an activist group of architects and other intellectuals organized to protect "sensitive" areas and sites, the "Committee for the Protection of the Hellenic Landscape" founded in 1954.[24] By the time he completed his work on the Acropolis and Philopappou Hills, and until the end of his life, Pikionis published a multitude of texts about the relationship of architecture to nature and the "lessons" of anonymous dwellings; they still seem fresh and original and merit new scholarly attention.

Aris Konstantinidis and *Two "Villages" from Mykonos*

Aris Konstantinidis's strong presence in Greek cultural life was not only due to his few but influential built works, but also to the numerous critical writings he published throughout his career. His texts provide an ongoing critique of architecture as well as of the political and administrative structures that, for him, placed countless obstacles to an architect's work. The earliest of Konstantinidis's books was *Two "Villages" from Mykonos and Some More General Thoughts about Them*, published in 1947, closely followed by *The Old Athenian Houses*, also written during the 1940s and published in 1950. In these early texts Konstantinidis described his first encounter with the popular/vernacular:

22 Dimitris Pikionis, "Our Popular Art and Ourselves", p. 65.
23 Dimitris Pikionis, "A Sentimental Topography" (1935), in *Dimitris Pikionis, Architect 1887–1968*, p. 68.
24 For more on the work of this committee and Pikionis's involvement, see Yorgos Simeoforidis, "The Architects and the Attic Landscape 1953–1963" (To Attiko topio kai oi architektones 1953–1963], in Yiannis Aesopos, Olga Simeoforidi, and Yorgos Tzirtzilakis (eds.), *Dielefseis: Texts about Architecture and Metapolis*, Athens, Metapolis Press, 2005, pp. 113–127.

5.6 Dimitris Pikionis. Pikionis's conceptual connection between the outline of a Doric column and a notional undulation of a peasant woman's skirt as she moves around in a dance, is simply labeled "Doric Rhythm."
Source: Dimitris Pikionis, "A Sentimental Topography" [1935] in *Texts (Keimena)*, Athens, 1987.

25 *Two "Villages" from Mykonos and Some More General Thoughts about Them* [Dyo "choria" ap'ti Mykono kai merikes pio genikes skepseis mazi tous], Athens, 1947, p. 12.
26 Konstantinidis was a remarkable photographer. The last book published during his lifetime was a collection of photographs taken at different points throughout his life. Entitled "God-Built" *[Ta Theoktista]* from 1993, it includes images from Mykonos, perhaps taken around the time of the book discussed here.
27 "I feel something turning deep inside my heart – an unfolding – the memories and the fire still burn. Perhaps the hesitation, the surprise and the uncertainty together with the initial misguided disbelief. The first sweet meeting returns more strongly, the first kiss and the embrace – the many tight embraces – and the endless love-making with the whole of nature." From *Two "Villages" from Mykonos*, opening paragraph, p. 9.

the former addressed rural architecture, the latter was the first study in the Greek context of an *urban* domestic vernacular.

Konstantinidis began work on *Two Villages from Mykonos* soon after he returned from his studies in Munich in 1936 and before he was drafted to fight on the Albanian front in 1940 at the start of the Second World War. The slim, small format volume is a diatribe about the relationship of buildings to nature. Like the earlier *laographers*, Konstantinidis went to Mykonos to "listen" to the *laòs*, to get as close to the "humble man" as possible. He wrote:

> We say "popular" architecture and our imagination constructs an almost divine building. But what is the meaning of this word and what justifies its existence? And which of man's work on the earth is the work of the people – *popular* – and which isn't? And finally which part of ourselves is "the people" [*laòs*] and which isn't?[25]

At that time Mykonos had not yet been discovered by the jet-set vacationers, and still had – like many other mountainous rural areas in Greece – a relatively limited economy. Mykonians made their living primarily from fishing and from cultivating small agricultural plots. Konstantinidis studied two houses outside the dense main settlement of Mykonos (*chòra*), that the locals call "the village." Houses like the ones Konstantinidis studied were – and still are – found dotted along the island to accommodate shepherds who take their flocks there to graze or farmers who tend to isolated fields nearby. They are temporary dwellings, with only the most essential items for inhabitation.

What did Konstantinidis find in Mykonos? Even though at the start of the book the author declares that he would have liked his drawings to have "spoken" alone, his text is lengthy in comparison with the scarcity of sketches (four for each "village") that appear after the text, almost as an afterthought. And even though there are no photographs, the sketches are curiously framed as if they were camera views, drawn from such a distance so as to "fit" in the center of the frame, indicating Konstantinidis's keen photographer's eye.[26]

Most of all, Konstantinidis was interested in the ways in which these houses interact with the outdoors as the main subject of the book is the interaction of popular/vernacular buildings with nature. The plans show the outlines of courtyards and indicate paths and dry stone walls. Each sketch offers a perspective view with few details of surface materials and texture or other decorative elements. The sparse black and white lines are supposed to capture only "the essential": the rectangular masonry volumes, the overgrown vegetation, the elevated platform for sleeping at one side of the room with storage underneath, perhaps a piece of bedding hanging from a rail, the hearth always at one corner of the room, and some large jars leaning against it, probably where olive oil and wine were kept. We can also discern the construction of the ceiling made of wooden slats filled with reeds and, one imagines, as is the practice in the Cyclades to this day, topped with a special mix of soil with sand and then whitewashed. The equally laconic plans give us an indication of scale, orientation, the thickness of the stone walls, the differences in level inside the house, and openings and niches typically for storage of various household objects and icons.

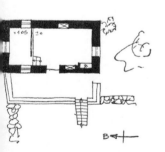

5.7 Aris Konstantinidis. Sketch and plan of a house in Mykonos.
Source: A. Konstantinidis, *Two "Villages" from Mykonos and Some More General Thoughts about Them*, Athens, 1947.

In bursts of youthful enthusiasm, Konstantinidis's accompanying text announced that upon landing on the island he began finding himself in "an endless love-making with the whole of nature."[27] He described a swim experienced as if a new baptism into nature, a rebirth or a reawakening. In Mykonos, the author tells us, he discovered the most "true" and therefore "beautiful" works of man, those of the local, "simple" and "innocent" dwellings:

> Reborn, as if a newborn again, you open yourself up to limitless space. And you run over the hills, the paths, the sandy beaches . . . you run to find the beauty of the architecture. The shiny stones that were so bright from afar, and that you thought were placed there by our Great Maker of the world, when you approach them you see that they are but small, affectionate, innocent works of man, created in the midst of his daily toil.[28]

Like Pikionis, Konstantinidis also juxtaposed ideas about language with architecture. As the description of the swim ends, Konstantinidis visited a chapel where, looking at the icons, he pronounced a renewed spirituality and faith in the "language of nature." After all, even though he is not considered a member of the Thirties Generation, Konstantinidis's formative period during his education were the 1930s. He too was writing against the background of the "language question," and was, even more than Pikionis, an ardent demoticist – an expert of the language of the "common people."

In fact, Konstantinidis made a point of formulating his views on nature and the vernacular in opposition to those of Pikionis. Although never mentioning the older architect by name, Konstantinidis's remarks betray a great deal of animosity against Pikionis and particularly towards Pikionis's own creative work. Although Konstantinidis never explicitly confronted Pikionis, there are enough clues in his texts indicating that he thought of him as too emotive, too sentimental, too artistic to be a "real" architect. Plkionis's work seemed too painterly to Konstantinidis's rigorous modernist eyes: the term "scenographic," already deployed in *Two "Villages" from Mykonos* as well as in many of his other books, was used by Konstantinidis as a charge against Pikionis. Konstantinidis was also critical of the larger project of the *laographers*, of their organized expeditions and exhibitions as well as their efforts to produce ethnographic studies, which he countered as "awkward," and furthermore as "tasteless concoctions, compassionate but hard-to-digest." He was particularly vehement against Aggeliki Chatzimihali who was charged with being "naïve" in her book.[29]

Were Konstantinidis's views about the relationship of nature to the Greek popular/vernacular dwelling all that different from those of Pikionis? Despite his oppositional stance – he implied that *only he* understood the "essential" in vernacular architecture – at its core Konstantinidis's argument is similar to Pikionis's: for both, popular/vernacular architecture is about the closeness of man to nature and to the indigenous landscape. "Humble men" not only achieve a perfect harmony between their buildings and their landscape but they also manage to create buildings that appear as if they are rooted to the ground and that are organically related to how people live their everyday lives. But whereas Pikionis suggested subtle observation, in this early book Konstantinidis argued that only if an architect becomes "one" with "the people"/*laòs* might he understand the "truth" about building.

This idea brought Konstantinidis to an impossible position. For how can someone from a highly educated cosmopolitan background identify on equal terms with "the people"? The rigid contrast between these two worlds, that of the "civilized" urban middle class and the rural peasant, reminds us of Adolf Loos's writings in the early part of the twentieth century. But whereas Loos never tried to become one with the "rooted" peasant, Konstantinidis

[28] Ibid., p. 10.
[29] Since there were no other women *laographers* working with buildings at the time, this rather cruel comment was clearly directed against her. No matter that Chatzimihali spent her whole life in isolated villages studying and collecting priceless materials and artifacts, for Konstantinidis she too did not truly understand what was essential about the vernacular, which according to him, needed "stronger [male?] hands." Ibid., p. 25.

5.8 Aris Konstantinidis. Guests' quarters, Xenia, Epidauros, 1962.
Source: A. Konstantinidis, *Projects + Buildings*, Athens, 1981.

recommended: "become *laòs* first yourself and then show the others what is valuable from your own people." And, "I say it again, if there is a goal, an ultimate destination in this whole effort, it is only this: that we should become *laòs* . . . so as to be *true* and great."[30] Taking the Loosian dialectic further, Konstantinidis wrote that the city contained "a restricted and artificial – mechanized – atmosphere where man has lost all contact with nature."[31] In contrast to this "artificial man" of the city, and departing from Loos (and Pikionis), Konstantinidis proposed that not only was the vernacular building an extension of the body, but that "popular" man *was* nature/landscape, and so when he builds, he recreates this nature in his buildings. Thus these "popular" buildings *become* landscape.[32]

In this early book, Konstantinidis often echoed his European education, adapting terminology and concepts from the North to the context of the South. The idea of building in "truth" and of being "true" to materials and to function, as well as reading popular humble Cycladic buildings as "rational" and "functional" is familiar to students of European modernism. His own interpretation of modernist ideas and the existing context of *laography*, no matter as he opposed it, led him to re-evaluate the Greek vernacular in very particular ways. For Konstantinidis undoubtedly believed that the *laòs* was the *only* source of reaching what is "true" and what is "Hellenic" – and at times the two were interchangeable.

In that sense, we realize that Konstantinidis's highest admiration for the "villages" of Mykonos was reserved exactly for their ability to be almost erased by nature. It is precisely this quality that he consistently tried to reproduce in

[30] Ibid., p. 26.
[31] Ibid., p. 14.
[32] Konstantinidis wrote: "the *man-laòs* [. . .] he too is a part of nature and has blossomed on the earth like the bush, the tree, the flower. And when he builds his dwelling it stands as an extension of his body and soul and property. He will present again anew the curves of the mountaintops, the sections of the landscape itself. So as in the end, he too will become landscape in his land – for man is also landscape, as long as he remains *laòs* and does not become alienated from nature." Ibid., p. 15.

his own work: from the landscaping of his very first project, a house in Elefsis (1938), to the Actors' Changing Rooms and Xenia guests' quarters at Epidauros (1958, 1960, and 1962), the Xenia Hotel in Mykonos (1960), and the Weekend House in Anavyssos (1962). Some of the ways in which he achieved a dialogue between his buildings and their specific natural environments was that the buildings, which tended to be low (single or at most two-stories high), always followed the topography of the site, no matter how uneven. He used local materials, especially stone, that was sometimes structural, and at other times acted as an infill in a reinforced concrete grid. The concrete grid was often whitewashed or was left un-rendered. Stone walls were almost always un-rendered so that not only did they blend with the colors of the surrounding landscape but they evoked popular/vernacular processes. Similarly, he was fond of using stone for landscaping, evoking the indigenous dry stone walls he studied in the Cyclades.

Another contribution that Konstantinidis brought to the discussion of the vernacular, was his admiration for contemporary "informal" structures. In the Mykonos book, Konstantinidis wondered how we may cultivate our "sense of the popular" so as to train our eyes and hands to build like "the people." At different points in his life he drew and photographed all kinds of self-made constructions, both in cities and in the countryside, temporary or permanent. From simply built bamboo-covered eating areas by the sea, to whitewashed single-room refugee housing. In these informal constructions Konstantinidis recognized a similar instinctive feeling for building well, and wrote with admiration that "popular men" understand how to build in this particular landscape whether in stone or in glass and concrete.

Whereas Pikionis comes across as a quiet and humble writer, it is characteristic of Konstantinidis's essays to have a passionate, even explosive tone. Even though his texts can be extremely subtle and perceptive, they are often riddled with contradictions, betraying a constant internal conflict. In this instance,

5.9 Aris Konstantinidis, Perspective, Xenia Hotel, Delos, 1962. Source: © Neohellenic Architecture Archives, Benaki Museum, Athens.

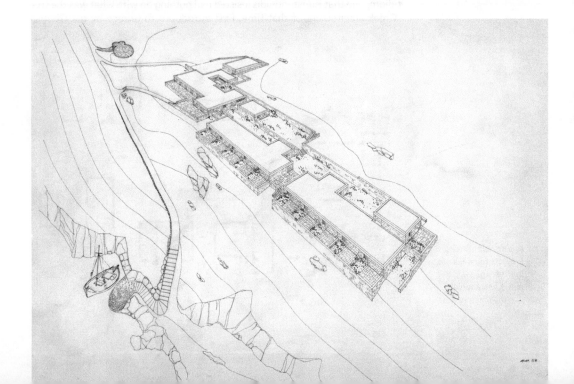

33 For close reading of that book within the context of twentieth-century Athenian urbanism and domestic culture, see Ioanna Theocharopoulou, Ph.D. Dissertation, 2007.
34 *Two "Villages" from Mykonos*, p. 33.
35 The influence of architects educated in France was less pronounced (Frederich Boulanger, Ernst Troumpe, and the urban planner Hebrard were some of the most prominent ones). Konstantinidis does not mention any of their works in particular. Rather he talks about "the Europeans" always within quotation marks as if he doesn't really believe in the existence of such beings or in order to emphasize the irony of Europe's conflicted relationship to Greece and to classical Greece.

despite the charges against the *laographers*, we can't help noticing that Konstantinidis, too, studied the vernacular using ethnographic methods, especially in his next book, *Old Athenian Houses*, which he was already working on during the 1940s. There he explored not only how pre-Independence Athenians built their houses and what those houses looked like in numerous photographs, sketches, and plans, but he also documented how they were inhabited, recording stories and rituals about a building type that was already becoming rapidly extinct.[33] Already in the book about Mykonos, Konstantinidis laid out a method that is unmistakably ethnographic, but which he calls "architectural":

> We shall review the architectural data: on the one hand man, on the other the landscape, climate and geography. We will study the manners, customs and rituals (for every particular geographical area), the landscape and agricultural production. We will try to understand the local economy . . . and religion. Also the songs, the prayers, the feasts, as well as all other expressions of the "popular" society and only then will we be able to say: these are the tools the "popular" person uses to build.[34]

What Konstantinidis called "old" Athenian houses, dated from the late eighteenth and early nineteenth centuries, the period just before Greek Independence in 1821. Studying them carefully with sketches and photographs, Konstantinidis found out that these houses were always composed of a courtyard and a series of rooms of one or two stories, placed around it. These houses were mostly built of wood and stone. When two stories high, there would usually be a glass loggia above and a semi-covered space below. Typical features included an external staircase, a well in the courtyard, and a high wall secluding and protecting the house from the gaze of passersby.

Konstantinidis contrasted these *Old Athenian Houses* with the neoclassical urban domestic buildings constructed after 1834. For Konstantinidis, neoclassicism was a German and more generally European-brought architectural idiom, one that Konstantinidis insisted had nothing do with what was the true Greek architecture of that time. First introduced to Greece by the German

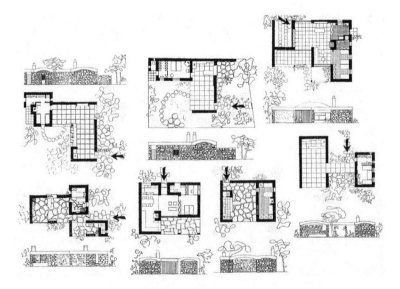

5.10 Aris Konstantinidis. Projects for weekend houses, 1942–45.
Source: A. Konstantinidis, *Projects + Buildings*, Athens, 1981.

architects and engineers who had accompanied the young Bavarian King, when Athens was chosen as the capital in 1834, neoclassicism quickly became the official architectural language of the new state.[35] The fact that neoclassicism was "imported" from the West was the focus of Konstantinidis's polemical and at times outright angry comments. The rediscovery of classical Greek architecture and the birth of neoclassicism in Europe coincided with greater accessibility of classical sites during the mid- and late-eighteenth centuries. The European cultural identification with ancient Greece was indeed nowhere more pronounced during the nineteenth century as in Germany.

As Konstantinidis's work suggests, aspects of Greek culture were idealized, mimicked, and appropriated in order to fulfill the European's own quest for origins. The idealization of ancient Greece was crucial in Philhellenism, the movement for independence initiated among diaspora Greeks and European

5.11 Aris Konstantinidis. Photograph and sketch of beach shelter structure.

Source: A. Konstantinidis, *Elements for Self-knowledge: Towards a True Architecture: Photographs, Drawings, Notes,* Athens, 1975.

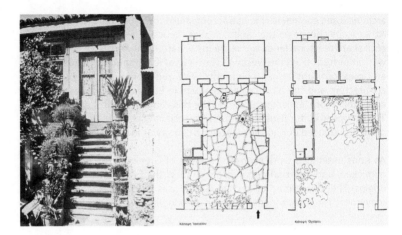

5.12 Aris Konstantinidis.
House in Athens.
Source: A. Konstantinidis,
The Old Athenian Houses,
Athens, 1950.

intellectuals in the late eighteenth century. This pattern is a trope of orientalism present in most colonial situations. But the difference in this case was that this modernity was somehow understood to have originated from Greece itself. And while the nineteenth-century Europeans had become Greeks, in their eyes post-Independence Greeks had turned into savages.

Yet while blaming the Germans and Europeans for misunderstanding the Greek architectural heritage, ironically, Konstantinidis probably had greater intellectual affinity with his European contemporaries than he was aware of. Indeed the *Old Athenian Houses* is an architectural manifesto, the genre through which European modernist artists and architects articulated their revolutionary ambitions and desires – and like other such documents of this kind, *Old Athenian Houses* is aggressive, political, and polemical. In addition, the very language and terminology Konstantinidis used to describe these houses was dominated by European and specifically German modernist thought. For instance, one of the ways in which he described these *Old Athenian Houses*, was by using the notion of "type," a concept that he adopted in a manner reminiscent of the Werkbund debates of 1914. Like these German thinkers, with whom he was probably familiar through his education, Konstantinidis also praised the "old" Athenian houses as having achieved the status of "the typical," that is the purely essential and functional in their architecture.[36] Like these European architects, Konstantinidis's studies of the *Old Athenian Houses* influenced his own projects of this period. Like them, he praised what he saw as the vernacular aspects of urban domestic architecture rather than the neoclassical buildings that were usually regarded as monuments. He thus endowed these humble houses that he chose to record with value. In his words, he sought to "recover" or "reawaken"[37] what he saw as an original Athenian architecture as if from sleep – or at least from the darkness of history, treating them as repositories of memory.[38]

Constantinos Doxiadis and the Question of the *Popular Architecture*

Any discussion of popular architecture in relation to early twentieth-century Greece has to include at least a mention of Constantinos Doxiadis. During the 1930s Doxiadis worked with Pikionis and other artists and architects of the Association for Hellenic Popular Art recording domestic vernacular architecture as a consultant; in the 1940s and especially as Undersecretary of Reconstruction (1945–51), Doxiadis collected and classified data about indigenous buildings

[36] Echoing Adolf Loos, in particular, Konstantinidis also wrote that "only the temple (house of God) and the tomb have the right to be monuments" (*Old Athenian Houses*, p. 27). Konstantinidis also discussed using contemporary materials and especially glass to "bring the landscape inside the house to the most hidden corners" (*Old Athenian Houses*, p. 45) in a manner reminiscent of Le Corbusier's writings and drawings.
[37] This is a trope used as an analogy of the whole state of Greek culture/ nation during the Ottoman occupation by intellectuals since the Greek Enlightenment. For instance, see George Seferis's phrase "the awakening of the race," in an essay dating from 1938–39, "Dokimes A," translated in George Seferis, *On the Greek Style. Selected Essays in Poetry and Hellenism*, Boston/Toronto, Little Brown 1966, p. 93.
[38] Yet in contrast to Konstantinidis's views in this book, I want to emphasize that by the end of the nineteenth and early twentieth centuries these humble neoclassical houses had *become* a new urban vernacular. This new popular/vernacular architecture had quickly been disseminated all around the country, always however associated (as Konstantinidis rightly pointed out), with the idea of national rebirth.

and settlements, both personally and by assigning research to his associates. Yet his contribution is almost unknown – if not deliberately obscured – in Greek architectural circles.[39]

An exact contemporary of Aris Konstantinidis, Constantinos Apostolos Doxiadis was a student, a teaching assistant, and later on a close friend and occasional collaborator of Dimitris Pikionis. Having studied at the Athens National Polytechnic School where he first encountered Pikionis, Doxiadis went to Berlin-Charlottenburg Technical University for one year to study for a Ph.D., returning to practice in Greece in 1937 (a year after Konstantinidis). Despite his young age – he was only 24 – Doxiadis soon became Chief Town Planning Officer for the Greater Athens Area.[40]

Finding almost no information he could rely on to proceed with his appointed task, Doxiadis convinced his superiors to include a special questionnaire section about housing, designed by him, to the 1940 National Census. He then organized a very large team to study this information. His team produced extensive surveys that encompassed both visual and written information in the form of "multi-dimensional tables" and "gave a highly interesting, original and very detailed picture of *ekistic* conditions in Greece" before the onset of the Second World War. The origin of this well-known term denoting "the science of human settlements" [from *oikos* = house], was coined by Doxiadis during the 1940s.[41] When Italy attacked Greece in October 1940, Doxiadis, like Aris Konstantinidis, fought on the Albanian front. Upon returning to Athens and resuming his government post under the occupying forces, Doxiadis founded an underground intelligence organization that became the "scientific" general staff of the resistance movement.[42]

There are at least three ways in which Doxiadis's activities enriched the discussion of the anonymous/popular/vernacular in the Greek context in the 1940s. His first contribution was the importance given to ethnography during his tenure in various government posts. Additionally to his other resistance activities during the period of occupation, Doxiadis organized a clandestine group the "Circle of Technologists" [*Kyklos Technikwn*] who met weekly to discuss the state of Greek – primarily rural – settlements and culture in a broader sense. The proceedings of these discussions were published as a journal, *Chorotaxia*, only one volume of which (from 1942) remains in the archives.

Both Konstantinidis and Aggeliki Chatzimihali participated in these "Circle" meetings. Chatzimihali presented research on "Popular Architecture and Popular Art"; there were presentations on the architecture of the Aegean islands, the architecture of Zagora in mainland Greece, and the architecture of farm houses. John Papaioannou, a musicologist and long-time collaborator of Doxiadis, presented research on climate and how it effects architecture and planning. Aris Konstantinidis, whose article in the surviving volume discussed the relationship between art and architecture, also talked about what he called "architecture without architects," noting that there we might discover "the *eternal* character of *all* architecture, that which is expressed differently in each age but that is in the end its most interesting aspect."[43] In addition, the renowned *laographer* Georgios Megas provided one of the first methodological theses about *laography*, as well as detailed studies of the material culture of the Northern rural countryside that included a great amount of detail about buildings.

Doxiadis's second contribution was at the level of language and terminology. An important new term, *Chorotaxia*, was to denote "planning," which as a

[39] The reason why Doxiadis's work has up to now remained obscure especially among Greek architectural historians has to do primarily with the onset of Civil War and the subsequent political polarization of intellectuals that lasted well into the 1970s, was accentuated during the Military Junta (1968–74), and certainly lasted until Doxiadis's death in 1975. Doxiadis was seen as belonging to the Right – even the ultra-Right – and was also suspected of espionage for the Americans and the British. In addition, Doxiadis left a huge archive that for many years remained inaccessible, but is now open. See the exhibition catalogue *Constantinos A. Doxiadis: Texts, Design Drawings, Settlements*, Athens, Benaki Museum, 2007.

[40] Doxiadis published his dissertation, completed in one year, as *Raumordnung im griechischen Stadtebau* (Heidelberg, Berlin, K. Vowinckel, 1937). It was translated into English by his colleague Jaqueline Tyrwitt as *Architectural Space in Ancient Greece*, Cambridge, The MIT Press, 1972. Konstantinidis probably worked under Doxiadis during this time as he was employed at the City Planning Department from March 1939 to the beginning of the war (1940) returning to work in this department until 1953.

[41] John Papaioannou "C.A. Doxiadis' Early Career and the Birth of Ekistics," in *Ekistics* 247, June 1976, p. 315. Even though some statistical information from this survey still exists, the bulk of this material was completely destroyed by fire during or after the war.

[42] See *Constantinos A. Doxiadis: Texts, Design Drawings, Settlements*, p. 339.

[43] Konstantinidis, *Chorotaxia* Journal, 1942, p. 7.

44 Papaioannou writing in *Ekistics* 247, June 1976, p. 314. I thank Mr. Panagis Psomopoulos, editor of *Ekistics*, for directing me to this issue.

45 The term *chorognosia* was yet another new term Doxiadis was trying to introduce along with other branches of this other "new science": "Anthropoecology," "Phytoecology," and "Zooecology" [*anthropooikología, phytooikología, zooecología*]: see *Chorotaxia* Journal, 1942, p. 3.

46 One direct attempt by Doxiadis to implement his ideas about the vernacular in the postwar period was the project of *Aspra Spitia* [White Houses], a small company town for "Aluminion de Grece" on a Peloponnesian coast near Delphi (1961–75). There Doxiadis Associates worked both as planners and as architects, developing certain standardized dwelling types, using local materials, and trying to recreate the feeling of "a Greek city of the past." Despite his efforts, and due in part to financial difficulties, Doxiadis did not manage to see this project completed before his death. For more on *Aspra Spitia*, see *Constantinos A. Doxiadis, Texts, Design Drawings, Settlements*.

47 *Thessalikai Oikiseis* [Dwellings from Thessaly], Athens, Ypourgion Anoikodomiseos, 1946.

discipline did not yet exist in Greece. The term literally means bringing order (*taxis*) to space (*choros*). It embodies an intentional ambiguity of which Doxiadis was very fond, namely it denoted the idea of planning at any scale – *chòros* = space, *chorió* = village, *chòra* = country. As his colleague John Papaioannou has shown, the idea for this term originated in his studies in Berlin. There he first became acquainted with the terms *Städtebau* (city building) and *Raumordnung* and *Landesplanung* (land use, territorial planning), none of which had exact equivalents in Greek. For Papaioannou the term *chorotaxia* "was meant as an exact translation of the German *Raumordnung* with a side glance at *Landesplanung*."[44] It was as if Doxiadis believed that if only a linguistic fit could be made between a Northern European concept to Greek, it would also bring about a successful real-life practice.

This new science of *chorotaxia* was comprised of "practical," "theoretical" parts, and also of another separate category, the omnibus term *chorognosia* meaning "country/land-knowledge", probably close to the German term *Landesplanung*. Whereas "practical" planning was about studying "details," i.e. architecture, town planning, periphery planning, and national planning, "theoretical" planning was about studying more general phenomena such as the economy, demography, organization of production, industry, population, administrative organization, etc. Lastly he saw *chorognosia* as "the soul" of administration since it had to do with the relationship of man to his environment.[45]

Related to *laography* and to *chorotaxia*, was the idea of the survey at different scales, including the regional, that was introduced in the Greek context by Doxiadis. Formulated by the Scottish planner, Sir Patrick Geddes during the late nineteenth century, the survey was partly envisioned as a way to study society and the effects of industrialization then taking place in Scotland. Doxiadis's own use of the survey encompassed *laography*: the surveys of his associates at the ministry, like those of Maria Zagorisiou in Crete and Mytilini, were primarily detailed studies of vernacular/popular architecture.

Whereas Pikionis and Konstantinidis used their research on the vernacular to enrich their own ideas about architecture, Doxiadis was more interested in the larger scale of settlements as well as in policy and the reconstruction of society.[46] But his studies of "anonymous," primarily rural architecture, helped him develop strategies for development. As Undersecretary of Reconstruction he published and personally introduced Megas's research in a separate booklet from the series he organized through the ministry.[47] Megas's and other *laographers'* methods of working had an enormous influence on Doxiadis who began to set up his own study of *Ekistics* using some of the very same methods and techniques as Megas, and who continued to study local popular civilization in the countries he was charged to plan for in the postwar period.

The study of popular/vernacular shelter was an extremely important aspect of Greek architectural culture during the first part of the twentieth century. The ways in which architects explored the question of the vernacular might have identified "the people" with a romantic idea of the nation and, at least to some extent, idealized them. At the same time the concept of *laography* and the methods of ethnographic research gave Greek architects some means to overcome irreconcilable opposites, particularly a way to bridge the ancient revered past and an uncertain but exciting *modern* future.

Through the question of popular/vernacular shelter, all three architects explored here were struggling with the issue of identity vis-à-vis the approaching modernization of Greek society. They agonized over what could be a new *Hellenic* architecture, and how to position themselves as intellectuals in regard to the *laòs*. Pikionis and Konstantinidis "read" characteristics and virtues of modern architecture into simple popular, primarily rural, shelter. They tried to find "roots" in a primal way of building, natural, even primitive, that was capable of providing *only the essentials* in everyday life – that was after all also a modernist quest par excellence. Doxiadis produced exhaustive surveys of popular architecture and recognized the contribution of ethnography enough so as to include ethnographic scholarship in his war-time discussions, survey questionnaires, and later on to use these expanded surveys in his work as a global planner. As most building still happens outside "the architect's influence," a renewed study of the popular/vernacular, raises the question of how to study non-architect-designed buildings and artifacts. Architectural history needs to open up this question more broadly. ■

5.13 a and b Constantinos Doxiadis. Apollonion settlement near Porto Rafti, Greece. View of the center (top); view of residential quarter (bottom). Initial design, from 1958; construction from 1969.
Source: © Constantinos A. Doxiadis Archives, Athens.

6

THE LEGACY OF AN ISTANBUL ARCHITECT

Type, Context and Urban Identity in the Work of Sedad Eldem

Sibel Bozdogan

Like other great world cities of the Mediterranean basin such as Naples, Palermo, or Cairo, Istanbul has been the subject of countless literary and visual accounts by travelers, Orientalists, photographers, and artists over many centuries. Along with the legendary silhouette of mosques and minarets crowning the hilltops, most of these representations have depicted a dense urban fabric of two- or three-story wooden houses along narrow winding streets, among ample greenery and gardens. For almost five centuries, these images have defined the city's unique urban form and identity, preserved more or less intact until about the mid-twentieth century.[1] Beginning in the 1950s and aggravated since the 1980s, the phenomenal growth, sprawl, and overbuilding of the city have resulted in a tragic and irreversible rupture of that historical continuity in the form of a transformed skyline, erosion of greenery, and rapid disappearance of old wooden houses.

Today, the discourse on the urban form and urban culture of Istanbul is largely a discourse of profound loss and nostalgia. Whereas intellectuals, poets, photographers, artists, and architectural historians struggle to keep this sense of loss alive, practicing architects have largely been indifferent to the plight of the city, if not directly complicit in it. The major exception to this is the life and career of the late Sedad Hakki Eldem (1908–88), arguably the most prominent and prolific Turkish architect of the twentieth century. As urban historian of Istanbul, teacher at the Academy of Fine Arts, and a prominent public figure involved with historical heritage and preservation efforts in Turkey, Eldem's contributions to our awareness of Istanbul's urban identity have been as significant as his work as a practicing architect, if not more so.

Elsewhere I have extensively documented Eldem's work and his compelling agenda for defining a modern Turkish architecture informed by tradition, historical precedent, and cultural continuity.[2] Here, I shall offer a critical reading of some projects in the urban context of Istanbul and in light of his stated theoretical and methodological premises. Through them, I shall suggest that, although Eldem represents a strong position against a universally posited avant-garde modernism that disregards culture, context, and history, it is still theoretically difficult to designate his work as "contextual" or "regionalist." Rather, Eldem can be seen as a *rationalist* architect who looks at tradition in order to abstract certain transhistorical and transregional "types" from it. As such, his architecture is ultimately *classical* and self-referential and, by the same token, "timeless" and "placeless," lending itself to formal and stylistic reappropriations in postmodern Turkey.

[1] Istanbul is one of the most depicted, mapped, engraved, and photographed cities in the world. A good collection of these images are reproduced in Sedad Hakkı Eldem, *Istanbul Anıları (Reminiscences of Istanbul)* and *Bogaziçi Anıları (Reminiscences of the Bosphorus)*, 2 volumes, Istanbul, Alarko Kültür Yayınları, 1979. A collection of Istanbul postcards was published as A. Eken (ed.), *Kartpostallarda Istanbul*, Istanbul, Municipality of Istanbul Publications, 1992. For a more recent general urban history see Doğan Kuban, *Istanbul: An Urban History*, Istanbul, Turkish Economic and Social History Foundation, 1996.

[2] See Sibel Bozdogan et al., *Sedad Eldem: Architect in Turkey*, Mimar Books, Singapore, Concept Media, 1987, reprinted by London, Butterworth, 1990.

6.1 (*Far left*) Sedad Eldem. Social Security Administration Complex (with the Valens aqueduct in the background), Zeyrek, Istanbul, 1962–64.
Source: Courtesy of the Aga Khan Trust for Culture, Geneva.

Documenting Istanbul and the Traditional Turkish House

Following his studies at the Academy of Fine Arts in Istanbul between 1924 and 1928, the young Sedad Eldem embarked on a two-year tour of Europe. In a recent article I argued that this period of time Eldem has spent traveling and sketching, the "vernacular" was a critical category for him – seen against a formulaic and placeless understanding of modernism and not yet instrumentalized for nationalist ends or Heimat-style discourses. He sketched houses inspired by very different vernaculars (from white Mediterranean cubes to adobe Central Anatolian houses) in a rich, inclusive palette irreducible to his later codified, exclusive "Turkish House" formula. Like Italian and Catalan architects of the 1930s who found the origins of modernism in Mediterranean traditions, Eldem believed that the vernacular traditions of the Balkans, Anatolia and the Mediterranean were "already modern".

Two beautiful 1928 sketches of the young Eldem give us a particular insight into his state of mind at the time. The first sketch shows a portico supported by slender columns in a seemingly arid landscape – Anatolia – with a slender woman figure (plate 32). The second one is a distinctly Mediterranean image: a verandah overlooking the blue sea with an antique broken torso to complete the figure (plate 31). These enigmatic, dream-like drawings accompany the notes of a young architect imagining about the dream-house that he will one day build for himself and his imagined woman. As such, they do invite complex psychoanalytical readings as the personal fantasies of a young Eldem searching for his identity – both personal and cultural – on the margins of Europe. At the same time, they represent Eldem's quest for a more lyrical, poetic and "situated" modernism, still connected to the classical and vernacular traditions of architecture in the Mediterranean basin, against the prevailing "machine age" discourse that informed canonic modernism at the time. This brief exploratory and contemplative period ended with his return to Turkey, and his "Mediterranean dream" gave way to the Nationalist project of "inventing the Turkish House tradition," i.e. his well-known and prolific career. The Mediterranean idea was largely forgotten, with the exception of two un-built projects (1941

6.2 Sedad Eldem. Halls in various Turkish building types.
Source: *Türk Evi Plan Tipleri* (Plan Types of Turkish Houses), Istanbul, 1954.

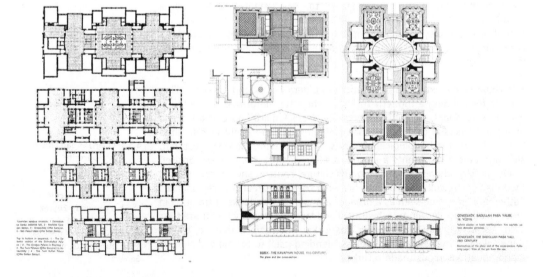

and 1976) that diverge from the rest of his canonic work, without however recapturing the brilliance of the 1928 sketches.[3]

Sedad Hakki Eldem was an "Istanbul architect" par excellence, not only by birth, residence, and work but also by his lifelong commitment to the city's architectural and urban heritage. He published numerous monographs on individual pavilions, kiosks, and houses of the late Ottoman period as well as a two-volume documentary of engravings and turn-of-the-century photographs that he nostalgically titled *Reminiscences of Istanbul: The Historical Peninsula* and *Reminiscences of the Bosphorus*, respectively. These are still the primary resources for scholars working on Istanbul's urban history in the eighteenth and nineteenth centuries. Perhaps more significantly, they provide indispensable background material towards a more informed appreciation of Eldem's own architecture.

To be an "Istanbul architect" was not the most popular thing at a time when the glory and importance of the Ottoman capital was eclipsed by the ethos of Ankara rising as the modern capital of the new Republic. Throughout the early Republican period (1923–50), with which Eldem's architectural training and early career coincided, Ankara was the primary focus of the new regime in its allocation of funds, privilege, and attention. More significantly, a set of ideologically charged and officially reproduced binary oppositions separated the two cities in the 1930s: Ankara as the new, modern, patriotic, nationalist capital of the "Kemalist Revolution," and Istanbul as the seat of the old, corrupt, imperial, and cosmopolitan empire. Although Eldem was a distinguished professional committed to and respected by the Republican regime, as the descendant of an elite Ottoman family in Istanbul, he never fully reconciled himself with the populism and revolutionary rhetoric of Ankara. Nor did he have much sympathy for the so-called "Ankara cubic" – a plain, austere Central European modernism introduced to the country primarily by Ernst Egli and Clemenz Holzmeister among other German-speaking architects commissioned by the new regime in the 1930s.[4]

Throughout his career Eldem argued that the most viable sources of a modern but national Turkish architecture had to be sought in the country's own traditions, in the civic and residential architecture of the Ottoman Empire. When he was a student at the Academy of Fine Arts in Istanbul between 1924 and 1928, he regarded the historical peninsula in Istanbul as his "real teacher." His most important and enduring insight was to approach the Ottoman tradition in a different way than the academic Ottoman revivalism or the "National Style" that dominated architectural education and practice in the 1910s and 1920s. Unlike the latter's focus on monumental religious buildings and their stylistic and decorative features, Eldem's interest was focused on houses, residential pavilions, and palaces. Instead of a preoccupation with stylistic motifs and classical composition, Eldem was interested in the plan types and constructional systems of Ottoman residential architecture and in the rational expression of these on the exterior façades. For him, this functional, structural, and formal rationality was the defining element of the traditional Ottoman "building culture," which manifested itself across different scales, programs, and budgets – from the imperial pavilions of Topkapi Palace to the vernacular wooden houses of the winding streets and poorer districts of Istanbul's historical neighborhoods. His earliest sketches of wooden houses and beautifully rendered drawings of the imperial pavilion (*Hünkar Kasrı*) attached to the seventeenth-century mosque, *Yenicami*, bear testimony to his intuitive feel for a basic "type" that was going to be the primary focus of his lifelong pedagogical

[3] This is an earlier article originally published in German in 2000. For a more recent article of mine titled "Another Sedad Eldem Trope: A Lyrical Anatolian/Mediterranean Modernism Against the Machine Age" (in Turkish), see the two volume publication *Sedad Hakki Eldem Retrospektif* (in Turkish), U.Tanyeli and B.Tanju (eds.), Istanbul, Ottoman Bank Research Center Publications, 2009. These volumes accompany a two part exhibition in Istanbul on Eldem's life and career on the occasion of the 100th anniversary of his birth. The parallel publication of Eldem's early sketches and travel diary (1928–30) has surely given us ample reason to rethink the canonic historiography of the architect.
[4] For the most recent and complete account of German-speaking architects working in Turkey in the early Republican period, see Bernd Nicolai, *Moderne und Exil: Deutschsprachige Architekten in der Turkei 1925–1955*, Berlin, Verlag fur Bauwesen, 1998.

5 Especially as expressed by Bruno Taut's famous words: "All nationalist architecture is bad but all good architecture is national." See Bruno Taut, *Mimari Bilgisi* (Architekturlehre), Istanbul, Academy of Fine Arts Publications, 1938, p. 333.

and professional program (plate 30). The wide overhanging eaves, modular repetition of windows, and the projection of the upper floors above a solid base captured in these early drawings would gradually and systematically find their way into Eldem's own work, becoming his trademark.

After more than half a century since its conception, Sedad Eldem's idea of a "modern" but distinctly "Turkish" architecture still offers the most theoretically elaborate program for reconciling tradition with modern architecture. His primary legacy is the theorization and codification of the "Turkish house" as a particular "type" and a recognizable "cultural artifact" spanning a time frame of about five hundred years and spread over the vast territories of the Ottoman Empire in Anatolia and the Balkan provinces. For Eldem, the most elaborate examples of the type are located in Istanbul and although many regional variants exist, certain constant characteristics make it a distinct type. These characteristics are the lifting of the main floor above a service/storage floor on the ground, a clear differentiation between the rooms (upper floor projections supported by brackets) and circulation spaces, rows of windows reflecting the timber frame structure and finally, a tile roof with overhanging eaves. Numerous examples of these traditional houses were studied and documented by Eldem's students in the National Architecture Seminar, which he established at the Academy of Fine Arts in Istanbul in 1934 and turned into a major institution with formative influences on an entire generation of young architects. Eldem's own *Türk Evi Plan Tipleri* (Plan Types of Turkish Houses) published in 1954 and his monumental *Türk Evi* (Turkish House), initially conceived in five volumes, the first of which was published in 1984, are based largely on the work of the National Architecture Seminar.

In *Türk Evi*, Eldem provides an elaborate typological matrix of house plans based on the shape, configuration, and location of the hall (*sofa* in Turkish), the main access space of the traditional house. The three generic types of houses are those with external halls, with internal halls, and with central halls, with the possibility of derivative connected types. For example, in Eldem's schema, even the grand imperial palaces in Istanbul like *Dolmabahçe* and *Çıragan* (which have highly eclectic façades of neo-classic and neo-Islamic elements, respectively) are in fact elaborate versions of the same basic plan type, repeating it along an axis parallel to the Bosphorus. In other words, for Eldem, plan type has a primacy over style and represents continuity even when styles change. There is also a roughly chronological basis to Eldem's classification. The external hall type is the earliest form (with some surviving examples from the seventeenth century), more common in Bursa, Edirne, Kütahya, and other early Ottoman cities, in which the *sofa* is an open terrace connected to the garden or courtyard. With the addition of rooms and the closing off of the external hall in the eighteenth century, especially in response to the urban conditions of Istanbul, the internal hall type was developed and was sometimes designated as the *karnıyarık* plan (literally "split belly"). The most elaborate variant of the same idea, the central hall type, proliferated in the nineteenth century, and with the arrival of Baroque influences upon the tastes of the Ottoman elite, oval-shaped central halls became popular, especially in the Bosphorus *yalıs*, which had formative influences on Eldem.

In the 1930s, when the term "international style" was anathema to the passionately nationalist climate in Turkey, most of Eldem's Turkish friends and German-speaking colleagues argued that good modern architecture, which responds to its context, was, by definition, "national" in an unselfconscious way.[5] Eldem, who was the leading proponent of a "National Architecture

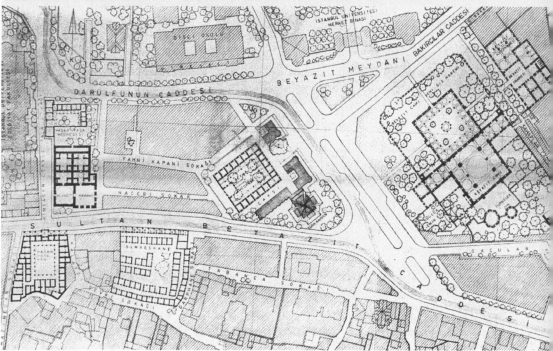

6.3 Sedad Eldem. Plan and model of intervention on Beyazit Square, Istanbul, 1938.
Source: Courtesy of the Aga Khan Trust for Culture, Geneva.

[6] Eldem wrote: "The traditional Turkish house is remarkably similar to today's conceptions of the modern house. Ample windows and light, free plan, priority of comfort over ostentatious display, honesty of materials, the relationship of the house to nature through terraces, courtyards and gardens. Aren't these the very qualities we look for in a modern house?" See Sedad Hakkı Eldem, "Türk Evi" (Turkish House), in *Sedad Hakkı Eldem: 50 Yıllık Meslek Jübilesi*, Istanbul, Academy of Fine Arts Publications, 1983, p. 19.

[7] The irony of which is the fact that, as many scholars point out, it was the wooden Turkish house that had formative influences on Le Corbusier's search for a "modern vernacular," culminating in his Villa Savoye of 1929. See Francesco Passanti, "The Vernacular, Modernism and Le Corbusier," in *Journal of Society of Architectural Historians* 56, no. 4, December 1997, pp. 438–451; and Adolf Max Vogt, *Le Corbusier: The Noble Savage*, Cambridge, The MIT Press, 1998.

Movement" in those years, proposed the corollary argument that in its simplicity, formal rationality, and structural logic the traditional Turkish house was "already modern."[6] In other words, Eldem's appreciation of tradition was not for the sake of positing the traditional against the modern, but rather for showing the profoundly "modern character" of traditional buildings and ultimately arguing for their validity and applicability towards a modern Turkish architecture. In fact, he openly admitted to having "discovered" the Turkish house in Europe in the late 1920s, after seeing the Wasmuth publication of Frank Lloyd Wright's prairie houses and looking closely at Le Corbusier's idea of lifting the house on *pilotis* above the ground floor level.[7]

At the same time, the traditional wooden house was by no means the only source of inspiration for Eldem. He also deeply admired the monumental stone architecture of Central Asia, pre-historic Anatolia, and Ottoman monuments, not for their decorative programs, but for what he saw as "the beauty of their

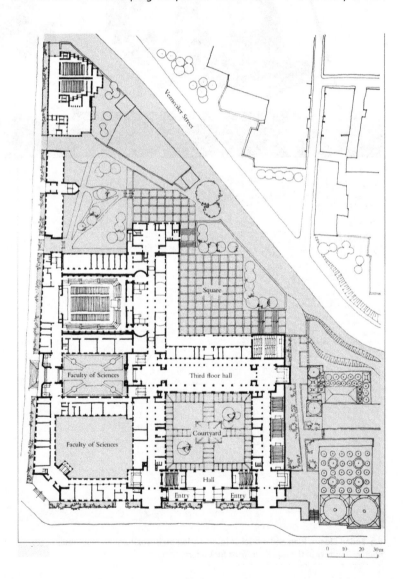

6.4 Sedad Eldem. Plan of the Faculty of Sciences and Literature, Istanbul University, 1942.
Source: Courtesy of the Aga Khan Trust for Culture, Geneva.

6.5 Sedad Eldem. Main
façade of the Faculty of
Sciences and Literature,
Istanbul University,
1942.
Source: Courtesy of the Aga
Khan Trust for Culture,
Geneva.

structure, space and massing." In the 1940s, these latter influences, combined with his admiration for the New German Architecture exhibition brought to Turkey by Paul Bonatz in 1943, unfolded in his work as a more monumental and overtly classical tendency, conforming to the nationalist cultural politics of the time. It was only after the dramatic transformation of Turkish politics and culture in the 1950s that Eldem dropped the term "nationalist" to designate his work and appropriated the term "regionalist" instead.

Building on the Historical Peninsula

Until as late as the mid-twentieth century, Istanbul's historic peninsula was characterized by a dense urban texture of houses and gardens punctuated by the contrasting scale and public character of imperial mosques, baths, and bazaars. Photographs reproduced in Eldem's *Reminiscences of Istanbul* testify to this tightly knit relationship between the more anonymous fabric and the larger monuments. In such areas as around Hagia Sophia, houses were literally huddled against the monuments before the nineteenth-century Ottoman modernizers cleaned and opened up the area around the mosque. In his recent urban history of Istanbul, Doğan Kuban argues that until the nineteenth century, public urban space did not exist in Ottoman and Islamic planning concepts and that the private was always more important than the public, which was "a residual space."[8] Whether this argument is historically accurate or not, it is well known that the modernization of the city in the late nineteenth century introduced efforts to open up urban spaces along European models and small-scale interventions to regularize the street patterns.[9] These new "European aspirations" of the Empire also brought proposals for "grand projects," like the French architect Bouvard's unimplemented 1902 scheme to reorganize Beyazit Square in a manner utterly alien to culture and topography.

Sedad Eldem's 1938 project for a small urban intervention for the same Beyazit Square can be read as a critical statement against the very idea of the "grand project" and in favor of restoring the historical character and scale of the Ottoman urban space. In this proposal, the walls of the Beyazit Mosque are restored; the *medrese* on the opposite side is surrounded by small shops in an

[8] Doğan Kuban, *Istanbul: An Urban History*, Istanbul, Turkish Economic and Social History Foundation, 1996, pp. 368–369.
[9] See Zeynep Çelik, *The Remaking of Istanbul: Portrait of an Ottoman City in the Nineteenth Century*, Seattle, University of Washington Press, 1986.

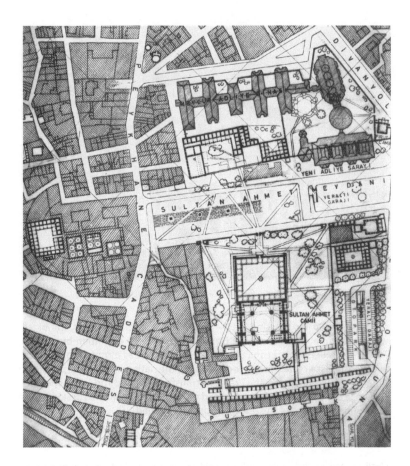

6.6 Sedad Eldem. Site plan, Istanbul Palace of Justice, 1948.
Source: Courtesy of the Aga Khan Trust for Culture, Geneva.

assembly of narrow streets and courtyards with a small yet prominently located coffeehouse.[10] The latter is a recurrent type in Eldem's career, repeated in the *Çamlıca* (1941) and *Taçşlık* (1948) coffeehouse projects. Although for Eldem, the idea of the city is associated with notions of order and discipline (hence his play on the word *polis* as both "city" and "police"), what he advocated was a specific order distilled through history and culture, not superimposed on the city in a grand gesture.[11] On the other hand, this sensitivity to the scale and history of the *medrese* is compromised in the Beyazit Square proposal by the vehicular traffic cutting through the square – a gesture of modern urbanism that can be seen as a reflection of the contradictory undercurrents in Eldem's thinking.

His first major built project on the historical peninsula is the Faculty of Sciences and Literature of Istanbul University (1942–43), designed in collaboration with Emin Onat (1908–61) and at the height of Eldem's close relationship with Paul Bonatz. The scheme is conceived as a system of quadrangles and open courtyards that were labeled as "*taçşlık*" to highlight the analogy to the stone-paved courtyards of traditional houses. The site plan illustrates a sensitivity to the historical context, especially the relationship of the main entry block along Ordu Caddesi to adjacent historical structures – the Beyazit Bath (*hamam*) and the Hasan Pasa Medrese with a stepped "inner street" between them culminating at the fountain (*sebil*) of the *medrese*. The two monumental façades of the scheme are arranged at right angles along the two main avenues to give a more urban and institutional façade to them. In contrast, the scheme "opens

[10] [Editor's note] During the Ottoman period, the *medrese* was a superior school or even university, located in the immediate surroundings of the mosques. These were not only religious complexes but also genuine centers of social life, which also grouped hamans, libraries, collective kitchens, etc.

[11] *Sedad Hakkı Eldem, 50 Yıllık Meslek Jübilesi*, p. 21.

up" at the back with a series of courtyards and open spaces towards the Vezneciler Caddesi, beyond which an old neighborhood was designated for preservation.

The entire project is the first large-scale demonstration of Eldem's nationalist agenda – a translation of his "Turkish house" paradigm from the residential scale to the scale of a monumental institutional building. The main façade of the building along Ordu Caddesi is particularly illustrative: it is an elongated version of Eldem's traditional Turkish house, blown-up in scale and lifted above a monumental colonnade on the ground level, making clear allusions to Paul Bonatz's Stuttgart Railway Station (1912–28). The materials and façade characteristics of the building – especially the alternating layers of brick and stone along the Recşit Paşa Caddesi elevation and in the courtyards – replicate the traditional Ottoman walling techniques that Eldem had studied as a student.

The next project, the Palace of Justice (1948–71), which engaged Eldem on and off for more than twenty years, is located in the heart of the historical peninsula

6.7 *Above* and *Below*: Sedad Eldem. Panoramic elevation of the project within the context, and site plan, Social Security Administration Complex, Zeyrek, Istanbul, 1962–64.
Source: Courtesy of the Aga Khan Trust for Culture, Geneva.

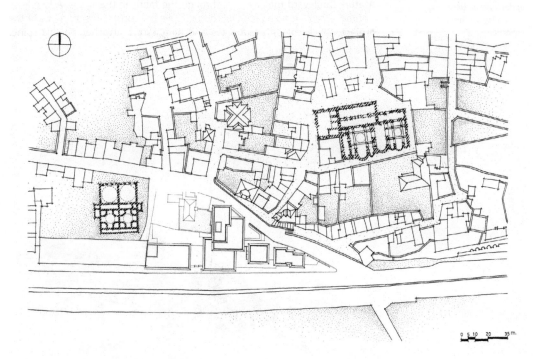

0 5 10 20   35 m.

on the Sultanahmet Square, in close proximity to major Byzantine and Ottoman monuments. It was designed in collaboration with Emin Onat as a competition entry in 1948, with Paul Bonatz as a member of the competition jury. What is urbanistically significant is the response of the scheme to its overpowering historical context in terms of scale and silhouette. The concern for the Sultanahmet Square elevation is evident on the drawings, especially in the careful adjustment of the roofline of the scheme behind the historical Ibrahim Paşa Palace on the square. The faint superimposition of the outline of the Blue Mosque on this elevation suggests an effort not to raise the new scheme above the level of the mosque's dome system. From this initial scheme, only the long backbone of the project behind the Ibrahim Paşa Palace was built, containing offices and courtrooms. The two larger blocks towards Divanyolu were not built when construction was interrupted due to archeological finds excavated on the site. Much later in 1978, Eldem proposed to raise the blocks above the level of the excavated ruins and to shelter the excavated Byzantine rotunda and church under light structures like a geodesic dome and a tent structure, respectively. These later (and unrealized) proposals are interesting, if not as successful for Eldem, as evidence of the profound problems of building in historical areas with layers of urban archeology to be reckoned with. In that respect, Istanbul, like Rome, is a "collage city" par excellence, and the multiplicity of layers (from Roman and Byzantine to Ottoman and Republican) complicates the issue of what exactly constitutes the city's urban identity.

Finally, the most acclaimed "contextualist" scheme of Eldem on the historical peninsula is the Social Security Administration Complex in Zeyrek (1962–64), the winner of a prestigious Aga Khan Award in 1986. The site is in close proximity to the Roman aqueduct and the Byzantine church of St. Pantocrator and is surrounded by one of the few remaining traditional neighborhoods of Istanbul, with its narrow streets and vernacular wooden houses. The complex of offices and shops are situated on a triangular lot where the Zeyrek slope meets the Atatürk Boulevard that was cut through the fabric in the 1940s. A two level "interior street" running parallel to the boulevard constitutes the spine of the project. Blocks of different sizes and heights are attached to this spine,

6.8 *Yalı* **houses.**
Source: A.I. Melling, *Voyage Pittoresque de Constantinople et des Rives du Bosphore,* Paris, 1819. Author's collection.

conforming to the topography of the site sloping upwards towards the old neighborhoods of Zeyrek. More than in any other project by Eldem, here we see the buildings actually "climbing the site" in fragmented blocks and abandoning the more monumental and "classical" expression of his other buildings on the peninsula. The explanation largely resides in chronology and the shift in the architectural culture at large, from the nationalist classicism of the 1940s to a more "humanized" and contextual modernism of the 1960s.

Along the Banks of the Bosphorus

In Istanbul, the houses of the wealthy Ottoman elite were primarily of two variants of the same type. The *konak*, also sketched and admired by Le Corbusier during his *Voyage d'Orient* of 1911, was a large house inside a garden, with only its upper floor visible from the street. The *yalı*, the primary source of inspiration for Sedad Eldem, was a uniquely Istanbul variant of the type, located on the water's edge along the Bosphorus and giving a full view of the house to the boats passing by. Among many other literary and visual accounts of these *yalıs* in sketches, engravings, and later postcards, Ignace Melling's *Voyage pittoresque de Constantinople et des rives du Bosphore* (1819) is an invaluable documentation of the eighteenth-century Bosphorus and was a source of inspiration for Eldem throughout his career. Scholars connect the proliferation of these *yalıs*, pavilions, and kiosks along the water in the eighteenth century to the development of new aesthetic sensibilities in the Empire and to the ritualistic significance of the Bosphorus as "a theater of life" in the manner of Venice's Grand Canal.[12] Melling's engravings bear testimony to the lightness and airiness of these structures with ample windows projecting above the water.[13] The most elaborate examples of these *yalıs*, like the Sadullah Pasa and Koçeoglu *yalıs* in Çengelköy from the eighteenth century or the Hasip Paşşa Yalısı in Beylerbeyi (nineteenth century), were meticulously studied and documented by Eldem. The oldest one of them, Amcazade Hüseyin Pasa *yalisi* (1689) was a particularly inspirational model. His most celebrated signature work, the Taçşlık Coffee House (1947–48) is a reinforced concrete replica of this *yalı*, not on the water's edge like the original but on a hill overlooking the Bosphorus on the opposite side.

Eldem's own designs for his early *yalıs* in the 1930s reflect his reliance upon the traditional plan typologies, especially the *karnıyarık* plan with the internal hall (*sofa*) clearly expressed on the outside. In the Ayaşlı Yalısı in Beylerbeyi of 1938, the *sofa* projects towards the sea above the ground floor, while in the Tahsin Günel Yalısı of the same year in Yeniköy, the *sofa* is differentiated by a curved and recessed façade. It is, however, after the late 1950s that Eldem's lifelong reputation as the signature architect of the Bosphorus *yalıs* was made. A paradigmatic example is the Suna Kıraç Yalısı in Vaniköy (1965), which continues the "inner *sofa* type" of the 1930s work, but elevates this idea to a pristine, almost Miesian expression with the "house-object" standing on a paved platform. This treatment of the house as a free-standing object on a platform or terrace is repeated in his Uşaklıgil Villa in Emirgan (1956–65), Bayramoglu Yalısı in Kandilli (1969–74), and later in his villa for Turkey's top industrialist, Rahmi Koç, on a Tarabya hill overlooking the Bosphorus. The latter was conceived as part of a series of villas, each designed as a free-standing object on its own terrace and separated from others by a series of terraces and garden walls. This attitude testifies to Eldem's "classical" rather than "contextual" premises.

On the other hand, wherever the constraints of the site did not allow a spacious application of the traditional plan types, Eldem could be more conforming to

[12] Shirine Hamadeh, "The City's Pleasures: Architectural Sensibility in Eighteenth Century Istanbul," Ph.D. Dissertation, MIT, 1998; Tülay Artan, "Architecture as a Theater of Life: Profile of the Eighteenth Century Bosphorus," Ph.D. Dissertation, MIT, 1988.
[13] Antoine Ignace Melling, *Voyage pittoresque de Constantinople et des rives du Bosphore*, Paris, 1819.

6.9 (*Above*) Sedad Eldem. Front view of Tacşlık Coffee House, Istanbul, 1947–48.
Source: Courtesy of the Aga Khan Trust for Culture, Geneva.

6.10 (*Above right*) Sedad Eldem. Suna Kıraç Yalı House, Vaniköy, 1965.
Source: Courtesy of the Aga Khan Trust for Culture, Geneva (photo Engin Yenal).

the topography and to the specificity of the site. An interesting example of this is Semsettin Sirer Yalısı in Yenikoy (1966–67) built on a narrow lot with an adjoining building and the program distributed over four different levels. While there is no recognizable traditional plan type or *sofa* in this *yalı*, the house steps down from the entry level of the street behind to the sea level in the front. Also an effort is made to match the height of the roof and upper balconies of the adjacent building.

The role of patronage is of great importance in Eldem's career along the Bosphorus. He was uniquely the architect of Istanbul's wealthiest and most elite sector of businessmen, industrialists, and professionals. In the same manner that the historical Bosphorus *yalıs* were built for the old Ottoman elite of prominent pashas, princesses, and dignitaries, Eldem's villas and *yalıs* were in particular demand by a new elite clientele with sophisticated tastes and a strong consciousness of historical heritage. Collectively, these villas and *yalıs*, along with others built in the same idiom by Eldem's colleagues and students, comprise a recognizable "Bosphorus style," seeking to reconstruct partial memories of Melling's picturesque Bosphorus wherever possible. However, although the architecture of individual *yalıs* along the edge of the water attain some measure of success in this enterprise, the dramatic transformation of the Bosphorus hills with high-rise apartments and rapidly diminishing greenery marks the failure of the enterprise in urbanistic terms. When compared with the old photographs, contemporary views of the Bosphorus, even with the celebrated Eldem *yalıs* in the foreground, testify to the limitations of Eldem's typological program when it is not complemented by and extended to a concern with urban morphology and urban context. After all his efforts of codifying an architecture that is informed by historical context and precedent, that context has rapidly and irreversibly disappeared in many parts of the city and his villas remain isolated objects.

The Question of Contextualism and Regionalism

As the leading modern Turkish architect whose work is directly informed by and responsive to Istanbul's cultural and historical heritage, Eldem is arguably a "contextualist" architect if the term is understood to be the opposite of "international style modernism" or, more recently, of "globalized post-modernism." By the same token, he is frequently characterized as a "regionalist" architect whose work represents something uniquely "Turkish" in the way that Hassan Fathy is an "Egyptian architect" or Luis Barragán is a "Mexican archi-tect." Eldem himself has often associated his work with the term "regionalism," especially after his earlier quest for a "national architecture" became ideologically problematic in the aftermath of the Second World War. However, I will propose that Eldem's typological approach and rationalist methodology differentiates him from the more *empirical* premises of an architecture that is shaped exclusively by the local context and regional considerations. Eldem's work is profoundly "at home" in Istanbul, informed by the city's historical heritage. But his program for a systematic codification of a modern Turkish architecture, based on Turkish precedents, was put forward as a much larger claim to represent the nation as a whole.

In an unorthodox, critical and, most importantly, *empirical* understanding of what modern architecture means, form is not supposed be an a priori stylistic choice, but a consequence of *rational* considerations of program, site, soil, climate, budget, and materials. It is very important to note that "rational" here designates simply "reasonable," that is, form as a "logical" response to given circumstances rather than to pre-given precedents or established rules. This was the definition of "rationalism" in the teachings of the German-speaking modernist architects in early Republican Turkey, Ernst Egli and Bruno Taut in particular, who regarded "context" as the key word to "nationalize" modern architecture in Turkey. By contrast, Eldem's program is best characterized as *rationalist* (or the opposite of *empirical* in philosophical terms) in the sense that he departs from the existence of certain culturally and historically established

6.11 Sedad Eldem. Rahmi Koç Villa, Tarabya, 1975–80.
Source: Courtesy of the Aga Khan Trust for Culture, Geneva.

14 As in the case of his Indian (1965–68) and Dutch (1973–77) embassy residences in Ankara.
15 Sedad Eldem, "Gelenekselle Yasçamak ve Yeniden Insça Etmek" in *Sedad Hakkı Eldem: 50 Yıllık Meslek Jübilesi*, p. 44.

a priori constructs whose validity persists over time. As in the case of his Bosphorus *yalıs* or his recurrent use of the tall slender columns, historical precedents that have inspired his work are abstracted into a set of basic "types" that transcend specific examples, specific programs, and specific historical periods. The central *sofa* plan type of the traditional wooden house and the modular grid regulating the elevation are, for example, major transhistorical and acontextual formal categories in Eldem's work, applicable to a modern villa on the Bosphorus, a coffeehouse in Istanbul, or an embassy building in Ankara.[14] Independent of site, program, or scale, Eldem's work displays its characteristic uniformity, making it a "signature style" against his own desire for "blending naturally with the context" in the way traditional buildings do.[15]

Few would question Eldem's strong preoccupation with historical and cultural context. Yet contextualism also involves the *physical* context: topography and urban form in particular. As I have already explained, with the exception of the Social Security offices, Eldem's buildings are in essence classical object-types – free-standing and complete in their own rationality. His sketch elevation for the Tarabya villas mentioned above shows the conspicuous object-ness of each villa, very different from the historical views of the same Tarabya shore and hills in which the overall impact is one of a continuous fabric or clusters of houses among greenery. Eldem is ultimately the designer of individual houses, *yalıs*, and villas, rather than of *housing* or urban fabrics. It cannot be overlooked that his interest in and documentation of traditional houses are predominantly limited to the analytical study of plan types and formal elements of individual houses, rather than studies in urban morphology in traditional towns. Largely missing from Eldem's own villas is the feeling of the traditional streets of Istanbul, Bursa, Safranbolu, Antalaya, and other Turkish cities, where ideal types are deformed, manipulated, and adapted to the street, the slope, the views, the property lines, and existing elements like trees and fountains.

"Regionalism" too is a difficult term to apply to Eldem's program, which was conceived and elaborated at the height of Turkish nation building under a unitary

6.12 Sedad Eldem. Sketch for a group of private villas overlooking the Tarabya Bay, Bosphorus, c.1970.
Source: Courtesy of the Aga Khan Trust for Culture, Geneva.

6.13 Sedad Eldem.
Semsettin Sirer Yalı
House, Yeniköy,
1966–67.
Source: Courtesy of the Aga
Khan Trust for Culture,
Geneva.

state. Regionalism, before everything else, is about *diversity* of expression, especially in a country like Turkey with at least five different geographical regions with different particularities of climate, terrain, local materials, and indigenous building traditions. Under the unique historical circumstances of Kemalist nation building however, the emphasis was on *uniformity* rather than diversity. Hence local and "sub-national" affiliations implied in a regionalist sensibility were as ideologically problematic as the supranational connotations of the "international style." Sedad Eldem expressed this as follows:

> Local architecture is not necessarily national architecture. People of a nation may be living in different regions and consequently building different houses but this does not make all of them national architecture.[16]

His Turkish house, the only one that qualified as "national architecture," was a highly developed and rationalized type spread over a vast geography of humid climates and fertile lands – hence the timber construction and pitched roofs. As distinct from other local vernaculars and building traditions, including stone and the mud brick/adobe of central, eastern and southeastern Turkey (and the Mediterranean basin of nearby Greece as well), it is an idealized type that deliberately transcends regional or local variants and evokes the character of "Turkishness" irreducible to these variants.

In conclusion, Eldem's work is ultimately less "contextualist" and "regionalist" than it is "classic" in the true etymological sense of the term, which means "authoritative works for study," "timeless," and open to formal and stylistic reappropriations beyond the life and career of the architect. If Eldem's idea of a tradition-conscious, modern architecture for Istanbul was based on a typological and formal reinterpretation of historical "originals," his own work constitutes the new "originals" today, in high demand by Istanbul's *nouveau riche*. Numerous developer schemes for exclusive villas on the Bosphorus and gated communities in the suburbs of Istanbul have proliferated in recent years, most of them featuring the "Turkish house" style initially popularized by Eldem. His characteristic overhanging roofs, projecting window bays on the upper level, and the modular rows of windows can now be seen in countless lesser examples, endlessly reproduced in ads for luxury villas. The villas of Kemer Country, the coding of which bears the signature of Duany Plater-Zyberk & Company, are only the most upscale, famous, and expensive of these developments, which are symptomatic of postmodern urbanism as Istanbul

[16] Eldem, "Türk Evi," in *Sedad Hakkı Eldem: 50 Yıllık Meslek Jübilesi*, p. 16.

17 On this point, see Sibel Bozdogan, "Vernacular Architecture and Identity Politics: The Case of the Turkish House," in *Traditional Dwellings and Settlements Review*, no. 2, Spring 1996, pp. 7–18.

joins other cities in the early twenty-first century global market system. Whereas Eldem's work was the product of a lifelong study of historical precedents with an analytical rigor, these more recent examples appropriate only the imagery of the "Turkish house" as an instant identity kit.[17] Perhaps the largest irony of Eldem's career is that after his quest for a culturally relevant, almost "anonymous" architecture that would "blend in" with Istanbul's traditional character, his buildings have ultimately become self-referential precious objects, context-free and repeatable. The traditional "Turkish house" is now just one stylistic choice among many (Kemer Country also has Italianate villas, English houses, and even American "log cabins"); and in today's Istanbul, the idea of a unified, tradition-conscious urban identity is increasingly fragmented by the plurality of class, social status, taste, cultures, and world view.   ∎

Part II
NORTH

40 Stuttgart. Weissenhofsiedlung, Araberdorf

7

THE ANTI-MEDITERRANEAN IN THE LITERATURE OF MODERN ARCHITECTURE

Paul Schultze-Naumburg's *Kulturarbeiten*

Kai K. Gutschow

In the heated battles to define modern architecture in Germany at the beginning of the twentieth century, well-chosen propaganda images played a vital role in shaping public opinion as well as the profession.[1] Architects on all sides of the debates used the nascent media culture of the day to make their often complex arguments memorable and easily understood. Many of the most potent images were created in the wake of Stuttgart's large Weissenhof housing exhibition of 1927, designed by an all-star cast of modern architects from around Europe. Walter Curt Behrendt's well-known book from the same year, for example, used a heroic, flag-waving view of the Weissenhof Siedlung to pronounce the "victory of the new building style."[2] Similar images were strategically placed on the covers and title pages of books by Ludwig Hilberseimer, Adolf Behne, and the German Werkbund to celebrate the arrival of modern architecture.[3]

Although less well known, German adversaries of the new style of architecture were just as effective in promoting their opposing messages, often with similar images, though in very different contexts. In his popular book, *Das Gesicht des deutschen Hauses* (The Face of the German House, 1929), for example, the German architect and critic Paul Schultze-Naumburg contrasted a view of the Weissenhof Siedlung with a picturesque view of a seaside village on the Greek island of Santorini.[4] For readers in search of the Mediterranean ideal in modern architecture, the images offer evidence of how closely related the whitewashed, asymmetrically sited, flat-roofed, rectangular prisms of modern architecture in Germany were to timeless forms of the Mediterranean vernacular. Similar comparisons with Italian vernacular architecture were later used by Italian modernists such as Giovanni Michelucci to demonstrate the Mediterranean roots and timeless values of their forms.[5]

But the context of Schultze-Naumburg's illustrations produced a very different reading. He offered the comparative photographic images as proof of the "foreign" and stylized forms of modern architecture. The new architecture, he argued, was "un-German" in its physiognomy, and incompatible with the rainy, snowy, and cold northern climate. He claimed that the flat roofs and simple cubic forms had been developed in the "Orient," in the heat of the Mediterranean, and that they were culturally inappropriate and functionally unfit for the hills of Stuttgart.[6] The parallels of modern architecture to foreign forms were, for Schultze-Naumburg, signs of a "disruption" or "derailment" of the natural evolution of good German architecture, and perhaps even indications of the "demise" of the soul of the German *Volk*.[7] His critique aligned with other conservative critics who lambasted the modernist housing development as an "Arab Village" or a "Little Jerusalem," or as "Bolshevik" in

[1] Parts of this essay were delivered at the 2001 SAH conference in Toronto; at "The Other Modern" conference in Capri, Italy, in 1998; and at the 1992 IASTE conference in Paris, France. Portions were published as "Schultze-Naumburg's *Heimat*: A Nationalist Conflict of Tradition and Modernity," *Traditional Dwellings and Settlements: Working Papers* 36, 1, 1992: 1–36.

[2] Walter Curt Behrendt, *Der Sieg des neuen Baustils*, Stuttgart, Akademischer Verlag Dr. Fritz Wedekind, 1927; translated by Harry Francis Mallgrave as *The Victory of the New Building Style*, Santa Monica, Getty, 2000.

[3] Ludwig Hilberseimer, *Internationale Neue Baukunst*, no. 2, Stuttgart, Verlag J. Hoffmann, 1927; Adolf Behne, *Eine Stunde Architektur*, Stuttgart, Akademischer Verlag Dr. Fritz Wedekind, 1928; Deutscher Werkbund (ed.), *Bau und Wohnung: die Bauten der Weissenhofsiedlung n Stuttgart*, Bücher der Form, Stuttgart, F. Wedekind, 1927.

[4] Paul Schultze-Naumburg, *Das Gesicht des deutschen Hauses*, Stuttgart, G. W. Callwey, 1929.

[5] Richard Etlin, *Modernism in Italian Architecture, 1890–1940*, Cambridge, The MIT Press, 1991, pp. 297–312; Giovanni Michelucci, "Fonti della moderna architettura Italiana," in *Domus* August 1932, pp. 460–461. See also in this volume the essay by Michelangelo Sabatino.

[6] In German, the "Orient" tended to mean the Near and Middle East, synonymous with much of the Arab-Islamic cultural world, and in the context of this book, the Eastern Mediterranean. Unlike the English

7.1 (*Far left*) Postcard of the Weissenhof as Arab Village, highlighting the "foreign" and "Mediterranean" nature of modern architecture.
Source: © Stadtarchiv Stuttgart, Sammlung Weissenhof.

word, it does not usually include East Asia, Southeast Asia, or South Asia. As Schultze-Naumburg used it, it often had an even more general meaning of "East," and seemed to include all that was east of the German and Austrian-Hungarian empires, down to the Caucasus and the eastern Mediterranean. For the influences of "the Orient" on modern architecture, see Simone Hain, "'Ex oriente lux'. Deutschland und der Osten," in Romana Schenider and Vittorio Magnano Lampugnani (eds.), *Moderne Architektur in Deutschland 1900 bis 1950: Reform und Tradition*, Stuttgart, Frankfurt, Hatje, 1992; Francesco Passanti, "The Vernacular, Modernism, and Le Corbusier," in *Journal of the Society of Architectural Historians* 56, no. 4, 1997, pp. 443, 449 n. 27; revised slightly in Maiken Umbach and Bernd-Rüdiger Hüppauf (eds.), *Vernacular Modernism: Heimat, Globalization, and the Built Environment*, Stanford, Stanford University Press, 2005.
[7] Schultze-Naumburg, *Das Gesicht des deutschen Hauses*, p. 5.
[8] Karin Kirsch, *The Weissenhofsiedlung. Experimental Housing Built for the Deutscher Werkbund, Stuttgart, 1927*, New York, Rizzoli, 1989, pp. 199–200; Richard Pommer and Christian Otto, *Weissenhof 1927 and the Modern Movement in Architecture*, Chicago, University of Chicago Press, 1991, pp. 138ff.; Barbara Miller-Lane, *Architecture and Politics in Germany, 1918–1945*, Cambridge, MA, Harvard University Press, 1985 (1st edn. 1968), pp. 125ff.
[9] Paul Schultze-Naumburg and Walter Gropius, "Wer hat Recht? Traditionelle Baukunst oder Bauen in neuen Formen. Zwei sich widersprechende Ansichten," in *Der Uhu* 2, no. 7, 1926, pp. 30–40, 103–113, here p. 40.
[10] Magdalena Bushart, *Der Geist der Gotik und die expressionistische Kunst*, Munich, Silke Schreiber, 1990.
[11] Paul Schultze-Naumburg, *Hausbau*, Kulturarbeiten 1, Munich, G. W. Callwey, 1903 (1st edn. 1901), p. 35.

spirit.[8] A famous photo montage sold as a postcard made visible these critiques, showing an "Arab" street market, complete with camels and lions, in the streets of the Weissenhof development.

These and other anti-Mediterranean critiques of modern architecture were but part of a long-running media campaign that Schultze-Naumburg had been maintaining both individually and in unison with some of Germany's most influential cultural reform organizations. As will be discussed in the essay below, the origins of these attacks, both the content and the graphic techniques, go back to the nineteenth-century discussions about German identity and national character, and in the case of Schultze-Naumburg, to the start of his career as an Arts and Crafts artist. What began as an attempt to work against the eclecticism and "soulless" design in the 1890s, soon took on profound implications for shaping the development of modern architecture in Germany. The attacks against foreign influences, and the associated propaganda techniques, became ever more harsh and polarizing after 1925, as the seemingly alien modern architecture and design gained footholds in Germany, not just with the avant-garde, but with municipal governments, non-profit housing associations, worker-clubs, and the general public. Although often framed in the modernist arguments about form and function, protests against the "New Building" (*Neues Bauen*) increasingly revealed a deep-seated nationalism, racism, and anti-Semitism, even where there were no overt Jewish or Mediterranean connections.

Just a few months before the Weissenhof exhibition, for example, the populist journal *Der Uhu* commissioned Schultze-Naumburg and Walter Gropius to debate their different positions on modern architecture in the article "Who is Right? Traditional building-art or building in new forms?" Schultze-Naumburg claimed that German architects had divided into two camps: those that consciously rejected their Nordic heritage for exotic precedents, and those that sought to rekindle time-tested German building conventions. The two positions were clearly illustrated in the comparative images throughout the article, pitting the "New Building" of Gropius, Mies van der Rohe, Le Corbusier, and Karl Schneider against some of Schultze-Naumburg's own country-house designs. In his text, Schultze-Naumburg, expressed frustration at seeing how many German architects "did not feel drawn through their bloodline, to the Nordic family of forms," and that so many modern houses around him were based on what he felt were "East Asian, Indian, or Negro" precedents.[9] The many modern artists and architects inspired by cultures from the "Orient," from the Far and Near East, and from the Mediterranean basin, only confirmed Schultze-Naumburg's opposition to the new architecture and bias against the Mediterranean.

Instead, Schultze-Naumburg implored Germans to reconnect to their own Nordic traditions. But what was "German" or "Nordic" architecture? The question has a long, complicated history, and is one of the key – but now often overlooked – questions that helped define the development of modern architecture in Germany. Germans since Goethe had promoted the Gothic as homegrown and suitably nordic in character, a sentiment revived in the twentieth century by Expressionist artists, Gropius's early Bauhaus, and others.[10] But Schultze-Naumburg conceded that Germans had always had a fascination with, and even a special penchant for, assimilating aspects of foreign and even exotic cultures, beginning with classicism in the Renaissance. He himself favored a simplified, bourgeois classicism, which he claimed had, over time, been "made German."[11] His single-minded attempt to revive local vernacular conventions

7.2 The Greek island of Mykonos above a view of the Weissenhof Siedlung, Stuttgart, with Hans Scharoun's house to the left. To the right, the large apartment building designed by Stuttgart-School architect Karl Beer, begun after the official Weissenhof project.
Source: Paul Schultze-Naumburg, *Das Gesicht des deutschen Hauses*, 1929.

for a modern German architecture caused him to overlook the fact that other critics saw classicism as a "Southern" import, not unlike Santorini. The Jewish modernist architect Erich Mendelsohn, who came under increasing attack by conservatives, later chided Schultze-Naumburg for conveniently "overlooking" the fact that the Mediterranean was the basis for all Western culture.[12]

The Search for a Modern Architecture

Schultze-Naumburg's indictment of Mediterranean architecture arose from a host of interrelated theoretical and personal beliefs. During the first decades of the newly established German Reich, a pervasive romantic nationalism led many artists and ideologues such as Schultze-Naumburg to "invent" traditions for the new country.[13] As a leader in the German Arts and Crafts movement, and the director of an important regional applied arts workshop, he also had a cultural and business interest in promoting local craft traditions. In a rapidly globalizing world, organizations such as the German Werkbund and the German Heimatschutzbund (Homeland Protection Association) – both of which he helped found – sought to define the hallmarks of what it meant to be "Made in Germany."[14] This trend eventually overlapped with a rising interest in cultural anthropology as well as eugenics as a way of sorting out what was "local" and "authentic."

[12] Erich Mendelsohn, "Neu-Athen," in *Berliner Tageblatt* no. 261, June 5, 1931; republished in Ita Heinze-Greenberg and Regina Stephan (eds.), *Erich Mendelsohn. Gedankenwelten. Unbekannte Texte zu Architektur, Kulturgeschichte und Politik*, Ostfildern-Ruit, Hatje-Kantz, 2000, pp. 118–119. See also the essay by Ita Heinze-Greenberg in this volume.
[13] Barbara Miller-Lane, *National Romanticism and Modern Architecture in Germany and the Scandinavian Countries*, Cambridge, Cambridge University Press, 2000; Jacek Purchla and Wolf Tegethoff (eds.), *Nation, Style, Modernism*, Cracow, Munich, Zentralinstitut für Kunstgeschichte, 2006.
[14] Frederic Schwartz, *The Werkbund*, New Haven, Yale University Press, 1996; Mark Jarzombek, "The Kunstgewerbe, the Werkbund, and the Aesthetics of Culture in the Wilhelmine Period," in *Journal of the Society of Architectural Historians* 53, no. 1, 1994, pp. 7–19; Mark Jarzombek, "The Discourse of a Bourgeois Utopia," in Francois Forster-Hahn (ed.), *Imagining Modern German Culture*, Studies in the History of Art, 53, Washington, DC, National Gallery of Art, 1996.

WER HAT RECHT?

Traditionelle Baukunst oder

Bauen in neuen Formen

Zwei sich widersprechende Ansichten
Von
Prof. Schultze-Naumburg
und
Walter Gropius, dem Leiter des „Bauhauses" in Dessau

Moderne Baukunst: Straßenfront des Wohnhauses Michaelsen bei Hamburg
in gekalktem Backstein. Von Architekt Karl Schneider

Traditionelle Baukunst: Landhaus Otto von Mendelssohns bei Potsdam
Von Professor Schultze-Naumburg

Der Kampf um die Entwicklung der Baukunst wogt hin und her. Vertreten einer traditionellen Architektur stehen Architekten gegenüber, die grundsätzlich jede überlieferte Form verwerfen. Während die neue Form sich für neue Schöpfung der Technik von selbst ergibt, ist z. B. die Frage noch unentschieden, ob auch unsere Wohnhäuser radikal in neuen Formen gebaut werden müssen. Wir geben je einem prominenten Vertreter beider Richtungen das Wort.

7.3 Cover page of the article "Who is Right?" by Schultze-Naumburg and Gropius comparing the *Neues Bauen* to a more traditional country house.
Source: *Der Uhu*, vol. 2, 1926.

Schultze-Naumburg's own attempt to define a German modern architecture began just before the turn of the century, when as a 29-year-old German painter, designer, and critic he complained, "We have no modern house."[15] By modern he meant "realistic . . . [in tune with] the ideals of our own time."[16] In contrast to the sham architecture of the mid- to late nineteenth century, which he felt too often merely copied historical architecture, he sought modern (from the Latin *modo* meaning "of the day") buildings that were functional, clear, contemporary, and local. Set on his mission, Schultze-Naumburg launched a thirty-year propaganda campaign to create a reformed architecture specific to, and appropriate for, modern Germany.

He began with the premise that good art and architecture grow naturally out of a specific combination of place, culture, and time. He speculated that over a long period of time, generations of anonymous designers, craftsmen, and end-users defined a vernacular tradition that derived from the most fundamental physical as well as spiritual ideals and needs of the local people (*Volk*). Where architectural elements could not be tied to specifically German traditions, Schultze-Naumburg postulated affinities to a broader "Nordic" race, culture, and climate that included England, Scandinavia, and greater Germany. In the course of this natural evolution, specific forms were adapted constantly to changing needs and conditions, but the overall essence resisted the swings of style, fashion, and the willful manipulation by individuals. Functional and material needs of the moment were always met, he proclaimed, balanced with the immaterial qualities necessary to create an appropriate home.

15 Paul Schultze-Naumburg, *Häusliche Kunstpflege*, Leipzig, Eugen Diederichs, 1899, p. 1.
16 Ibid., pp. 1–3.

At the heart of Schultze-Naumburg's early campaign to define a modern architecture lay his multi-volume *Kulturarbeiten* (Cultural Works) books, begun in 1900, and which opened with the following statement:

> The purpose [of these books] is to work against the terrible devastation of our country in all areas of visible culture. Through a constant repetition of good and bad examples, the books are to force even the most untrained eyes to compare and to think. Furthermore, they are to reawaken an awareness of the good work done before the mid-nineteenth century, and in such a way help to re-connect and to continue the clear working methods of *tradition*.[17]

For Schultze-Naumburg, the way to a modern German house could be found by using local traditions as a guide, and not images from abroad, as he proposed modern architects had done at the Weissenhof. Clues for continuing traditions were to be found in the most recent "healthy" epoch of German architecture, the vernacular architecture from "around 1800," before the onset of eclectic styles in the mid-nineteenth century.

He made his point more forcefully with a graphic and didactic comparison of two ordinary houses. In considering an older residence near his own home in Saaleck, in central Thuringia, he wrote:

> The one is a simple garden house, no architectural masterpiece, just a plain, friendly house as was completely natural in the eighteenth century [when it was built]. But what grace, what presence, what a *truthful* expression throughout, from the door to the topmost rooftile . . . [The roof's silhouette] is the complete reflection of its function, the bearer of a lofty, airy chamber from which to look out over river and valley beyond.[18]

[17] Schultze-Naumburg, *Hausbau*, n.p. A nearly identical preface was inserted into every volume of the *Kulturarbeiten*, as each was intended to be but an elaboration of the central idea. For biographical information on Schultze-Naumburg and the only extended investigations to date on the *Kulturarbeiten* see the very uncritical Norbert Borrmann, *Paul Schultze-Naumburg 1869–1949. Maler. Publizist. Architekt*, Essen, R. Bacht, 1989; Vittorio Magnano Lampugnani, "From the 'Kulturarbeiten' to the Deutscher Werkbund," Part I of "A History of German Modern Architecture," in *A+U*, no. 259, April 1992; Julius Posener, "Kulturarbeiten," in *Berlin auf dem Wege zu einer neuen Architektur: das Zeitalter Wilhelms II*, Studien zur Kunst des 19. Jahrhunderts, vol. 40, Munich, Prestel, 1979, slightly revised in "Kulturarbeiten," *Arch+*, 72, pp. 35–38.

[18] Paul Schultze-Naumburg, "Kulturarbeiten I," in *Der Kunstwart* 14, no. 1, 1900, pp. 23–24, later in Schultze-Naumburg, *Hausbau*, pp. 14–15.

7.4 The first didactic comparison from Schultze-Naumburg's *Kulturarbeiten*, showing a garden house from "around 1800" that Schultze-Naumburg admired on the left; and a suburban villa from the outskirts of Berlin that he abhorred on the right.
Source: Paul Schultze-Naumburg, *Hausbau*, Kulturarbeiten 1, 1904.

19 Ibid., p. 24.
20 Ibid.
21 Stanford Anderson, "Introduction: Style-Architecture and Building-Art: Realist Architecture as the Vehicle for a Renewal of Culture," in Hermann Muthesius, *Style-Architecture and Building Art: Transformations of Architecture in the Nineteenth-Century and its Present Conditions*, Santa Monica, Getty, 1994, pp. 5ff, 14ff.
22 Schultze-Naumburg's work has been compared to the work of Christopher Alexander, Robert Stern, and Leon Krier; see Borrmann, *Paul Schultze-Naumburg*, pp. 226, 241 n. 898–900; P. Peters, "Robert Stern und der moderne Traditionalismus," in *Baumeister* 83, no. 7, July 1986, pp. 44–61.
23 On the modern and seemingly prescient environmental ideas espoused by Schultze-Naumburg and the *Heimatschutz* organizations, see William H. Rollins, *A Greener Vision of Home. Cultural Politics and Environmental Reform in the German Heimatschutz Movement, 1904–1918*, Ann Arbor, University of Michigan Press, 1997; Matthew Jefferies, "Back to the Future? The *Heimatschutz* Movement in Wilhelmine Germany," in *Politics and Culture in Wilhelmine Germany. The Case of Industrial Architecture*, Oxford and Washington, DC, Berg, 1995; B. Ringbek, "Architektur und Städtebau under dem Einfluß der Heimatbewegung 1918–1945," in Edeltraud Klueting (ed.), *Antimodernismus und Reform. zur Geschichte der deutschen Heimatbewegung*, Darmstadt, Wissenschaftliche Buchgesellschaft, 1991; Christian F. Otto, "Modern Environment and Historical Continuity: The *Heimatschutz* Discourse in Germany," in *Art Journal* 43, no. 2, 1983, pp. 148–157.
24 Borrmann, *Paul Schultze-Naumburg*; Stephanie Barron (ed.), *Degenerate Art. The Fate of the Avant-Garde in Nazi Germany*, Los Angeles, LACMA, 1991.
25 Rolf Peter Sieferle, "Heimatschutz und das Ende der Romantischen Utopie" *Arch+*, no. 81, 1985, pp. 38–42.
26 "Cultural Despair" is a phenomenon with a vast literature, very little of it directly related to architecture or the visual arts. On cultural criticism in Germany see the bibliographic essay by Armin Mohler, *Die Konservative Revolution in Deutschland, 1918–1932*, Darmstadt, Wissenschaftliche Buchgesellschaft, 1989; George L. Mosse, *The Crisis of German Ideology. Intellectual Origins of the Third Reich*, New York, H. Fertig, 1981 (1st edn. 1964); Fritz Stern, *The Politics of Cultural Despair: A Study in the Rise of a Germanic Ideology*, New York, Doubleday, 1961. The *Kulturarbeiten* are not mentioned in any of these works, though Schultze-Naumburg, *Der Kunstwart*, and the *Heimatschutz* organizations were implicated.
27 Kenneth Frampton, *Modern Architecture, A Critical History*, London, Thames and Hudson, 1992, pp.

He admired the straightforward, honest craftsmanship, the functional forms, the fitting relation to the surrounding German landscape, and what he considered a timeless beauty. His analysis of the house covered every level of detail, always in a praiseworthy tone, luring the reader into trusting the inherent goodness of the older, local vernacular architecture of central Germany. He was careful to point out that the two *trompe-l'oeil* windows painted on the upper floor were unfortunate, though characteristic, late nineteenth-century additions.

In comparing the older garden house with a typical villa recently built in one of the mushrooming suburbs of metropolitan Berlin, he decried:

> And now the other. Why do we laugh so? It's not funny, but terribly sad. ... It is the *type* of house that is visible everywhere, hundreds and thousands of them ruthlessly sprouting out of the ruins of a fine, honest, civil, common culture. Yes, it is this "elegant" little house that can be found here in the suburbs of Berlin and nearly everywhere else today.[19]

He proceeded to criticize its abundant and "useless" ornament, rebuking the mixture of "foreign" classical styles that had been "pasted on" by the greedy, speculative builder, and also condemned the smaller, less pleasant, and less functional rooms inside.[20] He commented on a lack of *Sachlichkeit*, or straightforwardness in the design, by which he meant that ideals of clarity and common-sense function had not been rigorously applied in determining the forms of the house.[21] His critique also extended to the siting of the houses: the one rooted in the German landscape, the other part of a carelessly organized subdivision.

This leading comparison introduced the major architectural themes and propaganda methods that Schultze-Naumburg promoted throughout the populist and polemical *Kulturarbeiten*, which he published between 1900 and 1929. His critical view of the international architectural profession, his advocacy of local craft and tradition to combat contemporary architectural ills, and his proselytizing manner have led some historians to see the *Kulturarbeiten* as important links from the vernacular classicism of the nineteenth century to postmodernism and the present.[22] Others have praised the books for first helping draw public attention to the beauty of ordinary, vernacular cultural landscapes, as well as the environment. Schultze-Naumburg's writings were, in fact, instrumental in efforts to establish some of the earliest grassroots national historic preservation movements as well as *Heimatschutz* (homeland protection) organizations supporting the conservation and rehabilitation of man-made and natural environments.[23]

Most often, however, the *Kulturarbeiten* are analyzed in the dark light of Schultze-Naumburg's later, more ideologically motivated writings that made him one of the most rabidly conservative and influential ideologues of Nazi art and architecture.[24] Historians see these early books either as the last gasps of a romantic, backward-looking nineteenth-century historicism,[25] or as proto-Nazi keystones of German anti-modernism, suffering from what Fritz Stern has called the "pathology of cultural despair."[26] Standard histories of modern architecture find Schultze-Naumburg's entire life work, even the early *Kulturarbeiten*, infected with a reactionary, conservative thought that led in a deterministic manner to Nazi architectural ideology.[27]

As part of an effort to trace the anti-Mediterranean sentiments in Schultze-Naumburg's later works, I will argue against interpreting the *Kulturarbeiten* deterministically as cases of "cultural despair" or as Nazi architecture *avant-le-lettre*. Although the *Kulturarbeiten* were without a doubt important precedents to the Nazi ideology that Schultze-Naumburg later helped formulate, their content and format set the stage for a whole range of modern architects and critics who worked during the heyday of the modernist avant-garde in Weimar Germany. They illustrate perfectly one of the paradoxes of this period in Germany: that reformers who maintained very similar architectural theories around the turn of the century went on to espouse radically different ideological and architectural positions by 1933. The line dividing the progressive, forward-looking camp of modern architecture from the conservative, reactionary backward-looking camp, was not nearly as neat as historians working under the specter of Fascism, Stalinism, and the Cold War have at times led us to believe.[28]

By focusing on Schultze-Naumburg's earlier written works, rather than his traditionalist architectural designs or the context of his late eugenic writings, this essay relocates his embrace of local culture and latent anti-Mediterranean attitude within turn-of-the-century debates about modern architectural reform in Germany, in the crux between tradition and progress that led *not only* to a conservative nationalism, *but also* to a functionalist modern architecture after World War I.[29] It demonstrates how Schultze-Naumburg's theories developed out of, and in the long run were instrumental in shaping, a trend in German modern architecture away from foreign traditions and eclectic styles, and towards a valuation of region and place as an important determinant of modern architecture. It thus forms part of a growing body of literature that questions the dominant narrative of modern architecture as based primarily in "functionalism" and "internationalism," and reinforces the revisionist thinking that has begun to reevaluate the importance of place and the vernacular in the formation of modern architecture.[30]

I will focus on three themes to make this point. The first is Schultze-Naumburg's criticism of the contemporary built environment, which he saw as contaminated by "foreign" elements and equated with a weakened national psyche. The second theme involves the identification of a set of timeless ideals and a healthy national tradition within the German *Heimat* (homeland) upon which to graft further development. Third is the need to harness the positive advances wrought by modernization in order to create an architecture both respectful of timeless German tradition and culture, and able to embrace the modern, contemporary world.

Criticism in the *Kulturarbeiten*

Schultze-Naumburg shared with contemporary advocates of a realist and *sachlich* architecture, as well as with later modernist architects and propagandists, a disgust of late nineteenth-century architecture and design. The *Kulturarbeiten* combated three interrelated developments through a concerted effort of criticism and negation. First and foremost, they worked against the stylistic historicism, ornamental eclecticism, and foreign influences that reached its high point in Germany during the building boom of the *Gründerzeit* (founder times), the prosperous years immediately following German unification in 1871. As a new country, and a mix of many cultural groups, he felt Germans were particularly susceptible to being enamored and influenced by foreign ideas.[31]

Instead of imitating the Gothic or the Renaissance styles of the distant past or distant shores, Schultze-Naumburg advocated adopting "realistic" ideals in

217–218; Nikolaus Pevsner, *Pioneers of Modern Design: From William Morris to Walter Gropius*, Harmondsworth, Penguin, 1960 (1st edn. 1936), p. 33.

[28] Miller-Lane, *Architecture and Politics in Germany, 1918–1945*.

[29] On architectural reform in turn-of-the-century Germany see Kai Buchholz (ed.), *Die Lebensreform: Entwürfe zur neugestaltung von Leben und Kunst um 1900*, 2 vols., Darmstadt, Institut Mathildenhöhe, Häusser, 2001; Kevin Repp, *Reformers, Critics, and the Paths of German Modernity*, Cambridge, MA, Harvard University Press, 2000; Gerhard Kratzsch, *Kunstwart und Dürerbund. Ein Beitrag zur Geschichte der Gebildeten im Zeitalter des Imperialismus*, Göttingen, Vandenhoeck u. Ruprecht, 1969.

[30] Umbach and Hüppauf (eds.), *Vernacular Modernism*; Purchla and Tegethoff, *Nation, Style, Modernism*; Jennifer Jenkins, *Provincial Modernity: Local Culture and Liberal Politics in Fin-de-Siècle Hamburg*, Ithaca, Cornell University Press, 2003.

[31] Schultze-Naumburg, *Das Gesicht des deutschen Hauses*, p. 15.

[31] Schultze-Naumburg, *Häusliche Kunstpflege*, pp. 1–3.

[33] Paul Schultze-Naumburg, *Dörfer und Kolonien, Kulturarbeiten* 3, Munich, G. W. Callwey, 1908 (1st edn. 1903), pp. 123–125.

[34] Schultze-Naumburg, *Hausbau*, p. 23; Paul Schultze-Naumburg, *Die Kultur des weiblichen Körpers als Grundlage der Frauenkleidung*, Leipzig, Eugen Diederichs, 1901.

[35] Schultze-Naumburg, *Dörfer und Kolonien*, p. 37.

[36] Schultze-Naumburg, *Hausbau*, pp. 35, 154–157. He later published a book on the flat roof controversy: *Flaches oder geneigtes Dach?*, Berlin, Seger and Cramer, 1927; see Richard Pommer, "The Flat Roof: A Modernist Controversy in Germany," *Art Journal* 43, no. 2, 1983, pp. 158–169.

[37] Schultze-Naumburg, *Hausbau*, n.p. The German Werkbund later attempted to reform a similarly vast spectrum of cultural artifacts when Muthesius sought to reform everything "vom Sofakissen zum Städtebau" (from pillows to cities); Muthesius, "Wo stehen wir?," *Jahrbuch des Deutschen Werkbundes 1912*, Jena, Eugen Diederichs, 1912, p. 16.

[38] All volumes of the *Kulturarbeiten* were published by the official Kunstwart publisher G. W. Callwey in Munich: volume 1, *Hausbau*, editions 1901, 1904, 1907, 1912; volume 2, *Gärten*, editions 1902, 1905, 1909; *Ergänzende Bilder zu Band 2: Gärten*, editions 1905, 1910; volume 3, *Dörfer und Kolonien*, editions 1903, 1908; volume 4, *Städtebau*, editions 1906, 1909; volume 5, *Kleinbürgerhäuser*, editions 1907, 1911; volume 6, *Das Schloß*, 1910. The last three volumes together were also titled *Die Gestaltung der Landschaft durch die Menschen*: volume 7 = Part I, "Wege und Strassen," "Die Pflanzenwelt," editions 1915, 1928; volume 8 = Part II, "Geologische Aufbau der Landschaft," "Wasserwirtschaft," editions 1915, 1928; volume 9 = Part III, "Industrie," "Siedlungen," editions 1917, 1928. All three parts were also published together as a single volume in 1922 and 1928.

[39] These earlier serialized essays, much like the *Kulturarbeiten*, were first published in *Der Kunstwart*, and later as books. They brought Schultze-Naumburg fame and the large readership which made the *Kulturarbeiten* so successful. See Paul Schultze-Naumburg, "Über Kunstpflege im Mittelstande," in *Der Kunstwart*, 11, no. 1, 1897, pp. 226ff; later published in Schultze-Naumurg, *Häusliche Kunstpflege*; and Paul Schultze-Naumburg, *Kunst und Kunstpflege*, Leipzig, Eugen Diederichs, 1901.

[40] Paul Schultze-Nuamburg, *Der Städtebau*, Kulturarbeiten 4, p. 442.

[41] Schultze-Naumburg, *Hausbau*, n.p.; Paul Schultze-Naumburg, "Entwicklung und Ziele des Heimatschutzes in Deutschland," in *Heimatschutz* 7, no. 4, 1911, p. 131.

accord with the present and the local.[32] He complained repeatedly about the *unsachlich* (non-straightforward) forms that were invented for situations where none were needed in recent architecture. The misapplication of pseudo-historical ornament, he felt, had led to a confusion of building types and styles throughout modern Germany and led him to complain: "Workers' houses were like palaces, palaces like Swiss chalets, farm houses like prisons, prisons like churches, churches like train stations."[33]

Second, Schultze-Naumburg railed against the many experimental attempts to concoct totally new architectural styles at the turn of the century such as Art Nouveau, the Secession style, and the German Jugendstil. These styles avoided overt copying of past forms and were ostensibly attuned to the modern world, but he saw them as arbitrary, unnatural, and inorganic developments on German soil. By completely skirting all conventions of established, and what Schultze-Naumburg called "*wahrhaftig*" (truthful) architecture they became superficial fads, superseding each other in rapid succession, like insipid changes in clothing fashions, and thus inappropriate for a modern national architecture.[34] By the time Schultze-Naumburg published the last editions of the *Kulturarbeiten*, he would come to see the abstract, white forms of the modern movement or "New Building," as it was called in Germany, in the same light: as an artificially concocted style that had little relation to local functional and cultural needs.

Third, Schultze-Naumburg confronted what he perceived to be the low quality and impoverished "schematic" architecture that characterized the vast majority of ordinary buildings recently constructed through the German landscape.[35] As he walked around his home town he felt the newer architecture lacked the spirituality, harmoniousness, and honest functionality of older buildings. The ugly, mass-produced, artificial building materials and ornament emoted an uncaring, cold-hearted sense of expediency. He felt unnatural forms such as the flat roof ignored sound craft traditions and were doomed to fail in the German climate.[36]

Schultze-Naumburg's critique extended well beyond merely architecture, to a particularly broad implementation of the romantic philosophy of *Gesamtkunstwerk* (total work of art) and the Arts and Crafts movement that had infiltrated Germany from England. The *Kulturarbeiten* addressed "all areas of visible culture," the whole German landscape, built and natural, the material, environmental, and cultural.[37] Beginning with a volume on the German house, the central theme of architectural reform efforts of his day, he divided his comprehensive analysis into a variety of sub-fields, each covered by one volume.[38] When combined with earlier essays on the domestic interior, taste in the fine arts, and women's fashion, the spectrum covered nearly all that had been shaped by German hands.[39]

This all-encompassing approach led Schultze-Naumburg to deduce from two photographs of a bridgehead in Saale taken from the same spot fifteen years apart, for example, that the physiognomy of the whole German cultural landscape had been gradually decaying. He urged his readers not to be complacent, to fight against the tendency to see all existing developments as "equally logical and therefore justified," a mentality that he claimed would "lead to the mentality of the Oriental, who merely passively awaits his fate."[40] If these developments persisted, he felt, Germany would soon have "the raw and unhappy face of a depraved nation where the purpose of life itself has wasted away."[41] Although targeting the exotic and Arabic "Orient" more than the Mediterranean, such attempts to separate the Germanic "North" from the lazy "South," and the active and artistically passionate "West" from the "primitive" and passive "East," were common in the writings of reformers of the day, although often reversed in terms of their biases.[42]

Such early physiognomic correlations of visual culture and national identity implicated not only aesthetic, but also social values. Schultze-Naumburg took his cues from German cultural critics such as Ferdinand Tönnies and Julius Langbehn, as well as English Arts and Crafts reformers such as Augustus W. N. Pugin, John Ruskin, and William Morris, whose writings were widely translated in Germany. He equated the ravaged built environment with a weak national character and failed national destiny. He blamed the decay in the German landscape on a whole array of societal forces: the unscrupulous greed of building speculators, the rampant modernization associated with industrialization and laissez-faire capitalism, bureaucratic building and planning officials, overly academic architectural schooling, and the importation of styles from the South, particularly the Renaissance. He attacked the rise of a soulless and alienating *Gesellschaft* (society) and materialistic *Zivilisation*, and blamed them for the destruction of an organic *Gemeinschaft* (community) and harmonic *Kultur* that had characterized the old German *Heimat* he so cherished.[43]

The *Um 1800* Vernacular

Seeking more timeless, cultured principles in contrast to the deplorable eclecticism and over-ornamentation of the materialistic late nineteenth century, Schultze-Naumburg insisted in 1905 that:

> true architectural design must be possible *without* ornament. The worth and significance of our buildings is totally independent of the ornament applied. The only important points are the layout of the overall building complex, proper use of good materials, and simplicity and honesty of expression.[44]

Anticipating some of the aesthetic asceticism and functionalism of later modern architecture, he aspired to an architecture that was unornamented and straightforward. Much like the contemporary ideas of Adolf Loos and museum director Alfred Lichtwark, he sought a "realist" and "*sachlich*" (objective) architecture that would act as a "seed" for the development of "modern" design.[45]

He found such a seed in the simple, tectonic forms and distilled classicism of the vernacular architecture of the late eighteenth-century Baroque or Biedermeier period still visible in the landscape all around them. Building on the nostalgic concepts of *Heimat* first developed by Romantic writers such as W. H. Riehl and the Grimm brothers in the late eighteenth century, he felt that traditions from the period between 1780 and 1840 provided the most recent, and therefore most accessible, example of a timeless way of building that was truthful and German, pure and functional.[46] With clear nationalist undertones, Schultze-Naumburg claimed that German Biedermeier traditions from this period around 1800 were natural, integrated into the common culture, and more accessible to the ordinary citizen than contemporary architecture.

Perhaps the single most widely referenced example of vernacular classicism from the period around 1800 was Goethe's unassuming but culturally resonant garden house in Weimar, just up the river from Schultze-Naumburg's own

[42] Expressionist architects such as Bruno Taut, by contrast, ascribed great creativity and communal fortitude to Eastern art in comparison to the moribund and decadent art of the West; see Simone Hain, "'Ex oriente lux'. Deutschland und der Osten."

[43] On the *Gemeinschaft/Gesellschaft* dichotomy see Ferdinand Tönnies, *Community and Society*, trans. by C. Loomis, New York, Harper and Row, 1963 (*Gemeinschaft und Gesellschaft*, 1887). The related *Kultur/Zivilisation* split had its origins in German idealist thinkers around 1800, such as Kant and Wilhelm von Humboldt. See Stern, *The Politics of Cultural Despair*, p. 246.

[44] Paul Schultze-Naumburg, *Die Entstellung unseres Landes*, Flugschriften des Bundes Heimatschutz, 2, Meiningen, Bund Heimatschutz, 1908 (1st edn. 1905), p. 60.

[45] Mannhardt, *Alfred Lichtwark*; Mallgrave, "From Realism to *Sachlichkeit*," pp. 298–304; Hamann and Hermand, *Stilkunst um 1900*, pp. 440–464.

[46] *Heimat* (root of the related terms *Heimatschutz*, and *Heimatstil*), is a difficult term that can best be translated as "homeland" or "hometown." The nostalgic term connotes a Germanic past that encompasses a whole world view that was at the core of Schultze-Naumburg's conception of a healthy culture. The stable, almost unchanging form of the pre-industrial German *Heimat* was neither urban nor rural but somewhere in between. It was a closed system – nested webs of relationships that nurtured a harmonious culture and a society with an intimate sense of tradition and values. A strong sense of self-sufficiency led to a pride in regional identity and differentiation. A natural pragmatism avoided excess and constantly adapted to changing forces, although the primary purpose of the hometowns seemed to be to uphold conventions: drastic change was anathema. See Peter Blickle, *Heimat: A Critical Theory of the German Idea of Homeland*, Rochester, NY, Camden House, 2002; Celia Applegate, *A Nation of Provincials: The German Idea of Heimat*, Berkeley, University of California Press, 1990.

Wohnmaschine

Goethes Gartenhaus

7.5 Paul Schmitthenner's comparison of Hans Scharoun's house at the Weissenhof Siedlung, labeled "Machine for Living," on the left, and Goethe's beloved garden house in Weimar, on the right.
Source: Paul Schmitthenner, *Baugestaltung: Erste Folge*, 1932.

47 Goethe's garden house in the royal park in Weimar was actually an earlier Baroque construction, first occupied by Goethe in 1776, and modified only slightly by the cultural hero. Schultze-Naumburg referred often to Goethe and his houses, but never actually illustrated the garden house in the *Kulturarbeiten*. Its popularity after the turn of the century can be traced to the importance of Weimar as a place of artistic and cultural reform. See Paul Mebes, *Um 1800: Architektur und Handwerk im letzten Jahrhundert ihrer traditionellen Entwicklung*, Munich, F. Bruckmann, 1908; Wolfgang Voigt, "Vom Ur-Haus zum Typ: Paul Schmitthenners 'deutsches Wohnhaus' und seine Vorbilder," and Hartmut Frank, "Heimatschutz und typologisches Entwerfen. Modernisierung und Tradition beim Wiederaufbau von Ostpreußen 1915–1927," both in Schneider and Lampugnani, *Modern Architektur in Deutschland 1900 bis 1905*. Paul Schmitthenner popularized the building in his teaching in Stuttgart as well as in his book *Baugestaltung: Erste Folge, Das deutsche Wohnhaus*, Stuttgart, K. Wittmer Verlag, 1932.
48 Schultze-Naumburg, *Enstellung unseres Landes*, p. 10.

home in Saaleck.[47] Its pure forms, elegant proportions and detailing, neat and tidy appearance, and general informality revealed a natural serenity, honesty, and logic. Like so many of Goethe's writings, his garden house embodied the core values of the old bourgeois culture that Schultze-Naumburg feared was being destroyed in Germany. It was neither flamboyant nor ornamental, but rather efficient, practical, and functional, akin to the somewhat Spartan landscape of Germany, and therefore still appropriate, according to the twentieth-century critic. Goethe's house was used by tradition-oriented critics as an ideal to oppose both nineteenth-century eclecticism and modern architecture after World War I. But the minimal, unornamented, white stucco house was no doubt an important precedent for traditionalists and modernists alike. The connections to the universally admired cultural hero Goethe, as well as to the period around 1800, when German nationalism and the awareness of a unique German, bourgeois culture first began to emerge in the face of Napoleonic oppression, were key to its appeal. Not unlike the Colonial Revival in the Americas around this same time, the vernacular architecture from around 1800 had important political undertones in the newly unified Germany still in search of its own cultural identity.

Although Goethe's house was seen as a prototypical example of the German Biedermeier, Schultze-Naumburg focused primarily on more anonymous, vernacular examples in order to arrive at general principles, not individual expressions. He sought the typical, not the extraordinary. He avoided "those art historically catalogued monuments that have been recognized as the pinnacle of higher artistic development" in favor of the "inconspicuous and daily fare used by the *Volk*."[48] Schultze-Naumburg's contemporary, Adolf Loos, had a similar distaste for "fashionable" design and maintained a reverence for, and trust in, the timeless traditions and styles of the ordinary craftsman over the willful styles of any artist or architect.[49] Both reformers felt that a modern house would arise not through the experimentation of high-style architects, but rather by connecting to a simple, tectonic building tradition that was completely connected to the common culture. Where Schultze-Naumburg focused on local German culture, however, Loos professed culture to be evolving towards more uniform and international ideals, borrowing freely from England, the United States, as well as ancient Egypt. This bias towards the local and ordinary was visible in all of Schultze-Naumburg's early work. The domestic reform movement and grassroots *Heimatschutz* organizations that he helped found sought to revive a German culture from the bottom up. They recognized the need to reach beyond the small circle of cultured professionals who already understood these ideas and to convert the ordinary *Volk*. In line with his content, Schultze-Naumburg targeted the common man, and wrote:

> Our wish is also to win over the people – the townsmen, the farmer, the workers . . . from the street paver, to the old lady who cultivates flowers on her window ledge . . . all those that work most closely in shaping the face of our nation.[50]

[49] Burkhardt Rukschcio and Roland L. Schachel, *Adolf Loos. Leben und Werk*, Vienna, Residenz Verlag, 1987, pp. 50–51, 115–121; Adolf Loos, "Architektur," *Der Sturm*, 1910, excerpted in A. Opel (ed.), *Über Architektur: Ausgewählte Schriften die Originaltexte*, Vienna, Georg Prachner Verlag, 1995.
[50] Schultze-Naumburg, *Hausbau*, n.p., 2–3.

BIELEFELD   KL. KESSELSTRASZE

STUKSHOF BEI LANGFUHR

7.6 Two vernacular houses from "Around 1800". Source: Paul Mebes, *Um 1800*, 1920, 3rd edition.

51 Ibid., pp. 2, 23.
52 Stanford Anderson has described this "covert," "domesticated," and "quotidian" classicism in great detail; see Stanford Anderson, "The Legacy of German Neoclassicism and Biedermeier: Behrens, Tessenow, Loos and Mies," *Assemblage* 15, 1991, pp. 63–87; Stanford Anderson, "Architecture in a Cultural Field," in Taisto Makela and Wallis Miller (eds.), *Wars of Classification: Architecture and Modernity*, New York, Princeton Architectural Press, 1991; see also Heyden, *Biedermeier als Erzieher.*
53 Hermann Muthesius, *Style-Architecture and Building Art. Transformations of Architecture in the Nineteenth Century and its Present Condition*, Santa Monica, Getty, 1994 (orig. 1902), p. 53.
54 Mebes, *Um 1800*; Frank, "Heimatschutz und typologisches Entwerfen"; Edina Meyer, *Paul Mebes. Miethausbau in Berlin 1906–1938*, Berlin, Seitz, 1972, pp. 148ff.
55 Mebes, *Um 1800*, vol. 2, p. 15 n.1.
56 Kenneth Frampton, "The Classical Tradition and the European Avant-Garde: Notes on France, Germany and Scandinavia 1912–37," in Simo Paavilainen (ed.), *Nordic Classicism 1910–1930*, Helsingfors, Finlands arkitekturmuseum, 1982.
57 Anderson, "The Legacy of German Neoclassicism and Biedermeier"; Anderson, "Architecture in a Cultural Field."
58 Heinrich Tessenow, *Der Wohnhausbau*, Munich, G. W. Callwey, 1909 (2nd edn. 1914, 3rd edn. 1927); Marco de Michelis, *Heinrich Tessenow, 1876–1950. Das architektonische Gesamtwerk*, Stuttgart, Deutsche Verlags-Anstalt, 1991.
59 Walter Curt Behrendt, *Kampf um den Stil im Kunstgewerbe und in der Architektur*, Stuttgart, Deutsche Verlags-Anstalt, 1920, p. 81; Walter Curt Behrendt, Preface, in Paul Mebes, *Um 1800*, pp. 11–12; Kai K. Gutschow, "Revising the Paradigm: German Modernism as the Search for a National Architecture in the Writings of W. C. Behrendt," M.Arch. thesis, University of California, Berkeley, 1993.
60 Behrendt, *Kampf um den Stil*, pp. 80–83. Schultze-Naumburg attended an applied arts college and the art academy in Karlsruhe from 1886 to 1893, when he moved to Munich to start his own private painting school. In 1895 he joined the Munich Secession, and in 1897 moved briefly to Berlin before moving to Saaleck in Thuringia in 1901.
61 Behrendt, preface, in Mebes, p. 11.

More so than the German Werkbund he later helped found, Schultze-Naumburg sought to reach beyond training consumers and reforming high art and industrial production. He insisted that true cultural reform begins at the grassroots level, with the design of ordinary houses, "the only object on which the average person is artistically engaged."[51] Far from being merely private matters, the vernacular houses and interiors of the *Heimat* were the ultimate embodiment of a nation's culture.

The anonymous, domesticated classicism from around 1800 that Schultze-Naumburg promoted and helped reintroduce in his *Kulturarbeiten* soon became a standard reference in a flood of publications by designers, critics, and reformers throughout Germany.[52] Hermann Muthesius, in his important book *Style-Architecture and Building Art* from 1902, concluded that the architecture from around 1800 "could serve as a model for contemporary conditions."[53] The movement received a name and a tremendous popularity boost with the publication of Paul Mebes's 1908 picture book *Um 1800. Architektur und Handwerk im letzten Jahrhundert ihrer traditionellen Entwicklung* (Around 1800: Architecture and Craft in the Last Century of their Traditional Development), which illustrated vernacular and high-style architecture from this period.[54] Like Schultze-Naumburg, Mebes intended his book as a didactic tool to help contemporary architects "re-connect" to the spirit of simple, honest construction around 1800. He cited the *Kulturarbeiten* as one of the central forces that brought this period of architectural history back into contemporary consciousness, and he republished several of Schultze-Naumburg's photographs.[55]

The *Um 1800* vernacular that Schultze-Naumburg helped reintroduce was part of a more generalized "call to order" coursing throughout Europe in all the arts before and after World War I, and key to the development of modern architecture.[56] But Schultze-Naumburg's far-reaching influence on these developments is unmistakable. Heinrich Tessenow, who began his architectural career working in Schultze-Naumburg's Saalecker Werkstätten workshops in 1904, was one of the first to implement what Stanford Anderson has called a "covert classicism."[57] Tessenow's drawings, including many of Goethe's garden house, his popular book *Der Wohnhausbau* (House Building) of 1909, and actual built works such as those in the garden city of Hellerau, helped set the tone for the reformed, modern classicism that dominated the work of architects as diverse as Peter Behrens, Paul Schmitthenner, Bruno Taut, Ludwig Mies van der Rohe, and others in the Werkbund before and after World War I.[58] The similarity of their early work is astounding in light of the divergent paths these architects took in the 1920s.

In an early appraisal of this *Um 1800* architecture, Walter Curt Behrendt praised Schultze-Naumburg and the movement he helped spawn.[59] This unity of architects working towards a common goal, Behrendt observed, was the first step towards a new, modern style for Germany. Moreover, the logic and rationality of this simple classicism provided basic rules of proportion, tectonics, and construction techniques that were easily followed, especially by the many artistic reformers who were not architects by profession such as Henri Van de Velde, Behrens, and even Schultze-Naumburg himself.[60]

For Behrendt, although the *Um 1800* architecture had close connections to Goethe and the rise of German nationalism, it was at its core a foreign "import," from the Mediterranean "South."[61] He complained that Classicism had become a meaningless "international style," a "world language," reaching beyond all

7.7 Mies van der Rohe's Riehl House in Potsdam/ Babelsberg, 1907, in the style from "Around 1800."

Source: *Moderne Bauformen* 9, 1910.

borders, even to the colonial style of America. As a result, he saw the *Heimatstil* and *Um 1800* classicism as signs of the unfortunate "cosmopolitan" and "international-izing" tendencies growing in Germany. Echoing Schultze-Naumburg's *Kulturarbeiten*, he lamented that local, regional, and national identities were slowly being destroyed in favor of this "*Großstadtstil*," and that "instinctive, folk traditions of art are no longer tenable," no longer "able to uphold long-standing national art traditions". He lamented that in the hands of inferior, academically trained architects, the classicism inspired by *Um 1800* was too often only a meaningless simplification of nineteenth-century styles, a dignified reaction to eclecticism but not a model appropriate for the modern world.[62]

To justify his taste for the Biedermeier in the face of such critiques, Schultze-Naumburg provided a complicated argument that classicism had been "Germanized" by the great Prussian architects Gilly and later Schinkel. In the resulting "Prussian Style," as it was later christened in a book by Arthur Moeller van den Bruck, the classicism of the ancient Greeks was appropriated, fused with indigenous forms and ideals, and converted to a Germanic ideal.[63] Nordic simplicity and power had been combined with classical rule and proportion. Such a translation from a "Southern" to a German style was possible, according to the author, since all truly great cultural developments evolved out of the combination of opposite principles, "as when father and mother combine to produce a child."[64]

[62] Walter Curt Behrendt "Die deutsche Baukunst der Gegenwart," in *Kunst und Künstler* 12, no. 5, 1914; Behrendt, *Kampf um den Stil*, pp. 81–83.
[63] Arthur Moeller van den Bruck, *Der Preussische Stil*, Munich, Piper, 1916.
[64] Schultze-Naumburg, *Hausbau*, p. 35; Behrendt, preface in Mebes, pp. 9–11.

⁶⁵ Schultze-Naumburg, *Die Entstellung unseres landes*, n.p.
⁶⁶ Wilhelm Bode, "Paul Schultze-
Naumburgs Bauten," in *Dekorative
Kunst* 16, 1908, pp. 234–237.
⁶⁷ Schultze-Naumburg, *Hausbau*,
p. 5.
⁶⁸ Borrmann, *Paul Schultze-
Naumburg*, p. 60; Andreas Knaut,
"Paul Schultze-Naumburgs Kulturtheorie um 1900," in Jürgen John
(ed.), *Kleinstaaten und Kultur in
Thüringen*, Cologne, Böhlau, 1994,
p. 547; Ludwig Bartning, *Paul
Schultze-Naumburg. Ein Pionier
deutscher Kulturarbeit*, Munich,
G. D. W. Callwey, 1929, p. 5.
⁶⁹ Bode, "Paul Schultze-Naumburgs
Bauten."

Although there are formal similarities, the principles outlined in the *Kulturarbeiten* differed on some key points from much of the *Um 1800* and much of the *Heimatstil* architecture actually built, including by Schultze-Naumburg himself. He was adamant that his books not be thought of as promoting "antiquarian ideals" or as pattern books of examples to be copied.⁶⁵ Instead he hoped that his readers would study the pictures and comparisons and derive from them an appreciation of the rich *Heimat* tradition. Through the photographs of the German *Heimat* in the *Kulturarbeiten*, he attempted to recapture an older spirit or method, and transfer its vitality in the creation of a renewed modern architecture. Both Mebes and Schultze-Naumburg, at least in their rhetoric, insisted on the *approach* and conventions of such buildings from 1800, not on the borrowing of *forms* or styles. Although Schultze-Naumburg eventually became fervently anti-modernist, and his architecture was revivalist, contemporaries were aware that the earlier *Kulturarbeiten* demonstrated a clear embrace of contemporary ideas.⁶⁶ They were not advertising another revival or a historicist application of traditional details, but rather a sympathetic, evolving *continuation* of known local building traditions and national types.

Progress, Type, and Modernity

Although the *Kulturarbeiten* did react to and draw attention to many of the negative developments of modernity and the perceived loss of German bourgeois *Kultur*, they were not wholly anti-modern or merely reactionary. Despite his love for tradition, Schultze-Naumburg often turned to the modern world for design answers and inspiration. In the preface of *Hausbau* from 1901, for example, he wrote poetically of the technological sublime he saw in the railroad locomotive:

> Is there a truer or more powerful expression of energy functionally harnessed than the train? When this monstrosity approaches with glowing eyes; when it shoots through the large curve in the track, and later in the station sits coughing and all out of breath as it takes on the additional loads . . . is this not beautiful? Beauty is everywhere that powerful function is forced totally into existence.⁶⁷

These words recall the fascination with trains by the Impressionists a few years earlier, but also anticipate the glorification of speed and power by the Italian Futurists and the rest of the machine aesthetic of the avant-garde that coalesced a decade later.

Schultze-Naumburg's admiration for modern technology translated to his personal life as well. He outfitted his houses with all the most modern electronics, and was one of the first people to own an automobile in Germany, replacing it regularly with the newest model.⁶⁸ Living not far from Jena, he was a great fan of Zeiss cameras and lenses, the most modern in the world. One critic even hypothesized that some day Schultze-Naumburg would be the first artist to travel in his own airplane.⁶⁹ These new industrial products satisfied his demands of *Sachlichkeit*: they achieved a perfect fit of form, function, and beauty.

His admiration of functional, technological products is fundamental to understanding the primary purpose of the *Kulturarbeiten*: to determine and re-establish a specifically German cultural heritage built on tradition that might serve as a basis for a similar sense of modern design in architecture. Schultze-

Naumburg sought to: "*reconnect* to the last good traditions, not in order to substitute for further development, but precisely to make possible this development from a solid foundation." Only when this foundation was secured would further true, organic, and modern development be possible, "based on the updated circumstances of the times."[70]

These views were in many ways typical of the most progressive reformers and architects of his day. Adolf Loos, for example, maintained a similar trust in convention when he insisted that the Egyptian stool was a perfect resolution of its function, and thus did not need reinventing or redesigning.[71] As a result, several of Loos's chair designs from 1899 on were based on copies of Egyptian originals produced by Liberty & Co. in England, and his essays consistently praise the traditions of craftsmen's work.[72] In the Berlin Expressionist journal *Der Sturm*, Loos in 1910 seemed to echo Mebes and Schultze-Naumburg when he wrote of "the need to *reconnect* to the interrupted chain of development [around 1800]."[73]

As a means to this end, Schultze-Naumburg searched for origins, what he called the "*Ur-haus*," that would be the foundation, or "seed," to which the further development of German architecture could be "re-attached."[74] He became fascinated by what he considered to be a unique and powerful building type, the "German farmhouse." According to Schultze-Naumburg, the original German farmhouse was a rural, free-standing, half-timber structure, no ornament, a large pitched roof covered in clay tile, often with eyebrow windows:

> The house was of utmost simplicity and of the finest proportions, the honest expression of materials, the comforting distribution of rooms and building elements, and a sincere expression of comfort and home. Had we continued this tradition with updates and adaptations, we would have today what the English have: the national house. For us then, that would be: *the German house.*[75]

The late eighteenth-century German farmhouse, according to Schultze-Naumburg, responded not only to the harsh Nordic climate, but also to the specific sensibility of the semi-rural German *Heimat* and its people. Although the primary purpose of the farmhouse and the *Heimat* seemed to be to uphold tradition, a natural pragmatism avoided excess and constantly adapted to changing forces. New standards of technology and hygiene, as they were developed by industry, were always incorporated into the original. He contended that "earlier artisans did not simply copy stylistic details, but restructured them into sleek, functional forms so thoroughly, that they created the best buildings that we have in Germany."[76] This anonymous evolutionary process also provided lessons about avoiding experimentation for novelty's sake: "earlier artisans were wary to invent on their own that which could only be the product of communal work, the type." Fanciful inventions such as those of the Jugendstil, or later the *Neues Bauen*, were seen as counterproductive to a natural historical evolution and thus to a modern house.[77]

The idea of an anonymous, local architectural type that insured the stability of traditions but evolved naturally to include alterations, modernizations, and perfection over time has its roots in nineteenth-century German theory going back to the Biedermeier epoch and the work of Goethe and Schinkel, but also in Gottfried Semper's theories and late nineteenth-century reformers such as Lichtwark and Richard Streiter.[78] Interest in national and vernacular typologies was also part of the European-wide Arts and Crafts movement to invent traditions

[70] Schultze-Naumburg, *Hausbau*, pp. n.p., 10–11; Schultze-Naumburg, *Dörfer und Kolonien*, pp. 38–39, 204–205.
[71] Stanford Anderson, "Critical Conventionalism in Architecture," in *Assemblage* 1, 1986, pp. 7–23.
[72] Hubert Locher, "'Enough of the Original Geniuses! Let us Repeat Ourselves Unceasingly!' Adolf Loos, the New and 'The Other'," *Daidalos* 52, 1994, p. 79; Rukschcio and Schachel, *Adolf Loos. Leben und Werk*, pp. 32, 33.
[73] Loos, "Architektur," p. 82
[74] Schultze-Naumburg, *Dörfer und Kolonien*, pp. 16, 19.
[75] Schultze-Naumburg, *Dörfer und Kolonien*, p. 33; Schultze-Naumburg, *Hausbau*, p. 112.
[76] Schultze-Naumburg, *Hausbau*, p. 112.
[77] Schultze-Naumburg, *Dörfer und Kolonien*, p. 32.
[78] Barry Bergdoll, *Karl Friedrich Schinkel: An Architecture for Prussia*, New York, Rizzoli, 1994; Werner Oechslin, *Stilhülse und Kern: Otto Wagner, Stilhülse und Kern: Otto Wagner, und der evolutionäre Weg zur Modernen Architektur*, Zurich, Berlin, ETH, Ernst and Sohn, 1994; translated as *Otto Wagner, Adolf Loos, and the Road to Modern Architecture*, Cambridge, Cambridge University Press, 2002.

79 Umbach, "The Deutscher Werk-bund"; Purchla and Tegethoff, *Nation, Style, Modernism*; Miller-Lane, *National Romanticism*.

80 Muthesius, *Style-Architecture and Building Art*, p. 90; Passanti, "The Vernacular, Modernism, and Le Corbusier."

81 Winfried Nerdinger (ed.), *100 Jahre Deutscher Werkbund, 1907–2007*, Munich, Prestel, 2007; Frederic Schwartz, *The Werkbund*, New Haven, Yale University Press, 1996.

82 Giuliano Gresleri, *Le Corbusier, Viaggio in Oriente*, Venice, Marsilio Editori, 1984; Beatriz Colomina, "Le Corbusier and Duchamp: The Uneasy Status of the Object," in Makela and Miller (eds.), *Wars of Classification*, p. 47.

83 Julius Posener, "Müller-Wulckows: Deutsche Architektur und die Suche nach einer nationalen Kultur," in Gerd Kuhn (ed.), *KonTEXTe. Walter Müller-Wulckow und die deutsche Architektur von 1900–1930*, Königstein im Taunus, Langewiesche, 1999; Werner Oechslin, "Politisches, allzu Politisches . . . 'Nietzschlinge,' der 'Wille zur Kunst' und der Deutsche Werkbund vor 1914," in Hermann Hipp and Kurt von Beyme (eds.), *Architektur als politische Kultur: philosophia practica*, Berlin, D. Reimer, 1996.

84 Schultze-Naumburg, *Häusliche Kunstpflege*, p. 2; Schultze-Naumburg, *Hausbau*, pp. 11,12.

85 Schultze-Naumburg, *Hausbau*, pp. 88–89.

7.8 Comparison of Richard Riemerschmid's "modern" house near Munich that updated timeless traditions (*left*) and a typical historicist farmhouse (*right*). Source: Paul Schultze-Naumburg, *Hausbau, Kulturarbeiten* 1, 1904.

and to codify the various national houses in order to counter foreign influences and the anonymity of mass production through regional differentiation.[79]

As Francesco Passanti has shown, this idea of an anonymous vernacular type had profound implications for the development of modern architecture.[80] Muthesius's turn-of-the-century analysis of the English house and his call for the development of a specifically German house were part of this same effort as Schultze-Naumburg's. A few years later, the idea of the "type" would become central to Muthesius and other Werkbund reformers in their attempts to influence German design towards a modern, exportable standard.[81] After being adopted by the Werkbund, an institution Schultze-Naumburg helped found, it was transformed slightly by Muthesius into an active rather than a passive process, whereby architects purposefully created conventional types. It was in part Le Corbusier's familiarity with these German architectural ideas, including Schultze-Naumburg's, that led him and others to reject the elitism of high art in favor of anonymous, collective production as the basis upon which to theorize the *objet type* and modern architecture more generally.[82] Indeed, this need to determine a modern, national architecture was behind much architectural reform in Germany until well into the 1920s.[83]

Although he gave credit to William Morris and the English Arts and Crafts movement for starting international reform efforts towards simpler, more vernacular forms in domestic architecture, Schultze-Naumburg demanded as early as 1899 that the Germans develop their own national house and architecture.[84] The *Kulturarbeiten* advocated picking up where such honest, German *Heimat* buildings had left off in 1840, appropriating the advances wrought by industry since then, and continuing the German traditions. Where functions had not radically changed, as was the case with the "German house," he felt the basic type should be maintained. This was the case with one of the few positive examples of contemporary architecture illustrated in the early *Kulturarbeiten*, Richard Riemerschmid's own house near Munich. Schultze-Naumburg praises how this "good modern house . . . fits perfectly into the *Heimat* conditions, develops old traditions but with new forms in which the old traditions have been updated for new conditions."[85]

When new building types had to be invented, Schultze-Naumburg insisted that care should be taken to express their functions fully, simply, and objectively. This had been the case, he claimed, with the concrete grain silo, a relatively

BEISPIEL

GEGENBEISPIEL

new building type, at least with this massive scale and new material. Much as he admired the modern locomotive, Schultze-Naumburg praised the modern industrial vernacular of concrete silos as early as 1908, well before Gropius, Le Corbusier, or even the populist *Illustriete Zeitung* heralded the *Sachlichkeit* of these simple, functional volumes.[86]

By the time Schultze-Naumburg published the last volume of the original *Kulturarbeiten* series in 1917, and certainly by the time the last editions were released in 1929, he announced that the architectural situation had begun to improve in Germany. Influenced by the nationalism and technological pride of a country at war and the modern developments of Wilhelmine Germany,

[86] Schultze-Naumburg, *Enstellung unseres Landes*, pp. 25, 35; Paul Schultze-Naumburg, "Industrie," part V of *Die Gestaltung der Landschaft durch die Menschen*, Kulturarbeiten vol. 9, Munich, G. W. Callwey, 1917, p. 40; Jarzombek, "The Discourse of Bourgeois Utopia," p. 133. The popular image of German concrete grain silos in Landshut was first published in *Süddeutsche Zeitung*; and in W. Klatte, "Zur Umgestaltung des Fabrikwesens," *Heimatschutz* 4, 1–3, 1908, fig. 9. The idea of celebrating the "beauty" of technology was becoming increasingly common, as Henri van de Velde, Alfred Gotthold Meyer, and Josef August Lux all wrote books and essays expressing similar views.

Abbildung 31. Maschinenzentrale in Bad Nauheim. Entworfen von der Großherzogl. Baubehörde unter Leitung des Großherzogl. Bauinspektors Jost und unter Mitwirkung des Reg.-Baumstr. Kraft und Reg.-Bauführers Marr.

Abbildung 32. Getreide-Silo in Landshut. Entworfen und ausgeführt von der Firma Luipold u. Schneider, Stuttgart

7.9 Positive examples of recent industrial buildings, including concrete grain silos in Landshut, designed by Luitpold & Schneider of Stuttgart.
Source: Paul Schultze-Naumburg, *Die Entstellung unseres Landes*, 1908.

87 Schultze-Naumburg, "Industrie,"
pp. 29–32.
88 Ibid., p. 37.
89 See the chapter in this volume
by Benedetto Gravagnuolo.
90 Passanti, "The Vernacular,
Modernism, and Le Corbusier."

Schultze-Naumburg illustrated the concrete silos, Behrens' AEG Turbine Factory, and several Krupp industrial works as exemplars of a new, praiseworthy architecture.[87] In these situations, he argued, Germany had been forced by a competitive world market to rid itself of the historicist straightjacket and to build simple functional buildings. He praised Behrens and other designers for helping elevate these designs beyond the merely functional, turning them into valued artifacts of *Kultur*, rather than merely products of *Zivilization*. For Schultze-Naumburg, true design and the creation of authentic architecture was not the domain of overly rational engineers and purveyors of *Zivilisation*, but rather in the realm of *Kultur*.[88] An effort by cultured architects and the entire German nation was now necessary to develop the same purity and simple functionalism in a modern German house and the rest of the German landscape.

Schultze-Naumburg's fascination with modern technology is key to understanding his contribution to the development of modern architecture. His love of vernacular architecture, both new and old, industrial and domestic, is part of a long architectural tradition that stretches back to Schinkel's trips to England and Italy, and Adolf Menzel's paintings of industrial Berlin, and extends forward to Josef Hoffmann's trip to Capri and Le Corbusier's "Voyage d'Orient."[89] But Schultze-Naumburg fundamentally changed the lessons to be taken from the vernacular. In the past, architects had absorbed primarily aesthetic lessons such as the informal, variegated massing of Italian hill towns, or the unadorned structural rationalism of Manchester factories. Schultze-Naumburg, however, focused on process and the development of authentic architecture that continued the architectural typologies and culture of the *Heimat*, rather than on mere form. It was this lesson that Le Corbusier and the moderns would take from him.

The emphasis on process over form in Schultze-Naumburg challenges some of the dichotomies that several scholars have proposed to understand the pre-war period's difficult mix of modernity and tradition. Passanti, for example, has differentiated the "vernacular modernism" of Muthesius and the *Heimatstil*, from the "modern vernacular" of Le Corbusier and the modern movement.[90] The former, he claims, sought to update strictly local conventions and typologies to accommodate modern lifestyles, but for the most part retained the formal model of the local vernacular. In contrast, the latter rejected the forms of the local vernacular, but sought to emulate their evolutionary process to create a new, modern vernacular, a family of functional forms that were constantly updated and built on each other. In the context of the essays in this volume, the former sought to continue German and Nordic formal traditions as the path to modern architecture, while the latter took their lessons from the Mediterranean and Southern vernaculars and applied them more abstractly to generate an "international" architecture. Although Schultze-Naumburg's conservative architectural designs, as well as the photos of *Um 1800* architecture that fill the *Kulturarbeiten*, identify him as part of the Muthesius camp, his fascination with modern technology and the associated forms clearly also aligns him with aspects of Le Corbusier's "modern vernacular."

In his insightful studies of the subtle variations in the use of tradition and convention in pre-World War I architecture, Stanford Anderson has created a similar dichotomy between the ideas of Schultze-Naumburg and Muthesius, and modern architects such as Loos and Le Corbusier. He contrasted Schultze-Naumburg's embrace of only a single cultural patrimony – and with

BEISPIE

Abbildung 22

Strasse in Augsburg. Bei-
spiel für gute gerade Strassenführung mit Abschluss

GEGENBEISPIE

Grundriss
zu Abbildung 22

Grundriss
zu Abbildung 23

Abbildung 23

Beispiel für schlechte gerade
Strassenführung ohne Abschluss

7.10 A comparison of two urban streetscapes: the human-scaled and bounded alley of the Fuggerei in Augsburg, above, and the endless and dreary modern street, below.
Source: Paul Schultze-Naumburg, *Städtebau, Kulturarbeiten 4*, 1906.

it the rejection of foreign influences – with Loos's more critical approach that he calls "critical conventionalism," which embraces elements of multiple traditions and conventions according to modern needs.[91] Although Schultze-Naumburg was clearly more conservative and less catholic in his studies of precedents than the dominant architects of the international avant-garde, the fundamental lessons he drew from the vernacular and modern technological products were nearly identical. Schultze-Naumburg's admonition against copying the past, or even the neighbors, and against the arbitrary and willfully new fashions of much modern design, even foreshadow critiques expressed only much later by modernists such as Adolf Behne and Le Corbusier, as the fascination with the machine started to blend with interests in the natural and the local.[92]

91 Anderson, "Critical Convention-alism in Architecture"; Anderson, "The Legacy of German Neo-classicism and Biedermeier."
92 Adolf Behne, "Dammerstock," in *Die Form* 5, no. 6, 1929; reprinted in Kristiana Hartmann (ed.), *Trotzdem Modern*, Brunswick, Vieweg, 1994.

[93] A contemporary review by Muthesius raved about the simple, powerful format and message of the book which could be understood and should be read by all; Hermann Muthesius, "Culturarbeiten" [*sic*] *Zentralblatt der Bauverwaltung* 22, no. 103, December 27, 1902, p. 641. Le Corbusier too acknowledged their "enormous" influence, even on his own work; see Leo Schubert, "Jeanneret, the City, and Photography," in Stanislaus von Moos and Arthur Rüegg (eds.), *Le Corbusier before Le Corbusier. Applied Arts, Architecture, Painting, Photography, 1907–1922*, New Haven, Yale University Press, 2002. Another review in the *Berliner Tageblatt* by Fritz Stahl from 1910 reads, "I wish a million copies of this book would go in circulation," cited in Paul Schultze-Naumburg, *Das Schloß*, Kulturarbeiten 6, Munich, G. W. Callwey, 1910, p. 310. Lewis Mumford contended that the *Kulturarbeiten* were "A work of fundamental importance upon the artful and orderly transformation of the environment by man. One of the original documents of its generation"; Lewis Mumford, *City in History: Its Origins, its Transformations, and its Prospects*, New York, Harcourt, Brace and World, 1961, p. 622. Posener commented that their influence "can hardly be exaggerated"; Posener, *Berlin auf dem Wege*, p. 191.
[94] A similar example is Le Corbusier's essays in *L'Esprit nouveau* that culminated in his book *Vers une architecture* (1923). See Maria Rennhofer, *Kunstzeitschriften der Jahrhundertwende in Deutschland und Österreich 1895–1914*, Augsburg, Bechtermünz Verlag, 1997.
[95] Ferdinand Avenarius, editorial, *Der Kunstwart* 10, no. 1, 1896, p. 1.
[96] See Maria Rennhofer, *Kunstzeitschriften der Jahrhundertwende in Deutschland und Österreich 1895–1914*, Augsburg, Bechtermünz Verlag, 1997.
[97] Annette Cirè and Haila Ochs, *Die Zeitschrift als Manifest*, Basle, Birkhäuser. Cirè and Ochs, 1991; Jacques Gubler (ed.), "Architecture in Avant-garde Magazines," special issue of *Rassegna* 4, no. 12, 1982.
[98] Kratzsch, *Kunstwart und Dürerbund*; Bernd Kulhoff, *Bürgerliche Selbstbehauptung im Spiegel der Kunst: Untersuchungen zur Kulturpublizistik der Rundschauzeitschriften im Kaiserreich (1871–1914)*, Bochum, Brockmeyer, 1990.
[99] Schultze-Naumburg, *Die Entstellung unseres Landes*.
[100] Ibid., pp. 6, 64; Schultze-Naumburg, "Entwicklung und Ziele des Heimatschutze in Deutschland," p. 135.
[101] Schultze-Naumburg, ibid., p. 136.

Aligning Medium and Message

Arguably the most modern aspect of the *Kulturarbeiten* and the feature that had the most influence on the development of modern architecture was the publication format. These books were not typical nineteenth-century treatises, historical discourses, or theoretical essays for architectural professionals or elite art lovers. They were propaganda: inexpensive picture books, mass media with some populist shock value, intended to make simple points to a very large audience. The handy, octavo-sized books were available in either soft or hard cover, purchased through subscription or at news stands. More like cheap novels than traditional architectural texts, they enjoyed almost instant success and set an important precedent for modern architectural publishing.[93] By adding images and rearranging the basic material into different editions, Schultze-Naumburg was able to publish nine volumes in at least seven different editions between 1902 and 1929, making it one of the longest running architectural titles of its day.

In order to insure a large readership for his ideas, Schultze-Naumburg published the first sections of the *Kulturarbeiten* books in serialized format in the popular magazine *Der Kunstwart* (Warden of the Arts), where he himself served as art editor.[94] Founded in 1887 by Ferdinand Avenarius, this magazine's nationalist edge assured a sympathetic audience, as it too was dedicated to "all the important questions and dilemmas concerning the arts of the day," and tried to combat "all that was false, artificial, and spurious in German art."[95] It was part of a late nineteenth-century explosion of bourgeois art and cultural magazines throughout Europe that provided key fora in the fights for the renewal of culture and insured the eventual success of modern art and architecture in Germany.[96] These journals were the direct antecedents to the many avant-garde architectural publications that helped promote modern architecture after World War I.[97]

The *Kulturarbeiten* and *Der Kunstwart*, in turn, were but pieces of a larger group of interrelated publications and organizations that circulated Schultze-Naumburg's ideas. As a founding member and leading ideologue of many of the important pre-war reform organizations such as the Dürerbund, the Heimatschutzbund, the Munich Secession, the Deutsche Gartenstadt Gesellschaft (German Garden City Association), and the Werkbund, he was in a key position to disseminate his message as widely as possible.[98] While publishing the *Kulturarbeiten* series, he wrote many articles with similar messages in other newspapers and magazines, often referring readers back to the series. In a small booklet called *Die Entstellung unseres Landes* (The Devastation of our Country), part of a popular pamphlet series produced by the Heimatschutzbund, for example, he voiced nearly the same arguments as in the *Kulturarbeiten*, using some of the same photographs and comparisons.[99]

As part of his widespread, grassroots campaign to save the German cultural landscape and establish a modern house, Schultze-Naumburg announced in 1905: "the main emphasis of our work in the future has to be propaganda, to insure a better understanding and vision."[100] His propaganda educated a broad public about his ideas, maligned opposing views, and countered allegedly false "counter-propaganda." He waged real press wars, replete with a bellicose vocabulary, which featured "campaigns," "fighters," "enemies," and "strikes" against contemporary architecture and forces such as the tar roofing-paper manufacturers, who opposed his calls for more aesthetic roof shapes and roofing materials.[101]

The divisiveness of these battles was echoed in the discursive method of his books: a simple and persuasive technique of contrasting paired photographs. He stated explicitly in the preface that the "propagandistic and didactic power of these books was based exclusively on the example/counter-example method."[102] Each pair was labeled "*Beispiel*," (example) – usually older buildings from around 1800 – and "*Gegenbeispiel*," (counter-example) – usually more recent architecture. Each pair was meant to demonstrate a specific point with clear lessons. He admitted that he wanted to force the viewer not only to make judgments of "ugly and beautiful," but also to associate these with a "right and wrong" – both in the sense of "morally good and bad," and "useful and not useful."[103] The pedagogical contrasts were repeated and often verged on the pedantic, but the themes were clear even to the most unsophisticated reader. After some initial words of guidance the author expected the images to speak for themselves.[104]

Schultze-Naumburg's use of photographs, technical images, mechanically reproduced as mass medium, proved to be a powerful and effective means to capture and promote the valued aspects of the traditional *Heimat* and the modern house. An avid amateur photographer and one of the first people to use the new portable camera developed by Zeiss, he created one of the largest photographic collections of German vernacular architecture of his day, some 2,500 images from which appeared in the *Kulturarbeiten* alone.[105] The use of countless, carefully chosen paired photographs rather than difficult prose, architectural plans, or hand drawings allowed him to reach the large, diverse audience he targeted with a definite and easily understood message. Although photographs had been used in large architectural pattern books before, they were still novel in such inexpensive books in 1900, especially to his lower- and middle-class readers. The medium and sheer number of photographs of ordinary, familiar buildings from all over Germany reinforced his message with reassuring, seemingly objective, evidence.

The comparative technique afforded many value-laden variations, including before–after, old–new, right–wrong, and rural–urban, all supporting the central thesis. As a painter who took most of his own photographs, Schultze-Naumburg felt free to alter and improve his photographs in order to achieve maximum effect. Viewing angle, lighting, context, and at times even retouching of the images, subtlely reinforced his arguments. The positive examples tended to be inviting, frontal views of older buildings in rural or natural settings, on a sunny day with dappled shadows, a hedge and a beautiful tree framing the view and site. The negative examples were often awkward, oblique views of new, historicist structures on a gray day or in full shade, with unsightly advertising or utility lines marring the view, and visual access to the image and the site often impeded by ugly paving or industrial fencing in the foreground. When he added short captions in later editions, he usually gave the name and hometown of the positive image, like a familiar friend, while leaving the negative one anonymous and placeless, with the connotation that it could be anywhere in Europe and did not belong in Germany. In the positive examples he defined the materials and forms more clearly, cleaned blemishes, and made the buildings literally more "painterly," a quality he admired in the actual buildings of the *Heimat*.[106] In negative views he emphasized the crass ornament and ugly fencing with aggressive scratches of his pen.

Such a graphic, comparative method was, of course, not new or unique to Schultze-Naumburg. Its origins in architecture go back at least to French and English architectural theory of the eighteenth and early nineteenth century. Pugin's moralizing book *Contrasts* (1836), which Schultze-Naumburg may have

[102] Schultze-Naumburg, *Hausbau*, n.p.
[103] Ibid.
[104] Schultze-Naumburg, *Dörfer und Kolonien*, n.p. The *Kulturarbeiten*'s volume 2 on gardens and volume 5 on palaces were actually made up exclusively of photographs. Schultze-Naumburg intended them to serve merely as further examples of points and issues already discussed.
[105] Schultze-Naumburg, "Künstlerische Photographien," in *Der Kunstwart* 13, no. 18, 1900, pp. 201–203. Some photos in the *Kulturarbeiten* were borrowed from the publisher, others from Hermann Muthesius and Otto Bartning. Most likely this was only a selection from a much larger collection, an invaluable resource of the vernacular landscape in Germany. Unfortunately the collection has been lost; Borrmann, *Paul Schultze-Naumburg*, p. 26; Posener, *Berlin auf dem Wege*, p. 190. Knaut, "Paul Schultze-Naumburgs Kulturtheorie um 1900," p. 545, notes that Schultze-Naumburg was given his first camera by his publisher Avenarius.
[106] Schultze-Naumburg, *Hausbau*, p. 96.

[107] Pugin's books may have been influenced by the famous "Red Books" of Humphry Repton, showing before-and-after views for his landscape designs, which also sought to fight against the ills of the industrialized landscape; Stephen Daniels, *Humphry Repton: Landscape Gardening and the Geography of Georgian England*, New Haven, Yale University Press, 1999. Interesting examples parallel to Schultze-Naumburg occur in the American *Ladies Home Journal* (e.g. Feb. 15, 1911), part of the American domestic reform movement, also with roots in Pugin and the English Arts and Crafts movement.

[108] Wölfflin's first comparative work was *Renaissance und Barok* (1888), with subsequent editions, and other books such as *Klassische Kunst* (1899) and *Kunstgeschichtliche Grundbegriffe* (1915) all based on the comparative analysis of form. Wölfflin was listed as a board member of Schultze-Naumburg's Dürerbund, along with an impressive list of prominent German intellectuals. See Kratzsch, *Kunstwart und Dürerbund*, p. 466.

[109] Ulyz Vogt-Göknil, "Polarisation der Stile als Methode der Architekturrepresentation," in V. Rentsch (ed.), *Das architektonische Urteil: Annäherungen und Interpretationen von Architektur und Kunst*, Basel, Birkhäuser, 1989; Paul Brandt, *Sehen und Erkennen: Eine Anleitung zur vergleichenden Kunstbetrachtung*, Leipzig, F. Hirt & Sohn, 1911; Werner Oechslin, "A Cultural History of Modern Architecture," *a+u*, 235, 1990, pp. 50–64.

[110] Martin Warnke, "Bau und Gegenbau," in Hipp and Seidl, *Architektur als politische Kultur*.

[111] Kai K. Gutschow, "Example-Counterexample: The Role of Visual Comparisons in Creating a Modern German Architecture," unpublished paper at 13th Berkeley Symposium "Interdisciplinary Approaches to Visual Representation", March 16, 2002.

[112] Paul Schultze-Naumburg and Walter Gropius, "Wer hat Recht? Traditionelle Baukunst oder Bauen in neuen Formen. Zwei sich widersprechende Ansichten," pp. 30–40, 103–113; Werner Hegemann, "May und Schultze-Naumburg," in *Wasmuths Monatshefte für Baukunst* 11, 1927, pp. 108–127.

known through Muthesius and a general interest by German reformers in the English Arts and Crafts movement, contains both similar graphic comparisons and an ideology of nostalgia for a more wholesome past.[107] But Schultze-Naumburg did not look back exclusively to a pre-industrial past as did Pugin, and his plethora of real-life photographs drove home the points much more realistically than Pugin's pen and ink fantasies.

The philosophical dichotomies *Kultur/Zivilisation* and *Gemeinschaft/Gesellschaft* that Schultze-Naumburg delineated also made comparisons a natural tool. The influence of the art historian Heinrich Wölfflin, who was developing the comparative method of art historical research used to determine the development of formal stylistic traits during these same years, cannot be discounted.[108] In her analysis of the contemporary architectural and cultural historians Josef Strzygowski, Wilhelm Worringer, and Oswald Spengler, the historian Ulyz Vogt-Göknil has even suggested that the comparative method was indispensable to any critical discussion of architecture during this period.[109] Martin Warnke has suggested even more broadly that most architecture through history has been built in "competition" or "ideological opposition" to other buildings, making comparisons fundamental to the design process, and to interpretation.[110]

Schultze-Naumburg and Modern Architecture

In the heated ideological battles to redefine German culture and promote distinct visions of modern architecture, architects and writers of all convictions increasingly resorted to simple juxtaposed photographs and eventually the related technique of photo-collage to reinforce their architectural ideas.[111] The techniques reached their most provocative extremes in the late 1920s and early 1930s. Popular illustrated magazines such as *Der Uhu* as well as professional journals such as Werner Hegemann's *Wasmuths Monatshefte* ignited public opinion and fanned the flames of these battles.[112] In a clear

7.11 Aerial view of Bruno Taut's Hufeisersiedlung in Berlin-Britz, with the conservative *Heimat* architecture crossed out as unacceptable, although Taut's rowhouses had similar pitched roofs.
Source: Bruno Taut, *Bauen*, 1927.

Abb. 155
GEHAG-SIEDLUNG BRITZ, Hufeisen. — Gärten und Straßen unfertig

response to the *Heimatschutz* campaigns, for example, the progressive architect Bruno Taut edited an aerial of his own housing development to highlight where the enemy camp lay. The critics Adolf Behne and Sigfried Giedion used similar techniques. The more conservative Stuttgart architect Schmitthenner maligned Hans Scharoun's mechanistic "machine for living" at the Weissenhof housing exhibit, and compared it unfavorably to Goethe's beloved garden house.[113]

As Schultze-Naumburg's message and technique of reform began to take hold after the first decade of the century, however, he himself relied ever less on such straightforward visual comparisons.[114] As his colleague Ferdinand Avenarius wrote, the "crass technique" which "had been necessary to open people's eyes," was by then no longer quite as essential because of the changes that it had already begun to effect.[115] In the greatly revised and reissued edition of the last three volumes of the *Kulturarbeiten* from 1929, for example, Schultze-Naumburg juxtaposed the Weissenhof with Santorini, or Ernst May's and Bruno Taut's housing developments with old prisons and more "schematic" developments. Rather than good–bad comparisons, these pairs operated through guilt by association – both were seen as negative. The book's cover, however, still contrasted Le Corbusier's "foreign" looking Weissenhof duplex with a grand old house from the *Heimat*. Either way, his antipathy towards the stylized *Neues Bauen* was obvious.

It was, in part, in reaction to the effectiveness of Schultze-Naumburg's publicity effort that many modern architects launched their own campaigns. More than just promoting certain reforms, I contend that his early use of photographic comparisons and partisan arguments played a decisive role in pushing German architects – including himself – into the opposing and increasingly polarized camps described in his 1926 *Der Uhu* article. Modern architects of all persuasions mined his propaganda for disparate causes. Conservatives clung to the romantic, nationalist, and anti-Mediterranean spirit recalled by the early nineteenth century, to the values of handcrafted construction, and to the forms of older German vernacular traditions such as the pitched roof. More progressive architects valued the emphasis on international trends, tectonic construction, the lack of ornament, and simple functional forms, but also the vernacular's tendency constantly to update itself to accommodate new conditions, even industrialization.

Eventually, the German architecture from "around 1800" represented for both camps not just an aesthetically and symbolically appropriate past, but the basis for a homegrown, modern German architectural aesthetic that no longer relied on history and a classical, Mediterranean precedent. In rebuttal to Schultze-Naumburg's article in *Der Uhu*, for example, the young modernist Hugo Häring sought to claim the mantle of "homegrown" for modern architects. He even stooped to the same kinds of racist arguments, but now in reverse. He proclaimed that Schultze-Naumburg's *Um 1800* classicism represented an intrusion into Nordic culture, "a foreign element, derived from the Orient, Greece, and Rome," and thus "more closely associated with Mongoloid and Negro blood," than the architecture of the New Building.[116] Häring complained that traditional house builders were in fact the purveyors of a "Greek and Latin" heritage, and as a result were "outfitting the Nordic landscape with an architecture of Mediterranean peoples" that did not belong in "our Nordic cultural landscape." The "purism" and purity of modern architecture was now closely associated with cultural and even racial purity. Both camps, modernists and traditionalists, were increasingly anti-Mediterranean.

[113] Schmitthenner, *Baugestaltung*.
[114] Schultze-Naumburg, *Gesicht des deutschen Hauses*; Paul Schultze-Naumburg, *Kampf um die Kunst*, Nationalsozialistische Bibliothek, vol. 36, Munich, Frz. Eher Nachf., 1932.
[115] Avenarius, editorial; Ferdinand Avenarius, "Beispiel und Gegen-beispiel," in *Der Kunstwart* 25, no. 12, 1912, p. 410.
[116] Hugo Häring, "Die Tradition, Schultze-Naumburg und wir," in *Die Form* 1, no. 8, May 1926, p. 180.

[117] His proto-Nazi writings after World War I include: *Kunst und Rasse*, Munich, J. F. Lehmann, 1928, 1935, 1938, 1942; the official Nazi pamphlet *Kampf um die Kunst*; *Rassengebundene Kunst*, Erfurt, K. Stenger, 1934; *Die Kunst der Deutschen*, Stuttgart, Deutsche Verlags Anstalt, 1934, 1936; *Kunst aus Blut und Boden*, Leipzig, E. A. Seemann, 1934; and *Nordische Schönheit*, Munich, J. F. Lehmann, 1937, 1943. On eugenics, see for example the advertisements for books on eugenics by the conservative J. F. Lehmann Verlag in Munich in the back of Schultze-Naumburg, *Kunst und Rasse*, such as H. Günther, *Rasse und Stil* (1926); the very popular H. Günther *Rassenkunde des Deutschen Volke*, which was continually reprinted from 1923–43; L. Clauß, *Rasse und Seele* (1926); and *Siedlungskunde des deutschen Volkes* (1927). The American social activist Margaret Sanger and many others used similar theories of eugenics in her arguments for birth control and other social ills; e.g. Margaret Sanger, *Women and the New Race*, New York, Brentano's, 1920.

[118] Borrmann, *Paul Schultze-Naumburg*; Konrad Nonn, "Die Kulturarbeit Schultze-Naumburgs," in *Zentralblatt der Bauverwaltung*, 59, no. 23, 1939, pp. 633–639.

[119] Jarzombek, "The Kunstgewerbe, the Werkbund, and the Aesthetics of Culture in the Wilhelmine Period"; Jarzombek, "The Discourse of a Bourgeois Utopia."

[120] K. Michael Hays, "Tessenow's Architecture as National Allegory: Critique of Capitalism or Proto-fascism," *9H: On Rigor*, 1988, pp. 54–71; also in *Assemblage* 8, Feb. 1989, pp. 105–124.

Although Schultze-Naumburg's propaganda techniques and the rejection of the stylishly modern and the Mediterranean in 1929 were similar to the messages in the *Kulturarbeiten* from 1900, the message of late books such as *Das Gesicht des deutschen Hauses* had begun to change dramatically. Eventually a growing xenophobia, outright racism, and blatant anti-Semitism led Schultze-Naumburg to condemn diversity and all foreign ideas in favor of Germanic "purity." His pre-war writings did refer to a German nationalist architecture and a common Nordic spirit, and did make connections between architecture and bourgeois nationalist politics in the *Um 1800* period. But, as we have seen by looking occasionally at the work of Muthesius and Loos, similar ideas could be found in a broad spectrum of reformers of the day. After World War I, Schultze-Naumburg's ever greater politically motivated conflation of architecture, physiognomy, and national identity began to alter not just the tone of his writings, but his target audience. He found increasing ideological support in popular theories of eugenics that were circulated all over the world, and financial and political support in the right-wing factions that were blossoming in Germany.[117] These eventually led him to close personal associations with Adolf Hitler, Alfred Rosenberg, and the top Nazi ideologues.[118] His writings changed from focusing on architectural and cultural reform, to promoting specific political and racial agendas.

But even with the dogmatic adherence to German traditional rural forms and an extremely racist and nationalist ideology in his late writings and in his architectural designs, attempts to bind his turn-of-the-century reform efforts to the Nazi ideology that actually crystallized only decades later can be greatly misleading. Mark Jarzombek, for example, awkwardly sidesteps the well-documented progressive influence of the Werkbund and publications such as the *Kulturarbeiten* on modern architecture, when he implicates the reformers in a carefully scripted bourgeois plot to find a suitable nationalist identity for modern Germany through the applied arts.[119] The attention to quality, craft, and a harmonious design culture promoted by the Werkbund, Jarzombek claims, helped set in place and legitimate highly stereotypical ideas about art, architecture, and an aesthetic culture which, in the decades after World War I, were exploited by reactionary cultural critics such as Schultze-Naumburg and other Nazis. Here Muthesius and Behrens are analyzed alongside Schultze-Naumburg as examples of Stern's "cultural despair." Similarly, by labeling Tessenow's earliest pre-World War I ideas "proto-fascist" rather than simply a popular and romantic "critique of capitalism," K. Michael Hays risks making his history more operative than factual.[120] Such arguments are easily tainted by anachronisms and teleological arguments. They overlook changing political and cultural contexts, and minimize the role of changing contexts and audiences.

Schultze-Naumburg's nationalist rhetoric and polarizing use of stark contrasts in the *Kulturarbeiten* helped set the tone and direction for subsequent architectural polemics in modern Germany. By focusing his critiques exclusively on Germany and denigrating foreign imports, especially those from the Orient and the Mediterranean, Schultze-Naumburg's *Kulturarbeiten* were instrumental in shaping a trend for much of German modern architecture away from classical and foreign traditions and eclectic styles — many of which were associated with the Mediterranean. Instead German architects increasingly valued region and place as prime determinants of modern architecture. Although clearly influenced by precedents and developments from abroad, the development of modern architecture in Germany remained at its core a nationalist and anti-Mediterranean one. ■

7.12 Adolf Behne's comparison of a stuffy Wilhelmine-era parlor and women's fashion, the functionally furnished "Co-op Zimmer" by Hannes Meyer, and the "New Man" in sporty tennis outfit.

Source: Adolf Behne, *Eine Stunde Architektur*, 1928.

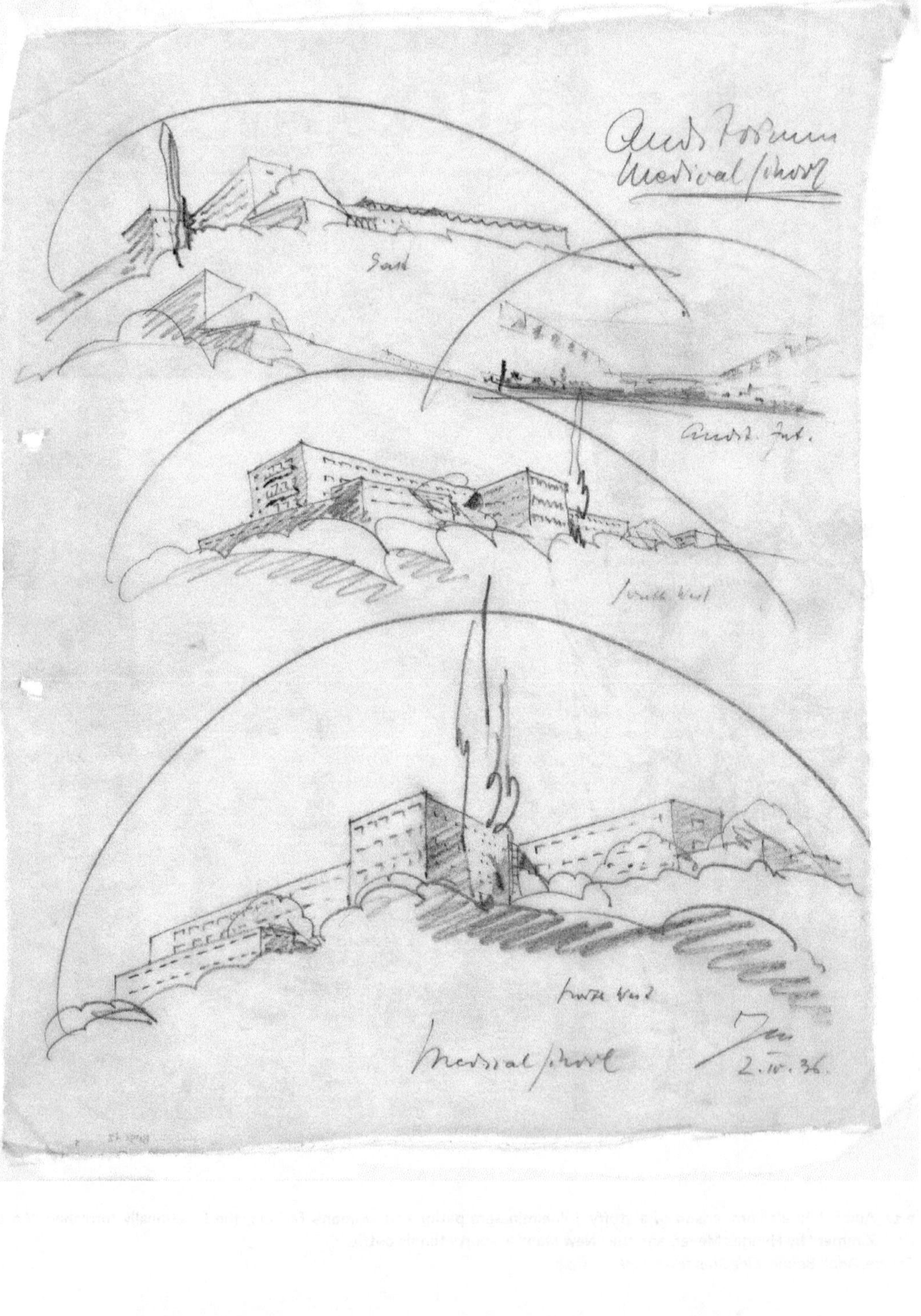
Arch Forum
Medical school
Medical school
2.IV.36.

8

ERICH MENDELSOHN'S MEDITERRANEAN LONGINGS

The European Mediterranean Academy and Beyond in Palestine

Ita Heinze-Greenberg

The closure in 1932 of the Bauhaus in Dessau was spearheaded by architect Paul Schultze-Naumburg, the influential member of the *Kampfbund für deutsche Kultur* (a nationalistic association dedicated to the fight for German culture). At the very same time modernism was being challenged in Germany, Berlin-based architect Erich Mendelsohn, together with the French painter Amédée Ozenfant and the Dutch publisher and architect Hendricus Theodorus Wijdeveld, conceived the Académie Européenne Méditerranée (AEM) as a European art school on the Mediterranean shores of southern France. Although the idea ultimately remained on paper as an unrealized utopia, it was an ambitious enterprise, which progressed far beyond the stage of conceptual plans. Potential financial sponsors were secured, an appropriate building plot was purchased, artists from different disciplines and from various European countries had signed contracts as future academy teachers, and beautifully designed brochures with the teaching curriculum were already printed in five languages. Beyond that, an impressive list of celebrities from science, politics, and the arts joined the advisory committee as members, starting with Albert Einstein, followed by Paul Valéry, Frank Lloyd Wright, and Igor Stravinsky. The teaching program listed all the arts, including music, film, and dance, thus displaying an innovative multidisciplinary character. It would have been a kind of Bauhaus on the Côte d'Azur. But the Académie Européenne Méditerranée had more on its agenda: it presented – shortly before its crisis – a "borderless" vision of Europe, for which the Mediterranean culture would supply a unifying and universalist identity. Above all, it was about a reassessment of modern art and its nexus with the values of classical and vernacular traditions. Or as Mendelsohn put it in one of his smart *bons mots*: "We'll leave it to the Schultzes from Naumburg to ignore the Mediterranean as the father of the international Western theory of style."[1]

The initiator of the original academy project was Hendrik Wijdeveld (1885–1987). He is best known for his long-standing commitment as the editor of the journal *Wendingen*, the voice of the Amsterdam School, a loose group of architects gathered around the leading young architect Michel de Klerk.[2] "*Dutchy*," as his friends named Wijdeveld, was the term for a "jack-of-all-trades." He was acquainted with all the influential people of the international art scene, and for several years he had pursued the idea of bringing together his numerous contacts and focusing them on one special project: starting an international art school.

In the second half of the 1920s, Wijdeveld developed a scheme for "*een internationale werkgemeenschap*" (an international work community) in Holland, to be established in the idyllic landscape around the lakes of Loosdrecht, near

[1] Erich Mendelsohn, "Neu-Athen," *Berliner Tageblatt*, June 1931, p. 14.
[2] For an evaluation of Wijdeveld's architectural works and townplanning projects, see Mariëtte van Stralen, "De Landhuizen van H.Th. Wijdeveld," in *Forum* 37, 3–4, January 1995, pp. 3–144; Jean-Paul Baeten and Aaron Betsky, *Ontwerp het onmogelijke. De wereld van architect Hendrik Wijdeveld (1885–1987)*, Rotterdam, NAi Uitgevers, 2006.

8.1 (*Far left*) Erich Mendelsohn. Hadassah University Medical Center, Mount Scopus, Jerusalem, *c.*1935. Perspectives of the medical school and auditorium.
Source: © The Museum of Modern Art/Licensed by SCALA/Art Resource, New York.

[3] Hendrik Th. Wijdeveld, *Naar een internationale werkgemeenschap*, Santpoort, C. A. Mees, 1931; also published in German translation: *Eine internationele Arbeitsgemeinschaft*, Santpoort, C. A. Mees.

[4] Ibid., pp. 13–16, author's translation from the German edition.

[5] Since 1926 a joint school project was a subject in the correspondence between Frank Lloyd Wright and Wijdeveld. In 1931 Wright invited Wijdeveld to Spring Green to take over coequal partnership in setting up the Taliesin Fellowship. A contract was drawn up (Wijdeveld Archives, Nederlands Architectuurinstituut in Rotterdam (NAi, WIJD B 26.198), but not implemented. However, Wijdeveld's potential employment as the fellowship's schoolmaster was still discussed in 1933 (NAi, WIJD B 4.13).

[6] Wijdeveld's extensive correspondence includes letters written in Dutch, German, French, and English (NAi, WIJD).

[7] Louise Mendelsohn, *My Life in a Changing World*, unpublished memoirs, San Francisco, pp. 274–276. Copies of the manuscript are held in the Mendelsohn Archive, Staatliche Museen zu Berlin – Preussischer Kulturbesitz, Kunstbibliothek Berlin, and in the Getty Research Institute for the History of Art and the Humanities, Department of Special Collections and Visual Resources, Los Angeles, Erich and Louise Mendelsohn Papers, 1887–1992.

[8] Wim de Wit. (ed.), *The Amsterdam School*, Cambridge, MA, The MIT Press, 1983, p. 168.

[9] Letter from F. L. Wright to Lewis Mumford, Spring Green, Dec. 9, 1931; in Bruce Brooks Pfeiffer and Robert Wojtowicz (eds.), *Frank Lloyd Wright + Lewis Mumford. Thirty Years of Correspondence*, New York, Princeton Architectural Press, 2001, p. 122.

Utrecht. He published his program in the form of an attractive, hardcover booklet, including two different architectural designs.[3] Accordingly, his art school was conceived as a non-academic work community, where teachers and students, architects, artists and craftsmen, would all live and work together. They would learn together through doing, dining together in a communal hall, and taking part in cultural and sporting activities, or at a smaller scale, agricultural activities aimed at rendering the community self-sufficient. These more romantic communitarian inclinations were counterbalanced with a clear allegiance to the latest production systems and an enthusiastic embrace of technology and industry.

All these aspects suggested a strong Bauhaus influence, namely from both the Weimar and the Dessau period. Nevertheless, while Gropius had to fix his school fees for foreign students studying at the *Staatliches Bauhaus* at double those for German students, Wijdeveld strongly emphasized the international character in the agenda of his project:

> Young people from all parts of the world come to live and work there and they will be immersed in the internationalism that will reign there in all its variations. . . . Scientists and artists from Europe and America, from Asia and other parts of the world will not only be our guests, but will also become permanent collaborators.[4]

The initiative generated great interest, but seemingly more abroad than at home. Although Wijdeveld had deemed Holland's role in the European discourse to be a crucial one, the project attracted primarily influential partners from other countries, among them Frank Lloyd Wright from America,[5] Erich Mendelsohn from Germany, and Amédée Ozenfant from France. Mendelsohn and Ozenfant succeeded finally in persuading Wijdeveld to exchange the lakes of Loosdrecht for the Mediterranean, the blue sea and the yellow sun of the South, and above all to go back to the cradle of a timeless, classical and vernacular tradition. Thus already from the beginning of 1931, it became assumed that the Mediterranean shore of France was the right location for this future international work community.

The Founding Triumvirate of the Mediterranean Academy

At the time Mendelsohn, Wijdeveld, and Ozenfant began to collaborate all three of them were in their forties and at the peak of their careers. They were very different in character and each of them spoke his own artistic language. Yet, they were ready to contribute each his own special ability to the project: Mendelsohn contributed his powerful capability to translate ideas into reality, Wijdeveld his imaginative enthusiasm, and Ozenfant his theory based on Mediterranean thought. Together they formed an interesting triumvirate of future academy directors.

Starting with the father of the idea, Wijdeveld was a widely traveled cosmopolitan, who spoke several European languages.[6] He had spent his youth in South Africa, and had worked in various architectural offices in Holland, England, and France before he opened his own practice in Amsterdam in 1914. Friends remembered him as a great enthusiast, who easily made contacts.[7] Wim de Wit called him the "most exuberant of all the Amsterdam School architects."[8] And Frank Lloyd Wright depicted Wijdeveld in a letter to Lewis Mumford as "a lyrical egoist," who "makes my egocentricity look like a single color in the spectrum while he has them all. This surprised me. I thought I was the limit."[9]

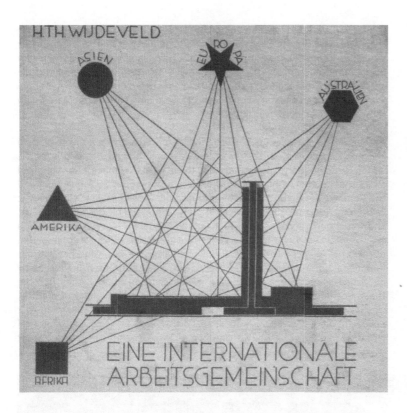

8.2 Hendrik Th. Wijdeveld.
 Cover of the German
 edition of his
 Internationale
 Werkgemeenschap
 [International Work
 Community].
Source: H. Th. Wijdeveld,
Eine internationale
Arbeitsgemeinschaft,
Santpoort, 1931.

8.3 Hendrik Th. Wijdeveld.
 Perspective drawing of
 his projected school
 building, second version,
 1929.
Source: Author's collection.

In any case, Wijdeveld must have been an exceptional person, a great visionary and dreamer with astonishing physical strength and mental powers. He would eventually reach the age of 102. When he was 85, he wrote that he still felt full of energy for tackling every new task.[10] Mendelsohn has left us one of the most wonderful descriptions of Wijdeveld:

> I have seen him dancing on the wall surrounding ancient Jerusalem to the syncopated beats of Arab workmen, and to the smiling motion of the surf on the silver sand of France's Côte d'Azur.[11]

Mendelsohn's acquaintance with Wijdeveld goes back to the years shortly after World War I. Correspondence between the two men started in 1920, when Wijdeveld invited Mendelsohn to publish his works in *Wendingen*. Some months later, in February 1921, Mendelsohn's sketches filled a whole issue. In addition Wijdeveld organized two lecture tours around Holland for Mendelsohn, in 1921 and 1923.[12] When Mendelsohn traveled to Palestine early in 1923, Wijdeveld spontaneously accepted his invitation to accompany him. Their mutual understanding developed into a very cordial friendship, and it was at Wijdeveld's home in Amsterdam where Mendelsohn and his wife Louise found refuge, when they escaped from Germany on the last day of March in 1933.[13]

Erich Mendelsohn (1887–1953) is still best known for his architectural debut, the Einstein Tower in Potsdam, which catapulted him into the headlines, and helped him to establish one of the busiest architectural offices in Germany. By the time he got involved in the academy project, he could look back on an impressive oeuvre, mainly large-scale projects for industry and commerce, and a number of private residences.[14] His biggest building under construction at

[10] Letter from H. Th. Wijdeveld to Hermann Finsterlin, n.p., 31 June 1971, NAi, WIJD B 32.7.
[11] H. Th.Wijdeveld, *Time and Art*, Hilversum, Rotting's Printing Works, 1947, p. 9.
[12] According to the documents at NAi WIJD, the correspondence between Mendelsohn and Wijdeveld started with a letter from Wijdeveld of 5 June 1920, NAi, WIJD B 28.9–11.
[13] Louise Mendelsohn, *My Life*, p. 255.
[14] For an overview on Mendelsohn's architectural oeuvre, see Regina Stephan (ed.), *Eric Mendelsohn. Architect 1887–1953*, New York, Monacelli Press, 1999.

15 Ita Heinze-Greenberg, "'I Often Fear the Envy of the Gods'. Success, House and Home," in Regina Stephan (ed.), *Mendelsohn*, pp. 170–181; and "Das Haus Am Rupenhorn in Berlin von Erich Mendelsohn," in Christoph Hölz (ed.), *Freiräume. Häuser, die Geschichte machten 1920 bis 1940*, München, HypoVereinsbank, 1998, pp. 74–93.

the time of the AEM was the Columbus House, a towering office building on the Potsdamer Platz in Berlin. Furthermore, he had just finished realizing his own home, *Am Rupenhorn*, on Berlin's Lake Havel, and had moved there with his wife and daughter a few months earlier. This newly built family refuge spoke a restrained language of classical elegance and moderation, a far cry from Mendelsohn's first dynamic works in Germany.[15] It was decorated with three murals executed by Ozenfant.

Amédée Ozenfant (1886–1966) was a multitalented artist: apart from holding an important position in the ranks of Cubist painters, he was also a prolific writer. He acted as the spokesman of all those artists in France who supported a classical tradition within modernism. Already in 1916, Ozenfant had founded the journal *L'Élan*, and in it published his widely read article "Notes sur le Cubisme" (Notes on Cubism) which strongly expressed his desire to clean up, and somehow rationalize, cubism. It was an appeal for a new order and for a return, within the avant-garde, to principles of classical order. He continued to develop his *"rappel à l'ordre"* (Call to Order) after the war, together with his famous co-author Charles-Edouard Jeanneret, alias Le Corbusier. In their jointly published essay "Après le Cubisme" (After Cubism) of 1918 they laid the theoretical foundation for Purism, which could be called a kind of purified, classical cubism. Until 1925, the two artists worked together on the further development of these ideas, both in their artistic works and in their theoretical writings, mostly published in the journal they co-edited entitled *L'Esprit*

8.4 Mendelsohn's house *Am Rupenhorn* with the mural by Amédée Ozenfant.
Source: Erich Mendelsohn, *Neues Haus – Neue Welt*, Berlin, 1932.

nouveau. Purism was the artistic expression of the re-establishment of an order, a kind of mathematical lyricism, which was intended to integrate itself into a natural, universal cosmic order. Its source of reference was the classical and vernacular tradition of the Mediterranean.[16] Ozenfant broadened these ideas in his widely noted, controversial book *Art*, which was published in Paris in 1928, and three years later translated into German, as well as into English under the title *Foundations of Modern Art*.[17]

Mendelsohn's decision to commission Ozenfant expressed his choice of a Mediterranean sensitivity for his house. In particular the large mural for the reception hall, entitled *Musik und die bildenden Künste* (Music and the Plastic Arts) and considered as Ozenfant's last Purist painting – with motifs such as the harp and the earthen vessel, seemed like the introduction to Mendelsohn's Mediterraneanism.[18] Having already known his works and writings for some years, Mendelsohn's initial personal contact with Ozenfant was probably made during his first visit to Paris, early in 1929.[19] A year later, in 1930, Ozenfant came to stay for several weeks at Mendelsohn's newly built home, *Am Rupenhorn*, in order to execute his murals. This provided an excellent opportunity for the two men to get to know each other more closely, resulting in a deep mutual respect. Ozenfant's exuberant eulogy about Mendelsohn's house, published in 1932 in the trilingual book *New House – New World*, testifies to how far they followed similar artistic approaches.[20] It may be assumed that the culture and tradition of the Mediterranean world was the subject of many talks between these two artists. Ozenfant surely told stories about his recent journeys to Greece and the Near East, which in turn probably reminded Mendelsohn of his own happy trip together with Wijdeveld to Palestine and the neighboring countries in 1923. It may have awoken in Mendelsohn atavistic feelings for the Eastern shore of the Mediterranean. Ozenfant perhaps also gave Mendelsohn the initial impulse to visit Greece, which he did in spring 1931.[21] The journey turned out to be an overwhelming experience for Mendelsohn, Greece becoming a new source of inspiration for his thinking and his architectural understanding. After his journey he wrote six very poetic essays for the *Berliner Tageblatt*, which gave testimony to his newly discovered love, the powerful impact Greece had on him. He called Athens "Europe's mother" and the Mediterranean the "father of the international Western theory of style."[22]

Ozenfant was the only one among the future school directors with teaching experience. In 1924 he had founded, together with Fernand Léger, the Académie Moderne in Paris, and later in 1932, he opened his own art school, the Académie Ozenfant, which had a branch in London from 1936 onwards until he transferred the school entirely to New York. The Académie Ozenfant, which he established in the same building as his famous studio built by Le Corbusier, at 53 avenue Reille, focused on "dessin, peinture, sculpture" [drawing, painting, sculpture]. The program promised that these courses would be supplemented by interdisciplinary lectures, given by art critics, architects, engravers, poets, and musicians. Furthermore, it also offered introductions to different philosophical and scientific concepts. The underlying pedagogical idea was to lead each student to discover his own talents and style, free from any pressure exerted by the master.[23] Ozenfant envisaged his art school as an "international centre of artistic culture."[24] Thus, his concept coincided with Wijdeveld's, and subsequently with the fundamental points of the Mediterranean Academy program, which was written down less than one year later. Ozenfant probably saw both academy projects as complementary enterprises. Since, however, he was preoccupied with setting up his own school in Paris, it was primarily Wijdeveld and Mendelsohn who were first active in getting the project in southern France up and running.

[16] See Charles Harrison and Paul Wood (eds.), *Art in Theory 1900–1990. An Anthology of Changing Ideas*, Oxford, Cambridge, MA, Blackwell, 1996, pp. 217–245; and Gottfried Boehm, "Amédée Ozenfant and Le Corbusier: Works of Purism," in Gottfried Boehm, Ulrich Mosch, and Katharina Schmidt (eds.), *Canto d'Amore. Classicism in Modern Art and Music 1914–1935*, Bern, Benteli Verlags AG, 1996, pp. 334–335.
[17] Amédée Ozenfant, *Art*, Paris, Jean Budry, 1928; English edition: *Foundations of Art*, London, John Rodker, 1931.
[18] Susan L. Ball, *Ozenfant and Purism. The Evolution of a Style 1915–1930*, Ann Arbor, MI, UMI Research Press, 1981, p. 147.
[19] Louise Mendelsohn writes in her memoirs, *My Life*, p. 867, that she and her husband knew Ozenfant and his works from the various issues of *L'Esprit nouveau*. When it came to the decoration of their home they decided for Ozenfant's Purism, since "Eric and I loved those pure forms which Ozenfant balanced so harmoniously in color and subject."
[20] Erich Mendelsohn, *Neues Haus– Neue Welt*, Berlin, Mosse, 1932 (reprint Berlin, Gebr. Mann, 1997).
[21] Mendelsohn received an invitation from the German Archeological Institute in Athens, whose director was Prof. Georg Karo, a very good friend of Mendelsohn's early patroness Baroness Elsa von Bissing.
[22] Four of the six articles are reprinted in Ita Heinze-Greenberg and Regina Stephan (eds.), *Eric Mendelsohn. Gedankenwelten. Unbekannte Texte zu Architektur, Kulturgeschichte und Politik*, Ostfildern-Ruit, Hatje Cantz, 2000, pp. 116–123.
[23] Printed announcement of the Académie Ozenfant at 53 Avenue Reille, Paris, 4 January 1932; author's collection.
[24] Ibid: "L'Académie Ozenfant sera, en quelque sorte, à Paris, un centre international de culture artistique."

25 Letter Erich Mendelsohn to Louise Mendelsohn, Lyons, 8 August 1932, machine-typed copy by Louise Mendelsohn in author's collection.
26 Letter Erich Mendelsohn to Louise Mendelsohn, Hyères, 11 August 1932, machine-typed copy by Louise Mendelsohn in author's collection.
27 Letter Erich Mendelsohn to Louise Mendelsohn, Cavalière, 13 August 1932, machine-typed copy by Louise Mendelsohn in author's collection.
28 Prospectus of the Académie Européenne Méditerranée, 1933, Mendelsohn Archive, Staatliche Museen zu Berlin, no number; and NAi WIJD.
29 NAi, WIJD holds an extensive correspondence with the potential academy teachers.
30 For further information on Eric Gill, see Fiona MacCarthy, Eric Gill, London/Boston, Faber and Faber, 1989.
31 For further extensive information on Serge Chermayeff, see Alan Powers, Serge Chermayeff: Designer, Architect, Teacher, London, RIBA Publications, 2001.

The Implementation of the Academy Project

In summer 1932, Mendelsohn and Wijdeveld traveled from Paris down the river Rhône to tour the Mediterranean coast of southern France, in search of a suitable site on which to build the future academy. Mendelsohn wrote letters to his wife every day or other short travelogues, which are full of enthusiasm for the Mediterranean experience and the academy project. On August 8, 1932:

> One drinks, drowns in Beaujolais and is – saved. Germany is far behind us, and the midi in front of our nose. We already smell olives, macchia [scrub] and the fragrance of summer.[25]

And three days later:

> We are taking every winding lane to discover every single beautiful place – driving down the coast, entering private properties, awarding marks to them and noting these on the maps.[26]

And again two days later:

> We are seeing a lot, because we sense that the birth of reality is dependent on the right site.[27]

At the beginning of 1933 the triumvirate decided to buy a building plot of one hundred hectares at Cavalière in the bay between Cap Nègre and Pointe du Rossignol, halfway between Cannes and Marseille. It was to occupy magnificently situated grounds, secluded from all distractions of the Riviera, yet on the international lines of communication. The financing of the whole project was to be assured by a limited liability company. The total costs were estimated at three million French francs.[28] Parallel to searching for an appropriate building site Mendelsohn, Wijdeveld, and Ozenfant tried to find suitable and capable future teachers for the academy. The list of staff who accepted an invitation to teach shows that the triumvirate of directors succeeded in winning over renowned artists from various European countries as heads of the different departments.[29]

Through Ozenfant's personal contacts they won over Paul Bonifas (1893–1967) from Switzerland for the ceramic department and the Spanish artist Pablo Gargallo (1881–1934) as head of the sculpture department. Bonifas had enjoyed professional education in pottery, etching, engraving, and music. At the beginning of the 1920s he had worked as general secretary of the journal L'Esprit nouveau, with Ozenfant and Le Corbusier. Gargallo, a friend of Picasso from his Barcelona period, worked in Paris and was represented by the famous gallery of Leon Rosenberg.

Two artists from England joined in: Serge Chermayeff (1900–96) and Eric Gill (1882–1940). The latter, who was to take over the faculty of typography, was one of England's most successful sculptors and typographers. Gill had a very ambivalent dazzling character: coming from the Arts and Crafts tradition, he himself founded three handicraft-based communities, in which he succeeded to fuse religion, art, and sex.[30] Chermayeff was an artistic figure not less intriguing. Born near Grozny in Chechnia he grew up in London with a period abroad in South America. After a short career as a professional dancer he had specialized with great success in interior decoration and was thus chosen by the triumvirate to head the future department of interior design.[31] Finally the German musician Paul Hindemith (1895–1963) joined the list of staff members. Since 1927 he had been teaching at the Berlin Academy of Music. His reputation was that of a revolutionary who had developed into a scholar of classical Modernism.[32]

With this number of eminent artists the circle of future staff members was closed for the time being. The three directors themselves were to take over the departments of architecture (Mendelsohn), theatre (Wijdeveld), and painting (Ozenfant). Additional courses such as Dance, Textiles, Photography and Film, were to be implemented at a later date.

Even more impressive than the list of the future teaching staff was the composition of the board of honorary members. It reads like namedropping from a contemporary edition of *Who's Who*. With Albert Einstein at its head, this committee was composed of well-known men from science, politics, and the arts, and one woman, Hélène de Mandrot de Sarraz, initiator of the International Congress of Modern Architecture (CIAM); other names on the impressive list of internationally known personalities were the prominent architects Hendrik Petrus Berlage, August Perret, Charles Herbert Reilly, Raymond Unwin, Henry van de Velde, and Frank Lloyd Wright, the British stage designer Edward Gordon Craig, the German theatre director Max Reinhard, the French writer and poet Paul Valéry, and the musicians Leopold Stokovsky and Igor Stravinsky.[33]

The next step involved advertising the whole project. Lavishly designed brochures and booklets were printed in French, English, Dutch, German, and Spanish, five hundred copies in each language to be distributed among interested circles throughout Europe.[34] They provided information about the ambitious goals of the academy and were enriched by enchanting photos of the site. The brochure's text opened with general statements about the character of the projected Académie Européenne Méditerranée (AEM). The school's goal was defined as forging a Golden Mean between the stultifying effects of the traditional academic training and the freedom of private study, possibly leading to individual eccentricity. The term 'academy' was used to make clear that modernism was not understood as a break with tradition, but rather as an organic development rooted in the past.

The union of tradition and innovation was felt in the content of the courses, as well as in the didactic forms themselves. Rather than radically breaking with conventional teaching methods, the program of study was built on traditional ideas. New creative pedagogical and artistic approaches did not replace the old ones, but were added to them. If the academy had been realized according to the program described in the brochure, the AEM would have doubtlessly developed into a centre of the collected *experience* of the Modern Movement, in contrast to the Bauhaus, which became the focus of the collected *experiments* of modernism. Moreover, the European identity was stressed in the text of the brochure and emphasized in maps, which idealistically drew together a European cultural unity, which stood in harsh contrast with existing and emerging political divisions of the time. Two reasons were given to justify the choice of site: first, the excellent Mediterranean climate, and second its cultural situation as a "historical cradle and home of the principles of faith, law, and form."[35] Ultimately, the academy enterprise was about a geographical shift in modernism, back towards the Mediterranean roots that had inspired so many contemporaries, with Le Corbusier at the top of the list. It was a movement away from the Northern European – if one dares to say Protestant/Calvinist – pragmatism with political as well as aesthetic implications. Its agenda affirmed nothing less than Mediterranean Europe's central role in the cultural world.

[32] In a letter from Cavalière on 1 September 1933, Mendelsohn wrote to his wife: "I have heard that Hindemith has been dismissed on account of his Jewish wife. So he is safe for the Academy," in Oskar Beyer, *Eric Mendelsohn. Letters of an Architect*, London/New York/Toronto, Abelard-Schuman, 1967, p. 136.

[33] Prospectus (note 29).

[34] Today copies are to be found in various archives. Up to now the author could locate some of them at the KB Berlin, at the NAi WIJD, and at the Avery Library, Columbia University. There are two different versions: one is a lavishly designed square-formatted booklet including beautiful photos of the Mediterranean coast, the other has the form of a simple prospectus.

[35] Prospectus (note 29).

ACADÉMIE EUROPÉENNE MÉDITERRANNÉE
CAVALIÈRE, Cap Nègre, Le Lavandou (Var), FRANCE
Siège social provisoire, 10, rue des Marronniers, Paris, XVI

¶ LA Société Anonyme 'Académie Européenne Méditerranée' a été
constituée le 27 juin 1933. Le but de la Société est la création d'une
Académie d'art au bord de la Méditerranée. L'Académie enseignera
l'architecture–la peinture–la sculpture et la céramique–le tissage–la
typographie–le théâtre–la musique et la danse–la photographie et le
cinéma.
La Société a nommé comme directeurs de l'Académie les architectes
H. Th. Wijdeveld (Amsterdam), Erich Mendelsohn (Berlin) et le
peintre Amédée Ozenfant (Paris).

8.5 Page of the Mediterranean Academy (AEM) brochure showing the location of the academy's plot at Cavalière.
Source: Mendelsohn-Archive, Staatliche Museen zu Berlin – Preussischer Kulturbesitz, Kunstbibliothek.

The *Pensée Midi*

The Mediterranean has fascinated Northern Europeans for centuries. Goethe wrote, for instance, in his travel-book *Italienische Reise* (Italian Journey) (1786–88):

> Everyone is in the street, sitting in the sun, so long as it shines. The Neapolitan believes that he owns Paradise. He has a very sad notion of Northern countries: . . . always snow, wooden houses, great ignorance; but plenty of money.[36]

Of the three future directors of the AEM, it was Mendelsohn in particular who time and again reflected this North–South contrast. His travel notes from the Côte d'Azur give witness to his exalted mood; thus from Ajaccio in autumn 1931:

> The Mediterranean contemplates and creates; the North winds itself up and labours. The Mediterranean lives; the North defends itself.[37]

And about Corsica he wrote:

> Here one can grow old without work. . . . No comforts – just sun, no desires – just being.[38]

[36] Johann Wolfgang von Goethe, Hamburger edition in 14 volumes, ed. by Erich Trunz, vol. 11, München, 1994, p. 184.
[37] Letter Erich Mendelsohn to Louise Mendelsohn, Ajaccio, 29 October 1931, machine-typed copy by Louise Mendelsohn in author's collection.
[38] Letters Erich Mendelsohn to Louise Mendelsohn, Paris, 2 November 1931, in Oskar Beyer, *Erich Mendelsohn. Briefe eines Architekten*, München, Prestel, 1961, reprint: Basel, Berlin, Boston, Birkhäuser, 1991, p. 84.

Mendelsohn, who used to call himself *"ein Orientale aus Ostpreußen"* (an Oriental from East Prussia), not only felt an allegiance to both circles of perception, but also felt their diverging forces in himself.[39] On the one hand he had strong atavistic feelings towards the Eastern shore of the Mediterranean; on the other hand he strongly stood by his Prussian background. It was just the ambivalence of familiarity and otherness that opened new dimensions for him. He reflected on the Mediterranean as an involved outsider. His letters from those years were enchanting odes to the Mediterranean Sea. From Hyères in August 1932:

> Water, like pellucid blue glass, transparent. Imaginary points in the distance, mist, haze and unconsciousness. Two hundred metres of solitary cove surrounded by worldly enclave of an unknown pleasure – of a way of life – of a form of pleasure, which is perceived within us from the beginning to the end.[40]

And from Cavalière in May 1933:

> How splendid, this fresh sea wind. Of a tender heat, feminine. The sky, the islands, the sea, immerse themselves in the same marvel of this distant blue, which makes me at the same time feel alive and serene. The background of that nostalgia that has been with me since I was a child and which has carried me through time, which gives meaning to my awareness of space, to the harmony of mass, to the relation of each part to the whole, to the equilibrium of the three dimensions.[41]

And again from Cavalière in June 1933:

> Six days beside the Mediterranean, we feel a piece of antiquity becoming part of us, inadvertently distancing us from the north, from the change of temperature and of feelings – to that balance of life which doesn't know any excess weight.[42]

Life on the shores of the Mediterranean is depicted as a great sensual experience of happiness, the vital stimulus being attributed to the three gods of the Mediterranean: the sun, the sea, and the sky. It is what the French call the *pensée midi* which literally means "meridian thinking." But it encompasses so much more. It is the Mediterranean philosophy of harmony and measure, of oneness with nature, of Southern light as the source of thinking, of the appeal to measure as the centre of existence, of the inner stability of the Mediterranean world as the cradle of form, together with an exuberant homage to the culture of Greek Antiquity and Italian Renaissance, the philosophy behind the vital spirit of the classical era and its heritage.

The *pensée midi* leads to several of the greatest contemporary French thinkers, and above all to Paul Valéry. His *Eupalinos, ou l'architecte* seems to be omnipresent in the academy project. Eupalinos – the historic figure was an engineer from Megara, noted for building the aqueduct tunnel of Samos around 550 BC – is the central figure of Valéry's famous essay of 1921–23, which he cast in the form of the Platonic dialogue.[43] The subject of the dialogue is the arts – painting, literature, dance, music, sculpture and, above all, architecture – together with their relations to one another and their impact on man. It is Valéry's credo about form, about man as a creator in the image of God, about how to turn a shapeless pile of stones into a world of precise forces, of sacred balanced order set in the landscape of the Greek Mediterranean tradition.

[39] Letter Erich Mendelsohn to Louise Mendelsohn, Herrlingen, 26 August 1923, in Oskar Beyer, *Briefe*, p. 54.
[40] Letter Erich Mendelsohn to Louise Mendelsohn, Hyères, 12 August 1932, in Oskar Beyer, *Briefe*, p. 85.
[41] Letter Erich Mendelsohn to Louise Mendelsohn, Cavalière, 30 May 1933, machine-typed copy by Louise Mendelsohn in author's collection.
[42] Letter Erich Mendelsohn to Louise Mendelsohn, Cavalière, 3 June 1933, machine-typed copy by Louise Mendelsohn in author's collection.
[43] Paul Valéry, *Eupalinos ou l'architecte, précédé de L'ame de la danse*, Paris, Gallimard, 1923. First published in *Nouvelle Revue Française*, no. 90, 1 March 1921, pp. 237–285. English translation: *Eupalinos, or The Architect*, London, Oxford University Press, 1932.

44 Paul Valéry, "Inspirations méditerranéennes," in Jean Hytier (ed.),
2 vols, I, Paris, Gallimard, 1957–77,
pp. 1086ff.
45 Paul Valéry, *Regards sur le monde
actuel*, Paris, Gallimard, 1931.
46 Paul Valéry, "Le Centre Universitaire Méditerranéen," in *Regards sur
le monde actuel & autres essays*, Paris,
Gallimard, 1945, pp. 301 ff.; first published as a booklet under the title
*Projet d'organisation du Centre
Universitaire méditerranéen à Nice*,
Nice, Université Aix, 1933. See also
Willy-Paul Romain, *Paul Valéry
et la Méditerranée*, Lourmarin de
Provence, Fondation de Lourmarin
Laurent-Vibert et Association des
Amis de Lourmarin, 1987.
47 Mendelsohn surely knew Rainer
Maria Rilke's translation of Valéry's
Eupalinos, which was published in
1927 by the Insel Verlag in Leipzig.
Apart from that, André Gide, a lifelong close friend of Valéry, was at
least once guest in Mendelsohn's
home *Am Rupenhorn* in Berlin. Ozenfant drew his inspirations from the
very same resources as Valéry. In
1916 he had excerpts of Plato's dialogue *Philebus* reprinted in *L'Élan*.
48 Letters from Erich Mendelsohn
to his wife Louise, Paris, 22 August
1933 and Paris, 30 August 1933,
machine-typed copies by Louise
Mendelsohn in author's collection.

8.6 Hendrik T. Wijdeveld.
Draft plan for the
academy buildings in
Cavalière, January 8,
1934.
Source: Wijdeveld-
Archive, Nederlands
Architectuurinstituut (Nai),
Rotterdam.

The formation of spirit and intellect from the Mediterranean Sea, and the
heritage of the Mediterranean classicism was one of Valéry's central themes.
He called this the *"Inspirations méditerranéennes"* (Mediterranean inspirations),
which became the title of an autobiographical essay.[44] In other writings Valéry
added an important socio-political concept to the emotional and intellectual
notion, by perceiving the Mediterranean as the spiritual centre of Europe. In an
anthology of essays, published in 1931 under the title *Regards sur le monde
actuel*, which included his "Notes sur la Grandeur et la Decadence de l'Europe"
[Notes on the Rise and Fall of Europe] he described the fate of Europe as
dependent on the preservation of its original culture as developed by the
Mediterranean.[45] Without its Mediterranean centre of creative forces, Valéry
did not see any chance of survival for Europe, for its identity, integrity, and
unity.

In 1933, the French minister of education, Anatole de Monzie, appointed
Valéry as administrative director to the Centre Universitaire Méditerranéen
(Mediterranean University Centre), then being established by the French
government in Nice. Valéry defined this centre's purpose as the analysis
and preservation of Mediterranean culture's immense intellectual and
humanitarian contribution to civilization.[46] It seems worthwhile to bring
attention to the fact that the AEM project dates from exactly the same time.
Given Valéry's membership in its advisory committee, one may well conclude
that the academy project developed along the intellectual lines of Valéry's
ideas. We might even come to understand the academy as an ideological,
albeit not institutional, branch of his university project. It may be assumed that
Valéry's works were well known to the three future principals.[47] In any case
they shared a romantic view of the Mediterranean as the cradle of Western
culture, and contrasted its timeless values with the shortcomings of the
industrialized West.

The Great Fire

We see here the most outstanding intellectuals involved in advancing ideas of
a European Union, for which the classical Mediterranean culture would supply
a unifying and universal identity. Europe's political reality, however, was directed
by pan-European forces of a different kind, ones which would deny poets and
thinkers like Valéry – in 1941 the Vichy regime stripped him of his job as the
director of the Mediterranean University Centre – or artists like Wijdeveld,
Ozenfant, and Mendelsohn the right to continue such work. These forces also
worked towards forging a new European identity by referring to a new
Classicism, but a completely different story grew out of this.

Back to the chronology of the academy: after Mendelsohn escaped Germany
at the end of March 1933, he focused all his energy on the AEM. For the
next few months he was the driving force behind it, putting the idea of
the academy into action. He was especially successful in finding sponsors,
and preparations for the actual start on the site in Cavalière were going ahead
at full speed. Late in August 1933, however, following a journey to England
to recruit new sponsors, Mendelsohn informed Wijdeveld of his decision to
settle in England and to establish an office in London together with Serge
Chermayeff.[48] This news must have been a terrible shock for Wijdeveld.
Although Mendelsohn repeatedly pointed out that his move would not
necessarily put an end to his active participation in the academy enterprise, it
nevertheless sealed the fate of this promising project. Without doubt,
Mendelsohn had been the powerful motor for the entire program during the

decisive period of spring and summer 1933. He had also functioned as an important mediator between Wijdeveld, the enthusiast, and Ozenfant, the purist. Without a fully committed Mendelsohn, Ozenfant and the rest of the teachers gave notice, and some of the putative sponsors withdrew their offers.[49] In a letter to Eric Gill, Wijdeveld described the unhappy development:

> After several months of preparing, planning, visiting France, buying grounds, only one man had to do the job. Mendelsohn, who had fled from Berlin, took refuge in our home in Amsterdam, had no office, no work, could have started at once in Cavalière. His character however made him longing to live and work in the midst of the crowd and work out his projects alone. He suddenly went to London, then to Palestine. (. . .) Ozenfant is a real Frenchman and would surely have come to Cavalière, if he could take Paris with him. The Chermayeffs it seemed also needed the glittering light of a Métropole! Left alone, Hindemith and Gargallo withdrew. So we, my wife and youngest son, started alone.[50]

A handful of students accompanied the Wijdeveld family to Cavalière.[51] Later on the group was joined by a young German landscape architect Reinhold Lingner (1902–68), who took charge of landscape design and gardening. In addition he took on responsibility for training the students in these disciplines.[52] During the winter months of 1933–34 Wijdeveld prepared at least three different designs for the future academy campus, all on a more modest scale than had originally been anticipated. Two simple old stone houses existed on the grounds, standing side by side. Wijdeveld intended to retain these, using one as the gardener's living quarters and the other as a communal dining room with an adjoining kitchen. The new, purpose-built structures were to be three spacious studios (for architecture, painting, and sculpture respectively), ten single-room residences for students, a large garage, and a small administration unit. The drawings suggested an architectural treatment – one might call it restrained modern – to fit the character of the existing stone buildings. Only the ten flat-roofed cabins, "cellules pour une personne" (literally "cells for one person"), each standing on its own in the midst of shrubs and woodland, with a large glazed wall open to the South, the Mediterranean, reveals a Corbusian imprint. The school's principal buildings were arranged around a semicircular open-air theatre and a shared garden, both of central importance in Wijdeveld's concept of a living-and-working community.[53]

Yet, the plans were destined to remain on paper, an unfulfilled utopia. Its fate seems to anticipate the historical development in a remarkable way. In summer 1934, vast parts of the academy grounds were destroyed by a big fire, leaving behind black earth covered with ashes. Wijdeveld wrote:

> A big fire . . . We saw the catastrophy [sic] with great dread. The mountains between Le Lavandou and Le Rayol turned into a grey mass. The large slopes surrounding our site are covered with burnt wood. . . . It all looks like a vast battlefield. Under these circumstances the continuation of our academy project looks impossible. . . . Fate has decided. [54]

In retrospect Ozenfant furnished the woeful end of the project with wishes for sanguine future prospects:

> Thus a fine project went up in smoke; one day others will take it up again and will build a staging post of optimism and beauty in the Côte d'Azur, this old Greek colony, and potentially a new Attica.[55]

[49] Louise Mendelsohn, *My Life*, pp. 28off.
[50] Letter from H. Th. Wijdeveld to Eric Gill, Holland, December 1936, NAi, WIJD B 4.16.
[51] Nothing is known of their identities, and very little about the artistic training or other activities that actually took place on the academy's grounds.
[52] Lingner stayed at Cavalière for about a year, when he returned to Germany. After World War II he became one of the most famous and influential landscape architects in the German Democratic Republic, as well as a profilic teacher, both as head of the landscape department at the Institut für Bauwesen der Akademie der Wissenschaften and as professor of landscape design at the Landwirtschaftlich-Gärtnerische Fakultät der Humboldt-Universität.
[53] Plans at NAi, WIJD A34 are dated from 2 November 1933, 20 November 1933, 8 January 1934. Wijdeveld's booklet *Time and Art* (note 12), p. 13 has three additional tiny perspective drawings which seem to belong to an earlier planning stage. There are no plans for the AEM by Mendelsohn.
[54] Letter H. Th. Wijdeveld to the members of the limited liability company, Cavalière, 22 June 1934, Mendelsohn Archive, KB Berlin, no number.
[55] Amédée Ozenfant, *Mémoirs*, Paris, Seghers, 1968, p. 299.

56 Letter from Erich Mendelsohn to Louise Mendelsohn, Cavalière, 30 May 1933, in Oskar Beyer, *Briefe*, p. 90.
57 On Tel Aviv, see for instance Irmel Kamp-Bandau, Winfried Nerdinger, and Pe'era Goldman (eds.), *Tel Aviv Modern Architecture, 1930–1939*, Tübingen, Wasmuth, 1994; Neal Payton, "Modern Architecture and Traditional Urbanism: Patrick Geddes and the Plan for Tel Aviv," *The New City* 3, Fall 1996, pp. 4–25.
58 Eric Mendelsohn, *Twenty Years of Building in Tel Aviv* (1940), manuscript of an unpublished(?) review, Staatliche Museen zu Berlin, Kunstbibliothek, B IV 5a/1. Also see Alona Nitzan-Shiftan, "Contested Zionism – Alternative Modernism: Erich Mendelsohn and the Tel Aviv Chug in Mandate Palestine," in *Architectural History* 39, 1996, pp. 147–180.
59 Letter Erich Mendelsohn to Julius Posener, Capri, 30 March 1937, in Oskar Beyer, *Letters of an Architect*, p. 148.
60 Memories of Hans Schiller, Mendelsohn's long-standing assistant in Jerusalem as well as in San Francisco, quoted according to Louise Mendelsohn, *My Life*, p. 604.

Mendelsohn's Mediterranean Home

Although Mendelsohn, determined by pragmatic considerations, had left the academy project for new professional opportunities in England, the Mediterranean experience stayed as an ever-inspiring spark on his mind. Unmistakably mingled with all of his declarations of love towards the Mediterranean were his longings towards the "land of his fathers" on the Eastern shore. In a letter to his wife Louise written in May 1933 he confessed: "The Mediterranean is a first step towards a return to that country, to that final stage where we both belong. One is glad to know that."[56]

This was written after Erich and Louise Mendelsohn had fled from Germany at the end of March 1933. One and a half years later Mendelsohn opened his office in Jerusalem. Faced with the *Neues Bauen* that was making Tel Aviv into an international metropolis that reflected the European origin of its inhabitants, he warned against precipitate, one-sided adherence to Western standards.[57] He never tired of criticizing the Western tendencies of his architect colleagues against a social and cultural background:

> As far as this land is concerned its dwellings are much too strongly oriented to European patterns. Too much imitation exists and too little independent spirit of invention. The climate of Palestine and the lifestyle of its inhabitants, closely bound to nature, require us to free ourselves from this normal ground plan in order to achieve coolness and a larger scale for the interior. This purpose is fulfilled by the hall, which is the refreshing center of the Arab town house and the one-room stone tent of the sedentary Bedouins in Es-Salt. Open balconies, for example, serve no function in a subtropical climate, while trees next to the façade are more effective for producing shade and more pleasant in appearance. Thus much remains to be done.[58]

To his colleagues in the country he recommended that they should study the whole range of traditional vernacular Mediterranean architecture before building in Palestine.[59] He himself translated whatever he had experienced and learned on his extensive journeys throughout the Mediterranean countries into his architecture in Israel. Especially his first built project, the Weizmann residence in Rehovot, gives testimony of his credo. Villa Weizmann was planned and built between 1934 and 1936. At that time Chaim Weizmann was the president of the Zionist World Organization. Thus, the house was conceived not so much as a private family refuge, but rather as a place where Weizmann could receive official guests from all walks of life and from all over the world. In retrospect one could call it a house for a president-to-be in a state-to-be. According to one of Mendelsohn's axioms, "good architecture is designed around the corner."[60] He defined the relation between man and architecture as a dynamic process, as the tension between moved and moving energy. Now the element of motion can reside with either the object or the viewer, meaning either the object "moves" in front of a static viewer or the latter moves around a static object. These were the two possibilities that were explored in futurism and cubism. Mendelsohn's extroverted German architecture spoke the futurist language. There, his curved concrete masses seem to swing around corners with long ribbon windows floating horizontally.

The closed walls of the Weizmann house, on the other hand, mediate a static character in their introversion and geometric tranquility. In order to nonetheless produce a sense of dynamic tension, Mendelsohn used a device that recalled the perspective play of the cubists: he moved the viewer around his object,

8.7 Erich Mendelsohn.
    **Weizmann House,
    Rehovot, 1934–36.**
Source: Mendelsohn-Archive,
Staatliche Museen zu Berlin –
Preussischer Kulturbesitz,
Kunstbibliothek.

8.8 Erich Mendelsohn. Plans
    and schematic site plan,
    **Weizmann House,
    Rehovot, 1934–36.**
Source: *Architectural Review*,
October 1937.

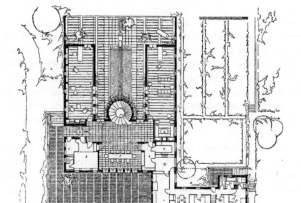

GROUND FLOOR PLAN

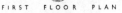

FIRST FLOOR PLAN

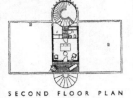

SECOND FLOOR PLAN

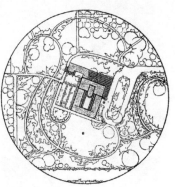

61 Susan King, "Interview with Mrs. Eric Mendelsohn," in *The Drawings of Eric Mendelsohn*, Berkeley, Berkeley University Art Museum, 1969, p. 26.

here in a literal, physical sense. Mendelsohn developed a carefully calculated perspective program for the house; a number of sketches showed him exploring various views of the house from different angles. In particular, he designed the approach to the house as a winding path presenting proudly all sides of his monument to the visitor. Before entering the interior of the house through the main door, the visitor has already seen all the façades and corner views of Israel's White House.

In this play of changing perspectives, Mendelsohn appears to have been inspired by the architecture of classical Greece. He had visited Greece for the first time – as we heard already on Ozenfant's recommendation – only three years before, in spring 1931. Louise remembered:

> he never thought much about Greek architecture until he saw it with his own eyes. The Acropolis in Athens overwhelmed him. He was especially impressed by the way in which the approach is so calculated and integrated with the entire complex.[61]

Thus in his first built project for the "old–new" land, Mendelsohn – one of the prophets of the machine age in Germany – returned to the ancient roots of the Mediterranean. The complex consists of four interlocking blocks arranged symmetrically along an east–west axis around an open inner courtyard. Two essential elements violate the strict symmetry: a service wing attached to the northeast corner, and the entrance to the house, shifted out of axis to the south front. This solution shows the bravura typical of Mendelsohn's early work: the transformation of a symmetrical composition into an asymmetrical experience.

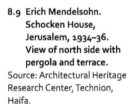

8.9 Erich Mendelsohn. Schocken House, Jerusalem, 1934–36. View of north side with pergola and terrace.
Source: Architectural Heritage Research Center, Technion, Haifa.

Likewise, the Weizmann house represents a fine example for applied nautical symbolism. The clear, symmetrical hierarchy of the long, low blocks recalls the longitudinal section of a ship. The projecting, semicircular stair tower with its continuous ribbon window beneath the roofline suggests a captain's bridge,

while the small round windows, the oculi of the main representative rooms, resemble the portholes of a steamer. Allusions to ship building in modern architecture are well known. Recall the work of Le Corbusier, Hans Sharoun, Ernst May, or Antonio Sant'Elia for example. Most of those allusions are based on a glorification of functionality and the machine aesthetic. In the Weizmann house, however, other meanings associated with the image of the ship came into play, such as: departure and voyage to faraway destinations, escape and deliverance, movement towards a utopia, hope for a "brave new world." The archetypal motif associated with these meanings is the ark of Noah. Almost all literary utopias use the ship motif in one form or another. The Weizmann house symbolizes a Noah's ark that has alighted on Mount Ararat, laden with hopes for a better society in a new homeland.

During the same period 1934–36, Mendelsohn designed the house of another important man in Jewish circles in Palestine, Salman Schocken.[61] Despite the typological similarities with the Weizmann house, the Schocken residence could not have been more different. Located in the northeast section of Rehavia, a garden city planned in the early 1920s by Richard Kauffmann, the house presented itself as a typical town house integrated into the structure of the villa suburb.[63] Each house is the portrait of its patron and his role in society. Weizmann was a politician who represented the Zionist movement; accordingly, his country house was laden with symbols representing a public political mission. Schocken, on the other hand, avoided the public eye; as the organizing power of the Zionist movement in the background, he was best and most comfortable planning from his desk. His residence was free from symbolic superstructure; it was designed from the inside out.

The asymmetrical building is subjected to the graduated rhythm of vertical glass doors and a horizontal band of loggias, consolidated into a homogeneous composition by the repetition of motifs such as round projecting forms (terrace, balcony, swimming pool) and pergolas (east side of the south terrace, north terrace, porch of roof garden). The long narrow structure, like all subsequent buildings in Jerusalem, was a concrete construction with stone facing on the exterior. The almost forty-centimeter thick masonry was produced using a customary method in Jerusalem: two layers of stone were built up and then filled with cement or concrete, with reinforcement iron girders at important bearing points. Mendelsohn's handling of the yellowish-gold Jerusalem stone is especially striking in the careful treatment of the door and window frames. In calculating the cut of the stone, he placed great emphasis on the continuation of the primary lines around the building at the same height. In this use of natural stone, Mendelsohn followed the old Jerusalem building tradition, on which both the Ottoman and the British building codes had been based.[64]

Since both Weizmann and Schocken were involved in the affairs of the new Hebrew University on Mount Scopus, it was clear that Mendelsohn would be the university's new man. Sir Patrick Geddes conceived the first masterplan in 1919, and a couple of buildings in an oriental formal vocabulary tainted with a European accent were built. In the 1930s, the time was ripe for a revision and a significant expansion of the program. In 1937, Mendelsohn made a model of the new Scopus masterplan, which was shown at the world exposition in Paris the same year, not far away from the pavilions of Hitler's Germany, Stalin's Russia, and the pavilion of the ailing Spanish Republic where *Guernica* sounded a lamentation against war and fascism. In this context, Mendelsohn's model represented the most important witness of the Jewish old–new homeland and its intellectual and cultural renaissance. Here, against the background of an

[61] On the Schocken family and Mendelsohn's relations with them in Germany and Palestine, see Regina Stephan, *Eric Mendelsohn*, op. cit.
[63] Richard Kauffmann was a former fellow student with Mendelsohn and a pupil of Theodor Fischer at the Technische Hochschule in Munich. In 1921 he emigrated to Palestine where he became the most important settlement planner, with projects including 150 *moshavim* and *kibbutzim*.
[64] See Michael Lewis, "The Stones of Jerusalem," in *Journal of Jewish Art* 2, 1975, pp. 72ff.

**8.10 Erich Mendelsohn.
Hadassah University
Hospital, entrance,
Jerusalem, c.1936.**
Source: Archives of the
Hebrew University, Jerusalem.

approaching inferno, the concept of learning and erudition – deeply anchored in the Jewish tradition – brought the only glimmer of hope for the future.

Mendelsohn's design, however, was gradually rubbed away between the bureaucratic demands of the British Mandate government, the pragmatism of the university administration, and the egotistical wishes of American donors. The only structures realized under his direction were the Hadassah University Medical Center and two other modest buildings. In spite of this failure, the Hadassah Center became the symbol of the university, and the entrance with the three domes the architectural logo of the hospital. Mendelsohn wrote:

> We are on Mount Scopus in Jerusalem looking down to villages three-thousand-years old or is it six thousand, who knows? Everywhere little domed stone houses. So I adopted the form of the dome."[65]

[65] Manuscript of an interview by Prof. J. Murphy (Washington University School of Architecture) with Eric Mendelsohn, March 13, 1944, KB, E.M. Archives, B IV A.

Undoubtedly, the three domes represent a homage to the Arab architecture he repeatedly praised for its native sense of harmony. Yet, rather than copying, he quoted – and since the quotation was torn from its original context, he felt free to play with it uninhibitedly, translating the traditional masonry dome into concrete, relieving it from its function as a space-enclosing element by positioning it over an open passageway, and tripling it.

"Palestine and the World of Tomorrow"

Mendelsohn's Zionist utopia was a vision about an open Middle East – a Semitic Commonwealth – with possibilities for him to build in Cairo, Damascus, Amman, and Beirut. The pragmatic nationalism of the country's politics was a stage too narrow for him: "Judea is heavenly, but too small for me," he wrote to a friend.[66] To those who continued building up the "Promised Land," he left behind a study about *Palestine and the World of Tomorrow*, which is remarkable for its farsightedness and actuality. In his writing, he locates Palestine at the interface of two old cultural regions, the Arab-Semitic and the Mediterranean. He calls upon the Mediterranean people to contemplate and reflect on their own rich culture, instead of running after "golden calves." He does not get tired warning in ever new and original linguistic images against a sell out of their traditional values for the sake of money and so-called progress:

> The Mediterranean peoples get no profit from the exploitation of their enigmatic splendour for the sake of the European-American pseudo-styles. They sell the copyright of their genuine creations for the tips left behind by romantic artists, snobs and eager archaeologists. They get no royalties for their unique creations, being listed into a pattern book of architectural details and decorations . . .
> The mismanagement and exploitation of their forests leads to the sterilization of the mountains of Greece and the hills of Judea. The arrogance that despises those who prefer spiritual benediction to the blessings of technology, leads to the sterilization of human endeavour. The decline of the creative power of the Mediterranean and the loss of its political importance are in close and continuous relation to each other. Palestine is only a part of this process.[67]

With letters of recommendation by no less important persons than Henry Morgenthau and Lewis Mumford Mendelsohn entered into the "Land of Unlimited Possibilities."[68] After arriving in America in 1941, Mendelsohn stayed in New York for some years, but then moved to the West Coast. From San Francisco he wrote to his old friend Oskar Beyer in December 1951:

> I build, teach at the University, live in my ideas and from the stillness, which gives birth to everything – in a country I trust; in a state that unites the breath of the Mediterranean – my limited early home – the breeze of the boundless Pacific; on a hill in a city whose situation comes closest to the Bay of Corinth, the Bay of Naples and Crete's Merabelo Bay.[69] ■

[66] Letter Erich Mendelsohn to Chaim Yaski, 1936, quoted according to Gilbert Herbert, "The Divided Heart: Erich Mendelsohn and the Zionist Dream," in *Erich Mendelsohn in Palestine*, Haifa, Technion, 1987, reprint 1994, p. 13.
[67] Eric Mendelsohn, *Palestine and the World of Tomorrow*, Jerusalem, 1940, pp. 6f.
[68] Letter Henry Morgenthau to the Secretary of State, 23 December 1940; letter Lewis Mumford to Secretary of State, 7 December 1940, Mendelsohn Archive, Staatliche Museen zu Berlin, Kunstbibliothek, IV 8.
[69] Letter Erich Mendelsohn to Oskar Beyer, San Francisco, 24 December 1951, in Oskar Beyer, *Letters of an Architect*, pp. 175f.

Acknowledgments
This essay is a revised version of the author's earlier article: "An Artistic European Utopia at the Abyss of Time: The Mediterranean Academy Project, 1931–34," in *Architectural History* 45, 2002, pp. 441–482. The essay at hand includes new research data and insights resulting from the author's expanded current research on the very same subject conducted under the auspices of the *Zentralinstitut für Kunstgeschichte*, München, funded by the *Deutsche Forschungsgemeinschaft* (DFG). The final section is borrowed from my chapter "'I am a free builder.' Architecture in Palestine 1934–41," in Regina Stephen (ed.), *Eric Mendelsohn. Architect 1887–1953*, New York, Monacelli Press, 1999.

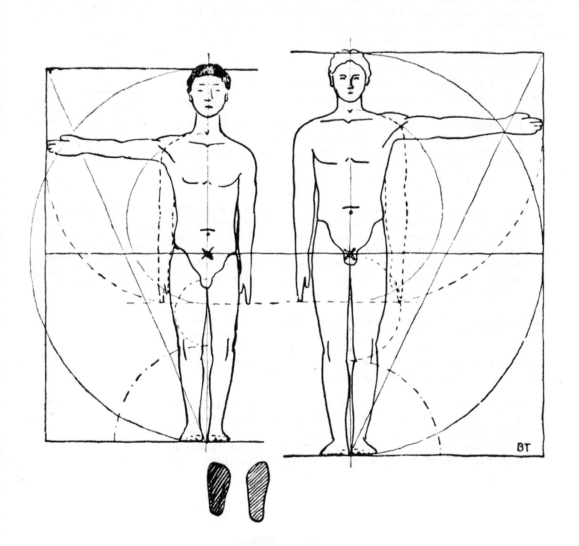

Plate 24 Salvador Dalí. *Portrait of Luis Buñuel*, 1924.
Source: Museo Nacional Centro de Arte Reina Sofía, Madrid. Erich Lessing/Art Resource, New York. © 2009 Artists Rights Society (ARS), New York/Salvador Dalí, Gala-Salvador Dalí Foundation.

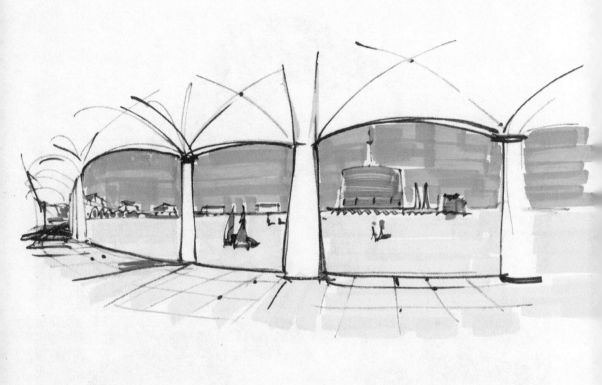

Plate 25 Alejandro de la Sota. Sketch of the square and church in Entrerríos, Mérida, c.1956.
Source: © Fundación Alejandro de la Sota, Madrid.

Plate 26 Joan Miró. *La Masía* (The Farm), 1921–22.
Source: National Gallery of Art, Washington DC. © 2009 Successió Miró/Artists Rights Society (ARS), New York/ADAGP, Paris.

Plate 27 Le Corbusier. Drawing of Marseille, August 1931.
Source: © 2009 Artists Rights Society (ARS), New York/ADAGP, Paris/FLC.

**Plate 28 Le Corbusier. Drawing of Fort l'Empereur,
Algiers, 1933.**
Source: © 2009 Artists Rights Society (ARS), New York/
ADAGP, Paris/FLC.

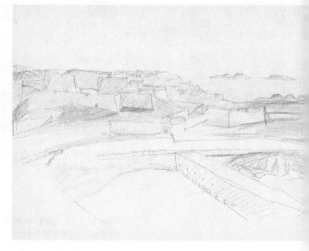

**Plate 29 Le Corbusier. Drawing of Fort Saint-Nicholas,
Marseille, 1933.**
Source: © 2009 Artists Rights Society (ARS), New York/ADAGP,
Paris/FLC.

Plate 30 Sedad Eldem. Detail from Hünkar Kasri (Imperial Pavilion), Yenicami, Istanbul. Survey drawing, 1927.
Source: Courtesy of the Aga Khan Trust for Culture, Geneva.

Plate 31 (*Top right*) Sedad Eldem. "Mediterranean Dream House, 1928".
Source: Courtesy of the Aga Khan Trust for Culture, Geneva.

Plate 32 (*Bottom right*) Sedad Eldem. Sketch for "The Spirit, House, and Nature," 1928.
Source: Courtesy of the Aga Khan Trust for Culture, Geneva

Plate 33 Dimitris Pikionis. Experimental School, Thessaloniki, Preliminary drawing, 1935.
Source: © Neohellenic Architecture Archives, Benaki Museum, Athens.

Plate 34 (*Below*) Dimitris Pikionis. Aixoni Settlement, Glyfada, Elevations of houses,
Preliminary drawing, 1953–55.
Source: © Neohellenic Architecture Archives, Benaki Museum, Athens.

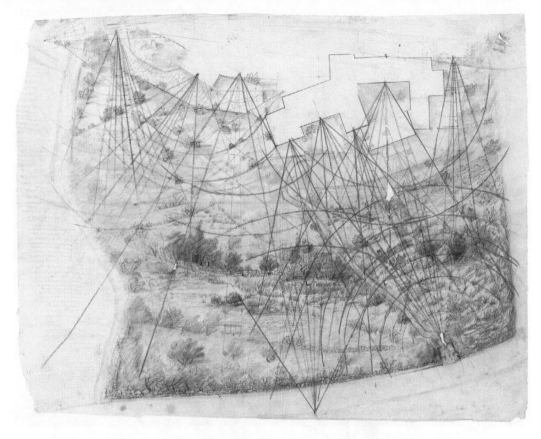

Plate 35 (*Above*) Dimitris Pikionis. Aixoni Settlement, Glyfada, Preliminary site drawing, 1953–55.
Source: © Neohellenic Architecture Archives, Benaki Museum, Athens.

**Plate 36 Dimitris Pikionis.
            Delphi Centre,
            Perspective, 1934.**
Source: © Neohellenic
Architecture Archives,
Benaki Museum, Athens.

**Plate 37 Bruno Taut. Sketch
            of a Japanese
            vernacular house.**
Source: From Bruno Taut,
Houses and People of Japan,
Tokyo, 1937.

Plate 38 Gunnar Asplund. Tunis travel sketch, Perspective view of a street, 1914.
Source: © Arkitekturmuseet Stockholm, photo Nikolaj Alsterdal.

Plate 39 (*Top left*) Gunnar Asplund. Sketch depicting the interior of a Pompeian house, 1914.
Source: © Arkitekturmuseet Stockholm, photo Nikolaj Alsterdal.

Plate 40 (*Bottom left*) Jacques Ignace Hittorf. Reconstruction of the Temple of Empedocles at Selinus, 1830.
Source: From Jacques Ignace Hiittorf, *Atlas. Restitution du temple d'Empédocle à Sélinonte ou l'architecture polychrôme chez les Grecs*, Paris, 1851.

Plate 41 (*Bottom right*) Henri Labrouste. Drawing inscribed "Agrigentum, 1828."
Source: Académie d'architecture, Paris.

Plate 42 Gunnar Asplund. The Stockholm Exhibition of 1930, night view, 1930.
Source: © Arkitekturmuseet Stockholm, photo Matti Östling.

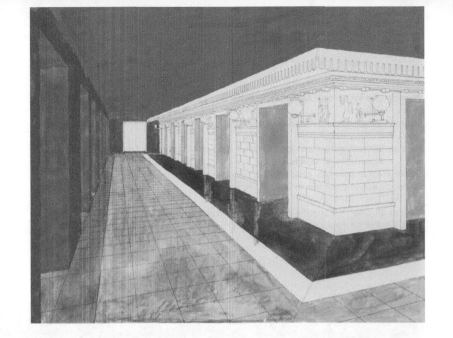

Plate 43 (*Top left*) Gunnar Asplund. Skandia Cinema, perspective view of ground level corridor, 1923.
Source: © Arkitekturmuseet Stockholm, photo Nikolaj Alsterdal.

Plate 44 (*Bottom left*) Gunnar Asplund. Skandia Cinema, Perspective view of the interior of the auditorium looking toward the film screen, 1923.
Source: © Arkitekturmuseet Stockholm, photo Nikolaj Alsterdal.

Plate 45 (*Below*) Bernard Rudofsky. Oia, Santorini, 1929.
Source: Research Library, The Getty Research Institute, Los Angeles.

Plate 46 Gio Ponti and Bernard Rudofsky. Aerial perspective of San Michele Hotel, Capri, 1938.
Source: © Archivio Gio Ponti, CSAC, Parma.

Plate 47 (*Below left*) **Gio Ponti. Ideal vacation villas, elevation, 1939.**
Source: From *Stile* 8, August 1941. © Archivio Gio Ponti, CSAC, Parma.

Plate 48 (*Below right*) **Gio Ponti. Ideal vacation villas, section, 1939.**
Source: From *Stile* 8, August 1941. © Archivio Gio Ponti, CSAC, Parma.

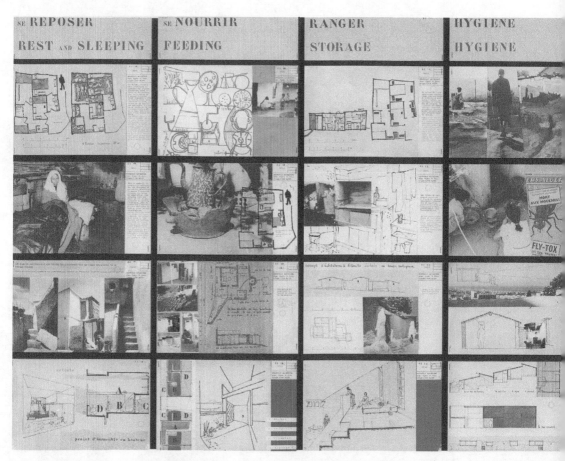

Plate 49 CIAM-Algiers, Roland Simounet and Michel Emery. Bidonville Mahieddine Grid [partim], 1953.
Source: © CIAM Archives, Institut für Geschichte und Theorie der Architekturg/eTH Zürich.

Plate 50 (*Overleaf*) Bernard Rudofsky. Naïve perspective of the Procida house, *c.*1935.
Source: *Domus* 123, March 1938.

9

BRUNO TAUT'S TRANSLATIONS OUT OF GERMANY

TOWARD A COSMOPOLITAN ETHICS IN ARCHITECTURE

Esra Akcan

The stronger the belief that East and West belong together, the stronger the energy to get to know the foreignness in one's nature. With the growth of this energy, the melancholy will sink down to the grave it deserves.[1]

My two intentions in this essay are to exemplify a cultural practice that complicates the received notions about modernism's relation with "non-Western" countries by using a theoretical framework that I call translation, and to discuss the conceptual distinctions between hybridity and cosmopolitan ethics.[2] To accomplish this, I focus on the theoretical writings of the German-born architect Bruno Taut in Japan and Turkey, and analyze his own house in Istanbul through the lens of these theories.

Even though recent scholarship has established that the architecture of the early twentieth century was much more complex, diverse, and multifaceted than what the initial proponents of postmodernism were willing to acknowledge, the relation of modernism to the world at large is still a growing field of research.[3] The customary account about the impact of modernist architectural movements on countries that remain outside the imaginary borders of Europe and North America usually condemns modernism for monotonous "International Style" blocks, devoid of local specificity. While this account may seem to hold true for the majority of cities around the world, it hardly explains the intentions of many modern architects themselves, and certainly not of Taut. The reaction to this alleged homogenization of the world through modernization is usually interpreted as "regionalist" architecture. It is thus far too common to treat modern architecture in "non-Western" countries as an oscillation between the regional and the modern, the national and the international. However, such a bipolar analysis remains on the surface in coming to terms with the complexities of cross-cultural relations in this period. The increased geographical mobility, collaboration, and confrontation between professionals from different countries throughout the twentieth century have continuously produced new hybrids and dialectical relations. In this sense, there is no pure regional or international style of expression, no pure architecture produced at a location completely closed to other locations. The definition of the local is always in flux. Nor can there be an architecture that is produced at some abstract space outside the forces of any local condition. Understanding modern architecture therefore requires an explanatory concept that challenges the common dichotomies such as international versus national style or modernist versus regionalist building. As a conceptual framework that explains modernization in terms of the interaction between different places and nation-states, *translation* discusses the mutual dependence and interaction between different countries, and traces the flows of people, ideas, images,

[1] Bruno Taut, "Japans Kunst. Mit europäischen Augen gesehen," Manuscript of 1936, Nachlaß Taut, Baukunst Sammlung, Mappe 1. Nr 14. BTS 323. p. 24, Akademie der Künste, Berlin.

[2] For more discussion on this theory of translation, see Esra Akcan, "Modernity in Translation. Early Twentieth Century German-Turkish Exchanges in Land Settlement and Residential Culture," Ph.D. Dissertation, Columbia University, 2005. Also see the extensive bibliography on "translation" (note #1) in the first publication of this essay in *New German Critique* 99 33 no. 3, Fall 2006, pp. 7-39. I would like to thank my committee Kenneth Frampton, Andreas Huyssen, Mary McLeod, Gayatri Spivak, Sibel Bozdogan, and Barry Bergdoll for their helpful comments on my dissertation, which constitutes the groundwork of this essay.

[3] Postmodernism in architecture usually connotes a different meaning than "postmodern condition" (Jameson and Harvey) or "postmodern thought" (Lyotard). See in particular the first manifestoes of postmodernism in architecture, Robert Venturi, *Complexity and Contradiction in Architecture*, New York, Museum of Modern Art, 1966; Aldo Rossi, *The Architecture of the City*, Cambridge, The MIT Press, 1982 [1966]; also see Charles Jencks, *The Language of Post-Modern Architecture*, London, Academy Editions, 1987.

9.1 (*Far left*) Bruno Taut. Comparative diagram for the human body (East–West).

Source: Bruno Taut, *Houses and People of Japan*, Tokyo, 1937.

⁴ Bruno Taut, Letters from Istanbul, Manuscripts in Nachlaß Taut, Baukunst Sammlung, BT–Slg–01–9 bis 13, BT–Slg–01–142, Akademie der Künste, Berlin.
⁵ Paul Scheerbart, Glass Architecture, New York, Praeger, 1972 (translated from Glasarchitektur, 1914); Bruno Taut, Die Stadtkrone, Jena, Verlag Eugen Diederichs, 1919; Bruno Taut, Alpine Architektur, Hagen, Folkwang-Verlag, 1919; Bruno Taut, "Ex Oriente Lux: Call to Architects" (1919), in Tim and Charlotte Benton (eds.), Form and Function, London, Crosby Lockwood Staples, 1975, pp. 81–82. Also see Simone Hain, "Ex oriente lux," in Vittorio Magnano Lampugnani and Romana Schneider (eds.), Moderne Architektur in Deutschland 1900 bis 1950. Expressionismus und Neue Sachlichkeit, Stuttgart, Verlag Gerd Hatje, 1994, pp. 133–160.
⁶ Rosemarie Bletter, "Bruno Taut and Paul Scheerbart's Vision. Utopian Aspects of German Expressionist Architecture," Ph.D. Dissertation, Columbia University, 1973; Rosemarie Bletter, "The Interpretation of the Glass Dream – Expressionist Architecture and the History of the Crystal Metaphor," in Journal of the Society of Architectural Historians 40, March 1981, pp. 20–43; Rosemarie Bletter, "Expressionism and the New Objectivity," in Art Journal 43, no. 2, Summer 1983, pp. 108–120.
⁷ Taut, Die Stadtkrone, p. 82.

information, and technologies across geographical space, as well as their varying degrees and modes of transformations at the new destinations. Translation is thus the *study of a field* that explores and evaluates different experiences of the foreign, of the "other," of what had yet remained outside, in a given context, at a given moment. It is through translation that a country opens itself to the foreign, modifies and enriches itself, while negotiating its domestic norms with those of the other. However, translation is not removed from the geographical distribution of power. It can hardly be considered a neutral exchange between equals, or a "bridge" between cultures that are smoothly translatable. Translation must thus be treated as a contested zone where geographical differences are discovered, reconciled, or opposed and where conflicts between Westernization and nationalization are negotiated or intensified.

Taut was one of the few architects of the modern period who were consciously engaged in understanding these tensions and potentials inherent in cross-cultural translations. Exiled from Germany in 1933, he spent three years in Japan and two years in Turkey until his death in 1938. Living abroad gave him a unique opportunity to reflect on the problems of modernization outside Europe. Taut had taken an interest in "non-Western" architecture long before he moved to Japan and Turkey. Curiosity about the "East" is obviously not a value in itself, since this hardly qualifies anything unless its distinction from the Orientalist interest (in Edward W. Said's sense) of numerous painters, poets, or writers can be specified. What makes Taut a revealing case is his intellectual growth over the years and the resulting transformations in his approach throughout his career. Taut considered his architectural engagements in Japan and Turkey as continuous experiences.⁴ Therefore, his career after leaving Germany and his last theoretical statements can hardly be understood without discussing their gradual development in all three countries. By tracing Taut's letters, diaries, and manuscripts in Japan and Turkey, this essay suggests the reconstruction of a theory that might be called a cosmopolitan ethics in architecture.

Ex Oriente Lux: Germany, 1919–33

Taut's early texts (the ones usually attributed to his "expressionist period") were full of references to Asia.⁵ As Rosemarie Bletter has demonstrated, the glass utopias of Paul Scheerbart and Taut or the latter's Glass Pavilion for the Werkbund Exhibition in 1914 were more than technocratic impulses to explore the potentials of a new material. On the contrary, as Taut and Scheerbart were also aware, glass had a long history as the metaphor of sacred, spiritual, and romantic sources, including Asian ones.⁶ In *Die Stadtkrone* (written during the war and published in 1919) Taut illustrated examples of cities with a "city crown" from all over the world to show how an "organic unity" could be achieved in urban settlements, in contrast to the "chaos" of the modern European cities. Taut's examples included medieval, Indian, Chinese, and Ottoman cities, as well as a comparison between Ebenezer Howard's Garden City and the Chinese city of Küfu. For Taut, this comparison proved that "all rational men end up with similar principles" although he ranked the Garden City slightly higher for its potential to guide modern settlements.⁷ Through this comparison Taut was not just adding one more example from the East to his list. The assertion that the Garden City's principles could be observed in a Chinese city claimed a universal truth to the model he was promoting, without any evidence of communication between the two or in-depth analysis of the Chinese example. Here an example from the East became a vehicle to prove the alleged universality of the architect's own principles, rather than being evaluated in its own right.

In *"Ex oriente lux"* (*The Sun Rises from the East*, 1919), Taut's ideas about the East as the "savior of Europe" were most radically asserted.

> Kill the European, kill him, kill him, kill him off! Sings St. Paulus [Scheerbart]
> . . .
> Each tiny part of the great culture from the fourth to the sixteenth century in Upper India, Ceylon, Cambodia, Amman, Siam and on Indulines – what melting of form, what fruitful maturity, what restraint and strength and what unbelievable fusion with plastic art! . . . Bow down in humility, you Europeans!
> Humility will redeem you. It will give you love, love for the divinity of the earth and for the spirit of the world. You will no longer torment your earth with dynamite and grenades, you will have the will to adorn her, to cultivate and care for her – culture![8]

The forcefulness of Taut's prose needs to be understood within the bellicose context of the First World War. By offering dozens of architectural examples from non-European countries as a proof of redemption, Taut not only continued his social utopian position in assigning a sanctifying value to architecture, but also turned his gaze eastward for this purpose. Taut's anti-war ideas must have motivated his search for a model of peace and harmony in the Orient that he could not find in modern European cities at the dawn of the war.[9] This is not a type of common Orientalism that claims the superiority of the West, nor does it claim any desire to control, manipulate, or dominate the Orient. However, another sort of Orientalist undertone is still present here. The idea about the Orient's saving power in times of crisis is one of the basic symptoms of Orientalism, still in Edward Said's sense, in its seemingly affirmative face. This type of Orientalism not only distances the Orient as the ready-at-hand solution to be taken out of the medicine chest whenever "Western progress" is under

[8] Taut, *"Ex Oriente Lux,"* pp. 81–82.
[9] Boyd Whyte has also argued that Taut's interest in the "East" was directly linked to his disappointment with the events in Europe before and during the First World War. See Ian Boyd Whyte, *Bruno Taut and the Architecture of Activism*, Cambridge, Cambridge University Press, 1982. Taut's entry for the German-Turkish House of Friendship Competition in Istanbul in 1916 supports this point. Almost all entries were neo-classical with some Ottoman appliqués, and Taut's project was the most Ottoman of all. Here, Taut appeared to be denying the rejuvenation of forms that he had begun promoting in Germany. It seemed that for the young German architecture in this part of the world was to remain as eternal, authentic, untouched, exotic and thus non-historical as "it has always been."

9.2 Bruno Taut. Entry for the House of Friendship Competition, Istanbul, 1916.
Source: ODTU, *Mimarlık Fakültesi Dergisi* 1, no. 2, 1975.

[10] Bruno Taut, *Die Neue Wohnung. Die Frau als Schöpferin* (1924), Leipzig, Verlag Klinkhardt & Biermann, 1928. Reprinted as Manfred Speidel (ed.), Bruno Taut, *Die Neue Wohnung. Die Frau als Schöpferin*, Berlin, Gebr. Mann Verlag, 2001.

[11] Taut also noted how the division between sleeping and living spaces does not exist in the rooms (*oda*) of Ottoman vernacular houses. This was an organization that, he later suggested, could be plausible for small working-class houses in Germany. Ibid., pp. 21–23.

[12] Bruno Taut, "Nippon, mit europäischen Augen gesehen," Manuscript of 1933, Nachlaß Taut, Baukunst Sammlung, Akademie der Künste, Berlin; Bruno Taut, "Die Architektur des Westens mit ihrer Bedeutung für Japan," Manuscript for the Conference Series on 9, 10, 12, 13, 16, 17 July 1934, Kaiserlichen Universität Tokyo; Bruno Taut, *Fundamentals of Japanese Architecture*, Tokyo, Kokusai Bunka Shinkokai, 1935; Bruno Taut, *Japans Kunst*, Tokyo, Verlag Meiji Shobo, 1936; Bruno Taut, "Japanese Village," Manuscript (written in English) of 1936, Nachlaß Taut, BT–Slg–01–85, Baukunst Sammlung, Akademie der Künste, Berlin; Bruno Taut, "New Japan. What its Architecture Should Be," Manuscript of 1936, Nachlaß Taut, BT–Slg–01–86, Baukunst Sammlung, Akademie der Künste, Berlin; Bruno Taut, *Houses and People of Japan* (1937), Tokyo, Sanseido, 1958.

[13] Bruno Taut, *Houses and People of Japan*, op. cit. German version: Manfred Speidel (ed.), Bruno Taut, *Das japanische Haus und sein Leben* (1937), Berlin, Gebr. Mann Velag, 1997. "The Japanese House and its Homelife" is the title Taut used for the prospectus of 1935. (This prospectus is reprinted at the end of the German version).

[14] Taut, *Houses and People of Japan*, p. ii.

suspicion, but also treats the Orient as an exotic, unchanging, and harmonious dreamland deprived of progress, modernity, and the idea of history.

Taut's approach to these questions became much more refined in Japan and Turkey. The transformation had started before he was exiled from Germany, as exemplified in his book *Die Neue Wohnung. Die Frau als Schöpferin* (*The New House. Woman as Creator*, 1924).[10] The book's historical examples of Japanese and Ottoman vernacular houses held a specific place in Taut's formulation of the characteristics of modern dwellings. For instance, rooms without walls in Japan fascinated Taut. The movable partitions that continuously changed the division of space, and the sliding exterior walls that allowed different levels of continuity with the outside, inspired him to make flexibility an important principle of the modern dwelling. Taut also admired the built-in-the-wall closets of Ottoman vernacular houses (*Wandschränke*) that functioned as minimized service spaces, freeing the rest of the room. In his own modern dwellings during the Weimar period, the service spaces such as the kitchen, bath, and closets were inspired by the Ottoman closets and similarly handled as minimum boxes to be opened up and closed down, leaving the maximum space for the living sections.[11]

Melancholy of the East: Japan, 1933–36

The Japanese International Association of Architects invited Taut to Japan where he was mainly occupied with designing craft objects and researching the country's vernacular architecture. As opposed to his heavy responsibilities in Germany and later in Turkey, Taut had few opportunities to build in Japan and spent his time writing several books on Japanese architecture.[12] A new theory of architecture emerged from this research, which culminated in *Mimari Bilgisi* (*Lectures in Architecture*), a book written and published in Turkey just before Taut's death.

For most of his projects in exile, Taut did more than simply transport his German practice to new locations. His designs appeared so transformed that many scholars and colleagues interpreted this as a radical change. For instance, in Germany, Taut had been highly critical of the *Heimatstil* for nostalgically promoting the revival of values embodied in traditional German farmhouses. In Japan, however, after spending most of his time researching the region's vernacular architecture, he promoted the "Japanese houses" and the Katsura Palace as a guide to the properties of an appropriate modern architecture in that country.

Why would a visionary avant-garde designer promote a building practice based on the study of traditional vernacular houses? Is it possible that Taut, rather than advocate a nostalgic conservatism, tested the geographical limits of German modernism during his exile in Japan and Turkey and realized the necessity of translating his own ideas? The answer to these questions can be found in Taut's texts from the period, where, I suggest, Taut had two main intentions: to criticize the Western Orientalist perceptions of these regions, and to criticize the current modernization in Japan and Turkey.

Houses and People of Japan (the title was originally intended to be *The Japanese House and Its Homelife*, 1937) was the main book in which Taut delivered his research, written in the form of a diary chronicling a one-year sojourn in Japan.[13] Envisioned as a "contribution to international friendship,"[14] the book is a lively, detailed, interrogative representation of Taut's research on traditional "Japanese

9.3 Bruno Taut in front of his house in Japan.
Source: Taut Archiv, Akademie der Künste, Berlin.

houses," living habits, crafts, and clothes as well as their confrontation with the demands of modern living. Determined not to "go back as ignorant as . . . [he] came," Taut aspired to disclose and challenge the Western Orientalist views of Japan, which eventually led him to develop deeper thoughts on the notion of "non-Western" modernization.[15]

> I failed to see how the Japanese could possibly claim that their house is their castle. . . . But after all, these houses are nothing more than tents, though provided with roofs and structural refinements.[16]

These were the words Taut used to express his astonishment at his first visit to the house he would inhabit in Japan. In his deliberately ironic words, Taut bumps his head against the low door frames during his first day, has a hard time finding door handles and other such things, desperately looks for familiar furniture, and tries to get used to the "oddities" of his new habitat such as taking off his shoes before entering the house, surviving the hot water in the bathroom and the freezing temperature of the house, sleeping on mats, eating with chopsticks, and so on. About the houses and ways of living he passionately researched during the rest of his stay in Japan, Taut continued:

> But could it be called a room? It was really nothing more than an open hall, raised above the level of the ground. . . . The problem was where to eat, sleep, and work. . . . Furniture could hardly be used on the soft straw mats. . . . Where was I to work, and how was I to dispose my books and

15 Ibid., p. 40.
16 Ibid., p. 21.

17 Ibid., pp. 5–8.
18 Ibid., p. 175.
19 Ibid., p. 75.
20 Taut, "Japans Kunst. Mit europäischen Augen gesehen."
21 Ibid., pp. 12–13.
22 Esra Akcan, "Modernity in Translation;" Esra Akcan, "Melancholy and the 'Other'" www.eurozine.com
23 See most notably: Bruno Taut, "New Japan. What its Architecture Should be."

papers? . . . My wife was not less perturbed when she came to inspect the kitchen. . . . There was neither stove, nor gas, nor even a kitchen table . . . [In] this so-called kitchen . . . there was nothing else to see. . . . But how on earth were we to make ourselves at home?[17]

These words at the beginning of *Houses and People of Japan* are deliberately misleading. By repeating some of the Orientalist stereotypes, the architect was actually preparing the ground for criticizing European perceptions of Japan. Taut's real intentions are disclosed in the following pages of the book:

> What is still today the image of Japan, which – apart from a few connoisseurs – generally prevails among the masses of the West? Is it not that of a strange island whose singular inhabitants, contrary to the custom everywhere else, have introduced into art an affected elegance, faintness, dwarfish diminutiveness, irregularity, abnormality, oddity, in a word, whim . . . The West only saw what it understood, and relished it the more as it appeared to be an exotic, piquant curiosity.[18]

And further:

> The intention [of this book] has been to show that strange and unaccustomed ways have very natural and simple reasons. Whosoever looks at these ways as something exotic, behaves like a child in the zoo gaping in front of the glass cage of the boa constrictor. But such a sentimental and romantic approach to the unfamiliar is as unjust as it is unreasonable, since human beings all over the world are endowed with an equal amount of reason.[19]

The West, which "only saw what it understood" deemed the East nothing more than an "exotic" fairyland, distant and strange, abnormal and odd. During his life in the "Orient," Taut's Orientalist hymns were toned down. Furthermore, he also intuitively realized some of the basic problems of non-European countries under Westernization. For instance, based on the increasing number of suicides and the dark depictions of movies such as *Alpus Teisho*, Taut asserted in a chapter entitled "Melancholie," in his manuscript "Japans Kunst" ("Japan's Art," 1936), that a depressive mood and melancholy governed the Japanese artistic scene, about which he freely speculated throughout the manuscript.[20] Taut mainly talked about a fundamental dichotomy (*Zwiespalt*) that caused some sort of "depression" and "resignation." The recent indications of this dichotomy, the architect argued, were largely due to the perceived gap between the East and Europe, the declining state of Japanese tradition as a mere "exotic museum piece," and the perceived opposition between the traditional ways of living and European modernism.[21] Taut's choice of the word "melancholy" is more theoretically suggestive than it appears at first. It implies his intuitive recognition of one of the most pertinent cultural reactions to modernization in many "non-Western" countries. Melancholy is the tension that stems from the perceived inequality between "West" and "non-West" at the moment of cross-cultural translation – a condition that I have elsewhere explained in further detail as "the melancholy of the non-Western."[22]

Taut's observations in "Melancholie" can be additionally supported by analyzing his manuscripts and published pieces for Japanese journals, where the architect delivered his criticism and suggestions on modern architecture.[23] In *Houses and People of Japan* for instance, he discussed his confrontation with the contemporary modern problems of Japan in the chapter entitled "What Now?"

This chapter was written as an imaginary discussion with Mr. Suzuki, but it was actually a collage of real conversations between Taut and his Japanese colleagues.[24] It contained some phrases that may suggest Taut's relapse into the Orientalist hopes of his early career. Yet, this dream about the redemptive power of the Orient took place only momentarily in this conversation, since Taut's imaginary friend Mr. Suzuki warned him not to idealize the "glorious days of the past" and not to ignore the modern developments of Japan.[25] Besides, the fact that Taut was now in Japan obliged him to notice the country's expanding Westernization. Unlike the earlier accounts where the architect treated the Orient as non-historical and redemptive, Taut was now much

[24] This information is taken from Manfred Speidel's editorial note in *Daidalos*. Bruno Taut, "Houses and People of Japan" [Reprint of Chapter "What Now"], in *Daidalos* 54, December 1994, pp. 62–73.
[25] Taut, *Houses and People of Japan*, pp. 259–260.

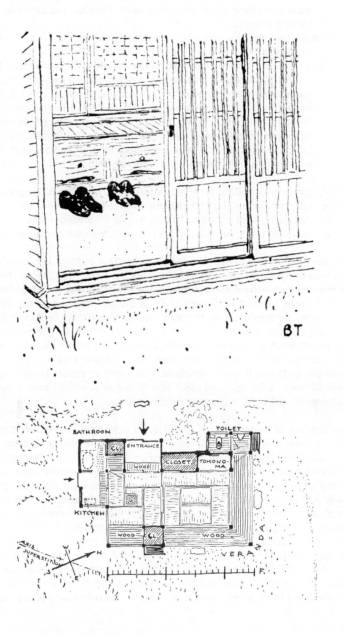

9.4 *Top* and *Bottom*: Bruno Taut. Drawings of Japanese houses.
Source: Bruno Taut, *Houses and People of Japan*, Tokyo, 1937.

26 Ibid., pp. 262–263 (my emphasis).
27 Ibid., pp. 177–178.
28 The discussion is introduced when Mr. Suzuki adds to the "catalogue of our progress" that Japanese people are getting taller. Taut objects to this statement by saying that "stature has nothing to do with genius" and that neither the proportions of the Japanese body nor the traditional way of sitting or sleeping have necessarily caused an unhealthier lifestyle (compared with European). To support his point, Taut says that he will throw away his spring mattress and lie on flat mats when he "gets home." (Taut never went back to Germany). Suzuki replies: "Well, this is amusing and interesting, I must say! . . . We generally think that the Western way of living is much more healthy. And there you come along, a European, telling us the contrary." Ibid., pp. 261–262.
29 Paul Bonatz brought Neufert to Turkey. I would like to thank Can Bilsel for this information.

more attentive to the development of modern architecture in Japan, as well as the actual problems emerging during this process. He assessed the main conflict as the dilemma between copying Western forms and searching for an alternative modernism. In "What Now?" Taut questioned both the enthusiasm for and reaction to Westernization:

> Taut: What I do mean is the admirable way in which the Japanese house has adapted itself to the special *climate of Japan* and is in harmony with local customs and daily occupations . . . And then, why is there nowhere that splendidly conceived veranda adapted to modern style building? Where are the broad gables, in Japan a most necessary thing to keep the large window openings shaded from sun and rain, since you must leave everything open during the heat. Terraces and balconies are *Western imitations*!
>
> Suzuki: Ah, well, you may be right. But then, you see, for modern life the old style of building is not suitable at all.
>
> Taut: Nobody said you were to imitate the old style completely! That would be as terrible a mistake as *slavish imitation of foreign styles*. But it does seem as if some of your countrymen *feel ashamed*, if their houses don't look exactly like every house in Paris or Berlin. This seems to lead others into reaction, causing them to construct their homes entirely in the old classical way, which is wrong too. After all, it can't be terribly difficult to find an arrangement for simultaneously shading roofs and providing light for the rooms inside.[26]

A feeling of insecurity, Taut observed, unsettled his Japanese colleagues. In a previous part of the text, Taut had already criticized the "European reception rooms" that were placed in modern houses, despite the disfavor of their owners, just because they were "consider[ed] necessary . . . to please the Europeans."[27]

The theme of inferiority was also repeated when Taut and Suzuki talked about the Japanese people's desire to be taller, since they took the European height as the human standard and considered the "Western way of living" "much more healthy."[28] Thus ideologies of Eurocentrism traveling to the Orient constructed the Western body (that itself varies and should not be standardized) as the ideal human norm. The "Oriental" himself – Suzuki – believed in the superiority myth of this Western norm. If the ideal European masculine body was considered a universal norm, then we can assert that a regional and particular truth had been universalized during modernization. Therefore, the "non-Western" subjects could speak of a feeling of inferiority caused by the lost natural right of belonging to this universality.

The ideology of ergonomics influenced world architecture more than it might be imagined. From graphic standard books such as *Neufert*, generations of architects worldwide learned and applied several physical standards to their modern furniture, kitchens, bathrooms, and stairs.[29] These modern norms were based on the dimensions and proportions of the idealized white masculine body *à la* Vitruvius, and ignored racial or gender differences. In this sense, Taut's diagram comparing the idealized European and Japanese bodies can be assessed as a groundbreaking, yet overlooked, comment on the politics of ergonomics. With this diagram, which appeared both in *Houses and People of Japan* and in the original (Turkish) version of *Mimari Bilgisi* (figure 9.1), the architect admitted that his initial uneasiness in moving about his house in Japan, because of the low door frames, "uncomfortable" heights of the door handles, and the like, was not caused by a lack of refinement in ergonomic design but was a matter of difference. Today, this diagram must be considered as an unheard warning against the ideology of standardization based on European and North American norms. Rather than take the "Western man's" body as the human standard, this diagram challenges the notion of *a* universal norm by representing two norms. Unlike the white man's body, the Japanese masculine body does not fit into a geometric square when his arms are wide open. While the white man's legs are half of his whole body, the Japanese man's legs are proportionately not the same. Even though Taut's comparative diagram ignores gender or racial differences, it must be considered as a step towards de-universalizing the Western masculine body as the standard of ergonomic design. So already by the mid-1930s Taut's intuitive realization of the "non-Western" subject's distance from the ego-ideal led him to one of the most critical contributions on the state of architectural standardization.

Houses and People of Japan was a study of the vernacular architecture in Japan and its implications for the modern period (plate 37). Apart from the research on Japanese architecture, the book opened multiple perspectives for Taut's thinking. For instance, it led him to reflect on the definition of architecture as an institutionalized profession. In various passages Taut commented on the distinction between the mason and the architect, which still remains one of the main criteria where the professionalization of architecture, and the distinction between "Architecture" and "vernacular building" are under dispute.[30] Rather than suggest a hierarchical difference between a craftsman and an architect, vernacular and modern architecture, Taut was interested in improving the standardization of architectural materials in relation to the legacy of Japanese mats, which he considered an example of pre-industrial standardization.[31] At another point, Taut started to formulate a typological matrix of the Japanese house according to its historical development.[32] Even more so, he increasingly commented on the importance of climate for shaping architecture after his research on the Japanese vernacular.[33]

For our purposes, the most relevant is Taut's definition of the Japanese vernacular, or more specifically the farmhouses (*Bauernhaus*) as "cosmopolitan" buildings. In his piece "The Japanese Village" Taut claimed that the Japanese farmhouse was both "national" and "international."[34] In *Houses and People of Japan*, he collected an impressive number of comparative images of farmhouses from Japan and another European country that looked strikingly identical. Putting a picture of a house in Japan next to a curiously similar one from Austria, Germany, Italy, Serbia, Sweden, and Switzerland, the architect drew the reader's attention to a provocative body of evidence. Even though he admitted that the reasons for these striking similarities had to be explained after some research, he did not retreat from claiming that the "cosmopolitanism" of the Japanese farmhouse, as well as the "universality" of peasant life, could well have created this resemblance:

> The Japanese farmer, who does not speak to the world with words, speaks through his houses. He is the Japanese nation and his tongue is a *cosmopolitan* one. And being *cosmopolitan* it has *universal power*. . . . The cosmopolitan mind of the peasants shows itself in its sociability and in their tolerance of different kinds of wishes or inclinations. Nevertheless, there is ever the same spirit, which unites all the many variations and produces an aesthetic whole.[35]
> The organism of the Japanese house very naturally originates from the life and work of the country folk. However much climate and types of agriculture differ, the peasants all over the world are fundamentally alike.

30 Bruno Taut, *Houses and People of Japan*, pp. 173, 193.
31 Ibid., pp. 206–208.
32 Ibid., p. 121.
33 He said, for instance: "Thus it was the climate that built the Japanese house, more especially the summer. . . . To keep the body in its normal balance there is no better means than the life in a Japanese house. . . . Otherwise one would have to use expensive apparatus to give the same airing effect. But such ventilation is artificial and can only be used temporarily." Taut, *Houses and People of Japan*, p. 72.
34 "Anyone who undertakes a closer study of the Japanese village, should not be stuck by any impression of seemingly 'exotic' strangeness. Rather, except for some Japanese specialties such as floor-mats and paper-windows, he will feel that all species of farmhouse throughout the world reflect themselves in the Japanese farmhouse. . . . The Japanese farmhouse is thus an enigma in itself. It is remarkable indeed that here, in contrast to any machinery of war or peace, is a cultural phenomenon born of the very soil of Japan, and which is absolutely national, though the various forms of this same culture in all its details and variations happen to be quite international." From Bruno Taut, "The Japanese Village."
35 Ibid., pp. 112–113.

Left : Japan   Right : Switzerland

Left : Japan   Right : The Balkans (Serbia)

Left : Japan   Right : Italy

9.5 Bruno Taut. Page from *Houses and People of Japan*, comparing Japanese and European vernacular houses.
Source: Bruno Taut, *Houses and People of Japan*, Tokyo, 1937.

. . . Farmhouses all over the world once had the same open fireplace as is found nowadays in Japan. . . . A kettle hung or stood over the fire at which the people gathered together to warm themselves, and dry their wet clothes, the fireplace being the central point for the family and the household.[36]

The validity of these assertions is naturally suspect, yet my point is not about the historical evolution or geographical expansion of these houses themselves, but about Taut's aspirations in interpreting them. The architect's choice of the word *cosmopolitanism* here, as opposed to, say, *nationalism,* is crucial. During the same period, the revival of national vernacular types, such as the discourse of the German farmhouse, was abruptly becoming a tool for the cultural politics of National Socialism. A similar danger was also becoming more and more evident in other countries, including Turkey, because of the rise of chauvinistic nationalism. In contrast, Taut was promoting the study of vernacular architecture to disclose the architectural principles not of nationalism but of cosmopolitanism. What could have motivated Taut to see a cosmopolitan chord in Japanese vernacular buildings? If he were trying to differentiate his own interest in the vernacular from the architects of the German *Heimatstil,* and if he were trying to prove the similarity between farmhouses of different nations, why did he refrain from using words such as *international?* The implicit answers to these questions can be found in Taut's next book, *Mimari Bilgisi.*

Melancholy of the East: Turkey, 1936–38

On September 30, 1936, Martin Wagner, Taut's colleague from the Weimar housing reform who was in Turkey at the time, sent a telegram to Japan, directing Taut to depart "immediately" for Turkey. After Hans Poelzig's sudden death just before making it to Turkey, Wagner convinced the authorities to invite Taut instead.[37] Taut's work in Turkey would later disappoint his friends and a number of architectural historians. For instance, Wagner himself complained in a letter to Walter Gropius about Taut's steps back from modern architecture:

> As everyone who gets old, Taut is stuck with Renaissance principles and he can't find a way towards the New! I am very disappointed. . . . It is a shame for such an avantgardist.[38]

To give another example, Paul Bonatz relied on Taut's use of the traditional Almaşık constructional system on the exterior walls of the Faculty of Languages, History and Geography building in Ankara, as support for his own position advocating nationalism in architecture.[39] Were these judgments correct? Did Taut start promoting a nationalist *Heimatstil* in Turkey after criticizing such a development in Germany during the 1920s? What was the visionary architect of the German Expressionist utopias – the designer of ten thousand worker and middle-class houses in over twenty *Siedlungen* and urban housing blocks, the promoter of pure, functional, flexible, and efficient houses for the modern dwellers of Germany – really pursuing in Turkey?[40]

As soon as he arrived, Taut was given serious responsibilities. He became the head of both the Department of Architecture at the Academy of Fine Arts and the Department of Construction in the Ministry of Education. In letters to architects Ernst May and Hans Scharoun, Wagner claimed that Taut's career in Turkey was not a bright one, since he was able to get commissions "only" for a few buildings,[41] and since he "turned all teachers and patrons against him"

[36] Ibid., pp. 116–117.

[37] After receiving the news, Taut wrote in his diary: "Bums!!! Schluss mit Japan." (Bum!!! End with Japan.) Ten days later, on October 10, Taut arrived in Turkey. Bruno Taut, "Tagebuch – Japan," Manuscript dated 16 July 1936–02 November 1936. Nachlaß Taut, BTS 01–75, pp. 20–21, Baukunst Sammlung, Akademie der Künste, Berlin.

[38] Martin Wagner, Letter to Walter Gropius. 29 August 1937, quoted in Manfred Speidel, "Bruno Taut. Wirken und Wirkung," in *Atatürk için Düsünmek. Iki Eser: Katafalk ve Anıtkabir. Iki Mimar: Bruno Taut and Emin Onat,* Istanbul, Milli Reasürans, 1997.

[39] Paul Bonatz, *Leben und Bauen,* Stuttgart, Engelhornverlag Adolf Spiemann, 1950.

[40] See Kurt Junghanns, *Bruno Taut, 1880–1938,* Milan, Franco Angeli, 1978; Luciana Capaccioli, *Bruno Taut. Visione e Progetto,* Bari, Delado Libri, 1981; Bettina Zöller-Stock, *Bruno Taut. Die Innenraumentwürfe des Berliner Architekten,* Stuttgart, Deutsche Verlags-Anstalt, 1993.

Also see Sibel Bozdogan, "Against Style: Bruno Taut's Pedagogical Program in Turkey, 1936–1938," in Martha Pollak (ed.), *The Education of the Architect. Historiography, Urbanism and the Growth of Architectural Knowledge,* Cambridge, London, The MIT Press, 1997, pp. 163–192; Bernd Nicolai, *Moderne und Exil. Deutschsprachige Architekten in der Turkei 1925–1955,* Berlin, Verlag für Bauwesen, 1998; Esra Akcan, "Öteki' Dünyanın Melankolisi. Bruno Taut'un Doğu Deneyimi," in *Domus,* February–March 2001, pp. 36–41.

[41] In a letter to Hans Scharoun, Wagner wrote: "Bruno Taut did not receive big or rewarding tasks here. Now, he is building only a school in Ankara, plans two Ministries, a big Opera house for 1,200 people. He also contributed a nice sketch for the Parliament for a competition. But it is not yet confirmed that these projects will be realized." From Martin Wagner, Letter to Hans Scharoun, 30 December 1937, Nachlaß Scharoun, Mappe. 6.3, Baukunst Sammlung, Akademie der Künste, Berlin; Martin Wagner, Letter to Ernst May, 12 March 1937, Nachlaß Wagner Doc. 26, Baukunst Sammlung, Akademie der Künste, Berlin.

[42] Martin Wagner, Letter to Ernst May, 10 February 1939, Nachlaß Wagner Doc. 26, Baukunst Sammlung, Akademie der Künste, Berlin.

[43] See Asım Mutlu, *Anılarda Mimarlık*, Istanbul, YEM, 1995; Ömer Gülsen (ed.), "Erinnerungen an Bruno Taut," in *Bauwelt* 75, no. 39, 1984, pp. 1675–1684.

[44] Taut's diary in Istanbul illustrates that he spent almost all of his time working either on building designs or on revising the academy's architectural program. See Bruno Taut, "Istanbul Journal," Manuscript, Nachlaß Taut, Mappe III, 18, Baukunst Sammlung, Akademie der Künste, Berlin; Bruno Taut, Letters to Karl and Li Crayl, Nachlaß Taut, BTS–01–337, Baukunst Sammlung, Akademie der Künste, Berlin.

[45] In a letter to Ueno, Taut wrote: "Where is homeland? Answer: Building. Where is Happiness? Answer: Building [Sheerbart]" (trans. by author), Bruno Taut, Letter to Ueno, 9 August 1938, Nachlaß Taut, BT–Slg–01–13, Baukunst Sammlung, Akademie der Künste, Berlin.

[46] "Istanbul Journal," Entry on 4 June 1938, p. 125.

[47] Taut's report to the Ministry of Education. Manfred Speidel Archive.

[48] Bruno Taut, Letter to Schüttes, 17 March 1938. I would like to thank Manfred Speidel for providing this document for me.

[49] Bruno Taut's public lecture in Istanbul at the Opening of the architect's Exhibition on 4 June 1938. Published as Bruno Taut, "Ansprache zur Eröffnung der Taut – Ausstellung in Istanbul am 4.6.1938," in *Bruno Taut 1880–1938*, p. 260.

[50] Taut changed Egli's program at the Academy, and concentrated on social issues such as social housing projects. See Sibel Bozdogan, "Against Style: Bruno Taut's Pedagogical Program in Turkey, 1936–1938."

[51] The last words he wrote in his diary were about his students at the Academy, seeking permission for them to work in the school until 9 p.m. Taut, "Istanbul Journal," Entry on 13 December 1938, p. 144.

[52] Taut summarized his position as a "search for synthesis between old tradition and modern civilization." From Taut, "Ansprache zur Eröffnung der Taut – Ausstellung in Istanbul am 4.6.1938," p. 260.

[53] Taut, *Houses and People of Japan*, pp. 2–3.

[54] Ibid., pp. 53–54.

[55] Ibid., p. 239.

[56] Ibid., p. 53.

[57] Taut, "New Japan. What its Architecture Should be," Bruno Taut, in *Mimari Bilgisi*, Istanbul, Güzel Sanatlar Akademisi, 1938. German version: Tilmann Heinisch and Goerd Peschken (eds.), Bruno Taut, *Architekturlehre*, Hamburg, VSA, 1977.

[58] Taut, *Mimari Bilgisi*, p. 89.

[59] Ibid., p. 166.

[60] Ibid., pp. 43, 157,

[61] Ibid., p. 166.

by committing lots of "faux pas" at the Academy.[42] Even though Taut's relations with his Turkish colleagues at the Academy were not always smooth,[43] the architect's own diary and letters indicate that he was often intensely busy but content with his work,[44] and that he had a fulfilling life in finding his "homeland" and "happiness" in architecture, not necessarily in a specific country.[45] Taut was also one of the first German architects whose work was extensively covered in the Turkish architectural journal *Arkitekt*, where the young Turkish architects had been attacking their "foreign" colleagues for lacking the necessary background to create the "new Turkish architecture." Taut nevertheless soon won their appreciation, as his correspondence with the journal's editor Zeki Sayar, suggests.[46]

Taut designed numerous schools in Ankara, Istanbul, Izmir, and Trabzon. These built projects are usually known as his only designs in Turkey, yet his diary and a report to the Ministry of Education indicate that he worked on over twenty buildings, most of which remained pending upon his death.[47] Taut collaborated with several assistants and colleagues from Germany such as Grimm (who had worked in Taut & Hoffmann's office), Mundt, Franz Hillinger (who had worked with Taut for Gemeinnützige Heimstätten AG), and Margarete Schütte-Lihotzky and Wilhelm Schütte (whom Taut himself invited to Turkey; they collaborated in a couple of projects at the Turkish Ministry of Education).[48] He organized a large and well-received exhibition of his lifetime work at the Istanbul Academy in 1938.[49]

Taut was also extremely influential as a teacher and prepared a reformed pedagogical program for the Academy.[50] As his diary suggests, Taut was in touch with many of the young and established architects of Turkey, working closely with them either at the Academy or in the design and drawings of his own projects. Again, from his diaries and letters, we understand that Taut spoke German and French with his Turkish colleagues, and German, French, and English with his Japanese friends, yet he also learned some Turkish as well as Japanese. Shortly after designing the catafalque of Atatürk, Taut died suddenly in December 1938 in Turkey. He had been suffering from asthma.[51]

When Taut came to Turkey he found himself under similar pressures that he had observed in Japan. Just like in Japan, he reacted against blindly copying forms from both "Western" modernism and an anachronistic past.[52] In *Houses and People of Japan, Fundamentals of Japanese Architecture*, and *New Japan. What its Architecture Should Be*, Taut had already disparaged examples of imported European modernism in Japan. Strolling down the road between Yokohama and Tokyo was "a cold shower of disillusionment" for him because of "the ludicrous would-be modernity of the tin façades,"[53] the "many ugly things, many 'modern' things and much trash" as the legacy of a "frantic importation of Western civilization."[54] Instead of improving the structural conditions, the modern works had augmented the risk of earthquake and fire in big cities.[55] The modern houses had none of the traditional vernacular sensitivity to climate.[56] The statistics showed that one-third of the school-age children in Tokyo were sick, because of the "falsely-built houses."[57] In his publications in Turkey, Taut did not hide his hostility for similar architectural practices, either. He openly criticized the "house as a machine,"[58] imported "cubic architecture" that "put boxes on needles,"[59] profit-oriented, mechanized American skyscrapers,[60] and "degenerated" modernism.[61] Yet this does not mean that the architect advocated a traditionalist vision. He was equally against a blind "imitation of old styles" that was motivated as a reaction to the "slavish imitation of foreign styles."[62] In Japan, Taut had concluded:

For more than seventy years now Japan had been importing Western civilization with all her might. But what had happened during those seventy years could not be compared to a natural growth. . . . One would have to give the Japanese time. Perhaps they have to make even more mistakes yet before they finally solve their problem of cultural synthesis. The day will come when foreign plant will have taken root in the new soil. But for the time being, *enthusiasm for foreign taste* will be followed by corresponding reactions in the direction of an *uninspired 'Nipponism.'*[63]

Taut's stance in Turkey was similar. In letters to his Japanese friends, the architect wrote that he "remains faithful fighting against" the architectural approach "named as *cubic*" in Turkey.[64] Taut's insightful observations of modernism's basic dilemmas outside Europe should not be swiftly dismissed as easy generalizations. On the contrary, Taut's remarks can be theoretically suggestive in disclosing typical conditions. As long as modernism was perceived as a "universal" form of expression, then, we should be able to speak about the reaction of a subject that was gauged by his or her ability to catch up with this modernism as a style. The "slavish imitation of foreign styles" and "uninspired" nativism Taut observed as two dead-end paradigms of modern architecture in Japan and Turkey can rightly be interpreted as nothing but the two faces of this reaction. Here the subject oscillates between fascination for and resistance towards the "West." In the phase of "slavish imitation of foreign styles," there was an attachment to the "West" as a substitute for the deprived right of sharing this notion of "universality." In the phase of "uninspired" nativism, there was a resistance against the "West" or "universality" that it supposedly embodied, and an attachment to the traditional forms as a substitute for lost glorious days. It was these days of the past that were perceived not to have been ruined by the feeling of insecurity. Three decades earlier, Taut had observed the same dilemma that Frantz Fanon outlined as the two basic but unproductive responses of the Algerian subject to the perceived "inferiority of his culture." The subject either "unfavorably criticizes his own national culture" or "takes refuge" in passionately defending it.[65]

Rather than perceive this dilemma as a struggle between two groups with opposite positions, it is usually more helpful to conceive it as a tension that exists simultaneously in one or a group of individuals. In other words, "slavish imitation of foreign styles" and "uninspired" nativism, fascination and resistance to the "West" are the two faces of the same condition – a condition that I call the melancholy of the "other."[66] On the one hand, accusing *all* regionalist tendencies for their chauvinism and anachronism would have failed to suggest an alternative to the hegemonic Westernization of "non-Western" contexts. These accusations would have ignored the strategic and emancipatory potential in the provisional promotion of regional or national expressions in these regions. On the other hand, underlining some supposedly fixed identities with increasing inflexibility would have fallen into essentialist definitions, myths of origins and would have maintained the segregation of the "non-West" from the "West." Taut's suggestion to resolve this fundamental dilemma was nothing less than an aspiration to construct a cosmopolitan ethics in architecture.

Toward a *Weltarchitektur*: Turkey, 1937–38

During 1937, Taut noted in his diary that he was working on the manuscript of a book that he later described as his "great work." This book first appeared in Turkish as *Mimari Bilgisi* (1938, *Lectures on Architecture*), shortly before the architect's death.[67] Because the German version, *Architekturlehre*,[68] did not appear until 1977, and was published without figures, the Turkish version is the

[62] Taut, *Houses and People of Japan*, p. 263.
[63] Ibid., p. 265 (my emphasis).
[64] Bruno Taut, Letter to Tokugen Mihara, undated, Nachlaß Taut, BT–Slg–01–145/2, Baukunst Sammlung, Akademie der Künste, Berlin.
[65] Frantz Fanon, *The Wretched of the Earth*, New York, Grove Press, 1963, p. 237.
[66] This dilemma, I suggest, is caused by the melancholy of the "non-Western" subject itself. The lost object here that causes melancholy remains centered on the natural right to belong to the condition of "universality" (an ideal of the early twentieth century). The oscillation between fascination and resistance to the "West" is similar to the melancholic condition in which the ego, in Freudian terms, swings between love and hatred. For more discussion see Esra Akcan, "Modernity in Translation."
[67] Though it was a theoretical work, Taut referred to historical examples from many parts of the world including Europe, the United States, Japan, Turkey, and Africa. Taut, *Mimari Bilgisi*.
[68] The book later appeared under the title *Architekturlehre* (Lectures in Architecture) in German, though Taut may have considered titling the German version as *Architekturgedanken* (Thoughts on Architecture). Erica Taut, Letters to Isaburo, 1 February 1939, Nachlaß Taut, BTS–01–16, BTS–01–17, Baukunst Sammlung, Akademie der Künste, Berlin.

⁶⁹ Taut, *Mimari Bilgisi*, pp.45–46.
⁷⁰ Ibid., pp. 85–86, German version, p. 69 (my emphasis).
⁷¹ Bruno Taut, *Modern Architecture*, London, Studio Limited, 1929.
⁷² Taut, *Mimari Bilgisi*, p. 334.
⁷³ Ibid., pp. 4–5, 24.
⁷⁴ Ibid., p. 62.
⁷⁵ Ibid., p. 65, also see p. 74.
⁷⁶ Ibid., p. 92.

only one that expresses Taut's precise intentions. Taut's main criticism in this book was the generalization of Modern Architecture as a style across the globe:

> The world is increasingly getting uniform and homogenous, just like the soldiers who carry uniform weapons in uniform clothes.[69]
> When technology *dominates* the house, machines, equipments, mechanical utilities, and the like that can be used anywhere in the world conquer the environment. . . . This brings a situation where buildings all around the world look like machines that can be used without changing its shape in relation to place. This results in commonplace architecture, that is, the numberless modern buildings whose pictures we see in all magazines. . . . Architecture is thus confronted with such devastation that it will take too long to recover. If this was just an aesthetic delusion, it would not be too wrong. However, *nature, in our case climate*, will take its revenge on this terrifying negligence: it will soon be understood that a building that is convenient for one country is not so for another.[70]

The latter quotation is one of the earliest criticisms of what was thereafter called the International Style. In *Modern Architecture* written in 1929 in Germany, Taut had already warned his colleagues about the danger of homogenization across the world through modernization.[71] Taut was one of the first architects to realize that the International Style was motivating the spread of European modernism, by claiming a universal character for a form of expression that originated from a limited region. Yet, he was also well aware of the reactionary threat of nationalism taking command in countries such as his native one. *Mimari Bilgisi* was full of passages that severely criticized advocates of nationalism, whether they expressed themselves in modern or historical forms. "Whether the architects are forced to create national architecture through modern expressions" as in "Fascist Italy" or "they are forced to use historical styles. . . . Both of the results are a disaster."[72]

How did Taut think, then, that he could reconcile the two forces at the very heart of the dilemma he had unveiled? Though he was against treating the Western man's body as a global norm, he was still immersed in the belief that architecture could embody universality. *Mimari Bilgisi* was an attempt to define universal principles of architecture in a way that would integrate geographical and cultural differences. By exemplifying "Greek Temple," "Gothic Cathedral," "Turkish Mosque," and "Japanese House," Taut defined the main principles of architecture *as technique, construction, function*, and finally *proportion*, which stood, for him, above the other three.[73] Then Taut opened a category that would respond to geographical differences: climate. According to Taut, almost all external conditions of architecture were a function of climate[74] and in each design, the four abstract principles had to be made concrete to achieve a climate-specific building. Climate not only gave "a specificity, a tonality, a musical color to the building," but also, Taut asserted, mirrored the ethnic differences in body proportions and human expressions.[75] In other words, climate was not only a functional matter for him, as it was for most European architects, but a much broader – even a metaphysical – issue. What distinguishes Taut's notion of climate is that he conceived it as a category to help attain universality, rather than regionalism: "the more architectural forms are appropriate to the climate, light and air of their place, the more they are universal."[76]

In making this statement, Taut was suggesting that climate-specificity forged a "universal" architecture that was "non-European," an architecture that captured what might be called, perhaps, a non-Eurocentric universality.

According to Taut, the idea of nature was universal, it could be applied worldwide; it was the earth itself. Climate, on the other hand, was both a fact of nature, something of the earth, and it was also place-specific. Thus climate, it followed for Taut, was the foundation for a non-Eurocentric universal architecture. Taut's stay in Japan and Turkey led him to test the geographical limits of Western European modernism, and to advocate a theory of modern architecture that would challenge the universalizing claims of modernization (in the sense of the importation of Western modernism), but nevertheless safeguard a notion of universality. In this way, Taut was able to maintain the importance he had assigned to nature as a guide for architecture during his early career in Germany.[77] While he had not elaborated a category of difference in nature then, he was now interpreting climate as the thing that came to terms with geographical diversity.

Taut criticized those who rejected foreign influences in rejuvenating domestic norms.[78] Yet, he advocated a foreign influence that would be, he said "no false Internationalism, no uniformalization (*Weltuniformierung*) of the world, no dullification (*Langweiligmachen*) of the whole earth," but a hybridization that would "make both sides richer."[79] In *Mimari Bilgisi*, he used the word *Allerweltsarchitektur* to criticize the homogenizing tendencies of Modern Architecture.[80] If Taut was against internationalism or uniformalization of the world, which word did capture his intentions? What would be a construct that could open a country to foreign influences, without totally assimilating its domestic norms within the norms of the foreign? Can it be that the "cosmopolitan" farmhouse that Taut so willingly defended in *Houses and People of Japan* was a preview of what he aspired to see rejuvenated through contemporary architecture? The word *cosmopolitan* not only assures openness to the foreign, but it also defies the Orientalist segregations between "East" and "West." The possibility that a "cosmopolitan farmhouse" exists must have been the very evidence for Taut against the persistence of the geographical divide. In his own words, only when one "gets to know the foreignness in one's own nature," can one have the vigor to send "melancholy . . . down to the grave it deserves." Only when a culture opened itself to the foreign with "the belief that East and West belong together," could it challenge melancholy.[81]

Taut's frank confrontation with and eventual denunciation of the Orientalist perceptions about non-European countries, as well as of the consequences of the spread of European modernism, led him to his search for a cosmopolitan ethics. While the architect genuinely criticized the dissemination of the International Style to countries such as Japan and Turkey, he was equally critical of the rising nationalist discourses. In an attempt to reconcile his aspiration for a universally valid set of architectural principles with his aspiration for the vitality of cultural differences, Taut emphasized the idea of the cosmopolitan and the determinative value of climate. In this, his theory in-progress sought ways to differentiate *Allerweltsarchitektur* – defined as the exportation of European modern architecture to the rest of the world – from his aspiration for what might be called a cosmopolitan *Weltarchitektur*.

Cosmopolitan Self: Cosmopolitan House (Istanbul, 1938)

Would a European ever want to build in Europe a Japanese house with European workmen? If one would work on the bridge of cultures, this is only possible by an awakened understanding of foreign singularities and by showing how the human spirit works logically and reasonably although its conceptions may vary completely from place to place. . . . In this way

77 Bruno Taut, "The Earth is a Good Dwelling." For more on Taut's ideas on nature see Rosemarie Bletter, "Bruno Taut and Paul Scheerbart's Vision. Utopian Aspects of German Expressionist Architecture."
78 Already in "Japans Kunst" Taut had argued that a fruitful modern architecture in Japan would be the result of a synthesis with European influences. Taut, *Japans Kunst*, p. 206.
79 Ibid., p. 206.
80 Taut, *Mimari Bilgisi*, p. 46.
81 Taut, "Japans Kunst. Mit Europäischen Augen Gesehen," p. 24.

9.6 Bruno Taut. Sketch for "Concealing the Front: Cubic Façades in Japan."
Source: *Mimari Bilgisi* [Lectures on Architecture], Istanbul, 1938.

[82] Taut, *Houses and People of Japan*, p. 40.

[83] Bruno Taut, Letter to Walter Segal, 2 March 1937, quoted in Speidel, "Bruno Taut. Wirken und Wirkung," p. 57.

[84] Bruno Taut, Letter to Kurata, 6 November 1937, quoted in Speidel, "Bruno Taut. Wirken und Wirkung," p. 57.

[85] Bruno Taut, "Türk Evi, Sinan, Ankara," in *Her Ay*, no. 2, 1938, pp. 93–94 (my emphasis).

we become aware of the same spirit whose various products are merely the consequence of different premises.[82]

Visitors are usually shocked when they first see the house Taut designed for himself in Ortaköy, Istanbul (1938). Like his own house in Dahlewitz which was built to embody the principles of the "rational house," Taut's house in Istanbul strikes one as slightly off. The building stands out like a floating lighthouse over a dense sea of trees on the slopes overlooking the Bosphorus. Taut's house often provokes surprise for its symbolic gestures. Local people commonly refer to it as the "Japanese house." If the multiple layers of eaves are meant to be references to pagodas, what exactly do they mean in Turkey? Why Japan in Turkey? Why a reference to any symbol from any country, whatsoever? What happened to the avant-garde designs inspired by Expressionist utopias, or the social housing projects with flat roofs?

Based on the previous discussion, one may view Taut's house (and other projects in Turkey and Japan) from a different angle. The initial sense of shock on seeing the house then gives way to considering it as, oddly enough, both traditionalist and out of place. Taut himself recognized this building as an important realization of his later thought. In his letters from Turkey to Walter Segal and Kurata, for instance, he wrote about his enthusiasm to "show how to apply theory into practice"[83] and to design buildings that would stand as "samples of my architectural understanding today."[84]

One enters the house from the back and moves forward to the main octagonal living room with high ceilings. The view and light of the Bosphorus stream through the windows situated at two different heights across the space. The narrow built-in wooden stair at one corner of the living room leads up to the study. This smaller octagonal room looks like the tower of the house from the exterior and has an inclined ceiling in the interior as in a Seljuk tomb. It is also surrounded almost on all sides with windows at table height overlooking the Bosphorus.

Rather than cover over the foreign, or totally domesticate an imported idea, or still, rather than assimilate and contain it as if it had no foreignness, Taut was explicit in expressing the legacy of Japan in his house. This house has an estranging, foreignizing effect, but a totally different one from the other foreign buildings that had become commonplace in Turkey by the time of his arrival. In a country wide open to foreign influences from its West, but equally closed to the ones from its East, building a "Japanese house" was definitely a critical and original gesture. The house integrated elements from Germany and Turkey as well. Its similarity to two of Taut's 1925 projects in Germany (his own house in Dahlewitz and Haus K) cannot be left unmentioned. In all houses Taut differentiated the service spaces from the main living halls, whose circular plans were meant to capture the maximum opening to the outside. The organization of the plan and the tripartite massing of Haus K is especially similar to the house in Ortaköy. In the latter, sun-shading devices replace the terraces. As a matter of fact, the more one looks at Taut's Ortaköy house from different angles, the more complicated the building becomes. From some viewpoints, the multilevel hanging eaves look like pagodas. But seen from other perspectives, they do not look dissimilar to the vernacular houses of Istanbul. One realizes that the eaves in Taut's house were designed as sun-shading devices for the double-height windows of the interior. This use of sun-shading devices at the mid-level of a double-height window was actually very common in the traditional vernacular buildings of the region, commonly referred to as "old Turkish houses." In an interview for a Turkish magazine, Taut was asked to comment on the "modern Turkish house." His answer was concerned with a residential modernism that explicitly condemned both the copy of modern European houses, and the "kitsch" imitation of traditional ones. He suggested instead the filtering of the principles of both through the category of climate. Taut's definition for the "modern Turkish house" was in reality a description of his own house in Istanbul:

> [The modern Turkish house will be born] whenever the architects free themselves from the fashion of cubic style that has become an ordinary practice here. Only then will the principles of modern architecture be applied with a freedom of thought. Both for houses and for some other buildings *climate* will be given priority, and thus some characters of the traditional Turkish house will be applied automatically, such as *shading eaves*, *pavilion* like structures, and *double-height windows* in rooms with high ceilings. Among these windows, the ones at the bottom will provide the view and necessary illumination for the house; the ones at the top will give a harmonious, sweet light to the whole room. . . . To be sure, one should avoid direct copies. Otherwise, this attempt will turn into a sentimental romanticism, namely a misunderstood nationalism. The result will be the ugly pretension called *kitsch*.[85]

As this quotation suggests, Taut regarded his Ortaköy house also as a particular continuation of the memory of vernacular architecture in Turkey. From his diary, we understand that Taut had just studied a typical wooden

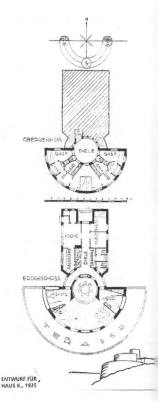

ENTWURF FÜR HAUS K., 1925

9.7 Bruno Taut. Plan of Haus K, Germany, 1925.
Source: Winfried Nerdinger, *Bruno Taut, 1880–1938: Architekt zwischen Tradition und Avantgarde*, Stuttgart, 2001.

9.8 Bruno Taut's personal house in Ortaköy, 1938.
Source: Photo Esra Akcan.

86 In the vernacular house of Edirne, Taut was interested in the principle of what he called *Wohnveranda* (semi-open sofa) and living space in the second floor. From Bruno Taut, "Istanbul Journal," Entry on 20 January 1938, p. 95.
87 Djelal Essad, *Constantinople. De Byzance a Stamboul*, Paris: Librarie Renouard H. Laurens, 1909; Celal Esad, 1912, in Dilek Yelkenci (ed.), *Eski Istanbul*, Istanbul, Çelik Gülersoy Yayınları, 1989; Celal Esad, *Türk Sanatı*, Istanbul, Akgam Matbaası, 1928. Celal Esad Arseven, *L'Art Turc. Depuis son origine jusqu'à nos Jours*, Istanbul, Devlet Basimevi, 1939.
88 Taut, *Die Neue Wohnung*, p. 21.
89 For instance: Taut, "Istanbul Journal," Entry on 10 May 1938, 30 June 1938.
90 Taut, *Mimari Bilgisi*, pp. 92–93. Also see pp. 151–152.
91 Bruno Taut, "Ansprache zur Eröffnung der Taut – Ausstellung in Istanbul am 4.6.1938," p. 260. Rosemarie Bletter also suggests that the humanism of Kant, developed particularly in "Perpetual Peace" strongly influenced the young Taut. Rosemarie Bletter, "Bruno Taut and Paul Scheerbart's Vision. Utopian Aspects of German Expressionist Architecture."

house during his trip to Edirne with Celal Esat,[86] the leading art historian at the Academy who was one of the first to draw attention to the term "Turkish house" as an important category of art history.[87] Long before he left Germany, Taut had already included a lengthy description of an Oriental *oda* (room) in his book *Die Neue Wohnung*.[88] At the Academy, he had already become familiar with Sedad Eldem's National Architecture Seminar. In his diary, Taut also referred briefly to Eldem's idea of *milli mimari* (national architecture), based on the modernized interpretation of vernacular houses.[89] The double-height windows of the "Turkish house" were a topic of interest for Taut in his book *Mimari Bilgisi*, where he claimed that the proportions of these windows were taken from nature.[90]

Conclusion

During his opening talk at the Istanbul Academy Taut had linked his own intellectual growth to the influence of Immanuel Kant's humanism.[91] Perhaps it is only fitting, then, that Taut, who shared his hometown with Kant, was striving to establish a cosmopolitan ethics in architecture. Taut's theory on what might be called *Weltarchitektur* was neither complete nor an ahistorical ready-at-hand solution. Needless to say, today it would be questionable to glorify Taut's position as the "therapy" for melancholy, as he might have liked to see it. The overemphasis on the redemptive value of climate as a critical position against Eurocentrism is, naturally, an exaggeration, even if not totally irrelevant. Nevertheless, Taut was one of the first architects to engage with the tough problems of a world characterized by increased connections and negotiations between different geographies. What stands out in Taut's late career is his openness to hybrid influences from a variety of regions and his willingness to translate those influences. But hybridity in itself is not adequate to distinguish his theoretical suggestion, nor does it sufficiently show Taut's continuing relevance. His still-engaging contribution needs to be understood, I suggest, in terms of a cosmopolitan aspiration.

I would therefore like to differentiate the concept of a hybrid artifact from one that embodies cosmopolitan ethics. I define *hybrid* as a de facto product of modern times, where there are no "pure national," or "pure Western" and "pure Eastern" artifacts, because of the constant translations between countries. While this hybridization has been amplified under globalization, it is definitely not a recent phenomenon; indeed we can trace it as early as our historiographical tools allow us, even though it has established itself in different political and economic contexts with accelerating intensity. The architects of the modern period also translated the foreign into the local and the local into the foreign on so many occasions that after a while there were only hybrids, making a much more nuanced understanding of translation necessary. The opinions of most architects have been shaped by the assigned local or global association to forms, rather than by the existence of pure local or pure global forms themselves. Hybrid artifacts are testimonies to the paradigmatic existence of translations between countries. There are many of them.

However, being a hybrid in itself does not prevent the ideological separation between "West" and "non-West," nor is it an antidote to chauvinistic nationalism or ethnocentrism. Hybrid artifacts are the prerequisites of a cosmopolitan ethics, but they alone are not capable of achieving it. There are many historical examples of buildings (or any type of artifacts) that were explicit and legible hybrids, but that were well attached to the official chauvinistic nationalist ideologies of their countries or used as propaganda tools by the same ideologies. Having a mixed palette of influences from numerous parts of the world is hardly a value in itself in the modern world.

The hybrid escapes its potential risk of maintaining separatist ideologies or fundamentalist identity politics only when it is coupled with a cosmopolitan ethics. Cosmopolitan law and hospitality were the two prerequisites for what Kant called "perpetual peace," a peace that annihilates the possibility of any future war.[92] Placed in the context of his writings as a whole, Kant's pursuit cannot be reduced merely to a legal formula for a global federation of lawful states, which one might falsely deem accomplished in such failed institutions as the League of Nations or the United Nations. Rather, Kant's aspiration must have also been towards an ethics that identifies an individual's response to the idea of an inclusive universal community. I am aware that the reference to Kant may at first seem to bring back the hierarchical assertion of European Enlightenment values. Kant's text has been challenged on numerous grounds, especially for its hidden Eurocentrism in the sense of the philosopher's ambition to extend his own legal structures to the rest of the world under the mask of perpetual peace.[93] Many critics have also rightly questioned the relevance of this text for discussing a post-national world order, if there were to be one, since Kant's own constitutional definitions came out of a world where the modern category of a nation-state itself was not yet well established.[94] Besides, Kant was not promoting an all-encompassing single world-state.[95] I would nevertheless like to maintain the category of cosmopolitan *ethics* as an aspiration, even if ways to achieve it without repeating Eurocentrism have yet to be defined. This cosmopolitanism need not necessarily be idealist, absolute, or timeless as it is sometimes perceived in the conventional Kantian version; but it may rather be redefined as a historically constituted and conscious aspiration reached *after* experience, a "project" after the recognition of the pitfalls of anti-cosmopolitan, exclusionary ideologies, or separatisms based on nation, ethnicity, race, or something else. In this sense, a cosmopolitan ethics that would be relevant for the world *today* is an aspiration for what Bruce Robbins defined as a "genuine striving toward common norms and mutual translatability," an aspiration that sees the potentials in the global circulation of goods, images, and ideas, in immigration and transport, namely in hybrid cultural formations, but is not satisfied with them.[96]

Against the objections that cosmopolitanism must necessarily impose Eurocentric modernist values, I used a modern case study as a counterexample. Namely, Taut's simultaneous aspiration for a non-Eurocentric cosmopolitan architecture may stand as a case in point, even if it is a premature one. On the one hand, the cosmopolitan ethics and perpetual peace that Taut must have discovered through Kant were the ultimate task of modernism as the heir of the Enlightenment. On the other hand, many of Taut's writings and projects aimed to construct an alternative against the homogenizing tendencies of what he called *Allerweltsarchitektur*, which exported European modernism to the whole world. It is for this reason that I interpreted the architect's last theoretical statement as one that sought not only for a challenge against Eurocentric modernization, not only for hybridity, but also for a cosmopolitan ethics. ∎

[92] Immanuel Kant, "Perpetual Peace. A Philosophical Sketch," in H. Reiss (ed.), *Political Writings*, Cambridge, Cambridge University Press, 1991, pp. 93–130 [1795]. For informative essays, see especially Allen W. Wood, "Kant's Project for Perpetual Peace," in P. Cheah and B. Robbins (eds.), *Cosmopolitics. Thinking and Feeling beyond the Nation*, Minneapolis, University of Minnesota Press, 1998, pp. 59–76; Jürgen Habermas, in C. Cronin and P. de Greiff (eds.), *The Inclusion of the Other: Studies in Political Theory*, Cambridge, The MIT Press, 2001, pp. 165–203; Martha Nussbaum, in J. Cohen (ed.), *For Love of Country: Debating the Limits of Patriotism*, Boston, Beacon Press, 1996.
[93] See for instance Jacques Derrida, *Adieu to Emanuel Levinas*, Stanford, Stanford University Press, 1999; David Harvey, "Cosmopolitanism and the Banality of Geographical Evils," in *Public Culture*, 12, 2000/2, pp. 529–564; Walter Mignolo, "The Many Faces of Cosmo-polis: Border Thinking and Critical Cosmopolitanism," in C. Breckenridge, S. Pollock, H. Bhabha, and D. Chakrabarty (eds.), *Cosmopolitanism*, Durham and London, Duke University Press, 2002, pp. 157–187.
[94] Pheng Cheah and Bruce Robbins (eds.), *Cosmopolitics*.
[95] Kant declared that such a single world-state would result in a "soulless despotism." From Emmanuel Kant, "Perpetual Peace," p. 113.
[96] Bruce Robbins, "Actually Existing Cosmopolitanism," in P. Cheah and B. Robbins (eds.), *Cosmopolitics*, pp. 12–13.

Acknowledgment
This essay was originally published in *New German Critique* 99 33, no. 3, Special Issue on "Modernism after Postmodernism," Fall 2006. All translations from German and Turkish belong to the author unless otherwise noted.

1-11-BERLHA

10

MEDITERRANEAN RESONANCES IN THE WORK OF ERIK GUNNAR ASPLUND

TRADITION, COLOR, AND SURFACE

Francis E. Lyn

Tunis, this is the most amusing I have come across in the twenty-eight years of my existence! . . . Above our heads a sky clear and deep the like of which I have never seen, such a tone in color that I am constantly imagining the sky as a vast blue painted dome.[1]

Erik Gunnar Asplund was born in Stockholm, Sweden, on September 22, 1885, and lived there until his death on October 20, 1940. In 1905 he began his architectural studies at the Royal Institute of Technology in Stockholm, and in 1910, when it seemed clear that the next step in his education was to attend the National Academy of Fine Arts, he and a number of fellow students decided instead to set up their own free academy. This academy would be called the Klara Skola. Citing displeasure with the program and faculty offered at the National Academy, they approached four of the most prominent Swedish architects of the time – Erik Bergman, Ivar Tengbom, Carl Westman, and Ragnar Ostberg – to become their tutors.[2] These were architects who were already heavily influenced by a radical shift in Swedish architectural discourse, toward a more romantic nationalist paradigm. According to Luca Ortelli, the Klara Skola was "a sort of liberal institution which drew on the greatest exponents of that tendency for its teachers."[3]

With the emergence of the Skansen Outdoor Museum of Agrarian Life, the newly established architectural profession began to develop the view that architecture needed to be emancipated from the nineteenth-century conflict between classical form and technology. This view was, in effect, the cause for the emergence of the movement called National Romanticism, and later, National Realism. This movement called for a return to "genuine materials and national character," and would ultimately have a clear influence on Asplund.[4]

Throughout his early career, Asplund made numerous visits to the Swedish interior to study its "folk" architecture, and undoubtedly preferred this, its "popular" architecture, to its monuments.[5] In his notebooks from a journey he made in 1912, there are representations of humble rural buildings, which confirmed his deep-seated belief in Swedish vernacular architecture.[6] The transcendent forms, materials, textures, and colors that he recorded never arrived in his work as quotations, but instead became transformed, to manifest new meaning. Simultaneously, among his Scandinavian contemporaries one could witness the breaking down of orders and the attenuation of proportions – examples of transgressions that went by the name of Swedish Grace[7] and whose refined simplification prefigured Modernism's formal idiom.[8]

It also seems clear that Asplund never really accepted the notion of an "International Style" or technology as a means of expression at face value.

[1] Erik Gunnar Asplund in Tunis in 1914, as quoted in Luca Ortelli, "Heading South: Asplund's Impressions," *Lotus International* 68, 1991, p. 31.

[2] On those architects, see Simo Paavilainen, *Nordic Classicism, 1910–1930*, Helsingfors, Finlands arkitekturmuseum, 1982.

[3] Luca Ortelli, "Heading South: Asplund's Impressions," p. 23.

[4] Claes Caldenby, "Time, Life and Work: An Introduction to Asplund," in *Asplund*, Claes Caldenby and Olof Hutlin (eds.), New York, Rizzoli International, 1985, p. 9. For the National Romanticism movement in Scandinavian countries, see Barbara Lane Miller, *National Romanticism and Modern Architecture in Germany and the Scandinavian Countries*, Cambridge, Cambridge University Press, 2000.

[5] The Swedish term "folk," however, reflects a greater nuance than the English word. In Sweden the concept of Folk is culturally conservative, and politically progressive, and connotes the freedom, equality, and solidarity inherent in the French Republican concept *le peuple*. At the same time it encompasses a broader range of society than in France. The percentage of Folk in Sweden was larger than that of *le peuple* in France, and more of Sweden's than France's bourgeoisie had sprung from this class. See Michelle Facos, *Nationalism and the Nordic Imagination: Swedish Art of the 1890s*, Berkeley, University of California Press, 1998, pp. 4–5.

[6] Caldenby, p. 23.

[7] Caldenby, p. 27.

[8] Eva Rudberg, "Aalto in Sweden," *Alvar Aalto – Toward a Human Modernism*, Munich, Prestel Verlag, 1999, p. 92.

10.1 *(Far left)* Gunnar Asplund. Woodland Cemetery, Perspective view of entryway, c.1935–40.
Source: © Arkitekturmuseet Stockholm, photo Nikolaj Alsterdal.

⁹ Michelle Facos, p. 3.
¹⁰ Claes Caldenby, "Beginnings," *Lectures and Briefings from the International Symposium on the Architecture of Erik Gunnar Asplund*, Christina Engfors (ed.), Stockholm, The Swedish Museum of Architecture and the Royal Academy of Fine Arts, 1986, p. 9.
¹¹ Christina Engfors and E. G. Asplund, *Architect, Friend and Colleague*, Stockholm, Arkitektur Forlag, 1990, p. 68.
¹² Erik Gunnar Asplund as quoted in *Gunnar Asplund Architect 1885–1940*, Gustav Holmdahl, Sven Ivar Lind, and Kjell Odeen (eds.), Stockholm, Ab Tidskriften Byggmastaren, 1950, p. 16.

Rather he used these notions as a way to explore a new reading of space and place relative to the new requirements of a rapidly changing and developing society. This attitude seems to have developed out of a consciousness that was in fact pervasive in Swedish National Romantic theory. According to Michelle Facos, "National Romanticism in Sweden distinguished itself from the same movement elsewhere and from mere nationalism by promulgating a modernist worldview embracing change, not a static pastoral/agrarian vision, which characterized culturally conservative movements elsewhere."[9] So, in Asplund's work, the reading of modernity that developed was not dogmatic, but rather a pragmatic one which was entirely place-derived.

In the summer of 1910, before beginning his studies at the Klara Skola, Asplund went on a three-month long study trip to Germany, which resulted later in an article on the use of concrete as a façade material. According to Claes Caldenby, this seems to be "a first step in the gradual turning away from the orthodoxy of natural materials."[10] Although he disparaged the artificial use of this new material (i.e., imitating granite or limestone) he did accept in the end the notion of cladding as legitimate. Another important point that this trip suggests is that Asplund must have been at least conversant in German, and would probably have been aware of the recent theories and methods concerning cladding that were being considered in Germany, Austria, and France. Asplund's student Goran Sidenbladh remarks that Asplund expected that his students be well versed in current literature, both German and French. So relative to these new theories as well as Asplund's requirement for a literate body of students, it seems reasonable to postulate that he should have been familiar with the writings of Gottfried Semper.[11] Clearly, around that time, the very theories that Semper had proposed were being questioned, and Asplund himself called for "truth" in architecture. In his article about concrete, he stated, "Advocates of the sound modern principle of truth in architecture are inclined to reject the whole of this new form of material, because it can only be an imitation of natural stone."[12] So here, and later in his career, he questioned the notion of surface as a legitimate rationale for the making of architecture. Yet, as in the Skandia Cinema (and to a lesser degree, several of his other projects), he would at times rationalize the use of the articulation of surface as architecture, and eventually accept it as an appropriate point of departure for the manifestation of a work of architecture.

At the turn of the century, the notions of surface articulation as a means of expression of architectural truth were becoming codified. Numerous architects had begun to investigate the separation of the skin of the building from its structure and Asplund's interests concerning these matters seemed clearly aligned with his continental contemporaries. So by the time he made his trip to the South, many of the fundamental components of his development as an architect were probably already in place. His interest in cladding and surface articulation, and his understanding of the importance of place were already clearly defined. This trip did not make him the architect that he was to become, but seemed rather to affirm certain beliefs that he already had, and to inspire new ways of interpreting the world in which he would build.

In 1913–1914, Asplund traveled to France, Italy, and the Mediterranean. The importance of his trip to the South, and its relevance to the architecture that he produced over the next several decades, have been discussed in numerous articles by various scholars (Ortelli, Caldenby, and Wrede, to name just a few). It was a trip in the tradition of the grand tour, but also one that was self-initiated and self-financed. So it was more in the spirit of the trips that students

10.2 Gunnar Asplund. Girgenti (now Agrigento) panoramic travel sketch, perspective view from northwest, 1914.

Source: © Arkitekturmuseet Stockholm, photo Nikolaj Alsterdal.

of the École des Beaux Arts had made to Greece in the early part of the nineteenth century, before academic acceptance of the islands was achieved. As a result, his Italian journey can be better understood as "experiential" rather than as "academic." Unlike the official trips of the academies, it had more to do with his personal interests. He had no reports to make, no *envois*, so to speak. Instead, his records consisted of volumes of journals filled with notes and sketches made as he traveled throughout Italy and the Mediterranean. These journals offer a glimpse of various concerns and issues that were to develop in his work.[13]

Asplund traveled first to Paris, where he felt completely out of place, and quickly moved on to Italy and Tunisia (plate 38). There he visited Rome, Palermo, Girgenti, Syracuse, Taormina, Tunis, Naples, Pompeii, Paestum, then north back to Rome, through the regions of Perugia, Umbria, Tuscany, and finally to Venice. On this trip he was sure to have seen many of the same things that students of the École des Beaux Arts such as Abel Blouet and Henri Labrouste had recorded a century earlier. In Pompeii he is moved by the street of tombs at the foot of Vesuvius and enchanted by its decorations; at Syracuse, the theatres and their relationship to the landscape; and in Tunis and Taormina, the festive atmosphere and the people. In his journals, continual references to color and the festive way of life are made:

> *Palermo*: "strong in colors and great in indolence. . . . Boys are splashing. . . . in the blue waters, the harbor is filled with masts and gaily-colored boats."
> *Girgenti*: "Greek temples and the deep blue sea . . . the roads and rocks a burning yellow."

[13] There is no English translation of his travel notes. See the illustrated Spanish version: Erick Gunnar Asplund, *Escritos 1906–1940 – Cuaderno de viaje a Italia en 1913*, El Escorial, El Croquis Editorial, 2002.

14 Erik Gunnar Asplund as quoted in
Gunnar Asplund Architect 1885–1940,
pp. 20–27.
15 Le Corbusier as quoted in William
J. R. Curtis, *Modern Architecture Since
1900*, London, Phaidon Press, 1982,
p. 166.
16 Benedetto Gravagnuolo, *Adolf
Loos*, New York, Rizzoli, 1988, p. 148;
also see Benedetto Gravagnuolo's
essay in this book.
17 Bjorn Linn, Introduction to Dan
Cruikshank (ed.), *Erik Gunnar Asplund*,
London, The Architects' Journal,
1988, p. 13.

Pompeii: "Large surfaces of color are often to be seen, but always picked out with thin lines and ornamentation in other colors, taking nothing away from the main coloring, but rather playing into it. The large pale walls sparsely divided by thin lines, garlands, small graceful columns, and the like are a delight to me. Deep yellow skirting, especially if one imagines it against a dark floor and light panels, is good (plate 39)."[14]

Asplund's insistence on color is one of the aspects that made his journals from the South different and unique. Most of his contemporaries chose, instead, to focus on the "whiteness" and abstract quality of the Mediterranean. In 1911 Le Corbusier wrote of the Italian portion of his travels:

Italy is a graveyard where the dogma of my religion now lies rotting. All the bric-a-brac that was my delight now fills me with horror. I gabble elementary geometry; I am possessed by the colour white, the cube, the sphere, the cylinder, and the pyramid.[15]

Likewise, commenting on Adolf Loos's Scheu House of 1912, Benedetto Gravagnuolo wrote of the "pure, radical and extremely modern shape of this stepped white shell . . . [that] gives rise to the invention of a new typological model for extensive residential building outside . . . the Mediterranean."[16]

Asplund's interest in the Northern vernacular had certainly made him well aware of the importance of color in the national context. His delight in the surfaces and colors observed during his trip to the South would soon betray the strategies that he would later employ in a number of his projects. Bjorn Linn states that by "the second half of the 1910's, Asplund's architectural style was becoming clear. He had assimilated his Italian studies and combined them with his deep empathy for the Swedish countryside and tradition of small town building in wood."[17] Yet, the possibility exists that the importance of surface and color in his work might also have been derived from a reading of Semperian theory and from the debates on the discovery of color in ancient temples that began about a century before his trip. It also seems reasonable to suggest that circumstances relative to social and cultural changes, as well as technological advances in construction (some of which developed out of Semperian theory) played a significant role in Asplund's development.

By revisiting the issues of color and surface explored by nineteenth-century French scholars, and conflating them with Asplund's own architectural discoveries both in Sweden and during his trip to the South, this essay seeks to establish one of the significant paradigms within which he would work for much of his career. By investigating a number of his most important projects (Villa Snellman, the Royal Chancellery Project, the Woodland Cemetery and Chapel, the Stockholm Public Library, the Gothenberg Law Courts Annex, his summer house at Stennäs, and the Skandia Cinema), I hope that his strategies of layered imagery, coupled with surface manipulation to render both cultural and architectural meaning, will be revealed.

The Debate about Polychromy

The first appearance of polychromy in the study of architecture came in the first decades of the nineteenth century at the peak of the Romantic Movement, and revolved around the fact that ancient Greek temples had been externally painted. Stuart and Revett, in their first volume of their *Antiquities of Athens*, published in 1762, had noted painted decorations on the frieze of the Temple of Ilissus. It was not, however, until 1815 that a general interest in the use of color in antiquity came to the forefront. That year, Antoine-Chrysostome Quatremère de Quincy (who would later become the permanent secretary of the Academie des Beaux Arts) published his observations on the use of color on antique sculpture, in an essay titled *Jupiter Olympien, ou l'art de la sculpture antique considérée sous un nouveau point de vue; ouvrage qui comprend un essai sur le goût de la sculpture polychrome.*[18] It was a work that studied the use of ivory, semi-precious and precious stones, gold, bronze, and paint in ancient Greek sculpture. The text, which was readily accepted, had a number of illustrations. One of these was a hand-colored plate in which the sculpture, naturally, included color. What is perhaps more significant is the fact that the surrounding architecture remained uncolored, thus retaining the "purity" that Winckelmann and other eighteenth-century scholars had aspired to. This aspiration was in fact pervasive throughout the eighteenth-century. According to Harry Francis Mallgrave in his introduction to his translation of Gottfried Semper's *The Four Elements of Architecture*, this aesthetic form had by the end of the century been extended to every fine art. But in the first few decades of the nineteenth century, the growing interest in classical studies in conjunction with the new discoveries of color being applied to antique works caused this "white" view of architecture to be thoroughly challenged.[19]

In 1834, Gottfried Semper – who had traveled around the Mediterranean region between 1830 and 1833 – published his pamphlet titled *Preliminary Remarks on Polychrome Architecture and Sculpture in Antiquity.*[20] The pamphlet came on the heels of the great polychrome debate that was taking place in the academies and which was centered primarily on Jacques-Ignace Hittorff's colored renderings of Temple B at Selinus, displayed in Paris in 1824 and published, with considerable negative reactions, in *Architecture antique de la Sicile* (1827–30) (plate 40). Hittorff was clearly concerned with archaeology, yet his interest was also contemporary. He regarded paint as a protective substance and saw it very adapted to the Parisian and northern light as a means of emphasizing form.[21] As a result, the debate became a major catalyst for the Grand Prix winners' interest in ancient Greek polychromy. No longer did the *pensionnaires* of the Villa Medici wish to remain in Italy.[22] It was not until 1845, however, that travel to Greece was officially sanctioned by the École. Prior to this, students such as Abel Blouet could only undertake projects in Greece outside of their official duties or after their five-year stay in Rome. Such trips would prove to be among the most consequential for the polychrome argument.

In 1828, Henri Labrouste studied three temples during his fourth year as a *pensionnaire* in Paestum, a Greek and later Roman colony site south of Naples. In his *envois*, the renderings were reserved, with coloring limited to the corona. While executing the Paestum *envoi*, Labrouste was concurrently working on a series of reconstructions of ancient cityscapes. Particularly interesting is the one that is inscribed "Agrigentum, 1828" on the back (plate 41). It is a watercolor fantasy in which polychromy is "laid over the architecture substructure as a shell."[23] Each monument within the representation is painted distinct from the other. This polychromy emphasizes the relationship to the Attic models. Half columns are painted to stand out from the wall, as if they were free-standing.[24] A line of triglyphs is painted on a red wall behind a gate. We understand this detail as painted because Labrouste shows the paint chipping off the stuccoed wall. Labrouste seems to be suggesting that the carved motifs that were to follow "had their origin in the effort to make permanent the more primitive and immediately meaningful painted and attached adornment."[25] Yet, polychromy had a wider significance for Labrouste. Color became an element

[18] See Antoine-Chrysostome Quatremère de Quincy, *Jupiter Olympien, ou l'art de la sculpture antique considérée sous un nouveau point de vue; ouvrage qui comprend un essai sur le goût de la sculpture polychrome*, Paris, 1815.

[19] Harry Francis Mallgrave, Introduction to Gottfried Semper, *The Four Elements of Architecture and Other Writings*, New York, Cambridge University Press, 1989, pp. 4–5. On the debate on polychromy, see in particular David Van Zanten, "Architectural Polychromy: Life in Architecture," in Robin Middleton (ed.), *The Beaux Arts and Nineteenth Century French Architecture*, Cambridge, The MIT Press, 1982, pp. 197–215; Neil Levine, "The Romantic Idea of Architectural Legibility: Henri Labrouste and the neo-Greek," in Arthur Drexler (ed.), *The Architecture of the Ecole des Beaux-Arts*, Cambridge, The MIT Press, 1977, pp. 325ff.

[20] Gottfried Semper, *Vorläufige Bemerkungen über bemalte Architektur und Plastik bei den Alten* (Hamburg-Altona, 1834). Later, he published his most important work, *Der Stil in den technischen und tektonischen Künsten oder Praktische Ästhetik*, 1861–63, in English: *Style in the Technical and Tectonic Arts, or Practical Aesthetics*, Getty Research Institute, Los Angeles, 2004.

[21] His theory was first published in his *Mémoire sur l'architecture polychrome chez les Grecs* (1830). In 1831, he published his renderings of the Temple of Empedocles in Selinunte (Selinus), which became the center of his polychrome theory. Hittorff's friend Franz Christian Gau presented ancient Egyptian architecture as colored in his plates of *Antiquités de la Nubie* (1821–27).

[22] See Neil Levine, "The competition for the Grand Prix in 1824," in Robin Middleton (ed.), *The Beaux Arts and Nineteenth Century French Architecture*, Cambridge, The MIT Press, 1982, pp. 139–173.

[23] Ibid., p. 199.

[24] Ibid.

[25] Ibid.

26 Harry Francis Mallgrave, "Introduction," p. 9.
27 Ibid., p.15.
28 Gottfried Semper, *Preliminary Remarks on Polychrome Architecture and Sculpture in Antiquity*, New York, Cambridge University Press, 1989, p. 63.
29 One need only look to the ancient Okthorp farmhouses, buildings Asplund was sure to have known, to understand the relationship of the type to this new house that he was designing. These buildings, which included a farmhouse and a number of barns, typically enclosed a rectangular farmyard. This farmyard was understood to be primarily a private space, separated from the public realm by the farmhouse. The Okthorp farmstead at the Skansen Open Air Museum in Stockholm was the first one of the kind in the world, started in 1891 by Artur Hazelius. Its foundation was contemporaneous with the National Romanticism movement that was at its height during Asplund's formative years. Peter Blundell Jones, "House at Stennas," in Dan Cruikshank (ed.), *Erik Gunnar Asplund*, pp. 123–124.

of "regional" reading of architecture where buildings would respond to regional conditions – in particular, the type of materials – and to particular functional, historical, and cultural conditions of the place.

Semper continued on these arguments in his *Preliminary Remarks* on polychromy of 1834. Where Hittorff had set the stage for the argument of color as a basic element of antique architecture, as an "order" that could be used in all of classical architecture, Semper used color as a point of departure to describe a theory that had its essence in the surface, where the surface could be understood as architecture. Like Labrouste, he had a "vernacular' vision of polychromy, as a response to and an effect of natural surroundings. He felt that in his naïve brilliance polychromy was democratic. At the same time, he followed Bronsted's argument regarding polychromy in ancient Greek wooden temples, which suggests that the painted pattern was a substitute for the missing plastic form, that "color [was] used to create an illusion as a substitute for sculptural effects."[26] Semper, however, felt that color held formal and symbolic meaning together. This idea resulted from his belief that decoration in monumental architecture was the direct descendant of natural artifacts hung or draped on a structural framework.[27] He states:

> Plain constructions were consecrated for an ennobling purpose, for worship for example. Decorations of a more definite religious meaning (not always designated) were appropriately attached to the outside walls and interiors of the sanctuaries: suspended flowers, festoons, branches, sacrificial implements, weapons, the remains of sacrificial victims, and other mythical symbols. With the further development of worship and concomitant with increasing artistic activity, they became fixed as typical symbols. No longer were they simply fastened to the walls in their natural state, according to local traditions and their destination; they were represented artistically and thereby incorporated into the monuments themselves as a characteristic part.[28]

From this point, Semper went on to further develop a theory that would culminate in his book *The Four Elements of Architecture* (1851), and *Der Stil in den technischen und tektonischen Künste* (1860–63). Of particular interest is his discussion of the essence of the wall. Here he describes the history of the wall from its beginning as a hedge fence, which would later develop into the weaving of mats, which could in turn be hung from a structural framework. The framework becomes incidental. What is more important to Semper is the surface of the textile that makes the space; that makes the architecture. He furthers this argument by stating that even after having arrived at masonry walls, upon which textiles could be hung as surface decoration, this masonry wall is still only an incidental structural framework to support the surface articulation.

The Impact of the Mediterranean Journey and Other Influences

In a large number of Asplund's most important works, the notions of spatial extension, of the inversion of space, of bringing the outside in, and of spatial and structural ambiguity assert themselves as primary themes. These themes, which were informed by both his interest in the Scandinavian vernacular as well as his Mediterranean tour, allowed for the manifestation of an architecture that went beyond a simple derivation of form from style, structure, or function. Consequently, Asplund developed an ever more complex design paradigm, in which the manipulation of surface and color, layered over these primary thematic strategies, began to emerge as a significant motif.

In one of the first commissions he received after returning from his trip to the Mediterranean, the Villa Snellman (1917–18), Asplund designed a house that is typologically related to the traditional one and one-half room deep Swedish house and the traditional Swedish farmhouse. Through a reinterpretation of that type and a careful strategy of manipulation of the thresholds between interior and exterior, Asplund derives a new and ambiguous reading of public versus private and ultimately creates a hybrid courtyard space that is neither public nor private.[29] This ambiguity is suggestive of an overall attitude towards the architecture of the house – that is, Asplund's desire to create a building where multiple readings might be formulated based on one's interaction with the house.

Further emphasis of this notion is made by his introduction of spatial extension. On the interior of the house he plays with slight shifts of the walls, with the alignment of windows, and a number of other devices that suggest a desire to create the reading of spaces expanding one into another, and beyond to the exterior.[30] In the end, this pulling of the skin and the maneuvering of spaces within the building (a direct result of the necessity to change the structural system from heavy masonry to light wood and stucco), betray a desire to separate surface from structure. Proportional strategies learned in Italy – the

[30] See Val Warke's essay "The Plight of the Object" for a more in depth analysis of the planning of the interior of this house and its relationship with the exterior façades, in *Cornell Journal of Architecture* 3, 1987, pp. 78–95.

10.3 **Gunnar Asplund (with Ture Ryberg). Competition entry for the Chancellery in Stockholm, general plan, 1922.**
Source: © Arkitekturmuseet Stockholm, photo Nikolaj Alsterdal.

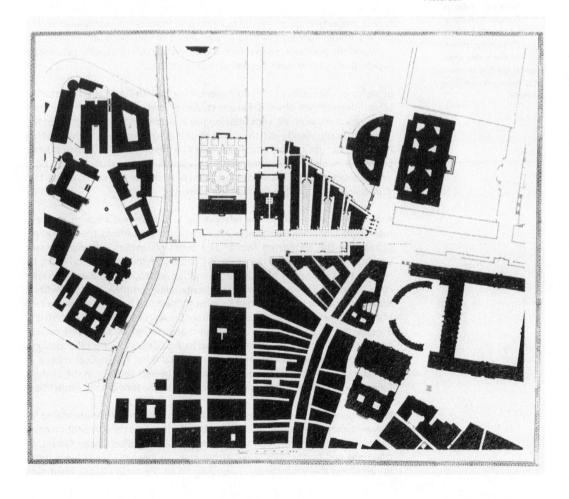

10.4 Gunnar Asplund (with Ture Ryberg). Competition entry for the Chancellery in Stockholm, elevation on the water, 1922.
Source: © Arkitekturmuseet Stockholm, photo Nikolaj Alsterdal.

façade proportions seem indeed to be derived from Italian farmhouses visited outside Rome – allowed him to further refine the relationship between the walls and the openings, so that he could ultimately create a subtle yet concise façade strategy that went beyond stylistic concerns.

In his Royal Chancellery Competition entry (1922; with Ture Ryberg), Venetian urban influences are obvious. Façade studies of *palazzi* emerge ghostlike from the pages of his journals, with their loggias and porticos floating lightly on the canal. Stairs slip silently into the water, almost as a premonition of the strategy he would later use in the Chancellery project. In this project, the urban influence of Venice is clearly demonstrated. An almost medieval quality of tight interconnectedness is manifested in paths destined for the water, as shifting axes weave back into the fabric of the context.

Asplund further reinforces the relationship to the context through a careful manipulation of scale. Designed primarily as two large buildings, the Chancellery appears on the waterfront façade as a series of smaller buildings. Equally significant is his departure from this very context. In the competition entry, he renders the Chancellery as a series of Venetian *palazzi*, and imbues them with color. Although this project is urbanistically quite complex, the competition drawings impart an impression of extreme flatness and begin to suggest a kind of stage set that is significantly different from the rest of Stockholm's waterfront. This masterful design, with its careful manipulation of scale and surface articulation, is suggestive of strategies that he would use in several other designs, including the projects for Gotaplatsen and Gustaf Adolf Torg in Gothenberg. In particular, he also seems to have used this "stage-set" strategy in the Skandia Cinema in Stockholm, which was designed around the time of this competition.

In the Woodland Cemetery (1915–40; with Sigurd Lewerentz), references to his Italian journey are again obvious. Stuart Wrede describes the competition entry as "a composition drawn partly from Nordic and Mediterranean landscape traditions and partly from burial archetypes. All these elements were freely mixed . . . in the promenade . . . leading up to the main chapel, lined with

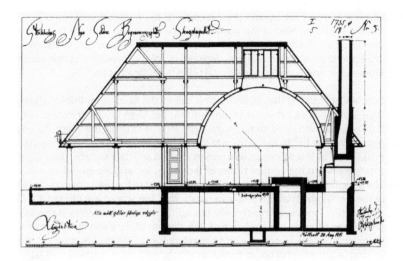

10.5 Gunnar Asplund.
Section, Woodland
Chapel, Woodland
Cemetery, Enskede,
1918–20.
Source: © Arkitekturmuseet
Stockholm, photo Nikolaj
Alsterdal.

tombs and sarcophagi like Pompeii's Via Sepulchra, and set amid a fir forest."[31] So the overlapping of Northern and Southern sensibilities, combined with the derivation of imagery from nineteenth-century German Romantic painting sets up a dialectic in which the symbols and images from various places coincide, yet seemingly concede to one another to manifest a sublime landscape, rich in spirit and meaning, as the narrative of death exerts itself as the mound, the pyramid, and the Way of the Cross.

The Woodland Chapel (1918–20) is a building rich in symbol. A wooden roof, whose construction emanates from traditional Swedish roof design, takes the shape of a dark and heavy pyramid, set above white columns whose proportions are derived from the trunks of the surrounding pine trees. At the base of this pyramid, the Angel of Death greets the mourner. Beyond this threshold, a low portico leads the mourner into the main space of the chapel. Because of its short dimension and the close spacing of the columns, one gets a sense of being alone in the woods. The space is in fact a continuation of the surrounding woods. The formal geometry of the space, however, allows a simultaneous monumentality to emerge. Movement continues through the space of the portico, through the metal-clad doors, and further through the gates, to finally arrive at a space that is intimately and ultimately expansive: the chapel. In this space we might postulate a transformation of the Temple of Vesta in Rome where the lightness of its peripteral colonnade is inverted to create a bright space with a dome that, according to Asplund, was to "hover weightlessly above the squat portico and entrance."[32] This inversion foreshadows a strategy that we would later see in the small vestibule adjacent to the lobby of the Skandia Cinema. By tautly stretching plaster over a light wooden frame and by carefully manipulating the light on this large white surface, he does indeed allow the dome to hover above the space, effectively dematerializing it. The space becomes a clearing in the woods, an exterior room, whose sky is a dome.

In the Woodland Crematorium (1935–40), resonances of his travels to the South are also revealed. Upon approaching the portico to the crematorium, one encounters perhaps the most sublime work of modern landscape architecture as a street in Pompeii is conflated with the Greek temples of Agrigento

[31] Stuart Wrede, The Architecture of Erik Gunnar Asplund, Cambridge, The MIT Press, 1980, p. 27.
[32] Erik Gunnar Asplund as quoted in Elias Cornell "The Sky as a Vault," in Claes Caldenby and Olof Hutlin (eds.), Asplund, p. 23.

and Paestum, all set against the backdrop of the mythical yet tangibly real Nordic woodland. Within the portico and the Chapel of the Holy Cross, this symbolic complexity is reinforced as traditional and modern detail and form engage representations of hope, depicted in John Lundquist's "Resurrection Monument" and Sven Erixson's mural titled "Life, Death, Life."

In a similar fashion, the round lending hall of the Stockholm Public Library (1918–27) reads as a drum over which a skin has been tautly stretched, with tiers of books veneered to the surface, telling the story of this place. As one approaches the hall from the main entrance, scenes from the *Iliad* are depicted in bas-relief by Ivar Johnsson on a remarkably flat and dark surface. Their scale, small relative to the vertical thrust of the space, imparts a sense of intimacy. These pictorial representations are in direct contrast to the real books presented in the lending hall, where it is understood that the stories are primarily told with words. Passing symmetrically placed, dark, lateral, curving staircases, one moves towards the lending hall. The rhythm of dark and light, as at the Woodland Chapel, is again used to great dramatic effect. Approaching the lending hall, the tiers of books appear as a flattened surface, perhaps wallpaper, perhaps a painted pattern. Not yet books and not yet tangible, they become symbolic elements, beckoning the reader, their mystery waiting to be revealed.

In the Gothenburg Law Courts Annex (1913–37), thinness and lightness prevails, as surfaces seem to delaminate and floors and stairs seemingly hover in space.

10.6 Gunnar Asplund. Perspective view of the portico, Woodland Crematorium, Woodland Cemetery, Enskede, c.1935–40. This view describes Asplund's masterful conflation of tradition and modernity, of vernacular and classical, in the portico of the Crematorium.
Source: © Arkitekturmuseet Stockholm, photo Nikolaj Alsterdal.

10.7 Gunnar Asplund. Perspective view of the interior, Woodland Crematorium, Woodland Cemetery, 1935. Note the simplicity and surface articulation in sharp contrast to the tectonic expression developed for the portico.
Source: © Arkitekturmuseet Stockholm, photo Nikolaj Alsterdal.

One might conjecture that these manipulations of surface might have been derived simply from Asplund's desire to create a modernist, mannered interior. But it is also important to note that his use of a structural system of columns and girders allowed for this clear expression of a new age in Sweden to occur. Almost invisible on the interior, these columns and girders are revealed in few places, most explicitly, perhaps, in their support of the floor and stair adjacent to the large glazed courtyard wall. All other surfaces – the plaster and the veneers – seem to be in constant movement, floating and hovering above the stone floor. On the exterior of the building, the manipulation of the skin again is evident. By deliberately expressing the structure of the building, Asplund allows the infill panels to be read as symbolic screens. By creating an asymmetrical fenestration pattern within these panels, we are made to understand the deference of the newer structure to the old, the one kneeling, perhaps to the other. So the manipulation of the skin in this building is not simply a mannerist expression of a modernist building. Rather, it is used as a symbolic gesture describing the relationships of the parts, just as the bas-reliefs, perhaps, hint at the events behind the surface.

The Stockholm Exhibition (1928–30) arguably marks the point of crystallization of Asplund's modernist tendencies that had begun several years earlier. These tendencies began to appear in a limited fashion in projects such as the competition entry for the Swedish Pavilion at the Paris Exhibition and the Stockholm Public Library. Indeed, Asplund's rendering for the marketplace at the base of the Stockholm Public Library (1928) reveals quite clearly the direction that he would pursue for the remainder of his career. There were also a number of functionalist buildings by various architects that were projected in the years leading up to the exhibition, but few were completed by 1930.[33]

33 Eva Rudberg, *The Stockholm Exhibition, 1930: Modernism's Breakthrough in Swedish Architecture*, Stockholm, Stockholmia Forlag, 1999, pp. 32–33.

[34] Erik Gunnar Asplund as quoted in *Gunnar Asplund Architect 1885–1940*, p. 23.
[35] Peter Blundell Jones, "House at Stennas," in Dan Cruikshank (ed.), *Erik Gunnar Asplund*, pp. 123–124.

This remarkable expression of a new age in Swedish design would present a singular architectural vision that was related to the various cultural shifts that had recently occurred, including the development of the new bourgeois culture, as well as technological shifts in the production and manufacture of goods and crafts (plate 42). There were also significant influences from Asplund's contemporaries in France and Germany who by this time had already clearly established formal vocabularies aligned with technology and the new spirit. But unlike these contemporaries, Asplund would not forgo ideas related to place or tradition, even in the face of a functionalist ideology. Rather we see an overlapping of these tendencies, where the formal expression is tempered by a site planning strategy that is, arguably, quite traditional. Here he creates streets, plazas, squares, and monuments and organizes them in a way that responds intimately to the context and that is somewhat reminiscent of a small town. This strategy is in stark contrast to projects such as Le Corbusier's *Ville Radieuse* (1933), where context and scale were irrelevant. Color was also strikingly used throughout the scheme to establish a festive atmosphere that was important to the exhibition's success. This seems likely to have been derived (at least in part) from Asplund's observations of a festival in Taormina. He writes in his journal: "It was the last day of carnival there, with colored lanterns and comic motley figures and a big orchestra on the square, and the starry sky above, and the rumble of the sea below."[34] By allowing the stark modernity of his functional display pavilions to be dressed in a festival clothing – colorful banners, flags, lights, signs, flowers, and trees – Asplund extended the conversation to a wary public, and boldly ushered in a new modernist sensibility in Swedish design.

In his house at Stennäs (1937), one of his last projects before he died, Asplund revisits many of the issues he dealt with in projects described earlier in this essay. In earlier schemes for this house, he had divided the house into three blocks, with cross passages running in the short dimension of the house. This organizational strategy seems clearly aligned with the traditional Swedish houses encountered at the Okthorp farmstead at the Skansen Open Air Museum, just outside of Stockholm.[35] But it seems possible that this scheme might also have been derived from observations of farmhouses outside Rome, where interconnected volumes of individual vernacular buildings are common. This notion seems particularly clear when comparing the massing of both the

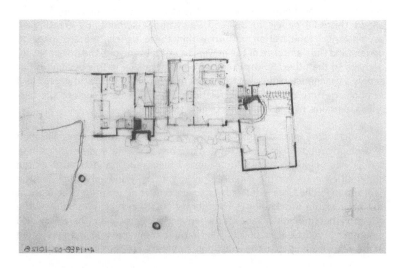

10.8 Gunnar Asplund. Preliminary floor plan, family summer house at Stennäs, 1936.
Source: © Arkitekturmuseet Stockholm, photo Nikolaj Alsterdal.

Villa Snellman and the final version of his house at Stennäs, to the farmhouse that Asplund saw and recorded near the Villa Madama in Rome.

One enters the house at Stennäs through a sort of courtyard, which, like at the Villa Snellman, is defined by the two volumes of the house and a natural feature, a large granite bluff. Similar to the Villa Snellman, the space has a clear reading of a room. Asplund reinforces the reading by locating a fireplace (the scale of which suggests an interior condition) on the outside of the house, creating again the condition of ambiguity between interior and exterior. Within the house, scales of elements and types of materials change in order to challenge their interiority. Large brick steps, reminiscent of the seats of the Greek theatre at Syracuse, are placed beside an enormous fireplace in the living room and face the majestic view of the fjord. In his journal, Asplund wrote:

> The Greek theatre is imposing in effect and size. The same fine gravity as the temples. The key to it all is the open space with the heavens above, all assembled round the stage, the plain and the sea. A simplicity of conception and great unity, with the purpose and meaning binding it all, to give it architectural fullness.[36]

Within this context, Asplund also challenged contemporary notions of space. The idea that a definition of space was no longer absolute (an interior, for example, was no longer necessarily just an interior), was clearly evidenced in his work. Simo Paavilainen, in his notes from the 1985 Asplund symposium, describes "how richly and abundantly Asplund . . . builds houses within interiors and exteriors within houses."[37] This kind of inversion happens not as clever architectural trickery, but perhaps as a means to investigate certain trends that were current, in particular the need to define a bourgeois culture that was radically changing and rapidly developing at the end of the nineteenth century.[38] Simultaneously, certain design strategies which were derived from his trip to the Mediterranean began to have quite specific effects on his work, while the evolution of building technologies in Scandinavia created yet another set of paradigms within which to work.

The Skandia Cinema

In the Skandia Cinema in Stockholm, the importance of Asplund's explorations of expansive space, tradition, symbol, color, surface, and their relationship to his travels become perhaps most apparent. For Asplund the theatre held great significance. Speaking again of the Greek theatre at Taormina he wrote:

> It is difficult to imagine a situation more steeped in devotion and gravity. One is struck by the lordly solemnity and the greatness of spirit that must have attuned the ideas and feelings of the ancients for art, both the art of the theatre and the art of sculpture, the one made to provide the framework for the other.[39]

Significant in this passage is his linking of sculpture with theatre, both arts presented in three dimensions. Film on the other hand is a medium and an art presented in two dimensions, and as such the articulation of the Skandia Cinema might be interpreted as a play on this idea.

The Skandia Cinema was designed between 1922 and 1923 (plates 43, 44). It was a commission that involved the construction of a theatre within an

10.9 Gunnar Asplund. Interior view, family summer house at Stennäs, 1936–37.
Source: © Arkitekturmuseet Stockholm, photo Sune Sundahl.

[36] Erik Gunnar Asplund as quoted in Luca Ortelli "Heading South: Asplund's Impressions," p. 31.
[37] Simo Paavilainen as quoted in Colin St. John Wilson, "Gunnar Asplund and the Dilemma of Classicism," in Vicky Wilson (ed.), *Gunnar Asplund 1885–1940: The Dilemma of Classicism*, London, AA Publications, 1988, p. 11.
[38] At the turn of the century, certain characteristic themes of the burgeoning bourgeois culture were taking shape. Time became a linear concept rather than cyclic, and nature became a refuge from the rational demands of urban life. The home and the family became the cornerstone of society and as such became a microcosm of the dichotomy of bourgeois society, between private and public. Claes Caldenby, "Time, Life and Work: An Introduction to Asplund," p. 9.
[39] Erik Gunnar Asplund as quoted in *Gunnar Asplund Architect 1885–1940*, pp. 23–24.

[40] Erik Gunnar Asplund as quoted in Elias Cornell, "The Sky as a Vault" in Claes Caldenby and Olof Hutlin (eds.), *Asplund*, p. 25.
[41] Gottfried Semper, *The Four Elements of Architecture*, trans. by Harry Francis Mallgrave and Wolfgang Herrmann, New York, Cambridge University Press, 1989, p. 102.
[42] Ibid.
[43] Harry Francis Mallgrave, Introduction to Gottfried Semper, *The Four Elements of Architecture*, p. 2.
[44] Erik Gunnar Asplund as quoted in Elias Cornell, "The Sky as a Vault," p. 25.
[45] Ibid., p. 28.

existing building. According to Asplund, "the main emphasis during the process of composition was on the viewpoints clearly stated by the client, who is experienced in this field: the desire of the audience for a gay, unrealistically splendid setting for the fantasy world of film, its need for cozy intimacy."[40] From the outset, the cinema was understood as a place that was to be for the gathering of people, specifically the new bourgeoisie. This setting in many ways is based in his trip to Tunis and Taormina in the first few months of 1914. In his diaries of his trip, Asplund describes the public squares that he visited, where people gathered in a festive atmosphere. They were gatherings that could be described as almost primal.

These notions described by Asplund are clearly aligned with Gottfried Semper's conception of "the first and most important, the moral element of architecture."[41] Here Semper states that:

> The first sign of human settlement and rest after the hunt, the battle, and wandering in the desert is today, as when the first men lost paradise, the setting up of the fireplace and the lighting of the reviving, warming . . . flame. Around the hearth the first groups assembled; around it the first alliances formed; around it the first crude religious concepts were put into the customs of a cult.[42]

Harry Francis Mallgrave elaborates on this theme. He states that, according to Semper, the origin of monumental architecture is in the festive celebration and improvised festival of apparatus.[43] These ideas are clearly identifiable in the Skandia Cinema, where we encounter ideas about gathering around a source of light. The curtains of the stage are down-lit and shimmer before being transformed into the pictures on the screen; the flame shimmers, just as the story is told around the fire.

In his articulation of walls, ceilings, and floors, Asplund again manages to make Semperian references. Throughout the design, the idea of bringing the exterior in and then turning the inside out is consistently reified. The flooring in the portico, for instance, is articulated in a stone paving that in color references the pavement on the exterior. Of this space Asplund states:

> The portico is intended to convey by architectural means the transition between the serious beautiful weathered façade by Scholander and the colorful, somewhat strident modernity of the cinema. Its walls and coffered ceilings accordingly are treated in the dark grayish-brown tone of the façade and the asphalt of the outside pavement enters in the guise of flooring.[44]

Through a deliberate use of color, Asplund has been able to manipulate a space in such a manner that its reading is completely controlled. He has brought the outside in, and in so doing has set the theme for the entire project.

Beyond the portico is the lobby, which again shows evidence of surface manipulation. Within the small rotunda, which is adjacent to the lobby, Asplund creates a space that may be seen as emblematic of the design of the entire project. Here is a space simply for the display of "pictures (preferably drawings) honoring – and advertising – famous celebrated film stars. . . . In the pale grey plaster of the roof there is a compluvium, wreathed in a chaste, gilded tracery, through which one can see a dark nothingness."[45] Again, through very specific articulation, Asplund creates a space that is the result of the modulation of surfaces, which in the end are signifiers, and therefore, make the architecture.

The most obvious of these signifiers are the pictures of the film stars. Without these elements, the strength of its overall conception would be diminished.

[46] David Van Zanten, "Architectural Polychromy: Life in Architecture," p. 198.

When looking at this space, the references to Labrouste's reconstruction of the Basilica at Paestum may at first be unclear. Upon further investigation, however, it becomes evident that because Asplund was also designing a place for assembly, a basilica of sorts, it might be appropriate to explore some of the same issues with which Labrouste had dealt. In the context of architectural history and theory, it is also important to note that Asplund must, indeed, have been aware of the works of Labrouste and the importance of works such as his Bibliothèque Sainte Geneviève and its influence on the development of modernist paradigms in architecture, particularly as it relates to systems of structure and surface articulation.

In Labrouste's longitudinal section of the Basilica, he has dismissed all of the subtleties of the orders so that only a structural diagram remains (a skeleton, so to speak), with the walls of the Basilica in another rendered plane. According to David Van Zanten, Labrouste shows these walls as no longer being temple walls, but rather walls of an assembly hall, which have their own accumulations of decorations: inscriptions recording events, vignettes, the rules of assembly, and military trophies. With this rendering, Labrouste shows the withering form vocabulary of the Greek temple which in turn evolves into another *decorative* vocabulary, which clothes the skeleton of the old architecture with the flesh of a new one.[46]

At the Skandia Cinema, not unlike Labrouste's conception of an architecture derived from a manipulation of surface, Asplund conceives of a small rotunda where the new decorative vocabulary, the sign, takes on the role of architecture. Beyond being simply a picture gallery, the space develops its own meaning based on its decoration. It is the sign here that gives the space significance, and indeed this space becomes emblematic of the strategy that Asplund was to employ throughout the project.

Beyond the lobby, Asplund placed a corridor. This space, again, has indications of a play between interior and exterior. Walls are colored differently (the outer walls dark green, the inner walls white) to permit a clearer reading of their interiority and exteriority. But it is not perhaps until we reach the interior space of the auditorium that we understand the full impact of Semper's theories on Asplund. Here he has created a space that is a genuine illusion but which is also understood as genuine architecture. The architecture is the decoration.

In order to create a more intimate yet dramatic atmosphere within the auditorium, specific formal manipulations were applied. Balcony barriers were made as large as possible to give the sense of nearness; and the rear and side galleries at the upper level were detached from one another to give the impression of a longer room. More significant, however were the scalar shifts in decorative elements. This design strategy served to link the architecture of the cinema to the "architecture of cinema" – one component of which includes the manipulation of scale for dramatic effect. The oversized Pompeian motifs applied to the balcony barriers – a derivation of the decorations that Asplund had admired during his trip to Italy – served to transform the scalar relationship of the audience to the space. A second example is the corridor on the upper floor, which surrounds the entrances to the balconies. Here, again, Asplund plays an elaborate game of scalar manipulation. On the doors to the balconies (where again the colors and motifs are derived from Pompeian decorations),

47 Erik Gunnar Asplund as quoted in Elias Cornell, "The Sky as a Vault," p. 26.
48 Ibid., p. 27.
49 Alvar Aalto as quoted in Stuart Wrede, p. 94.

he manipulates the scales of elements: this time however, reducing them in order to make the corridor feel larger and to perhaps suggest the fantasy of the film that the audience would soon experience.

And finally there is the ceiling. Asplund here elaborates on the theme of expansive space within the realm of a completely enclosed room. The electric stars along with the sky, which was "achieved by means of a blackish-blue barrel vault painted al fresco," are referred to by Asplund paradoxically as an entirely un-architectural idea that effectively creates the atmosphere of a festivity beneath a night sky.[47]

One could argue that film is a Semperian ideal. As the house lights are dimmed, and the story begins, the flat surface of the screen becomes the viewers' entire focus. It is a media that is entirely two dimensional and deals simply with the telling of stories by the light. The Skandia Cinema, through all the manipulations of its surfaces, is a representation of this ideal. According to Asplund,

> The distinctive character of the cinema, which may well emerge from the impersonal purely mechanical representation of life in the performances, from their repetition during the hours of the evening, from their ready availability and the democratic informality of the audience, this distinctive character has yet to acquire an altogether suitable costume.[48]

Inherent in the building's typology are inferences that have more to do with surface articulation than with any kind of formal structure. Erik Gunnar Asplund, with great ability, manipulated these ideas to create an architectural masterpiece that was unprecedented. It was neither structure nor decoration, and at the same time it was both. Alvar Aalto stated, "I had the impression that this was an architecture where ordinary systems hadn't served as parameters. Here, the point of departure was man, with all the innumerable nuances of his emotional life and nature."[49]

10.10 Gunnar Asplund. Perspective view of upper level corridor, Skandia Cinema, Stockholm, 1923.
Source: © Arkitekturmuseet Stockholm, photo Nikolaj Alsterdal.

At the time when Asplund was building, the use of color in Sweden was certainly nothing new. The beloved wooden farmhouses of the countryside had for centuries been dressed in a deep red. But changes in the application of color were also occurring, which had to do with the development of new methods of construction and new materials, a direct result of industrialization of the timber trade so important to the region. At this time, according to Henrik O. Andersson, "wooden and stone architecture were drawing closer to one another. . . . Plank houses were often dressed with plaster, and similar tones were often chosen for the oil paint applied to the woodwork as for the plaster color layer."[50] This transformation of the skin of the building, from one in which the paint was applied as a means of protection for the highly crafted woodwork to an application of a skin, is very clearly aligned with the development of early twentieth-century architectural thought. No longer was architectural form derived from hewn timber and the resultant tectonic expression associated with this method of construction. Instead, standardized building elements that were fabricated in the factory would allow more freedom of expression. With the development of new plastering techniques and materials, the range of colors also changed.

For Asplund, however, these were not the only reasons for rethinking the surface. Because of his clear understanding of context and place, his under-standing of the numerous changes in society and building techniques at the turn of the century, and his proficiency at combining all of these conditions, Asplund was able to manifest an architecture that achieved a level of complexity that many of his contemporaries could only aspire to.

Asplund's trip to the South affected him viscerally, and clearly affected the work that he would ultimately produce. He used these impressions to derive new meaning in a completely different context. These derivations become clearer when understood relative to the context of the pedagogy of travel. As with Blouet and Labrouste, Asplund used his travels to discover something about the places he visited that were not yet known. Labrouste had reorganized the historic timeline of the temples at Paestum as a means to explore and discover a new conception of architectural evolution. In his reconstruction of Agrigentum, Labrouste uses the drawing as a means to explore an idea about the importance of surface to place. Asplund uses these very techniques to discover new meaning and form in real architectural projects. By recombining time and place Asplund creates an architecture that is neither old nor new. It is understood rather as timeless and placeless – and yet simultaneously entirely of its time and of its place. The Way of the Cross is not Pompeii revisited; the Skandia Cinema is not a square in Tunis or Italy. And yet by applying these images to a new context in a new age, and through a quite deliberate manipulation of surface, Asplund was able to manifest an architecture that expresses the methods and materials with which he worked as well as the society for which he built. ∎

[50] Henrik O. Andersson, "Swedish Architecture around 1920" in Simo Paavilainen (ed.), *Nordic Classicism 1910–1930*, p. 125.

11

BERNARD RUDOFSKY AND THE SUBLIMATION OF THE VERNACULAR

Andrea Bocco Guarneri

When Bernard Rudofsky (1905–88) entered the Technische Hochschule in Vienna in 1923, the ideas and language of the *Neues Bauen* (New Architecture) were already well diffused and recognized. While Otto Wagner and Adolf Loos had laid out the theoretical basis and produced the built examples that had pioneered the way to a *Neues Bauen*, Josef Frank was, in the mid-1920s, the sole Viennese architect to bear the trademark "Modern Movement" – witness his house at the Stuttgart Weissenhofsiedlung of 1927, the only one by an Austrian architect.[1] During this time, a student at the Technische Hochschule would have received a solidly modern education from the point of view of technology and structural principles. Moreover, the stylistic struggle between historicizing formalism and *Neues Bauen* was much less violent there than in most other European academies. Post-World War I Vienna teemed with new construction that was clearly modern but shied away from the radical avant-garde, infatuated with the myth of the machine. In other words, an "other modern," professionally made and free of vociferation, was being built. It was no coincidence that, at the end of his first year at the university, the 18-year-old Rudofsky embarked on a journey to Germany to discover the new works and visit the first Bauhaus exhibition in Weimar. From there, he went north to Sweden, again with the intention to study the most recent buildings of Asplund, Lewerentz, and other modern-classicists.[2]

Rudofsky started his career in the studio of Otto Rudolf Salvisberg in Berlin (1928–30) and worked with Theiss & Jaksch Architects in Vienna in the two following years.[3] The works he collaborated on in those years demonstrated a mature vocabulary, imbued with the new techniques and methods of composition that the generation of the 1880s – including Emil Fahrenkamp, Clemens Holzmeister, and Josef Frank – had established. Like most Viennese architects who were born around the turn of the twentieth century or those slightly older – among those, Plischke, Neutra, Kiesler, Wlach, Augenfeld, Sobotka, Kleiner, Bayer, Strnad, Haerdtl, and Wenzel – Rudofsky intensely experienced the ongoing cultural transformation and became one of its actors. In the early 1930s, the perception was that Vienna teaching the merits of a new "architecture without architects" – namely, that the works of Viennese architects put forth the importance of the "domestic" and showed a disposition to welcome an array of decorative elements and daily objects, in "modern" buildings as well, that appeared to be the very choice of the residents and that continued the tradition of quality in the applied arts.[4]

It is critical to underscore that the great polemicist and reformer Adolf Loos did not intend to create an "alternative" culture, but rather to open up Viennese culture and import new elements that he judged positively.[5] As for Josef Frank, at the time of the founding texts of the movement, he affirmed the importance

[1] "From the point of view of the main current of modern architecture, the Viennese trends were at once precursory and marginal": from Hermann Czech, "Introduzione," in Josef Frank, *Architettura come simbolo*, Bologna, Zanichelli, 1986. German edition: Josef Frank, *Architektur als Symbol. Elemente deutschen neuen Bauens*, Wien, Scholl, 1931, reprinted in 1981 with the introduction by Hermann Czech.

[2] For more on Rudofsky, see Andrea Bocco Guarneri, *Bernard Rudofsky: A Humane Designer*, Wien/New York, Springer, 2003; and Architekturzentrum Wien (ed.), *Lessons from Bernard Rudofsky: Life as a Voyage*, Basel/Boston, Birkhäuser, 2007.

[3] On the importance of Otto Rudolph Salvisberg, see Claude Lichtenstein, *Otto Rudolph Salvisberg, die andere Moderne*, Zürich, Gta Verlag, 1985.

[4] Lisa Licitra Ponti, *Gio Ponti. The Complete Works, 1923–1978*, Cambridge, The MIT Press, 1990, p. 47.

[5] The review founded and directed by Adolf Loos – only two issues were published in 1903 – was significantly titled *Das Andere: Ein Blatt zur Einführung abendlischer Kultur in Oösterreich*. See the published texts in Adolf Loos, *Trotzdem*, Innsbruck, Brenner-Verlag, 1982 [1931]. On Loos, see Benedetto Gravagnuolo, *Adolf Loos: Theory and Works*, New York, Rizzoli, 1988; and Richard Bösel and Vitale Zanchettin, *Adolf Loos 1870–1933: architettura, utilità e decoro*, Milan, Electa, 2006.

11.1 *(Far left)* Bernard Rudofsky. Sketch for a patio house [inverted]. Source: The Bernard Rudofsky Estate, Vienna. © Ingrid Kummer.

[6] Josef Frank, *Architektur als Symbol*, op. cit. Also see *Josef Frank, Architect and Designer: An Alternative Vision of the Modern Home*, New Haven, Yale University Press/Bard Graduate Center for Studies in the Decorative Arts, 1996.

[7] "Apocalyptic" thinkers like Johan Huizinga and Lewis Mumford, and radical critics of modernity like William Morris were fundamental influences in the formation and development of Rudofsky's vision of architecture. See also Peter Blundell Jones, *Modern Architecture through Case Studies*, Oxford, Architectural Press, 2002.

[8] Claudio Magris, *Danubio*, Milano, Garzanti, 1986, p. 220. In English, Claudio Magris, *Danube*, New York, Farrar, Straus, Giroux, 1989.

[9] Bernard Rudofsky, *Behind the Picture Window*, New York, Oxford University Press, 1955, p. 7.

[10] Bernard Rudofsky, "Introduzione al Giappone," I, 4 of the manuscript (English original version not published). Published in Italian translation in *Domus* 319, June 1956, pp. 45–49.

[11] Cesare De Seta, "L'Italia nello specchio del Grand Tour," in Cesare De Seta (ed.), *Annali 5 – Il paesaggio, Storia d'Italia*, Torino, Einaudi, 1982; Fernand Braudel, "L'Italia fuori d'Italia: due secoli e tre Italie," in *Storia d'Italia*, vol. II, Torino, Einaudi, 1974.

[12] Eduard Sekler, *Josef Hoffmann: The Architectural Work*, Princeton, Princeton University Press, 1985. Hoffmann, "Architektonisches von der Insel Capri – Ein Beitrag für malerische Architekturempfindungen," in *Der Architekt* III, 1897, pp. 13–14; reproduced in Sekler, p. 479.

[13] See for instance Joseph Rykwert, *On Adam's House in Paradise: The Idea of the Primitive Hut in Architectural History*, New York, MoMA, 1972.

[14] Frank Lloyd Wright, *Ausgeführte Bauten und Entwürfen von Frank Lloyd Wright*, Berlin, Wasmuth, 1910.

of sentimental (i.e., psychological) values and the commodity of the dwelling.[6] Here, it is possible to identify a major difference between the heterogeneous group of architects established at the First International Congress of Modern Architecture (CIAM) in 1928 and the "Viennese Modern." I argue that in Viennese culture following the fall of the Empire, the ethical sense of a profession primarily interested in the satisfaction of the resident, and a critical and anti-dogmatic spirit were much more developed.[7] As Claudio Magris wrote: "Vienna . . . was . . . [a] place of a general skepticism in regard to the universal and the system of values."[8]

Rudofsky shared that skepticism with many of his compatriots; hence, he was no real advocate of the new credo of the modern. He was probably sympathetic with the life-reform movement and the polemical spirit of Karl Kraus. Likewise, there are no documents that would accredit direct contacts with Adolf Loos; yet it would be difficult to deny that, in his lectures and teaching, there was no greater influence from any other thinker. Aphorisms such as "complexity has never been a virtue,"[9] or "remember: art means to omit," could very well be by Loos himself.[10]

The Voyage to the Mediterranean

For centuries, and particularly since the discovery of Herculaneum and Pompeii, most genuine artistic education included the grand tour to Italy.[11] From the end of the eighteenth century onwards, the curiosity of the voyager expanded its subject, from famous and well-known monuments to the "anonymous" architecture of small towns and villages. Wolfgang von Goethe, in his letters to Alexander von Humboldt and in his *Italienische Reise*, was the first to comment on the importance of the "everyday" architecture, the comprehension of which was essential to the understanding of the classical. Later in the nineteenth century, the new moral values that filtered out from the pages of William Morris and John Ruskin were instrumental in furthering a growing interest in vernacular architecture.

During his trip to Italy (1896), Josef Hoffmann spent much time studying and drawing the traditional buildings of Campania. Beyond their sheer visual appeal, he interpreted them based on a sentimental "morality," suggestive of an immutable country life, outside of history, and derived from the hypothetical absence of intellectual speculation and the innate attraction of affability and serenity.[12] On the basis of architectural theory, particularly that of Gottfried Semper, it was possible to "read" the rural dwelling – specifically that of exotic and backward regions such as the south of Italy – as directly descendent, without substantial modification over the centuries, of a primeval idea of architecture.[13] Moreover, these constructions showed a direct relation between needs (usually considered "elementary") and design solutions (at times seen as "instinctive" or "spontaneous"), in contrast with academic architecture, its repertory of styles, and its formalistic methods of composition.

In the prestigious European edition of his works known as the *Wasmuth Portfolio* of 1910, Frank Lloyd Wright held that the observation of traditional buildings constituted the basis of any serious study of the art of architecture. Between these buildings and architecture (thought of as an art of the elite), there existed a similar relationship to the one linking tale and popular music with literature and classical music.[14] For Wright as well as many other architects, the basic principles and the very forms of vernacular architecture were increasingly legitimate tools of modern composition.

11.2 Roofs and chimneys in Oia, Santorini, 1929.
Source: Photo Bernard Rudofsky, The Bernard Rudofsky Estate, Vienna. © Ingrid Kummer.

Rudofsky was familiar with these texts, and had, since he was a child, a great desire to travel. The downfall of the monarchy left him with the feeling of not belonging to any definite world, and prompted him not to take root early. Every summer from 1923 onwards, he spent three months on the road. His first trip to the South was in 1925 (to Bulgaria and Turkey, Istanbul, Asia Minor, and the Black Sea); in 1926, 1927, and 1931, he visited Italy; in 1929 he returned to the Black Sea, visited Istanbul again, and traveled across Greece, from Athens to the Cycladic Islands (plate 45). He sojourned on the island of Santorini, whose traditional architecture became the subject of the doctorate dissertation he defended in 1931 under the title *Eine primitive Betonbauweise auf den südlichen Kykladen* (A primitive type of concrete construction in the southern Cyclades). The following year, he moved to Italy, living first in Capri, then in Naples and Procida.[15]

In the loci of the literary tradition – Goethe, Pierre Loti, and many others – Rudofsky did not look for the myth of the origin, which excited the intellectual curiosity of the moderns at that moment, or for the monuments codified in academic canon. Rather he wanted to experience the things by himself and on their very location. He did not travel to develop a creative poetics, but to collect images and stories, objects and customs.

Rudofsky relocated on the banks of the Mediterranean at the very moment that modernist architects were discovering its esthetical and ethical consonance with their own programs. During the 1930s, Le Corbusier was working on

[15] Rudofsky moved incessantly during those years, staying in New York for nine months. He went back to Vienna, moved to Naples, and eventually left for Buenos Aires and then Rio in 1938. Beyond his exhibitions, his greatest success was the famous Bernardo Sandals, designed from 1946 to 1965. Their technical concept was a development of the traditional Capri sandal, studied by Rudofsky during his years on the island. Beyond architecture, the study of shoes and human feet (particularly of women) was Rudofsky's main interest.

[16] See the essay by Benedetto Gravagnuolo in this book and the extensive bibliography cited. Particularly important is the essay by Silvia Danesi, "Aporie dell' architettura italiana in periodo fascista—mediterraneità e purismo" in Silvia Danesi and Luciano Patetta (eds.), *Il razionalismo e l'architettura in Italia durante il fascism*, Milano, Electa, 1976, pp. 21–28.

Roberto Pane was right to affirm, "if we consider that a part of the modern architecture done abroad derives, in more or less obvious ways, from our rural architecture, it appears quite legitimate for us to research our own roots on our own land. . . . Compared to the houses of Procida, the allegedly 'new' works by Le Corbusier become a somewhat timid game of volumes, specially if they are put in parallel with the messianic descriptions that accompany them." From Roberto Pane, "Tipi di architettura rustica in Napoli e nei Campi Flegrei," in *Architettura e arti decorative* VII, fasc. XII, August 1928, pp. 529–543.

[17] See Josep M. Rovira, *José Luis Sert. 1901–1983*, Milano, Electa, 2000. See Jean-François Lejeune's essay in this volume.

[18] "The tourist industry made a clean sweep of one of the most ingenious human activities, the intelligent pursuit of adventure. (. . .) Much as modern mass communications helped to weaken the barriers of national prejudice, they have taken the edge off the happier moments of travel. Bernard Rudofsky, *Introduzione al Giappone III*, p. 1 of the manuscript. The text was published in *Domus* 330, May 1957, pp. 36–38. The original English version was first published in Andrea Bocco Guarneri, *Bernard Rudofsky*, pp. 217–20.

[19] From Bernard Rudofsky, "How to Travel without Being a Tourist," unpublished article, c.1978.

[20] Bernard Rudofsky, Architecture without Architects: *A Short Introduction to Non-pedigreed Architecture*, New York, Museum of Modern Art, 1964; Bernard Rudofsky, *The Prodigious Builders: Notes Toward a Natural History of Architecture with Special Regard to those Species that are Traditionally Neglected or Downright Ignored*, New York-London, Harcourt Brace Jovanovich, 1977; Bernard Rudofsky, *Streets for People: A Primer for Americans*, Garden City, NY, Doubleday, 1969.

[21] William Morris, Paul Schultze-Naumburg, Adolf Loos, Rudolf Steiner, and Bruno Taut were illustrious precedents of architects and philosophers whose focus of attention went from architecture to the daily aspects of human life. Rudofsky read and appreciated their works. We also know that during his stay in Berlin he assimilated the lessons of the *Lebensreform* movement initiated in the late nineteenth century. That movement dealt with physical exercise and body health in the fields of food, clothing, and housing.

imposing the forms of the "Mediterranean order" as an authentic source of modern architecture, while the Italian Rationalists exalted the popular architecture of the Gulf of Naples as a contradictory tool of conciliation between the new style and the autarchic rhetoric of the Fascist regime.[16] Meanwhile, the Catalan modernists had rediscovered in the "everyday architecture" of the Balearic Islands (Ibiza, Majorca, Minorca, etc.) the elements necessary to affirm their right to participate in the new international trends.[17]

Beyond exotic romanticism, the vision for an "authentic life," and ideological consideration, it is his anthropological and architectural curiosity that enticed Rudofsky to travel and search for a new way of life. During the following decades, he wrote many theoretical and methodological essays about the "art of traveling," which had increasingly degraded to a product of mass-consumption, devoid of emotion, discovery, or surprise.[18] In his books and teachings, Rudofsky always stimulated his public to develop "a healthy appetite for architecture" by observing and taking pleasure in it, as he had done since a student during his Mediterranean travels. It was then that he discovered that the existential experience of the essence of architecture was not academic but domestic:

> the ruined houses and gardens of Pompeii have exactly nothing in common with the cabalistic system of classical Orders.[19]

Likewise, a large segment of his reflection about architecture – illustrated in *Architecture without Architects* (1964) and narrated in *The Prodigious Builders* (1977) and *Streets for People* (1969) – analyzed and dignified what he called "the dough, the bread," i.e., the everyday architecture, which constitutes the major part of the urban fabric, substituting for a moment the stage to the "formal construction."[20]

It is also important to point out that Rudofsky's attraction to the Mediterranean was primarily a physical one. He was interested in describing, and in personally leading, a healthy life. He committed himself to exploring all modalities of life (*Lebensweise*) and material culture in its totality: wardrobe dress, alimentation, and dwelling constituted for him an inseparable whole to which he applied the appropriate attempts at reform, through the practice of the project and the scientific vulgarization.[21] The latter – at times affectionate, at times caustic – was based on the consideration that "we don't know how to live."[22]

Dwelling as Theory and Practice

For Rudofsky, the main problem of contemporary architecture was the concept of residence: "The residence has been, and still is, viewed . . . as an inanimate thing, as [if] it could be detached from the life of its occupants."[23] Like Adolf Loos, he was interested in understanding how edifices were inhabited. He was also obsessed with the quality of material life – something that had nothing to do with "luxury," and even less with consumerism. "Loos was an architect" – Joseph Rykwert has observed – "who was possessed by the immediate quality of life, in which man put up rooms and spaces, by the quality of the smells, the quality of texture, the quality of every sensation."[24] Likewise, Rudofsky was a convinced hedonist and an Epicurean aristocrat, in the sense of "a minority of uncontaminated humans with their minds intact."[25] This definition was close to the one proposed by Gio Ponti:

> Modernity is an aristocracy of choice; it is the adoption of a measured simplicity that marries the most educated exigencies; it is an attitude of living, thinking, knowing and judging.[26]

Such a vision was shared by many architects. At the beginning of the century, Frank Lloyd Wright had found in Italy and in traditional Japan – as Rudofsky would find later – the true place of the "joy of living."[27] Likewise, Schindler once declared, "the sense of perception of architecture is not the eyes, but the joy of living."[28] According to Esther McCoy, he "called the work of De Stijl and Bauhaus groups an expression of the minds of a people who had lived through the First World War clad in uniforms, housed in dugouts, forced to utmost efficiency and meager sustenance, with no thought for joy, charm, warmth."[29] And in Richard Neutra's opinion, "nobody can fulfill the wishes of other people, take care of them, and do them so much good, as someone who creates the physical environment of their activity and of their recreation."[30]

Gio Ponti dedicated the first issue of Domus with his poetic statement about the house as the place of happiness.[31] As for Josef Frank, the house had "to make its inhabitants happy by its very existence, and had to bring them pleasure in every one of its parts."[32] Frank represented the opinion that principles without human feeling would "of necessity create extremes," that stood in opposition with the real life and thus would result in our contemporary "cannibal architecture."[33]

In Vers une architecture, Le Corbusier stated that, "we deserve compassion, because we live in indignant houses, which destroy our health and our morale."[34] He also gave a series of operative prescriptions, perhaps derived from the Reform movement, and that coincided in part with those later proposed by Rudofsky.[35] From the article "Des yeux qui ne voient pas. Les avions" (The eyes that do not see. The aircrafts), which in spite of the fact that the title was dedicated to housing and dwelling, most critics only retained the celebrated slogan "The house is a machine for living" and not the most profound suggestions from the Manuel de l'habitation.[36] The same Le Corbusier, who certainly did not believe that the nouvelle habitation consisted of the mere satisfaction of elementary physical needs, designed projects of collective settlements and wrote pages in which the new way of life appeared at once immaterial, overly intellectual, and vaguely poetic.

Yet, in the long run, only Siegfried Giedion and Rudofsky, among the modern critics, investigated the trivial matters of domestic life. Giedion focused his attention on the development of the services and their impact on daily life and the evolution of architecture.[37] Rudofsky, on the other hand, was convinced that the activities of human beings inside the house were not mechanical, and thus he emphasized the material quality of the existence.[38] The substance of Rudofsky's philosophy can be summarized in the powerful yet contradictory binomial Sparta/Sybaris: the exercise of Epicureanism is nothing less than a moral choice that includes an order and a rule. Here, the concordance with Ponti could not be more complete, "The style . . . is, precisely, discipline."[39]

The Mediterranean "Outdoor Room"

The architectonic production of Bernard Rudofsky was quantitatively limited, and it did not demonstrate a particular interest in formal experimentation. His buildings are neutral containers for people and activities, which fill them with life. For Rudofsky, the personality of a house is expressed by variations around a pattern and the way of life of its inhabitants, not by formal originality. In parallel, the example of the Japanese codification of gestures allowed him to develop his theory of a minimalist architectonic purism of a monastic stamp. For him, when the occupants do not have to concentrate their energy on the

[32] His major works in that field are the exhibition at MoMA New York in 1944–45, Are Clothes Modern? and its catalogue: Bernard Rudofsky, Are Clothes Modern?: An Essay on Contemporary Apparel, Chicago, P. Theobald, 1947; also see Bernard Rudofsky, Behind the Picture Window, New York, Oxford University Press, 1955.
[33] Bernard Rudofsky, "Notes on Patios," in New Pencil Points XXIV, June 1943, p. 46 [44–47].
[24] Joseph Rykwert, Introduction to Adolf Loos, Ins Leere Gesprochen, Wien-München, Herold, 1960, p. xxviii.
[25] Bernard Rudofsky, Are Clothes Modern?, p. 230
[26] Gio Ponti, "Falsi e giusti concetti nella casa," in Domus 123, March 1938, p. 1.
[27] Frank Lloyd Wright, Ausgeführte Bauten und Entwürfe, p. 2.
[28] From one of Schindler's note-books, quoted in Esther McCoy, Five California Architects, New York, Reinhold, 1960, p. 149.
[29] Esther McCoy, p. 153.
[30] Richard Neutra, Introduction to the Italian edition of Esther McCoy, Richard Neutra, Milano, Il Saggiatore, 1961, p. 13.
[31] Gio Ponti, "La casa all'italiana," Domus 1, 1928, p. 1.
[32] Josef Frank, Architektur als Symbol, p. 174.
[33] Ibid., p. 113.
[34] Le Corbusier, Vers une architecture, Paris, Crès, 1923, p. 6. In English, Toward an Architecture, Los Angeles, Getty Research Institute, 2007.
[35] See Marco De Michelis, "La casa della riforma della vita" in Georges Teyssot (ed.), Il progetto domestico. La casa dell'uomo: archetipi e prototipi, Milano, Triennale di Milano/Electa, 1986.
[36] Le Corbusier-Saugnier (Le Corbusier and Amédée Ozenfant), "Manuel de l'habitation," a part of their article "Des yeux qui ne voient pas . . . II: Les Avions," in L'esprit nouveau 9, June 1921, n.p.
[37] Sigfried Giedion, Mechanization Takes Command, New York, Oxford University Press, 1948.
[38] Bernard Rudofsky, Behind the Picture Window.
[39] Gio Ponti, "Verso funzioni nuove", in Domus 82, October 1934, p. 3.

⁴⁰ Daria Guarnati (ed.), *Aria d'Italia*, monographic issue titled "Espressione di Gio Ponti", Milano, 1954, pp. 23–36.
⁴¹ Rudofsky even demonstrated the properties of a white wall that becomes polychrome and decorated thanks to the ever-changing color of the daylight and the shadows projected on it by the foliage. This is a convincing example of his practice, which, though in apparent consonance with the modern movement, derived fundamentally from the experience of living.
⁴² The careful reading of *Architecture without Architects*, and even more so *The Prodigious Builders* could furnish a great quantity of arguments that we don't have the possibility to explore in this essay.
⁴³ Rudofsky, *Behind the Picture Window*, pp. 159, 194.
⁴⁴ Neutra "could not imagine that there are people who need seclusion, monastic silence, doors one can close, the environment only visible if desired and only in parts, windows with the appearance of framed pictures." From Manfred Sack, *Richard Neutra*, Zürich/London, Verlag für Architektur, 1992, p. 26.
⁴⁵ Bernard Rudofsky, "Notes on Patios," *The New Pencil Points* XXIV, June 1943, pp. 44–47.
⁴⁶ Bernard Rudofsky, "The Bread of Architecture", in *Arts and Architecture* 69, October 1952, pp. 27–29, 45.
⁴⁷ It is possible that Rudofsky may have been influenced by the atrium of the experimental house *am Horn* designed for the 1923 Bauhaus exhibition in Weimar by Georg Muche in association with Walter Gropius, and that he visited. See Duncan Macintosh, *The Modern Courtyard House*, London, Architectural Association/Lund Humphries, 1973, p. 25. Another possibility is the Oiva Kallio's Oivala Atrium House in Helsinki, 1925, very similar to *am Horn* but in wood. Both marked a modernized evolution of the typical atrium house of Italic origin, and can be seen as the precedents for Rudofsky's first two houses with central patio in Capri (1932) and Procida (1935).

architecture – be it in the form of creative endeavor or of visual distraction – then they can dedicate it to the intensity of their life.

The impossibility of simulating a primordial innocence in a modern architectural project did not exclude the possibility to borrow from the vernacular architecture and the frugal way of life of its inhabitants, a dignity, a reserve, and a wisely controlled naïveté. At the same time, his works made explicit his profound knowledge of traditional Mediterranean architecture: on the one hand, the sublimation of specific formal and constructive elements; on the other, the formulation of specific principles of composition. Gio Ponti summarized it with directness and concision: "The Mediterranean taught Rudofsky, Rudofsky taught me."[40]

The modernist lexicon of simple volumes, smooth, plane, and orthogonal – in fact, the language learnt during his formative period – is enriched by traits which confer human qualities to dwellings. It does not negate the materiality of the walls and, when it is necessary, as in Brazil, the utility of sloped roofs. The purity of volumes, the white stucco, and hand-painted ceramics adapt themselves to the site rather than do it violence; they give ample views of the landscape without imposing on the residents an excess of solar penetration or thermal dispersion.[41] The propitious details of Rudofsky's houses – the angle of a garden, a pergola, a basin for the bath, a bed, a cabinet, or a simple wall – are modeled on ways of life and domestic activities. They are able to create those small and tranquil effects of intimacy that characterize the genuine "architecture without architects," as Ponti also conceived of it.[42]

Rudofsky's experience of the Mediterranean focused on the pure concept of "room" as a fundamental architectonic entity. According to him, the most decisive perceptual quality of an architectural space was its being enclosed by walls. The enclosure gives concrete dimension to a human dwelling and defines its intimate character. Those spaces that are enclosed by walls but without roofs would be considered rooms as well. What counted was privacy. The gardens – like in Pompeii and Japan – were also seen as peaceful and self-contained outdoor rooms. That concept led him to fight against the large glass walls that exemplify the language of International Style architecture, although he valued them as being "inexplicably beautiful."[43] In the Californian villas of Richard Neutra, for instance, the relationship to nature is a dominating one; in other words, nature performs as a filmic background to architecture.[44] Likewise, the need for spatial seclusion was a principle that was formulated by many masters of the modern in their single-family houses – but contradicted in their large housing projects and the models of mass-produced houses. But for Rudofsky, it was the most important commandment that the architect had to observe and realize.

To the exploration and the promotion of the "outdoor room," he dedicated one of his most argumentative essays, which was also one of the first he published in America.[45] The centrality of these principles of privacy and of the "outdoor room" can be seen in many of his works, from the "atrium" of the house in Procida to the patios of his critically acclaimed Brazilian houses, and, above all, the garden for the Italian émigré artist and sculptor Costantino Nivola in Amagansett, New York, which afforded him the opportunity to write some of his most beautiful pages.[46] These principles were not only directly derived from domestic Mediterranean architecture, but also from modernist experimentations that were being realized at that time.[47]

11.3 Bernard Rudofsky.
       Sketch of an "outdoor
       room".
Source: *Interiors*, May 1946,
cover. Source: Research
Library, The Getty Research
Institute, Los Angeles.

During his collaboration with the magazine *Domus* in 1938, he published various aphorisms on the theme of the "outdoor room" and examples of houses with patios collected from Guido Harbers's book on residential gardens.[48] In one of his characteristic drawings, a sketch used as an editorial in *Domus*, Rudofsky depicted a garden, surrounded by high walls and laid out as a living room – even the piano is present.[49] For him, these open rooms – small and three-dimensionally defined – possessed, beyond their "obvious advantages, invaluable immaterial merits." He remarked, "the Persian word *Paradise* means a garden of pleasure surrounded by walls."[50] This concept contained for Rudofsky the entire idea of the house.

According to Gaston Bachelard's *Poetics of Space*, the house is, in its intimacy, the perfect expression of character, the place that can reveal the fullness of "being"; it gives rise to physical and erotic sensations.[51] Instead of creating

[48] Bernard Rudofsky, "Problema", in *Domus* 123, March 1938, p. xxxiv; "Variazioni" in *Domus* 124, April 1938, p. 14. Also see Guido Harbers, *Der Wohngarten: Seine Raum- und Bauelemente*, München, Callwey, 1933.
[49] Bernard Rudofsky, "Problema", p. xxxiv. Rudofsky reused such drawings for the cover of an *Interiors* issue, reproduced here above.
[50] Bernard Rudofsky, "Der wohltemperierte Wohnhof," in *Umriss* 10, 1/1986, pp. 5–20.
[51] Gaston Bachelard, *Poetics of Space*, New York, Orion Press, 1964.

model houses that he would present as umpteenth, megalomaniacal "definitive solutions," Rudofsky looked for his own way. He decided to publish his rich baggage of experience and discovery, in order to let the public use it and exploit it at will. His main agenda was to extract architecture out of the territories of theory, easily dominated by the initiated, to make it human and to place it at the level of the real life. As Giancarlo De Carlo wrote, "architecture is too important to be left to the architects."[52]

Buildings in Naples and in Brazil

Rudofsky's genuine manifesto on dwelling was the project for his own house on Procida, published in *Domus* in 1938.[53] The plans were conceived in the years 1934–35 during his investigation of Neapolitan vernacular architecture, when he discovered in Procida the place marked by his destiny.[54] However, as the military authority prevented construction on the chosen spot, the house was inevitably downgraded to the status of a starting point of his theoretical discourse – a "theoretical touchstone."[55] Attilio Podestà proposed that, in this project, Rudofsky showed "a spiritual position that comprehends the morality of building as a spontaneous product of heart and spirit." When Rudofsky

52 Giancarlo De Carlo, "Il pubblico dell'architettura," in *Parametro* 5, 1970, p. 4.
53 Bernard Rudofsky, "Non ci vuole un nuovo modo di costruire, ci vuole un nuovo modo di vivere," in *Domus* 123, March 1938, pp. 6–15.
54 Bernard Rudofsky, "Scoperta di una isola," in *Domus* 123, March 1938, pp. 2–5.
55 Bernard Rudofsky, "Non ci vuole un nuovo modo di costruire ci vuole un nuovo modo di vivere," p. 6.

"cannot convert refinement in spontaneity, he transmutes it into poetry."[56] Podestà also observed one of the finest aspects of his architecture, "the various shades of white on the stucco walls create an endlessly rich and ever-changing polychromy."[57]

The site was located on a high point of the island, and dominated the maritime landscape in the southeast direction. It was encircled by a garden wall, which functioned also as a perimeter wall. At the site's center was the main square-shaped building, with the rooms located around a central patio. The fourth side was covered yet open in order to connect the patio with the surrounding garden. A smaller edifice at the southern edge, almost on the cliff, functioned as a summer *triclinium*. The main building was very simple – one single floor and a flat roof, almost no windows (most were sliding doors), and no corridors. All the rooms were connected along a ring-like sequence. There was little furniture, responding nevertheless in a rigorous manner to an unusual way of dealing with the functions of dwelling. The master bedroom, for instance, had no furniture at all, but rather had a floor entirely made up of mattresses. Its cubic volume was made more intimate by a mosquito-net suspended from the center of the ceiling. The bathroom was equally sparse, with only a tub built in the ground. The corporal functions associated with bathing were relegated to an adjacent room. The patio floor was to be paved with tiles or left as grass.

Both the classicizing drawings illustrating the *Domus* article and the form of the Roman atrium conveyed the radical way of dwelling that the house suggested as well as Rudofsky's profound distancing from contemporary habits. He also indicated the type of clothing to give to the body the most appropriate postures.[58]

The circumstances that led to his proposal for the Hotel San Michele at Anacapri (1938), also unbuilt, were quite different. The commission was originally given to Gio Ponti, who Rudofsky first met in 1934, becoming his associate at the end of 1937.[59] The site was high on the island at the edge of a tall cliff, on the northern coast of Capri, a short distance from Axel Munthe's villa San Michele. The solution was a "village-hotel" – a typology that would later become typical in resort architecture. Each room was a small detached house, with its own mini-kitchen; some were coupled. Each room was designed with a specific decoration or physical characteristic.[60] The common services were conceived as a town center located around a square (plates 46, 47, 48).[61]

In the purity of the almost spontaneous project, one can discern a possible "architecture without architect," as co-designer Gio Ponti promoted it in those years – *Domus* made use of that expression in the 1930s for the interior decoration work of several Austrian architects like Hoffmann, Frank, Wlach, Strnad, and Haerdtl. The vernacular character of the project related to diverse sources: the living myth of architecture in Capri – a discussion initiated twenty years earlier following the preservation efforts led by Edwin Cerio;[62] the contemporary idyll between the Modern and the Mediterranean; Rudofsky's own research; and the policy of autarchy that governed Italian politics in the late 1930s. The inscription in the landscape recalled the local villages. The solidity of the walls and the curvature of the vaults were structural, climatically responsive, traditional and poetic at the same time. The comfort was carefully studied, with multiple variations in order to guarantee a healthy and regenerating stay for every guest. In the proposal reappeared extravagancies befitting the eccentric atmosphere of Capri and the function of resort

[56] Attilio Podestà, "Una casa a Procida dell'architetto Bernard Rudofsky," *Casabella* X, 117, September 1937, pp. 12–17.

[57] Ibid., p. 15.

[58] Personally, I doubt that Rudofsky would have eaten dinner lying down on a *triclinium*, even in his summer-house.

[59] Rudofsky had already worked on seaside hotel projects; this experience might explain why Ponti called him from Milan and invited him to work together. Among those projects was the small hotel for Procida, at times known as "Rio di Raia delle Rose." Another one for Positano was made up of free-standing rooms on a steeply terraced terrain. See Andrea Bocco Guarneri, *Bernard Rudofsky*, op. cit.

[60] Here one must admit that the village-like resort has become one of the archetypes that have destroyed the coasts of the Mediterranean during the last decades. Proliferation has been the problem, not the type itself; moreover, the craftsmanship displayed in the documents for the Hotel San Michele has no equivalent in the postwar quasi-industrial modes of construction.

[61] In Capri, the concept of an edifice made up of independent buildings with distinct names had a precedent: one of the most famous houses of the island, Edwin Cerio's village-house *Il Rosaio*, 1929. See Giuseppe Capponi, "Architettura e accademia a Capri: Il Rosaio di Edwin Cerio," in *Architettura e arti decorative*, December 1929, pp. 177–188.

[62] See the many writings of Edwin Cerio on Capri. Of particular interest is Edwin Cerio (ed.), *Il convegno del paesaggio*, Capri, Le Pagine dell'Isola, 1923 (reedition: Capri, Edizioni La Conchiglia, 1993).

[63] This idea was inspired by Japan. See Bernard Rudofsky, "Introduzione al Giappone (I)", in *Domus* 319, June 1956, pp. 45–49.

architecture – the large tubs excavated from the floor, in rooms separated from the toilets; built-in beds; staircases in masonry, covered with painted ceramic tiles; private gardens and terraces, screened by canopies; interior windows and vistas; and entry closets where arriving guests were to change into new clothes specially designed by the architects.[63]

Another seaside house was designed for a site near Positano, perhaps for the developer and builder Campanella. Although unrealized, it was extensively

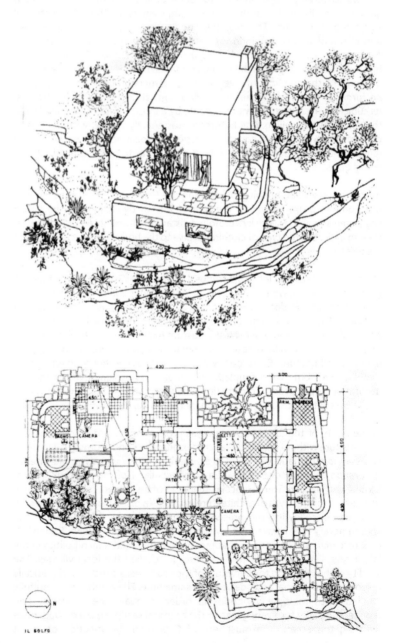

11.5 Bernard Rudofsky and Gio Ponti. Perspective of the *Stanza della Parete nera* [Plan of the Black Wall] and plan of the two *Stanze degli Angeli* [Rooms of the Angels]. Hotel San Michele, unbuilt, Anacapri, c.1938.
Source: Archivio Gio Ponti, Centro Studi e Archivio della Communicazione, Università di Parma.

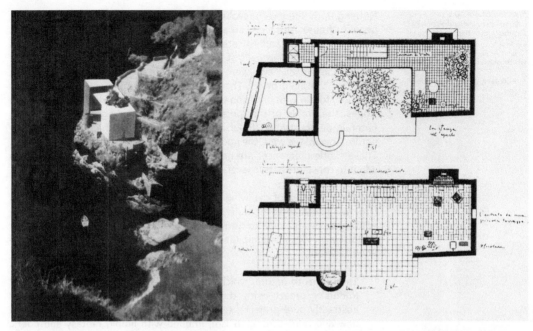

11.6 Bernard Rudofsky
and Luigi Cosenza.
Photomontage of the
model and plans, Villa
Campanella, unbuilt,
Positano, c.1936.
Source: Domus 109, 1937.

published in *Domus* in 1937.[64] The project combined the elements of radical domesticity of the Procida house with the minimalism of the hotel in Capri. *Domus* wrote that the house showed no signs of "the exhibitionist bourgeois house," but was "a honest construction for the pure and happy evasion from the city life . . . without polemical ideas and without utopia."[65]

The house, sited on a rocky outcropping, consisted of two volumes: one covered with stucco, the other in apparent calcareous stone. It offered a repertory of minimal "sheltering" spaces. There was the "covered dwelling", a room totally enclosed by walls, covered by a roof, and with a closeable door; there were rooms whose perimeter envelope was left incomplete (the entrance and hearth area downstairs and the "open-air room" upstairs). Finally, there was the main room whose area was perceptually determined by the volumes of the other rooms, by its flat roof, pierced to allow the growth of a fig tree and a magnolia tree, and by a background wall, which provided the only element of safe anchoring. Such a room was not much more than a portico, which symbolized shelter, while providing shade and a view of the sea. All rooms of the house displayed the same Spartan care, both in terms of materials (calcareous stone or lava, ceramics from Vietri), and basic comfort (the small cozy hearth, the open-air shower).

Rudofsky's only built house in the region was the Villa Oro in Naples, in collaboration with Luigi Cosenza. The site was very narrow, plunging vertically into the sea. Almost exclusively related to the sea, the house was built wide at the horizon and perfectly oriented to catch the sun throughout the day. The project was completed at the start of the summer 1935; yet, construction was delayed for a year because of the Ethiopian War. Rudofsky, back from the United States where he had resided for a couple of months, took over the project in the second half of 1936. Cosenza was in charge of the construction; one year later, the house was completed.[66]

64 "Una villa per Positano e per . . . altri lidi, "*Domus* 109, January 1937, pp. 11–17.
65 Ibid., pp. 12–13.
66 On Cosenza, see Alfredo Buccaro and Giancarlo Mainini (eds.), *Luigi Cosenza oggi, 1905–2005*, Napoli, Clean, 2006; Inken Baller, Evelyn Hendreich, and Gisela Schmidt-Krayer (eds.), *Villa Oro: Luigi Cosenza, Bernard Rudofsky, 1937 Neapel*, Berlin, Westkreuz, 2008.

[67] Attilio Podestà, "Una casa a Procida dell'arch. Bernard Rudofsky," *Casabella* 117, September 1937, pp. 12–17.
[68] Lisa Ponti, "Le piú desiderabili ville del mondo," in *Domus* 234, 1949, p. 4.
[69] Rudofsky, "Notes on Patios," p. 45.

Nothing from Rudofsky's revolutionary way of life did really transpire in this beautiful house. Although courageously modernist, it is merely an attractive, bourgeois home: a sophisticated articulation of neat, white cubic volumes supported by retaining walls of tuff. A series of gardens and terraces – some hidden, some in full view – were recovered from the slopes with the ingenious obstinacy of wine growers. The volumes, one per room as in the vernacular tradition, follow with precision the curves of the site and the two converging slopes: the profile of the roofs parallels the ascending panoramic street, faithfully demonstrating Rudofsky's acceptance of the limitations imposed by nature. Toward the west, the house has three floors; to the east, there are two. These subtle differences are generally imperceptible, playfully arranged to adapt to constant shifts in level.

The most intimate of the living rooms, at the lowest level, opens through a large window cut into the walls of tuff: its pavement represents a map of the entire gulf (from Licola to Sorrento with Capri, Ischia, Procida) painted by Rudofsky on Vietri ceramic tiles in his characteristic naïve style. As Attilio Podestà wrote,

> The return to nature, which the architects Luigi Cosenza and Bernard Rudofsky preach with their words and the example ... of their abstractly pure projects, tends to realize itself in the suggestion of a new and refined romanticism, imbued with limpid fantasy and poetic qualities. Its Mediterranean character admittedly reflects the environmental value, but its ambiguity is overcome in the rigor of a conscious modernity.[67]

Following his escape to Latin America, in December 1938, Bernard Rudofsky moved to São Paulo to work at an art gallery, founded and directed by the German immigrant, Theodor Heuberger. Between 1939 and 1940, he designed and built for Europeans who had immigrated to Brazil, the Casa Hollenstein in Minais Gerais, the Frontini and Arnstein Houses in São Paulo, and three unbuilt houses. The two houses he built in São Paulo were particularly significant for their treatment of the private sphere, the unlimited respect for the life of inhabitants, and the clever exploitation of the possibilities that both the local climate and vegetation offered. Yet, for his Brazilian clients, he only partially implemented his theories. The rooms in his completed houses ended up rather conventional, and the architect focused his attention on the gardens that he laid out as civilized spaces for a refined life. As Lisa Ponti wrote, his Brazilian projects were primarily dedicated "to provide the residents with a delicious life in the smallest things."[68]

The Casa Arnstein (1939–41) distinguished itself with the savant articulation of the gardens; in practice, every room had its own outdoor counterpart. A particular attention was given to the colors of the flowers during the four seasons, as well as to the selection of trees made to attract butterflies and hummingbirds. In contrast, the Casa Frontini (1939–41) was surrounded by one single garden, but possessed a paved and furnished interior court. The entire house surrounds it, with a cheerfully rhythmic arcade. In agreement with his theory, Rudofsky avoided giving these houses a genuine façade; he decided to create buildings

> that lack the outer dress to which our civilization attaches such exaggerated importance. The architecture is merely a shell for its owner . . . it is hardly noticeable in its unobtrusiveness.[69]

11.7 Bernard Rudofsky and Luigi Cosenza. View of the terraces of Casa Oro, Naples, 1935–37.
Source: Research Library, The Getty Research Institute, Los Angeles.

70 Quoted in Bernard Rudofsky, "Three Patio Houses," *Pencil Points* 24, June 1943, p. 54.

71 Philip L. Goodwin, *Brazil Builds*, New York, Museum of Modern Art, 1943, p. 100.

72 Sacheverell Sitwell, "The Brazilian Style," in *Architectural Review* 95, March 1944. Rudofsky left Brazil for New York in April 1941, after learning that he was one of the winners of the Museum of Modern Art's pan-American *Organic Design* competition.

73 The translation of Bernard Rudofsky's article title for the house in Procida: "Non ci vuole un nuovo modo di costruire ci vuole un nuovo modo di vivere." The motto also became the subtitle of his last book, *Sparta/Sybaris: Keine neue Bauweise, eine neue Lebensweise tut not*, Salzburg, Residenz, 1987.

74 Walter Gropius, *Social Premises for the Minimum Dwelling of Urban Industrial Population*, 1929. Also see Gropius, *Die Wohnung für das Existenzminimum*, Frankfurt, Englert and Schlosser, 1930.

75 Bernard Rudofsky, "On Architecture and Architects. An address delivered at the invitation of the Fogg Museum, at the Boston Museum of Art, in the course of the exhibition of Brazilian Architecture *Brazil Builds*," in *The New Pencil Points* 24, April 1943, p. 63.

Both houses received enthusiastic acclaim. Philip L. Goodwin wrote, for instance, that they were "living places of people sure of themselves by education and experience, designed by one who understood both them and his job thoroughly."[70] And he continued:

> There is no such homogenous and successful example of the modern house-garden in the Americas. . . . During three years of architectural work in Brazil, Rudofsky built some houses, which were considered the best of the American continent.[71]

As Sacheverell Sitwell wrote,

> Rudofsky's design makes inspired use of the tropical flowers and foliage, and of their shadows on the walls. The form of the trees has an effect of intoxicating richness against the cool control and serenity of the architecture.[72]

Even though Rudofsky postulated the interpretation of architecture as the receptacle for life, his solutions in plan remained very far from an organic esthetic of the dwelling as shell: it is my opinion that he meant life as organic, and architecture as inorganic. From the point of view of composition, his architectonic oeuvre fits in the style of the moderns, without particular originality. It manifested itself in plain, simple, clearly delineated, and Cartesian volumes. Throughout his career Rudofsky had a limited number of occasions to design buildings. Perhaps for this reason he remained unswerving in the use of the architectonic forms that characterized his works of the 1930s and 1940s.

Moreover, it must be unfortunately acknowledged that, with the exception of the house in Procida (1935), his proposals of reform of the domestic environment did not produce results, not even in his own buildings. His ideas proved to be too radical to be imposed upon his occasional clients in Italy, Brazil, or then in the United States. This appears as a failure for somebody who had repeatedly declared that "we don't need a new way of building, we need a new way of life."[73]

Rudofsky and Modernism

Rudofsky distanced himself from many modernist architects, primarily because he did not believe in a definitive solution to the housing question, which was born of illuminist-positivistic thinking and faith in the constancy of human desires. To declare immutable over time and place the human spirit and its material needs was the philosophical prerequisite to the planetary homogenization of the "international style." In the same manner, Gropius's affirmation of the universality of the *Existenzminimum* was justified by the "impending equalization of life requirements under the influence of travel and world trade."[74]

Until the 1940s, Rudofsky remained convinced that a modern revolution in lifestyle could be helped through the figure of the architect, who would be an "advocate of a better life."[75] However, his articles written for *Domus* in the 1930s already denounced architects who imposed their own choices on the residents and who did not radically question the premises that form the basis of consolidated practices. His hopes that the ethical principles of modernity would inform and modify the practice of architecture were definitely shattered during the 1950s.

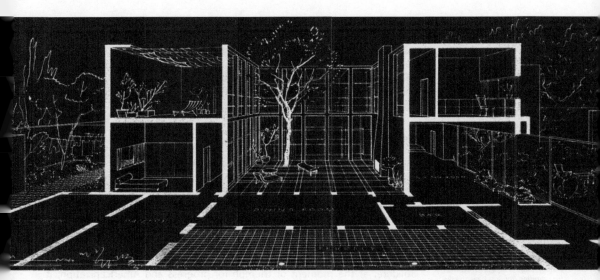

11.8 Bernard Rudofsky.
Perspective section
of Frontini House,
São Paulo, Brazil,
c.1939–41.
Source: The Bernard Rudofsky
Estate, Vienna. © Ingrid
Kummer.

The tone changed over time. In his two groundbreaking theoretical texts *Are Clothes Modern?* (1947) and *Behind the Picture Window* (1955), he suggested, in contrast with his following texts, alternative solutions to the criticized practices. After the 1950s, he gradually noticed that he was leading a solitary combat (perhaps from the very beginning), his goals changed, and his attacks became sharper. In the face of the standardization of place and buildings, and his being totally ignored by the architectural world, in the final chapter of *Streets for People* he declared that architects were the accomplices, if not the direct cause, of the bad quality of public as well as private spaces. He proposed the formulation of "ethical precepts for the performance of the profession," in the manner of the Hippocratic oath taken by physicians.[76]

According to Rudofsky, the architects have accepted, absorbed, and eventually promoted the interests of developers, thus forgetting what should be the main object of their endeavors – the well-being of the residents:

> The house as a machine for living ought to be run by a more dependable, more predictable inmate than man. . . . Assuming that in the future we shall be able to live the life of humans, the house of man will have to become once more an *instrument for living*, instead of a machine for living.[77]

As a result, during the last decades of his life, he crusaded to establish a direct contact with the public, through exhibitions and books, and to make useful suggestions for improving their material life. He was well aware that "at the end of a long historical process of reduction of the fact of dwelling to a simple function . . . the public has become satisfied with the consumption of symbols while losing entirely the 'act of living.' "[78] Nevertheless, he continued to wish that the solution could be found through the awareness and activism of the dwellers:

> I rarely address an audience of architects, if only because I consider them a hopeless breed, and a threat to humanity. I prefer to speak to laymen instead, since it is from them that any re-orientation in the field of architecture must come.[79]

[76] Bernard Rudofsky, *Streets for People*, pp. 337–342.
[77] Bernard Rudofsky, *Behind the Picture Window*, pp. 200–201.
[78] Antonio Tosi, *Ideologie della casa: contenuti e significati del discorso sull'abitare*, Milano, Franco Angeli, 1980, pp. 41–42.
[79] Bernard Rudofsky, *Back to Kindergarten*, unpublished lecture in Copenhagen, April 8, 1975, p. 1 of manuscript.

[80] Ivan Illich et al., *Disabling Professions*, London/Salem, M. Boyars, 1977.
[81] For a thorough analysis of *Architecture without Architects* within the context of the American architectural debate in the 1960s, see Felicity Scott, "Architecture without Architects," *Harvard Design Magazine*, Fall 1998, pp. 69–72. She writes: The reception . . . was facilitated by the catalogue's peculiar capacity to act as a not-fully-determined screen upon which so many contemporary issues could be projected. From fear of a technological progress gone awry, to the sense of a growing urgency for preservation, community, and regional identity, and even to a comparison with the New Monumentality in architecture, these photographs continued to evoke pressing issues."
[82] Bernard Rudofsky, *The Prodigious Builders*, p. 235.
[83] "Such projects as Friedrick Kiesler's Endless House exist, and have existed for centuries. You just have to take the time to look for them." Bernard Rudofsky, unpublished lecture, Bennington, VT. In doctoral thesis he demonstrated the logical and technical continuity between the "primitive concrete-like construction" of Santorini and the modern vault structures out of concrete.
[84] Giuseppe Pagano and Guarniero Daniel, *Architettura rurale italiana*, Milano, Hoepli, 1936, p. 6.
[85] Ibid., p. 76.

Rudofsky – an enemy of the "experts" – would have shared Ivan Illich's radical critique of the "disabling professions" that have expropriated people's awareness and abilities, attributing the right to know, act, or prescribe exclusively to ever more powerful, highly self-referential technocratic castes. Nothing was more distant from him than the figure of the architect as global designer, demiurge of the happiness of others, a technician and an artist, as the modernist architects propagandized it.[80]

Architecture without Architects

Another focal point of Rudofsky's relation with modernism was his ongoing research on vernacular architecture. Already in 1931, he had exhibited his photographs of spontaneous architecture, mostly taken in Santorini, in the Austrian section of the *Deutsche Bauaustellung Berlin*. The same year, he exhibited twenty-six watercolors at the Wiener Künstlerhaus. Two decades later, the exhibition *Architecture without Architects* – an idea he had already suggested in 1941 – stood in a completely different context. At a place and at a time, where the concept of "anonymous" bordered on ethnographic folklore, at the moment of triumph for progress and Americanization, it was sort of indecent to even deal with spontaneous architecture. Yet, the exhibition opened in 1964 in the "temple" in which the International Style was launched, the Museum of Modern Art in New York.[81] The show was enormously successful and circulated among eighty-four different venues for twelve consecutive years, thus making it in all probability the longest-running project in MoMA's Department of Architecture and Design. The catalogue was translated in seven languages and sold, in the United States alone, more than one hundred thousand copies in the first twenty years. Following the heavy polemics, it became Bernard Rudofsky's point of entry into architectural history.

For Rudofsky, vernacular architecture represented the first phase of architectural history. It was crucial yet until then neglected. In it the archetypes of construction were still visible and alive, not abstract, often ideological, concepts deriving from subsequent reconstruction. Thus it could not be judged with academic criteria – "The vernacular is much more than a style; it is a code of good manners that has no parallel in the urban world." It is the fruit of "an unconscious genius . . . free from the hysteria of the planners."[82]

He underlined its valuable common sense of addressing practical problems, and its comprehension of the limitations inbuilt in nature and architecture itself. He argued that the study of the vernacular could liberate the people from the cramped world of formal and commercial architecture, which was becoming more and more homogeneous and monotonous. This repertoire was the richest supply of inspiration for the people of the industrial age, and it was rich in technically advanced solutions.[83]

Rudofsky, as Giuseppe Pagano in Italy, had the same starting point: the idea of a "sound and honest rural architecture,"[84] "free from every fashion, filled with a modest and anonymous beauty, [that] teaches us how to conquer time and to overcome the decorative and stylistic variations of the past."[85] Interestingly, this theoretical predisposition could also be found in Adolf Loos's famous essay *Architektur*:

> The farmhouse is, contrary to the architect's house, a work of nature, not of men. It is beautiful – as do the animals who let themselves be guided by

their instinct. . . . Yes, it is beautiful, as are beautiful the rose or the thistle, the horse and the cow.[86]

The sensibility of Rudofsky toward vernacular architecture was also comparable to Le Corbusier's appreciation of the architecture he encountered in Italy, Turkey, Greece, Spain, and Algeria, or of rural buildings of villages like Vézelay. Like his predecessors and Rudofsky himself in his following texts, Le Corbusier recognized in each of these houses, built by "men in tune with fundamentals," "a center of happiness, of serenity . . . founded upon the solid rock of fundamental truth." Their architectonic solutions "are full of life; intelligent, economical, constructive, painstaking, sound; they are amiable and polite; architecturally speaking, they are courteous neighbors." In brief, they boasted the qualities that constitute "the stuff of architecture."[87]

Overall, Rudofsky spoke little about the protagonists of modern architecture, and when he did during the 1970s, it was not in flattering terms. With a few of them he maintained a reciprocal relationship of admiration: Gio Ponti, Pietro Belluschi, Serge Chermayeff, and Le Corbusier, with whom he differed in terms of "exhibitionism" but was connected by sensibility and common ideas:

> Modern architecture's prophets and pioneers, whose doctrines went unchallenged for years, were almost invariably men of parochial mind, untraveled, and loath to venture beyond their drawing board. Their foremost aim was to homogenize the world of architecture by impressing upon it a vapid "International Style". Enamored of mechanization, addicted to waste, they considered nations that depended mainly on the utilization of sun-, wind- and water-power hopelessly primitive. . . . One summer, curiosity led me to Weimar where the first Bauhaus exhibition had just opened. This was my first premonition of the ill wind that was to blow over the field of architecture. Weimar, and later Dessau, I found, had all the charm of a reformatory for juveniles.[88]
> By sheer contrast, Le Corbusier's early writings and early buildings were a revelation to me. His Latin elegance of reasoning, his native sophistication, made the ponderous pronouncement of his Teutonic colleagues seem boring. Besides, painter and sculptor that he was, he greatly admired the freely modeled houses of the Greek islands and North African towns.[89]

In *Architecture without Architects* and *The Prodigious Builders*, Rudofsky complained about the impoverishment of architecture because of the disappearance of cultural diversity. His critique paralleled Claude Lévi-Strauss's discourse in the anthropological field.[90] Rudofsky and Lévi-Strauss pursued the same goals, to demonstrate the cultural wealth of the world, "to walk the longer road" in order to return to the origins and to rediscover humankind.[91] Both theorized the employment of elements of foreign cultures for the renewal of the Western civilisation.[92] The comparative analysis of various cultural experiences, which recognizes the critical adoption and adaptation of foreign principles, practices, and objects, was at the basis of Rudofsky's book *Behind the Picture Window* (1955), and the later exhibitions *Now I Lay Me Down to Eat* (1980) and *Sparta/Sybaris* (1987), each accompanied by a homonymous catalogue.[93]

In spite of the important merits of *Architecture without Architects*, it has been noted by many, and in detail by Paul Oliver, that Rudofsky's approach to the conception of vernacular architecture was methodologically deficient (due to

[86] Adolf Loos, *Trotzolen*, p. 93.
[87] Le Corbusier, *Sur les quatre routes*, Paris, Gallimard, 1941. In English, *The Four Routes*, London, Dobson, 1947.
[88] For a general context, see the quotation from Schindler given previously in this essay from Esther McCoy in *Five California Architects*, p. 153.
[89] Bernard Rudofsky, unpublished lecture at the Walker Art Center, Minneapolis, 1981.
[90] See the lecture at UNESCO, 1971, with the title "Race et culture," in Claude Lévi-Strauss, *Le regard éloigné*, Paris, Plon, 1973. In English, *The View from Afar*, New York, Basic Books, 1985.
[91] See "Il giro più lungo, ovvero il senso dell'antropologia," in Francesco Remotti, *Antenati e antagonisti*, Bologna, Il Mulino, 1986.
[92] Claude Lévi-Strauss, *Tristes tropiques*, Paris, Plon, 1955, p. 381. In English, *Tristes Tropiques*, New York, Atheneum, 1973.
[93] Bernard Rudofsky, *Sparta-Sybaris*; Bernard Rudofsky, *Now I Lay Me down to Eat: Notes and Footnotes on the Lost Art of Living*, Garden City, NY: Anchor Press-Doubleday, 1980.

94 See for instance Paul Overy, "A Touch of Mediterranean Senti-mentality," *The Times*, September 10, 1974; Michel Ragon, *L'Architecte, le Prince et la Démocratie*, Paris, Michel, 1977.

95 "The images of architecture with-out architects appealed to the period's growing discontent with the devastation of the urban and rural environment, to its liberationist and anti-colonial politics, and to the uneasiness felt by some regarding the ever increasing commodification of everyday life. The carefully con-structed images even aroused the sentiment that one was being shown not only an alternative, but somehow a 'natural,' 'essential,' or 'true' archi-tecture which existed beyond representation." Felicity Scott, "Architecture without Architects," pp. 69–72.

96 Bernard Rudofsky, *The Kimono Mind*, Garden City, NY, Doubleday, 1965, p. 260.

97 See Robert Goldwater, *Primitivism in Modern Art*, Cambridge-London, The Belknap Press of Harvard University Press, 1986. The quote is from John Maass, "Where Architec-tural Historians Fear to Tread," in *Journal of the Society of Architectural Historians* 28, March 1969.

98 See Sally Price, *Primitive Art in Civilized Places*, Chicago, University of Chicago Press, 1989.

99 Karsten Harries, in *The Ethical Function of Architecture*, Cambridge, The MIT Press, 1997, p. 285, remarks that recent texts, "like Marvin Trachtenberg and Isabelle Hyman's *Architecture, from Prehistory to Post-Modernism: The Western Tradition* (1986) or Spiro Kostof's *A History of Architecture: Setting and Rituals* (1985) broaden the picture considerably but don't really change it." The "Pevsnerian" distinction between "architecture" and "building" persists.

a lack of historical and cultural contextualization) and that it belonged to the category of "idealistic" interpretation. In *Architecture without Architects* (but less so in *The Prodigious Builders*), the reading of the fascinating "spontaneous" constructions remained almost always formal and estheticizing. Curiously, while Rudofsky dedicated so much attention to the study of domestic architecture, his own exhibition displayed mostly exterior photographs. His approach, based upon formal and functional analogies, showed minimal interest for the symbolic values, the cultural context, the psychological-cultural foundations of the taboos, and other anthropological factors.

Over the years, Rudofsky continued to make clear, especially in light of its unexpected success, that he did not mean to propose "architecture without architects" as the apotheosis of the architectonic art and that the polemic value of his research had to be put into the context of the contemporary cultural debate. Undoubtedly, he had no prescriptive intention. However, due to either the occasional dogmatic overtone of his statements in *Architecture without Architects*, or the fact that the time was ripe to launch the final attack against what remained of the cultural establishment of modern architecture (1966 saw the publication of *Complexity and Contradiction* by Robert Venturi), Rudofsky became one of the heroes of anti-modernism.[94] More or less consciously, he provided theoretical ammunition for the development of the environmental movement, the mimesis of the vernacular lexicon, the care for the well-being of the resident, the centrality attributed to the collective and the concept of community, self-construction, or, simply, for all of those who wanted to radically distance themselves from the forms of late-modernist architecture.[95]

In all his writings, he encouraged his readers to direct their attention not only to the few outstanding objects – the "masterpieces," the upper class dresses, the chairs that are exhibited in the museums of modern art and so on – but rather to the architecture, objects, and garments of everyday, conceived for work, and carrying "the unselfconscious beauty of utilitarian things."[96] As a result, his largest merit relies in having performed in architecture what many enlightened thinkers – authors, travelers, painters – had done already with exotic primitive arts: they "discovered" and publicized them in such a manner that it was no longer possible to ignore them. As happened before, particularly in the early 1900s in Paris, with the growing interests of ethnographers and artists for "primitive" art, "the work of Rudofsky has enlarged the field of the history of art."[97]

The fact that a category defined as "primitive" (or dialectal) was questioned at all was clearly the result of a general advancement in the scope and ambitions of architectural and urban research, particularly in terms of the ever-increasing awareness of historical and cultural differences.[98] After *Architecture without Architects*, it became increasingly difficult to restrict architecture to the products of professionals ("pedigreed" architects, as Rudofsky wrote in the subtitle of the book), and to dedicate the history of architecture exclusively to those buildings "that housed the principal actors in formal history."[99]

The liberty with which Rudofsky placed side by side, kites and nomad tents, termite habitat and dovecotes, cemeteries and cave dwellings, could shock cool and rational individuals who looked for genuine scientific method. Yet, that did not alter the validity and freedom of the comparison, of which he was intimately convinced and with which he mainly aimed at discussing general and profound matters of architecture. The wealth of material he presented in his exhibitions was meant, first and for all, to stimulate the imagination of the visitor. Reading *Streets for People* – a book that enticed a whole generation to fight for pedestrian rights and human cities – Gio Ponti, for instance, invited his readers to become "friends, lovers, and connoisseurs" of architecture.[100]

In retrospect, one must recognize Rudofsky's influence upon a whole generation of architects who used *Architecture without Architects* and his other books as an opportunity to escape the formalism of the Moderns. Even if he can't be considered a real forerunner of a particular theory, he certainly was an early fighter toward a psychologically enjoyable, healthy, and thus ecological environment. To sum it all, Rudofsky's position was an unstable balance between modernity and anti-modernity. These two opposing tendencies coexisted throughout his career, and he was clearly marked by this profound contradiction. ∎

[100] Gio Ponti, "Rudofsking," in *Domus* 486, May 1970, p. 54.

Acknowledgment
This text has been adapted from Andrea Bocco Guarneri, "Bernard Rudofsky – zum Wohle der Zivilisation," in Matthias Boeckl (ed.), *Visionäre und Vertriebene. Österrechische Spuren in der modernen amerikanischen Architektur*, Berlin, Ernst und Sohn, 1995, pp. 170–187, and the lecture "The Sublimation of Modern Architecture through Bathing in the Mediterranean" he gave in Capri, in March 1998, during the symposium *The Other Modern*.

12

CIAM, TEAM X, AND THE REDISCOVERY OF AFRICAN SETTLEMENTS

BETWEEN DOGON AND BIDONVILLE

Tom Avermaete

My instinct tells me that there are today a few who are across the brink of another sensibility – a sensibility about cities, a sensibility about human patterns and collective built forms. Looking back to the fifties it was then that the brink was crossed, it was then that architectural theory convulsed, then that the social sciences suddenly seemed important. A change of sensibility is what I now think Team X was all about.[1]

The significant interest for urban and rural settlements of the Mediterranean side of the African continent amongst architects working in Europe and North America in the 1950s and 1960s is a well-known phenomenon. The motivations were diverse. For a small group of European architects Africa became a true working terrain, often described as a "laboratory of experimentation," on which the most modern architectural and urban concepts could be tested. This was for instance the case for French architects that were active in Morocco and Algeria and could elaborate experimental projects throughout the colonial territories during the 1950s and even after independence.[2] Often these projects were published in influential architectural periodicals as is exemplified by the special issues *Maroc* and *Afrique du Nord* of *L'Architecture d'aujourd'hui*, in 1951 and 1955 respectively.

These secondary sources became for a much broader group of European architects the vectors along which they developed an interest in African architecture. Besides periodicals and books, large international meetings such as the 1953 meeting in Aix-en-Provence of the Congrès Internationaux d'Architecture Moderne (CIAM IX) and later exhibitions like Udo Kultermann's *Neues Bauen in Afrika* (1966, Berlin) were important propellers of this new attention. Many study trips to Africa were made by practicing European and North American architects, as well as architectural students – trips that more often than not had major repercussions for architectural and urban design strategies. Publications on African settlements also emerged during that period from a variety of methodological angles, including Erwin Gutkind's contributions to *Architectural Design* on indigenous African houses, Aldo van Eyck's articles in *Forum* and *Architectural Forum* on the Dogon, Amos Rapoport's *House Form and Culture*, and other publications in *L'Architecture d'aujourd'hui* and the Helsinki-based periodical *Le Carré Bleu*.[3]

This renewed interest for the African continent has often been depicted as a curiosity. It has been described as a late romantic and orientalist gaze on Africa, and discussed as a moment of bewilderment in which European and North American architects turned their view to traditional African architecture with

[1] Peter Smithson, "The Slow Growth of Another Sensibility: Architecture as Townbuilding," in James Gowan (ed.), *A Continuing Experiment. Learning and Teaching at the Architectural Association*, London, Architectural Press, 1973, p. 56.
[2] For an introduction to these different projects, see for instance Udo Kultermann, *Neues Bauen in Afrika*, Tübingen, Ernst Wasmuth, 1963; and Maurice Culot and Jean-Marie Thiveaud (eds.), *Architectures Françaises Outre-Mer*, Liège, Mardaga, 1992.
[3] See for instance Aldo van Eyck, "Bouwen in de Zuidelijke Oazen," in *Forum* 8, no. 1, 1953, pp. 28–38; Aldo van Eyck, "Architecture of the Dogon," in *Architectural Forum*, September 1961, pp. 116–121; Aldo van Eyck, "Dogon: mand-huis-dorp-wereld," in *Forum* 17, July 1967, pp. 30–50; Bernard Rudofsky, *Architecture Without Architects: A Short Introduction to Non-Pedigreed Architecture*, New York, Museum of Modern Art, 1964; Georges Candilis, Shadrach Woods, and Alexis Josic, "Fort Lamy," in *Le Carré Bleu*, January 1965, unpaginated; Amos Rapoport, *House Form and Culture*, Englewood Cliffs, Prentice-Hall, 1969.

12.1 *(Far left)* ATBAT-Afrique. Compagnie Immobilière Franco-Marocaine, housing scheme for the Carrières Centrales, 1951–55 (photograph of 1958).
Source: Ministère de l'habitat, photographic archives, Rabat.

4 For an elaborate introduction to this group see: Max Risselada and Dirk van den Heuvel, *Team 10: A Utopia of the Present*, Rotterdam, Nai Publishers, 2005.
5 For a detailed description of this grid see Eric Mumford, *The CIAM Discourse on Urbanism, 1928–1960*, Cambridge, The MIT Press, 2000; and Tom Avermaete, *Another Modern: The Postwar Architecture and Urbanism of Candilis–Josic–Woods*, Rotterdam, Nai Publishers, 2005.

the erroneous expectation of finding solutions for their modern problems. This depiction as a marginal and trivial *excursus* within the development of modern architecture has wrongfully obscured the specific character and the diversity of approaches that this "turn to Africa" – more exactly, the African side of the Mediterranean – encompassed.

Looking back, the interest in Africa may nowadays appear as anachronistic. In the middle of the 1950s, the moment that Dutch, French, and English architects were designing historically large and sophisticated architectural and urban projects for the built environment in their rapidly modernizing countries, they developed an interest in the vernacular architecture of Africa. Yet, I would like to argue that the publications of the future Team X members epitomized an important epistemological shift in the development of the modern movement that resulted from the installation of a more meaningful relationship between European architectural thinking and African architectural realities. Aldo van Eyck's interest for Saharan settlements, George Candilis's and Shadrach Woods's reflections on the traditional Moroccan villages in the Atlas Mountains, and Herman Haan's motion pictures of Dogon villages and culture, are but a few articulations of this relationship.

Though these examples look comparable at first sight, the relationships they suggest between Europe and Africa are rather diverse. It is possible to look upon all those publications as case studies that allow us to distinguish between at least two major currents of attitudes in the North–South nexus. In an attempt to sketch an alternative image of this interest for Africa within the modern movement, my essay focuses on what can be considered as one of the key protagonists in modern architectural thinking of the 1960s – Team X. This group of "young Turks" that included among others Alison and Peter Smithson from the United Kingdom, Aldo van Eyck and Jacob Bakema from the Netherlands, and Georges Candilis and Shadrach Woods from France conjured up an important transformation in the thinking and the subsequent collapse (in 1959) of the CIAM organization.[4]

Team X: Born from an Interest for the South

The story of the young Team X architects cannot be told without reflecting upon the special role that North Africa played within their ventures. After all, the architects working in Morocco and Algeria radically altered the course of CIAM at the ninth meeting in 1953 in Aix-en-Provence and laid the foundation for what became Team X. As a result, and without exaggeration, it can be sustained that Team X emerged from the establishment of a meaningful relationship between the South and the North.

In particular, the presentations and debates related to the so-called CIAM "Grid" or *Grille* accelerated the schism between older and younger members of CIAM. In 1946 Le Corbusier had introduced the system of the CIAM Grid – a large matrix composed according to fixed CIAM categories that allowed for the presentation of a modern urban project in a standard fashion.[5] Le Corbusier believed that the grid was one of the tools by which different modern design solutions could be compared and thus would offer the basis for finding universal solutions for the future city. However, instead of showing a hyper-modern design for a new urban neighborhood as was normally done in CIAM Grids, the two representative North African groups at CIAM IX chose to focus on a completely different urban environment: the so-called bidonvilles or shanty-towns in Casablanca and Algiers. These informal shack settlements that were being constructed completely without the involvement of architects were, indeed, rising at a very fast pace in the peripheries of North African cities as a result of colonial modernization.

The CIAM-Morocco group included about fifteen architects among whom were Pierre Mas, Michel Écochard, and Georges Candilis. It presented two grids: Mas and Écochard's GAMMA (*Groupe d'Architectes Modernes Marocains*) Grid on "Moroccan Housing," and the ATBAT (Atelier des bâtisseurs)-Afrique presentation "Habitat for the Greatest Number Grid,"[6] prepared by Candilis. These grids represented investigations of the bidonville known as Carrières Centrales in the Moroccan city of Casablanca. It was composed of a large series of sketches, photographs, and collages that documented the living conditions in the old medina and in the bidonville as well as details about the renovation schemes presented by the Planning Department, including a study of the designs for collective housing based upon the patio system.[7]

The second group of North African architects, the CIAM-Algiers group under the leadership of architects Roland Simounet and Michel Emery, presented the so-called Bidonville Mahieddine Grid, that focused on the bidonville Mahieddine in the outskirts of Algiers. The grid showed a very detailed study of the reasons for the emergence of the area, the sanitary and health problems that it brought to the fore, photographic and graphic analyses of the way that the bidonville was used and lived in, as well as design proposals for new housing units that were to replace the shantytown (plate 49).

Alison Smithson, one of the participants to CIAM IX, noticed that both of the North African grids caused a lot of upheaval. The actual reason for this turmoil was according to Smithson not to be found in the composition of the grids, which virtually conformed to the standard *Grille*, but rather in their actual content.[8] In these grids there was no reference to pure forms, appealing aesthetics, and rich architectural traditions, but rather to the messy everyday urban environment – the bidonville – that emerges from poverty and necessity. Presenting the ordinary and often despised reality of the bidonville as if it were a valuable urban environment was perceived by modern masters such as Le Corbusier and Gropius as the crossing of an important boundary. Indeed, some of the old guard CIAM architects perceived this presentation as a negative deviation from CIAM's original goal that encompassed the delineation of radically modern and universal design solutions. To the contrary, for a whole group of other architects, like Alison and Peter Smithson, Aldo van Eyck and Jaap Bakema, Georges Candilis and Shadrach Woods, this "deviation" represented the beginning of a new path for the modern movement.

The Bidonville as a Site of Negotiation

In the GAMMA/ATBAT-Afrique grids and the Bidonville Mahiedinne Grid, the shabby built environment of the bidonvilles in Casablanca and Algiers stands at the center of attention.[9] It is no coincidence that the French architects that were not just traveling and visiting, but working in the midst of the North African territory, primarily depicted the bidonville as the locus of daily struggles with dwelling, diseases, and sanitary conditions. Though many of these (often very young) French architects had moved to Morocco and Algeria in order to realize their architectural ambitions on the *tabula rasa* of the colonial territory, one cannot overlook the empathic perspective on the harsh reality of the bidonville that the GAMMA Grid and the Bidonville Mahiedinne Grid adopted.

[6] The Grid was composed of five parts: 1. *Introduction et bidonville* by Mas; 2. *Planification et Urbanisme* by Écochard; 3. *L'ordre et construction* by Godefroy and Mas; 4. *La concentration horizontale* by Beraud and Godefroy; 5. *La concentration verticale* by Bodiansky, Candilis, Kennedy, Piot, and Woods.

[7] For an introduction to the GAMMA Grid see Jean-Louis Cohen and Monique Eleb, *Casablanca. Colonial Myths and Architectural Ventures*, New York, Monacelli Press, 2002.

[8] Alison Smithson, *Team 10 Meetings*, New York, Rizzoli, 1991, p. 19.

[9] For a discussion of the Bidonville Mahiedinne Grid see Zeynep Çelik, "Learning from the Bidonville," *Harvard Design Magazine*, Spring/Summer 2003, no. 18, pp. 70–74.

12.2 (*Overleaf*) Georges Candilis and Shadrach Woods. Panels (selection) of the GAMMA Grid, presented at CIAM IX, Aix-en-Provence, 1953.
Source: Ministère de l'habitat, photographic archives, Rabat.

MAROC 210-I
HABITAT DU PLUS GRAND NOMBRE

Le Bidonville

Vie collective.

Collective life.

MAROC 211-I
HABITAT DU PLUS GRAND NOMBRE

Le bidonville

Développement de la vie
sociale.

Naissance d'un esprit
collectif national : le na-
tionalisme.

Development of social
life.

Birth of a collective
nationalist "moroccan"
spirit.

MAROC 210-II
HABITAT DU PLUS GRAND NOMBRE

Le Bidonville

Dans le bidonville, les
mosquées sont plus nom-
breuses que partout
ailleurs.

In the shanty town,
mosques are more numerous
than any where else.

MAROC 210-III
HABITAT DU PLUS GRAND NOMBRE

Le bidonville

Recherches décoratives
dans la construction.

Search for decoration
in construction.

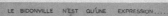

LE BIDONVILLE N'EST QU'UNE EXPRESSION . . . . . .

LE PROBLEME HABITAT
EST PLUS VASTE

— RESORPTION DES BIDONVILLES

— DECONGESTION DES MEDINAS

— SOLUTION A L'ACCROISSEMENT

DEMOGRAPHIQUE CONSTANT

MAROC 211-III
HABITAT DU PLUS GRAND NOMBRE

Le bidonville

Shanty town are one as-
pect the housing problem
is larger.

We implies :
— resorption of shanty-
towns.
— decongestion of
Medinas.
— the solution to cons-
tant demographic ex-
tension.

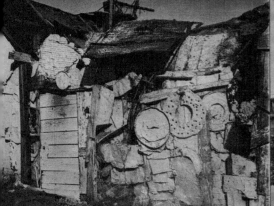

[10] See for instance Bruno de Rotalier, "Les yaouleds (enfants des rues) de Casablanca et leur participation aux émeutes de décembre 1951," in *Revue d'histoire de l'enfance irrégulière*, no. 4, 2002, pp. 20–28.

[11] For this specific approach to rural areas see E. Mauret, "Problèmes de l'équipement rural dans l'aménagement du territoire," in *L'Architecture d'aujourd'hui* 60, June 1955, pp. 42–45.

Since the First World War, the bidonville or shantytown was an integral part of North African cities such as Casablanca and Algiers. The bidonville was the figure par excellence in which the colonial situation with its uneven development of urban areas (considered merely as points of fabrication and transportation of products) and rural areas (regarded as blank territories that offered raw materials) comes to the fore. It was an urban zone in which the newcomers from the countryside were absorbed and in which their daily struggles with dwelling literally became visible. From reports of the period we also know that the bidonville was often the initial locus of protest and action against the colonial power. In 1952, the year of the fortieth anniversary of the Moroccan Protectorate and the moment that the ATBAT-Afrique architects pursued their research initiatives, the bidonville of the Carrières Centrales (called "Karyan central") was the center of riots against the colonial power.[10]

Against this background it should come as no surprise that young left-oriented and engaged architects such as Georges Candilis and Roland Simounet represented the bidonville as an urban environment that was remarkable because of the persistence and symbolic power of its dwelling and building practices. Dwelling practices of preparing meals, sleeping, gathering, and building practices of constructing shacks, as well as collective practices of gathering, going to the mosque, and selling goods and food, were all depicted in great detail. It was especially the persistence and adaptive capacity of traditional dwelling practices that struck the young European architects who commented on them in the texts of the panels.

In order to illustrate this particular perspective with regard to the socio-economic practices of the bidonville, the French architects relied upon a tradition of anthropological research that had been developed at among others the *Service de l'Urbanisme* (Planning Department) in Casablanca, Morocco. After the Second World War, these urban services of the French Protectorate initiated large programs for the investigation of indigenous dwelling patterns in towns and villages. From 1947 onwards, the *Service de l'Urbanisme* set up a research methodology that consisted primarily of a mobile unit or *atelier ambulant* – consisting of an engineer, an urban designer, a topographer, and two draftsmen – that literally traveled through the country to investigate dwelling culture in a truly ethnological manner.[11]

The *atelier ambulant* can be considered as the exponent of a different attitude towards architectural and urban design. If in the pre-war period the studio had been the point of departure for the "master-architect," in the postwar period the everyday reality of the terrain was the field of initial action for the "architect-ethnologist." The *Service de l'Urbanisme* introduced an idea of architectural and urban design that took as its point of departure the thorough and detailed analysis of dwelling typologies, of their underlying logics and their uses. Besides the drawings, the *Service de l'Urbanisme* used the relatively new technique of aerial photography as a way to make an inventory of the characteristics of everyday environments.

The most interesting aspect of the investigations led by the young French architects is that they did not remain limited to the terrain of traditional rural environments. The everyday urban spaces of the bidonville of Casablanca or Algiers were investigated in a similar ethnological fashion through drawings and photographs. By using this approach the architects of GAMMA/ATBAT-Afrique and CIAM-Algiers were able to depict the bidonville as the substance of daily practices of dwelling and building, as the material through which inhabitants leave the most rudimentary symbolic and spatial traces in the built environment. The bidonville was depicted as the locus of symbolic and spatial struggles.

Moreover, this particular mode of analysis portrayed the bidonville as a meeting point between a so-called "traditional culture" that was still part of everyday dwelling habits and the modern culture of cities like Algiers and Casablanca with their movie houses, cars, stores, and industries. The GAMMA Grid panels of the Moroccan architects also recognized certain ambivalent qualities of the bidonvilles.[12] For instance, the ATBAT-Afrique architects emphasized that the bidonvilles represented a radical departure from traditional rural dwelling conditions, as indicated in the panel with the subscript "Psychological causes of the movement towards towns – Desire of the individual to escape from rural patriarchy? – Town = Eldorado?"[13] Simultaneously, however, they underlined the enduring quality of traditional dwelling culture within the modern urban environment of the bidonville. They demonstrated how the courtyard typology of the shelters echoed the traditional courtyard houses in the Atlas Mountains, while their integration in a dense urban fabric functioned much as a modern urban environment. This contemporaneous presence of traditional and modern elements within the bidonville made Candilis and Woods believe that the dwelling environment could deal with the field of tensions between tradition and modernity that modernization created. It explains why one of the panels of the GAMMA Grid depicts the bidonvilles as interesting "new forms [that] appear in industrial cities."

The search for new forms that corresponded to a new way of living was at the center of the research by the GAMMA and the CIAM-Algiers groups. However, answers were not searched for within the rich and longstanding "grand vernacular tradition," but rather in the transient and ordinary vernacular environment of the bidonville itself – specifically because of its capacity to negotiate between traditional and modern patterns of living. According to the architects the bidonville opened up perspectives to rethink future dwelling environments on colonial territories and beyond. In the Bidonville Mahiedinne Grid, the CIAM-Algiers formulated it as such:

> Here, under the poverty of the used materials, the house is a spontaneous expression of life. It is molded on the human being, breathes with him and preserves, even in its rotting carcass, the dignity of living lines and proportions.
> But contemporary life implies techniques which, for reasons of economy, lead to standardized structures based on Western conceptions (échelle occidentale de vie).
> In an era when a mechanized civilization is permeating the whole world, will the Oriental be able to avoid being caught up in the machine and preserve unspoiled his primitive freshness?
> It is up to us to provide the basic and indispensable structural elements, which can afford to these people the possibility to give new expression to their own traditional conceptions. And perhaps in that creative expression we too shall find ourselves again.[14]

Beyond the grid panels, the projects and realizations presented at CIAM IX were highly regarded as a "new way of thinking" about the city, its neighborhoods, spaces, and typologies. The mix of individual patio houses (which were compared to the old houses of the medinas) and the three collective housings by ATBAT-Afrique, in contrast to the adjacent bidonvilles, were praised by Alison and Peter Smithson:

[12] For an elaborate description see Monique Eleb, "An Alternative to Functionalist Universalism: Écochard, Candilis and ATBAT-Afrique," in Sarah Williams Goldhagen (ed.), Anxious Modernisms: Experimentation in Postwar Architectural Culture, Cambridge, The MIT Press, 2001.
[13] Panel 208-I, Grid elaborated by the Service de l'Urbanisme for CIAM IX, Aix-en-Provence, 1953, in CIAM Collection at the gta/ETH.
[14] Bidonville Mahiedinne Grid, in CIAM Collection at the Fondation Le Corbusier, Paris.

15 From Alison and Peter Smithson,
"Collective Housing in Morocco," in
Architectural Design 25, no. 1, January
1955, p. 2. Quoted by Jean-Louis
Cohen and Monique Eleb, p. 332.
16 Ibid., p. 339.
17 On the work of Aldo van Eyck,
see Francis Strauven, *Aldo van Eyck:
The Shape of Relativity*, Amsterdam,
Architectura and Natura, 1998.
18 Aldo van Eyck, "Dogon: mand-
huis-dorp-wereld," p. 53. Also see
note 3 in this essay.
19 Francis Strauven, *Aldo van Eyck*,
p. 350.

We regard these buildings in Morocco as the greatest achievement since Le Corbusier's Unité d'habitation at Marseilles. Whereas the Unité was the summation of a technique of thinking about "habitat" which started forty years ago, the importance of the Moroccan buildings is that they are the first manifestations of a new way of thinking. For this reason they are presented as ideas; but it is their realization in built form that convinces us that here is a new universal.[15]

Even though they were not that well suited to the living conditions of Moroccan Muslims, the new "photogenic buildings of Carrières Centrale . . . denoted a paradigm shift between the universalist approach of modern architecture and an ambition to adapt to local cultures and identities that characterized the Team X generation."[16]

The Sahara, the Dogon and the Rootedness of the Grand Vernacular

In 1953, the year of the CIAM IX meeting, architect Aldo van Eyck (1918–99) published a memorable article in the Dutch Architectural periodical *Forum*.[17] In this article under the title "Building in the Southern Oases" (*Bouwen in de Zuidelijke Oasen*), the Dutch architect presented a photographic report of the travels to different settlements in the oases of the Algerian Sahara that he made together with the Dutch COBRA artist Corneille and the archi-tect Herman Haan in 1951 and 1952. Seven years later, van Eyck travelled to Mali to study and photograph the Dogon settlements that he had discovered in Marcel Griaule's account in *Le Minotaure* (1931–1933). Van Eyck later described these traditional settlements as the reminders of a long-lasting tradition that

> do not differ that much from the situation five thousand years ago. These are the same laboriously formed stones . . . the same spaces around an interior court; the same embryonic intimacy; the same absolute transition of dark to light.[18]

Though van Eyck's interest for this traditional architecture has often been explained as an interest in primal architectural forms, a central issue in his work at the time – and also the most important characteristic of his article – was his understanding of the settlements as material articulations of an "intelligible tradition." Van Eyck's comments on the photographs depicted the building structures in the Sahara as the result of an age-old tradition of building that is rooted in knowledge about local materials and climate, and that touches upon basic human needs and results in primal forms of architecture.

For van Eyck the building tradition of the settlements in the oases was as intelligible as the other architectural traditions that he was confronted with in his education as a European architect. Moreover, he considered this intelligibility complementary to other traditions that Western architectural thinking had brought to the fore: the classical and the modern tradition. This became obvious in the presentation that van Eyck made at the last official CIAM congress in Otterlo (Netherlands) in 1959. In this meeting he presented a diagram, the Otterlo Circles. For van Eyck these two circles were a criticism of the modern avant-garde, who had:

> been harping continually on what is different in our time to such an extent that it has lost touch with what is not different, with what is always essentially the same.[19]

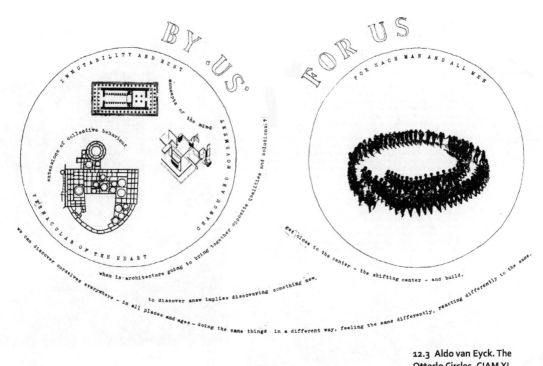

12.3 Aldo van Eyck. The Otterlo Circles, CIAM XI, 1959.
Source: NAI Collections and Archives, Rotterdam.

In the left circle ("by us") the Dutch architect represented three architectural traditions through three drawings: the Parthenon or the Acropolis of Athens, a construction by Van Doesburg, and a group of houses in the Aoulef villages in the Algerian Sahara. Later van Eyck would denote the different traditions respectively as "immutability and rest," "change and movement," and the "vernacular of the heart." The right circle ("for us") showed a spiral-like group of men and women. Commenting on the left circle he wrote:

> I have been in love with all three for years, with the values divided between them. I can't separate them any more. I simply can't. They complement each other; they belong together. Add San Carlo alle Quatro Fontane, not just to avoid the trinity, and we can start reconciling them – the essence not the form – in an endless sequence of possibilities that really fit man.[20]

With his Otterlo Circles van Eyck wanted to suggest and illustrate that if contemporary architecture attempted to respond to the complete human identity, then it had to engage with the basic values that the different architectural traditions had brought to the fore throughout the ages. The Aoulef villages in the Sahara played a key role in this perspective. They were, according to van Eyck, the expression of an architecture that engaged directly with the symbolical aspirations and needs of the inhabitants. This concept of a "vernacular of the heart" would be further developed in two articles in the periodicals *Forum* and *Via* in which the Dogon villages – built up from dirt and mud – were used as an example.[21]

In these articles van Eyck illustrated his fascination for the important role of mythology within the Dogon society. Inspired by the work of anthropologists like Marcel Griaule and Ruth Benedict, he explained how Dogon time and space are partitioned with a large variety of symbols.[22] The Dogon regards the world

[20] Ibid., p. 351.
[21] Aldo van Eyck, "Dogon: mand-huis-dorp-wereld," p. 53.
[22] Van Eyck's primary sources to understand these villages was the well-known work of Marcel Griaule, and in particular: Marcel Griaule, *Dieu d'eau: Entretiens avec Ogotommêli*, Paris, 1948 (In English: *Conversations with Ogotommêli: An Introduction to Dogon Religious Ideas*, London/New York, Oxford University Press, 1965); M. Griaule and G. Dieterlin, "The Dogon," in Daryll Forde (ed.), *African Worlds*, London, 1954, pp. 83–110; as well as the contributions of Griaule to the surrealist magazine *Minotaure*. Another source of inspiration was the work of the American anthropologist Ruth Benedict, *Patterns of Culture*, New York, Houghton-Mifflin, 1934.

GALLERY

Architecture of the Dogon

At a long bend of the Niger River in Northeastern Africa, in the rocky band of geography which lies between the parched Sahara and the soggy tropical plains, is one of the most compact complete civilizations of that tenaciously historical continent. It is the land of the Dogon, an area about twice the size of Maryland, dotted with small villages which sit like stage sets on small hard plateaus or cliffsides with deposits of arable land around them—like cupcakes in a gigantic baking tin. Aldo van Eyck, a Dutch architect, has long been fascinated by the buildings of these villages. The structures are well-designed shields against the severe climate; their groupings are a precise physical parable of the communal organization which characterizes the code of life here; most of all, the forms of the architecture itself are a stirring dramatization of both the tangible and traditional needs. The photographs and captions which appear on these six pages, and the text which follows, are by Architect van Eyck.—ED.

Since Marcel Griaule inaugurated the study of the Dogon in 1930 a vast amount of writing has been dedicated to these remarkable people whose extremely integrated social and religious pattern of life has withstood the onslaught of the modern world in a way quite unprecedented. The spiritual tenacity and integrity of the Dogon have certainly no rival in Africa today.

Their territory lies 200 kilometers due south of Timbuktu in the bend of the River Niger. The present population, estimated at approximately 250,000, lives in some 700 small communities spread over an area of 50,000

continued on page 186

Main village square in Yugo No, a typical cliff-debris-type village. Note buobab trees and plain in the distance.

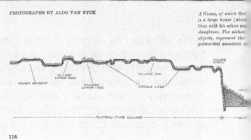

115

12.4 Pages from Aldo van Eyck's article "Architecture of the Dogon," 1961.
Source: *Architectural Forum*, September 1961.

[23] Geneviève Calame-Griaule, *Ethnologie et language. La Parole chez les Dogons*, Paris, 1965, p. 27 (In English: *Words and the Dogon World*, Philadelphia, Institute for the Study of Human Issues, 1986).
[24] *Forum*, July 1967; English version in *Via* 1, 1968, p.15 and also republished in Charles and Gorges Baird (eds.), *Meaning in Architecture*, New York, Braziller, 1969, pp. 170–213. Also see Aldo van Eyck, "A Miracle of Moderation," in *Via* 1, pp. 96–125. On Van Eyck's presentation in Otterlo, see Francis Strauven, *Aldo van Eyck*, pp. 346–354.

as "a gigantic human organism, and all its parts as being reproductions of the same image on a smaller or larger scale."[23] For van Eyck the Dogon way of making settlements represented a way of re-finding a meaningful relationship to the built environment; it was a way of locating or rooting the human being within his environment. In his opinion,

> [the Dogon] made the world system graspable, they brought the universe within their measurable confines; they made the world a habitable place, they brought what was "outside," "inside."[24]

Van Eyck's interest for the North African vernacular, and more particularly the connotations of rootedness that it received in his "vernacular of the heart" discourse, cannot be disconnected from the alienation that the postwar urban environments in Europe brought about. The effect on people of this "architecture for the greatest number" was one of the main concerns of Team X. In response to the alienation and psychological distress Van Eyck offered a view on "grand vernacular" architecture – that is, a vernacular that transcends its modest origins to be something that is larger than life. North Africa appeared in his publications as the territory of a grand everyday architectural tradition that represents longstanding customs and organizations. The Sahara settlements and the Dogon villages were presented as built environments that consist of meaningful primary forms, not *"unheimlich"* (uncanny) as most of the European dwelling environments, but rather habitable and in a certain harmony. For van Eyck these built environments had succeeded "to solve problems appertaining between man and cosmos, man and environment, man and man, and finally man in terms of himself."[25]

At the same Otterlo congress, van Eyck displayed a project by Piet Blom, his student at the Amsterdam Academy. The project was titled "The Cities Will Be Inhabited Like Villages" and van Eyck placed the motto "vers une casbah organizée" (toward an organized casbah) next to it. In doing so he put into question the Western tradition as the only way to resolve modern problems and made clear reference to the North African settlements and their value of model for contemporary urban design.[26]

Mat-Building

The distinct perspectives on African settlements, respectively as sites of negotiation with modernity and "grand vernacular," resulted also in specific architectural concepts. In this respect the article "How to Recognize and Read Mat-Building. Mainstream Architecture as it Developed towards the Mat-Building" that Alison Smithson published in 1974 in *Architectural Design* is revealing.[27] In this article Smithson attempts to outline the relation between certain experiences in vernacular African architecture and some of the architectural and urban concepts developed by some Team X architects in Europe. In particular, Smithson defined the architectural tendency of Mat-Building as follows:

> Mat-building can be said to epitomise the anonymous collective; where the functions come to enrich the fabric, and the individual gains new freedoms of action through a new and shuffled order, based on interconnection, close-knit patterns of association, and possibilities for growth, diminution, and change.[28]

The faculty of buildings to allow for appropriation and to accommodate changing building practices was one of the most important characteristics of the principle of Mat-Building theory. To underline this quality, Smithson referred explicitly to the "lessons" that were drawn from African settlements:

> Still existing in the simple Arab town, an interchangeability, in which the neutral cube contains a calm cell that can change; from home to workshop; green-grocery to paraffin store; an alley of houses in whose midst is a baker, made into a Souk by simple expedient of adding pieces of fabric over the public way . . . as needs grow.[29]

Out of this perspective Alison Smithson made a distinction between two seminal Mat-Building structures, Aldo van Eyck's Orphanage in Amsterdam (1957–60) and Candilis–Josic–Woods's Berlin Free University (from 1963), because these two projects represented a different way of organizing and composing space. While van Eyck's orphanage in Amsterdam is based on the so-called "configurative principle" that structurally assembles similar architectural elements, the Berlin Mat demonstrates another organizing principle. In van Eyck's orphanage, it is the repetition of "plain sameness"; in the Berlin Mat of the Free University, the "apparent sameness is the carrying order," writes Smithson.[30]

[25] Aldo van Eyck, *The Child, the City, and the Artist*, 1962 (unpublished stenciled book), p. 252.
[26] See Eric Mumford, "The Emergence of Mat or Field Buildings," in Hashim Sarkis and Pablo Allard (eds.), *Le Corbusier's Venice Hospital and the Mat-Building Revival*, Munich/New York, Prestel, 2001, pp. 66–67.
[27] Alison Smithson, "How to Recognize and Read Mat-Building. Mainstream Architecture as it Developed towards the Mat-Building," in *Architectural Design*, no. 9, 1974, pp. 573–590.
[28] Ibid, p. 573.
[29] Ibid., p. 576.
[30] Ibid.

12.5 Aldo Van Eyck. Aerial view of Orphanage, Amsterdam, 1955-60.
Source: From *Aldo Van Eyck: Works*, Birkhaüser, 1999.
© Photo Aldo Van Eyck.

31 See Francis Strauven, *Aldo van Eyck*.
32 Alison Smithson, "How to Recognize and Read Mat-Building," p. 575.

Undeniably, in the model of density that Alison Smithson denoted with her Mat metaphor, sameness is not an issue. Density is considered here to be the inextricable weaving of diverse built and functional entities at different scale levels, as it can be perceived in traditional African settlements. It is understood as the capacity to interlace the different architectural and functional elements into a close-knit fabric. Alison Smithson recognized this attitude in the *Pastoor van Ars Church* (1963–69), another project by Aldo van Eyck. Within a traditional closed architectural volume several urban figures were juxtaposed: chapels, sloping street ("via sacra") and meeting place ("crypt"), all united in the church's austere architectonic form.[31] Smithson held that the interrelation and weaving of urban figures result in the building's capacity to invite different forms of appropriation and thus different practices. Precisely, this "overlay of patterns of use: the disintegration of rigidity through this meshing . . . make this a nugget of *mat*-architecture."[32]

Likewise, the Free University Berlin by Candilis–Josic–Woods is a meshing of urban and architectural figures. The superimposition of the layer of *tracés* and the layer of *espaces ouverts* results in an orthogonal tissue. Interior streets, squares, and bridges are interlaced with gallery spaces, outdoor patios, terraces, and ramps. A primary weave or fabric of infrastructural elements is the result. In between the threads of this primary fabric, a large variety of architectural

12.6 Georges Candilis, Alexis Josic, Shadrach Woods. Model of the competition project showing the courtyards and the layers of the web, Freie Universität Berlin (Free University Berlin), 1963.
Source: Avery Library Special Collections, Columbia University, New York.

and programmatic entities can be woven. Auditoria, offices, laboratories, and seminar rooms are nestled among the primary infrastructural threads. The ensuing product is a dense, two-dimensional patch of urban fabric that stands midway between an architectural building and an urban project.

During the first decades after the Second World War, the built environment in Western Europe became increasingly subject to the control of the welfare state and the consumer society. Hence, for several European avant-garde architects the active participation of inhabitants in their environment was considered of prime importance. Within the Team X circle this idea of participation took on different forms. Giancarlo De Carlo organized animated meetings with the future inhabitants of his Terni project, and Shadrach Woods wrote manifestos with such challenging titles as *Urbanism is Everybody's Business* and *What U can DO*.[33] In the case of the Mat-Building projects, participation was understood as the intentional withdrawal of architectural design in order to open the possibilities for appropriation and identification. It is out of this perspective that Alison Smithson wrote that dense mats were not only considered as "the right living pattern for our way of life, and the equipment that serves it, but also . . . the right symbols to satisfy our present cultural aspirations."[34]

The Mat does not symbolize this faculty of appropriation and identification through linguistic preconditions or through the adoption of a certain kind of style, but rather through its very materiality. It is the tissue of the Mat, its material of clustered and interrelated spaces, that symbolizes the possibility of appropriation. Hence, the Mat turns out to be a design strategy aimed, through the introduction of a density that was discovered in Africa, at establishing a more cultured relationship between modern man and physical space. The conception of the Mat as an urban tissue that invites appropriation, illustrates an understanding of built space as a platform for, and the result of, spatial practices.

A New Perspective on the Modern Movement

When Aldo van Eyck attended the presentation of the two North African grids at CIAM IX he considered them as a turning point that allowed the thirty-year-old organisation to leave its narrow Occidental viewpoint. The minutes of the meeting made clear that the Dutch architect analyzed the grids as attempts to discard the Western rationalistic bias in order to gain access to the general-human archaic values that survived in the North African cultures. Van Eyck held that:

> Through both their artifacts and their habitats, these civilizations testify to the primary human capacity for self-expression in elementary forms charged with multiple meanings: pregnant forms that simultaneously voice the local natural condition, a social structure and cosmological views.[35]

Despite van Eyck's attempt to project his personal perspective on the studies of the GAMMA and CIAM-Algiers groups, it is clear that within the confines of Team X very different attitudes towards African vernacular emerged. The story of Team X illustrates that the interest for the South in the architectural culture of the 1950s and 1960s surpasses romantic views, fascination, and bewilderment, but is rather the expression of a fundamental search within the modern movement for an approach of the built environment that goes beyond Occidental rationalistic concepts.

[33] Shadrach Woods and Joaquim Pfeufer, *Stadtplannung geht uns alle an. Urbanism is Everybody's Business. L'urbanistica come problema di interesse collettivo*, Stuttgart, K. Kramer, 1968; Shadrach Woods, "What U Can Do," *Architecture at Rice*, no. 27, Spring 1970.
[34] Alison Smithson and Peter Smithson, *Ordinariness and Light. Urban Theories 1952–1960 and their Application in a Building Project 1963–1970*, Cambridge, The MIT Press, 1970, p. 161.
[35] Francis Strauven, *Aldo van Eyck*, p. 255.

36 See Aldo van Eyck, "De Pueblos," in *Forum* 16, no. 3, pp. 95–114, 122–123.

The Dogon and the bidonville – the grand and the ordinary vernacular – represent two sides of a broad spectrum of approaches to African settlements. These two sides make clearly distinguishable approaches but nevertheless share a common basis. After all, just like van Eyck, the architects of the CIAM-Algiers and the ATBAT-Afrique/GAMMA groups were searching for new architectural forms that would comply with the aspirations and needs of contemporary dwelling. However, while van Eyck was searching for a symbolic dimension in the long-lasting values of Dogon architecture – it is useful to remember that van Eyck also traveled to the Indian settlements of Taos, New Mexico – the GAMMA and CIAM-Algiers architects focused on the ordinary vernacular of the *bidonville* and its capacity to negotiate between tradition and modernity.[36]

These approaches to African vernacular did not remain limited to the circles of Team X. Throughout the architectural culture of the 1950s and 1960s they appeared and reappeared as defining elements of the North–South nexus, be it in mitigated forms. The spin-off appears so large that it might form one of the basis elements for a substantial revision of the historiography of the Modern Movement as we know it. At least, it reminds us that the development of the Modern Movement in architecture is not only a matter of avant-garde projects but also of attitudes to the vernacular, as well as of shared stories of migration, encounter, and exchanges between the African Mediterranean and Europe.■

12.7 Yona Friedman. *La Ville Spatiale* [The Spatial City], 1958/1962. Photomontage of interwoven city, on photograph by Bernard Rudofsky of vernacular village in Southern Italy (from *Architecture without Architects*).
Source: From Sabine Lebesque and Helene Fentener van Vlissingen, *Yona Friedman – Structures Serving the Unpredictable*, Rotterdam, NAi Publishers, 1999.

INDEX

#0334 - 020816 - C32 - 246/174/19 - PB - 9780415776349